ACCOUNTING PRINCIPLES

CANADIAN EDITION

ACCOUNTING PRINCIPLES

▶ **JERRY J. WEYGANDT** *Ph.D., C.P.A.*

Arthur Andersen Alumni Professor of Accounting
University of Wisconsin
Madison, Wisconsin

▶ **DONALD E. KIESO** *Ph.D., C.P.A.*

KPMG Peat Marwick Emeritus Professor of Accountancy
North Illinois University
DeKalb, Illinois

▶ **BARBARA TRENHOLM** *M.B.A., F.C.A.*

University of New Brunswick
Fredericton, New Brunswick

In collaboration with

▶ **DONALD C. CHERRY** *M.B.A., C.M.A.*

Dalhousie University
Halifax, Nova Scotia

 JOHN WILEY AND SONS CANADA, LTD

Toronto • New York • Chichester • Weinheim • Brisbane • Singapore

To my students — past, present, and future

Canadian Cataloguing in Publication Data
Weygandt, Jerry J.
    Accounting principles

1st Canadian ed.
Includes index.
ISBN 0-471-64252-5 (v.1)
ISBN 0-471-64253-3 (v.2)
ISBN 0-471-64254-1 (v.3)

1. Accounting. I. Keiso, Donald E. II. Trenholm, Barbara A. III. Title.

HF5635.W38 1998   657'. 044   C98-932431-1

Production Credits

Acquisitions Editor: John Horne
Publishing Services Director: Karen Bryan
Developmental Editor: Karen Staudinger
Marketing Manager: Carolyn J. Wells
Copy Editor: Leah Johnson
Proofreader: Jane Broderick
Design & Typesetting: Interrobang Graphic Design Inc.
Cover Photo Credits: First Light
Printing & Binding: Tri-Graphic Printing Limited

Printed and bound in Canada
10 9 8 7 6 5 4 3 2 1

John Wiley & Sons Canada, Ltd.
22 Worcester Road
Etobicoke, Ontario M9W 1L1
Visit our website at: www.wiley.com/canada

BRIEF CONTENTS

CONTENTS - VOLUME TWO

• • • • • ▶ **Concepts for Review**

Ottawa Hostel Has Payroll Locked Up

OTTAWA, Ont.—Today, the Ottawa International Hostel is a godsend for budget travellers to the nation's capital. But for over a hundred years the historic downtown building housed only involuntary guests—as the Carleton County Jail. Renovated and reopened as a hostel in 1973, it retains a few traces of its previous incarnation, such as bars on the dormitory room doors—and, some say, the ghost of a 19th-century inmate who was unjustly condemned to death.

If there is a ghost on the premises, he's not on the payroll, according to Cheri Gillis, the Hostel's Executive Assistant. The payroll *does* include 18 dedicated staff members. At the Hostel, as in almost every organization, making sure the pay arrives promptly, regularly, and in the correct amount is a crucial aspect of operations.

Four of the staff members, including Ms. Gillis, are full-time employees whose salaries are determined by contracts approved by the Hostel's Board of Directors. The rest are hired through a verbal agreement and paid by the hour, their work time tracked by having them sign in and out in a log book.

In most cases, employees' income tax, Employment Insurance, and Canada Pension Plan contributions are deducted from their paycheques. "A few part-time hourly employees—mostly students—arrange not to have deductions made at source, by filling out Revenue Canada's Personal Tax Credit (TD1) form."

Ms. Gillis explains that the exact calculations of deductions are made by Comcheq, a firm that handles the details of payroll deductions and payment. Workers' Compensation premiums, however, are paid by the Hostel directly. The firm also takes care of making the actual payments of wages—in most cases through direct deposit, which is increasingly popular in many organizations. A few employees, however, prefer to have cheques sent to the Hostel for pickup. Every employee receives a cheque stub. For every pay period, the Hostel receives both detailed and summary reports.

"Comcheq saves us a lot of time and makes our lives easier," Ms. Gillis emphasizes. But the Hostel management must still handle staffing and timekeeping, as well as plan and monitor the payroll budget. Also—Comcheq takes no responsibility for the ghost! ◀

CHAPTER • 11

CURRENT LIABILITIES AND PAYROLL ACCOUNTING

▶ **STUDY OBJECTIVES** ◀

After studying this chapter, you should be able to:

1. *Explain a current liability and identify the major types of current liabilities.*
2. *Explain the accounting for various current liabilities.*
3. *Describe the accounting and disclosure requirements for contingencies.*
4. *Discuss the objectives of internal control for payroll.*
5. *Compute the payroll for a pay period.*
6. *Describe employer payroll costs.*
7. *Identify the steps in recording the payroll.*

Whether it be accommodations like the Ottawa International Hostel, a pizza parlour like Pizza Delight, a public accounting firm like Grant Thornton, or a large multinational company like BCE Inc., all enterprises have liabilities for payroll. In addition, they have many other types of liabilities. These include the purchase of supplies on account, the borrowing of money on a bank loan, and the obligation to pay interest. Liabilities are classified as current or long-term on the balance sheet. We will explain current liabilities in this chapter and long-term liabilities in Chapter 16. The organization of this chapter is as follows:

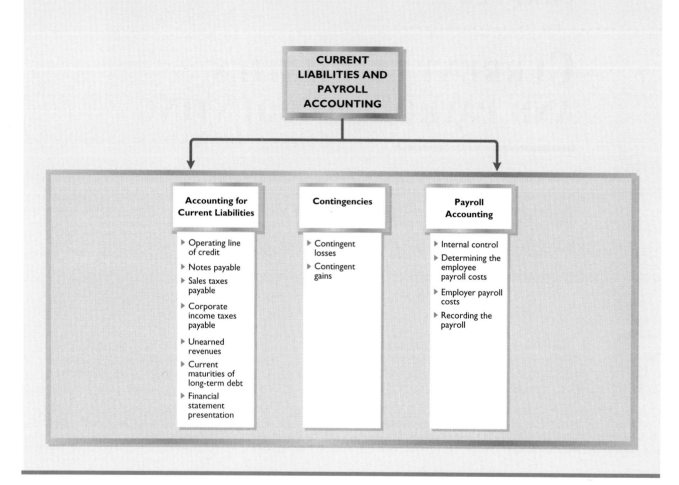

Accounting for Current Liabilities

STUDY OBJECTIVE

1

Explain a current liability and identify the major types of current liabilities.

As explained in Chapter 4, a **current liability** is a debt that is likely to be paid: (1) within one year (or the operating cycle, if longer), and (2) from existing current assets (e.g., cash) or through the creation of other current liabilities. Debts that do not meet both criteria are classified as long-term liabilities.

►Accounting in Action ► *Business Insight*

Procurement cards have cut administrative workloads significantly and sped up the payment of current liabilities. These cards work much the way credit cards do: They allow low-value goods and services to be purchased and paid quickly. With fewer purchase orders and subsequent cheque payments, transaction volume drops and less than one day passes between when a purchase is made and when it is paid for. After introducing VISA and MasterCard procurement cards, Siemens Canada Limited, a worldwide leader in electronics and technology, was able to reduce the number of its vendors from 3,000 to 500 and its accounts payable clerks from four to one.

Companies must carefully monitor the relationship of current liabilities to current assets. This relationship is critical in evaluating a company's liquidity, or short-term debt-paying ability, as discussed in Chapter 4. A company that has more current liabilities than current assets is usually the subject of some concern, because the company may not be able to make its payments when they become due.

Current liabilities include operating lines of credit, notes payable, accounts payable, accrued liabilities such as sales taxes, income taxes, salaries and wages, and interest payable, unearned revenues, and current maturities of long-term debt. The entries for accounts payable and adjusting entries for some current liabilities have been explained in previous chapters. Other types of current liabilities that are frequently encountered are discussed in the following sections.

Operating Line of Credit

Current assets (such as accounts receivable) do not always turn into cash at the exact time that current liabilities (such as accounts payable) must be paid. Consequently, most companies have an operating line of credit at their bank (a demand loan) to help them manage temporary cash shortfalls. This means that the company has been preauthorized by the bank to borrow money, up to a preset limit, when it is needed.

Air Canada, for example, has a $560-million line of credit. An Air Canada spokesperson said, "It's good policy to have additional cash available if we need it." Security or collateral is usually required by the bank as protection in the event of default on the loan. Collateral normally includes some, or all, of the company's current assets (e.g., accounts receivable or inventories) or a floating charge debenture over other assets of the company. We discuss debentures in Chapter 16.

Line of credit borrowings are normally on a short-term basis, repayable immediately upon request—that is, on demand—by the bank. In reality, however, repayment is seldom demanded without notice. A line of credit makes it very easy for a company to borrow money: it doesn't have to make a call or visit its bank to actually arrange the transaction. The bank simply covers any cheques written in excess of the bank account balance, up to the approved credit limit.

A number of companies show a negative, or overdrawn, cash balance at year end as a result of using their line of credit. This amount is usually termed **bank indebtedness**, **bank overdraft**, or **bank advances**. No special entry is required to record the overdrawn amount. The normal credits to cash will simply accumulate and be reported as a current liability with suitable note disclosure. Interest is usually charged on the overdrawn amount at a floating rate, such as prime plus,[1] and payable monthly.

STUDY OBJECTIVE 2

Explain the accounting for various current liabilities.

[1] Prime is the interest rate that banks charge their best customers. This rate is usually increased by a specified percentage that reflects the risk profile of the company.

An extract from a recent annual report of Andrés Wines shows how bank indebtedness is reported. They do not report any current asset cash balance. Instead, they present a current liability related to cash:

Illustration 11-1

Disclosure of bank indebtedness

ANDRÉS WINES LTD.	
LIABILITIES	
CURRENT LIABILITIES	
Bank indebtedness (Note 4)	1,065,677

Note 4 adds that Andrés has a $24 million operating line of credit, with accounts receivable and inventories that serve as collateral for this demand loan.

Notes Payable

The line of credit described above is similar to a note payable. Notes payable are obligations in the form of written promissory notes. In Chapter 8, Illustration 8-7, a promissory note was exhibited. To the payee of the note, Wilma Company, this was a note receivable; to the maker of the note, Fred Company, it was a note payable. Notes payable are the inverse of notes receivable, and the accounting is similar.

Notes payable are often used instead of accounts payable. This gives the lender written documentation of the obligation in case legal action is needed to collect the debt. Notes payable usually require the borrower to pay interest, and are frequently issued to meet short-term financing needs.

Notes are issued for varying periods. **Those due for payment within one year of the balance sheet date are classified as current liabilities.** Most notes are interest bearing. To illustrate the accounting for notes payable, assume that the Caisse Populaire agrees to lend $100,000 on March 1, 1999, to Chek Lap Kok Co. through a $100,000, 6%, note payable due June 27, 1999, 120 days hence. Chek Lap Kok Co. will receive $100,000 cash and make the following journal entry:

March 1	Cash	100,000	
	Notes Payable		100,000
	(To record issuance of 6% note due June 27 to the Caisse Populaire)		

Interest accrues over the life of the note, and must be recorded periodically. If Chek Lap Kok Co. prepares financial statements quarterly, an adjusting entry is required to recognize interest expense and interest payable of $493.15 ($100,000 x 6% x 30/365) at March 31. The adjusting entry is:

March 31	Interest Expense	493.15	
	Interest Payable		493.15
	(To accrue interest for one month on Caisse Populaire note)		

Helpful hint The account Interest Expense relates to notes payable, while Interest Revenue relates to notes receivable.

In the March 31 financial statements, the current liability section of the balance sheet will show notes payable of $100,000 and interest payable of $493 (rounded for financial statement presentation). In addition, interest expense of $493 will be reported under Other Expenses and Losses in the income statement.

At maturity (June 27), Chek Lap Kok Co. must pay the face value of the note ($100,000) plus $1,972.60 interest ($100,000 x 6% x 120/365). But first the interest must be brought up to date for the preceding three months, since interest was last recorded on March 31 ($1,479.45 = $100,000 x 6% x 90/365). The entries to record the accrual of interest and payment of the note and accrued interest follow:

June 27	Interest Expense	1,479.45	
	Interest Payable		1,479.45
	(To accrue interest for April, May, and June)		
	Notes Payable	100,000.00	
	Interest Payable ($493.15 + $1,479.45)	1,972.60	
	Cash ($100,000 + $1,972.60)		101,972.60
	(To record payment of Caisse Populaire note and accrued interest)		

Sales Taxes Payable

As consumers, we are well aware that many of the products we purchase at retail stores are subject to sales taxes. The taxes are expressed as a stated percentage of the sales price. As discussed in Chapter 5, sales taxes may take the form of **goods and services tax (GST)**, **provincial sales tax (PST)**, or **harmonized sales tax (HST)**. Federal GST is assessed at 7% across Canada. Provincial sales tax rates vary as shown in Illustration 11-2 and are subject to change:

Illustration 11-2

Provincial sales tax rates

Province	Provincial Sales Tax Rate
Alberta	0%
British Columbia	7%
Manitoba	7%
Northwest Territories	0%
Ontario	8%
Prince Edward Island	10%
Quebec	7.5%
Saskatchewan	7%
Yukon	0%

In Newfoundland and Labrador, Nova Scotia, and New Brunswick, the PST and GST have been combined into one 15% harmonized sales tax.

The retailer (or selling company) collects the tax from the customer when the sale occurs, and periodically (normally monthly) pays the GST (or HST) collected to the Receiver General of Canada and PST collections to the provincial Minister of Finance or Treasurer, as the case may be. In the case of GST and HST, collections may be offset against payments, in which case only the net amount owing (recoverable) must be paid (refunded).

The amount of the sale and the amount of the sales tax collected are usually rung up separately on the cash register. The cash register readings are then used to credit Sales and Sales Taxes Payable. For example, assuming that the March 25 cash register readings for Comeau Company show sales of $10,000, federal sales taxes of $700 (7% GST rate), and provincial sales taxes of $1,000 (sales tax rate of 10%), the entry is:

Case in point Watch as sales are rung up at local retailers, to see whether the sales tax is computed separately.

March 25	Cash	11,700	
	Sales		10,000
	GST Payable		700
	PST Payable		1,000
	(To record daily sales and sales taxes)		

When the taxes are remitted to the Receiver General and Minister of Finance/Treasurer, GST and PST (or HST) Payable is debited and Cash is credited. The company does not report sales taxes as an expense; it simply forwards the amount paid by the customer to the government. Thus, Comeau Company serves only as a **collection agent** for the respective government. In fact, some governments regard sales taxes as funds held in trust by companies that collect them.

Some businesses account for their sales on a tax-inclusive basis—they do not separate sales taxes from the price of the goods purchased. When this occurs, sales taxes must still be recorded separately from sales revenues. To determine sales, total receipts can be divided by 100% plus the sales tax percentage. To illustrate, assume that, in the above example Comeau Company records total receipts of $11,700. Because the amount received from the sale is equal to 100% of the sales price plus 17% (7% + 10%) of sales, or 1.17 times the sales total, we can compute sales as follows:

$$\$11,700 \div 1.17 = \$10,000$$

Helpful hint In Quebec the PST is called QST and both the GST and the QST are sent to the provincial Minister of Finance.

Thus, the sales tax amounts of $700 and $1,000 are found by either: (1) subtracting sales from total receipts ($11,700 – $10,000), or (2) multiplying sales by the respective sales tax rates ($10,000 × 7% and $10,000 × 10%).

In some provinces, PST is charged on GST. For example, in Quebec a $100 sale would include $7 GST (7%) and $8.02 PST [($100 + $7) × 7.5%]. The escalated sales tax rate is 15% [($7 + $8.02) ÷ $100] rather than the anticipated 14.5% (7% GST + 7.5% PST). It is important to be careful when extracting sales tax amounts from total receipts because of the varying rate combinations that may be in use.

►Accounting in Action ► *Business Insight*

Sales taxes do not apply exclusively to retail companies. They also apply to other types of businesses, such as manufacturing companies, service companies, and public utilities. The extent and complexity of the taxes has increased so much that Canada now has the dubious distinction of having one of the world's most complicated sales-tax systems. Some movement was made to embrace the principles of a single rate, a common base, and one administration with the institution of the HST in several Atlantic Canada provinces in 1997. However, much more work needs to be done. Catherine McCutcheon, Tax Partner and Head of Arthur Andersen's Commodity Tax Practice, comments: "We have a patchwork of complex sales-tax systems in Canada. What we need is consistency across the country. Only with uniformity and simplicity will we be able to realize the projected cost savings of $100 million for provincial governments and between $400 and $700 million for business."

Corporate Income Taxes Payable

Case in point Revenue Canada collects more than $12 billion of income tax from corporations each year.

For many corporations, income tax can be a significant cash outflow. The combined federal and provincial income tax rate averages 45% of income for large businesses and 20% for small businesses. Income taxes are calculated annually based on the income of the corporation, but must be paid monthly. Therefore, the year end current liability on the balance sheet is usually much less than the income tax expense that is reported for the period on the income statement. Most small businesses have three months (two months for larger companies) after year end to pay any balance due without penalty (or to request any refund), and six months after their fiscal year end to file their completed income tax return, called a T2.

The final determination of income tax expense and liability (or receivable) usually results in an adjusting entry. Assume that Landriault Ltée. expects to earn $150,000 of taxable income. At a 20% tax rate, their estimated income taxes will be $30,000. Landriault pays monthly instalments to Revenue Canada in the amount of

$2,500. At year end, Landriault actually reports taxable income of $200,000. The total tax liability is therefore $40,000 ($200,000 x 20%). If Landriault has already recorded and remitted $30,000 of tax, the required adjusting entry will be:

Income Tax Expense	10,000	
Income Tax Payable		10,000
(To adjust estimated income tax expense to actual)		

Landriault's income statement will report income tax expense in the amount of $40,000, and the balance sheet will report a current liability, due three months after year end, of $10,000.

Unearned Revenues

A magazine publisher such as Macleans may receive a customer's cheque when magazines are ordered, while an airline such as Canadian Airlines may receive cash when it sells tickets for future flights. How do these companies account for unearned revenues that are received before goods are delivered or services are rendered?

1. When the unearned revenue is received, Cash is debited, and a current liability account identifying the source of the unearned revenue is credited.
2. When the revenue is earned, the unearned revenue account is debited, and an earned revenue account is credited.

To illustrate, assume that Superior University sells 1,000 season hockey tickets at $200 each for its 25-game home schedule. The entry for the sales of season tickets is:

Sept. 6	Cash	200,000	
	Unearned Hockey Ticket Revenue		200,000
	(To record sales of 1,000 season tickets)		

Unearned Hockey Ticket Revenue is reported as a current liability in the balance sheet. As revenue is earned, a transfer from unearned revenue to earned revenue occurs. As each game is completed, Superior makes the following entry to recognize 1/25 of the revenue:

Sept. 25	Unearned Hockey Ticket Revenue	8,000	
	Hockey Ticket Revenue		8,000
	(To record hockey ticket revenues earned)		

Unearned revenue is significant for some companies. In the airline industry, tickets that are sold for future flights can represent an important proportion of total current liabilities. At Canadian Airlines, advance ticket sales recently totalled $201.4 million, or 26% of its current liabilities.

Current Maturities of Long-Term Debt

Companies often have a portion of long-term debt that comes due in the current year. For example, assume that Wynneck Construction issues a five-year, $25,000 note payable on January 1, 1999. This note specifies that each January 1, starting January 1, 2000, $5,000 of the note should be paid. When financial statements are prepared on December 31, 1999, $5,000 should be reported as a current liability and $20,000 as a long-term liability.

It is not necessary to prepare an adjusting entry to recognize the current maturity of long-term debt, if the proper statement classification of each liability account is recognized when the balance sheet is prepared.

Financial Statement Presentation

As indicated in Chapter 4, current liabilities are the first category under liabilities on the balance sheet. Each of the principal types of current liabilities is listed within the category. In addition, the terms of operating lines of credit, notes payable, and other information concerning the individual items are disclosed in the notes to the financial statements.

Current liabilities are usually listed in **order of liquidity**, by maturity date. In reality, though, it is often difficult to determine which specific obligations should be listed in which order. A more common, and entirely satisfactory, method of presenting current liabilities is to list them by **order of magnitude**, with the largest obligations first. Many companies, as a matter of custom, show bank loans, notes payable, and accounts payable first, regardless of amount. The following excerpt from a recent balance sheet of Cominco Ltd., a natural resource company headquartered in Vancouver, illustrates this practice:

Illustration 11-3

Balance sheet presentation of current liabilities

Helpful hint For another example from a current liability section, refer to the Second Cup balance sheet in Appendix A.

COMINCO LTD.	
Current Liabilities (thousands)	
Bank loans and notes payable	$ 38,621
Accounts payable and accrued liabilities	279,772
Income and resource taxes	10,108
Long-term debt due within one year	77,893
	406,394

ontingencies

....

STUDY OBJECTIVE
·········· **3** ··········
Describe the accounting and disclosure requirements for contingencies.

The examples of current liabilities in the preceding section are **definitely determinable**, with no uncertainty about their existence, amount, or timing. Other liabilities, however, depend upon the occurrence or non-occurrence of a future event. This event confirms either the existence of the liability, the amount payable, the payee, and/or the date payable. These are called **contingent losses** or **contingent liabilities**.

A contingency exists when it is not known if a current situation will result in a gain or loss. Although contingent gains exist, contingent losses are far more common. *Financial Reporting in Canada* reports that 60% of the 200 public companies surveyed disclosed contingent losses. No company reported only contingent gains, although 6% disclosed both contingent gains and contingent losses.

Contingent Losses

With notes payable, interest payable, accounts payable, and sales taxes payable, we know that an obligation exists to make payment. We know how much is owed and when it is due. But suppose your company is currently involved in a dispute with Revenue Canada over the amount of the company's income tax liability. Do you have to report the disputed amount on the balance sheet as a liability? Or suppose your company is the defendant in a lawsuit in which an adverse decision might result. How should this situation be reported?

The answers to these questions are difficult, because these liabilities are dependent—contingent—upon some future event. In other words, a contingent loss is a potential liability that may become an actual liability in the future. The principle of **conservatism** requires that loss contingencies be accrued by a debit to an expense account and a credit to a liability account if **both of the following conditions are met:**

1. The loss is **likely** (the chance of occurrence is high); and
2. The amount of the loss can be **reasonably estimated**.

►Accounting in Action ► *Business Insight*

 An interesting example of a contingent loss is frequent flyer points that are accumulated for free air travel. Frequent flyer award programs are so popular that North American airlines are estimated to owe participants nearly 26 million domestic round-trip tickets, at a typical cost of 25,000 points. That's enough to fly more than 1 trillion kilometres. Other, less conservative, estimates range as high as 5 trillion. To the airlines, any of these estimates are significant potential liabilities. They know they owe it, and to whom, but they don't know when—or even if—the points will be redeemed.

Source: Globe and Mail, February 25, 1997, C12.

Recording a Contingent Loss

Product warranties are a good example of a contingent loss that should be recorded in the accounts. Warranty contracts may lead to future costs for replacement or repair of defective units without charge to the customer, for a specified period of time after the product is sold. Generally, a manufacturer such as Black & Decker knows that some warranty costs will be incurred. Moreover, on the basis of prior experience with the product (or similar products), the company usually can make a reasonable estimate of the anticipated cost of servicing (honouring) the warranty.

The accounting for warranty costs is based on the **matching principle**. To comply with this principle, **the estimated cost of honouring product warranty contracts should be recognized as an expense in the period in which the sale occurs**. To illustrate, assume that in 1999 Hermann Manufacturing Company sells 10,000 washers and dryers at an average price of $600. The selling price includes a one-year warranty on parts. Based on past experience, it is expected that 500 units (5%) will be defective, and that warranty repair costs will average $100 per unit. In the year of sale, warranty contracts are honoured on 300 units at a total cost of $30,000.

At December 31, it is necessary to accrue the estimated warranty costs on the 1999 sales. The computation is as follows:

Number of units sold	10,000
Estimated rate of defective units	× 5%
Total estimated defective units	500
Average warranty repair cost	× $100
Estimated product warranty liability	**$50,000**

Helpful hint Another example of a contingent loss is toxic waste. Corporations have increasingly been held liable for toxic waste cleanup. Some expect that insurance will cover these costs, but insurance companies are arguing that: (1) intentional discharges are not covered, and (2) general liability policies were never meant to cover this type of situation.

Helpful hint The balance in Warranty Expense is always the estimated expense that arises from the sales of that period. In terms of matching, the effects are the same as if the percentage of sales method were used to estimate uncollectible accounts receivable.

The adjusting entry, therefore, is:

Dec. 31	Warranty Expense	50,000	
	Estimated Warranty Liability		50,000
	(To accrue estimated warranty costs)		

The entry to record repair costs incurred in 1999 to honour warranty contracts on 1999 sales is shown in summary form below:

Jan. 1– Dec. 31	Estimated Warranty Liability	30,000	
	Repair Parts / Wages Payable		30,000
	(To record honouring of 300 warranty		
	contracts on 1999 sales)		

Warranty expense of $50,000 is reported under selling expenses in the income statement, and the estimated warranty liability of $20,000 ($50,000 - $30,000) is classified as a current liability on the balance sheet.

In the following year, all expenses incurred to honour warranty contracts on 1999 sales should be debited to Estimated Warranty Liability. To illustrate, assume that 20 defective units are replaced in January 2000, at an average cost of $100 in parts and labour. The summary entry for the month of January 2000 is:

Jan. 31	Estimated Warranty Liability	2,000	
	Repair Parts / Wages Payable		2,000
	(To record honouring of 20 warranty		
	contracts on 1999 sales)		

Disclosure of Contingent Losses

When a contingent loss is **likely** but cannot be reasonably estimated, or if it is not determinable—neither likely nor unlikely—only disclosure of the contingency is required. Examples of contingencies that may require disclosure are pending or threatened lawsuits, threat of expropriation of capital assets, and loan guarantees. If a contingency is **unlikely**—the chance of occurrence is slight—disclosure is desirable if the event could have a substantial negative effect on the financial position of the company.

The disclosure should identify the nature of the item and, if known, the amount of the contingency and the expected outcome of the future event. Disclosure of the potential liability is usually accomplished through a note to the financial statements, as illustrated by the following:

Illustration 11-4

Disclosure of contingent loss

Canadian Airlines Corporation
14. Contingencies
The Corporation and its subsidiaries are involved in a number of legal proceedings. In the opinion of the Corporation's counsel, no significant liabilities are expected to arise from these proceedings.

Contingent Gains

Examples of contingent gains include refunds from Revenue Canada which may result from an income tax reassessment, or potential legal action which is likely to occur in your favour. Gain contingencies are treated even more conservatively than loss contingencies—they are simply not recognized. They are not recorded until cash or other resources are realized.

Contingent gains that are **likely** should be disclosed in the notes to the financial statements. No disclosure is required for gain contingencies that are **unlikely**; however, disclosure of gain contingencies for which the probability is not determinable may be desirable.

Accounting offers many examples of losses recognized in advance of gains. The rationale used is **conservatism**, to ensure that any negative effect on creditors and investors is reflected in the financial statements. Critics of this inconsistent approach denounce the lack of symmetry in the treatment of gains and losses. Illustration 11-5 summarizes the differing treatment of contingent losses and gains:

Probability of Occurrence	Contingent Loss		Contingent Gain	
	Accrue	Disclose	Accrue	Disclose
Likely and reasonably estimable	X			X
Likely but not estimable		X		X
Neither likely nor unlikely (not determinable)		X		X
Unlikely		X		

Illustration 11-5

Accounting treatment of contingencies

Before You Go On . . .

►Review It

1. What are the two criteria for classifying a debt as a current liability?
2. What entries are made for an interest-bearing note payable?
3. How are sales taxes recorded by a retailer?
4. Identify three examples of unearned revenue.
5. What are the accounting guidelines for contingent losses and gains?

►Do It

You, and several classmates, are studying for the next accounting examination. They ask you to answer the following questions: (1) How is sales tax recorded? (2) When should a contingency be recorded in the accounts?

Reasoning: To answer the first question, you must remember that sales taxes are not revenue; they are monies collected on behalf of the government. To answer the second question, you need to know the criteria for recording and disclosing contingent losses and gains.

Solution:

(1) GST Payable and PST Payable (or HST Payable) are recorded as current liabilities. They are periodically remitted to the government. Sales taxes are calculated at the appropriate percentage(s) of sales, which vary provincially.

(2) A contingent loss should be recorded when it is *likely* to happen and the amount can be *reasonably* estimated. Otherwise, it should be disclosed in a note. A contingent gain is never recorded, but may be disclosed in a note to the statements.

Related exercise material: BE11–1, BE11–2, BE11–3, BE11–4, BE11–5, E11–1, E11–2, E11–3, E11–4, and E11–5.

Payroll Accounting

Payroll and related fringe benefits often add up to a substantial percentage of current liabilities. In addition, employee compensation is often the most significant expense that a company incurs. For example, Air Canada recently reported total employees of 20,035 and labour costs of $1.1 billion, which is 25% of total operating expenses. Add to labour costs employee benefits such as health insurance, dental coverage, life insurance, disability insurance, and so on, and you can see why proper accounting and control of payroll are so important.

It should be emphasized that payroll accounting involves more than paying employees' wages. Companies are required by law to maintain payroll records for each employee, to report and remit payroll deductions, and to respect many provincial and federal laws regarding to employee compensation. Accounting for payroll has become much more complex as a result of these regulations.

The term payroll covers all salaries and wages paid to employees. Managerial, administrative, and sales personnel are generally paid salaries, which are often expressed in terms of a specified amount per month or per year. For example, in the opening story, four of the staff members at the Ottawa International Hostel are paid salaries. In contrast, part-time employees, store clerks, factory employees, and manual labourers are normally paid wages, which are based on a rate per hour or on piecework (such as per unit of product). Frequently, the terms salaries and wages are used interchangeably.

The term payroll does not include payments made for personal service by professionals such as accountants, lawyers, and architects. Such professionals are independent contractors, and payments to them are called **fees**, rather than salaries or wages. This distinction is important, because government regulations relating to the payment and reporting of payroll apply only to employees.

Internal Control

STUDY OBJECTIVE

4

Discuss the objectives of internal control for payroll.

Internal control was introduced in Chapter 7. As applied to payroll, the objectives of internal control are: (1) to safeguard company assets against unauthorized payment of payroll, and (2) to ensure the accuracy and reliability of the accounting records for payroll.

Unfortunately, irregularities often result if internal control is lax. Overstating hours, using unauthorized pay rates, adding fictitious employees to the payroll, keeping terminated employees on the payroll, and distributing duplicate payroll cheques are all methods of stealing from a company. Moreover, inaccurate records will result in incorrect paycheques, financial statements, and payroll reports.

Payroll activities involve four functions: hiring employees, timekeeping, preparing the payroll, and paying the payroll. For an internal control system to work effectively, these four functions should be assigned to different departments or individuals. To illustrate these functions in more detail, we will examine the case of Academy Company and one of its employees, Mark Jordan.

Hiring Employees

In large organizations, the human resources department is responsible for posting job openings, screening and interviewing applicants, and hiring employees. From a control perspective, this department provides important documentation and authorization. When Mark Jordan was hired by Academy Company, the human resources department prepared an authorization form detailing the terms of the position (Shipping Clerk), the approved pay rate ($10 per hour), and other relevant information (e.g., starting date).

Hiring Employees

Human resources department documents and authorizes employment.

The authorization form was then sent to the payroll department, where it was used to place the new employee on the payroll. The human resources department must ensure the accuracy of this form, since one of the most common types of payroll fraud is the addition of fictitious employees to the payroll.

►Accounting in Action ► *Business Insight*

Padding the payroll is not a new idea. In 1930, Abitibi's Sturgeon Falls, Ontario, plant closed. The mill was the only source of employment, and by 1932 the town of Sturgeon Falls was destitute. At that time, employment insurance did not exist but federal and provincial governments paid 85% of welfare relief costs. Civic officials, desperate for relief for their town, padded the welfare payroll with horses. "Owners couldn't buy feed for their horses, so the horses were given jobs by the town," explained one witness to the enquiry commission. One retailer noted, "The town had to have money, and [to avoid starvation] there did not appear to be any other way to get it."

Source: Report of the Royal Commission into Unemployment and Relief at Sturgeon Falls, March 1933.

The human resources department is also responsible for authorizing: (1) changes in pay rates during employment, and (2) terminations of employment. In each instance, the authorization should be in writing, and a copy of the change in status should be sent to the payroll department.

Timekeeping

Another area in which internal control is important is timekeeping. In the opening story, part-time employees at the Ottawa International Hostel use a log book to record their hours. Another means of recording time worked is by "punching" a time clock. The time of arrival and departure are automatically recorded by the employee when he or she inserts a time card into the clock. The time card for Mark Jordan is shown in Illustration 11-6.

Timekeeping

Supervisors monitor hours worked through time cards and time reports.

In large companies, time-clock procedures are often monitored by a supervisor or security guard to make sure an employee punches only one card. At the end of the pay period, the employee's supervisor is required to approve the hours shown by signing the time card. When overtime hours are involved, approval by a supervisor is usually mandatory to guard against unauthorized overtime. The approved time card is then sent to the payroll department. For salaried employees, a manually prepared weekly or monthly time report kept by a supervisor may be used to record time worked.

Illustration 11-6

Time card

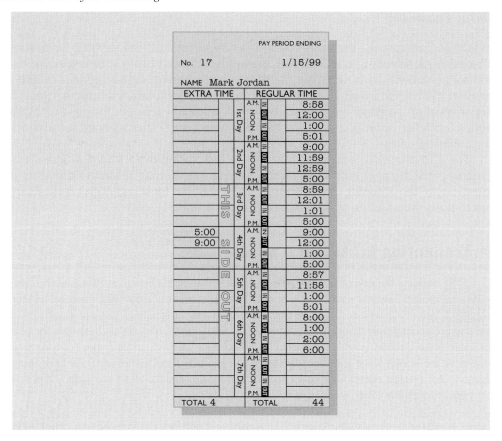

Preparing the Payroll

Preparing the Payroll

Two (or more) employees verify payroll amounts; supervisor approves.

The payroll department uses two sources of input to prepare the payroll: (1) personnel department authorizations, and (2) approved time cards. Because of the numerous calculations involved in determining gross wages and payroll deductions, it is customary for a second payroll department employee, working independently, to verify all amounts, and for a payroll department supervisor to approve the payroll. The payroll department is also responsible for preparing (but not signing) payroll cheques, maintaining payroll records, and preparing payroll reports.

Paying the Payroll

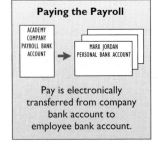

Paying the Payroll

Pay is electronically transferred from company bank account to employee bank account.

The payroll is the responsibility of the controller's department, or an independent payroll service bureau such as the one used by the Ottawa International Hostel. Often, wages and salaries are transferred electronically by means of direct deposit to each employee's bank account. The controller (or Comcheq on behalf of the Ottawa International Hostel) provides the bank with a list of individual payroll amounts to be posted to each employee's account. The bank withdraws (credits) the total payroll amount from the company's bank account and deposits (debits) each employee's pay into their own personal bank account. **Payment by direct deposit minimizes the risk of errors in cheque preparation**. It is also cost effective and very efficient.

   If payroll cheques are used, payroll cheques should be prenumbered and accounted for to maintain good internal control. Cheques must be signed by the controller (or a designated agent), and their distribution to employees should be controlled by the accounting department. Cheques may be distributed by the controller or a designated paymaster.

   If the payroll is paid in currency, it is customary for a second person to be designated to count the cash in each pay envelope, and for the paymaster to obtain a signed receipt from the employee upon payment. Thus, if alleged discrepancies arise, adequate safeguards exist to protect each party involved.

►Accounting in Action ► *Business Insight*

 Payroll processing is considered by many business owners to be a tedious and painful chore fraught with legal and tax headaches. As a result, service bureaus that process payrolls are very popular. One such example is Ceridian Corporation, a global leader in payroll services. They issue over 100 million payroll cheques a year for companies such as the CIBC and the TD Bank.

Companies appreciate the advantages that service bureaus such as Ceridian offer—relatively low cost, simplicity, confidentiality, accuracy, fast turnaround, and up-to-date information changes in payroll deduction rates and regulations.

Determining Employee Payroll Costs

Determining the payroll costs for employees involves computing: (1) gross earnings, (2) payroll deductions, and (3) net pay.

STUDY OBJECTIVE
········· **5** ·········
Compute the payroll for a pay period.

Gross Earnings

Gross earnings are the total compensation earned by an employee. There are three major types of gross earnings, or pay: wages, salaries, and bonuses.

Total **wages** for an employee are determined by multiplying the hours worked by the hourly rate of pay. In addition to the hourly pay rate, most companies are required by law to pay hourly workers a minimum of one and one-half times the regular hourly rate for overtime work in excess of 44 hours per week. Moreover, many employers pay overtime rates for work done at night, on weekends, and on holidays.

Assume that Mark Jordan's authorized pay rate is $10 per hour. The computation of Mark's gross earnings (total wages) for the 48 hours shown on his time card for the weekly pay period ending January 15 is as follows:

Case in point StatsCan recently reported that nearly 20% of Canadian employees worked overtime. About 60% of those did so without additional pay. Unpaid overtime for teachers was the highest of any occupation.

Illustration 11-7

Computation of total wages

Type of Pay	Hours	×	Rate	=	Gross Earnings
Regular	44	×	$10	=	$440
Overtime	4	×	15	=	60
Total wages					**$500**

This computation assumes that Jordan receives one and one-half times his regular hourly rate ($10 x 1.5) for his overtime hours. Union contracts often require that overtime rates be as much as twice the regular rates.

The **salary** for an employee is generally based on a monthly or yearly rate, rather than on an hourly rate. These rates are then applied to the payroll periods used by the company. Most executive and administrative positions are salaried and do not receive overtime pay. At the Ottawa International Hostel, overtime does not apply to the full-time staff.

Many companies have bonus agreements for management personnel and other employees. Bonus arrangements may be based on such factors as increased sales or net income. Bonuses may be paid in cash and/or by granting executives and employees the opportunity to acquire shares of stock in the company at favourable prices (called stock option plans). Bonuses have become very lucrative, as companies attempt to retain the services of key executives—so lucrative, in fact, that they have come under intense public scrutiny.

Case in point Bonuses to CEOs in Canada averaged 56% of their salary in a recent year.

▶Accounting in Action ▶ *Business Insight*

Robert Gratton, CEO of Power Financial Corp., led the 1997 salary stakes with more than $27 million in executive compensation. Of this amount, less than $1.8 million was salary and $2 million was in the form of a bonus. The remainder consisted of stock options and other perks. Compare this to the average pay earned by CEOs in 1997 in Canada, $660,000; the US, $1.4 million; in Japan, $600,000; and in Brazil, $1 million. And, for a reality check, note that it would take the average Canadian employee, earning $30,000 a year, 900 years to earn as much as Robert Gratton earned in one year.

Source: Report on Business Magazine, July 1998, 88.

Payroll Deductions

As anyone who has received a paycheque knows, gross earnings are usually very different from the amount actually received. The difference is attributable to payroll deductions. **Employee payroll deductions do not result in an expense to the employer.** The employer is only a collection agency, and it subsequently transfers the deductions to the government or other agency (such as an insurance company or the United Way). The designated collection agency for the federal government is known as the **Receiver General**, a division of Revenue Canada.

Payroll deductions may be mandatory or voluntary. The former are required by law and include Canada Pension Plan (CPP) contributions, employment insurance (EI premiums), and personal income taxes. The latter are at the option of the employee. Illustration 11-8 summarizes the types of payroll deductions:

Illustration 11-8

Payroll deductions

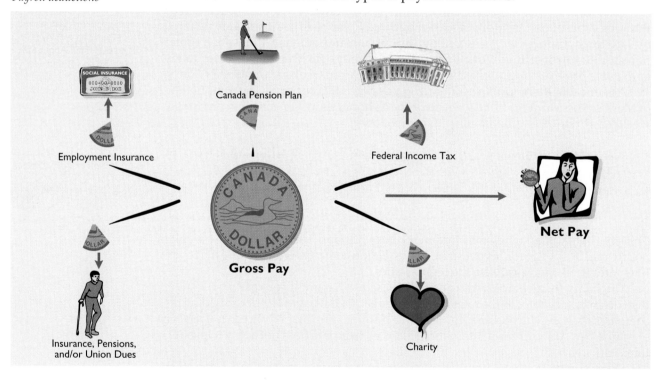

Canada Pension Plan.   All employees between the ages of 18 and 70, except those employed in the Province of Quebec, must contribute to the Canada Pension Plan (CPP). Quebec administers its own, similar program, the **Quebec Pension Plan (QPP)**. These plans provide supplemental disability, retirement, and death benefits to qualifying Canadians.

The contribution rates and pensionable earnings amounts are set by the federal government, and change intermittently. At the time of this writing, employee contributions under the *Canada Pension Plan Act* were 3.2% of pensionable earnings. Pensionable earnings deduct a basic yearly exemption ($3,500) and impose a maximum ceiling ($36,900), which change annually. The exemption and ceiling are prorated to the relevant pay period; that is, they may be applied weekly (/52), bi-weekly (/26), or monthly (/12).

Mark Jordan's CPP contributions for the weekly pay period ending January 15 are $13.85, calculated as follows:

> Pay period: Weekly
> Earnings: $500
> Basic yearly CPP exemption: $3,500
> Prorate basic exemption per week: $3,500 ÷ 52 = $67.31
> Weekly deduction: $500 − $67.31 = $432.69 × 3.2% = $13.85

In addition to withholding employee deductions to remit to the Receiver General, companies must contribute on behalf of their employees. We will discuss the employer's contributions later in this chapter.

Employment Insurance.   The Canada Pension Plan applies to all employees, whether self-employed or employed by others. Employment insurance, however, is paid, or collected by, only those employees who are not self-employed. **Employment insurance (EI)** is designed to provide income protection for a limited period of time to employees who are temporarily laid off, who are on parental leave, or who lose their jobs. EI also provides support measures to help the unemployed get jobs. As with the CPP, the benefits are financed by premiums taken from employees', and employers', earnings.

Under provisions of the *Employee Insurance Act*, the employer is currently required to pay a premium of 2.7% on insured earnings, to a maximum earnings ceiling of $39,000. In most cases, insured earnings are gross earnings plus any taxable benefits. There is no specified yearly exemption. The employment insurance premium for Mark Jordan for the January 15 payroll is $13.50 ($500 x 2.7%).

Personal Income Taxes.   In accordance with the *Income Tax Act*, employers are required to withhold income taxes from employees each pay period. The amount to be withheld is determined by three variables: (1) the employee's gross earnings, (2) the number of credits claimed by the employee for herself or himself, his or her spouse, and other dependents, and (3) the length of the pay period. To indicate to Revenue Canada the number of credits claimed, the employee must complete a Personal Tax Credits Return (TD1). There is no limit on the amount of gross earnings subject to income tax withholdings. The higher the earnings, the higher the amount of taxes withheld.

The calculation of personal income tax withholdings is complicated. The best way to determine how much should be withheld from an employee's wages for federal and provincial income taxes is to use payroll deductions tables supplied by Revenue Canada.

Payroll Deductions Tables.   **Payroll deductions tables** indicate the amount of income tax that should be withheld from gross wages based on the number of credits claimed. Separate tables are provided for weekly, bi-weekly, semi-monthly, and monthly pay periods, and vary by province. The portion of the withholding tables for Mark Jordan (assuming he earns $500 per week) is shown in Illustration 11-9. For a weekly salary of $500 with claim code 4, the federal and New Brunswick provincial income taxes to be withheld are $76.20.

Helpful hint   If CPP contributions remain at their current levels, the plan will go bankrupt by 2015.

Case in point   Combined federal and provincial personal income tax rates range approximately from 25% to 50%, depending on the province of residence.

New Brunswick Federal and Provincial Tax Deductions Weekly (52 pay periods a year)											Nouveau-Brunswick Retenues d'impôt fédéral et provincial Hebdomadaire (52 périodes de paie par année)

Pay Rémunération		If the employee's claim code from the TD1(E) form is Si le code de demande de l'employé selon le formulaire TD1 (F) est										
		0	1	2	3	4	5	6	7	8	9	10
From De	Less than Moins de	Deduct from each pay Retenez sur chaque paie										
457.	465.	121.55	86.95	82.70	74.20	65.75	57.25	48.75	40.30	31.80	23.35	14.85
465.	473.	123.65	89.05	84.80	76.30	67.85	59.35	50.85	42.40	33.90	25.45	16.95
473.	481.	125.75	91.15	86.90	78.40	69.95	61.45	52.95	44.50	36.00	27.55	19.05
481.	489.	127.85	93.25	89.00	80.50	72.00	63.55	55.05	46.60	38.10	29.65	21.15
489.	497.	129.95	95.35	91.10	82.60	74.10	65.65	57.15	48.70	40.20	31.75	23.25
497.	505.	132.05	97.40	93.20	84.70	76.20	67.75	59.25	50.80	42.30	33.85	25.35
505.	513.	134.15	99.50	95.30	86.80	78.30	69.85	61.35	52.90	44.40	35.90	27.45
513.	521.	136.25	101.60	97.40	88.90	80.40	71.95	63.45	55.00	46.50	38.00	29.55
521.	529.	138.35	103.70	99.50	91.00	82.50	74.05	65.55	57.10	48.60	40.10	31.65
529.	537.	140.45	105.80	101.60	93.10	84.60	76.15	67.65	59.20	50.70	42.20	33.75

Illustration 11-9

Payroll deductions tables

Canada Pension Plan Contributions Weekly (52 pay periods a year)		
Pay Rémunération		CPP RPC
From–De	To–À	
494.65	494.95	13.68
494.96	495.26	13.69
495.27	495.58	13.70
495.59	495.89	13.71
495.90	496.20	13.72
496.21	496.51	13.73
496.52	496.83	13.74
496.84	497.14	13.75
497.15	497.45	13.76
497.46	497.76	13.77
497.77	498.08	13.78
498.09	498.39	13.79
498.40	498.70	13.80
498.71	499.01	13.81
499.02	499.33	13.82
499.34	499.64	13.83
499.65	499.95	13.84
499.96	500.26	13.85
500.27	500.58	13.86
500.59	500.89	13.87
500.90	501.20	13.88
501.21	501.51	13.89
501.52	501.83	13.90
501.84	502.14	13.91
502.15	502.45	13.92
502.46	502.76	13.93
502.77	503.08	13.94

Employment Insurance Premiums		
Insurance Earnings Rémunération assurable		EI premium Cotisation d'AE
From–De	To–À	
496.86	497.22	13.42
497.23	497.59	13.43
497.60	497.96	13.44
497.97	498.33	13.45
498.34	498.70	13.46
498.71	499.07	13.47
499.08	499.44	13.48
499.45	499.81	13.49
499.82	500.18	13.50
500.19	500.55	13.51
500.56	500.92	13.52
500.93	501.29	13.53
501.30	501.66	1354
501.67	502.03	1355
502.04	502.40	13.56
502.41	502.77	13.57
502.78	503.14	13.58
503.15	503.51	13.59
503.52	503.88	13.60
503.89	504.25	13.61
504.26	504.62	13.62
504.63	504.99	13.63
505.00	505.37	13.64
505.38	505.74	13.65
505.75	506.11	13.66
506.12	506.48	13.67
506.49	506.85	13.68

As CPP and EI vary by wage level and are complicated by minimum and maximum earnings and other caveats, the easiest way to determine these payroll deductions is to use these same tables, furnished by Revenue Canada. As indicated in the tables, CPP and EI contributions are $13.85 and $13.50, respectively. These are the same amounts calculated earlier manually. Whether you calculate employee payroll deductions manually or by using the tables, care should be taken to ensure that you are using the appropriate guide, as rates, exemptions, and other regulations can, and do, change often.

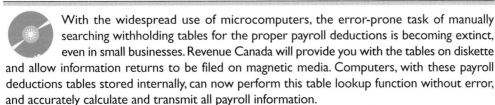

►Technology in Action

With the widespread use of microcomputers, the error-prone task of manually searching withholding tables for the proper payroll deductions is becoming extinct, even in small businesses. Revenue Canada will provide you with the tables on diskette and allow information returns to be filed on magnetic media. Computers, with these payroll deductions tables stored internally, can now perform this table lookup function without error, and accurately calculate and transmit all payroll information.

Voluntary Deductions. Employees may voluntarily authorize withholdings for charitable, retirement, and other purposes. All voluntary deductions from gross earnings should be authorized in writing by the employee. The authorization(s) may be made individually or as part of a group plan. Deductions for charitable organizations such as the United Way, or for financial arrangements such as Canada Savings Bonds and repayment of loans from company credit unions, are made individually. In contrast, deductions for union dues, extended health insurance, life insurance, and pension plans are often made on a group basis. For the purpose of illustration, we will assume that Jordan has voluntary deductions of $10 for the United Way and $5 for union dues.

Net Pay

Net pay is determined by subtracting payroll deductions from gross earnings. For Mark Jordan, net pay for the weekly pay period ending January 15 is $381.45, computed as follows:

Gross earnings		$500.00
Payroll deductions:		
CPP	$13.85	
EI	13.50	
Income taxes	76.20	
United Way	10.00	
Union dues	5.00	118.55
Net pay		$381.45

Illustration 11-10

Computation of net pay

►Accounting in Action ► *International Insight*

It is sometimes a surprise for employees to see how little they take home from their pay, after all the withholdings. Net pay as a percentage of gross pay averages 73% for the Canadian workforce. It is slightly higher for Americans, at 74%, and much higher for Japanese workers, at 84%.

Source: CGA Magazine, May 1997, 41.

Before we learn how to journalize employee payroll costs and deductions, we will turn our attention to specific *employer* payroll costs. After this discussion, we will record the total employee and employer payroll costs for Academy Company.

Employer Payroll Costs

STUDY OBJECTIVE
············ **6** ············
Describe employer payroll costs.

While **employee** payroll deductions do not create an expense for their employers, **employer** payroll contributions do. Payroll costs for businesses and institutions, like the Ottawa International Hostel, result from three costs **levied on employers** by the federal and provincial governments. The federal government mandates CPP and EI employer contributions. The provincial governments mandate employer funding of a Workplace Health, Safety and Compensation Plan. Each of these contributions, plus such items as paid vacations and pensions, are collectively referred to as employee benefits. The cost of these benefits in many companies is substantial. In Air Canada, for example, benefits total 15% of salary and wage costs, and 4% of total operating expenses.

Canada Pension Plan

We have seen that each employee must contribute to the Canada Pension Plan. The employer must also **match** each employee's CPP contribution. The matching contribution results in **payroll** or **employee benefits expense** to the employer. The employer's contributions are subject to the same rate and maximum earnings applicable to the employee. The account, CPP Payable, is used for both the employee's and the employer's CPP contributions.

Employment Insurance

Employers are required to contribute 1.4 times employees' EI deductions during a calendar year. The account EI Payable is used to recognize this liability.

Workplace Health, Safety and Compensation

Helpful hint   CPP and EI premiums are paid by both the employer and the employee. Workers' compensation is paid entirely by the employer.

The Workplace Health, Safety and Compensation Plan provides supplemental benefits for workers who are injured or disabled on the job. The cost of this program is paid entirely by the employer; the employee is not required to make contributions to this plan. Employers are assessed a rate—usually between 1% and 10%—of their gross payroll, after consideration of employee risk of injury and past experience.

Additional Employee Benefits

In addition to the three payroll contributions described above, employers have other substantial employee benefit costs. Two of the most important are paid absences and post-employment benefits. In addition to these, some provinces impose other payroll costs. For example, Ontario has a payroll tax.

Paid Absences.   Employees may have the right to receive compensation for future absences when certain conditions of employment are met. The compensation may pertain to paid vacations, sick pay benefits, and paid holidays. When the payment of such compensation is **probable**, and the amount can be **reasonably estimated**, a liability should be accrued for paid future absences. When the amount cannot be reasonably estimated, the potential liability should be disclosed. Ordinarily, vacation pay is the only paid absence that is accrued; the other types of paid absences are disclosed only in notes to the statements.

Entitlements to paid absences can be large and have thus gained the attention of employers'. Consider the case of an assistant superintendent of schools who worked for 20 years and rarely took a vacation or sick day. A month or so before she retired, the school district discovered that she was due nearly $30,000 in accrued benefits. The liability, however, had never been accrued.

Post-Employment Benefits.   Post-employment benefits are payments by employers to retired or terminated employees, or to employees who are on leave, for: (1) supplemental health care, dental care, and life insurance, and (2) pensions. For many years, the accounting for post-employment benefits was on a pay-as-you-go cash basis, meaning that no expense or liability was accrued in advance. However, both types of post-employment benefits are now accounted for on the accrual basis.

Post-Employment Health Care, Dental Care, and Life Insurance Benefits.   Providing supplemental medical and related health care benefits for retirees and terminees—at one time an inexpensive and highly effective way of generating employee goodwill—has turned into one of corporate Canada's most worrisome financial problems. Runaway medical costs, early retirement, and increased longevity are sending the liability for these benefits through the roof for many companies.

Employers must use the **accrual basis** in accounting for post-employment health-care, dental-care, and life-insurance benefits. It is important to **match** the cost of these benefits with the periods in which the employer benefits from services of the employee.

Pension Plans.   A pension plan is an agreement whereby an employer provides benefits (payments) to employees after they retire or leave the company. The provisions of provincial pension acts establish the minimum contribution that registered companies must make each year. The company uses the accrual basis of accounting in recognizing pension expense for the year. When a company's cash payment to the pension plan is less than the pension expense for the period, the difference between the accrued liability and the amount contributed is reported as a **current liability** in the balance sheet. Pension expense is reported as an **operating expense** in the income statement. Further consideration of the accounting for post-employment benefits and pension plans is left for more advanced courses.

> **Helpful hint**   These costs should be expensed during the working years of the employee, because that is the period during which the company benefits (i.e., the matching principle).

Recording Employer Payroll Costs

The various types of employer payroll costs have been briefly previewed in this section. These costs are usually recorded at the same time as the employee payroll costs. In the following section, we will learn how to record both the employee and employer payroll costs.

Before You Go On . . .
▶Review It

1. Identify two internal control procedures that are applicable to each payroll function.
2. What payroll deductions are: (a) mandatory, and (b) voluntary?
3. What payroll costs are levied on employers?
4. Should the cash or accrual basis of accounting be used in accounting for paid absences and post-employment benefits?

Related exercise material: BE11–6 and BE11–7.

Recording the Payroll

STUDY OBJECTIVE
••••••••••• **7** •••••••••••

*Identify the steps in
recording the payroll.*

Recording the payroll involves maintaining payroll department records, recognizing payroll expenses and liabilities, paying the payroll, and filing and remitting payroll deductions.

Maintaining Payroll Department Records

Employers must provide each employee with a Statement of Remuneration Paid (Form T4), following the end of each calendar year, to file with their personal income tax return. This statement shows employment income, CPP contributions, EI premiums, and income tax deducted for the year, in addition to other voluntary deductions. To produce this statement, an employer must maintain a cumulative record of each employee's gross earnings, deductions, and net pay during the year. The record that provides this information and other essential data is the **employee earnings record**. Mark Jordan's employee earnings record for the month of January is shown in Illustration 11-11, including the pay details computed in Illustration 11-10 for the week ending January 15:

Illustration 11-11

Employee earnings record

ACADEMY COMPANY
Employee Earnings Record
For the Year 1999

Name	Mark Jordan
Social Insurance Number	113-114-468
Date of Birth	December 24, 1962
Date Employed	September 1, 1995
Date Employment Ended	
Job Title	Shipping Clerk

Address	2345 Mifflin Avenue
	Fredericton
	New Brunswick E3B 6K1
Telephone	506-459-3354
E-mail	jordan@nbnet.nb.ca
Claim Code	4

1999 Period Ending	Total Hours	Gross Earnings				Deductions						Payment	
		Regular	Overtime	Total	Cumulative	CPP	EI	Income Taxes	United Way	Union Dues	Total	Net Amount	Cheque #
1/8	46	440.00	30.00	470.00	470.00	12.89	12.69	67.85	10.00	5.00	108.43	361.57	974
1/15	48	440.00	60.00	500.00	970.00	13.85	13.50	76.20	10.00	5.00	118.55	381.45	1028
1/22	47	440.00	45.00	485.00	1,455.00	13.37	13.10	72.00	10.00	5.00	113.47	371.53	1077
1/29	46	440.00	30.00	470.00	1,925.00	12.89	12.69	67.85	10.00	5.00	108.43	361.57	1133
Jan. Total		1,760.00	165.00	1,925.00		53.00	51.98	283.90	40.00	20.00	448.88	1,476.12	

A separate earnings record is kept for each employee and is updated after each pay period. The cumulative payroll data on the earnings record are used by the employer to: (1) determine when an employee has reached the maximum earnings subject to CPP and EI premiums, (2) file information returns with Revenue Canada (as explained later in this section), and (3) provide each employee with a statement of gross earnings and withholdings for the year on the T4 form. In the opening story about the Ottawa International Hostel, Comcheq prepares detailed and summary reports that include employee earnings records.

In addition to employee earnings records, many companies find it useful to prepare a payroll register to accumulate the gross earnings, deductions, and net pay per employee for each pay period. It provides the documentation for preparing a pay cheque for each employee. The payroll register is presented in Illustration 11-12, with the data for Mark Jordan shown in the wages section. In this example, Academy Company's total payroll is $17,210, as shown in the gross pay column:

Illustration 11-12

Payroll register

ACADEMY COMPANY
Payroll Register
For the Week Ending January 15, 1999

Employee	Total Hours	Earnings			Deductions						Paid		Accounts Debited	
		Regular	Overtime	Gross	CPP	EI	Income Taxes	United Way	Union Dues	Total	Net Pay	Cheque #	Office Salaries Expense	Wages Expense
Office Salaries														
Aung, Ng	44	638.00		638.00	18.26	17.23	177.75	15.00		228.24	409.76	998	638.00	
Canton, Matthew	44	649.00		649.00	18.61	17.52	146.40	20.00		202.53	446.47	999	649.00	
Mueller, William	44	583.00		583.00	16.50	15.74	107.45	11.00		150.69	432.31	1000	583.00	
Subtotal		5,200.00		5,200.00	136.03	150.80	1,194.00	120.00		1,600.83	3,599.17		5,200.00	
Wages														
Caton, Rejean	44	440.00	30.00	470.00	12.89	12.69	76.30	18.00	5.00	124.88	345.12	1025		470.00
Jordan, Mark	48	440.00	60.00	500.00	13.85	13.50	76.20	10.00	5.00	118.55	381.45	1028		500.00
Milroy, Lee	47	440.00	45.00	485.00	13.37	13.10	80.50	10.00	5.00	121.97	363.03	1029		485.00
Subtotal		11,000.00	1,010.00	12,010.00	302.60	348.29	2,640.20	301.50	115.00	3,707.59	8,302.41			12,010.00
Total		16,200.00	1,010.00	17,210.00	438.63	499.09	3,834.20	421.50	115.00	5,308.42	11,901.58		5,200.00	12,010.00

Note that this record is a listing of each employee's payroll data for the pay period. In some companies, a payroll register is a journal or book of original entry, and postings are made directly to ledger accounts from the register. In other companies, the payroll register is a supplementary record that provides the data for a general journal entry and subsequent posting to the ledger accounts. In the Academy Company situation, the latter procedure is followed. The main payroll report provided by Comcheq for the Ottawa International Hostel is the payroll register.

►Technology in Action

In addition to the entry to record the payroll, the output for a computerized payroll system would include: (1) a payroll listing to support the electronic funds transfer between the company's bank account and those of its employees, or, alternatively, payroll cheques, (2) a payroll cheque register, sorted by cheque and department, and (3) updated employee earnings records, which become the source for monthly and annual reporting of wages to Revenue Canada.

Recognizing Payroll Expenses and Liabilities

Payroll expenses for employees' payroll costs only exist for salaries and wages and employer's contributions, not for employee deductions. Employee payroll deductions are not an expense to the company, since they have been collected on behalf of the government or other third party. They remain a current liability to the company until remitted.

There are payroll expenses and a related current liability for the employer's share of contributions, to social security programs such as CPP, EI, and workers' compensation—and to other employee benefits, such as vacations or pensions. The following two sections discuss these payroll costs.

Employee Payroll Costs. From the payroll register in Illustration 11-12, a journal entry is made to record the employee portion of the payroll. For the week ending January 15, the entry is:

Jan. 15	Office Salaries Expense	5,200.00	
	Wages Expense	12,010.00	
	CPP Payable		438.63
	EI Payable		499.09
	Income Taxes Payable		3,834.20
	United Way Payable		421.50
	Union Dues Payable		115.00
	Salaries and Wages Payable		11,901.58
	(To record payroll for the week ending January 15)		

Specific liability accounts are credited for the mandatory and voluntary deductions made during the pay period. Separate expense accounts are used for gross earnings, because office workers are on a salary and other employees are paid on an hourly rate. In other cases, there may be additional debits such as Store Salaries and Sales Salaries. The amount credited to Salaries and Wages Payable is the sum of the individual cheques the employees will receive.

Employer Payroll Costs. Employer payroll costs are usually recorded when the payroll is journalized. The entire amount of gross pay ($17,210 = $5,200 + $12,010) shown in the payroll register in Illustration 11–12 is subject to each of the three employer payroll costs mentioned earlier: CPP, EI, and Workers' Compensation. For the January 15 payroll, Academy Company's CPP is $438.63 ($438.63 × 1). Its EI premium is $698.73 ($499.09 × 1.4).

Assume that Academy Company is also assessed workers' compensation at a rate of 1%. Their compensation expense for the week would therefore be $172.10 ($17,210 × 1%). For vacation pay, assume that Academy Company employees accrue vacation days at an average rate of 4% (equivalent to two weeks vacation) of the gross payroll. The accrual for vacation benefits in one pay period—one week—is $688.40 ($17,210 × 4%).

Accordingly, the entry to record the payroll costs or employee benefits associated with the January 15 payroll is:

Jan. 15	Employee Benefits Expense	1,997.86	
	CPP Payable		438.63
	EI Payable		698.73
	Workers' Compensation Payable		172.10
	Vacation Pay Payable		688.40
	(To record employer payroll costs on January 15 payroll)		

Case in point Employee benefits total about 27% of Siemens Canada's payroll.

The liability accounts are classified as current liabilities, since they will be paid within the next year. Employee Benefits Expense is often combined with Salaries and Wages Expense on the income statement, and classified as an operating expense.

Payment of the Payroll

Payment of salaries and wages by cheque is made from either the employer's regular bank account or a payroll bank account. Each cheque is usually accompanied by a detachable **statement of earnings** document that shows the employee's gross earnings, payroll deductions, and net pay.

Following payment of the payroll, the cheque numbers are entered in the payroll register. The entry to record payment of the payroll for Academy Company is as follows:

Jan. 15	Salaries and Wages Payable	11,901.58	
	Cash		11,901.58
	(To record payment of payroll)		

As noted earlier, in many cases payroll cheques are no longer issued. Instead, the amounts are transferred to—or deposited directly into—the employee's bank account. The entry to record the payroll would be the same for the company, whether paid by cheque or by direct deposit.

> **Case in point** Many companies use a separate bank account for payroll. Only the total amount of each period's payroll is transferred, or deposited, into that account prior to distribution. This helps the company determine if there are any unclaimed amounts. This is another example of an imprest fund, first introduced with petty cash in Chapter 7.

Filing and Remitting Payroll Deductions

Preparation of information returns is the responsibility of the payroll department; payment of the deductions is made by the controller's department. Much of the information for the returns is obtained from employee earnings records.

For the purposes of reporting and remitting, companies combine withholdings of CPP, EI, and income tax. **The withholdings must be reported and remitted monthly** on a Statement of Account for Current Source Deductions (Form PD7A), no later than the 15th day of the month following the month's pay period. There are allowable variations from the pattern of monthly remittances. For example, large employers must remit more often, and smaller companies with perfect payroll deduction remittance records can remit quarterly. Workplace Health, Safety and Compensation is remitted quarterly to the Workplace Health, Safety and Compensation Commission. Remittances can be made by mail or through deposits to any Canadian financial institution. When payroll deductions are remitted, payroll liability accounts are debited and cash is credited.

Other information returns must be filed by the last day of February each year. In addition, as noted previously, employers must provide employees with a Statement of Remuneration Paid, T4, by the same date.

> **Alternative terminology** The commission is known as the Workers' Compensation Board (or similar) in some provinces.

►Accounting in Action ► *Ethics Insight*

The owner of a newly restored Victorian hotel, nestled in a small town, skipped payment of withholding taxes for three quarters because of cash-flow problems. Before long, he received a call from Revenue Canada. After months of haggling, the hotel owner was told that unless he paid the amount owed, Revenue Canada would be forced to liquidate the hotel, land, and dozens of antiques in the inn, which had taken him and his wife years to acquire.

As this story indicates, cash-hungry small businesses are often tempted to skip or delay payment of withholding taxes. Increasingly, Revenue Canada is cracking down on such cheaters. Penalties for late payment or nonpayment can be devastating. Penalties equal 10% of withholdings owed for deductions not remitted. Interest is also charged from the day the payment was due. And in cases where the failure to remit was done knowingly, penalties of 20% can be applied, with interest added, to the unpaid balance. Under extreme cases, the government can padlock the doors, seize assets, and hold the officers, directors, or certain other employees personally responsible for the penalties.

What happened to the hotel owner? Rather than lose years of hard work, he is now working on a repayment plan.

Before You Go On . . .

▶ *Review It*

1. What account titles are used to record employee payroll costs, assuming only mandatory payroll deductions are involved?
2. What account titles are used in recording employer payroll costs?

▶ *Do It*

On February 15, the payroll supervisor determines that the bi-weekly gross earnings in the Rebagliati Company are $70,000. Employee deductions include $2,030 CPP, $2,065 EI, $17,500 personal income taxes, and $1,000 dental insurance. You are asked to record the employee and employer payroll costs for this period, and the payment of all payroll liabilities. For the employer's payroll contributions, there is no Workplace Health, Safety and Compensation Plan, pension plan, or vacation pay to record at this point.

Reasoning: For the employee payroll costs, the gross payroll forms the expense. The total salaries and wages liability to employees is reduced by employee deductions, each of which forms its own liability. They are later paid to various collecting agencies on behalf of the employees.

In recording employer contributions, you should remember that the employer only has responsibility for the company's share of CPP and EI. They must match the employee's CPP contributions and contribute 1.4 times the employee's EI premiums. The employer also has full responsibility for any Workplace Health, Safety and Compensation. In this case, however, there is none.

Solution:

The entry to record the employees' payroll costs is:

Feb. 15	Salaries and Wages Expense	70,000	
	CPP Payable		2,030
	EI Payable		2,065
	Income Taxes Payable		17,500
	Dental Insurance Payable		1,000
	Salaries and Wages Payable		47,405
	(To record payroll for the bi-weekly period ending Feb. 15)		

The entry to record the employer's payroll costs is:

Feb. 15	Employee Benefits Expense	4,921	
	CPP Payable ($2,030 x 1)		2,030
	EI Payable ($2,065 x 1.4)		2,891
	(To record employer's payroll costs on Feb. 15 payroll)		

The entry to pay the liabilities, on their respective due dates, is:

	Salaries and Wages Payable	47,405	
	CPP Payable ($2,030 + $2,030)	4,060	
	EI Payable ($2,065 + $2,891)	4,956	
	Income Taxes Payable	17,500	
	Dental Insurance Payable	1,000	
	Cash		74,921
	(To record payment of payroll and related liabilities for the bi-weekly period ending Feb. 15)		

Related exercise material: BE11–8, BE11–9, BE11–10, E11–6, E11–7, E11–8, and E11–9.

▶ *A Look Back at the Ottawa International Hostel*

Refer back to the story about the Ottawa International Hostel at the beginning of the chapter and answer the following questions:

1. In addition to income taxes withheld from employees, what employer payroll costs are remitted by the Hostel to the Receiver General, or other third parties?
2. For each of the four payroll functions, give examples of internal control procedures used by the Ottawa International Hostel.
3. Cheri Gillis definitively states that there is no ghost on the payroll. To what is she referring?

Solution:

1. In addition to the amounts withheld for federal and provincial income taxes, the Ottawa International Hostel must match the Canada Pension Plan contributions withheld from employees, and pay 1.4 times the employees' Employment Insurance premiums. It also pays Workers' Compensation costs.
2. *Hiring*: Contracts are issued to full-time employees, and their pay must be approved by the Board of Directors.

   Timekeeping: A time log is used for hourly employees, although no mention is made of controls used to ensure accurate recording of this log.

   Preparing the payroll: An independent service bureau has the responsibility of preparing and paying the payroll. Comcheq prepares useful reports for review by the Hostel including a payroll record for each employee.

   Paying the payroll: The majority of the payments are made by direct deposit. The few payroll cheques that are generated by Comcheq are distributed directly to employees by a designated employee of the Hostel. This employee would personally know the other employees, because of the small size of the staff.
3. One of the most common types of payroll fraud is the addition of fictitious employees (e.g., a ghost) to the payroll. In a small organization like the Hostel, this is not a very high internal control risk, as all employees are known.

◤ *Summary of Study Objectives*

1. *Explain a current liability and identify the major types of current liabilities.* A current liability is a debt that is likely to be paid: (1) within one year or the operating cycle, whichever is longer, and (2) from existing current assets or through the creation of other current liabilities. The major types of current liabilities are operating lines of credit, notes payable, accounts payable, sales taxes payable, unearned revenues, the current portion of long-term debt, and accrued liabilities such as corporate income taxes, salaries and wages, and interest payable.

2. *Explain the accounting for various current liabilities.* Operating lines of credit assist companies in covering temporary bank overdrafts, and are repayable upon demand. Interest is normally paid and recorded monthly on these demand loans.

When an interest-bearing promissory note payable is issued, interest expense is accrued over the life of the note. At maturity, the amount paid is equal to the face value of the note plus accrued interest.

Sales taxes payable are recorded at the time the related sales occur. The company serves as a collection agent for the taxing authority. Sales taxes are not an expense to the company.

Corporate income taxes are usually estimated in advance, paid monthly, and adjusted to the actual balance owing at year end when taxable income for the year is finalized.

Unearned revenues are initially recorded in an unearned revenue account. As the revenue is earned, a transfer from unearned revenue to earned revenue occurs. The current maturities of long-term debt should be reported as a current liability in the balance sheet.

3. *Describe the accounting and disclosure requirements for contingencies.* Contingent losses: If it is probable that the contingency will happen (if it is likely to occur) and the amount is reasonably estimable, the liability should be recorded in the accounts. However, if the contingency is probable but the amount is not estimable, or if the likelihood is not determinable, then the contingency should be disclosed in the notes to the statements. Contingent gains: Contingent gains that are likely should be disclosed in the notes. Contingent gains are never recorded in advance of realization, due to the principle of conservatism.

4. *Discuss the objectives of internal control for payroll.* The objectives of internal control for payroll are: (1) to safeguard company assets against unauthorized payments of payrolls, and (2) to ensure the accuracy and reliability of the accounting records for payrolls.

5. *Compute the payroll for a pay period.* The computation of the payroll involves gross earnings, payroll deductions, and net pay.

6. *Describe employer payroll costs.* Employer payroll costs consist of CPP, EI, and workers' compensation. These costs are usually accrued at the time the payroll is recorded by debiting Employee Benefits Expense and crediting separate liability accounts for each type of tax. Additional benefits associated with wages are paid absences (paid vacations, sick pay benefits, and paid holidays), and post-employment benefits (health care, dental care, life insurance, and pensions). Both types of benefits should be accounted for on the accrual basis.

7. *Identify the steps in recording the payroll.* In recording employee payroll costs, salaries (or wages) expense is debited for gross earnings, individual tax and other liability accounts are credited for payroll deductions, and salaries (wages) payable is credited for net pay. In recording employer payroll costs, Employee Benefits Expense is debited for the employer's share of CPP, EI, workers' compensation, vacation pay, and any other benefits provided. Each benefit is credited to its respective current liability account.

GLOSSARY

Bonus Compensation to management personnel and other employees, based on factors such as increased sales or net income. (p. 475).

Canada Pension Plan (CPP) Contributions designed to provide workers with supplemental retirement, disability, and death benefits. (p. 476).

Collateral Property pledged as security for a loan. (p. 463).

Contingent gain A potential receivable that may become an actual receivable in the future. (p. 470).

Contingent loss A potential liability that may become an actual liability in the future. (p. 469).

Demand loan A loan repayable on demand by the bank. (p. 463).

Employment insurance (EI) Premiums that provide benefits and assistance for a limited time period to employees when they are no longer employed. (p. 477).

Gross earnings Total compensation earned by an employee. Also known as gross pay. (p. 475).

Net pay Gross earnings less payroll deductions. (p. 479).

Payroll deductions Deductions from gross earnings to determine the amount of a paycheque. (p. 476).

Payroll deductions tables Tables that outline the amount to deduct from an employee's pay for CPP, EI, and income tax. (p. 477).

Payroll register A payroll record that accumulates the gross earnings, deductions, and net pay by employee for each pay period. (p. 482).

Pension plan An agreement whereby an employer provides benefits to employees after they retire. (p. 481).

Post-employment benefits Payments by employers to retired or terminated employees for health and dental care, life insurance, and pensions. (p. 481).

Salaries Specified amounts per month or per year paid to executive and administrative personnel. (p. 472).

Wages Amounts paid to employees based on a rate per hour or on piecework. (p. 472).

DEMONSTRATION PROBLEM

Cornerbrook Company had the following selected transactions:

Feb. 1 Signs a $50,000, 180-day, 9% note payable to the Canadian Imperial Bank of Commerce, receiving $50,000 in cash.

10 Cash register receipts total $43,200, which includes GST of $2,630 and PST of $3,005.

28 The payroll for the month consists of Sales Salaries $32,000 and Office Salaries $18,000. CPP and EI contributions are $1,335 and $1,450, respectively. A total of $8,900 in income taxes is withheld. The salaries are paid on March 1.

28 The following adjustment data are noted:

1. Interest expense has been incurred on the note.

2. Employer payroll costs include CPP and EI, at the rates stated in the chapter. The company also pays for a dental plan for its employees, at a monthly cost of $500.

3. Some sales were made under warranty. Of the units sold under warranty this month, 350 are expected to become defective. Repair costs are estimated to be $40 per unit.

Instructions

(a) Journalize the February transactions.

(b) Journalize the adjusting entries at February 28.

Solution to Demonstration Problem

(a) Feb. 1

Cash		50,000	
Notes Payable			50,000
(Issued 180-day, 9% note to the CIBC)			
10 Cash		43,200	
Sales			37,565
GST Payable			2,630
PST Payable			3,005
(To record sales and sales taxes payable)			
28 Sales Salaries Expense		32,000	
Office Salaries Expense		18,000	
CPP Payable			1,335
EI Payable			1,450
Income Taxes Payable			8,900
Salaries Payable			38,315
(To record February salaries)			

(b) Feb. 28

Interest Expense ($50,000 x 9% x 27/365)		333	
Interest Payable			333
(To record accrued interest for February)			
28 Employee Benefits Expense		3,865	
CPP Payable			1,335
EI Payable (1.4 x $1,450)			2,030
Dental Plan Payable			500
(To record employee benefits costs for February)			
28 Warranty Expense (350 x $40)		14,000	
Estimated Warranty Liability			14,000
(To record estimated product warranty liability)			

Problem-Solving Strategies

1. Employee deductions for CPP, EI, and income tax reduce the Salaries Payable.

2. Employer contributions to CPP, EI, and the dental plan create an additional expense.

3. Warranty costs are expensed in the period in which the sale occurs.

SELF-STUDY QUESTIONS

Answers are at the end of the chapter.

(SO 1) 1. The time period for classifying a liability as current is one year or the operating cycle, whichever is:

   a. longer.
   b. shorter.
   c. probable.
   d. possible.

(SO 1) 2. To be classified as a current liability, a debt must be expected to be paid:

   a. out of existing current assets.
   b. by creating other current liabilities.
   c. within two years.
   d. either (a) or (b).

(SO 2) 3. Julie Gilbert Company borrows $88,500 on September 1, 2000, from the Bank of Nova Scotia by signing an $88,500, 6% note due September 1, 2001. What is the accrued interest at December 31, 2000?

   a. $1,760.
   b. $1,770.
   c. $1,328.
   d. $5,310.

(SO 2) 4. Reeves Company has total proceeds from sales of $4,515. If the proceeds include sales taxes of 15%, the amount to be credited to Sales is:

   a. $4,000.
   b. $3,926.
   c. $5,192.
   d. $3,838.

(SO 3) 5. A contingency should be recorded in the accounts when:

   a. It is probable the contingency will happen but the amount cannot be reasonably estimated.
   b. It is possible the contingency will happen and the amount can be reasonably estimated.
   c. It is probable the contingency will happen and the amount can be reasonably estimated.

   d. It is reasonably possible the contingency will happen but the amount cannot be reasonably estimated.

(SO 3) 6. At December 31, Hanes Company prepares an adjusting entry for a product warranty contract. Which of the following accounts is/are included in the entry?

   a. Miscellaneous Expense.
   b. Estimated Warranty Liability.
   c. Repair Parts/Wages Payable.
   d. Both (a) and (b).

(SO 4) 7. The department that should pay the payroll is the:

   a. Timekeeping department.
   b. Human Resources department.
   c. Payroll department.
   d. Controller's department.

(SO 5) 8. J. Barr earns $14 per hour for a 40-hour week and $21 per hour for any overtime work. If Barr works 45 hours in a week, gross earnings are:

   a. $560.
   b. $630.
   c. $735.
   d. $665.

(SO 6) 9. Employer payroll costs do not include:

   a. Employment Insurance.
   b. Canada Pension Plan.
   c. Income taxes deducted from employees' earnings.
   d. Workers' Compensation.

(SO 6) 10. Which of the following is not an employee benefits expense?

   a. Post-retirement pensions.
   b. Paid absences.
   c. Paid vacations.
   d. Salaries.

QUESTIONS

1. Li Feng believes a current liability is a debt that is likely to be paid in one year. Is Li correct? Explain.

2. St. Lawrence Company obtains $25,000 in cash on July 1 by signing a 9%, 180-day, $25,000 note payable to the National Bank. St. Lawrence's fiscal year ends on September 30. What information should be reported for the note payable in the annual financial statements?

3. (a) Your roommate says, "Sales taxes are reported as expenses in the income statement." Do you agree? Explain.

(b) Hard Walk Café has cash proceeds from sales of $10,700. This amount includes $700 of sales taxes, in the form of GST. Give the entry to record the proceeds.

4. Aurora University sold 1,000 season football tickets at $90 each for its five-game home schedule. What entries should be made: (a) when the tickets were sold, and (b) after each game?

5. What is a contingent loss? Give an example of a contingent loss that is usually recorded in the accounts.

6. Under what circumstances is a contingent loss recorded in the accounts? Under what circumstances is a contingent loss disclosed only in the notes to the financial statements?

7. Under what circumstances is a contingent gain disclosed in the notes to the financial statements? Are there circumstances in which a contingent gain can be recorded in the accounts?

8. You are a newly hired accountant with Steeples Company. On your first day, the controller asks you to identify the main internal control objectives related to payroll accounting. How do you respond?

9. What are the four functions associated with payroll activities?

10. What is the difference between gross pay and net pay? Which amount should a company record as wages or salaries expense?

11. Are the income taxes withheld from employee pay cheques expense for the employer? Explain your answer.

12. Distinguish between the three main types of payroll deductions, and give examples of each.

13. What are the primary uses of the employee earnings record?

14. Identify the main types of employer payroll costs.

15. Identify three additional types of employee benefits commonly associated with employees' compensation.

16. What are paid absences? How are they accounted for?

17. What are the two types of post-retirement benefits? During what years should the employer's costs of these post-retirement benefits be expensed?

18. What have most companies used as the basis of accounting for the employer's cost of post-retirement health-care and life-insurance benefits? What basis is now required? Explain the basic difference between these methods in accounting for post-retirement benefit costs.

BRIEF EXERCISES

BE11–1 Fresno Company has the following obligations at December 31: (a) a note payable for $100,000 due in two years, (b) a 10-year mortgage payable of $200,000, payable in 10 $20,000 annual payments, (c) interest payable of $15,000 on the mortgage, and (d) accounts payable of $60,000. For each obligation, indicate what portion (if any) should be classified as a current liability.

Identify whether obligations are current liabilities.
(SO 1)

BE11–2 Romez Company borrows $60,000, from the bank on July 1, 1998, by signing a $60,000 10% note payable due on July 1, 1999. Prepare the journal entries to record: (a) the proceeds of the note, and (b) accrued interest at December 31, 1998, assuming adjusting entries are made only at the end of the year.

Prepare entries for an interest-bearing note payable.
(SO 2)

BE11–3 Grandy Auto Supply does not segregate sales and sales taxes at the time of sale. The register total for March 16 is $9,975. All sales are subject to 15% Harmonized Sales Tax. Compute the sales tax payable, and make the entry to record the sales and the sales tax payable.

Compute and record sales taxes payable.
(SO 2)

BE11–4 Concordia University sells 3,000 season basketball tickets at $60 each for its 12-game home schedule. Give the entry to record: (a) the sale of the season tickets, and (b) the revenue earned by playing the first home game.

Prepare entries for unearned revenues.
(SO 2)

BE11–5 On December 1, Irma Company introduces a new product that includes a one-year warranty on parts. 1,000 units are sold in December. Management believes that 4% of the units will be defective and that the average warranty costs will be $60 per unit. Prepare the adjusting entry at December 31 to accrue the estimated warranty cost.

Prepare adjusting entry for warranty costs.
(SO 3)

BE11–6 Lukas Company has the following payroll procedures:

1. A supervisor approves overtime work.
2. The Human Resources Department prepares hiring authorization forms for new employees.
3. A second Payroll Department employee verifies payroll calculations.
4. The Controller's Department pays the employees.

Identify the main payroll function for each procedure.

Identify various payroll functions.
(SO 4)

Compute gross earnings and net pay.
(SO 5)

BE11–7   Pat Broka's regular hourly wage rate is $14, and she receives an hourly rate of $21 for work in excess of 40 hours. During a January pay period, Pat works 43 hours. Pat's income tax withholding is $80 and she has no voluntary deductions. Compute Pat Broka's gross earnings and net pay for the pay period.

Record a payroll and payment of wages.
(SO 5, 7)

BE11–8   Data for Pat Broka are presented in BE11–7. Prepare the journal entries to record: (a) Pat's pay for the period, and (b) the payment of Pat's wages. Use January 15 for the end of the pay period and the payment date.

Record employer payroll costs.
(SO 6, 7)

BE11–9   In January, gross earnings in the Nigel Company totalled $50,000, from which $1,375 was deducted for the Canada Pension Plan, $1,450 for Employment Insurance, and $15,300 for income tax. Prepare the entries to record the January payroll, including the employee benefit costs.

Record vacation pay benefits.
(SO 6, 7)

BE11–10   At Welch Company, employees are entitled to one day's vacation for each month worked. In January, 50 employees worked the full month. Record the vacation pay liability for January, assuming the average daily pay for each employee is $120.

EXERCISES

Prepare entries for interest bearing notes.
(SO 2)

E11–1   On May 31, Cairo Company borrows $50,000 and issues a 180-day, 9% note due on November 27.

Instructions

(a) Prepare the entry on May 31.

(b) Prepare the adjusting entry on June 30.

(c) Prepare the entry at maturity, assuming monthly adjusting entries have been made through October 31.

(d) What was the total financing cost (interest expense)?

Journalize sales and sales taxes.
(SO 2)

E11–2   In providing accounting services to small businesses, you encounter the following situations pertaining to cash sales:

1. Nash Company rings up sales and sales taxes separately on its cash register. On April 10, the register totals are sales $25,000, GST $1,750, and PST $1,750.
2. Pontiac Company does not segregate sales and sales taxes. Its register total for April 15 is $13,780, which includes 7% GST and 7% PST.

Instructions

Prepare the entry to record the sales transactions and related taxes for each client.

Journalize unearned subscription revenue.
(SO 2)

E11–3   Westwood Company publishes a monthly sports magazine, *Fishing Preview*. Subscriptions to the magazine cost $24 per year. During November 1999, Westwood sells 6,000 subscriptions, which begin with the December issue. Westwood prepares financial statements quarterly and recognizes subscription revenue earned at the end of the quarter. The company uses the accounts Unearned Subscription Revenue and Subscription Revenue.

Instructions

(a) Prepare the entry in November for the receipt of the subscriptions.

(b) Prepare the adjusting entry at December 31, 1999, to record subscription revenue earned in December of 1999.

(c) Prepare the adjusting entry at March 31, 2000, to record subscription revenue earned in the first quarter of 2000.

Journalize entries regarding warranty costs.
(SO 3)

E11–4   Redland Company sells automatic can openers under a 90-day warranty for defective merchandise. Based on past experience, Redland estimates that 3% of the units sold will become defective during the warranty period. Management estimates that the average cost of replacing or repairing a defective unit is $10. The units sold and units defective that occurred during the last two months of 1999 are as follows:

Month	Units Sold	Units Defective Prior to Dec. 31
November	30,000	600
December	32,000	400

Instructions

(a) Determine the estimated warranty liability at December 31 for the units sold in November and December.

(b) Prepare the journal entries to record the estimated liability for warranties, and the costs (assume actual costs of $10,000) incurred in honouring the 1,000 warranty claims as of December 31.

(c) Give the entry to record the honouring of 500 warranty claims in January, at an average cost of $10 per claim.

E11–5 Paddy O'Day Company has the following liability accounts after posting adjusting entries: Accounts Payable $62,000, Unearned Ticket Revenue $24,000, Estimated Warranty Liability $18,000, Interest Payable $12,000, Mortgage Payable $120,000, short-term Notes Payable $80,000, and Provincial Sales Taxes Payable $10,000.

Prepare the current liabilities section of the balance sheet; comment on liquidity.
(SO 1, 2, 3)

Instructions

(a) Prepare the current liability section of the balance sheet, assuming $30,000 of the mortgage is payable next year.

(b) Comment on Paddy O'Day Company's liquidity, assuming total current assets are $300,000.

E11–6 Rose Reed's regular hourly wage rate is $12, and she receives a wage of 1.5 times the regular hourly rate for work in excess of 40 hours. During a March weekly pay period Rose worked 42 hours. Her gross earnings prior to the current week were $19,000. Rose lives in New Brunswick and has a claim code of 5 for tax deductions. Her only voluntary deduction is for group insurance at $10 per week.

Compute payroll amounts and record payment to employee.
(SO 5, 7)

Instructions

(a) Compute the following amounts for Rose's wages for the current week:

1. Gross earnings.
2. Income tax deduction.
3. Canada Pension Plan contribution.
4. Employment Insurance premium.
5. Net pay.

(b) Record Rose's pay, assuming she is an office worker.

E11–7 Ahmad Company has the following data for the weekly payroll ending January 31.

Prepare payroll register; journalize payroll and employee benefits expense.
(SO 5, 6, 7)

Employee	Hours Worked M T W T F S	Hourly Rate	Income Tax WithHolding	Health Insurance
A. Hope	8 8 9 8 10 0	$10	$ 74	$10
B. Innes	8 8 8 8 8 2	12	87	15
C. Stone	9 10 8 8 9 0	12	118	15

Employees are paid 1.5 times the regular hourly rate for all hours worked in excess of 40 hours per week. Ahmad Company must make payments to the Workers' Compensation Plan equal to 2% of the gross payroll.

Instructions

(a) Prepare the payroll register for the weekly payroll.

(b) Prepare the journal entry to record the payroll and Ahmad's employee benefits.

Compute missing payroll amounts; journalize the payroll and its payment.
(SO 5, 6, 7)

E11–8   Selected data from the February payroll register for Tia Yue Company are presented below, with some amounts intentionally omitted.

Gross earnings:	
Regular	(1)
Overtime	$1,050
Total	(2)

Deductions:	
Canada Pension Plan	303
Employment Insurance	324
Income taxes	(3)
Union dues	139
United Way	300
Total deductions	(4)
Net pay	8,294
Accounts debited:	
Warehouse wages	4,900
Store wages	(5)

Employment Insurance premiums are 2.7% of gross earnings.

Instructions

(a) Fill in the missing amounts.

(b) Calculate the company's contributions for the Canada Pension Plan and Employment Insurance.

(c) Journalize all aspects of the February payroll, and the payment of the payroll.

Prepare journal entries for employee benefits.
(SO 6, 7)

E11–9   Roanoke Company has two benefit plans for its employees:

1. It grants employees two days of vacation for each month worked. Ten employees worked the entire month of March at an average daily wage of $120 per employee.
2. The company provides supplementary medical-care insurance for its employees. The cost is $50 per employee per month, and is paid on the 15th of the following month.

Instructions

Prepare the adjusting entries at March 31.

PROBLEMS

••

Prepare current liability entries, adjusting entries, and balance sheet presentation.
(SO 1, 2, 3)

P11–1   On January 1, 1999, the ledger of Calcutta Company contains the following liability accounts:

Accounts Payable	$42,500
Provincial Sales Tax Payable	5,600
Unearned Service Revenue	15,000

During January the following selected transactions occurred:

Jan.   1 Borrowed $15,000 in cash on a 120-day, 10%, $15,000 note.

       5 Sold merchandise for cash totalling $8,550, which included 7% GST and 7% PST.

   12 Provided services for customers who had made advance payments of $8,000. (Credit Service Revenue.)

   14 Paid the Provincial Treasurer for sales tax collected in December of 1998, $5,600.

   20 Sold 500 units of a new product on credit at $52 per unit, plus 7% GST and 7% PST. This new product is subject to a one-year warranty.

   25 Sold merchandise for cash totalling $12,540, which included sales taxes (7% GST and 7% PST).

Instructions

(a) Journalize the January transactions.

(b) Journalize the adjusting entries at January 31 for: (1) the outstanding note payable, and (2) estimated warranty liability, assuming warranty costs are expected to equal 8% of sales of the new product.

(c) Prepare the current liability section of the balance sheet at January 31, 1999. Assume no change in Accounts Payable.

P11–2 Sure-Value Hardware has four employees who are paid on an hourly basis plus time-and-a-half for all hours worked in excess of 40 a week. Payroll data for the week ended March 15, 1999 are presented below:

Prepare payroll register and payroll entries.
(SO 5, 6, 7)

Employee	Hours worked	Hourly Rate	Income Tax Witholdings	United Way
A. Pima	40	$13.00	$ 90	$5.00
C. Zuni	42	13.00	110	5.00
E. Hopi	44	13.00	142	8.00
G. Mohav	46	13.00	148	5.00

The first three employees are sales clerks (store wages expense) and the other employee performs administrative duties (office wages expense).

Instructions

(a) Prepare a payroll register for the weekly payroll.

(b) Journalize the payroll on March 15, 1999, and the accrual of employee benefits expense.

(c) Journalize the payment of the payroll on March 16, 1999.

(d) Journalize the payment on March 31, 1999, of the amounts payable to Revenue Canada and the United Way.

P11–3 The payroll procedures used by three different companies are described below:

Identify internal control weaknesses in three companies and recommend inprovements.
(SO 4)

1. In Hamid Company, department managers interview applicants and, on the basis of the interview, either hire or reject the applicants. When an applicant is hired, the applicant fills out a TD1 form (for income tax deduction purposes). One copy of the form is sent to the human resources department and one copy is sent to the payroll department, as notice that the individual has been hired. On the copy of the TD1 sent to payroll, the managers manually indicate the hourly pay rate for the new employee.

2. In Lindy Company, each employee is required to mark the hours worked on a time card. At the end of each pay period, the employee must have this time card approved by the department manager. The approved card is then given to the payroll department by the employee. Subsequently, the controller's department pays the employee by cheque.

3. In Selina Company, clock cards and time clocks are used. At the end of each pay period, the department manager initials the cards, indicates the rates of pay, and sends them to payroll. A payroll register is prepared from the cards by the payroll department. Cash equal to the total net pay in each department is given to the department manager, who pays the employees in cash.

Instructions

(a) Indicate the weakness(es) in internal control in each company.

(b) For each weakness, describe the control procedure(s) that will provide effective internal control. Use the following format for your answer:

Weaknesses   **Recommended Procedures**

P11–4 Selected payroll procedures of Chen Wee Company are described below:

Identify internal control weaknesses within a company and recommend improvements.
(SO 4)

1. Employees are required to record hours worked on clock cards by "punching" a time clock. At the end of each pay period, the clock cards are collected by the department manager. The manager prepares a payroll register in duplicate and forwards the original to payroll. In payroll, the summaries are checked for mathematical accuracy and a payroll supervisor pays each employee by cheque.

2. Two clerks in the payroll department divide the payroll alphabetically. One clerk has employees A to L and the other has employees M to Z. Each clerk computes the gross earnings, deductions, and net pay for employees in their section and posts the data to the employee earning records.

3. The payroll cheques are manually signed by the chief accountant and given to the department managers for distribution to employees in their department. The managers are responsible for ensuring that any absent employees receive their cheques.

Instructions

(a) Indicate the weaknesses in internal control.

(b) For each weakness, describe the control procedures that will provide effective internal control. Use the following format for your answer:

Weaknesses   Recommended Procedures

Journalize payroll transactions and adjustments for related costs.
(SO 5, 6, 7)

P11–5   The following payroll liability accounts are included in the ledger of Carlos Costa Company on January 1, 1999:

Canada Pension Plan Payable	$1,324.40
Employment Insurance Payable	1,811.00
Income Taxes Payable	5,400.00
Workers' Compensation Payable	1,954.00
Union Dues Payable	250.00
Canada Savings Bonds Payable	500.00
Vacation Pay Payable	2,420.00

In January, the following transactions occurred:

Jan. 10   Sent a cheque for $250 to the union treasurer, for union dues.

12   Issued a cheque for $8,535.40 to the Receiver General for CPP, EI, and income taxes.

15   Purchased Canada Savings Bonds for employees by writing a cheque for $500.

20   Paid the amount due to the Workers' Compensation Plan.

31   Completed the monthly payroll register, which shows office salaries $14,600, store wages $15,400, CPP withheld $890.50, EI withheld $830.10, income tax withheld $5,850 union dues withheld $275, United Way contributions $300, and net pay $21,854.40.

31   Prepared payroll cheques for the net pay and distributed the cheques to the employees.

At January 31, the company also makes the following accruals pertaining to employee compensation:

1. CPP, in an amount equal to the employees' contributions, and EI, in an amount equal to 1.4 times the employees' contributions.
2. Workers' Compensation Plan: 7% of the gross payroll.
3. Vacation pay: 4% of gross earnings.

Instructions

(a) Journalize the January transactions.

(b) Journalize the adjustments pertaining to employee compensation at January 31.

Prepare entries for payroll and benefit costs; calculate liability balances resulting from payroll transactions and adjustments.
(SO 5, 6, 7)

P11–6   The following payroll liability accounts are included in the ledger of Amora Company on January 1, 1999:

Canada Pension Plan Payable	$1,520.00
Income Tax Withholdings Payable	6,240.00
Employment Insurance Payable	2,133.50
Workers' Compensation Payable	1,754.40
Union Dues Payable	370.00
Canada Savings Bonds Payable	210.00
Vacation Pay Payable	3,171.10
United Way Donations Payable	400.00
Salaries and Wages Payable	0.00

In January, the following transactions occurred:

Jan. 10 Sent a cheque to the union treasurer, for union dues.

   12 Issued a cheque to the Receiver General, for the amounts due.

   17 Issued a cheque to the United Way.

   20 Paid the Workers' Compensation Plan.

   31 Completed the monthly payroll register, which showed office salaries $14,600, store wages $18,400, CPP withheld $1,009, EI withheld $891, Income Tax withheld $6,630, union dues withheld $385, United Way contributions $400, and Canada Savings Bonds deductions $210.

   31 Prepared payroll cheques for the net pay, and distributed the cheques to employees.

At January 31, the company also made the following adjustments pertaining to employee compensation:

   CPP and EI, at the rates specified in the chapter, Workers' Compensation, in an amount equal to 6% of the gross payroll, and vacation pay: 4% of gross earnings.

Instructions

(a) Enter the beginning balances in T accounts, and post the January transactions to them.

(b) Journalize and post the adjustments pertaining to employee compensation at January 31.

(c) Calculate the balances in the payroll liability accounts, as of January 31.

P11–7 For the year ended December 31, 1999, Valley Electric Company reports the following summary payroll data:

Prepare entries for payroll, including employee benefit costs. (SO 5, 6, 7)

Gross earnings:	
Administrative salaries	$180,000
Electricians' wages	370,000
Total	$550,000

Deductions:	
CPP contributions	$ 15,577
Income taxes	122,694
EI contributions	14,250
United Way contributions	13,066
Dental insurance premiums	2,063
Long-term disability insurance	1,375
Company pension plan	17,500
Total	$186,525

Valley Electric Company's payroll costs include: CPP, EI, and Workers' Compensation. The latter amounts to $11,000 for the current year.

In addition, the company matches the employees' contributions to the long-term disability insurance plan and the company pension plan, and pays the entire cost of a medical insurance plan. The latter amounts to $24,400 for the current year.

Instructions

(a) Prepare a summary journal entry, at December 31, for the full year's payroll.

(b) Journalize the entry at December 31 to record the employee benefit costs for the year.

(c) Calculate the company's total payroll—related expense for the year.

P11–8 The following are selected transactions of Eldorado Company. Eldorado prepares financial statements quarterly.

Journalize and post note transactions; show financial statement presentation. (SO 2)

Jan. 12 Purchased merchandise on account from McCoy Company for $15,000, terms n/30.

Feb. 11 Issued a 10%, $15,000 note due April 22 to McCoy Company in payment of account.

Mar. 31 Accrued interest for 48 days on the McCoy note.

Apr. 22 Paid the face value and interest on the McCoy note.

July   17   Purchased equipment from Scottie Equipment by paying $11,000 in cash and signing a 10%, 90-day note for $24,000.

Sept. 30   Accrued interest on the Scottie note.

Oct.   15   Paid the face value and interest on the Scottie note.

Dec.   9   Borrowed $10,000 from the Toronto-Dominion Bank by issuing a 9% note due March 15.

Dec.   31   Recognized interest expense on the Toronto-Dominion Bank note.

Instructions

   (a)   Prepare journal entries for the above transactions and events.

   (b)   Post to the accounts, Notes Payable, Interest Payable, and Interest Expense.

   (c)   Show the balance sheet presentation of Notes Payable and Interest at December 31.

   (d)   What is total interest expense for the year?

Calculate missing payroll amounts; prepare all related journal entries.
(SO 5, 6, 7)

P11–9   Selected data from a payroll register for Czech Company are presented below, in alphabetical order, with some amounts intentionally omitted.

Accounts debited:	
Store wages	$ (1)
Warehouse wages	9,800
CPP deductions	606
EI deductions	(2)
Group insurance plan	400
Income taxes	(3)
Net pay	16,588
Overtime earnings	(4)
Regular earnings	21,900
Total deductions	7,812
Total gross earnings	(5)
Union dues	230
United Way	600

EI premiums are 2.7% of the gross payroll.

Instructions

   (a)   Fill in the missing amounts.

   (b)   Journalize the payroll, including the employer's portion of CPP and EI.

   (c)   Journalize the payment of the payroll to the employees, and the remittance of the amounts due to the Receiver General.

*B*roadening *Your Perspective*

F*INANCIAL* *REPORTING* PROBLEM

Refer to the financial statements of The Second Cup Ltd. and the Notes to Consolidated Financial Statements in Appendix A.

Instructions

Answer the following questions about the company's current and contingent liabilities:

(a) What were The Second Cup's total current liabilities at June 28, 1997? What was the increase/decrease in total current liabilities from the prior year?
(b) What were the components of total current liabilities on June 28, 1997?
(c) Explain why "Deposits" would be considered liabilities.
(d) Does The Second Cup report any contingent liabilities? If so, where are they disclosed?
(e) Explain the nature of The Second Cup's contingent liabilities.
(f) What is the total amount for which The Second Cup is contingently liable under subleases during the five-year period 1998–2002?
(g) Comment on the significance of The Second Cup's contingent liabilities, given your answers to (e) and (f), above.

D*ECISION* CASE

Quicko Processing Company provides word-processing services for clients and students in a university community. The work for clients is fairly steady throughout the year, but the work for students peaks significantly in December and April as a result of term papers, research project reports, and dissertations.

Two years ago, the company attempted to meet the peak demand by hiring part-time help. However, this led to numerous errors and considerable customer dissatisfaction. A year ago, the company hired four experienced employees on a permanent basis, instead of using part-time help. This proved to be much better in terms of productivity and customer satisfaction. However, it has caused an increase in annual payroll costs and a significant decline in annual net income.

Recently, Sue Stone, a sales representative for Hiawatha Services Inc., made a proposal to the company. Under the plan, Hiawatha Services would provide up to four experienced workers at a daily rate of $100 per person for an eight-hour workday. (Hiawatha workers are not available on an hourly basis.) Quicko Processing would have to pay only the daily rate for the workers used.

The owner of Quicko Processing, Denise Denby, asks you, as the company's accountant, to prepare a report on the expenses that are pertinent to the decision. If the Hiawatha plan is adopted, Denise will terminate the employment of two permanent employees who are each earning an average annual salary of $28,000. The remaining permanent employees also each earn an annual income of $28,000. Quicko Processing pays Canada Pension Plan contributions and Employment Insurance premiums, as specified in the chapter, and Workers' Compensation Plan payments equal to 1.5% of the gross payroll. In addition, Quicko Processing pays $40 per month for each employee for medical and dental insurance.

Denise indicates that if the Hiawatha Services plan is accepted, her needs for workers will be as follows:

Months	Number of Workers	Working Days per Month (for each worker)
January–March	2	20
April–May	3	25
June–October	2	18
November–December	3	23

Instructions

(a) Prepare a report showing the total costs associated with maintaining permanent workers versus the payroll expenses associated with adopting the Hiawatha Services plan.
(b) What other factors should Denise consider before finalizing her decision?

COMMUNICATION ACTIVITY

Consider the case of a movie theatre which sells thousands of gift certificates per year. The certificates can be redeemed at any time—they have no expiry date. Some of them are never redeemed (because they are lost or forgotten, for example).

The owner of the theatre has raised a number of questions with respect to the accounting for these gift certificates.

Instructions

Prepare a memorandum to answer the following questions asked by the owner.
   (a) Why is a liability recorded when these certificates are sold? After all, they bring customers into the theatre—where they spend money on snacks and drinks, etc. Why should something which helps generate additional revenue be treated as a liability?
   (b) How should the gift certificates which are never redeemed be treated? At some point in the future, can the liability related to them be eliminated? If so, what type of journal entry would be made?

GROUP ACTIVITY

The following topics are discussed in the section on Accounting for Current Liabilities: (1) operating lines of credit, (2) notes payable, (3) sales taxes payable, (4) corporate income taxes payable, (5) unearned revenues, and (6) current maturities of long-term debt and financial statement presentation.

Instructions

With the class divided into six groups, each group should choose one topic and prepare a presentation to explain to the class the key points about the assigned topic.

ETHICS CASE

Jack Johnson owns and manages the Spicy-Saucer Restaurant, a 24-hour restaurant near the city's medical complex. Jack employs nine full-time employees and 16 part-time employees. He pays all of the full-time employees by cheque, the amounts of which are determined by Jack's public accountant, Clara Hankes. Jack pays all of his part-time employees in cash that he withdraws directly from his cash register. Clara has repeatedly urged Jack to pay all employees by cheque. But, as Jack has told his competitor and friend, Bud MacKenzie, who owns the Tasty Diner, "First of all, my part-time employees prefer the cash over a cheque, and, secondly, I don't withhold or pay any taxes or workers' compensation on those wages, because they go totally unrecorded and unnoticed."

Instructions

   (a) Who are the stakeholders in this situation?
   (b) What are the legal and ethical considerations regarding Jack's handling of his payroll?
   (c) Clara Hankes is aware of Jack's payment of the part-time payroll in cash. What are her ethical responsibilities in this case?
   (d) What internal control principle is violated in this payroll process?

CRITICAL THINKING

►*A Real-World Focus: Ault Foods Limited*

Ault Foods is a major Canadian dairy products company whose brand names include Black Diamond, Sealtest, Häagen-Dazs, Parlour, Cheestrings and Lactantia. Its annual report for the fiscal year ended April 26, 1997, included the following information (with all amounts reported in thousands of dollars) regarding contingencies, in a note accompanying the financial statements:

16. CONTINGENT LIABILITIES

In fiscal year ended April 27, 1996, the Company received income tax reassessments from Revenue Canada, Taxation covering the fiscal years ended April 30, 1988 to 1991. These reassessments disallowed capital losses claimed by Ault on two transactions, as well as disagreeing with the inventory-valuation method used by the Company. The Company has since been advised that Revenue Canada Taxation does not intend to pursue its challenge of the inventory-valuation method.

The Company continues to disagree with the disallowed capital losses portion of the reassessments, and Notices of Objection have been filed. Both management and tax counsel believe the Company has substantial arguments to support its position; however, the ultimate outcome of the objections is not determinable at this time.

The tax and interest relating to the assessed amounts for the objected items totals $8,500 for the four years. In addition, should the Federal tax reassessments be upheld, the Ontario Ministry of Revenue would be entitled to reassess on the same basis, thereby resulting in a potential additional liability, including interest, of $3,600.

Pursuant to a requirement of the Income Tax Act (Canada), the Company has funded $5,100 of the total amount reassessed. In addition, $2,300 in net refunds relating to fiscal years 1992 and 1993 have been applied against the 1988–91 reassessments. These amounts have been included in "Income and Other Taxes Receivable" on the consolidated balance sheet, pending the outcome of the Company's appeal. If the Company's Notices of Objection are ultimately upheld, these amounts, plus interest, will be refunded. Any tax reassessments upheld will be charged to net earnings.

The Company gave a form of guarantee for a portion of the bank indebtedness of La Llanura, a Mexican dairy, in the amount of $3,500 as at April 26, 1997. The Company is contingently liable for the principal and interest on a U.S. dollar denominated bank loan, plus the principal portion regarding a Mexican peso denominated bank loan. In 1997, the Company increased the provision of $3,000 made in 1995 to $3,500, representing the maximum exposure with respect to these guarantees. Notwithstanding these provisions, the Company is contesting its contingent liability related to the Mexican peso denominated loan.

Instructions

(a) Do the income tax reassessments described above represent a contingent loss or a contingent gain for Ault Foods?

(b) Of the total amount of $12.1 million ($8.5 million federally plus $3.6 million provincially) that is contested, Ault has already "funded," or left on deposit with Revenue Canada pending settlement of the appeal, $7.4 million ($5.1 million plus $2.3 million)—as required under the *Income Tax Act*.

If Revenue Canada's position is upheld, what will the company do about the $7.4 million that is recorded as receivable? What will it do about the remaining $4.7 million?

(c) Does the situation regarding the bank indebtedness guarantees represent a contingent loss or a contingent gain for Ault Foods?

(d) If Ault is successful in contesting its contingent liability related to the Mexican peso denominated loan, what will it do with respect to the $3.5 million provision that has been made?

ACCOUNTING ON THE WEB

Payroll deductions for CPP contributions, EI premiums, and income tax withheld are remitted periodically to Revenue Canada. This case explores Revenue Canada's website, viewing payroll deduction guides and forms.

Instructions

Specific requirements for this Internet case are available on-line at www.wiley.com/canada/weygandt.

Answers to Self-Study Questions
1. a 2. d 3. a* 4. b 5. c 6. b 7. d 8. d 9. c 10. d

* The precise answer, using days, is $88,500 × 6% × 121/365 = $1,760. If months are used, the answer is $88,500 x 6% x 4/12 = $1,770. Since this is just an accrual, rather than a payment, the latter (choice b) would be acceptable.

Before studying this chapter, you should understand or, if necessary, review:

a. *The organization primarily responsible for setting accounting standards in Canada. (Ch. 1, p. 11)*

b. *The going concern assumption, the monetary unit assumption, the economic entity assumption, and the time period assumption. (Ch. 1, pp. 11–13 and Ch. 3, p. 93)*

c. *The cost principle, the revenue recognition principle, and the matching principle. (Ch. 1, p. 11 and Ch. 3, pp. 93–94)*

As We Go On-line, Do Promotion Costs Go Off-track?

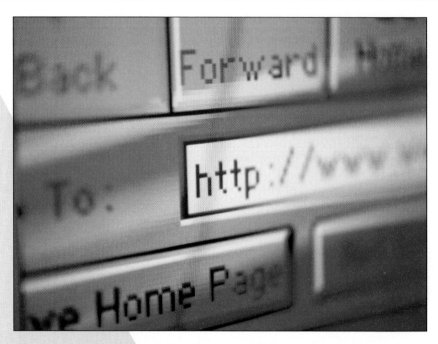

As more and more people in Canada and around the world "get wired," ISPs—Internet Service Providers—are experiencing phenomenal growth. For example, at an Ontario ISP called Internet Direct, established in 1992 and best known for its TUCOWS software, sales have grown recently by 200% to 300% per year.

The two biggest and best known ISPs in North America, America Online (known in Canada as AOL Canada) and CompuServe, have also grown rapidly in the 1990s. But just how successful they appear depends, in part, on how they choose their accounting principles.

ISPs compete with one another to win new subscribers through such techniques as mail solicitation, billboard and subway advertising, and free trial memberships. Such promotion is expensive—in one recent year, for example, America Online spent over $54 million on subscription acquisition.

The choice of how to treat such costs can make a significant difference in a company's bottom line. America Online treats these costs as an investment undertaken to acquire assets—in this case, customers. It capitalizes these costs and amortizes them over 18 months. If America Online had expensed—rather than capitalized—its $54 million of promotion costs, it would have reported a net loss of $9 million, rather than a net income of $9 million. CompuServe, by contrast, expenses client-acquisition costs as they occur.

CompuServe's controller contends that to use America Online's methods is to taint or dilute actual earnings. Most smaller companies seem to agree. At Internet Direct, for example, where advertising and marketing account for a significant 13% of total costs, accounting head Loretta Hoi says emphatically, "We expense all such costs right now."

America Online defends its accounting practices by citing the principle of matching expenses with revenues. Similarly, magazine publishers often capitalize the costs of direct-mail campaigns for attracting subscribers. One test of the wisdom of this policy may be the long-term loyalty of subscribers. If most clients attracted through the costly marketing campaigns stay with the company, then the cost of the campaign can more reasonably be seen as an investment in acquiring the most valuable assets of all—customers. ◀

CHAPTER 12

ACCOUNTING PRINCIPLES

▶ STUDY OBJECTIVES ◀

After studying this chapter, you should be able to:

1. *Explain the meaning of generally accepted accounting principles and identify the key items of the conceptual framework.*
2. *Describe the basic objectives of financial reporting.*
3. *Discuss the qualitative characteristics of accounting information and elements of financial statements.*
4. *Identify the basic assumptions used by accountants.*
5. *Identify the basic principles of accounting.*
6. *Identify the constraints in accounting.*
7. *Explain the purpose of international accounting standards.*

It is important that general guidelines be available to resolve accounting issues such as that faced by America Online and other Internet service providers in the opening story. Without these basic guidelines, each enterprise would have to develop its own set of accounting practices. If this happened, we would have to become familiar with every company's peculiar accounting and reporting rules in order to understand their financial statements. Thus, it would be difficult—if not impossible—to compare the financial statements of different companies.

This chapter explores the basic accounting principles that are considered in developing specific accounting guidelines. The organization of the chapter is as follows:

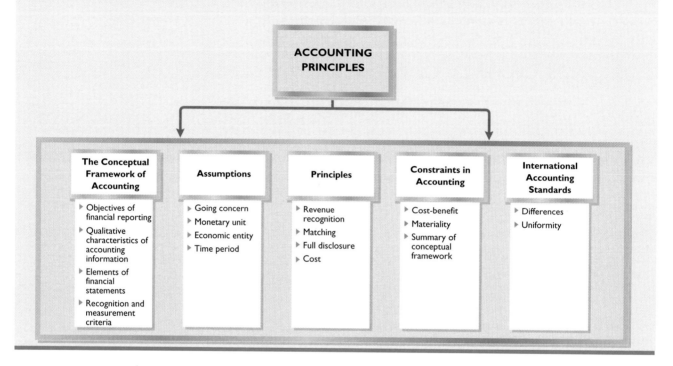

▼The Conceptual Framework of Accounting

STUDY OBJECTIVE

············▼············

Explain the meaning of generally accepted accounting principles and identify the key items of the conceptual framework.

The accounting profession has established a set of standards and rules that are recognized as a general guide for financial reporting purposes. This recognized set of standards is called generally accepted accounting principles (GAAP). "Generally accepted" means that these principles have substantial authoritative support. Such support has come through the Canadian Institute of Chartered Accountants (CICA), which has the primary responsibility for standard setting in Canada. Provincial securities commissions and federal and provincial incorporating acts have named the CICA as the official promulgator of generally accepted accounting principles. This means that GAAP have the force of law for incorporated and publicly traded companies.

Before 1988, the conceptual foundation for accounting standards in Canada was more implicit than explicit, and it was often found by examining practices of countries other than our own. In 1988, a comprehensive conceptual framework was developed and presented in the *CICA Handbook*, a looseleaf binder of accounting and auditing recommendations and guidelines, published by the CICA.

Section 1000 of the *Handbook,* Financial Statements Concepts, organizes the concepts that underlie the development and use of accounting principles by enterprises in the public and private sectors. These concepts provide guidance in choosing what to present in financial reports, making decisions among alternative ways of reporting economic events, and selecting appropriate ways of communicating such information. This increases the usefulness of financial statements and provides an understanding of the limitations of accounting. The framework outlined in this Section is intended to help:

1. Ensure that existing standards and practices are coherent and consistent.
2. Provide a structure to permit quick response to new issues.
3. Increase the understandability, relevance, reliability, and comparability of financial reporting results.

It is impossible to create accounting principles for all existing and future situations. The conceptual framework has therefore become especially important in situations where standards do not exist: it helps professionals determine which accounting alternatives fall outside of the framework and are not acceptable accounting treatments. The conceptual framework also guides the development of new accounting principles.

The CICA has set up an Emerging Issues Committee (EIC) whose purpose is to review, on a timely basis, emerging accounting issues that might receive different or inappropriate accounting treatment in the absence of official guidelines. Nearly 90 abstracts of issues have been published by the EIC to provide guidance on topics ranging from accounting for new financial instruments to accounting for the costs of modifying software for the year 2000. Over time, these abstracts go through a rigorous standard setting process and, if they are approved, they will become recommendations for external reporting in the *CICA Handbook*.

Section 1000 refers the user to the Emerging Issues Committee as a reference source for matters that are not covered by a *CICA Handbook* recommendation or that are not covered by general practice. When dealing with such matters, an accountant should also consider principles for similar situations dealt with in the *CICA Handbook* or in the guidelines from other countries. If guidance cannot be found from these sources, one should refer to the broad theoretical concepts that underlie accounting practices, which can be found in Section 1000, research studies, journals, and accounting texts.

► **Accounting in Action** ► *International Insight*

You should recognize that different religious, political, and cultural influences affect the accounting that occurs in many countries. For example, in the some Islamic countries religious tenets—such as the prohibition of interest charges—have been introduced into accounting practice. In Sweden, accounting is considered an instrument that shapes fiscal policy. In Europe, more emphasis is given to social reporting (information on employment statistics, health of workers, and so on), because employees and their labour organizations are strong and demand that type of information from management.

The CICA's conceptual framework consists of the following four major sections:

1. Objectives of financial reporting.
2. Qualitative characteristics of accounting information.
3. Elements of financial statements.
4. Recognition and measurement criteria (assumptions, principles, and constraints).

We will discuss each of these sections on the following pages.

Objectives of Financial Reporting

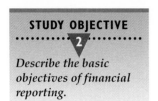

STUDY OBJECTIVE

2

Describe the basic objectives of financial reporting.

Determining the objectives of financial reporting requires answers to such basic questions as: Who uses financial statements? Why? What information do they need? How knowledgeable about business and accounting are the users of financial statements? How should financial information be reported so that it is best understood?

The conceptual framework helps in answering these questions. According to it, the objectives of financial reporting are to provide information that:

1. Is useful to those making investment and credit decisions.
2. Is helpful in assessing future cash flows.
3. Identifies the economic resources (assets), the claims to those resources (liabilities), and the changes in those resources and claims.

The conceptual framework also describes the characteristics that make accounting information useful.

Qualitative Characteristics of Accounting Information

STUDY OBJECTIVE

3

Discuss the qualitative characteristics of accounting information and elements of financial statements.

How does a company like Loblaw Companies, Canada's largest retail and food distributor, decide on the amount of financial information to disclose? In what format should its financial information be presented? How should assets, liabilities, revenues, and expenses be measured? **The primary criterion for judging such accounting choices is decision usefulness**. The accounting practice selected, or the policy adopted, should be the one that generates the most useful financial information for making a decision. To be useful, information should possess the following qualitative characteristics: understandability, relevance, reliability, and comparability.

Understandability

In order for the information provided in financial statements to be useful, it must be **understandable** by the users. Users are defined primarily as investors and creditors, in addition to other interested decision makers. Unfortunately, these users may vary widely in the types of decisions they must make and in their level of interest in the information. At one extreme is a sophisticated financier who carefully scrutinizes all aspects of the financial information. At the other extreme is an unsophisticated shareholder who may only scan the text and not study the numbers.

It is impossible to satisfy all users' needs with one general-purpose set of financial statements. It is therefore necessary to establish a base level of understanding to assist both the preparer of financial information and the user of it. **The average user is assumed to have a reasonable understanding of, and ability to study, accounting concepts and procedures, as well as general business and economic conditions**. If this level of understanding and ability does not exist, the user is expected to rely upon professionals with an appropriate level of expertise to assist them. With your study of this course, you are well on your way to becoming this average user!

Relevance

Accounting information is **relevant** if it makes a difference in a decision. Relevant information has predictive or feedback value, or both. **Predictive value** helps users forecast future events. For example, when Loblaw issues financial statements, the information in the statements is considered relevant because it provides a basis for forecasting (predicting) future earnings. **Feedback value** confirms or corrects prior expectations. When Loblaw issues financial statements, it not only helps to predict future events, but also confirms or corrects expectations about the company.

In addition, for accounting information to be relevant it must be **timely**. That is, it must be available to decision makers before it loses its capacity to influence decisions. Many people believe that by the time annual financial statements are issued—sometimes up to six months after year end—the information has limited usefulness for decision-making purposes. Timely *interim* financial reporting is therefore essential to relevant decision making.

Reliability

Reliability of information means that the information is dependable and free of error and bias. To be reliable, accounting information must be **verifiable**—we must be able to prove that it is free of error and bias. The information must also be a faithful representation of the economic substance, not just the form, of the transaction. If Loblaw reports a source of debt financing as equity rather than as a liability, then the statement is not a **faithful representation**. Accounting information must also be **neutral**—it cannot be selected, prepared, or presented to favour one set of interested users over another. Neutrality is affected by the use of conservatism in situations of uncertainty. **Conservatism** in accounting means that, when in doubt, the accountant should choose the method that will be least likely to overstate assets and revenues or understate liabilities and expenses. It does **not** mean the converse: to deliberately understate assets or revenues, or overstate liabilities or expenses.

To ensure reliability, external professional accountants audit financial statements, just as Revenue Canada audits tax returns for the same purpose.

Comparability

Accounting information about an enterprise is most useful when it can be compared with accounting information about other enterprises. **Comparability** results when different companies use the same accounting principles. For example, both CompuServe and Internet Direct expense, rather than capitalize, promotions costs.

Theoretically the methods used by companies to comply with an accounting principle should also be comparable. However, accounting practices include several methods of inventory costing and various amortization methods. At this point, comparability of methods is not required, even for companies in the same industry, as the opening story about Internet service providers demonstrates. Thus, McCain Foods and Maple Leaf Foods may, if they wish, choose to use different inventory costing and amortization methods in their financial statements. The only accounting requirement is that **each company must disclose the accounting methods used**. From the disclosures, the external user can determine whether the financial information is comparable.

Comparability is enhanced when accounting policies are used **consistently** from year to year. Thus, if a company selects FIFO as the inventory costing method in the first year of operations, it is expected to continue to use FIFO in succeeding years. When financial information has been reported on a consistent basis, the financial statements permit meaningful analysis of trends within a company.

▸Accounting in Action ▸ *Business Insight*

There is an old story that professors often tell students about a company looking for an accountant. The company approached the first accountant and asked, "What do you believe our net income will be this year?" The accountant said $4 million. The company asked the second accountant the same question, and the answer was, "What would you like it to be?" Guess who got the job? The reason we tell the story here is that, because accounting principles offer flexibility, it is important that you understand that: (a) different principles will yield different results, and (b) a consistent treatment must be provided from period to period—otherwise it will be very difficult to interpret financial statements. Perhaps *no* alternative methods should be permitted in accounting. What do you think?

A company *can* change to a new method of accounting if management can justify that the new method results in more meaningful financial information. In the year in which the change occurs, the change (and its impact) must be disclosed in the notes to the financial statements, so that users of the financial statements are aware of the lack of consistency. In addition, the past years of corporate performance must be presented as if the new method had been used.

The qualitative characteristics of accounting information are summarized in Illustration 12-1:

Illustration 12-1

Qualitative characteristics of accounting information

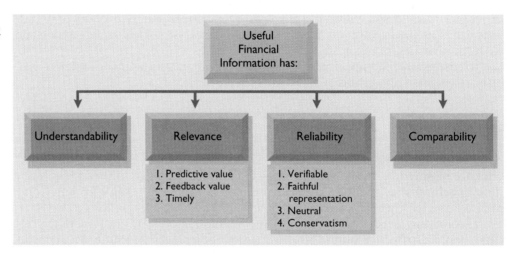

Trade-Offs Between Qualitative Characteristics

Many accounting choices require trade-offs between qualitative characteristics. For example, there is often a trade-off between relevance and reliability—that is, between ensuring that financial information is produced on a timely basis and verifying the accuracy of the information included. In order to produce financial statements annually, estimates are required. These estimates reduce the accuracy of the information provided. However, if we were to wait until estimates were no longer necessary for things like uncollectible accounts and useful lives of capital assets, the financial information would no longer be relevant. The conceptual framework does not always provide obvious solutions to accounting issues such as these; rather, it enables professionals to judge the appropriate balance between these characteristics in a particular situation.

Elements of Financial Statements

An important part of an accounting conceptual framework is a set of definitions that describe the basic components of financial reports. This set of definitions is referred to as the **elements of financial statements**. They include such terms as assets, liabilities, equity, revenues, and expenses.

Because these elements are so important, they must be precisely defined and universally understood and applied. Finding the appropriate definition for many of these elements is not easy. For example, how should an asset be defined? Should the value of a company's employees be reported as an asset on a balance sheet? Should the death of the company's president be reported as a loss? A good set of definitions should provide answers to these types of questions. Because you have already encountered most of these definitions in earlier chapters, they are not repeated here.

Recognition and Measurement Criteria

The objectives of financial statements, the qualitative characteristics of accounting information, and the elements of financial statements are very broad. However, because accountants and standard-setting bodies must solve practical problems, more detailed criteria are needed. **Recognition criteria help determine when items should be included or recognized in the financial statements. Measurement criteria outline how to measure or assign an amount to those items**. We have chosen to organize these criteria as assumptions, principles, and constraints.

Assumptions provide a foundation for the accounting process. **Principles** indicate how economic events should be reported in the accounting process. **Constraints** on the accounting process allow a relaxation of the principles under certain circumstances. Illustration 12-2 provides an outline of these recognition and measurement criteria. They are discussed in more detail in the following sections.

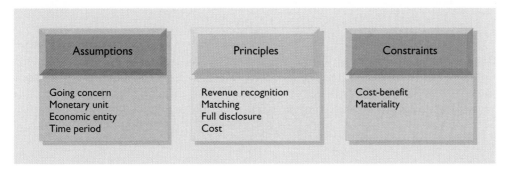

Illustration 12-2

Recognition and measurement criteria

Before You Go On . . .

►*Review It*

1. What are generally accepted accounting principles?
2. What are the basic objectives of financial information?
3. What are the qualitative characteristics that make accounting information useful? Give an example of a trade-off between qualitative characteristics.
4. Identify two elements of financial statements.

Related exercise material: BE12–1, BE12–2, BE12–3, BE12–4, BE12–5, and BE12–6.

ssumptions

STUDY OBJECTIVE
•••••••• ▼ 4 ••••••••

Identify the basic assumptions used by accountants.

Assumptions provide a foundation for the accounting process. You have already studied the major assumptions in preceding chapters—the going concern, monetary unit, economic entity, and time period assumptions. We will review them here briefly.

Going Concern Assumption

The going concern assumption assumes that the enterprise will continue to operate in the foreseeable future and will be able to realize assets and discharge liabilities in the normal course of its operations. The accounting implications of adopting this assumption are critical. If a going concern assumption is not used, then capital assets should be stated at their liquidation value (selling price less cost of disposal)—not at their historical cost. As a result, amortization of these assets would not be needed. In each period, these assets would simply be reported at their anticipated liquidation value. Also, without this assumption, the current/noncurrent classification of assets and liabilities would have little significance. Labelling anything as long-term would be difficult to justify.

Monetary Unit Assumption

▸ *International note*

In an action that sent shock-waves through the French business community, the CEO of Alcatel (a FF 130 billion international group involved in telecommunications systems and equipment) was taken into custody for an apparent violation of the economic entity assumption. Allegedly, the executive improperly used company funds to install an expensive security system in his home.

The monetary unit assumption states that only transaction data which can be expressed in terms of money should be included in the accounting records of the economic entity. For example, the death of a company president would not be reported in a company's financial records as a loss, because, among other reasons, the event cannot be expressed easily in dollars.

An important counterpart to the monetary unit assumption is the assumption that the unit of measure remains sufficiently stable over time. That is, any inflationary (or deflationary) effects are assumed to be minimal and are ignored.

Economic Entity Assumption

The economic entity assumption states that economic events can be identified with a particular unit of accountability. For example, it is assumed that the activities of Harvey's can be distinguished from those of Swiss Chalet, even though both are owned by the Toronto-based company Cara Operations.

▶Accounting in Action ▸ *Ethics Insight*

 A flamboyant Vancouver entrepreneur who made lots of money in real estate, then lost lots by dabbling in pro sports teams was convicted for theft, in what was essentially a violation of the economic entity assumption. The entrepreneur took $100,000 from an investor's trust fund in a real estate company, and used the money to pay a variety of personal expenses, such as credit card bills, brokerage fees, and a daughter's mortgage. The crown prosecutor in the case noted: "It's a very serious offence to take an investor's money [that] he's entrusted you with. It's not your money to do with as you wish—you can only use an investor's money for the purpose that he authorizes."

Source: *Globe and Mail*, February 26, 1997, B1.

Time Period Assumption

The **time period assumption** states that the economic life of a business can be divided into artificial time periods. Thus, it is assumed that the activities of business enterprises such as Abitibi Consolidated, Bombardier, or Imperial Oil, or any enterprise, can be subdivided into months, quarters, or a year for meaningful financial reporting purposes.

As discussed in Chapter 3, time periods of less than one year are referred to as interim periods. Periods of one year are known as fiscal years or, if extending from January through December, calendar years. Most large companies are required to prepare both interim and annual financial statements.

Before You Go On . . .

► *Review It*

1. What are the going concern assumption, the monetary unit assumption, the economic entity assumption, and the time period assumption?

Principles

From these fundamental assumptions of accounting, the accounting profession has developed principles that dictate how transactions and other economic events should be recorded and reported. In earlier chapters we discussed the cost principle (Chapter 1) and the revenue recognition and matching principles (Chapter 3). We now examine a number of reporting issues related to these principles. In addition, another principle, the full disclosure principle, is discussed.

STUDY OBJECTIVE
5

Identify the basic principles of accounting.

Revenue Recognition Principle

The **revenue recognition principle** says that revenue should be recognized in the accounting period in which it is earned. More specifically, revenue should be recognized as soon as:

1. The production and/or sales effort is substantially complete.
2. Revenues can be objectively measured.
3. Collection is reasonably assured (an estimate can be made of amounts anticipated to be uncollectible).
4. Material expenses can be determined and matched.

Applying this general principle, however, can be difficult. In Chapter 3, for example, we noted how difficult it was for Twentieth Century Fox to estimate their Star Wars revenues and match these revenues with expenses.

Another example is apparent in long-term construction situations. For example, Strait Crossing built the Confederation Bridge, linking the provinces of Prince Edward Island and New Brunswick. Construction commenced in 1992 and was completed in 1997. The bridge opened in June 1997 and started earning toll revenue immediately thereafter. Expenses were incurred starting in 1992, but no revenue was received until

1997. When should revenues be recorded, and how should they be matched to expenses, in situations such as this?

Another example is the past revenue recognition practices of the banking industry. The failure of the Canadian Commercial Bank was said to have been caused—in part—by its practice of recognizing revenue before collection was reasonably assured.

Depending upon the circumstances, the four criteria for revenue recognition can be satisfied at a number of points in time, ranging from some point during production to later collection of cash. The most common points of revenue recognition are:

1. At point of sale.
2. During production.
3. At completion of production.
4. Upon collection of cash.

Point of Sale

Helpful hint   Revenue should be recognized in the accounting period in which it is earned, which may not be the period in which the related cash is received. In a retail establishment, the point of sale is usually the critical point in the process of earning revenue.

When a sale is involved, revenue is usually recognized at the point of sale. The sales basis involves an exchange transaction between the seller and the buyer, and the sales price provides an objective measure of the amount of revenue realized. Consider a sale by the Great Canadian Bagel Company. At the point of sale, the customer pays the cash and takes (and eats!) the merchandise. The company records the sale by debiting Cash and crediting Sales Revenue. If the sale were on account rather than for cash (assuming the company accepts credit sales), and the customer had a good credit rating, the company would record the sale by debiting Accounts Receivable and crediting Sales Revenue. This is the most common point of revenue recognition for most goods and services. The product is complete and delivered, revenue can be objectively measured, collection has occurred or is reasonably assured, and expenses have been incurred.

During Production

Helpful hint   In accounting for long-term construction contracts, it is normally appropriate to use the percentage-of-completion method of revenue recognition because the critical event in the earning process is making progress towards completion. The ultimate sale and selling price are assured by the contract.

In long-term construction contracts, recognition of revenue is usually possible (and desirable) before the contract is completed. For example, assume that Warrior Construction Co. had a contract to build a dam for the Province of British Columbia for $400 million. Construction is estimated to take three years (starting early in 1998) at a construction cost of $360 million. If Warrior applies the point of sale basis, it will report no revenues and no profit in the first two years. However, when completion and sale take place, in 2000, Warrior will report $400 million in revenues, costs of $360 million, and the entire profit of $40 million. Did Warrior really produce no revenues and earn no profit in 1998 and 1999? Obviously not. The dam will be as good as sold when Warrior completes the project according to specifications. Although technically an exchange transaction (transfer of ownership) has not occurred until completion of the dam, the earning process is considered substantially completed at various stages as construction progresses.

In recognizing revenue, Warrior can apply the percentage-of-completion method. This method recognizes revenue and income over the life of a long-term project on the basis of reasonable estimates of the project's progress towards completion. Progress towards completion is measured by comparing the costs incurred in a period to the total estimated costs for the entire project. That percentage is multiplied by the total revenue for the project; the result is then recognized as revenue for the period. The formulas for this method are presented in Illustration 12–3. The costs incurred in the current period are then subtracted from the revenue recognized during the current period to arrive at the gross profit.

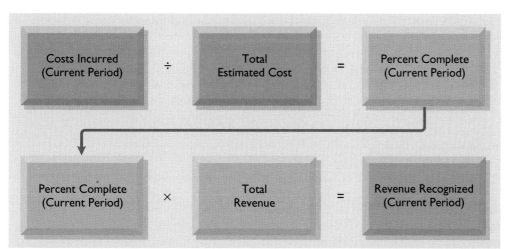

Let's look at an illustration of the percentage-of-completion method. Assume that Warrior Construction Co. has costs of $54 million in 1998, $180 million in 1999, and $126 million in 2000 on the dam project. The portion of the $400 million of revenue recognized in each of the three years is shown in Illustration 12-4:

Illustration 12-4

Revenue recognized—percentage-of-completion method

Year	Costs Incurred (Current Period)	÷	Total Estimated Cost	=	Percent Complete (Current Period)	×	Total Revenue	=	Revenue Recognized (Current Period)
1998	$ 54,000,000		$360,000,000		15%		$400,000,000		$ 60,000,000
1999	180,000,000		360,000,000		50%		400,000,000		200,000,000
2000	126,000,000					Revenue remaining to be recognized			140,000,000
Totals	$360,000,000								$400,000,000

Note that no estimate is made of the percentage of work completed during the final period. In the final period, all remaining revenue is recognized. In this example, the company's cost estimates were totally accurate: the costs incurred in the third year brought the total costs to $360,000,000—exactly what had been estimated. In reality, this does not always happen, and revisions of remaining estimates may be necessary as additional information becomes available.

The gross profit recognized each period is as follows:

Illustration 12-5

Gross profit recognized—percentage-of-completion method

Year	Revenue Recognized (Current Period)	−	Actual Cost Incurred (Current Period)	=	Gross Profit Recognized (Current Period)
1998	$ 60,000,000		$ 54,000,000		$ 6,000,000
1999	200,000,000		180,000,000		20,000,000
2000	140,000,000		126,000,000		14,000,000
Totals	$400,000,000		$360,000,000		$ 40,000,000

Billing practices of professional accounting firms are another example of recognizing revenue during production. If a firm undertakes a job for a client that lasts for more than one month, it is usual to bill the client monthly for the number of hours of service rendered and for any expenditures incurred to date.

Application of the percentage-of-completion method involves some subjectivity. Error is possible in determining the amount of revenue to be recognized and net income to be reported. But to wait until completion would seriously distort each period's financial statements. Naturally, **if it is not possible to obtain dependable estimates of costs and progress, then the revenue should be recognized at the completion date** and not by the percentage-of-completion method.

Completion of Production

Helpful hint The completion of production method is not applicable to ordinary manufacturing situations.

If Warrior Construction Co. was not able to estimate its costs with any degree of reliability, it would use the completed-contract method to report its revenue of $400 million, costs of $360 million, and profit of $40 million at the completion of production, in the year 2000. It is not until production is complete, in this case, that expenses and profit can be reasonably determined.

Collection of Cash

Another basis for revenue recognition is the receipt of cash. The cash basis is generally used only when it is very difficult to determine the revenue amount at the time of a credit sale because collection is so uncertain. One popular approach to the recognition of revenue using the cash basis is the instalment method.

Under the instalment method, each cash collection from a customer consists of: (1) a partial recovery of the cost of the goods sold, and (2) partial gross profit from the sale. For example, if the gross profit rate on the sale is 40%, each subsequent receipt consists of 60% recovery of the cost of goods sold and 40% gross profit. The formula to recognize gross profit is as follows:

Illustration 12-6

Gross profit formula— instalment method

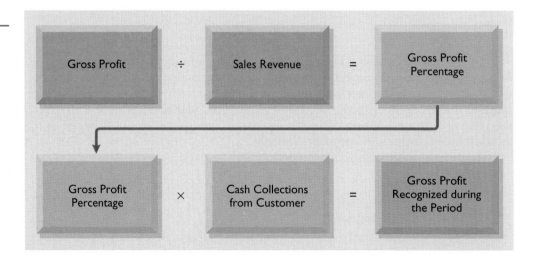

To illustrate, assume that in its first year of operations a Manitoba farm machinery dealer had instalment sales of $600,000 and a cost of goods sold on instalment sales of $420,000. Total gross profit is, therefore, $180,000 ($600,000 − $420,000), and the gross profit percentage is 30% ($180,000 ÷ $600,000). The collections on the instalment sales were as follows: first year, $280,000 (down payment plus monthly payments); second year, $200,000; and third year, $120,000. The collections of cash and recognition of the gross profit are summarized in Illustration 12-7 (interest charges are ignored in this illustration):

Illustration 12-7

Gross profit recognized—instalment method

Year	Gross Profit	÷	Sales Revenue	=	Gross Profit Percentage	×	Cash Collections from Customers	=	Gross Profit Recognized
1998	$180,000		$600,000		30%		$280,000		$ 84,000
1999	180,000		600,000		30%		200,000		60,000
2000	180,000		600,000		30%		120,000		36,000
Totals							$600,000		$180,000

Under the instalment method of accounting, gross profit is recognized in the period in which the cash is collected.

Matching Principle (Expense Recognition)

The expression "let the expense follow the revenue," shows that expense recognition is traditionally tied to revenue recognition. This practice is referred to as the **matching principle**. It says that expenses must be matched with revenues in the period in which efforts are taken to generate revenues. Expenses are not recognized when cash is paid, or when the work is performed, or when the product is produced; they are recognized when the labour (service) or the product actually makes its contribution to revenue.

Costs that will generate revenues only in the current accounting period are expensed immediately. They are reported as operating expenses in the income statement. Such costs include advertising, salaries, and repairs. These expenses are often called **expired costs**.

Costs that will generate revenues in future accounting periods are recognized as assets. For example, this is the basis on which America Online accounts for its subscription acquisition costs. Other examples are merchandise inventory, prepaid expenses, and capital assets. These costs represent **unexpired costs**. Unexpired costs become expenses in two ways:

1. **Cost of goods sold.** Costs carried as merchandise inventory are expensed as cost of goods sold in the period when the sale occurs. Thus, there is a direct matching of expenses with revenues.
2. **Operating expenses.** Unexpired costs become operating expenses through use or consumption (as in the case of capital assets and store supplies), or through the passage of time (as in the case of prepaid insurance and prepaid rent). Operating expenses contribute to the revenues of the period, but their association with revenues is less direct than for cost of goods sold.

These points about expense recognition are illustrated in Illustration 12-8.

> ► **Ethics note**
>
> Many appear to do it, but few like to discuss it. It's earnings management, and it's a clear violation of the revenue recognition and matching principles. Banks may time the sale of investments, or the expensing of bad debts to accomplish earnings objectives. Prominent companies such as GE have been accused of matching one-time gains with one-time charge-offs so that current-period earnings are not so high that they can't be surpassed next period.

Illustration 12-8

Expense recognition patterns

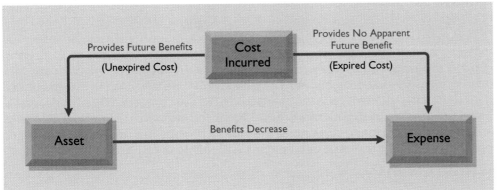

▶Accounting in Action ▸ *Business Insight*

Implementing expense recognition guidelines can be difficult. Consider, for example, the Casino Windsor, a gambling establishment located in Windsor, Ontario. How should the Casino report expenses that are related to the payoff of its progressive slot machines? Progressive slot machines, which generally have no ceiling on their jackpots, are capable of providing a lucky winner with all the money that many losers had previously put in. Payoffs tend to be huge but infrequent. The basic accounting question is: when it determines net income, should the Casino Windsor deduct (as an expense) the thousands of dollars sitting in its progressive slot machines from the revenue recognized during the accounting period? One might argue that no, you cannot deduct the money until it is won. However, a winning handle pull might not occur for many months, or even years. Although admittedly an estimate would have to be used, the better answer is to match these costs with the revenue recognized, assuming that an average payout period can be documented. And the revenue amounts can be significant. The Casino Windsor grosses more than $500 million annually! This example demonstrates how difficult it can be to apply the matching principle.

Full Disclosure Principle

The **full disclosure principle** requires disclosure of circumstances and events which make a difference to financial statement users. For example, most accountants would agree that Air Canada and other airlines, as described in Chapter 11, should disclose the cost of providing travel awards under their frequent flyer program so that interested parties are made aware of this contingent liability.

The full disclosure principle is achieved through two elements in the financial statements: the data they contain and the accompanying notes. The first note in most cases is a **summary of significant accounting policies**. The summary includes the methods used by the company where a choice is made among acceptable accounting policies. For example, the Second Cup Ltd.'s first note discloses, on page A14 in Appendix A, that they have chosen the FIFO method of inventory costing and the straight-line method of amortizing their capital assets.

The information that is usually disclosed in the notes to the financial statements generally falls into three additional categories. These categories follow the summary of significant accounting policies, which are to:

1. Provide supplementary detail or explanation (for example, a schedule of cost of goods sold).
2. Explain unrecorded transactions (for example, contingencies, commitments, subsequent events).
3. Supply new information (for example, information about related party transactions).

Financial statements were much simpler years ago, when many companies provided little additional information regarding the financial statements. In 1930, General Electric had no notes to the financial statements; today the parent company has over 30 notes to its statements! Why this change? A major reason is that the objectives of financial statements have changed. In the past, information was generally presented on what the business had done. Today the objectives of financial reporting are more future-oriented; accounting is trying to provide information that makes it possible to predict the probability, amount, and timing of future cash flows.

►Accounting in Action ► *Business Insight*

In response to alleged disclosure problems that led to the collapse of several trust companies, the Toronto Stock Exchange has proposed sweeping changes to how companies disclose information to shareholders and investors. Substantial fines for companies which misinform readers have also been proposed for the company in question (ranging from $1 million to 5% of capital stock), in addition to fines for corporate officials ($25,000 minimum) and their professional advisors ($1 million minimum).

Source: Globe and Mail, March 19, 1997, B1.

Cost Principle

As you know, the cost principle requires assets to be recorded at cost. Cost is used because it is both relevant and reliable. Cost is **relevant** because it represents the price paid, the assets sacrificed, or the commitment made at the date of acquisition. Cost is **reliable** because it is objectively measurable, factual, and verifiable. It is the result of an exchange transaction. Cost is the basis used in preparing financial statements.

The cost principle, however, has received much criticism. One criticism is that it is irrelevant. After acquisition, the argument goes, cost is not equivalent to market value or current value. For that matter, as the purchasing power of the dollar changes, so too does the meaning associated with the dollar that is used as the basis of measurement. Consider the classic story about the individual who went to sleep and woke up 10 years later. Hurrying to a telephone, she got through to her stockbroker and asked what her formerly modest stock portfolio was worth. She was told that she was a multimillionaire—her Hongkong Bank stock was worth $5 million and her Microsoft stock was up to $10 million. Elated, she was about to inquire about her other holdings when the telephone operator cut in with "Your time is up. Please deposit $100,000 for the next three minutes."

This story demonstrates that prices can and do change over a period of time, and that one is not necessarily better off when they do. Although the numbers in the story are extreme, consider some more realistic data that compare prices in 1978 with those 20 years later, in 1998.

Helpful hint Are you a winner or a loser if you hold cash during a period of inflation? A loser, because the value of the cash declines as inflation climbs.

	1978	1998
University tuition	$750	$3,400
Automobile (Cutlass)	$5,600	$30,000
Small bungalow (Maritimes)	$40,000	$100,000
McDonald's milk shake	$0.35	$1.49
First class postage stamp	$0.14	$0.45
Minimum wage (Province of New Brunswick)	$2.80/hour	$5.50/hour

Illustration 12-9

Example of changing prices

Despite the inevitability of changing prices during a period of inflation, the accounting profession still follows the **stable monetary unit assumption** (referred to earlier in this chapter) in preparing a company's primary financial statements. While admitting that some changes in prices do occur, the profession believes the unit of measure—the dollar—has remained sufficiently constant over time to provide meaningful financial information.

Before You Go On . . .

▶Review It

1. What are the revenue recognition principle, the matching principle, the full disclosure principle, and the cost principle?
2. Identify the four points of revenue recognition. Provide an example of a company or product that would use each different point of revenue recognition.

Related exercise material: BE12–7, BE12–8, BE12–9, E12–4, E12–5, and E12–6.

Constraints in Accounting

STUDY OBJECTIVE
···········**6**···········
Identify the constraints in accounting.

Constraints permit a company to modify generally accepted accounting principles without reducing the usefulness of the reported information. The constraints are cost-benefit and materiality.

Cost-Benefit Constraint

The cost-benefit constraint ensures that the value of the information exceeds the cost of providing it. Accountants could, in applying the full disclosure principle, disclose every financial event that occurs and every contingency that exists. However, providing additional information entails a cost, and the benefits of providing this information in some cases may be less than the costs.

Some believe that the benefits of applying GAAP to small businesses is not worth the substantial cost of both time and money. This has led to what is called the Big GAAP-Little GAAP controversy. Should there be one set of GAAP to which all businesses adhere, or should there be a different set for small businesses? The CICA is currently reviewing this matter, recognizing that the cost-benefit constraint often overrides the principle of one standard for all.

▶Technology in Action

Some accountants are reconsidering the current means of financial reporting. These accountants propose a database concept of financial reporting. In such a system, all the information from transactions would be stored in a computerized database to be accessed by various user groups. The main benefit of such a system is the ability to tailor the information requested to the needs of each user.

However, questions such as "Who should be allowed to make inquiries of the system?" "What is the lowest/smallest level of information to be provided?" and "Will such a system be better than the current means of disclosure?" must be answered before such a system can be implemented on a large scale.

Materiality Constraint

Materiality relates to an item's impact on a firm's overall financial condition and operations. An item is material when it is likely to influence the decision of a reasonably prudent investor or creditor. It is immaterial if its inclusion or omission has no impact on a decision maker. In short, if the item does not make a difference, GAAP does not have to be followed. To determine the materiality of an amount (that is, to determine its financial significance), the accountant usually compares it to such items as total assets, total liabilities, gross revenues, and net income.

To illustrate how the constraint of materiality is applied, assume that Yanik Co. purchases a number of low-cost capital assets, such as wastepaper baskets. Although the proper accounting would appear to be to amortize these wastepaper baskets over their useful lives, they are usually expensed immediately. This practice is justified because these costs are considered immaterial. Establishing amortization schedules for these assets is costly and time-consuming, and will not make a material difference in total assets and net income. Other applications of the materiality constraint are the non-disclosure of very minor contingencies, or the expensing of any capital assets under a certain dollar amount.

Summary of Conceptual Framework

As we have seen, the conceptual framework for developing sound reporting practices starts with a set of objectives for financial reporting, and follows with the development of qualities that make information useful. In addition, elements of financial statements are defined. Recognition and measurement criteria in the form of assumptions, principles, and constraints are then provided. These points are summarized in Illustration 12-10:

Illustration 12-10

Conceptual framework

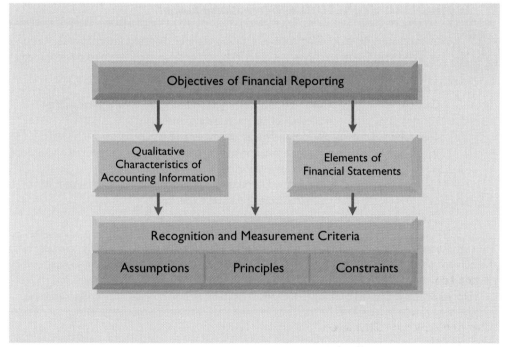

International Accounting Standards

World markets are becoming increasingly intertwined. Foreigners buy Canadian grain, drink Canadian water, heat with Canadian fuels, celebrate with Canadian Christmas trees, eat Canadian potatoes, fly in Canadian planes, defend their countries with Canadian ships, listen to CBC radio, and guzzle Canadian beer. Canadians, in turn, drive Japanese and U.S. cars (often built with Canadian auto parts), wear Italian shoes and Scottish woollens, drink Brazilian coffee and Indian tea, eat Swiss

STUDY OBJECTIVE

7

Explain the purpose of international accounting standards.

▸ *International note*

Canada sells more than 50% of its agricultural exports to the United States, 12% to Japan, 10% to the European Union, 6% to China, 2% to Mexico, and about 20% to nearly 200 other trading partners.

chocolate bars, smoke Cuban cigars, watch U.S. television, sit on Danish furniture, and use Arabian oil. The tremendous variety and volume of both exported and imported goods indicates the extensive involvement of Canadian business in international trade. Almost 40% of all Canadian-made goods and services are sold as exports, which is the highest percentage of all G7 countries. For many Canadian companies, the world is their market.

Firms that conduct their operations in more than one country through subsidiaries, divisions, or branches in foreign countries are referred to as **multinational corporations**. The accounting for multinational corporations is complicated, because differing accounting standards and foreign currencies are involved. These international transactions and operations must be translated into Canadian dollars.

Differences in Standards

As the world economy becomes globalized to the point where Canada is only one of several major players, many investment and credit decisions require the analysis and interpretation of foreign financial statements. Unfortunately, accounting standards differ from country to country. This lack of uniformity is the result of different legal systems, different processes for developing accounting standards, different governmental requirements, and different economic environments.

▶Accounting in Action ▸ *International Insight*

Research and development costs are an example of different international accounting standards. Compare how five countries account for research and development:

Country	Accounting Treatment
Canada	Some development expenditures may be capitalized; all research costs must be expensed.
Germany	All expenditures are expensed.
Japan	Expenditures for new products may be capitalized and amortized over five years.
United Kingdom	Some development expenditures may be capitalized; all research costs must be expensed.
United States	All expenditures are expensed.

Thus, a research and development expenditure of $100 million is charged totally to expense in the current period in the U.S. and Germany. This expense would be $20 million in Japan, while ranging from zero to $100 million in Canada and the United Kingdom.

Do you believe that accounting principles should be comparable across countries?

Uniformity in Standards

Much effort has been made to obtain uniformity in international accounting practices. In 1973, the International Accounting Standards Committee (IASC) was formed by an agreement of accounting organizations in Canada, the United States, the United Kingdom, Australia, France, Germany, Japan, Mexico, and the Netherlands. More than 140 accounting organizations from over 101 countries now participate in the development of international accounting standards.

To date, over 40 International Accounting Standards have been issued for IASC members to introduce to their respective countries. But, because the IASC has no enforcement powers, these standards are by no means universally applied. Countries weigh the benefits of uniformity in international financial reporting against the social and economic costs of changing local—and often legitimate—reporting practices. Today, many large multinational companies have found benefits in adhering to the international accounting standards. Celanese Canada and Mark's Work Wearhouse are but two examples of nearly 500 companies from around the world that issue financial statements in conformity with IASC standards. Thus, considerable progress has been made towards greater uniformity in international accounting.

Uniformity is also sought between Canada and the U.S. Since the U.S. is a major economic partner, and our borders have opened somewhat with free trade, harmonization of accounting practices has become more critical to serving the needs of the marketplace. The CICA and the Financial Accounting Standards Board in the U.S. are working closely with each other, in addition to with the IASC, to harmonize new accounting standards and to review the differences between existing ones.

Before You Go On . . .
►*Review It*

1. What are the cost-benefit constraint and the materiality constraint?
2. What is the purpose of the International Accounting Standards Committee?

Related exercise material: BE12–10, E12–1, E12–2, and E12–3.

►*A Look Back at America Online*

Refer back to the opening story and answer the following questions:
1. Internet Direct expenses its subscriber acquisition costs as incurred; America Online capitalizes these costs and amortizes them over 18 months. Are the concepts of comparability or consistency violated in this situation? Explain.
2. The controller for CompuServe stated that they do not want to taint or dilute their earnings by following America Online's accounting method. Explain this statement.

Solution:

1. Comparability results when different companies use the same accounting principles. In this case, comparability does not exist, because Internet Direct and America Online use different practices to account for subscriber acquisition costs. Consistency means that a company uses the same accounting principles and methods from year to year. Both companies are consistent as they continue to use the same accounting method from year to year.
2. CompuServe expenses its subscriber acquisition costs as incurred, as does Internet Direct. Their current period earnings are therefore conservatively reported (often referred to as high-quality earnings).

▼*Summary of Study Objectives*

1. *Explain the meaning of generally accepted accounting principles and identify the key items of the conceptual framework.* Generally accepted accounting principles are a set of rules and practices that are recognized as a general guide for financial reporting purposes. Generally accepted means that these principles must have substantial authoritative support. The key items of the conceptual framework are: (1) objectives of financial reporting, (2) qualitative characteristics of accounting information, (3) elements of financial statements, and (4) recognition and measurement criteria (assumptions, principles, and constraints).

2. *Describe the basic objectives of financial reporting.* The basic objectives of financial reporting are to provide information that is: (1) useful to those making investment and credit decisions, (2) helpful in assessing future cash flows, and (3) helpful in identifying economic resources (assets), the claims to those resources (liabilities), and the changes in those resources and claims.

3. *Discuss the qualitative characteristics of accounting information and elements of financial statements.* To be judged useful, information should possess the following qualitative characteristics: understandability, relevance, reliability, and comparability. The elements of financial statements are a set of definitions that can be used to describe the basic terms used in accounting.

4. *Identify the basic assumptions used by accountants.* The major assumptions are going concern, monetary unit, economic entity, and time period.

5. *Identify the basic principles of accounting.* The major principles are revenue recognition, matching, full disclosure, and cost.

6. *Identify the constraints in accounting.* The major constraints are cost-benefit and materiality.

7. *Explain the purpose of international accounting standards.* The International Accounting Standards Committee (IASC), of which Canada is a member, attempts to achieve uniformity in international accounting practices to facilitate trade in world markets.

GLOSSARY

Completed-contract method   When revenues or costs cannot be reliably estimated, revenue, expenses, and profit are recognized at the completion of production. (p. 514).

Cost-benefit   The constraint that the costs of obtaining and providing information should not exceed the benefits gained. (p. 518).

Cost principle   Accounting principle that assets should be recorded at their historical cost. (p. 517).

Economic entity assumption   Accounting assumption that economic events can be identified with a particular unit of accountability. (p. 510).

Full disclosure principle   Accounting principle that circumstances and events which make a difference to financial statement users should be disclosed. (p. 516).

Generally accepted accounting principles (GAAP)   A set of rules and practices, having substantial authoritative support, that are recognized as a general guide for financial reporting purposes. (p. 504).

Going concern assumption   The assumption that the enterprise will continue in operation long enough to carry out its existing objectives and commitments. (p. 510).

Instalment method   A method of recognizing revenue using the cash basis; each cash collection consists of a partial recovery of cost of goods sold and partial gross profit from the sale. (p. 514).

Matching principle   Accounting principle that expenses should be matched with revenues in the period when efforts are expended to generate revenues. (p. 515).

Materiality   The constraint of determining if an item is important enough to influence the decision of a reasonably prudent investor or creditor. (p. 518).

Monetary unit assumption   Accounting assumption that only transaction data capable of being expressed in monetary terms should be included in accounting records. (p. 510).

Percentage-of-completion method   When revenues and costs can be reliably estimated, revenue expenses and profit are recognized proportionately, using a percentage based on costs, as a long-term project is completed. (p. 512).

Revenue recognition principle   Accounting principle that revenue should be recognized in the accounting period in which it is earned (generally at the point of sale). (p. 511).

Sales basis   Recognition of revenue at point of sale. Alternatives to this method of recognition are the completed-contract, instalment, and percentage-of-completion methods. (p. 512).

Time period assumption   Accounting assumption that the economic life of a business can be divided into artificial time periods. (p. 511).

DEMONSTRATION PROBLEM 1

Wu Construction Company is under contract to build a condominium at a contract price of $2,000,000. The building will take 18 months to complete, at an estimated cost of $1,400,000. Construction began in November 1998 and will be finished in April 2000. Actual construction costs incurred in each year were: 1998, $140,000; 1999, $910,000; and 2000, $350,000.

Instructions
Compute the gross profit to be recognized in each year.

Solution to Demonstration Problem 1

Year	Costs Incurred (Current Period)	÷	Total Estimated Cost	=	Percent Complete (Current Period)	×	Total Revenue	=	Revenue Recognized (Current Period)
1998	$ 140,000		$1,400,000		10%		$2,000,000		$ 200,000
1999	910,000		1,400,000		65%		2,000,000		1,300,000
2000	350,000				Revenue remaining to be recognized				500,000
	$1,400,000								$2,000,000

Year	Revenue Recognized (Current Period)	−	Actual Cost Incurred (Current Period)	=	Gross Profit Recognized (Current Period)
1998	$ 200,000		$ 140,000		$ 60,000
1999	1,300,000		910,000		390,000
2000	500,000		350,000		150,000
	$2,000,000		$1,400,000		$600,000

Problem-Solving Strategies
1. Percent complete is determined by dividing costs incurred by total estimated costs.
2. Percent complete is multiplied by contract price to find revenue to be recognized.
3. Gross profit equals revenue recognized less actual costs incurred.
4. Percentage-of-completion method recognizes revenue as construction occurs—it is viewed as a series of sales.

DEMONSTRATION PROBLEM 2

Richard Inc. uses the instalment method to account for its sales. During its first year of operations, it had instalment sales of $900,000 and a cost of goods sold on instalments of $600,000. The collections on instalment sales were as follows: Year 1, $330,000; Year 2, $420,000; and Year 3, $150,000.

Instructions
Compute the amount of gross profit to be recognized each year.

Solution to Demonstration Problem 2

Year	Cash Collected	×	Gross Profit Percentage	=	Gross Profit Recognized
1	$330,000		33⅓%		$110,000
2	420,000		33⅓%		140,000
3	150,000		33⅓%		50,000
	$900,000				$300,000

Problem-Solving Strategies
1. Instalment method is used when cash collection is uncertain.
2. Calculate the gross-profit percentage.
3. Gross profit recognized each period equals cash collected times gross-profit percentage.

SELF-STUDY QUESTIONS

Answers are at the end of the chapter.

1. Generally accepted accounting principles are:
   a. a set of standards and rules that are recognized as a general guide for financial reporting.
   b. established by Revenue Canada.
   c. the guidelines used to resolve ethical dilemmas.
   d. fundamental truths that can be derived from the laws of nature.

(SO 2)   2. Which of the following is not an objective of financial reporting?

a. Provide information that is useful in investment and credit decisions.

b. Provide information about economic resources, claims to those resources, and changes in them.

c. Provide information that is useful in assessing future cash flows.

d. Provide information on the liquidation value of a business.

(SO 3)   3. The primary criterion by which accounting information can be judged is:

a. consistency.

b. predictive value.

c. decision-usefulness.

d. comparability.

(SO 3)   4. Verifiablity is an ingredient of:

	Reliability	Relevance
a.	Yes	Yes
b.	No	No
c.	Yes	No
d.	No	Yes

(SO 4,5,6)   5. Valuing assets at their liquidation value, rather than at their cost, is inconsistent with the:

a. time period assumption.

b. matching principle.

c. going concern assumption.

d. materiality constraint.

(SO 5)   6. Gonzalez's Construction Company began a long-term construction contract on January 1, 1999. The contract is expected to be completed in 2000 at a total cost of $20,000,000. Gonzalez's revenue for the project is $24,000,000. Gonzalez incurred contract costs of $4,000,000 in 1999. What gross profit should be recognized in 1999?

a. $800,000.

b. $1,000,000.

c. $2,000,000.

d. $4,000,000.

7. Glackin Company had instalment sales of $1,000,000 in their first year of operations. The cost of goods sold on instalment was $650,000, and Glackin collected a total of $500,000 on the instalment sales. Using the instalment method, how much gross profit should be recognized in the first year?   (SO5)

a. $140,000.

b. $175,000.

c. $350,000.

d. $500,000.

8. When a company's financial statements have been audited, this indicates that: (SO5)

a. the statements have been certified as correct by the public accounting firm that conducted the audit.

b. the financial statements have been prepared by a firm of public accountants, rather than by the company to which they pertain.

c. the financial statements have been checked by Revenue Canada, to ensure compliance with tax laws.

d. in the professional judgement of the public accounting firm that conducted the audit, the statements are not misleading.

9. The accounting term that refers to the tendency of accountants to resolve uncertainty in favour of understating assets and revenues is known as: (SO4,

a. the matching principle.

b. materiality.

c. conservatism.

d. the monetary unit assumption.

10. The organization that issues international accounting standards is the: (SO7)

a. Financial Accounting Standards Board.

b. International Accounting Standards Committee.

c. International Financial Standards Agency.

d. None of the above.

QUESTIONS

1. (a) What are generally accepted accounting principles (GAAP)? (b) What body provides authoritative support for GAAP in Canada?

2. What elements form the CICA's conceptual framework?

3. What are the basic objectives of financial reporting?

4. Identify the essential qualitative characteristics of accounting information.

5. Raynard Company substantially increased its net income in 1999 while keeping its unit inventory relatively the same. The president is very pleased with this. The chief accountant cautions him, however. She points out that, since Raynard changed from the Average Cost to the FIFO method of inventory valuation this year, there is a comparability problem and it would be difficult to determine whether the company's performance is better. Do you agree? Explain.

6. How is the concept of *consistency* related to the qualitative characteristic of comparability?

7. Why does it matter whether accountants assume an economic entity will remain a going concern?

8. When should revenue be recognized? Why is the

date of sale usually chosen as the point at which to recognize the revenue resulting from the entire producing and selling process?

9. Ryder Construction Company has a $200-million contract to build a bridge. Its total estimated cost for the project is $170 million. Costs incurred in the first year of the project were $34 million. Ryder appropriately uses the percentage-of-completion method. How much revenue and gross profit should Ryder recognize in the first year of the project?

10. Merchandise with a cost of $80,000 was sold during the year for $100,000. Cash collected for the year amounted to $40,000. How much gross profit should be recognized during the year, if the company uses the instalment method?

11. Distinguish between expired costs and unexpired costs.

12. Where does the accountant disclose information about an entity's financial position, operations, and cash flows?

13. The nature and amount of information included in financial reports reflects a series of judgemental trade-offs. What are the objectives of these trade-offs?

14. Sue Leonard is the president of Better Books. She has no accounting background, and cannot understand why current cost (or market value) is not used as the basis for accounting measurement and reporting. Explain what basis is used, and why.

15. Describe the two constraints inherent in the presentation of accounting information.

16. Your roommate believes that international accounting standards are uniform throughout the world. Is your roommate correct? Explain.

17. What organization establishes international accounting standards?

BRIEF EXERCISES

BE12–1 Indicate whether each of the following statements is true or false.

1. GAAP is a set of rules and practices established by the accounting profession to serve as a general guide for financial reporting purposes.
2. Substantial authoritative support for GAAP usually comes from two standard-setting bodies: the CICA and Revenue Canada.
3. "Generally accepted" means that these principles must have "substantial authoritative support."

Generally accepted accounting principles.
(SO 1)

BE12–2 Indicate which of the following items is (are) included in the CICA's conceptual framework. (Use "Yes" or "No" to answer this question.)

1. Analysis of financial statement ratios.
2. Objectives of financial reporting.
3. Qualitative characteristics of accounting information.

Items included in the conceptual framework.
(SO 1)

BE12–3 According to the CICA's conceptual framework, which of the following are objectives of financial reporting? (Use "Yes" or "No" to answer this question.)

1. Provide information that is helpful in assessing past cash flows and stock prices.
2. Provide information that is useful to those making investment and credit decisions.
3. Provide information that identifies the economic resources (assets), the claims to those resources (liabilities), and the changes in those resources and claims.

Objectives of financial reporting.
(SO 2)

BE12–4 Presented below is a chart showing the qualitative characteristics of accounting information. Fill in the blanks from (a) to (d).

Qualitative characteristics of accounting.
(SO 3)

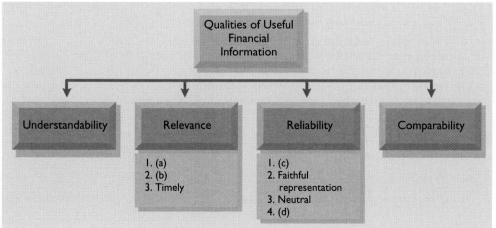

Qualitative characteristics of accounting.
(SO 3)

BE12–5   Using the qualitative characteristics of accounting established by the CICA's conceptual framework, complete each of the following statements:

  1. For information to be_____, it should have predictive or feedback value, and it must be presented on a timely basis.
  2. _____ is the quality of information that gives assurance that it is free of error and bias; it can be depended upon.
  3. _____ means using the same accounting principles and methods from year to year within a company.

Qualitative characteristics of accounting.
(SO 3)

BE12–6   Presented below is a set of qualitative characteristics of accounting information.

  (a) Predictive value.
  (b) Neutral.
  (c) Verifiable.
  (d) Timely.

Match these qualitative characteristics to the following statements:

  1. _____ Accounting information must be available to decision makers before it loses its capacity to influence their decisions.
  2. _____ Accounting information cannot be selected, prepared, or presented to favour one set of interested users over another.
  3. _____ Accounting information must be capable of being proven to be free of error and bias.
  4. _____ Accounting information should help users make predictions about the outcome of past, present, and future events.

Operating guidelines or concepts.
(SO 3, 4, 5)

BE12–7   Presented below are four concepts discussed in this chapter:

  (a) Time period assumption.
  (b) Cost principle.
  (c) Full disclosure principle.
  (d) Conservatism.

Match these concepts to the following accounting practices:

  1. _____ Recording inventory at its purchase price.
  2. _____ Using notes and supplementary schedules in the financial statements.
  3. _____ Preparing financial statements on an annual basis.
  4. _____ Using the lower of cost and market method for inventory valuation.

Revenue recognition— percentage of completion method.
(SO 5)

BE12–8   Hard Hat Construction Company was under contract to build a commercial building at a price of $4,000,000. Construction began in January 1997 and was finished in December 1999. Total estimated construction costs were $2,800,000. Actual construction costs incurred in each year were: 1997, $560,000; 1998, $1,820,000; 1999, $420,000. Compute the revenue to be recognized in each year, using the percentage-of-completion method.

Revenue recognition— instalment method.
(SO 5)

BE12–9   Waldo Co. uses the instalment method to determine its net income. During its first year of operations, it had instalment sales of $800,000 and a cost of goods sold of $600,000. The collections on instalment sales were as follows: Year 1, $360,000; Year 2, $440,000. Determine the gross profit recognized for Years 1 and 2.

Violation of accounting concepts.
(SO 3, 4, 5, 6)

BE12–10   The Emelda Company uses the following accounting practices:

  1. Inventory is reported at cost when market value is lower.
  2. Revenue on instalment sales is recognized at the time of sale.
  3. Small tools are recorded as capital assets and amortized.
  4. The income statement shows paper clips expense of $10.
Indicate the accounting concept, if any, that has been violated by each practice.

EXERCISES

•••

Identify the assumption, principle, or constraint that has been violated.
(SO 4, 5, 6)

E12–1   A number of accounting reporting situations are described below:

  1. Tercek Company recognizes revenue at the end of the production cycle, but before sale. The

price of the product, as well as the amount that can be sold, is not certain.

2. In preparing its financial statements, Seco Company omitted information concerning its method of accounting for inventories.

3. Shea Company uses the direct write-off method of accounting for uncollectible accounts.

4. Ravine Hospital Supply Corporation reports only current assets and current liabilities on its balance sheet. Capital assets and bonds payable are reported as current assets and current liabilities, respectively. Liquidation of the company is unlikely.

5. Barton Inc. is carrying inventory at its current market value of $100,000. Inventory had an original cost of $110,000.

6. Bonilla Company is in its fifth year of operation and has yet to issue financial statements.

7. Watts Company has inventory on hand that cost $400,000. Watts reports inventory on its balance sheet at its current market value of $425,000.

8. Steph Wolfson, president of the Classic Music Company, bought a computer for her personal use. She paid for the computer by using company funds and debited the "computers" account.

Instructions

For each of the above, list the assumption, principle, or constraint that has been violated, if any. List only one term for each case.

E12–2   Presented below are some business transactions that occurred during 1999 for Marietta Co.

Identify the assumption, principle, or constraint that has been violated, and prepare correct entries.
(SO 4, 5, 6)

(a) Equipment worth $90,000 was acquired at a cost of $72,000 from a company that had water damage in a flood. The following entry was made:

Equipment	90,000	
Cash		72,000
Gain		18,000

(b) The president of Marietta Co., George Winston, purchased a truck for personal use and charged it to his expense account. The following entry was made:

Travel Expense	18,000	
Cash		18,000

(c) An account receivable has become a bad debt. The following entry was made:

Allowance for Doubtful Accounts	7,000	
Accounts Receivable		7,000

(d) Merchandise inventory with a cost of $208,000 is reported at its market value of $260,000. The following entry was made:

Merchandise Inventory	52,000	
Gain		52,000

(e) An electric pencil sharpener costing $50 is being amortized over five years. The following entry was made:

Amortization Expense—Pencil Sharpener	10	
Accumulated Amortization—Pencil Sharpener		10

Instructions

In each of the situations above, identify the assumption, principle, or constraint that has been violated, if any, and discuss the appropriateness of the journal entries. Give the correct journal entry, if necessary.

E12–3   Presented below are accounting concepts, assumptions, principles, and constraints discussed in this chapter:

Identify the assumption, principle, or constraint related to various situations.
(SO 4, 5, 6)

(a) Economic entity assumption.
(b) Going concern assumption.
(c) Monetary unit assumption.
(d) Time period assumption.
(e) Cost principle.

(f) Matching principle.
(g) Full disclosure principle.
(h) Revenue recognition principle.
(i) Materiality.
(j) Cost-benefit.

Instructions

Identify by letter the accounting assumption, principle, or constraint that describes each situation below. Do not use a letter more than once.

1. Is the rationale for why capital assets are not reported at liquidation value. (Do not use the historical cost principle.)

2. Indicates that personal and business record-keeping should be separately maintained.

3. Ensures that all relevant financial information is reported.

4. Assumes that the dollar is the appropriate "measuring stick" for reporting on financial performance.

5. Requires that the accounting guidelines be followed for all significant items.

6. Separates financial information into time periods for reporting purposes.

7. Requires recognition of expenses in the same period as related revenues.

8. Indicates that market value changes after a purchase are not recorded in the accounts.

Determine the amount of revenue to be recognized.
(SO 5)

E12–4   Consider the following transactions of Kokomo Company for 1999:

1. Leased office space to Excel Supplies for a one-year period begininning September 1. The rent of $36,000 was paid in advance.

2. A sales order for merchandise that cost $9,000 and was sold for $12,000 was received on December 28 from Warfield Company. The goods were shipped FOB Kokomo's warehouse on December 31 and Warfield received them on January 3, 2000.

3. Signed a long-term contract to construct a building at a total price of $1,800,000. Total estimated cost of construction is $1,200,000. During 1999, the company incurred $300,000 of costs and collected $330,000 in cash. The percentage-of-completion method is used to recognize revenue.

4. Merchandise inventory on hand at year end amounted to $160,000. Kokomo expects to sell the inventory in 2000 for $180,000.

Instructions

For each item above, indicate the amount of revenue Kokomo should recognize in 1999. Explain.

Determine the gross profit for a construction project.
(SO 5)

E12–5   Qi Shen Construction Company currently has one long-term construction project. The project has a contract price of $150,000,000 with total estimated costs of $100,000,000. Qi Shen appropriately uses the percentage-of-completion method. After two years of construction, the following costs have been accumulated:

Actual cost incurred, Year 1	$30,000,000
Total estimated cost remaining after Year 1	70,000,000
Actual cost incurred, Year 2	50,000,000
Total estimated cost remaining after Year 2	20,000,000

Instructions

Determine the gross profit that should be recognized for each of the first two years of the construction contract.

Determine the gross profit, using the instalment and point-of-sale bases of revenue recognition.
(SO 5)

E12–6   Wabush Company sold equipment for $300,000 in 1998. Collections on the sale were as follows: 1998, $70,000; 1999, $190,000; 2000, $40,000. Wabush's cost of goods sold is typically 75% of sales.

Instructions

(a) Determine Wabush's gross profit for 1998, 1999, and 2000, assuming that Wabush recognizes revenue under the instalment method.

(b) Determine Wabush's gross profit for 1998, 1999, and 2000, assuming that Wabush recognizes revenue under the point-of-sale basis.

PROBLEMS

••

P12–1 Ava and Brad are accountants for Qwik Printers. They are having disagreements concerning the following transactions that occurred during the year:

Analyse transactions to identify principle or assumption violated; prepare correct entries.
(SO 4, 5)

1. Qwik bought equipment for $30,000, including installation costs. The equipment has a useful life of five years. Qwik amortizes equipment using the straight-line method. "Since the equipment as installed into our system cannot be removed without considerable damage, it will have no resale value, and therefore should not be amortized but, instead, expensed immediately," argues Ava.

2. Amortization for the year was $26,000. Since net income is expected to be low this year, Ava suggests deferring amortization to a year when there is more net income.

3. Qwik purchased equipment at a fire sale for $21,000. The equipment would normally have cost $26,000. Ava believes that the following entry should be made:

Equipment	26,000	
Cash		21,000
Gain on Purchase of Equipment		5,000

4. Ava says that Qwik should carry equipment on the balance sheet at its liquidation value, which is $20,000 less than its cost.

5. Qwik rented office space for one year, starting October 1. The total amount of $24,000 was paid in advance. Ava believes that the following entry should be made on October 1:

Rent Expense	24,000	
Cash		24,000

The company's fiscal year ends on December 31.

6. Land that cost $41,000 was appraised at $49,000. Ava suggests the following journal entry:

Land	8,000	
Gain on Appreciation of Land		8,000

Brad disagrees with Ava on each of the situations above.

Instructions

For each transaction, indicate why Brad disagrees. Identify the accounting principle or assumption that Ava would be violating if her suggestions were used. Prepare the correct journal entry for each transaction, if any.

P12–2 Presented below are a number of business transactions that occurred during the current year for Chita, Inc.:

Determine the appropriateness of journal entries, in terms of generally accepted accounting principles or assumptions.
(SO 4, 5)

1. An order for $70,000 has been received from a customer for products on hand. This order is to be shipped on January 9 next year. The following entry was made:

Accounts Receivable	70,000	
Sales		70,000

2. Because of a "flood sale," equipment obviously worth $300,000 was acquired at a cost of $250,000. The following entry was made:

Equipment	300,000	
Cash		250,000
Gain on Purchase of Equipment		50,000

3. Because the general level of prices increased during the current year, Chita, Inc. determined that there was a $40,000 understatement of amortization expense on its equipment and decided to record it in its accounts. The following entry was made:

Amortization Expense	40,000	
Accumulated Amortization		40,000

4. The president of Chita, Inc. used his expense account to purchase a pre-owned Mercedes-Benz 190 solely for personal use. The following entry was made:

Miscellaneous Expense	28,000	
Cash		28,000

5. Land was purchased on April 30 for $200,000 and this amount was entered in the Land account. On December 31, the land would have cost $230,000, so the following entry was made:

Land	30,000	
Gain on Land		30,000

Instructions

▸ In each of the situations above, discuss the appropriateness of the journal entries in terms of generally accepted accounting principles.

Recognize gross profit using the percentage-of-completion method.
(SO 5)

P12–3   Beaver Construction Company is involved in a long-term construction contract to build an office building at a total estimated cost of $30 million and a contract price of $40 million. Additional information follows:

	Cash Collections	Actual Costs Incurred
1998	$ 9,000,000	$ 4,500,000
1999	9,000,000	6,000,000
2000	12,500,000	12,000,000
2001	9,500,000	7,500,000

Instructions

Prepare a schedule to determine the gross profit in each year for the contract, using the percentage-of-completion method.

Recognize gross profit using the instalment method.
(SO 5)

P12–4   Beaver Construction sold apartments it had constructed to Mattson Management Company for $2.5 million. Beaver's cost to construct the apartments was $2 million. Beaver appropriately uses the instalment method. Additional information follows:

Year	Cash Collected
1998	$ 800,000
1999	1,200,000
2000	500,000

(a) Determine the gross profit for each year using the instalment method.

(b) Repeat (a) assuming the construction costs were $1.8 million.

Identify accounting assumptions, principles, and constraints.
(SO 4, 5, 6)

P12–5   Presented below are accounting assumptions, principles, and constraints discussed in this chapter.

(a) Economic entity assumption
(b) Going concern assumption
(c) Monetary unit assumption
(d) Time period assumption
(e) Full disclosure principle
(f) Revenue recognition principle
(g) Matching principle
(h) Cost principle
(i) Materiality
(j) Cost-benefit

Identify by letter the accounting assumption, principle, or constraint that describes each situation below. *Do not use a letter more than once.*

1. Assets are not stated at their liquidation value.
2. The death of the president is not recorded in the accounts.
3. Repair tools are expensed when purchased.
4. An allowance for doubtful accounts is established.
5. Market value changes subsequent to purchase are not recorded in the accounts.
6. Reporting must be done at defined intervals.
7. Revenue is recorded at the point of sale.
8. Small businesses do not have to comply with all GAAP when preparing financial statements.
9. All important information is presented in the footnotes or in the financial statements.
10. Indicates that personal and business record keeping should be separately maintained.

Recognize gross profit using the instalment method, with complexities.
(SO 4, 5)

P12–6   Crazy Carl's Deep Discount Furniture Store makes many of its sales on long-term instalment contracts, and accounts for these using the instalment method. During 1997, Crazy Carl's had

$840,000 of instalment sales; the related cost of goods sold was $588,000. The instalment contracts called for the customers' payments to be made as follows:

1997	$160,000
1998	$200,000
1999	$200,000
2000	$200,000
2001	$ 80,000

The company collected the payments for 1997 through 1999 exactly as scheduled above. However, in 2000 and 2001 things were quite different:

1. Collections in 2000 were only $180,000. Nevertheless, the company was hopeful that the amounts in arrears would soon be collected.
2. Collections in 2001 were only $50,000, and the company conceded that none of the amounts in arrears (neither the $20,000 from 2000 nor the $30,000 from 2001) would ever be collected.

Instructions

(a) Calculate the amount of gross profit to be recognized in the years 1997 though 1999.

(b) Calculate the amount of gross profit to be recognized in 2000. (Hint: Note that the overall gross profit expected to be earned on these instalment sales has not been changed by the year's events. Therefore, you can follow the usual instalment method procedures in this situation.)

(c) Calculate the amount of gross profit (if any) to be recognized in 2001. (Hint: Note that the overall gross profit earned on these instalment sales has been changed by this year's developments. Therefore, you should begin by calculating the overall gross profit actually realized on these sales, and then compare it to the cumulative amount recognized already, in the years 1997 through 2000.)

(d) ▭▭▭▷ Comment on the above results.

P12–7 Karim Construction Company has a contract for the construction of a new health and fitness centre, and is accounting for this project using the percentage-of-completion method. The contract amount is $2,000,000 and the costs of construction are initially expected to total $1,500,000.

Recognize gross profit using the percentage-of-completion method, with complexities. (SO 4, 5)

The actual costs incurred each year, the estimated remaining costs to complete the contract, and the expected total cost of the construction are shown below for the three-year life of the project:

Year	Actual Cost Incurred During the Year	Remaining Cost to be Incurred	Expected Total Cost
1998	$500,000	$1,000,000	$1,500,000
1999	$500,000	$ 500,000	$1,500,000
2000	$400,000	Contract completed	$1,400,000 (actual)

Instructions

(a) Calculate the amount of gross profit to be recognized in each of the years 1998 and 1999.

(b) Calculate the amount of gross profit (if any) to be recognized in 2000. (Hint: Note that the overall gross profit earned on the project is different from previously expected. Therefore, you should begin by calculating the overall gross profit actually realized on the contract, and then compare it to the cumulative amount that has already been recognized, in 1998 and 1999.)

(c) ▭▭▭▷ Comment on the above results.

P12–8 Some companies adopt a policy of writing off items such as intangible assets over a very short period of time, and defend this as "conservative" accounting practice.

Consider the nature of conservatism and the impact of conservative accounting policies. (SO 3)

Instructions

▭▭▭▷ Comment on this type of policy. Consider: (1) the intent of conservatism and (2) the effects of such a policy on net income, during both the period over which the asset is written off and subsequent periods.

Discuss various alternatives
regarding revenue recognition.
(SO 5)

P12–9   Consider the following events, which are listed in chronological order:

1. Dexter Maersk decides to buy a custom-made snowboard and calls The Great Canadian Snowboard Company to inquire about their products.

2. Dexter requests Great Canadian Snowboard to manufacture a custom board for him.

3. The company sends Dexter a purchase order to fill out, which he immediately completes, signs, and sends back.

4. Great Canadian Snowboard receives Dexter's purchase order and begins working on his board.

5. The Great Canadian Snowboard Company has its fiscal year end. At this time, Dexter's board is 75% completed.

6. The company completes the snowboard for Dexter and notifies him to take delivery.

7. Dexter picks up his new snowboard from the company and carefully takes it home.

8. Dexter tries the snowboard out and likes it so much that he carves his initials into it.

9. The Great Canadian Snowboard Company bills Dexter for the cost of the snowboard.

10. The company receives partial payment from Dexter, in the form of a cheque written on the back of an old envelope.

11. The company is relieved when Dexter's cheque is cleared by the bank.

12. The company receives payment of the balance due from Dexter, in cash.

Instructions

Discuss the following:

(a) When could The Great Canadian Snowboard Company record the revenue related to this snowboard? Consider several possible points, in light of the revenue recognition principle.

(b) Suppose that, with his purchase order, Dexter was required to make a down payment. Would that change your answer?

(c) Suppose that Great Canadian Snowboard had sold items to Dexter in the past, and had always been paid. Would that change your answer?

*B*roadening *Your Perspective*

FINANCIAL REPORTING PROBLEM

Refer to the Notes to Consolidated Financial Statements for The Second Cup Ltd., in Appendix A.

Instructions

Answer the following questions:

(a) One of the subsections of Note 1 describes The Second Cup's accounting policy regarding Store Pre-opening Costs. Explain how the company's treatment of these costs relates to (1) the matching principle, and (2) the going-concern or continuity assumption.

(b) Note 8 refers to the company's Provision For Coffee Plantation Store Closures. What accounting principles and constraints are reflected in this disclosure?

(c) Note 12 provides information concerning transactions with companies that are related (in terms of ownership) to The Second Cup. Why might it be important for readers of the financial statements to be aware of these transactions?

DECISION CASE

Hague Industries has two operating divisions—Devany Construction Division and Security Equipment Division. Both divisions maintain their own accounting systems and methods of revenue recognition.

Devany Construction Division

During the fiscal year ended November 30, 1999, Devany Construction Division had one construction project in progress. A $30,000,000 contract for construction of a civic centre was granted on June 19 and construction began on August 1, 1999. Estimated costs of completion at the contract date were $26,000,000 over a two-year period. By November 30, 1999, construction costs of $8,000,000 had been incurred.

The construction costs to complete the remainder of the project were reviewed on November 30, 1999, and were estimated to amount to only $16,000,000 because of an expected decline in raw materials costs.

Revenue recognition is based upon the percentage-of-completion method.

Security Equipment Division

Security Equipment Division works through manufacturers' agents in various cities. Orders for alarm systems, and down payments, are forwarded from the agents. The division ships the goods FOB factory directly to customers (usually police departments and security-guard companies). Customers are billed directly for the balance due, plus the actual shipping costs.

The firm received orders for $6,000,000 of goods during the fiscal year ended November 30, 1999. Down payments of $600,000 were received, and goods with a selling price of $5,000,000 were billed and shipped. Actual freight costs of $100,000 were also billed. Commissions of 10% of the product price are paid to the agents, after the goods are shipped to the customers. Such goods are warranted for 90 days after shipment, and warranty returns have been about 1% of sales.

Revenue is recognized at the point of sale by this division.

Instructions

(a) There are various methods of revenue recognition. Define and describe each of the following methods of revenue recognition, and indicate the circumstances under which each of them is in accordance with generally accepted accounting principles.
   1. Point of sale.
   2. Percentage-of-completion.
   3. Completed contract.
   4. Instalment sales.
(b) Compute the amount of *revenue* to be recognized in fiscal year 1999 for each operating division of Hague Industries, in accordance with generally accepted accounting principles.

COMMUNICATION ACTIVITY

Sue Federco has successfully completed her first accounting course and is now working as a management trainee for the National Bank during the summer. One of her fellow management trainees, Bill Harlow, is taking the same accounting course this summer and has been having a "lot of trouble." On a recent examination, for example, Bill became confused about inventory valuation methods and completely missed all the points on a problem involving this issue.

Bill's instructor recently indicated that the next examination will probably have a number of essay questions dealing with accounting principles. Bill is quite concerned about this for two reasons. First, he has never taken an accounting examination where essay answers are required. Second, Bill knows that he has to do well on the next examination in order to get an acceptable grade in the course.

Bill has therefore asked Sue to help him prepare for the next examination. Sue agrees, and asks Bill to develop a set of possible questions on the accounting principles material which they will disuss.

Instructions

Answer the following questions that were developed by Bill:

(a) What is a conceptual framework?

(b) Why is there a need for a conceptual framework in accounting?

(c) What are the objectives of financial reporting?

(d) If you had to explain "generally accepted accounting principles" to a non-accountant, what essential characteristics would you include in your explanation?

(e) What are the qualitative characteristics of accounting information? Explain each one.

(f) Identify the basic assumptions used in accounting.

(g) What are two major constraints involved in financial reporting? Explain both of them.

GROUP ACTIVITY
· ·

Assume that the CICA has decided to address the problem of information overload. It has agreed to eliminate one of the principles, assumptions, constraints, or qualitative characteristics listed below. This concept will be deleted from all textbooks and will no longer be considered important in accounting literature.

Instructions

With the class divided into groups, each group will be assigned one or more of the following:

Relevance	Revenue recognition
Reliability	Matching
Comparability	Full disclosure
Economic entity	Cost
Monetary unit	Materiality
Time period	Cost-benefit
Going concern	Understandability

(a) Discuss within your group why your specific concept(s) should not be eliminated.

(b) Pick a group leader who will present to the class the group's reasons why the CICA should not delete your group's concept(s).

(c) At the end of all the presentations, the class should vote on which concept to delete.

ETHICS CASE
· ·

When the CICA issues new accounting recommendations, the required implementation date is usually 12 months or more after the date of issuance, but early implementation is encouraged.

Kathy Johnston, accountant at Redondo Corporation, discusses with her financial vice-president the need for early implementation of a recently issued recommendation. She says it will result in a much fairer presentation of the company's financial condition and earnings. When the financial vice-president determines that early implementation of the new Handbook section would adversely affect reported net income for the year, he strongly discourages Kathy from implementing the recommendation until it is required.

Instructions

(a) Who are the stakeholders in this situation?

(b) What, if any, are the ethical considerations in this situation?

(c) What could Kathy gain by supporting early implementation? Who might be affected by the decision against early implementation?

CRITICAL THINKING

Consider the case of a company that reported the following capital assets in its financial statements at the end of:

	1998	1999	2000
Equipment, at cost	$100,000	$100,000	$100,000
Less: Accumulated amortization	30,000	40,000	50,000
Net book value	70,000	60,000	50,000
Buildings, at cost	$900,000	$900,000	$900,000
Less: Accumulated amortization	100,000	150,000	200,000
Net book value	800,000	750,000	700,000
Land, at cost	$200,000	$200,000	$200,000

The estimated current market values of these assets (after taking "wear and tear," age, etc., into consideration) were as follows:

	1998	1999	2000
Equipment	$ 75,000	$ 70,000	$ 65,000
Buildings	850,000	875,000	900,000
Land	300,000	325,000	350,000

Instructions

(a) Notice that the net book values of the capital assets shown on the financial statements are consistently below their current market values, and that the gap is widening each year. Discuss this situation, criticizing or defending it in light of: (1) generally accepted accounting principles, and (2) the likely implications (if any) for the users of the financial statements.

(b) The amounts shown for equipment and buildings in the financial statements indicate that the value of these assets is considerably less in 2000 than it was in 1998. Comment on the extent to which this is, or is not, a reasonable representation in light of the information presented regarding the current market values of the equipment and buildings. (Hint: You should consider—among other things—whether the increase in market values is likely to be temporary or permanent.)

(c) The amount shown for the land in the financial statements indicates that the value of this asset is the same in 2000 as it was in 1998. Comment on the extent to which this is, or is not, a reasonable representation, in light of the information presented regarding the current market value of the land. (Hint: Consider whether the owners of the business are "better off" in 2000 than in 1998 as a result of the increase in the current market value of the land.)

 ACCOUNTING ON THE WEB

This case reviews the mandates of two organizations—the Canadian Institute of Chartered Accountants and the International Accounting Standards Committee—which are responsible for the development of accounting principles used in financial reporting in Canada and worldwide, respectively. The structure and composition of their standard-setting boards and committees are also examined.

Instructions

Specific requirements of this Internet case are available on-line at www.wiley.com/canada/weygandt.

CUMULATIVE COVERAGE—CHAPTERS 8 TO 12

Nahas Company and Nordlund Company are competing businesses. Both began operations six years ago and are quite similar in most respects. The current balance sheet data for the two companies are as follows:

	Nahas Company	Nordlund Company
Cash	$ 50,300	$ 48,400
Accounts receivable	309,700	312,500
Allowance for doubtful accounts	(13,600)	-0-
Merchandise inventory	463,900	520,200
Capital assets	245,300	257,300
Accumulated amortization, capital assets	(107,650)	(189,850)
Total assets	$947,950	$948,550
Current liabilities	$440,200	$ 436,500
Long-term liabilities	78,000	80,000
Total liabilities	518,200	516,500
Owner's equity	429,750	432,050
Total liabilities and owner's equity	$947,950	$948,550

You have been engaged as a consultant to conduct a review of the two companies. Your goal is to determine which of them is in the stronger financial position.

Your review of their financial statements quickly reveals that the two companies have not followed the same accounting practices. The differences, and your conclusions regarding them, are summarized below:

1. Nahas Company has used the allowance method of accounting for bad debts. A review shows that the amount of its write offs each year have been quite close to the allowances that have been provided. It therefore seems reasonable to have confidence in its current estimate of bad debts.

   Nordlund Company has used the direct write off method for bad debts, and has been somewhat slow to write off its uncollectible accounts. Based upon an aging analysis and review of its accounts receivable, it is estimated that $24,000 of its existing accounts will probably prove to be uncollectible.

2. Nahas Company has determined the cost of its merchandise inventory on a LIFO basis, with the result that its inventory appears on the balance sheet at an amount that is below its current replacement cost. Based upon a detailed physical examination of its merchandise on hand, the current replacement cost of its inventory is estimated at $517,000.

   Nordlund Company has used the FIFO method of valuing its merchandise inventory, with the result that its ending inventory appears on the balance sheet at an amount that quite closely approximates its current replacement cost.

3. Nahas Company estimated a useful life of 12 years and a salvage value of $30,000 for its capital assets, and has been amortizing them on a straight-line basis.

   Nordlund Company has the same type of capital assets. However, it estimated a useful life of 10 years and a salvage value of $10,000, and has been amortizing its capital assets using the double-declining-balance method.

   Based upon engineering studies of these types of capital assets, you conclude that Nordlund's estimates and method for calculating amortization are the more appropriate.

4. Among its current liabilities, Nahas has included the portions of long-term liabilities that become due within the next year. Nordlund has not done so.

   You find that $20,000 of Nordlund's $80,000 of long-term liabilities are due to be repaid in the current year.

Instructions

(a) Revise the balance sheets presented above, so that the data are comparable and reflect the current financial position for each of the two companies.

(b) Prepare a brief report to your client, stating your conclusions.

Answers to Self-Study Questions

1. a 2. d 3. c 4. c 5. c 6. a 7. b 8. d 9. c 10. b

░░░░ ▶ **Concepts for Review**

Before studying this chapter, you should understand or, if necessary, review:

a. *The cost principle of accounting. (Ch. 1, p. 11)*
b. *The statement of owner's equity. (Ch. 1, p. 26)*
c. *How to make closing entries and prepare the post-closing trial balance. (Ch. 4, pp. 142–148)*
d. *The steps in the accounting cycle. (Ch. 4, p. 149)*
e. *The format of a classified balance sheet. (Ch. 4, pp. 155–156)*

Partners Come and Go, But the Beat Goes On

HALIFAX, N.S.—Cinnamon Toast Records may not be a household name, but the alternative pop bands such as Plumtree and Sloan that have appeared under its label are popular on campus and community radio stations across the country. Several have been nominated for East Coast Music Awards.

In 1992, Cinnamon Toast was founded as a partnership by four young music lovers in Halifax. "We weren't exactly very formal about it," says Walter Forsyth, one of the founding partners, "but we did draw up a partnership agreement— though I don't think we even typed it—setting out the mandate of the company and what the partners should expect to put into the business and get out of it. We agreed we would figure out what it was worth and split the assets equally."

Typed or not, the agreement's basic principles have become important over the years as the structure of Cinnamon Toast's ownership has changed. For example, one partner left after about a year. The departing partner's interest was bought out by the partnership, in accordance with the withdrawal clause in the agree-

ment. Fortunately for the remaining partners, although the label had produced one album, it hadn't realized a profit yet. Therefore, the value of the partnership assets hadn't changed very much.

Another time, a new partner joined by investing assets in the partnership, which brought an infusion of capital at a time when it was greatly needed. On another occasion, a departing partner paid a bonus to the remaining ones, recovering less than his original investment because the fair market value of the partnership assets was low.

Cinnamon Toast has found this flexibility to be only one advantage. Another advantage is the pooling of skills that has been facilitated—for a time, one of the partners was a

graphic designer, who was able to contribute to marketing material and album covers.

Today, the company is owned by three partners: Walter Forsyth, Colin MacKenzie, and Shawn Duggan. Their current catalogue lists five CDs and cassettes, plus a dozen seven-inch singles in good old-fashioned vinyl, which the bands use "like business cards." None of the partners expects to get rich from Cinnamon Toast—all have other sources of income—but they are serious players in the East Coast independent music scene.

Their advice to anyone thinking of forming a partnership? "Communication is essential. When money gets involved, things can get difficult. Strive for fairness." ◀

ACCOUNTING FOR PARTNERSHIPS

It is not surprising that the four music lovers who founded Cinnamon Toast Records decided to use the partnership form of organization. They saw the need for hands-on control of their product and its promotion. In this chapter, we will discuss reasons why the partnership form of organization is popular, and explain the major issues in accounting for partnerships. The organization of this chapter is as follows:

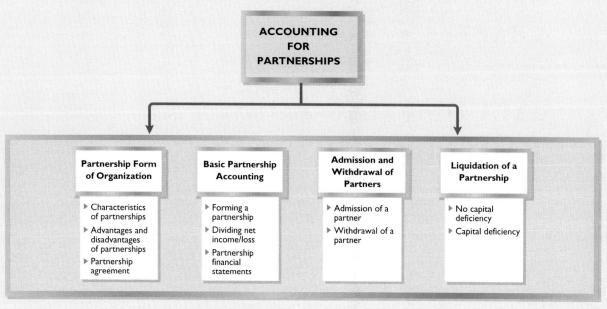

▼Partnership Form of Organization

All common law provinces in Canada have a *Partnership Act*, which provides the basic rules for the formation and operation of partnerships. These acts define a **partnership** as two or more people who carry on business with the intention of making a profit. This does not necessarily mean that you must make a profit—just that profit is your objective. Partnerships are common among retail establishments and small manufacturing companies. Similarly, if you enter a profession such as accounting, advertising, law, or medicine, you may find it desirable to form a partnership with other professionals in your field. Professional partnerships can vary in size from two to thousands of partners.

Characteristics of Partnerships

STUDY OBJECTIVE

Identify the characteristics of the partnership form of business organization.

Partnerships are fairly easy to form, as indicated in the opening vignette of this chapter. Although they can be formed by a verbal agreement, partners who have not put in writing the rights and obligations of the partners have found that the absence of a written agreement can sometimes lead to later difficulties. The principal characteristics of the partnership form of business organization are shown in Illustration 13-1, and are explained in the following sections.

Illustration 13-1

Partnership characteristics

Association of Individuals

The voluntary association of two or more individuals in a partnership may be based on an act as simple as a handshake. However, it is preferable to state the agreement in writing. A partnership is a legal entity for certain purposes. For instance, property (land, buildings, equipment) can be owned in the name of the partnership, and the firm can sue or be sued. **A partnership is also an accounting entity for financial reporting purposes.** Thus, the purely personal assets, liabilities, and transactions of the partners are excluded from the accounting records of the partnership, just as they are in a proprietorship.

The net income of a partnership is not taxed as a separate entity. Instead each partner's share is personally taxable. This share of income is recorded on the partner's personal income tax return and taxed at his or her personal tax rate, regardless of the amount withdrawn from the partnership during the year.

Mutual Agency

Mutual agency means that each partner acts for the partnership when doing partnership business. The action of any partner is binding on all other partners, even when partners exceed their authority, so long as the act appears appropriate for the partnership. For example, a partner of a grocery store who purchases a delivery truck creates a binding contract in the name of the partnership, even if the partnership agreement denies this authority. On the other hand, if a partner in a law firm were to purchase a snowmobile for the partnership, such an act would not be binding on the partnership because it is clearly unrelated to the activities of a law firm.

Helpful hint Because of mutual agency, an individual should be extremely cautious in selecting partners.

Limited Life

A partnership does not have unlimited life. A partnership may be ended voluntarily at any time when either a new partner joins the firm or a current partner withdraws. A partnership may be ended involuntarily if a partner either dies or is incapacitated. Partnership dissolution occurs whenever there is a change in the number of partners, regardless of the cause. Dissolution of a partnership does not necessarily mean that the business ends. If the continuing partners agree, operations can continue, without interruption, through the formation of a new partnership.

Unlimited Liability

Case in point Concern over unlimited liability is reduced in small partnerships in which partners work closely together and have faith in each other's competence and integrity.

Each partner is **jointly and severally (individually) liable** for all partnership liabilities. If one partner incurs a liability, the other partner(s) is (are) also held responsible. This is sometimes called **vicarious liability**. In addition, the **liability is unlimited** and so each partner's personal assets are also at risk. Creditors' claims attach first to partnership assets and then to the personal resources of any partner, regardless of that partner's equity in the partnership. To illustrate, assume that: (1) the Hasan & Machat partnership is terminated when the claims of company creditors exceed partnership assets by $30,000, and (2) L. Hasan's personal assets total $40,000 but B. Machat has no personal assets. Creditors can collect their total claims from Hasan regardless of Hasan's equity in the firm, even though Machat and Hasan may be equal partners. Hasan, in turn, has a legal claim on Machat, but this would be worthless because Machat has no assets.

►Accounting in Action ► *Business Insight*

 The legal liability of audit partners has been interpreted differently by the courts over the past two decades. This has left the auditing profession concerned about seemingly unlimited amounts of liability. Canadian accounting firms have experienced a dramatic increase in lawsuits. Practitioners were particularly unnerved by a series of suits, totalling more than $716 million. They were brought against the Coopers & Lybrand (as it was then named) accounting firm by the creditors and investors of a Montreal-based mortgage company.

Auditors heaved a huge sigh of relief when the Supreme Court of Canada recently ruled that while a duty of care is owed by auditors to their client, auditors are not generally liable to unknown third parties such as creditors, shareholders, and potential investors.

Canadian law also allows registration of limited partnerships under provincial legislation. In a limited partnership, one or more partners have unlimited liability and one or more partners have limited liability for the debts of the firm. The former are called **general partners** and the latter are called **limited partners**. The responsibility of limited partners for the debts of the partnership is limited to their investment in the firm. For the privilege of limited liability, the limited partner usually accepts less compensation than a general partner and has little or no influence over the affairs of the firm. This form of organization works well in large partnerships where the partners do not work together closely. In such cases, partners want some protection from liability caused by the acts of partners they may hardly know.

Co-ownership of Property

Partnership assets are owned jointly by all the partners. If the partnership is terminated, the assets do not legally return to the original contributor. Each partner has a claim on total assets equal to the balance in his or her respective capital account. This claim does not attach to specific assets that an individual partner contributed to the firm.

►Accounting in Action ► *Business Insight*

 Limited partnerships were very popular as income tax shelters in the 1980s. At that time, more than 4,000 limited partners invested in Journey's End hotels and motels across Canada. When Revenue Canada ended these tax shelters in the 1990s, these investments—often not good investments on their own—lost much of their appeal. Since then, limited partners have had difficulty selling these properties. Until recently, that is, when Journey's End Corp. offered up to $200 million to buy out 4,000 limited partners' interests in 55 properties located throughout eight provinces.

Source: Globe and Mail, June 24, 1997, B6.

Similarly, if a partner invests a building in the partnership that is valued at $100,000 and the building is later sold at a gain of $20,000, that partner does not personally receive the entire gain. Partnership net income (or net loss) is also co-owned. **If the partnership contract does not specify to the contrary, all net income or net loss is shared equally by the partners.** As you will see later, partners may agree to unequal sharing of net income or net loss.

Advantages and Disadvantages of Partnerships

Why do people choose to form partnerships? Often, it is to combine the **skills and resources of two or more individuals**. For example, the partners of Cinnamon Toast Records are able to share their knowledge of the music scene and divide operating responsibilities such as acquisition of new bands, promotion and marketing, and finance and accounting.

In addition, a partnership does not have to deal with the "red tape" that a corporation must face. That is, a partnership is **easily formed and is relatively free from governmental regulations and restrictions**. Decisions can be made quickly on important matters that affect the firm, whereas in a corporation, formal meetings with the board of directors and shareholders are often needed.

On the other hand, partnerships also have some major disadvantages: **mutual agency, limited life, and unlimited liability**. Unlimited liability is particularly troublesome to many individuals because they may lose not only their initial investment, but also their personal assets if those assets are needed to pay partnership creditors. As a result, partnerships often find it difficult to obtain large amounts of investment capital. That is one reason why the largest business enterprises in Canada are corporations, not partnerships.

The advantages and disadvantages of the partnership form of business organization are summarized in Illustration 13-2:

Advantages	Disadvantages
Combines the skills and resources of two or more individuals	Mutual agency
Easily formed	Limited life
Relatively free of governmental regulations and restrictions	Unlimited liability
Ease of decision making	

Illustration 13-2

Advantages and disadvantages of a partnership

Partnership Agreement

Ideally, the voluntary agreement of two or more individuals to form a partnership should be in the form of a written contract, known as the partnership agreement. The partnership agreement contains such basic information as the name and principal location of the firm, the purpose of the business, and the date of inception. In addition, different relationships that might exist among the partners are specified, such as the following:

1. Names and capital contributions of partners.
2. Rights and duties of partners.
3. Basis for sharing net income or net loss.
4. Provision for withdrawals of assets.
5. Procedures for submitting disputes to arbitration.
6. Procedures for the withdrawal, or addition, of a partner.
7. Rights and duties of surviving partners in the event of a partner's death.

The importance of a written contract—even a handwritten contract like that of Cinnamon Toast—cannot be overemphasized. If a partnership agreement does not exist, the provisions of the *Partnership Act* will apply, which may not conform to the wishes of the partners. The partnership agreement should be drawn with care and should attempt to anticipate all possible situations, contingencies, and disagreements. A poorly drawn contract may create friction among the partners and eventually cause the termination of the partnership.

Before You Go On . . .

►Review It

1. What are the distinguishing characteristics of a partnership?
2. What are the principal advantages and disadvantages of a partnership?
3. What are the major items in a partnership agreement?

Basic Partnership Accounting

We now turn our attention to the basic accounting for partnerships. The major accounting issues relate to forming the partnership, dividing net income or net loss, and preparing financial statements.

Forming a Partnership

STUDY OBJECTIVE
2
Explain the accounting entries for the formation of a partnership.

Each partner's initial investment in a partnership should be recorded at the **fair market value of the assets at the date of their transfer to the partnership**. The values assigned must be agreed to by all of the partners.

To illustrate, assume that T. M. Gan and C. K. Sin combine their proprietorships to start a partnership named Interactive Software. The firm will specialize in developing financial modelling software packages. Gan and Sin have the following assets prior to the formation of the partnership:

	Book Value		Market Value		Illustration 13-3
	Gan	Sin	Gan	Sin	*Book and market value of assets invested*
Cash	$ 8,000	$ 9,000	$ 8,000	$ 9,000	
Office equipment	5,000		4,000		
Accumulated amortization	(2,000)				
Accounts receivable		4,000		4,000	
Allowance for doubtful accounts		(700)		(1,000)	
	$11,000	$12,300	$12,000	$12,000	

The entries to record the investments are:

Helpful hint   The cost principle applies. Cash and the fair market value of non-cash assets are recorded at the date of acquisition. The fair market value is what the assets would have cost, if they had been purchased at that time.

Investment of T. M. Gan

Cash	8,000	
Office Equipment	4,000	
T. M. Gan, Capital		12,000
(To record investment of Gan)		

Investment of C. K. Sin

Cash	9,000	
Accounts Receivable	4,000	
Allowance for Doubtful Accounts		1,000
C. K. Sin, Capital		12,000
(To record investment of Sin)		

Note that neither the original cost of the equipment ($5,000) nor its book value ($5,000–$2,000) is recorded by the partnership. Instead, the equipment is recorded at its fair market value of $4,000. Since the equipment has not yet been used by the partnership, there can be no accumulated amortization. In contrast, the gross claims on customers ($4,000) are carried forward to the partnership, and the allowance for doubtful accounts is adjusted to $1,000 to arrive at a net realizable value of $3,000. A partnership may start with an Allowance for Doubtful Accounts account, because this balance pertains to existing accounts receivable that are expected to be uncollectible in the future. In addition, this procedure maintains the control and subsidiary relationship between accounts receivable and the accounts receivable subsidiary ledger.

►Accounting in Action ► *Business Insight*

 A partnership may be created without deliberate intent to do so. For example, the *Partnership Act* for British Columbia states that if you receive a share of income from a business you will be deemed a partner in the business unless evidence exists to the contrary. In B.C., then, it would be wise to have a formal agreement that specifies the partners of a firm. If not, you may be part of a partnership without knowing it!

After the partnership has been formed, the accounting for transactions is similar to the accounting for any other type of business organization. For example, all transactions with outside parties, such as the purchase or sale of merchandise inventory and the payment or receipt of cash, should be recorded in the same manner for a partnership as for a proprietorship.

The steps in the accounting cycle that are described in Chapter 4 for a proprietorship also apply to a partnership. For example, it is necessary to prepare a trial balance and to journalize and post adjusting entries. In addition, a work sheet may be used. There are minor differences in journalizing and posting closing entries and in preparing financial statements, as explained in the following sections. The differences occur because there is more than one owner in a partnership.

Dividing Net Income or Net Loss

Partnership net income or net loss is shared equally unless the partnership agreement specifically indicates a different division. As the same basis of division usually applies to both net income and net loss, it is customary to refer to the basis as the income ratio, the income and loss ratio, or the profit and loss ratio. Because of its wide acceptance, we will use the term **income ratio** to identify the basis for dividing both net income and net loss. A partner's share of net income or net loss is recognized in the accounts through closing entries.

Closing Entries

As with proprietorship, four entries are required in preparing closing entries for a partnership. The entries are:

1. Debit each revenue account for its balance and credit Income Summary for total revenues.
2. Debit Income Summary for total expenses and credit each expense account for its balance.
3. Debit Income Summary for its balance and credit each partner's capital account for his or her share of net income. Conversely, credit Income Summary and debit each partner's capital account for his or her share of net loss.
4. Debit each partner's capital account for the balance in that partner's drawings account, and credit each partner's drawings account for the same amount.

The first two entries are the same as in a proprietorship. The last two entries are different only because there are two or more capital and drawings accounts, and it is necessary to divide net income (or net loss) among the partners.

To illustrate the last two closing entries, we will assume that Interactive Software has a net income of $32,000 for 1999. The partners, T. M. Gan and C. K. Sin, share net income and net loss equally, and drawings for the year were Gan $8,000 and Sin $6,000. The last two closing entries are:

Dec. 31	Income Summary	32,000	
	T. M. Gan, Capital ($32,000 x 50%)		16,000
	C. K. Sin, Capital ($32,000 x 50%)		16,000
	(To transfer net income to partners'		
	capital accounts)		
Dec. 31	T. M. Gan, Capital	8,000	
	C. K. Sin, Capital	6,000	
	T. M. Gan, Drawings		8,000
	C. K. Sin, Drawings		6,000
	(To close drawings accounts		
	to capital accounts)		

As in a proprietorship, the partners' capital accounts are permanent accounts and the partners' drawings accounts are temporary accounts. Normally, the capital accounts will have credit balances and the drawings accounts will have debit balances. Drawings accounts are debited when partners withdraw cash or other assets from the partnership for personal use. For example, the partnership agreement may permit each partner to withdraw cash monthly for personal living expenses.

Income Ratios

As indicated earlier, the partnership agreement should specify the basis for sharing net income or net loss. The following are typical of the ratios that may be used:

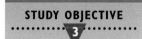

STUDY OBJECTIVE
··········▼··········
3

Apply various bases to divide net income or net loss.

1. A fixed ratio, expressed as a proportion (2:1), a percentage (67% and 33%), or a fraction (⅔ and ⅓).
2. A ratio based either on capital balances at the beginning of the year or on average capital balances during the year.
3. Salaries to partners and the remainder on a fixed ratio.
4. Interest on partners' capitals and the remainder on a fixed ratio.
5. Salaries to partners, interest on partners' capitals, and the remainder on a fixed ratio.

The objective is to agree to a basis that will equitably reflect the differences among partners in terms of their capital investment and service to the partnership.

A fixed ratio is easy to apply, and it may be an equitable basis in some circumstances. Assume, for example, that Hughes and Lane are partners. Each contributes the same amount of capital, but Hughes expects to work full time in the partnership, while Lane expects to work only half-time. Accordingly, the partners agree to a fixed ratio of ⅔ to Hughes and ⅓ to Lane.

A ratio based on capital balances may be appropriate when the funds invested in the partnership are considered the critical factor. Capital balances may also be equitable when a manager is hired to run the business and the partners do not plan to take an active role in daily operations.

The three remaining ratios (items 3, 4, and 5 in the list above) give specific recognition to differences that may exist among partners. These ratios provide salary allowances for time worked and interest allowances for capital invested. Then, any remaining net income or net loss is allocated on a fixed ratio. Some caution needs to be exercised in working with these types of income ratios. **These ratios pertain exclusively to the computations that divide net income or net loss.**

Salaries to partners and interest on partners' capitals are not expenses of the partnership. Therefore, these items are not used for the matching of expenses with revenues and the determination of net income or net loss. For a partnership, as with other entities, salaries expense is for the cost of services performed by employees, and interest expense relates to the cost of borrowing money from creditors. As owners, partners are not considered either employees or creditors. Thus, when the income ratio includes a salary allowance for partners, some partnership agreements permit the partner to make monthly withdrawals of cash based on their salary. In such cases, the withdrawals are debited to the partner's drawings account; they are *not* debited to salaries expense.

▶Accounting in Action ▸ *Business Insight*

Partners in public accounting firms can, and do, make substantial incomes. For example, a few senior partners may earn as much as $1,000,000. However, the average earnings of partners are more likely to be in the $150,000–$200,000 range. Note that the compensation of partners in most large partnerships differs in both form and substance from the compensation of a corporate executive. Partners are not guaranteed an annual salary, nor are they granted stock options. Compensation depends entirely on each year's operating results. Substantial investment is required of each partner. This capital is at risk for the partner's entire career—often 25–30 years—without an established return. Upon leaving, it is repayable to the partner without adjustment for inflation or appreciation in value.

Salaries, Interest, and Remainder on a Fixed Ratio

Under this income ratio (item 5 in the list on the preceding page), **salaries and interest must be paid before the remainder is divided according to the specified fixed ratio**. This is true even if the salary and interest provisions exceed net income or the partnership has suffered a net loss for the year.

To illustrate this basis for sharing income or loss, assume that Sara King and Ray Lee recently graduated from law school and are in the first year of their law practice. The partnership agreement provides for: (1) salary allowances of $8,400 to King and $6,000 to Lee, (2) interest allowances of 10% on capital balances at the beginning of the year, and (3) the remainder to be distributed equally. Capital balances on January 1 were King $28,000 and Lee $24,000. In 1999, partnership net income is $22,000. The division of net income is as follows:

Illustration 13-4

Division of net income

	Sara King	Ray Lee	Total
Net income			$22,000
Salary allowance	$8,400	$6,000	(14,400)
Interest allowance			
King ($28,000 x 10%)	2,800		
Lee ($24,000 x 10%)		2,400	(5,200)
Remaining income			2,400
King ($2,400 x 50%)	1,200		
Lee ($2,400 x 50%)		1,200	(2,400)
			0
Division of net income	$12,400	$9,600	$22,000

The entry to record the division of net income is:

Dec. 31	Income Summary	22,000	
	Sara King, Capital		12,400
	Ray Lee, Capital		9,600
	(To close net income to partners' capital accounts)		

To illustrate a situation in which the salary and interest allowances exceed net income or loss, assume that King and Lee report a net loss of $18,000. In this case, the salary and interest allowances are still allocated as illustrated. This creates a deficiency of $37,600, which is divided equally among the partners:

Illustration 13-5

Division of net loss

	Sara King	Ray Lee	Total
Net loss			($18,000)
Salary allowance	$8,400	$6,000	(14,400)
Interest allowance			
King ($28,000 x 10%)	2,800		
Lee ($24,000 x 10%)		2,400	(5,200)
Remaining deficiency			(37,600)
King ($37,600 x 50%)	(18,800)		
Lee ($37,600 x 50%)		(18,800)	37,600
			0
Division of net loss	($ 7,600)	($10,400)	($18,000)

The journal entry to record the division of the net loss would be:

Dec. 31	Sara King, Capital	7,600	
	Ray Lee, Capital	10,400	
	Income Summary		18,000
	(To close net loss to partners' capital accounts)		

Partnership Financial Statements

The financial statements of a partnership are similar to those of a proprietorship. The differences are related to the fact that a number of owners are involved in a partnership.

The income statement for a partnership is identical to the income statement for a proprietorship. The statement of equity for a partnership is called the statement of partners' capital. Its function is to explain the changes in each partner's capital account and in total partnership capital during the year. As in a proprietorship, changes in capital may result from three causes: additional capital investment, drawings, and net income or net loss.

The statement of partners' capital for King and Lee shown in Ilustration 13-6 is based on the division of $22,000 of net income in Illustration 13-4. The statement includes assumed data for the additional investment and drawings.

STUDY OBJECTIVE
4

Describe the form and content of partnership financial statements.

Illustration 13-6

Statement of partners' capital

KING AND LEE Statement of Partners' Capital For the Year Ended December 31, 1999			
	Sara King	Ray Lee	Total
Capital, January 1	$28,000	$24,000	$52,000
Add: Additional investment	2,000		2,000
Net income	12,400	9,600	22,000
	42,400	33,600	76,000
Less: Drawings	7,000	5,000	12,000
Capital, December 31	$35,400	$28,600	$64,000

The balance sheet for a partnership is the same as for a proprietorship, except in the equity section. In a proprietorship, the equity section of the balance sheet, called **owner's equity**, details a one-line capital account for the owner. In a partnership, the capital balances of each partner are shown in the balance sheet, in a section termed **partners' equity**. The partners' equity section for King and Lee would show the following:

Illustration 13-7

Partners' equity section of a partnership balance sheet

KING AND LEE Partial Balance Sheet December 31, 1999		
Total liabilities (assumed amount)		$115,000
Partners' equity		
Sara King, capital	$35,400	
Ray Lee, capital	28,600	64,000
Total liabilities and partners' equity		$179,000

Large partnerships, such as those found in international accounting firms, cannot report each individual partner's equity separately. For reporting purposes, these amounts are usually aggregated in the balance sheet.

Before You Go On . . .

▸*Review It*

1. How should a partner's initial investment of assets be valued?
2. What are the closing entries for a partnership?
3. What types of income ratios may be used in a partnership?
4. How do partnership financial statements differ from proprietorship financial statements?

▸*Do It*

LeMay Company reports net income of $44,000. The partnership agreement provides for salaries of $30,000 to L. Lee and $24,000 to R. May, with the remainder to be shared on a 60:40 basis, respectively. L. Lee asks for your help in dividing the net income between the two partners and in preparing the closing entry.

Reasoning: Salaries to partners and interest on partners' capital are not expenses of the partnership, and these items are not used to determine net income or net loss. To divide income, salaries are allocated and then the income ratios are applied to the remainder (a deficiency in this case). The closing entry for net income in a partnership is the same as in a proprietorship, except that more than one capital account is credited.

Solution: The division of net income is as follows:

	L. Lee	R. May	Total
Net income			$44,000
Salary allowance	$30,000	$24,000	(54,000)
Remaining deficiency			(10,000)
Lee (60% x $10,000)	(6,000)		
May (40% x $10,000)		(4,000)	10,000
			0
Division of net income	$24,000	$20,000	$44,000

The closing entry for net income therefore is:

Income Summary		44,000	
L. Lee, Capital			24,000
R. May, Capital			20,000
(To close net income to partners' capital accounts)			

Related exercise material: BE13–1, BE13–2, BE13–3, BE13–4, BE13-5, E13–1, E13–2, and E13–3.

Admission and Withdrawal of Partners

We have seen how the basic accounting for a partnership works. We now look at how to account for a common occurrence in partnerships—the addition or withdrawal of a partner.

Admission of a Partner

The admission of a new partner results in the **legal dissolution of the existing partnership and the beginning of a new partnership**. From an economic standpoint, however, the admission of a new partner (or partners) may be of minor significance to the continuity of the business. For example, in large public accounting or law firms, partners are admitted annually without any change in operating policies established by the continuing partners. **To recognize the economic effects, it is only necessary to open a capital account for each new partner.** The entries described below assume that the accounting records of the old partnership will be used by the new partnership.

A new partner may be admitted by either: (1) purchasing the interest of one or more existing partners, or (2) investing assets in the partnership, as shown in Illustration 13-8. The former affects only the capital accounts of the partners who are involved in transaction; the total capital of the partnership is not affected. The latter increases both net assets (total assets less total liabilities) and total capital of the partnership.

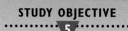

STUDY OBJECTIVE

5

Explain the effects of the entries when a new partner is admitted.

Illustration 13-8

Procedures in adding partners

Admission of Partner through:

1. Purchase of a Partner's Interest

2. Investment of Assets in Partnership

Purchase of a Partner's Interest

Helpful hint In a purchase of an interest, the partnership is *not* a participant in the transaction. For example, no cash is contributed to the partnership.

The admission by purchase of an interest of a partner in the firm is a personal transaction between one or more existing partners and the new partner. Each party acts as an individual, separate from the partnership entity. The price paid is negotiated and determined by the individuals involved. It may be equal to or different from the partners capital in the accounting records of the partnership. The purchase price passes directly from the new partner to the partner who is giving up part or all of his or her ownership claims. Any money or other consideration exchanged is the personal property of the participants and **not** the property of the partnership. After purchasing an interest, the new partner acquires the selling partner's capital interest and income ratio. A partner does not have to obtain the approval of the other partners to sell his or her interest. However, the *Partnership Act* says that the purchaser does not become a partner until he or she is accepted into the firm by the continuing partners.

Accounting for the purchase of an interest is straightforward. As far as the partnership is concerned, only the transfer of a partner's capital is recorded. **The partner's capital account is debited for the ownership claims that have been relinquished, and the new partner's capital account is credited with the capital equity purchased.** Total assets, total liabilities, and total capital remain unchanged, as do all individual asset and liability accounts.

To illustrate, assume that L. Carson agrees to pay $10,000 each to two partners, D. Arbour and D. Baker for one-third of their interest in the Arbour-Baker partnership. At the time of the admission of Carson, each partner has a $30,000 capital balance. Both partners, therefore, give up $10,000 (⅓ × $30,000) of their capital equity. The entry to record the admission of Carson is:

D. Arbour, Capital	10,000	
D. Baker, Capital	10,000	
L. Carson, Capital		20,000
(To record admission of Carson by purchase)		

Net assets will remain unchanged at $60,000 (net assets = equities), and each partner will now have a $20,000 capital balance. Note also that Arbour and Baker continue as partners in the firm but the capital interest of each has changed from $30,000 to

$20,000 ($30,000 – $10,000). The cash paid by Carson goes directly to the individual partners and not to the partnership.

Regardless of the amount paid by Carson for the one-third interest, the entry above would be exactly the same. For example, if Carson pays $12,000 each to Arbour and Baker for 33% of the partnership, the foregoing entry is still made.

Investment of Assets in a Partnership

The admission of a partner by an investment of assets is a transaction between the new partner and the partnership. It is often referred to simply as admission by investment. This transaction **increases both the net assets and the total capital of the partnership**. In the opening vignette, Cinnamon Toast admitted a partner by investment, which increased both assets and capital.

To illustrate, assume that instead of purchasing an interest, Carson invests $30,000 in cash in the Arbour-Baker partnership for a 33% capital interest. In such a case, the entry is:

Cash	30,000	
L. Carson, Capital		30,000
(To record admission of Carson by investment)		

Both net assets and total capital increase by $30,000.

Remember that Carson's one-third capital interest might not result in a one-third income ratio. Carson's income ratio should be specified in the new partnership agreement, and it may or may not be equal to the one-third capital interest.

The different effects of the purchase of an interest and admission by investment are shown in the comparison of the net assets and capital balances in Illustration 13-9:

Admission by Purchase of an Interest		Admission by Investment	
Net Assets	$60,000	Net Assets	$90,000
Capital		Capital	
D. Arbour	$20,000	D. Arbour	$30,000
D. Baker	20,000	D. Baker	30,000
L. Carson	20,000	L. Carson	30,000
Total Capital	$60,000	Total Capital	$90,000

Illustration 13-9

Comparison of admission by purchase of an interest and by investment

As indicated above, when an interest is purchased the total net assets and the total capital of the partnership do not change. However, when a partner is admitted by investment both the total net assets and the total capital change.

In the case of admission by investment, further complications occur when the new partner's investment differs from the capital equity acquired. When those amounts are not the same, the difference is considered a bonus either to the existing (old) partners or to the new partner.

Bonus to Old Partners. The existing partners may be unwilling to admit a new partner without receiving a bonus for both personal and business reasons. In an established firm, existing partners may insist on a bonus as compensation for the work they have put into the company over the years.

Two accounting-related factors underlie the business reason. First, total partners' capital equals the **book value** of the recorded net assets of the partnership. At the time the new partner is admitted, the fair market values of assets such as land

and buildings may be higher than their book values. Second, when the partnership has been profitable, goodwill may exist. However, the goodwill is not recorded among the assets not reflected in total partners' capital. In such cases the new partner is usually willing to pay the bonus to become a partner.

A bonus to old partners results when the new partner's capital credit on the date of admittance is less than his or her investment in the firm. The bonus results in **an increase in the capital balances of the old partners, and is allocated to them on the basis of their income ratios before the admission of the new partner**.

To illustrate, assume that the Bart-Simpson partnership, owned by Sam Bart and Homer Simpson, has total capital of $120,000 when Lisa Trent is admitted to the partnership. Lisa acquires a 25% ownership (capital) interest by making a cash investment of $80,000 in the partnership. The procedure for determining Trent's capital credit and the bonus to the old partners is as follows:

1. **Determine the total capital of the new partnership** by adding the new partner's investment to the total capital of the old partnership. In this case the total capital of the new firm is $200,000, computed as follows:

Total capital of existing partnership	$120,000
Investment by new partner, Trent	80,000
Total capital of new partnership	$200,000

2. **Determine the new partner's capital credit** by multiplying the total capital of the new partnership by the new partner's ownership interest. Trent's capital credit is $50,000 ($200,000 × 25%).

3. **Determine the amount of bonus** by subtracting the new partner's capital credit from the new partner's investment. The bonus in this case is $30,000 ($80,000 − $50,000).

4. **Allocate the bonus to the old partners on the basis of their income ratios**. Assuming the ratios are Bart 60% and Simpson 40%, the allocation is to Bart $18,000 ($30,000 × 60%) and to Simpson $12,000 ($30,000 × 40%).

The entry to record the admission of Trent is:

Helpful hint   (1) The debit to Cash is greater than the new partner's capital credit. (2) Credits to old partners' capitals are needed for equal debits and credits.

Cash	80,000	
Sam Bart, Capital		18,000
Homer Simpson, Capital		12,000
Lisa Trent, Capital		50,000
(To record admission of Trent and bonuses to old partners)		

Bonus to New Partner.   A bonus to a new partner results when the new partner's capital credit is greater than his or her investment of assets in the firm. This may occur when the new partner possesses resources or special attributes that are desired by the partnership. For example, when bank interest rates are high, the new partner may be able to supply cash that is urgently needed for expansion or to meet maturing debts. Alternatively, the new partner may be a recognized expert or authority in a relevant field. Thus, an engineering firm may be willing to give a world-renowned engineer a bonus to join the firm. Similarly, the partners of a restaurant may offer a bonus to a sports celebrity in order to add the athlete's name to the partnership.

A bonus to a new partner results in a **decrease in the capital balances of the old partners based on their income ratios before the admission of the new partner**. To illustrate, assume that Lisa Trent invests $20,000 in cash for a 25% ownership interest in the Bart-Simpson partnership. Using the procedures described in the preceding section, the computations for Trent's capital credit and bonus are as follows:

1.	Total capital of Bart-Simpson partnership		$120,000
	Investment by new partner, Trent		20,000
	Total capital of new partnership		$140,000
2.	Trent's capital credit (25% 3 $140,000)		$ 35,000
3.	Bonus to Trent ($35,000 2 $20,000)		$ 15,000
4.	Allocation of bonus:		
	From Bart ($15,000 × 60%)	$9,000	
	From Simpson ($15,000 × 40%)	6,000	$ 15,000

Illustration 13-10

Computation of capital credit and bonus to new partner

The entry to record the admission of Trent is as follows:

Cash	20,000	
Sam Bart, Capital	9,000	
Homer Simpson, Capital	6,000	
Lisa Trent, Capital		35,000
(To record Trent's admission and bonus)		

Withdrawal of a Partner

Now let's look at the opposite situation—the withdrawal of a partner. A partner may withdraw from a partnership **voluntarily**, by selling his or her equity in the firm, or **involuntarily**, by reaching mandatory retirement age or by dying. The withdrawal of a partner, like the admission of a partner, legally dissolves the partnership. The legal effects of a withdrawal may be recognized in accounting by dissolving the firm. However, it is customary to record only the economic effects.

As indicated earlier, the partnership agreement should specify the terms of withdrawal. The withdrawal of a partner may be accomplished by payment from partners' personal assets, or payment from partnership assets, as shown in Illustration 13-11. The former affects only the partners' capital accounts. The latter decreases total net assets and total capital of the partnership.

STUDY OBJECTIVE

••••••••••**6**••••••••••

Describe the effects of the entries when a partner withdraws from the firm.

Withdrawal of Partner through:

1. Payment from Partners' Personal Assets

2. Payment from Partnership Assets

Illustration 13-11

Procedures in partnership withdrawal

Payment from Partners' Personal Assets

The withdrawal of a partner when payment is made from the remaining partners' personal assets is **the direct opposite of admitting a new partner who purchases a partner's interest**. Withdrawal by payment from partners' personal assets is a personal transaction between the partners. Payment to the departing partner is made directly from the remaining partners' personal assets. **Partnership assets are not involved in any way, and total capital does not change**. Thus, the effect on the partnership is limited to a transfer of the partners' capital balances.

To illustrate, assume that Sam Bart, Lisa Trent, and Homer Simpson have capital balances of $25,000, $15,000, and $10,000, respectively, which total $50,000. Bart and Trent agree to buy out Simpson's interest. Each of them agrees to pay Simpson $8,000 in exchange for one-half of Simpson's total interest of $10,000. The entry to record the withdrawal is:

Homer Simpson, Capital	10,000	
Sam Bart, Capital		5,000
Lisa Trent, Capital		5,000
(To record purchase of Simpson's interest)		

Net assets and total capital remain the same, at $50,000 (Bart, Capital $30,000 + Trent, Capital $20,000). All that has happened is a reallocation of capital amounts. Note also that the $16,000 paid to Simpson is not recorded. Simpson's capital is debited for only $10,000, not the $16,000 that he received. Similarly, both Bart and Trent credit their capital accounts for only $5,000, not the $8,000 they each paid.

Payment from Partnership Assets

Using partnership assets to pay for a withdrawing partner's interest is the **reverse of admitting a partner through the investment of assets in the partnership**. Withdrawal by payment from partnership assets is a transaction that involves the partnership. **Both partnership net assets and total capital are decreased**.

Case in point Note these two points: (1) No adjusting entries to reflect market values, and (2) adherence to the cost principle and GAAP.

Many partnership agreements state that the amount paid should be based on the fair market value of the assets at the time of the partner's withdrawal. When this basis is used, some accountants believe that any differences between recorded asset balances and their fair market values should be recorded by an adjusting entry, and allocated to all partners on the basis of their income ratios.

This position has serious flaws, however. Recording the revaluations violates the cost principle, which requires assets to be stated at original cost. It is also a departure from the going concern assumption, which assumes the entity will continue indefinitely. The terms of the partnership contract should not dictate the accounting for the event.

In accounting for a withdrawal by payment from partnership assets:

1. Asset revaluations should not be recorded.
2. Any difference between the amount paid and the withdrawing partner's capital balance should be considered a bonus to the departing partner or a bonus to the remaining partners.

Bonus to Departing Partner.   A bonus may be paid to a departing partner when:

1. The fair market value of partnership assets is more than their book value,
2. There is unrecorded goodwill resulting from the partnership's superior earnings record, or
3. The remaining partners are anxious to remove the partner from the firm.

The bonus is deducted from the remaining partners' capital balances on the basis of their income ratios at the time of the withdrawal.

To illustrate, assume that the following capital balances exist in the RST partnership: Fred Roman $50,000, Dee Sand $30,000, and Betty Terk $20,000. The partners share income in the ratio of 3:2:1, respectively. Terk retires from the partnership and receives a cash payment of $25,000 from the firm. The procedure for determining the bonus to the departing partner and the allocation of the bonus to the remaining partners is as follows:

1. **Determine the amount of the bonus** by subtracting the departing partner's capital balance from the cash paid by the partnership. The bonus in this case is $5,000 ($25,000 − $20,000).
2. **Allocate the bonus to the remaining partners on the basis of their income ratios.** The ratios of Roman and Sand are 3:2. Thus, the allocation of the $5,000 bonus is: Roman $3,000 ($5,000 x ⅗) and Sand $2,000 ($5,000 x ⅖).

The entry to record the withdrawal of Terk is:

Betty Terk, Capital	20,000	
Fred Roman, Capital	3,000	
Dee Sand, Capital	2,000	
Cash		25,000
(To record withdrawal of, and bonus to, Terk)		

The remaining partners, Roman and Sand, will recover the bonus given to Terk as the undervalued assets are sold or used in the partnership.

Bonus to Remaining Partners. As in the Cinnamon Toast Records partnership, the departing partner may give a bonus to the remaining partners if:

1. Recorded assets are overvalued,
2. The partnership has a poor earnings record, or
3. The partner is anxious to leave the partnership.

In such cases, the cash paid to the departing partner will be less than the departing partner's capital balance. **The bonus is allocated (credited) to the capital accounts of the remaining partners on the basis of their income ratios.**

To illustrate, assume that, instead of the example above, Terk is paid only $16,000 for her $20,000 equity upon withdrawal from the RST partnership. In such a case:

1. The bonus to remaining partners is $4,000 ($20,000 − $16,000).
2. The allocation of the $4,000 bonus is: Roman $2,400 ($4,000 × ⅗) and Sand $1,600 ($4,000 × ⅖).

The entry to record the withdrawal is:

Betty Terk, Capital	20,000	
Fred Roman, Capital		2,400
Dee Sand, Capital		1,600
Cash		16,000
(To record withdrawal of Terk and bonus to remaining partners)		

Death of a Partner

The death of a partner dissolves the partnership, but provision generally is made for the surviving partners to continue operations. When a partner dies, it is usually necessary to determine the partner's equity at the date of death. This is done by: (1) determining the net income or loss for the year to date, (2) closing the books, and (3) preparing financial statements. The partnership agreement may also require an audit of the financial statements by independent auditors and a revaluation of assets by an independent appraisal firm.

The surviving partners may agree to either purchase the deceased partner's equity from their personal assets or use partnership assets to settle with the deceased partner's estate. In both instances, the entries to record the withdrawal of the partner are similar to those presented in previous illustrations.

To facilitate payment from partnership assets, some partnerships have life insurance policies for each partner, with the partnership as the beneficiary. The proceeds from the insurance policy on the deceased partner are then used to settle with the estate.

Before You Go On . . .

▸ Review It

1. How does the accounting for admission by purchase of an interest differ from accounting for admission by investing assets in the partnership?
2. Contrast the accounting effects of the withdrawal of a partner by payment from: (a) personal assets, and (b) partnership assets.

▸ Do It

Chandler, Phoebe, and Ross have a partnership. Each partner has a $40,000 balance in their capital account. Record journal entries for each of the independent events listed below:

1. Chandler, Phoebe, and Ross agree to admit Rachel as a new one-quarter interest partner. Rachel pays $10,000 in cash directly to each partner.
2. Chandler, Phoebe, and Ross agree to admit Rachel as a new one-quarter interest partner. Rachel contributes $40,000 to the partnership.
3. Phoebe withdraws from the partnership, and $30,000 of partnership cash is distributed to Phoebe. Chandler and Ross share income and losses equally.
4. Chandler and Ross agree to let Phoebe withdraw from the partnership. Each pays Phoebe $25,000 out of his personal assets.

Reasoning: You need to understand that admission (withdrawal) by purchase (sale) of an interest is a personal transaction between one or more existing partners and the new (withdrawing) partner. In contrast, admission (withdrawal) by investment (distribution) of partnership assets is a transaction between the new (withdrawing) partner and the partnership.

Solution:

1.	Chandler, Capital	10,000	
	Phoebe, Capital	10,000	
	Ross, Capital	10,000	
	Rachel, Capital		30,000
	(To record admission of Rachel by purchase)		

2.	Cash	40,000	
	Rachel, Capital		40,000
	(To record admission of Rachel by investment)		

3.	Phoebe, Capital	40,000	
	Cash		30,000
	Chandler, Capital		5,000
	Ross, Capital		5,000
	(To record withdrawal of Phoebe and bonus to remaining partners)		

4.	Phoebe, Capital	40,000	
	Chandler, Capital		20,000
	Ross, Capital		20,000
	(To record purchase of Phoebe's interest)		

Related exercise material: BE13–6, BE13–7, BE13–8, BE13–9, E13–4, E13–5, E13–6, and E13–7.

Liquidation of a Partnership

The liquidation of a partnership terminates the business. It entails selling the assets of the firm, paying liabilities, and distributing any remaining assets to the partners. Liquidation may result from the sale of the business by mutual agreement of the partners, from the death of a partner, or from bankruptcy. In contrast to the dissolution of a partnership, partnership liquidation ends both the legal and economic life of the entity.

Before the liquidation process begins; the accounting cycle for the partnership must be completed for the final operating period. This includes the preparation of adjusting entries, financial statements, and closing entries. Only balance sheet accounts should be open as the liquidation process begins.

The liquidation process may occur at a specific point in time, or it may occur over a period of time. In liquidation, the sale of non-cash assets for cash is called **realization**, and the difference between book value and the cash proceeds is called the **gain or loss on realization**. To liquidate a partnership, it is necessary to:

1. Sell non-cash assets for cash and recognize any gain or loss on realization.
2. Allocate any gain or loss on realization to the partners, based on their income ratios.
3. Pay partnership liabilities in cash.
4. Distribute remaining cash to partners, on the basis of their capital balances.

Each of the steps must be performed in sequence, because **creditors must be paid before partners receive any cash distributions**. Also, each step must be recorded by an accounting entry.

When a partnership is liquidated, all partners may happen to have credit balances in their capital accounts—a situation termed **no capital deficiency**. Alternatively, one or more of the partners' capital accounts may have a debit balance—a situation termed a **capital deficiency**. To illustrate each of these conditions, assume that the Ace Company is liquidated when its ledger shows the following assets, liabilities, and partners' equity accounts:

STUDY OBJECTIVE

7

Prepare the entries to record the liquidation of a partnership.

Illustration 13-12

Account balances prior to liquidation

Assets		Liabilities and Partners' Equity	
Cash	$ 5,000	Notes payable	$15,000
Accounts receivable	15,000	Accounts payable	16,000
Inventory	18,000	R. Aube, Capital	15,000
Equipment	35,000	P. Chordia, Capital	17,800
Accumulated amortization		W. Elliott, Capital	1,200
—equipment	(8,000)		
	$65,000		$65,000

No Capital Deficiency

The partners of Ace Company agree to liquidate the partnership on the following terms: (1) sale of the non-cash assets of the partnership to Moriyama Enterprises for $75,000, and (2) payment of partnership liabilities by the partnership. The income ratios of the partners are 3:2:1. The steps in the liquidation process are as follows:

1. The non-cash assets (accounts receivable, inventory, and equipment) are sold for $75,000. Since the book value of these assets is $60,000 ($15,000 + $18,000 + $35,000 – $8,000), a gain of $15,000 is realized on the sale. The entry is:

Cash	75,000	
Accumulated Amortization—Equipment	8,000	
Accounts Receivable		15,000
Inventory		18,000
Equipment		35,000
Gain on Realization		15,000
(To record realization of non-cash assets)		

Helpful hint   Unless the partnership agreement states the contrary, the income ratio also applies to realization gains and losses.

2. The gain on realization of $15,000 is allocated to the partners based on their income ratios, which are 3:2:1. The entry is:

Gain on Realization	15,000	
R. Aube, Capital ($15,000 × 3/6)		7,500
P. Chordia, Capital ($15,000 × 2/6)		5,000
W. Elliott, Capital ($15,000 × 1/6)		2,500
(To allocate gain to partners' capitals)		

3. Partnership liabilities consist of Notes Payable $15,000 and Accounts Payable $16,000. Creditors are paid in full by a cash payment of $31,000. The entry is:

Notes Payable	15,000	
Accounts Payable	16,000	
Cash		31,000
(To record payment of partnership liabilities)		

4. The remaining cash is distributed to the partners on the basis of their capital balances. After the entries in the first three steps are posted, all partnership accounts, including Gain on Realization, will have zero balances except for four accounts: Cash $49,000; R. Aube, Capital, $22,500; P. Chordia, Capital, $22,800; and W. Elliott, Capital, $3,700, as shown below:

Cash				R. Aube, Capital			P. Chordia, Capital			W. Elliott, Capital		
Bal.	5,000	(3)	31,000	Bal.	15,000		Bal.	17,800		Bal.	1,200
(1)	75,000			(2)	7,500		(2)	5,000		(2)	2,500
Bal.	49,000			Bal.	22,500		Bal.	22,800		Bal.	3,700

Illustration 13-13

Ledger balances before distribution of cash—no capital deficiency

The entry to record the distribution of cash is as follows:

R. Aube, Capital	22,500	
P. Chordia, Capital	22,800	
W. Elliott, Capital	3,700	
Cash		49,000
(To record distribution of cash to partners)		

After this entry is posted, all partnership general ledger accounts will have zero balances.

A word of caution: **cash should not be distributed to partners on the basis of their income-sharing ratios**. On this basis, for example, Aube would receive ³⁄₆, or $24,500, which would produce an erroneous debit balance of $2,000. The income ratio is a proper basis for allocating net income or loss and any gains or losses on realization of assets, but it is not a proper basis for making the final distribution of cash to the partners.

Helpful hint Zero balances after posting is a quick proof of the accuracy of the cash-distribution entry.

Capital Deficiency

A capital deficiency may be caused by recurring net losses, excessive drawings before liquidation, or losses from realization suffered during liquidation. To illustrate, assume that Ace Company is on the brink of bankruptcy. The partners decide to liquidate by having a going-out-of-business sale in which merchandise is sold at substantial discounts, and the equipment is sold at auction. Cash proceeds from these sales and collections from customers total only $42,000. Accordingly, the loss from liquidation is $18,000 ($60,000 book value − $42,000 proceeds). The steps in the liquidation process are as follows:

1. The entry for the realization of non-cash assets is:

Cash	42,000	
Accumulated Amortization—Equipment	8,000	
Loss on Realization	18,000	
Accounts Receivable		15,000
Inventory		18,000
Equipment		35,000
(To record realization of non-cash assets)		

Case in point These entries are the same as those in the No Capital Deficiency Section except for the loss on realization.

2. The loss on realization is allocated to the partners on the basis of their income ratios. The entry is:

R. Aube, Capital ($18,000 × ³⁄₆)	9,000	
P. Chordia, Capital ($18,000 × ²⁄₆)	6,000	
W. Elliott, Capital ($18,000 × ¹⁄₆)	3,000	
Loss on Realization		18,000
(To allocate loss on realization to partners)		

3. Partnership liabilities are paid. This entry is the same as in the previous example.

Notes Payable	15,000	
Accounts Payable	16,000	
Cash		31,000
(To record payment of partnership liabilities)		

4. After posting of the three entries, two accounts will have debit balances—Cash, $16,000 and W. Elliott, Capital, $1,800—and two accounts will have credit balances—R. Aube, Capital, $6,000, and P. Chordia, Capital, $11,800, as shown below:

Cash				R. Aube, Capital				P. Chordia, Capital				W. Elliott, Capital			
Bal.	5,000	(3)	31,000	(2)	9,000	Bal.	15,000	(2)	6,000	Bal.	17,800	(2)	3,000	Bal.	1,200
(1)	42,000					Bal.	6,000			Bal.	11,800	Bal.	1,800		
Bal.	16,000														

Illustration 13-14

Ledger balances before distribution of cash—capital deficiency

Elliott has a capital deficiency of $1,800. Therefore, Elliott owes the partnership $1,800 and Aube and Chordia have a legally enforceable claim against Elliott's personal assets. The distribution of cash is still made on the basis of capital balances. However, the amount will vary depending on how the deficiency is settled.

Payment of Deficiency

If the partner with the capital deficiency pays the amount owed to the partnership, the deficiency is eliminated. To illustrate, assume that Elliott pays $1,800 to the partnership. The entry is:

Cash	1,800	
W. Elliott, Capital		1,800
(To record payment of capital deficiency by Elliott)		

The cash balance of $17,800 ($16,000 + $1,800) is now equal to the credit balances in the capital accounts (Aube $6,000 + Chordia $11,800), and cash is distributed on the basis of these balances. The entry is:

R. Aube, Capital	6,000	
P. Chordia, Capital	11,800	
Cash		17,800
(To record distribution of cash to the partners)		

After this entry is posted, all accounts will have zero balances.

Nonpayment of Deficiency

If a partner with a capital deficiency is unable to pay the amount owed to the partnership, the partners with credit balances must absorb the loss. The loss is allocated on the basis of the income ratios that exist between the partners with credit balances. The income ratios of Aube and Chordia are 3:2 or ⅗ and ⅖, respectively. Thus, the following entry is made to remove Elliott's capital deficiency:

R. Aube, Capital ($1,800 × ⅗)	1,080	
P. Chordia, Capital ($1,800 × ⅖)	720	
W. Elliott, Capital		1,800
(To record write off of capital deficiency)		

The cash balance of $16,000 now equals the sum of the credit balances in the capital accounts (Aube $4,920 [$6,000 – $1,080] + Chordia $11,080 ([$11,800 – $720]). The entry to record the distribution of cash is:

R. Aube, Capital	4,920	
P. Chordia, Capital	11,080	
Cash		16,000
(To record distribution of cash to partners)		

After this entry is posted, all accounts will have zero balances.

Before You Go On . . .
▶ Review It

1. Identify the steps in liquidating a partnership.
2. What basis is used in making the final distribution of cash to the partners?

Related exercise material: BE13–10, E13–8, E13–9, and E13–10.

▶ A Look Back at Cinnamon Toast Records
• •

Refer back to the opening story about Cinnamon Toast Records, and answer the following questions:

1. Speculate as to why the four founders selected the partnership form of organization for their business, Cinnamon Toast Records.
2. What do you believe are the major items that should be written into the partnership agreement for Cinnamon Toast Records?
3. Explain the impact on the financial position of the partnership when one of the partners joined by investment. What about when one of the partners departed and paid a bonus to the remaining partners?

Solution:

1. The founders may have chosen to form a partnership, rather than a corporation, for a number of reasons. First, the partnership is formed (and reformed) much more quickly and easily, with little of the red tape associated with a corporation. Second, the partnership form allows skills and talents to be combined, which is a distinct advantage over a proprietorship. Third, since the partners work closely together to achieve the same goals, their concerns about the risk of unlimited liabilities resulting from inappropriate actions by the other partners are reduced.
2. The partnership agreement of Cinnamon Toast Records should specify the capital contributed by each partner, and the basis for sharing income and losses and for withdrawing funds from the partnership. In addition, it should specify a mechanism to resolve disputes, add or remove a partner, or deal with the death of one of the partners. A well-written partnership agreement can significantly reduce conflicts as the firm changes size.
3. Admission by investment will cause an increase in net assets (normally cash) and capital (an added capital account for the new partner) of the partnership.

> Purchase of a departing partner's interest will reduce the capital (departing partner's account is eliminated) and net assets (normally cash) of the partnership. In addition, the capital accounts of the remaining partners will be increased, proportionately, by the amount of the bonus (amount paid in excess of the departing partner's capital balance).

▶*Summary of Study Objectives*

1. *Identify the characteristics of the partnership form of business organization.* The principal characteristics of a partnership are: (a) association of individuals, (b) mutual agency, (c) limited life, (d) unlimited liability, and (e) co-ownership of property.

2. *Explain the accounting entries for the formation of a partnership.* When a partnership is formed, each partner's initial investment should be recorded at the fair market value of the assets at the date of their transfer to the partnership.

3. *Apply various bases for dividing net income or net loss.* Net income or net loss is divided on the basis of the income ratio, which may be: (a) a fixed ratio, (b) a ratio based on beginning or average capital balances, (c) salaries to partners and the remainder on a fixed ratio, (d) interest on partners' capitals and the remainder on a fixed ratio, and (e) salaries to partners, interest on partners' capitals, and the remainder on a fixed ratio.

4. *Describe the form and content of partnership financial statements.* The financial statements of a partnership are similar to those of a proprietorship. The principal differences are: (a) the statement of owners' equity is called the statement of partners' equity, and (b) each partner's capital is usually reported on the balance sheet.

5. *Explain the effects of the entries when a new partner is admitted.* The entry to record the admittance of a new partner by purchase of a partner's interest affects only partners' capital accounts. The entries to record the admittance by investment of assets in the partnership: (a) increase both net assets and total capital, and (b) may result in recognition of a bonus to either the old partners or the new partner.

6. *Describe the effects of the entries when a partner withdraws from the firm.* The entry to record a withdrawal from the firm when payment is made from partners' personal assets only affects partners' capital accounts. The entry to record a withdrawal when payment is made from partnership assets: (a) decreases net assets and total capital, and (b) may result in recognizing a bonus to either the departing partner or the remaining partners.

7. *Prepare the entries to record the liquidation of a partnership.* When a partnership is liquidated, it is necessary to record the: (a) sale of non-cash assets, (b) allocation of the gain or loss on realization, (c) payment of partnership liabilities, and (d) distribution of cash to the partners.

Gᴌᴏssᴀʀʏ

Admission by investment Admission of a partner by an investing of assets in the partnership. Both partnership net assets and total capital increase. (p. 553).

Admission by purchase of an interest Admission of a partner by means of a personal transaction between one or more existing partners and the new partner. It does not change total partnership assets or total capital. (p. 552).

Income ratio The basis for dividing both net income and net loss in a partnership. (p. 546).

Limited partnership A partnership in which one or more partners has unlimited liability and one or more partners has limited liability for the obligations of the firm. (p. 542).

Partnership An association of two or more persons to carry on as co-owners of a business for profit. (p. 540).

Partnership agreement A contract that expresses the voluntary agreement of two or more individuals in a partnership. (p. 544).

Partnership dissolution A change in the number of partners that does not necessarily terminate the business. (p. 541).

Partnership liquidation An event that ends both the legal and economic life of a partnership. (p. 559).

Statement of partners' capital The equity statement for a partnership that shows the changes in each partner's capital balance, and in total partnership capital during the year. (p. 549).

Withdrawal by payment from partners' personal assets Withdrawal of a partner by means of a personal transaction between partners. It does not change total partnership assets or total capital. (p. 556).

Withdrawal by payment from partnership assets Withdrawal of a partner by a transaction that decreases both partnership net assets and total capital. (p. 556).

DEMONSTRATION PROBLEM

On January 1, 1999, the capital balances in Hollingsworth Company are Lois Holly $26,000 and Jim Worth $24,000. In 1999, the company reports net income of $30,000. The income ratio provides for salary allowances of $12,000 for Holly and $10,000 for Worth, with the remainder to be distributed equally. Neither partner had any drawings in 1999.

In 2000, assume that the following independent transactions occur on January 1:

1. Donna Reichenbacher purchases one-half of Holly's capital interest for $25,000.
2. Marsha Mears is admitted with a 25% capital interest by a cash investment of $40,000.
3. Stan Wells is admitted with a 35% capital interest by a cash investment of $40,000.

Instructions

(a) Prepare a schedule showing the distribution of net income in 1999.

(b) Journalize the division of 1999 net income to the partners.

(c) Journalize each of the independent transactions that occurred on January 1, 2000.

Solution to Demonstration Problem

(a) Net income $30,000

Division of Net Income

	Lois Holly	Jim Worth	Total
Salary allowance	$12,000	$10,000	$22,000
Remaining income $8,000 ($30,000 − $22,000)			
Lois Holly ($8,000 × 50%)	4,000		
Jim Worth ($8,000 × 50%)		4,000	
Total remainder			8,000
Total division	$16,000	$14,000	$30,000

(b) 12/31/99   Income Summary   30,000

                   Lois Holly, Capital ($12,000 + $4,000)   16,000

                   Jim Worth, Capital ($10,000 + $4,000)   14,000

                     (To close net income to partners' capitals)

(c)   1.

   1/1/00   Lois Holly, Capital ($26,000 + $16,000) × 50%   21,000

                   Donna Reichenbacher, Capital   21,000

                   (To record purchase of one-half of Holly's interest)

                           2.

   1/1/00   Cash   40,000

                   Lois Holly, Capital   5,000

                   Jim Worth, Capital   5,000

                   Marsha Mears, Capital   30,000

                   (To record admission of Mears and bonus to old partners)

               Total capital after investment: $120,000

                 (Holly, $42,000, Worth $38,000,

                 Mears investment $40,000)

               Mears's capital credit (25% × $120,000) $30,000

               Bonus to old partners ($40,000 − $30,000) $10,000

               Allocation of bonus:

                   Holly ($10,000 × 50%) $ 5,000

                   Worth ($10,000 × 50%)   5,000   10,000

Problem-Solving Strategies

1. When distributing net income or loss, any allowances for salaries or interest must be allocated first, before the income-sharing ratio is applied to the remaining amount.

2. Admission of a new partner by purchase of an interest from an existing partner does not affect the partnership's assets, nor the capital accounts of the other partners.

3. Admission of a new partner by investment in the partnership brings new assets into the partnership, and may involve adjustments to the other partners' capital accounts (referred to as bonuses).

	3.		
1/1/00	Cash	40,000	
	Lois Holly, Capital	1,000	
	Jim Worth, Capital	1,000	
	Stan Wells, Capital		42,000
	(To record Wells's admission and bonus)		

Wells's capital credit (35% × $120,000)		$42,000
Bonus to Wells ($42,000 − $40,000)		$ 2,000
Allocation of bonus:		
Holly ($2,000 × 50%)	$ 1,000	
Worth ($2,000 × 50%)	1,000	$ 2,000

SELF-STUDY QUESTIONS

Answers are at the end of the chapter.

(SO 1)   1. Which of the following is *not* a characteristic of a partnership?
   a. Taxable entity.
   b. Co-ownership of property.
   c. Mutual agency.
   d. Limited life.

(SO 1)   2. The advantages of a partnership do *not* include:
   a. ease of formation.
   b. unlimited liability.
   c. little government regulation.
   d. ease of decision making.

(SO 2)   3. Upon formation of a partnership, each partner's initial investment of assets should be recorded at their:
   a. book values.
   b. original cost.
   c. market values.
   d. appraised values.

(SO 3)   4. The ABC Company reports net income of $60,000. If partners A, B, and C have an income ratio of 50%, 30%, and 20%, respectively, C's share of the net income is:
   a. $30,000.
   b. $12,000.
   c. $18,000.
   d. No correct answer is given.

(SO 3)   5. Using the data in (4), what is B's share of net income if the percentages are applicable after each partner receives a $10,000 salary allowance?
   a. $12,000.
   b. $20,000.
   c. $19,000.
   d. $21,000.

(SO   6. Which of the following statements about partnership financial statements is true?
   a. Details of the distribution of net income are shown in the statement of partners' capital.
   b. The distribution of net income is shown on the balance sheet.
   c. Only the total of all partner capital balances is usually shown in the balance sheet.
   d. The statement of owners' equity is called the statement of partners' capital.

(SO   7. R. Ranken purchases 50% of L. Lars's capital interest in the K & L partnership for $22,000. If the capital balances of Kim and Lars are $40,000 and $30,000, respectively, Ranken's capital balance after the purchase is:
   a. $22,000.
   b. $35,000.
   c. $20,000.
   d. $15,000.

(SO   8. Capital balances in the DEA partnership are D Capital $60,000, E Capital $50,000, and A Capital $40,000, and income ratios are 5:3:2, respectively. The DEAR partnership is formed by admitting R to the firm with a cash investment of $60,000 for a 25% capital interest. The bonus to be credited to A Capital in admitting R is:
   a. $10,000.
   b. $7,500.
   c. $3,750.
   d. $1,500.

(SO   9. Capital balances in the TERM partnership are T Capital $50,000, E Capital $40,000, R Capital $30,000, and M Capital $20,000, and income ratios are 4:3:2:1, respectively. M withdraws from the firm following payment of $29,000 in cash from the partnership.

E's capital balance after recording the withdrawal of M is:
a. $36,000.
b. $37,000.
c. $38,000.
d. $40,000.

10. In the liquidation of a partnership it is necessary to:

(1) distribute cash to the partners, (2) sell non-cash assets, (3) allocate any gain or loss on realization to the partners, and (4) pay liabilities. These steps should be performed in the following order:
a. (2), (3), (4), (1).
b. (2), (3), (1), (4).
c. (3), (2), (1), (4).
d. (3), (2), (4), (1).

(SO 7)

QUESTIONS

1. The characteristics of a partnership include the following: (a) limited life, and (b) co-ownership of property. Explain each of these terms.

2. Carla Cardosa is confused about the partnership characteristics of: (a) mutual agency, and (b) unlimited liability. Explain these two characteristics to Carla.

3. V.K. Nasser and T. Yoko are considering a business venture. They ask you to explain the advantages and disadvantages of the partnership form of organization.

4. S. Brown and D. Barclay form a partnership. Brown contributes land and a building with a book value of $50,000 and a fair market value of $65,000. He also contributes equipment with a book value of $52,000 and a fair market value of $57,000. The partnership assumes a $20,000 mortgage on the building. What should be the balance in Brown's capital account once the partnership is formed?

5. R. Hay, S. Innis, and L. Joyce have a partnership called Express Wings. There is a dispute among the partners because Hay has invested twice as much as the other two partners, and believes net income and net losses should be shared in accordance with the capital ratios. The partnership agreement does not specify the division of profits and losses. How will net income and net loss be divided?

6. S. Hark and R. Green are discussing how income and losses should be divided in a partnership they plan to form. What factors should be considered in determining the division of net income or net loss?

7. H. Astro and S. Sund share net income and net loss equally. (a) Which accounts are debited and credited to record the division of net income between the partners? (b) If H. Astro withdraws $30,000 in cash for personal use in lieu of salary, which accounts are debited and credited?

8. Partners R. Rowe and B. Zander are provided salary allowances of $30,000 and $25,000, respectively. They divide the remainder of the partnership income in a ratio of 60:40. If partnership net income is $50,000, how much is allocated to each partner?

9. Are the financial statements of a partnership similar to those of a proprietorship? Discuss.

10. Holly Canter decides to pay Mark Waller $30,000 for a one-third interest in the partnership of Waller and Rose. What effect does this transaction have on partnership net assets?

11. R. Minoa decides to invest $15,000 in a partnership for a one-sixth capital interest. How much do the partnership's net assets increase? Does Minoa also acquire a one-sixth income ratio through this investment?

12. Won Jang has a $37,000 capital balance in a partnership. She sells her interest to Karen Crest for $42,000 cash. What entry is made by the partnership for this transaction?

13. Rorey Rolf retires from the partnership of Suarez, Tanks, and Rolf. She receives $87,000 of partnership assets for her capital balance of $75,000. If the income-sharing ratios are 5:3:2, respectively, how much of Rolf's bonus is debited to Tanks's capital account?

14. Your roommate argues that partnership assets should be revalued in situations like those in question 13. Why is this generally not done?

15. How is a deceased partner's equity determined?

16. How does the liquidation of a partnership differ from the dissolution of a partnership?

17. Joe and Jean are discussing the liquidation of a partnership. Joe maintains that all cash should be distributed to partners on the basis of their income ratios. Is he correct? Explain.

18. In continuing their discussion, Jean says that even in the case of a capital deficiency, all cash should still be distributed on the basis of capital balances. Is Jean correct? Explain.

19. Mike, Larry, and Joan have income ratios of 5:3:2 and capital balances of $34,000, $31,000, and $28,000, respectively. Non-cash assets are sold at a gain. After creditors are paid, $109,000 of cash is available for distribution to the partners. How much cash should be paid to Larry?

20. Before the final distribution of cash, account balances are: Cash $24,000; R. Katz, Capital, $18,000 (cr); M. Moss, Capital, $12,000 (cr); and T. Zaret, Capital, $6,000 (dr). Zaret is unable to pay any of the capital deficiency. If the income-sharing ratios are 5:3:2, respectively, how much cash should be paid to Moss?

BRIEF EXERCISES

···

Journalize the entries in forming a partnership.
(SO 2)

BE13–1   R. Alfredo and B. Starr decide to organize the ALL-Star partnership. Alfredo invests $15,000 cash, and Starr contributes $10,000 cash and equipment having a book value of $3,500. The equipment has a fair market value of $4,000. Prepare the entry to record Starr's investment in the partnership.

Prepare a partial opening balance sheet for a partnership.
(SO 2, 4)

BE13–2   C. Held and G. Kamp decide to merge their proprietorships into a partnership called HeldKamp Company. The balance sheet of Kamp Co. shows:

Accounts Receivable	$15,000	
Less: Allowance for Doubtful Accounts	1,200	$13,800
Equipment	20,000	
Less: Accumulated Amortization	8,000	12,000

The partners agree that the net realizable value of the receivables is $12,500 and that the fair market value of the equipment is $11,000. Indicate how these items should appear in the opening balance sheet of the partnership.

Journalize the division of net income, using fixed income ratios.
(SO 3)

BE13–3   B&R Co. reports net income of $60,000. The income ratios are: B 60% and R 40%. Prepare the closing entry to distribute the net income.

Compute the division of net income, with salary allowances and fixed ratios.
(SO 3)

BE13–4   Met Co. reports net income of $50,000. Partner salary allowances are: M $10,000, E $5,000, and T $5,000. Indicate the division of net income to each partner, assuming the income ratio is 50:30:20, respectively.

Show the division of net income when the allowances exceed the income.
(SO 3)

BE13–5   S&T Co. reports net income of $20,000. Interest allowances are S $6,000 and T $5,000; salary allowances are S $15,000 and T $10,000; the remainder is shared equally. Show the distribution of income.

Journalize an admission by purchase of an interest.
(SO 5)

BE13–6   In ABC Co., capital balances are: Ali $30,000, Babson $25,000, and Carter $20,000. The partners share income equally. Daniel is admitted to the firm by purchasing one-half of Carter's interest for $12,000. Journalize the admission of Daniel to the partnership.

Journalize an admission by investment.
(SO 5)

BE13–7   In the EZ Co., capital balances are Edie $40,000 and Zane $30,000. The partners share income equally. Kerns is admitted to the firm with a 40% interest by an investment of cash of $42,000. Journalize the admission of Kerns.

Journalize a withdrawal paid by personal assets.
(SO 6)

BE13–8   Capital balances in DEB Co. are: Ditka $40,000, Embs $30,000, and Boyd $28,000. The partners share income equally. Ditka and Embs each agree to pay Boyd $12,000 from their personal assets, and each receive 50% of Boyd's equity. Journalize the withdrawal of Boyd.

Journalize a withdrawal paid by partnership assets.
(SO 6)

BE13–9   Data pertaining to DEB Co. are presented in BE13–8. Instead of payment from personal assets, assume that Boyd receives $32,000 from partnership assets in withdrawing from the firm. Journalize the withdrawal of Boyd.

Journalize the final cash distribution in a liquidation.
(SO 7)

BE13–10   After liquidating non-cash assets and paying creditors, account balances in the ARB Co. are: Cash $18,000, A Capital (Cr.) $9,000, R Capital (Cr.) $6,000, and B Capital (Cr.) $3,000. The partners share income equally. Journalize the final distribution of cash to the partners.

EXERCISES

···

Journalize the entry for the formation of a partnership.
(SO 2)

E13–1   Ted Karl has owned and operated a proprietorship for several years. On January 1, he decides to terminate this business and become a partner in the firm of Payne and Karl. Karl's investment in the partnership consists of $15,000 in cash and the following assets of the proprietorship: accounts receivable $14,000 less allowance for doubtful accounts of $2,000, and equipment $20,000 less accumulated amortization of $4,000. It is agreed that the allowance for doubtful accounts should be $3,000 for the partnership, and the fair market value of the equipment is $18,000.

Instructions
Journalize Karl's admission to the firm of Payne and Karl.

E13–2 R. Huma and W. How have capital balances on January 1 of $50,000 and $40,000, respectively. The partnership income-sharing agreement provides for: (1) annual salaries of $14,000 for Huma and $12,000 for How, (2) interest at 10% on beginning capital balances, and (3) remaining income or loss to be shared 70% by Huma and 30% by How.

Prepare a schedule showing the distribution of net income; journalize the closing entry.
(SO 3)

Instructions

(a) Prepare a schedule showing the distribution of net income, assuming net income is: (1) $45,000, and (2) $28,000.
(b) Journalize the allocation of net income in each of the situations above.

E13–3 In Salton Co., beginning capital balances on January 1, 1999, are M. Salz $20,000 and C. Toni $18,000. During the year, drawings were Salz $6,000 and Toni $3,000. Net income was $30,000, and the partners share income equally.

Prepare a statement of partners' capital and a partial balance sheet.
(SO 4)

Instructions

(a) Prepare the statement of partners' capital for the year.
(b) Prepare the partners' equity section of the balance sheet at December 31, 1999.

E13–4 T. Halo, K. Rose, and J. Lamp share income on a 5:3:2 basis. They have capital balances of $32,000, $24,000, and $21,000, respectively, when R. Zahn is admitted to the partnership.

Journalize the admission of a partner by purchase of an interest.
(SO 5)

Instructions

Prepare the journal entry to record the admission of Zahn under each of the following assumptions:
1. Zahn purchases 50% of Halo's equity for $19,000.
2. Zahn purchases 50% of Rose's equity for $10,000.
3. Zahn purchases 33% of Lamp's equity for $9,000.

E13–5 Joe Keho and Mike McLain share income on a 6:4 basis. They have capital balances of $90,000 and $70,000, respectively, when Ed Kehler is admitted to the partnership.

Journalize the admission of a partner by investment.
(SO 5)

Instructions

Prepare the journal entry to record the admission of Ed Kehler under each of the following assumptions:
1. Kehler invests $80,000 cash for a 25% ownership interest, with bonuses to the existing partners.
2. Kehler invests of $36,000 cash for a 25% ownership interest, with a bonus to the new partner.

E13–6 Mary Lane, Vera Miles, and Debra Noll have capital balances of $50,000, $30,000, and $20,000, respectively, and their income ratios are 5:3:2.

Journalize the withdrawal of a partner, with payment from partners' personal assets.
(SO 6)

Instructions

Journalize the withdrawal of Noll under each of the following independent conditions:
1. Lane and Miles agree to purchase Noll's equity by paying $15,000 each from their personal assets. Each purchaser receives 50% of Noll's equity.
2. Miles agrees to purchase all of Noll's equity by paying $20,000 cash from her personal assets.
3. Lane agrees to purchase all of Noll's equity by paying $23,000 cash from her personal assets.

E13–7 Dale Nagel, Keith White, and Dan Neal have capital balances of $95,000, $75,000, and $60,000, respectively. They share income or loss on a 5:3:2 basis.

Journalize the withdrawal of a partner, with payment from the partnership's assets.
(SO 6)

Instructions

Journalize the withdrawal of White under each of the following conditions:
1. White is paid $82,000 in cash from partnership assets, and a bonus is granted to him.
2. White is paid $68,000 in cash from partnership assets, and bonuses are granted to the remaining partners.

E13–8 Baylee Company at December 31 has cash $20,000, non-cash assets $100,000, liabilities $55,000, and the following capital balances: Bayer $40,000 and Leech $25,000. The firm is liquidated, and $120,000 in cash is received for the non-cash assets. Bayer and Leech have income ratios of 60% and 40%, respectively.

Calculate amounts paid to partners on the liquidation of a partnership.
(SO 7)

Instructions

Calculate how much will be paid to each of the partners, when the firm is liquidated.

Journalize transactions in a partnership liquidation.
(SO 7)

E13–9   Data for the Baylee partnership are presented in E13–8.

Instructions

Prepare the entries to record: (1) the sale of non-cash assets, (2) the allocation of the gain or loss on liquidation to the partners, (3) payment of creditors, and (4) distribution of cash to the partners.

Journalize transactions in a partnership liquidation with a capital deficiency.
(SO 7)

E13–10   Prior to the distribution of cash to the partners, the accounts in the MEL Company are: Cash $31,000, M Capital (Cr.) $18,000, E Capital (Cr.) $16,000, and L Capital (Dr.) $3,000. The income ratios are 5:3:2, respectively.

Instructions

(a) Prepare the entry to record: (1) L's payment of $3,000 in cash to the partnership, and (2) the distribution of cash to the partners.

(b) Prepare the entry to record: (1) the absorption of L's capital deficiency by the other partners, and (2) the distribution of cash to the partners.

PROBLEMS

Prepare entries for the formation of a partnership, and a balance sheet.
(SO 2, 4)

P13–1   The post-closing trial balances of two proprietorships on January 1, 1999, are presented below.

	Hamp Company		Vong Company	
	Dr.	Cr.	Dr.	Cr.
Cash	$ 13,000		$16,000	
Accounts receivable	17,500		26,000	
Allowance for doubtful accounts		$ 3,000		$ 4,400
Merchandise inventory	26,500		18,400	
Equipment	45,000		28,000	
Accumulated amortization—equipment		24,000		12,000
Notes payable		20,000		15,000
Accounts payable		20,000		31,000
L. Hamp, Capital		35,000		
P. Vong, Capital				26,000
	$102,000	$102,000	$88,400	$88,400

Hamp and Vong decide to form the Hamp-Vong Company with the following agreed-upon valuations for non-cash assets:

	Hamp Company	Vong Company
Accounts receivable	$17,500	$26,000
Allowance for doubtful accounts	4,500	4,000
Merchandise inventory	28,000	20,000
Equipment	25,000	18,000

All cash will be transferred to the partnership, and the partnership will assume all the liabilities of the two proprietorships. Further, it is agreed that Hamp will invest $20,000 in cash and Vong will invest $9,000 in cash.

Instructions

(a) Prepare separate journal entries to record the transfer of each proprietorship's assets and liabilities to the partnership.

(b) Journalize the additional cash investment by each partner.

(c) Prepare a balance sheet for the partnership on January 1, 1999.

P13–2 The post-closing trial balances of two proprietorships on January 1, 1999, are presented below.

Analyse transactions and prepare the balance sheet for a new partnership.
(SO 2, 4)

	Kreal Company		Donal Company	
	Dr.	Cr.	Dr.	Cr.
Cash	$ 6,500		$ 8,000	
Accounts receivable	15,000		23,000	
Allowance for doubtful accounts		$ 2,500		$ 4,000
Merchandise inventory	28,000		17,000	
Equipment	52,000		30,000	
Accumulated amortization—equipment		24,000		13,000
Notes payable		20,000		—
Accounts payable		25,000		37,000
R. T. Kreal, Capital		30,000		
A. C. Donal, Capital				24,000
	$101,500	$101,500	$78,000	$78,000

Kreal and Donal decide to form the Donal Kreal Company with the following agreed-upon valuations for non-cash assets:

	Kreal Company	Donal Company
Accounts receivable	$15,000	$23,000
Allowance for doubtful accounts	3,500	6,000
Merchandise inventory	30,000	21,000
Equipment	31,000	18,000

All cash will be transferred to the partnership, and the partnership will assume all the liabilities of the two proprietorships.

Instructions

Prepare a balance sheet for the partnership on January 1, 1999.

P13–3 At the end of its first year of operations, on December 31, 1999, the LMN Company's accounts show the following:

Journalize divisions of net income; prepare a statement of partners' capital.
(SO 3, 4)

Partner	Drawings	Capital
Lois Lang	$12,000	$30,000
Mary Mio	9,000	20,000
Sue Norton	6,000	10,000

The capital balance represents each partner's initial capital investment; net income or net loss for 1999 has not been closed to the partners' capital accounts.

Instructions

(a) Journalize the entry to record the division of net income for 1999 under each of the following assumptions:
1. Net income is $28,000 and income is shared 5:3:2.
2. Net income is $30,000; Lang and Mio are given salary allowances of $10,000 and $8,000, respectively, and the remainder is shared equally.
3. Net income is $25,200; each partner is allowed interest of 10% on beginning capital balances; Lang is given a $15,000 salary allowance, and the remainder is shared equally.

(b) Prepare a statement of partners' capital for the year under assumption (3) above.

P13–4 At the end of its first year of operations, on December 31, 1999, HRZ Company's accounts show the following:

Journalize divisions of net income; prepare a statement of partners' capital.
(SO 3, 4)

Partner	Drawings	Capital
Sue Horton	$23,000	$45,000
Tracey Rugen	14,000	30,000
Eileen Zak	10,000	25,000

The capital balance represents each partner's initial capital investment; net income or net loss for 1999 has not been closed to the partners' capital accounts.

Instructions

(a) Journalize the entry to record the division of net income for the year 1999 under each of the following assumptions:

1. Net income is $34,000; Horton and Rugen are given salary allowances of $15,000 and $10,000, respectively, and the remainder is shared equally.

2. Net income is $22,000; each partner is allowed interest of 10% on beginning capital balances; Horton is given a $15,000 salary allowance, and the remainder is shared equally.

(b) Prepare a schedule showing the division of net income under assumption (2) above.

(c) Prepare a statement of partners' capital for the year under assumption (2) above.

Journalize the admission of a partner under various assumptions.

(SO 5)

P13–5   At April 30, partners' capital balances in the ELM Company are: A. Ellis $50,000, C. Lazzeri $24,000, and W. Matt $16,000. The income-sharing ratios are 3:2:1, respectively. On May 1, the ELMO Company is formed by admitting N. Ortiz to the firm as a partner.

Instructions

Journalize the admission of Ortiz under each of the following assumptions:

1. Ortiz purchases 50% of Matt's ownership interest by paying Matt $9,000 in cash.

2. Ortiz purchases 50% of Lazzeri's ownership interest by paying Lazzeri $16,000 in cash.

3. Ortiz invests $35,000 cash in the partnership for a 40% ownership interest that includes a bonus to the new partner.

4. Ortiz invests $30,000 in the partnership for a 20% ownership interest and bonuses are given to the old partners.

Journalize the admission of a partner under various assumptions.

(SO 5)

P13–6   At April 30, partners' capital balances in NSW Company are: A. Nolan $60,000, D. Spoda $36,000, and T. Wise $14,000. The income-sharing ratios are 5:4:1, respectively. On May 1, the NSWO Company is formed by admitting M. Otton to the firm as a partner.

Instructions

(a) Journalize the admission of Otton under each of the following assumptions:

1. Otton purchases 33% of Spoda's ownership interest by paying Spoda $15,000 in cash.

2. Otton invests $60,000 for a 30% ownership interest.

3. Otton invests $40,000 for a 30% ownership interest.

(b) Assume that Spoda's capital balance is $32,000 after Otton is admitted to the partnership by investment. If Spoda's ownership interest is 20% of total partnership capital, what was Otton's cash investment and the bonus to the new partner?

Journalize the withdrawal of a partner under various assumptions.

(SO 6)

P13–7   On December 31, the capital balances and income ratios in the ART Company are as follows:

Partner	Capital Balance	Income Ratio
E. Atlas	$70,000	60%
P. Ross	30,000	30%
L. Tower	20,000	10%

Instructions

Journalize the withdrawal of Tower under each of the following assumptions:

1. Each of the remaining partners agrees to pay $12,000 in cash from personal funds to purchase Tower's ownership equity. Each receives 50% of Tower's equity.

2. Ross agrees to purchase Tower's ownership interest for $18,000 in cash.

3. From partnership assets, Tower is paid $29,000, which includes a bonus to him.

4. Tower is paid $17,000 from partnership assets, and bonuses to the remaining partners are recognized.

Journalize the withdrawal of a partner under various assumptions.

(SO 6)

P13–8   On December 31, the capital balances and income ratios in the BAG Company are as follows:

Partner	Capital Balance	Income Ratio
R. Beano	$60,000	50%
D. Alman	40,000	30%
P. Garth	32,000	20%

Instructions

(a) Journalize the withdrawal of Garth under each of the following assumptions:
   1. Each of the continuing partners agrees to pay $17,000 in cash from personal funds to purchase Garth's ownership equity. Each receives 50% of Garth's equity.
   2. Garth is paid $38,000 from partnership assets, which includes a bonus to him.
   3. Garth is paid $28,000 from partnership assets, and bonuses to the remaining partners are recognized.

(b) If Alman's capital balance after Garth's withdrawal is $43,000, what was the total bonus to the remaining partners and the cash paid by the partnership to Garth?

P13–9 The partners in Inland Lakes Company decide to liquidate the firm when the balance sheet shows the following:

Prepare entries for the liquidation of a partnership.
(SO 7)

INLAND LAKES COMPANY
Balance Sheet
April 30, 1999

Assets		Liabilities and Partners' Equity	
Cash	$24,000	Notes payable	$14,000
Accounts receivable	18,000	Accounts payable	24,000
Allowance for doubtful accounts	(1,000)	Wages payable	2,000
Merchandise inventory	30,000	T. E. Huron, Capital	24,000
Equipment	17,000	P. A. Erie, Capital	12,800
Accumulated amortization—equip.	(8,000)	C. R. Lake, Capital	3,200
Total	$80,000	Total	$80,000

The partners share income and loss 5:3:2. During the process of liquidation, the transactions below were completed in the following sequence:
   1. A total of $48,000 was received from converting non-cash assets into cash.
   2. Liabilities were paid in full.
   3. Cash was paid to the partners.

Instructions

(a) Prepare the entries to record the transactions. (Hint: Remember to distribute any gain or loss on realization to the partners' capital accounts.)
(b) Post to the cash and capital accounts.

P13–10 The partners in the JRS Company decide to liquidate the firm when the balance sheet shows the following:

Prepare entries for a partnership liquidation; capital deficiency.
(SO 7)

JRS COMPANY
Balance Sheet
May 31, 1999

Assets		Liabilities and Partners' Equity	
Cash	$ 27,500	Notes payable	$ 13,500
Accounts receivable	24,000	Accounts payable	27,000
Allowance for doubtful accounts	(1,000)	Wages payable	3,800
Merchandise inventory	34,500	M. Jagger, Capital	35,000
Equipment	21,000	K. Richards, Capital	20,000
Accumulated amortization—equipment	(5,500)	R. Simka, Capital	1,200
Total	$100,500	Total	$100,500

The partners share income and loss 5:3:2. During the process of liquidation, the following transactions were completed in the following sequence:
   1. A total of $53,000 was received from converting non-cash assets into cash.
   2. Liabilities were paid in full.
   3. Simka paid his capital deficiency.
   4. Cash was paid to the partners with credit balances.

Instructions

    (a) Prepare the entries to record the transactions.

    (b) Post to the cash and capital accounts.

    (c) Assume that Simka is unable to pay the capital deficiency.

        1. Prepare the entry to allocate Simka's debit balance to Jagger and Richards.

        2. Prepare the entry to record the final distribution of cash.

*B*roadening Your Perspective

DECISION CASE

Bart Holmar and Sally Izod, two professionals in the finance area, have worked for Advanced Leasing for a number of years. Advanced Leasing is a company that leases high-tech medical equipment to hospitals. Bart and Sally have decided that, with their financial expertise, they might start their own company to provide consulting services to individuals interested in leasing equipment. One form of organization they are considering is a partnership.

    If they start a partnership, each individual plans to contribute $15,000 in cash. In addition, Bart has a computer that originally cost $3,800, which he intends to invest in the partnership. The computer has a current market value of $1,800.

    Although both Bart and Sally are financial wizards, they do not know a great deal about how a partnership operates. As a result, they have come to you for advice.

Instructions

Answer the following questions:

    (a) What are the major disadvantages of operating a business as a partnership?

    (b) What type of document is needed for a partnership, and what should this document contain?

    (c) Both Bart and Sally plan to work full-time in the new partnership. Therefore they believe that net income or net loss should be shared equally. However, they are wondering how they can provide compensation to Bart for his additional investment of the computer. What would you tell them?

    (d) As indicated above, Bart and Sally have worked together for a number of years. Bart's skills complement Sally's and vice versa. If one of them dies, it will be very difficult for the other to maintain the business, not to mention the difficulty of paying the deceased partner's estate for his or her partnership interest. What would you tell them to do?

COMMUNICATION ACTIVITY

You are an expert in the field of forming partnerships. Bill Glass and Enid Hall want to establish a partnership to start up "Enid's Pasta Shop," and they are going to meet with you to discuss their plans. Prior to the meeting you will send them a memo discussing the issues they need to consider before their visit.

Instructions

Write a memo, in good form, to be sent to Bill and Enid. In it, provide an overview of the various aspects of a partnership agreement and the issues that need to be addressed in order for the agreement to be a well-thought-out document.

GROUP ACTIVITY

In groups of five or six students, form a partnership. Decide as a group what you will be selling or providing as a service.

Instructions

(a) Discuss what each member will contribute to the partnership, and what income-sharing ratio would be appropriate.

(b) Assume that one member of your group wishes to provide one-half of the total assets of the partnership but does not otherwise wish to participate in the partnership. Discuss how this would affect your partnership's income-sharing ratio.

ETHICS CASE

Susan and Karen operate a beauty salon as partners who share profits and losses equally. The success of their business has exceeded their expectations and it is operating quite profitably. Karen is anxious to maximize profits, and schedules appointments from 8 a.m. to 6 p.m. daily—even sacrificing some lunch hours to accommodate regular customers. Susan schedules her appointments from 9 a.m. to 5 p.m. and takes long lunch hours. Susan regularly makes significantly larger withdrawals of cash than Karen does, but she says, "Karen, you needn't worry; I never make a withdrawal without you knowing about it, so it is properly recorded in my drawings account and charged against my capital at the end of the year." Susan's withdrawals to date are double Karen's.

Instructions

(a) Identify the problems with Susan's actions, and discuss the ethical considerations of her actions.

(b) How might the partnership agreement be designed to accommodate the differences in Susan's and Karen's work and withdrawal habits?

CRITICAL THINKING
▶ *A Real-World Focus: Mergers of Accounting Firms*

The global merger of accounting and management consulting firms Coopers & Lybrand and Price Waterhouse resulted in the largest accounting and professional services partnership in the world, PricewaterhouseCoopers. In Canada, this merger brought together almost 1,000 partners, generating almost $1 billion in revenues. Worldwide, the combined firm employed more than 135,000 people—including more than 8,500 partners—in over 130 countries, with revenues of over $13 billion.

Instructions

(a) Explain how the assets and equities of the old partnerships would be transferred to the new partnership. At what values would the assets be recorded? How would the partners agree the values are fair?

(b) Describe the types of entries that would be necessary to record the formation of the new partnership.

(c) When mergers such as this occur, some partners of the old firms usually "retire." On what basis should cash payments to the withdrawing partners (in settlement of their partnership interests) be made?

ACCOUNTING ON THE WEB

This problem introduces some of the largest accounting firm partnerships.

Instructions

Specific requirements of this Internet case are available on-line at www.wiley.com/canada/weygandt.

Answers to Self-Study Questions
1. a 2. b 3. c 4. b 5. c 6. d 7. d 8. d 9. b 10. a

Concepts for Review

Before studying this chapter, you should understand or, if necessary, review:

a. *The content of the shareholders' equity section of a balance sheet. (Ch. 4, p. 155)*

b. *The content of the equity section of the balance sheet for a proprietorship (Ch. 1, pp. 25–26) and for a partnership. (Ch. 13, p. 550)*

c. *How to prepare closing entries for a proprietorship (Ch. 4, pp. 142–144) and for a partnership (Ch. 13, pp. 546–547)*

Have You Driven a Ford Lately?

OAKVILLE, Ont.—The Ford Motor Company of Canada is an integral part of the Ontario economy – just as its cars have been integral to Canadians' lives for almost a century. The history of this company and its parent, the first American auto giant, is full of interesting stories.

Henry Ford was a defiant visionary from the day Ford Motor Company was formed in 1904. His goal from day one was to design a car he could mass produce and sell at a price that was affordable to the working class. He accomplished this goal in short order and, by 1920, 60% of all vehicles on North American roads were Fords.

Henry Ford was intolerant of anything that stood between himself and success. In 1916, he decided that, to retain funds to finance expansion, the company would skip a dividend payment to its shareholders. When the shareholders sued, the Ford family purchased 100% of the outstanding shares, eliminating any outside interference. It was over 35 years before shares were again issued to the public.

Ford has continued to evolve over the years. Today there are nearly 1.2 billion shares of Ford stock publicly traded around the world. Almost 372,000 people are employed by Ford to serve customers in more than 200 countries and territories on six continents.

Yet many of the basic tenets Henry Ford promoted remain. In 1997, for example, Bobbie Gaunt became the first female president of Ford Motor Company of Canada. Meeting the customers' needs, Gaunt says, is paramount. Henry Ford knew that. And, just as the Model T was designed to appeal to a customer base that was huge for its time, the company's integrated global product cycle plan is to mass produce a car that can be sold around the world with only minor changes.◄

CHAPTER 14

CORPORATIONS: ORGANIZATION AND CAPITAL STOCK TRANSACTIONS

▶ STUDY OBJECTIVES ◀

After studying this chapter, you should be able to:

1. *Identify and discuss the major characteristics of a corporation.*
2. *Differentiate between contributed capital and retained earnings.*
3. *Record the issuance of common stock.*
4. *Differentiate preferred stock from common stock.*
5. *Prepare the shareholders' equity section of the balance sheet.*
6. *Compute return on equity.*
7. *Distinguish between book and market value per share.*

Incorporated companies like the Ford Motor Company of Canada have substantial resources. In fact, the corporation is the dominant form of business organization in terms of revenues, earnings, and employees. In this chapter we will explain the essential features of a corporation and the accounting for a corporation's capital stock transactions. In Chapter 15 we will look at other issues related to accounting for corporations. The organization of this chapter is as follows:

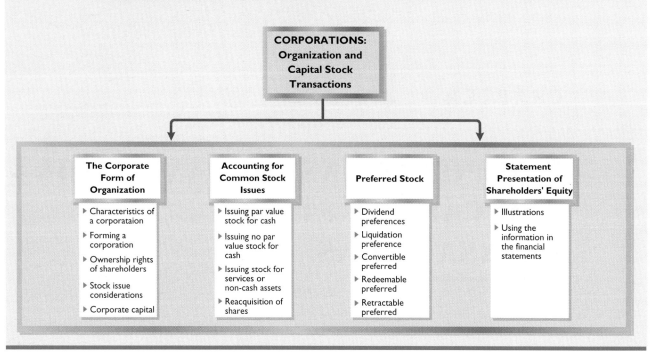

▼he Corporate Form of Organization

A corporation is a **legal entity separate and distinct from its owners**. As a legal entity, a corporation has most of the rights and privileges of a person. The major exceptions are privileges that can be exercised only by a living person, such as the right to vote, to hold public office, or to marry. Similarly, a corporation is subject to the same duties and responsibilities as a person—for example, it must abide by the laws, and it must pay taxes.

Corporations may be classified in a variety of ways. Two common bases are by purpose and by ownership. A corporation may be organized for the purpose of making a **profit**, or it may be **nonprofit** (also known as not-for-profit). Corporations for profit include such well-known companies as Cineplex Odeon Corp., Corel Corp., Imax Corp., Maple Leaf Foods Inc., and Rocky Mountain Bicycle Co. Ltd. Nonprofit corporations are organized for cultural, social, charitable, medical, educational, and religious purposes and include organizations such as Big Brothers/Big Sisters, Canadian National Institute for the Blind, Chamber of Commerce, Kelowna Curling Club, Red Cross, Society for the Prevention of Cruelty to Animals, and the University of New Brunswick.

Classification by **ownership** distinguishes between publicly held and privately held corporations. A publicly held corporation may have thousands of shareholders, and its stock is usually traded in an organized securities market such as the Toronto Stock Exchange. Most of the largest Canadian corporations are publicly held. Examples of publicly held corporations are BCE Inc., Canadian Pacific Ltd., MacMillan Bloedel Ltd., and Stelco Inc. In contrast, a privately held corporation, often referred to as a closely held corporation, usually has only a few shareholders and does not offer its stock for sale to the general public. Privately held companies are generally much smaller than publicly held companies, although there are notable exceptions such as the Jim Pattison and Irving groups of companies. A crown corporation is similar to a privately held company except that it is owned by the government. Atlantic Lotteries, Canada Post, Ontario Hydro, and BC Ferries are examples of crown corporations.

Characteristics of a Corporation

A number of characteristics distinguish a corporation from proprietorships and partnerships. The most important of these characteristics are explained below.

Separate Legal Existence

As an entity separate and distinct from its owners, the corporation acts under its own name rather than in the name of its shareholders. A corporation may buy, own, and sell property, borrow money, and enter into legally binding contracts in its own name. It may also sue or be sued, and it pays its own taxes.

In contrast to a partnership, in which the acts of the owners (partners) bind the partnership, the acts of the owners (shareholders) do not bind the corporation unless such owners are duly appointed agents of the corporation. For example, if you owned shares of Sleeman Breweries Ltd. stock, you would not have the right to purchase a brewery for the company unless you were appointed an agent of the corporation.

Limited Liability of Shareholders

Since a corporation is a separate legal entity, creditors ordinarily have recourse only to corporate assets to satisfy their claims. The liability of shareholders is normally limited to their investment in the corporation, and creditors have no legal claim on the personal assets of the owners unless fraud has occurred. Thus, even in the event of bankruptcy of the corporation, shareholders' losses are generally limited to their capital investment in the corporation.

Transferable Ownership Rights

Ownership of a corporation is in shares of capital stock, which are transferable units. Shareholders may dispose of part or all of their interest in a corporation simply by selling their stock. In contrast to the transfer of an ownership interest in a partnership, which requires the consent of each owner, the transfer of stock is entirely at the discretion of the shareholder. It does not require the approval of either the corporation or other shareholders. The transfer of ownership rights between shareholders normally has no effect on the operating activities of the corporation or on a corporation's assets, liabilities, and total equity. That is, the enterprise does not participate in the transfer of these ownership rights after it has issued the capital stock.

Ability to Acquire Capital

It is relatively easy for a large corporation to obtain capital through the issuance of stock. Buying stock in a corporation is often more attractive to an investor than investing in a partnership, because a shareholder has limited liability and shares of stock are

STUDY OBJECTIVE

I

Identify and discuss the major characteristics of a corporation.

Shareholders
Legal existence separate from owners

Shareholders
Limited liability of shareholders

Transferable ownership rights

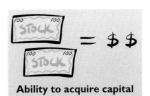

Ability to acquire capital

readily transferable. Moreover, many individuals can become shareholders by investing small amounts of money. For these reasons a successful corporation's ability to obtain capital is virtually unlimited.

Continuous Life

Continuous life

The life of a corporation is stated in its charter; it may be perpetual, or it may be limited to a specific number of years. If it is limited, the period of existence can be extended through renewal of the charter. Since a corporation is a separate legal entity, the life of a corporation and its continuance as a going concern are not affected by the withdrawal, death, or incapacity of a shareholder, employee, or officer. As a result, a successful enterprise can have a continuous and indefinite life. For example, the Hudson's Bay Co., Canada's oldest corporation, was founded in 1670 and is still going strong.

▸ *Ethics note*

The separation of ownership from management caused by the corporation form of organization can create an ethical dilemma for management. Managers are often compensated based upon the performance of the firm, and thus may be tempted to exaggerate performance by inflating income figures, or to emphasize short-term results to the detriment of long-term performance.

Corporation Management

Although shareholders legally own the corporation, as in Ford, they manage the corporation indirectly through a board of directors they elect. The board, in turn, formulates the operating policies for the company, and selects officers—such as a president and one or more vice-presidents—to execute policy and to perform daily management functions.

The organizational structure of corporations—if reasonably large—enables a company to hire professional managers to run the business. On the other hand, the separation of ownership and management prevents owners from having an active role in managing the company, which is difficult for some owners to accept.

▸Accounting in Action ▸ *Business Insight*

An interesting question is who runs a corporation—the shareholders or the board of directors? This issue has taken on increased importance because shareholders and boards of directors are often on opposite sides of the fence these days, especially when potential takeovers occur.

A classic example is the unfriendly takeover bid made by Paramount Communication Inc. for Time Inc. Paramount bid up Time's stock price substantially. Many shareholders said sell—but Time's board of directors had other plans. They were in the process of trying to make a friendly deal with Warner Communications. Some shareholders said, "Let's vote on what we should do." But Time decided to proceed without a shareholders' vote, even though the board of directors knew that the Warner deal would depress Time's stock price in the short term. They figured that many shareholders would prefer to accept the Paramount bid. The shareholders sued to overturn the deal with Warner Communications, but lost. The judge wrote, "Corporation law does not operate on the theory that directors, in exercising their powers to manage the firm, are obligated to follow the wishes of a majority of shareholders. In fact, the directors, not the shareholders, are charged with the duty to manage the firm."

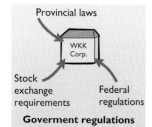

Goverment regulations

Government Regulations

Canadian companies may be incorporated federally, under the terms of the *Canada Business Corporations Act*, or provincially, under the terms of a provincial business corporations act. A federally incorporated corporation can carry on business in every province and territory. A provincially incorporated corporation, however, must obtain a licence to do business in other jurisdictions.

Federal and provincial laws specify requirements for issuing stock, the permitted distributions of earnings to shareholders, and the effects of retiring stock, as well as other procedures and restrictions. Similarly, securities laws govern the sale of capital stock to the general public. When a corporate stock is listed and traded on organized securities markets, the corporation must comply with the reporting requirements of these exchanges. Compliance with federal, provincial, and securities regulations increases the cost and complexity for the corporate form of organization, as do recurring fees.

Regulations are designed to protect the owners of the corporation. Unlike the owners of most proprietorships and partnerships, most shareholders do not participate in the day-to-day management of the company.

►Accounting in Action ► *Ethics Insight*

The collapse of the Calgary-based Bre-X company in 1997 represents the world's biggest mining hoax and stock disaster. It has raised questions that remain unanswered about the integrity of the world's stock markets and financial regulatory agencies. On top of that, the story has all the makings of a soap opera, including suicide, murder, adultery, greed, and conspiracy plots.

Bre-X collapsed after an independent audit found that their Indonesian gold discovery, proclaimed to be the world's largest, contained almost no gold. At the peak of its trading, Bre-X shares were worth $6 billion. Its shares are now worthless. The stock price moved like a yo-yo in response to information leaks on the Internet. Regulators halted trading, but unofficial markets outside the stock exchanges sprang up.

While there are many fingers being pointed in all directions to assign blame for this debacle, Canadian regulatory authorities and investors have learned two important lessons. "No one in Canada is protected from cyber sellers who post insider information or lies on the Internet. No one in Canada can be protected from a Jakarta newspaper with scurrilous information."

Source: Maclean's, June 2, 1997, 61.

Income Taxes

Neither proprietorships nor partnerships pay income taxes. Each owner's share of earnings is reported on his or her personal income tax return, and taxes are paid by the individual on this amount. Corporations, on the other hand, must pay federal and provincial income taxes as a separate legal entity. These taxes can be substantial, amounting to as much as 50% of taxable income.

However, there are tax redeductions available to some corporations. Deductions such as the manufacturing and processing profits deduction and the small business deduction can reduce the tax rate to between 20% and 25%. With eligible deductions, or other corporate tax incentives, this tax rate may be lower than the tax rate for the same amount of income earned personally.

In some circumstances, an advantage of incorporation is deferral of personal income tax payment. The shareholders of a corporation do not pay tax on the corporate earnings until they are distributed to them. Shareholders pay taxes on cash dividends, which are pro rata distributions of net income. Thus, many people argue that corporate income is taxed twice (double taxation)—at the corporate level and again at the individual level. This is not exactly true, however, as individuals receive a dividend tax credit to reduce the tax burden.

Case in point After income taxes, adjusted for the dividend tax credit, an individual gets to pocket only about 66% of the dividend. This rate will vary by province.

To determine whether incorporating will result in more or less taxes than those of a proprietorship or partnership, it is wise to seek expert advice. Income tax laws are complex, and care in tax planning is essential for any business venture.

From the foregoing, we can identify the following advantages and disadvantages of incorporation versus a proprietorship or partnership form of organization:

Illustration 14-1

Advantages and disadvantages of a corporation

Advantages	Disadvantages
Corporation management— professional managers	Corporation management— ownership separated from management
Separate legal existence	
Limited liability of shareholders	Increased costs and complexity to adhere to government regulations
Deferred or reduced taxes	
Transferable ownership rights	
Ability to acquire capital	Additional taxes
Continuous life	

It is worth noting that many of these advantages and disadvantages may be illusory, depending on the size of the entity. For example, in a small (private, closely held) corporation such as the Diab Corner Grocery Store Ltd., it is just as hard to sell shares of ownership, or to acquire capital, as it is for an unincorporated business. The limited liability feature also makes it harder for a small corporation to obtain loans currently. In such cases, lenders often require officers to personally guarantee the loans. In larger corporations, the separation of ownership and management provides a useful function for investors.

Forming a Corporation

▶ *International note*

As noted previously, corporations in Canada are identified by *Ltd., Inc.,* or *Corp.* In Brazil and France, the letters used are *SA* (Sôciedade Anonima, Société Anonyme); in Japan, *KK* (Kabushiki Kaisha); in the Netherlands, *NV* (Naamloze Vennootschap); in Italy, *SpA* (Società per Azioni); in Sweden, *AB* (Aktiebolag); and in the U.S., *Inc.*

In the UK, public corporations are identified by *Plc* (Public limited company), while private corporations are denoted by *Ltd.* The parallel designations in Germany are *AG* (Aktiengesellschaft) for public corporations and *GmbH* (Gesellschaft) for private corporations.

As previously mentioned, a company can incorporate federally under the *Canada Business Corporations Act,* or provincially. Each province has a *Corporations Act* governing the formation of a corporation. Three different methods of incorporation currently exist in Canada, although these differences are slowly being eliminated: (1) the federal government and the majority of provinces file **articles of incorporation,** (2) in other provinces you must **register** your company (British Columbia and Nova Scotia), or (3) obtain a **letters patent** (Quebec and Prince Edward Island). We will assume, for the purposes of this chapter, that the articles of incorporation method is used.

The initial step in the formation of a corporation is to file an application as required by the respective province's *Corporations Act.* The application contains the following types of information: (1) the name, purpose, and duration of the proposed corporation, (2) the amounts, kinds, and number of shares of capital stock to be authorized, (3) the address of the corporation's principal office, (4) the names and addresses of the incorporators, and (5) the shares of stock to which each has subscribed. Anyone can apply to incorporate a company, as long as he or she is over the age of 18, of sound mind, and not bankrupt.

After an incorporation fee has been paid and the application has been approved, a **charter** is granted. The issuance of the charter, specifically referred to as the **articles of incorporation,** creates the corporation.

The costs of forming a corporation are called organization costs. These costs include fees to underwriters for handling stock and bond issues, legal fees, incorporation fees, and promotional expenditures. Organization costs are capitalized by debiting an intangible asset entitled Organization Costs. It may be argued that organization costs have an asset life equal to the life of the corporation, which is indefinite. Many companies, however, **amortize these costs** over an arbitrary period of time, up to a maximum of 40 years. Some companies prefer to use what income tax regulations permit: the amortization of three-quarters of the cost of organization at a 7% rate on a declining balance basis. Other companies expense organization costs in the year of occurrence. Organization costs are generally immaterial in total, and amortization practice varies in accordance with the **materiality constraint** discussed in Chapter 12.

Ownership Rights of Shareholders

When chartered, the corporation may begin selling ownership rights in the form of shares of stock. The shares of the company are divided into different classes such as Class A, Class B, and so on. The rights and privileges assigned to each class of shares are stated in the articles of incorporation. These are usually differentiated by use of the generic terms **common stock** and **preferred stock**. When a corporation has only one class of stock, it has the rights and privileges of **common stock**. Each share of common stock gives the shareholder the ownership rights pictured in Illustration 14-2.

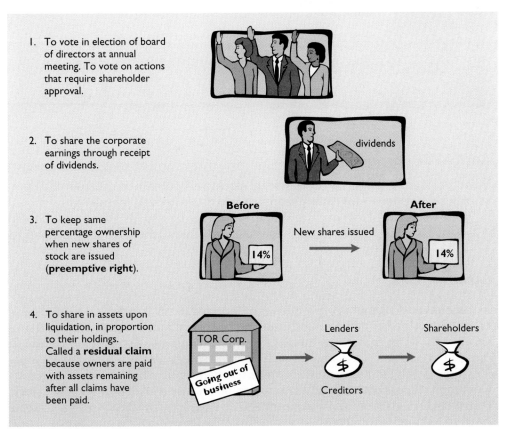

1. To vote in election of board of directors at annual meeting. To vote on actions that require shareholder approval.

2. To share the corporate earnings through receipt of dividends.

3. To keep same percentage ownership when new shares of stock are issued (**preemptive right**).

4. To share in assets upon liquidation, in proportion to their holdings. Called a **residual claim** because owners are paid with assets remaining after all claims have been paid.

Illustration 14-2

Ownership rights of shareholders

Case in point   A number of companies have eliminated the preemptive right, because they believe it makes an unnecessary and cumbersome demand on management.

Stock ownership is proven by a printed or engraved form known as a **stock certificate**. The face of the certificate shows the name of the corporation, the shareholder's name, the class and special features of the stock, the number of shares owned, and the signatures of duly authorized corporate officials. Certificates should be prenumbered to facilitate their accountability; they may be issued for any quantity of shares. Most stock certificates are preprinted with the relevant information. Some, especially in smaller corporations, provide space for the certificate details to be inserted as shown in Illustration 14–3.

Illustration 14-3

A stock certificate

Stock Issue Considerations

When considering the issuance (or sale) of stock, a corporation must answer a number of basic questions. How many shares should be authorized for sale? How should the stock be issued? At what price should the shares be issued? What value should be assigned to the stock? These questions are answered in the following sections.

Authorized Stock

The amount of stock that a corporation is **authorized** to sell is indicated in its charter. It may be specified as an unlimited amount or a certain number (e.g., 500,000 shares authorized). More than three-quarters of public companies with share capital in Canada have an unlimited amount of authorized shares. When a company incorporates, the total amount of authorized stock normally anticipates its initial and subsequent capital needs of a company. If a corporation has sold all of its authorized stock, it must obtain legislative approval to amend its charter before it can issue additional shares. The number of shares sold is commonly known as the number of shares issued. If these shares are held outside the company (see treasury stock on page 591), they are considered to be outstanding.

Helpful hint A memo entry is sometimes made in the general journal for the authorized shares.

The authorization of capital stock does not result in a formal accounting entry, since the event has no immediate effect on either corporate assets or shareholders' equity. However, disclosure of the number of shares of authorized stock is required in the shareholders' equity section. To determine the number of unissued shares that can be issued without amending the charter, the total shares issued are subtracted from the total authorized. For example, if Advanced Micro Corp. was authorized to sell 100,000 shares of common stock but issued only 80,000 shares, 20,000 shares would remain unissued. If Advanced Micro had an unlimited amount of common stock authorized, an unlimited number of shares would remain unissued.

Issuance of Stock

A corporation can choose to issue common stock either directly to investors or indirectly through an investment dealer (brokerage house) that specializes in bringing securities to the attention of prospective investors. ScotiaMcleod and RBC Dominion Securities are examples of two such investment firms. Direct issue is typical in closely held companies; indirect issue is customary for a publicly held corporation.

In an indirect issue the investment dealer, or group of dealers, may agree to **underwrite** the entire stock issue. In this case, the underwriter buys the stock from the corporation at a specified price, then resells the shares to investors. The corporation avoids any risk of being unable to sell the shares, and it obtains cash from the underwriter for immediate use. The investment dealer assumes the risk of reselling the shares but profits from an underwriting fee—the profits expected from a sales price to the public higher than the price paid to the corporation.[1] For example, Kolff Medical, maker of the Jarvik artificial heart, used an underwriter to help it issue common stock to the public. The underwriter charged a 6.6% underwriting fee on Kolff Medical's $20-million public offering.

How does a corporation set the price for a new issue of stock? Among the factors to be considered are: (1) the company's anticipated future earnings, (2) its expected dividend rate per share, (3) its current financial position, (4) the current state of the economy, and (5) the current state of the securities market. The subject can be complex and is usually taught in a finance course.

Market Value of Stock

The shares of publicly held companies are traded on organized exchanges at dollar prices per share established by the interaction between buyers and sellers. In general, the prices follow the trend of a company's earnings and dividends. However, factors beyond a company's control (such as the imposition of an embargo on oil, a quota on fish stocks, changes in interest rates, and the outcome of an election) may cause day-to-day fluctuations in market prices.

The volume of trading on national and international exchanges is heavy. More than 130 million shares are often traded daily on the Toronto Stock Exchange alone. For each listed security, financial press outlets such as *The Financial Post* report the highs and lows of the stock during the year, the total volume of stock traded on a particular day, the high and low prices for the day, and the closing market price, with the net change for the day. The same information is repeated for the entire week and it is preceded by earnings data for the company. A listing published on May 9, 1998, for The Second Cup Ltd. is shown below:

▶ *International note*

The United States has the largest market capitalization, $5.2 trillion, followed by Japan, $3.2 trillion, Britain, $1.4 trillion, Germany, $545 billion, France, $538 billion, Canada, $376 billion, and Hong Kong, $239 billion.

						——— Friday ———				——— Earnings data ———			——— Week ———			
52W high	52W low	Stock	Ticker	P/E	Vol. 00s	High /ask	Low /bid	Cls/ last	Net chg	fiscal	Interim EPS	12mth EPS	Vol 00s	High /ask	Low /bid	Cls/ last	Net chg
18.95	9.00	Second Cup	SKL	30.6	9	18.00	17.50	17.75	+0.25	Mar36W	0.61	0.58	138	18.00	17.00	17.75	+0.50

Illustration 14-4

Stock market price information

These numbers indicate that the high and low market prices for the last 52 weeks have been, respectively, $18.95 and $9.00. Ticker is the basic trading symbol used by the exchange. The price-earnings (P/E) ratio for The Second Cup Ltd. was 30.6, which

---

[1] Alternatively, the investment dealer or dealers may agree to enter into a **best efforts** contract with the corporation. In such cases, the dealer(s) agree(s) to sell as many shares as possible at a specified price, and the corporation bears the risk of unsold stock. Under a best efforts arrangement, the investment firm(s) receives a fee or commission for services rendered.

indicates that the market price ($17.75) is 30.6 times the Second Cup's earnings per share ($0.58). This ratio will be discussed further in Chapter 19. The trading volume for May 9 was 900 shares; the high, low, and closing prices for that date were $18.00, $17.50 and $17.75, respectively. The net change for the day was an increase of $0.25 per share over the previous day. Earnings information is given for the 36 weeks to March 1998. Interim earnings per share are $0.61, and annual earnings per share are $0.58. The remaining information summarizes the volume of shares traded; the high, low, and closing prices; and the change in price for the week.

When capital stock is traded on securities exchanges, already issued shares are sold by an existing shareholder to another investor. Consequently, these transactions have no impact on either a corporation's shareholders' equity section or its balance sheet.

▲Technology in Action

Giant, publicly held corporations could not exist without organized stock markets, and stock markets could not exist without massive computerization. Not too many years ago, tickers would run behind, or trading would completely halt, when trading volume was extremely high. Now, exchanges throughout the country operate efficiently with the computer technology that has largely replaced the colourful and clamorous floor traders.

Par and No Par Value Stocks

Case in point   Par is often associated with quality or excellence (as, for example, shooting par in golf). In the early 1920s there were many stock swindles because uninformed buyers couldn't resist buying $100 par value stock at $10 per share.

Par value stock is capital stock that has a specfic value per share which is stated in the corporate charter. The par value may be any amount selected by the corporation. Generally, the amount of par value is quite low, because filing fees vary with the amount of legal capital. For example, Ford Motor Company's common stock has a par value of $1.00.

Par value does not indicate of either the worth or the market value of the stock. Ford has a par value of $1.00, but its market price has recently reached nearly $100 per share. **The significance of par value is a legal matter**. Par value represents the **legal capital** per share that must be kept in the business for the protection of corporate creditors. That is, it is not available for withdrawal by shareholders. Thus, corporations are required to sell shares at par or above.

Par value stock has two significant drawbacks. As market prices increase further away from par values (as with Ford), creditors may be left with an inadequate cushion of protection if the company only retains assets equal to its minimum legal. On the other hand, if market prices fall below par value, corporations cannot use equity markets to raise capital, because they are not allowed to sell their stock under par. Because of these difficulties, many jurisdictions, such as the Province of Ontario and the federal government, have abolished par value shares in favour of no par value stock.

No par value stock is capital stock that has not been assigned a value in the corporate charter. If shares have no par value, the questionable practice of using par value as a basis for fair market value never arises. No par value stock is the most common form of stock today. It has been estimated that more than 90% of Canadian public companies now issue no par value stock.

In many provinces, the board of directors is permitted to assign a stated value to the no par shares, which becomes the legal capital per share. The stated value of no par stock may be changed at any time by the directors. Stated value, like par value, does not indicate the market value of the stock. When there is no assigned stated value, the entire proceeds received upon issuance of the stock are considered legal capital. Only a few companies in Canada use stated values, as for example, Sears Canada Inc.

The relationship of par and no par value to legal capital is shown below:

Stock	Legal Capital per Share
Par value	→ Par value
No par value with stated value	→ Stated value
No par value without stated value	→ Entire proceeds

Illustration 14-5

Relationship of par and no par value stock to legal capital

As will be explained later, each time stock is issued, a common stock account is credited for the legal capital per share.

Corporate Capital

Equity in a corporation is identified as **shareholders' equity**. The shareholders' equity section of a corporation's balance sheet consists of: (1) contributed capital, and (2) retained earnings (earned capital). The distinction between contributed capital and retained earnings is important from both a legal and an economic point of view. Legally, dividends can be declared out of retained earnings, but in most jurisdictions dividends cannot be declared out of contributed capital. Management, shareholders, and others examine earnings to evaluate the continued existence and growth of the corporation.

STUDY OBJECTIVE
••••••••••• **2** •••••••••••
Differentiate between contributed capital and retained earnings.

Contributed Capital

Contributed capital is the term used to describe the total amount of cash and other assets paid to the corporation by shareholders in exchange for capital stock. In a complex capital structure, other transactions may also affect contributed capital. Discussion of complex capital structures is left to an intermediate accounting course.

> capital from shareholders only.

Retained Earnings

Retained earnings is the cumulative net income (loss) that has been retained (i.e., not distributed to shareholders) in a corporation. Retained earnings are distributed to shareholders by way of dividends, which are discussed in detail later in this Chapter and in Chapter 15.

Net income is recorded in Retained Earnings by a closing entry in which Income Summary is debited and Retained Earnings is credited. For example, assume that net income for Delta Robotics Ltd. in its first year of operations is $130,000. The closing entry is:

Helpful hint Chapter 4 has a full explanation of closing entries for a proprietorship, Chapter 13 for a partnership.

> net income or (loss).

Income Summary	130,000	
Retained Earnings		130,000
(To close income summary and transfer net		
income to retained earnings)		

Helpful hint A net loss is closed by debiting Retained Earnings and crediting Income Summary.

Assume Delta Robotics has 100,000 authorized and 50,000 issued no par value common shares. These shares were issued for a total of $800,000 and no dividends were declared. The company's shareholders' equity section is as follows:

Illustration 14-6

Shareholders' equity section

Shareholders' equity		
Contributed capital		
Common stock, 100,000 no par value shares		
authorized, 50,000 issued and outstanding	$800,000	
Retained earnings	130,000	
Total shareholders' equity	$930,000	

The following illustration compares the equity accounts for a proprietorship, a partnership, and a corporation:

Illustration 14-7

Comparison of equity accounts

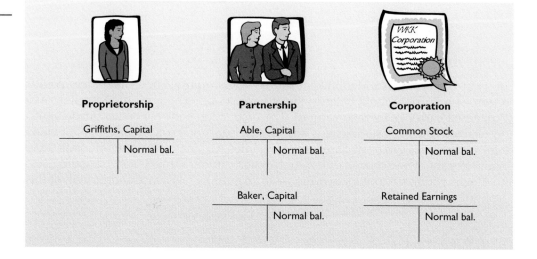

Before You Go On . . .

▸Review It

1. What are the advantages and disadvantages of a corporation compared to a proprietorship or partnership?
2. What rights are inherent in owning a share of common stock in a corporation?
3. Distinguish between authorized, issued, and outstanding stock.
4. Distinguish between par value, stated value, no par value, and fair market value.

▸Do It

At the end of its first year of operation, Dai-ichi Corporation has $750,000 from an issue of 25,000 no par value shares of common stock (unlimited number of shares authorized) and net income of $122,000. Prepare: (a) the closing entry for net income, and (b) the shareholders' equity section of the balance sheet at year end.

Reasoning: Net income is recorded in Retained Earnings by a closing entry in which Income Summary is debited and Retained Earnings is credited. The shareholders' equity section consists of: (1) contributed capital, and (2) retained earnings.

Solution:

(a)	Income Summary	122,000	
	Retained Earnings		122,000
	(To close income summary and		
	transfer net income to retained earnings)		

(b) Shareholders' equity
      Contributed capital
         Common stock
            Authorized: Unlimited
            Issued and Outstanding: 25,000 no par

value shares	$750,000	*$30/share*
Retained earnings	122,000	
Total shareholders' equity	$872,000	

Related exercise material: BE14–1 and BE14–2.

Accounting for Common Stock Issues

Let's now look at how to account for issues of common stock. The primary objectives in accounting for the issuance of common stock are to: (1) identify the specific sources of contributed capital, and (2) maintain the distinction between contributed capital and retained earnings. As shown below, **the issue of common stock affects only contributed capital accounts.**

STUDY OBJECTIVE
······· **3** ···········

Record the issuance of common stock.

Issuing Par Value Stock for Cash

As discussed earlier, par value does not indicate a stock's market value. Therefore, the cash proceeds from issuing par value stock may be equal to, or greater than, par value. The proceeds cannot be less than par value, since stock is prohibited from being issued at less than par value. When the issuance of common stock for cash is recorded, the par value of the shares is credited to Common Stock, and the portion that is above par value is recorded in a separate contributed capital account.

This contributed capital account is called by many names. We call it Contributed Capital in Excess of Par Value. It is also sometimes recorded as Premium, Contributed Surplus, Paid-In Capital, Additional Paid-In Capital, or Capital Surplus.

Helpful hint Contributed Capital in Excess of Par Value is not reported in the income statement, because it is not a gain.

To illustrate the issue of common stock, assume that Hydro-Slide, Inc., is authorized to issue 10,000 shares of $1 par value common stock. They issue 1,000 of these shares at par for cash. The entry to record this transaction is:

Cash	1,000	
Common Stock		1,000
(To record issuance of 1,000 shares of common stock at par)		

Note that the remaining authorized shares are not recorded until sold.

If Hydro-Slide, Inc., issues an additional 1,000 shares of the $1 par value common stock for cash of $5 per share, the entry is:

Cash	5,000	
Common Stock (1,000 × $1 par)		1,000
Contributed Capital in Excess of Par Value		
[1,000 × ($5 − $1)]		4,000
(To record issuance of 1,000 shares of common stock)		

The total contributed capital from these two transactions is $6,000 ($1,000 + $5,000), and the legal capital is $2,000 ($1,000 + $1,000). If Hydro-Slide, Inc., has retained earnings of $27,000, the shareholders' equity section is as follows:

Illustration 14-8

*Shareholders' equity—
contributed capital in excess
of par value*

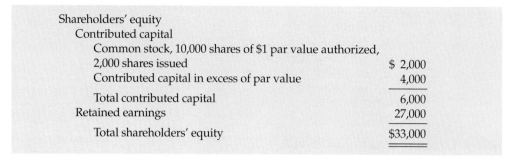

Shareholders' equity		
Contributed capital		
Common stock, 10,000 shares of $1 par value authorized,		
2,000 shares issued		$ 2,000
Contributed capital in excess of par value		4,000
Total contributed capital		6,000
Retained earnings		27,000
Total shareholders' equity		$33,000

Issuing No Par Value Stock for Cash

When no par common stock has a stated value, the entries are similar to those illustrated for par value stock. The stated value represents legal capital, and therefore is credited to Common Stock. In addition, when the selling price of no par stock exceeds stated value, the excess is credited to Contributed Capital in Excess of Stated Value. Contributed Capital in Excess of Stated Value is reported as part of contributed capital in the shareholders' equity section.

When no par stock does not have a stated value, the entire proceeds from the issue become legal capital and are credited to Common Stock. Thus, if Hydro-Slide does not assign a stated value to its no par stock, the issuance of the 1,000 shares at $5 per share for cash is recorded as follows:

Cash	5,000	
Common Stock		5,000
(To record issue of 1,000 shares of no par stock)		

In this instance, the amount of legal capital for Hydro-Slide is $5,000.

Issuing Stock for Services or Non-cash Assets

Stock may be issued for services (compensation to lawyers, consultants, and others) or for non-cash assets (land, buildings, and equipment). In such cases, a question arises about the cost that should be recognized in the exchange transaction. To comply with the **cost principle** in a non-cash transaction, **cost is the cash equivalent price**. Thus, cost is the **fair market value of the consideration given up**. If this amount is not determinable, we look to the **fair market value of the consideration received** to determine cost.

To illustrate, assume that the lawyers for the Panjer Corporation agree to accept 4,000 shares of no par value common stock in payment of their bill of $5,000 for services performed in helping the company to incorporate. At the time of the exchange, there is no established market price for the stock. In this case, the market value of the consideration received, $5,000, is the best (only) measure of the asset. Accordingly, the entry is:

Organization Costs	5,000	
Common Stock		5,000
(To record issuance of 4,000 shares of no par value stock		
to lawyers)		

As explained earlier in the chapter, organization costs are classified as an intangible asset in the balance sheet.

In contrast, assume that Schafer Research Inc. is a publicly held corporation whose no par value stock is actively traded at $8 per share. The company issues 10,000 shares of stock to acquire land recently advertised for sale at $90,000. On the basis of these facts, the best value is the market price of the consideration given, $80,000 (10,000 x $8). Thus, the transaction is recorded as follows:

Land	80,000	
Common Stock		80,000
(To record issuance of 10,000 shares of no par value stock for land)		

If, instead of a no par value, this stock had a par value of $5 per share, the land would not be recorded at the par value of the stock issued, $50,000. It would still be recorded at its fair market value of $80,000, and $30,000 would be recorded as contributed capital. **The par value of the stock is never a factor in determining the cost of the assets received, because it does not represent economic value**. This is also true of the stated value of no par stock.

Reacquisition of Shares

Companies can purchase their own shares on the open market. Why would they do this? A company may wish to reacquire its own shares for a number of reasons: to reduce dividend payments, to increase share value, to minimize the possibility of a hostile takeover, or for compliance reasons. Rogers Communications Inc. once repurchased more than 14 million of its own shares from foreign investors in order to maintain sufficient Canadian ownership to qualify for Canadian broadcasting licences.

When a federally incorporated company reacquires its own shares, the repurchased shares must be retired and cancelled. This effectively restores the shares to the status of authorized but unissued shares. Some provincially incorporated companies are also allowed to hold reacquired shares for future use. Shares for this purpose are called **treasury stock**. Treasury stock transactions are extremely rare in Canada, and are permitted only in restricted circumstances.

Accounting for the repurchase of shares is complex and best left for an intermediate accounting course.

▶**Accounting in Action** ▶ *Business Insight*

 Until 1971, Canadian companies were not permitted to repurchase their own shares. Why? Regulators feared officers and directors would use inside information to manipulate the price of stock. Repurchases are now allowed under strict guidelines and disclosure rules.

Before You Go On . . .
▶*Review It*

1. Explain the accounting for par, stated, and no par value common stock that is issued for cash.
2. Explain the accounting for the issuance of common stock for services or non-cash assets.

▶*Do It*

Victoria Corporation begins operations on March 1 by issuing 100,000 shares of no par value common stock for cash at $12 per share. On March 15, it issues 5,000 shares of common stock to its lawyers in settlement of their bill of $65,000 for organization costs. The stock continues to trade at $12 per share on March 15. Journalize the issuance of the shares.

Reasoning: When no par value shares are issued for cash, common stock is credited for the proceeds per share. When stock is issued for services, the cash equivalent price should be used, ideally of what was given up. In this case, the price is the market value of the shares. The shares are worth $60,000 (5,000 x $12) on the settlement date. Therefore, even though their bill is for $65,000, the lawyers are, in reality, accepting shares worth $60,000 in full payment of the account.

Solution:

Mar. 1	Cash	1,200,000	
	Common Stock		1,200,000
	(To record issuance of 100,000 shares at $12 per share)		
Mar. 15	Organization Costs	60,000	
	Common Stock		60,000
	To record issuance of 5,000 shares for lawyers' fees)		

Related exercise material: BE14–3, BE14–4, BE14–5, E14–1, and E14–3.

▼Preferred Stock

STUDY OBJECTIVE
•••••••••• 4 ••••••••••
Differentiate preferred stock from common stock.

To appeal to a larger segment of potential investors, a corporation may issue preferred stock in addition to common stock. **Preferred stock** has contractual provisions that give it a preference, or priority, over common stock in certain areas. Typically, preferred shareholders have priority over: (1) dividends, and (2) assets in the event of liquidation. However, they generally do not have voting rights.

▶Accounting in Action ▸ *Business Insight*

Companies are gradually eliminating having two classes of shares. Agra Inc., Laidlaw Inc., and SNC-Lavalin Group Inc. are recent examples of companies that have combined voting and non-voting stock into one class of shares with equal voting rights. James Bullock, CEO of Laidlaw, summed it up, "It was clearly inappropriate to have a situation where 15% of the shareholders had all of the votes." There is, however, at least one downside to this move for non-voting shareholders: They may gain the right to vote, but their equity decreases as voting shareholders demand an increasingly generous premium to give up their advantage.

Source: Financial Post, July 5, 1997, 12.

Like common stock, preferred stock may be issued for cash or for non-cash assets. It can also be reacquired. The entries for all these transactions are similar to the entries for common stock. Assume that Staudinger Corporation issues 10,000 shares of no par value preferred stock for $12 cash per share. The entry to record the issuance is:

	Cash	120,000	
	Preferred Stock		120,000
	(To record the issuance of 10,000 shares of no par value preferred stock)		

Preferred stock may be of either no par value or par value. As with common stock, no par value is most commonly issued. If preferred stock does have a par value, any excess proceeds received over par value should be recorded in a separate contributed capital account. When a corporation has more than one class of stock, each contributed capital account title should specifically identify the stock to which it relates (e.g., Contributed Capital in Excess of Par Value—Preferred Stock [or Class B], and Contributed Capital in Excess of Par Value—Common Stock [or Class A]). In the shareholders' equity section, preferred stock is presented first because of its dividend and liquidation preferences over common stock.

Dividend Preferences

As indicated before, corporate income is distributed to **preferred shareholders before it goes to common shareholders**. For example, if the dividend rate on preferred stock is $5 per share, common shareholders will not receive any dividends in the current year until preferred shareholders have received $5 per share. The first claim to dividends does not, however, guarantee dividends. Dividends depend on many factors, such as adequate retained earnings and availability of cash.

The per share dividend amount is always given as an **annual** amount, similar to interest rates. It will be stated either as a specified amount or as a percentage of the par value of the preferred stock. For example, Sun Ice Limited specifies a 9% dividend on its first preferred shares, whereas Trans Canada Pipelines Limited has a $2.80 dividend on one of its classes of no par value preferred stock. If the dividend is expressed as a percentage of par value, the annual per share dividend is computed by multiplying the dividend rate by the par value amount of the stock.

Cumulative Dividend

Preferred stock contracts often contain a cumulative dividend feature. This right means that preferred shareholders must be paid both current year dividends and any unpaid prior year dividends before common shareholders receive dividends. When preferred stock is cumulative, preferred dividends that are not declared in a given period are called **dividends in arrears**. To illustrate, assume that Staudinger's 10,000 no par value preferred shares have a $3.50 cumulative dividend. The annual dividend is $35,000 (10,000 x $3.50 per share). If dividends are two years in arrears, preferred shareholders will receive the following dividends (if sufficient cash) whenever dividends are next declared. The common shareholders will receive whatever is left over from the total declared amount.

Helpful hint *Funk & Wagnalls Canadian College Dictionary* defines cumulative as "gained or acquired by accumulation."

% or stated amount

Dividends in arrears ($35,000 x 2)	$ 70,000
Current year dividends	35,000
Total preferred dividends	$105,000

Illustration 14-9

Computation of total dividends to preferred stock

Dividends in arrears are not considered a liability. No obligation exists until a dividend is declared by the board of directors. However, the amount of dividends in arrears should be disclosed in the notes to the financial statements. Doing so enables investors to assess the potential impact of this future declaration on the corporation's financial position.

Dividends cannot be paid on common stock while any dividend on preferred stock is in arrears. The cumulative feature is what attracts investor to a preferred stock issue. When preferred stock is noncumulative, a dividend unpaid in any year is lost forever. Companies that are unable to meet their dividend obligations are not looked upon favourably by the investment community. When discussing one company's failure to pay its cumulative preferred dividend, a financial officer noted, "Not meeting your obligations on something like that is a major black mark on your record." The accounting entries for preferred stock dividends are explained in Chapter 15.

Participating Dividend

Preferred stock may also have a participating dividend feature. This right enables the preferred shareholder to share ratably (proportionately) with common shareholders in any dividends beyond the rate specified on the preferred stock. The participating feature only applies after common shareholders receive a rate of return on their shares equal to the specified dividend rate on preferred stock. The issuance of participating preferred stock is rare.

Liquidation Preference

Most preferred stocks have a preference on corporate assets if the corporation fails. This means that assets will be used to pay the preferred shareholder if the corporation goes bankrupt. This feature provides security for the preferred shareholder. The preference to assets may be for the legal capital of the shares or for a specified liquidating value. The liquidation preference is used in bankruptcy lawsuits that involve the claims of creditors and preferred shareholders.

Convertible Preferred

As an investment preferred stock is even more attractive when there is a conversion privilege. Convertible preferred stock permits the shareholder to convert preferred stock into common stock at a specified ratio.

Convertible preferred stock is purchased by investors who want the greater security of a preferred stock but who also desire the added option of conversion if the market value of the common stock increases significantly. To illustrate, assume that Ross Industries Inc. issues 1,000 shares of no par value convertible preferred stock at $100 per share. One share of preferred is convertible into 10 shares of no par value common (current market price $9 per share). At this point, it would not be advantageous for the holders of the preferred to convert, because they would exchange preferred stock worth $100,000 (1,000 x $100) for common stock worth $90,000 (10,000 x $9). However, if the price of the common stock were to increase above $10 per share, it likely would be advantageous for the preferred holders to convert.

To record the conversion, the amount paid for the preferred stock to appropriate common stock is usually transferred to appropiate common stock accounts. To illustrate, assume that the 1,000 shares of Ross Industries preferred are converted into 10,000 shares of common stock when the market values per share of the two classes of stock are $101 and $12, respectively. The entry to record the conversion is:

Preferred Stock	100,000	
Common Stock		100,000
(To record conversion of 1,000 shares of no par value		
preferred stock into 10,000 shares of no par value		
common stock)		

Helpful hint   Only shareholders' equity accounts are involved when conversion occurs. This transaction may be viewed as a realignment of a company's outstanding stock.

The book value of the preferred stock is used to record the conversion. **The conversion of preferred stock does not result in either gain or loss to the corporation. Note that the market values of the shares at the time of the transaction are not**

considered in recording the transaction. The reason is that the corporation has not received any assets equal to fair market value.

Redeemable Preferred

Many preferred stocks are issued with a redemption or call feature. Redeemable (or callable) preferred stock grants the issuing corporation the right to purchase the stock from shareholders at specified future dates and prices. The redemption feature offers some flexibility to a corporation by enabling it to eliminate this type of equity security when it is advantageous to do so. The **redemption or call price** is frequently slightly above the par or stated value of the shares, when such values exist. When preferred stock is redeemable, the call price tends to limit the market price of the shares.

Retractable Preferred

Retractable preferred stock is similar to redeemable or callable preferred stock except that the shareholder can redeem stock at their option instead of the corporation's. This usually occurs at an arranged price and date.

When preferred stock is retractable, the distinction between equity and debt begins to blur. Retractable preferred stock and debt have many similarities. They both offer a rate of return to the investor, and with the redemption of the stock they both offer a repayment of the principal investment. Because of these, and other innovative **financial instruments**, the CICA obliges companies to present these issues in accordance with their economic substance rather than their form. That is, retractable preferred stock would be presented in the *liability* section of the balance sheet rather than in the equity section, because it has more of the features of debt than of equity. Accounting for such financial instruments presents unique challenges to accountants. Further discussion of this topic is left to an intermediate accounting course.

Case in point The two features differ in terms of benefit. Retractable is at the option of the shareholder, whereas redeemable (callable) is at the option of the corporation.

Before You Go On . . .

► *Review It*

1. Compare the normal rights and privileges of common and preferred shareholders.
2. Distinguish between cumulative and noncumulative dividends.
3. Distinguish between convertible, redeemable, and retractable preferred stock.

Related exercise material: BE14–6, E14–2, E14–4, and E14–5.

Statement Presentation of Shareholders' Equity

In the shareholders' equity section of the balance sheet, contributed capital and retained earnings are reported, and the specific sources of contributed capital are identified.

Within contributed capital, two classifications are recognized:

1. **Capital stock**, which consists of preferred and common stock. Preferred stock is shown before common stock because of the additional rights it confers. Information about the legal value (e.g., par, no par, stated), shares authorized, shares issued, and shares outstanding is reported for each class of stock.

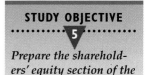

STUDY OBJECTIVE
·········· **5** ··········

Prepare the shareholders' equity section of the balance sheet.

2. **Additional contributed capital**, which includes the amounts paid over par or stated value, will result if par or stated values are specified. If the stock is no par value, there will be no additional contributed capital.

Illustrations

The shareholders' equity section of Zaboschuk Inc., shown in Illustration 14-10, includes most of the accounts discussed in this chapter. The disclosures for Zaboschuk's preferred stock indicate that the dividend rate is $9 per annum, 10,000 preferred shares of no par value have been authorized, and 6,000 shares are issued and outstanding. Although we do not know the original issue price of each share of preferred stock, we can compute the *average* issuance price of $128.33 per share ($770,000 ÷ 6,000). It is redeemable at a price of $120 per share.

The common stock has a $5 stated value with an unlimited amount of stock authorized to be issued; 400,000 shares have been issued to date and are outstanding.

Illustration 14-10

Shareholders' equity section

ZABOSCHUK INC. Partial Balance Sheet	
Shareholders' equity	
Contributed capital	
Capital stock	
$9 preferred stock, no par value, redeemable	
at $120, cumulative, 10,000 shares authorized,	
6,000 shares issued and outstanding	$ 770,000
Common stock, $5 stated value, unlimited	
shares authorized, 400,000 shares issued and	
outstanding	2,000,000
Total capital stock	2,770,000
Additional contributed capital	
Contributed capital in excess of stated	
value—common stock	860,000
Total contributed capital	3,630,000
Retained earnings	1,058,000
Total shareholders' equity	$4,688,000

In published annual reports, subclassifications within the shareholders' equity section are seldom presented. Moreover, the individual sources of additional contributed capital are often combined and reported as a single amount, and supplementary detail is given in the footnotes, as shown in Illustration 14-11:

Illustration 14-11

Published shareholders' equity section

Canadian National Railway Company (millions of dollars)	
Shareholders' equity (Note 9)	
Capital stock (Note 9)	$2,016
Contributed surplus	190
Retained earnings	1,211
	$3,417

In practice, the term contributed surplus is sometimes used instead of additional contributed capital, and earned surplus instead of retained earnings. The term surplus suggests that an excess amount of funds is available. Howver, this is not necessarily the case, and so **the term surplus should be avoided in accounting**.

►Technology in Action

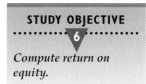

The Canadian Securities Administrators, representing provincial securities commissions, has proposed guidelines that will offer public companies the option of communicating with their shareholders on-line. The proposal recommends that companies be permitted to use cyberspace to publish their annual and interim reports and other documents traditionally mailed to shareholders. Companies would save substantial amounts in mailing costs, and investors would receive information on a more timely basis.

Source: Globe and Mail, June 14, 1997, B3.

Using the Information in the Financial Statements

There are many valuable ratios of information that can be determined from the shareholders' equity section of the balance sheet. Two of the most important are the return on equity ratio and the book value per share. Others include earnings per share and the price-earnings ratio, which we will discuss in Chapter 15.

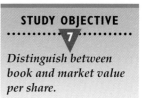

STUDY OBJECTIVE
••••••••••**6**••••••••••
Compute return on equity.

Return on Equity

Return on equity, also known as return on investment, is considered by many to be *the* most important measure of a firm's profitability and efficiency. It assesses revenues and expenses in comparison to the shareholders' investment. This ratio is used by management and investors to evaluate how many dollars were earned for each dollar invested by the owners. In essence, return on equity calculates the rate of return that the shareholders are earning on their investment. It can be used to compare investment in a specific company to alternative investment opportunities in the marketplace.

Return on equity is a widely published figure. In a recent year, banks reported an average return on equity of 20%, clothing stores 14%, and forestry companies 12%. The following illustration computes the return on equity ratio for Second Cup:

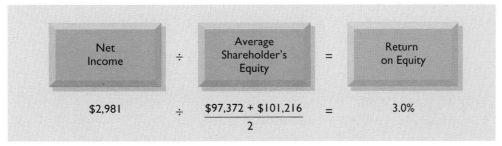

Illustration 14-12

Computation of return on equity

Book Value Per Share

You have already learned about several per share amounts in this chapter. Another important per share amount is book value per share. This per share amount represents **the equity a common shareholder has in the net assets of the corporation** from owning one share of stock. Since the net assets (assets less liabilities) of a corporation must be equal to total shareholders' equity, the formula for computing book value per share when a company has only one class of stock outstanding is:

STUDY OBJECTIVE
••••••••••**7**••••••••••
Distinguish between book and market value per share.

Illustration 14-13

Book value per share formula with no preferred stock

Thus, if the Fast Corporation has total shareholders' equity of $1,500,000 (Common Stock $1,000,000 and Retained Earnings $500,000) and 50,000 shares of common stock outstanding, book value per share is $30 ($1,500,000 ÷ 50,000).

When a company has both preferred and common stock, the computation of book value is more complex. Since preferred shareholders have a prior claim on net assets over common shareholders, their equity must be deducted from total shareholders' equity to determine the shareholders' equity that applies to the common stock. The computation of book value per share involves the following steps:

1. Compute the preferred shareholders equity. This equity is equal to the sum of the redemption price of preferred stock plus any cumulative dividends in arrears. If the preferred stock does not have a redemption price, the legal capital of the stock is used.

2. Determine the common shareholders' equity by subtracting the preferred shareholders' equity from total shareholders' equity. Since preferred shareholders ordinarily do not have a right to capital contributed in excess of redemption or par value, any amount over these values is assigned to the common shareholders' equity, in computing book value.

3. Divide common shareholders' equity by the number of shares of common stock outstanding to determine book value per share.

Illustration.   We will use the shareholders' equity section of Zaboschuk Inc., as presented in Illustration 14–10. Zaboschuk 's preferred stock is redeemable at $120 per share and cumulative. Assume that dividends on Zaboschuk 's preferred stock were in arrears for one year, $54,000 (6,000 × $9). The computation of preferred stock equity is:

Illustration 14-14

Computation of preferred shareholders' equity (Step 1)

Redemption price (6,000 shares x $120)	$720,000
Dividends in arrears (6,000 shares x $9)	54,000
Preferred shareholders' equity	$774,000

The computation of book value is as follows:

Illustration 14-15

Computation of book value per share with preferred stock (Steps 2 and 3)

Total shareholders' equity	$4,688,000
Less: Preferred shareholders' equity	774,000
Common shareholders' equity	$3,914,000
Shares of common stock issued and outstanding	400,000
Book value per share ($3,914,000 ÷ 400,000)	$ 9.78

Book Value versus Market Value. Book value per share seldom, if ever, equals market value. Book value is based on recorded historical costs; market value reflects the subjective judgement of thousands of shareholders and prospective investors about a company's potential for future earnings and dividends. Market value per share may exceed book value per share, but that correspondence does not necessarily mean that the stock is overpriced. Conversely, market value may also be less than book value. The correlation between book value and the company's market value per share is often remote, as indicated by the following recent data:

Case in point   Book value can obscure real value. Companies that have real estate, brand names, licences, or other properties worth more than cost are closely watched; therefore, the market value of the stock often reflects these hidden values.

Illustration 14-16

Book and market values compared

Company	Book Value	Market Value
George Weston Limited	$35.62	$55.50
Mark's Work Wearhouse Ltd.	1.31	5.00
Noranda Inc.	19.34	30.35
Second Cup Ltd.	7.08	18.00

Book value per share is useful for determining the trend of a shareholder's per share equity in a corporation. It is also significant in many contracts and in court cases, where the rights of individual parties are based on cost information.

Before You Go On . . .

► Review It

1. Identify the classifications within the contributed capital section and the totals that are stated in the shareholders' equity section of a balance sheet.
2. Explain how to compute return on equity.
3. What is the method for computing book value per share when there is: (a) only one class of stock, and (b) both preferred and common stock?

Related exercise material: BE14–7, BE14–8, E14–6, E14–7, and E14–8.

A Look Back at the Ford Motor Company

Refer back to the opening story about the Ford Motor Company and answer the following questions:

1. Why did Henry Ford originally choose to form a corporation rather than a sole proprietorship?
2. Why did the Ford Motor Company repurchase all of its shares?
3. What advantages and disadvantages of being organized as a corporation are illustrated by Ford?

Solution:

1. Henry Ford wanted to take full advantage of mass production. This would require large factories and many employees, which would in turn require considerable funds. The most efficient way to raise these funds was to issue stock.
2. The Ford Motor Company repurchased a massive amount of stock when Henry Ford's vision was found to be inconsistent with the wishes of the shareholders.

3. The history of the Ford Motor Company illustrates a number of the strengths and weaknesses of incorporation. Forming a corporation allowed for more efficient access to funds, and thus more rapid expansion. This was critical because, in the early 1900s, many companies were trying to manufacture cars for the North American market. However, by issuing shares Henry Ford gave up control of his firm. This led to a confrontation with shareholders in 1916, when the founder believed that it was in the company's best interest to retain funds in the firm rather than pay dividends. When outside shareholders have different objectives from those of a corporation's managers, the shareholders may force management to do things that hinder the firm's success.

Summary of Study Objectives

1. *Identify and discuss the major characteristics of a corporation.* The major characteristics of a corporation are: separate legal existence, limited liability of shareholders, transferable ownership rights, ability to acquire capital, continuous life, corporation management, government regulations, and entity income taxes.

2. *Differentiate between contributed capital and retained earnings.* Contributed capital is the total amount paid to acquire capital stock. Retained earnings is the cumulative net income retained (not distributed by way of dividends) in a corporation.

3. *Record the issuance of common stock.* When the issuance of par value common stock for cash is recorded, the par value of the shares is credited to the Common Stock account and the portion of the proceeds that is above par value is recorded in a separate contributed capital account. When no par common stock has a stated value, the entries are similar to those for par value stock. When no par does not have a stated value, the entire proceeds from the issue become legal capital and are credited to the Common Stock account.

4. *Differentiate preferred stock from common stock.* Preferred stock has contractual provisions that give it priority over common stock in certain areas. Typically, preferred shareholders have priority over: (1) dividends, and (2) assets in the event of liquidation. However, they usually do not have voting rights.

In addition, preferred stock may be convertible, redeemable, and/or retractable. A convertible preferred stock entitles the holder of the preferred stock to convert those shares to common stock in a specified ratio. The redemption feature grants the issuing corporation the right to purchase the stock from shareholders at specified future dates and prices. Retractable preferred stock gives the shareholder the option of selling their stock to the corporation, at specified future dates and prices.

5. *Prepare the shareholders' equity section of the balance sheet.* In the shareholders' equity section, contributed capital and retained earnings are reported and specific sources of contributed capital are identified. Within contributed capital, two classifications are shown: capital stock and additional contributed capital.

6. *Compute return on equity.* Return on equity is calculated by dividing net income by average shareholders' equity. It is an important measure of a firm's profitability and efficiency.

7. *Distinguish between book and market value per share.* Book value per share represents the equity a common shareholder has in the net assets of a corporation from owning one share of stock. Book value is based upon accounting values for assets and liabilities. Market value is an economic value, based upon what an investor is willing to pay for a share of stock. It is a subjective number, affected by the investor's financial position and perception of the future of the company.

GLOSSARY

Authorized stock The amount of stock that a corporation is authorized to sell, as indicated in its charter. This amount may be unlimited or specified. (p. 584).

Book value per share The equity a common shareholder has in the net assets of the corporation from owning one share of stock. (p. 597).

Contributed capital Total amount of cash and other assets paid in to the corporation by shareholders in exchange for capital stock. (p. 587).

Convertible preferred stock Preferred stock that the shareholder can convert into common stock at a specified ratio. (p. 594).

Corporation A business organized as a legal entity, separate and distinct from its owners, under corporation law. (p. 578).

Crown corporation A corporation owned by a government. (p. 579).

Cumulative dividend A feature of preferred stock that entitles the shareholder to receive current and unpaid prior year dividends before common shareholders receive any dividends. (p. 593).

Issued That portion of authorized stock that has been sold. (p. 584).

No par value stock Capital stock that has not been assigned a value in the corporate charter. All the proceeds from the sale of no par value stock are treated as legal capital. (p. 586).

Organization costs Costs incurred in the formation of a corporation. (p. 582).

Outstanding Capital stock that has been issued and is being held by shareholders. Issued stock is reduced by treasury stock (which is rare) held by the corporation to determine outstanding stock. (p. 584).

Participating dividend A feature of preferred stock that enables the shareholder to share ratably with common shareholders in any dividends beyond the rate specified on the preferred stock. (p. 594).

Par value stock Capital stock that has been assigned a value per share in the corporate charter, and is treated as the legal capital of the corporation. (p. 586).

Preferred stock Capital stock that has some contractual preferences over common stock. (p. 592).

Privately held corporation A corporation that has only a few shareholders and whose stock is not available for sale to the general public. (p. 578).

Publicly held corporation A corporation that may have thousands of shareholders and whose stock is usually traded on an organized securities market. (p. 578).

Redeemable (callable) preferred stock Preferred stock that grants the issuer the right to purchase the stock from shareholders at specified future dates and prices. (p. 595).

Retained earnings Net income after subtracting net losses and dividends distributed to shareholders since incorporation. If negative (i.e., a debit balance), it is called a deficit. (p. 587).

Retractable preferred stock Preferred stock that grants the shareholder the right to redeem the stock at specified future dates and prices. (p. 595).

Return on equity Net income expressed as a percentage of average shareholders' equity. (p. 597).

Stated value The amount per share assigned by the board of directors to no par stock that becomes legal capital per share. (p. 586).

DEMONSTRATION PROBLEM

The Rolman Corporation is authorized to issue 1,000,000 shares of no par value common stock and 100,000 shares of $50 par value 6% cumulative preferred stock. In its first year, the company has the following stock transactions:

Jan. 10 Sold 400,000 shares of common stock at $8 per share.

July 1 Issued 100,000 shares of common stock in exchange for land. The land had an asking price of $900,000. The stock is currently selling on the Montreal Stock Exchange at $8.25 per share.

Sept. 1 Issued 20,000 shares of preferred stock at par.

Dec. 1 Sold 4,000 shares of the preferred stock at $60 per share.

Instructions

(a) Journalize the transactions.
(b) Prepare the shareholders' equity section, assuming the company had retained earnings of $900,000 at December 31.

Solution to Demonstration Problem

(a) Jan. 10 Cash   3,200,000
       Common Stock   3,200,000
       (To record issuance of 400,000 shares of no par value stock)

July 1 Land   825,000
       Common Stock   825,000
       (To record issuance of 100,000 shares of no par value stock for land)

Sept. 1 Cash   1,000,000
       Preferred Stock   1,000,000
       (To record issuance of 20,000 preferred shares at $50 each)

Dec. 1 Cash   240,000
       Preferred Stock   200,000
       Contributed Capital in Excess of Par
       —Preferred   40,000
       (To record issuance of 4,000 shares of preferred stock at $60 each)

Problem-Solving Strategies

1. When shares are issued that have no par (or stated) value, the stock account is credited for the full amount of the proceeds.

2. When shares that have a par (or stated) value are issued, the stock account is credited for only the amount of the par (or stated) value; any excess is credited to an account for Contributed Capital in Excess of Par (or Stated) Value.

3. Separate accounts must be used for each type or class of shares.

4. In a non-cash transaction, the best available indication of fair market value should be used.

(b)   Shareholders' equity
         Contributed capital
           Capital stock
             Preferred stock, $50 par value, 6% cumulative, 100,000
               authorized, 24,000 shares issued and outstanding $1,200,000
             Common stock, no par value, 1,000,000 shares
               authorized, 500,000 shares issued and outstanding   4,025,000
           Additional contributed capital
             Contributed capital in excess of par value of preferred stock   40,000
                                                                                    _____
         Total contributed capital   5,265,000
         Retained earnings   900,000
                                                                                    _____
         Total shareholders' equity $6,165,000
                                                                                    ═══════════

SELF-STUDY QUESTIONS

Answers are at the end of the chapter.

(SO 1)   1. Which of the following is not a major advantage of a corporation?
         a. Separate legal existence.
         b. Continuous life.
         c. Government regulations.
         d. Transferable ownership rights.

(SO 1)   2. A disadvantage of a corporation is:
         a. limited liability of shareholders.
         b. additional taxes.
         c. transferable ownership rights.
         d. none of the above.

(SO 2)   3. Which of the following statements is *false*?
         a. Ownership of common stock gives the owner a voting right.
         b. The shareholders' equity section begins with contributed capital.
         c. The authorization of capital stock does not result in a formal accounting entry.
         d. Legal capital per share applies to par value stock but not to no par value stock.

(SO 2)   4. The account Retained Earnings is:
         a. a subdivision of contributed capital.
         b. net income kept in the corporation.
         c. reported as an expense in the income statement.
         d. closed to capital stock.

(SO 3)   5. ABC Corporation issues 1,000 shares of $10 par value common stock at $12 per share. In recording the transaction, credits are made to:
         a. Common Stock $10,000 and Gain on Sale of Shares Above Par Value, $2,000.

         b. Common Stock $12,000.
         c. Common Stock $10,000 and Contributed Capital in Excess of Par Value $2,000.
         d. Common Stock $10,000 and Retained Earnings $2,000.

(SO 4) 6. Preferred stock may have priority over common stock *except* in:
         a. dividends.
         b. assets in the event of liquidation.
         c. conversion.
         d. voting.

(SO 5) 7. Which of the following is *not* reported under additional contributed capital?
         a. Contributed capital in excess of par value.
         b. Common stock.
         c. Contributed capital in excess of stated value.
         d. All of the above are reported under additional contributed capital.

(SO 7) 8. The ledger of NWT, Inc., shows common stock and preferred stock. For this company, the formula for computing book value per share is:
         a. Total contributed capital divided by the number of shares of common stock outstanding.
         b. Common stock divided by the number of shares of common stock issued.
         c. Total shareholders' equity divided by the number of shares of common stock outstanding.
         d. Total shareholders' equity less preferred shareholders' equity divided by the number of shares of common stock outstanding.

QUESTIONS

1. Pat Kabza, a student, asks for your help in understanding the following characteristics of a corporation: (a) separate legal existence, (b) limited liability of shareholders, and (c) transferable ownership rights. Explain these characteristics to Pat.

2. (a) Your friend T.R. Cedras cannot understand how the characteristic of corporation management can be both an advantage and a disadvantage. Clarify this problem for T.R.
   (b) Identify and explain two other disadvantages of a corporation.

3. (a) The following terms pertain to the forming of a corporation: (1) charter, and (2) organization costs. Explain the terms.
   (b) Cary Brant believes a corporation must be incorporated federally if it wishes to operate in more than one province. Is Cary correct? Explain.

4. What are the basic ownership rights of common shareholders, in the absence of restrictive provisions?

5. (a) What are the two principal components of shareholders' equity?
   (b) What is contributed capital? Give two examples.

6. How do the financial statements for a corporation differ from the statements for a proprietorship?

7. The corporate charter of Letterman Corporation allows the issuance of a maximum of 100,000 shares of common stock. During its first two years of operations, Letterman sold 60,000 shares to shareholders and reacquired 7,000 of these shares. After these transactions, how many shares are authorized, issued, and outstanding?

8. Which is the better investment—common stock with a par value of $5 per share or common stock with a par value of $20 per share?

9. What factors help determine the market value of stock?

10. What effect does the issuance of stock at a price above par or stated value have on the issuer's net income? Explain.

11. Why is par value common stock usually not issued at a price that is less than par value?

12. Land appraised at $80,000 is purchased by issuing 1,000 shares of no par value common stock. The market price of the shares at the time of the exchange, based on active trading in the securities market, is $90 per share. Should the land be recorded at $80,000 or $90,000? Explain.

13. For what reasons might a company repurchase some of its stock?

14. Wilmor, Inc., purchases 1,000 shares of its own previously issued common stock. What effect does this transaction have on: (a) total assets, and (b) total shareholders' equity?

15. (a) What are the principal differences between common stock and preferred stock?
    (b) Preferred stock may be cumulative or participating, or both. Discuss these features.
    (c) How are dividends in arrears presented in the financial statements?

16. A preferred shareholder converts her convertible preferred stock into common stock. What effect does this have on the corporation's: (a) total assets, (b) total liabilities, and (c) total shareholders' equity?

17. What is the formula for computing book value per share when a corporation has only common stock?

18. WAT Inc.'s common stock has a book value of $29 and a current market value of $15. Explain why these amounts are different.

19. Indicate how each of the following accounts should be classified in the shareholders' equity section:
    (a) Common stock.
    (b) Contributed capital in excess of par value.
    (c) Retained earnings.
    (d) Contributed capital in excess of stated value.
    (e) Preferred stock.

BRIEF EXERCISES

BE14–1 Tracy Bono is studying for her accounting midterm examination. Identify for Tracy the advantages and disadvantages of the corporate form of business organization.

Advantages and disadvantages of a corporation.
(SO 1)

BE14–2 At December 31, Mile High Corporation reports revenues of $1,900,000 and expenses of $1,500,000. Prepare the entry to close the income summary account.

Closing entries for a corporation.
(SO 2)

Issuance of common stock.
(SO 3)

BE14–3   On May 10, Armada Corporation issues 1,000 shares of common stock for cash at $14 per share. Journalize the issuance of the stock, assuming (a) the stock has no par value, and (b) the stock has a par value of $10 per share.

Issuance of no-par value common stock.
(SO 3)

BE14–4   On June 1, Eagle Inc. issues 2,000 shares of no par common stock at a cash price of $7 per share. Journalize the issuance of the shares, assuming (a) the stock has no stated value, and (b) the stock has a stated value of $1 per share.

Issuance of stock in a non-cash transaction.
(SO 3)

BE14–5   Spiro Inc.'s no par value common stock is actively traded at a market value of $14 per share. Spiro issues 5,000 shares to purchase land advertised for sale at $80,000. Journalize the issuance of the stock in acquiring the land.

Issuance of preferred stock.
(SO 4)

BE14–6   Orford Inc. issues 5,000 shares of preferred stock for cash at $112 per share. The stock has no par value and a dividend rate of $8 per share. Journalize the issuance of the preferred stock.

Shareholders' equity section.
(SO 5)

BE14–7   Anita Corporation has the following accounts at December 31: Common Stock, no par, 5,000 shares issued, $50,000; Contributed Capital in Excess of Par Value $10,000; Preferred Stock, 8% cumulative $25 par, 800 shares issued, $20,000; and Retained Earnings $29,000. Prepare the shareholders' equity section of the balance sheet.

Book value per share.
(SO 7)

BE14–8   The balance sheet for Loren Inc. shows the following: total contributed capital $600,000, retained earnings $240,000, total shareholders' equity $840,000, common stock issued and outstanding 40,000 shares. Compute the book value per share.

Exercises

••

Journalize issuance of common stock under various assumptions.
(SO 3)

E14–1   During its first year of operations, the Bevis Corporation had the following transactions for its common stock:

Jan. 10   Issued 80,000 shares for cash at $5 per share.

July 1   Issued 30,000 shares for cash at $7 per share.

Instructions

    (a) Journalize the transactions assuming that the common stock has a par value of $5 per share.

    (b) Journalize the transactions assuming that the common stock is no par with a stated value of $1 per share.

    (c) Journalize the transactions assuming that the common stock is no par with no stated value.

Entries for issuance of common and preferred stock.
(SO 3, 4)

E14–2   Santiago Co. had the following transactions during the current period:

Mar. 2   Issued 5,000 shares of no par value common stock to lawyers as payment of a bill for $27,000 for services rendered in helping the company to incorporate.

June 12   Issued 60,000 shares of no par value common stock for used equipment that had originally cost $800,000 but currently had a book value of $300,000 and a fair market value of $375,000.

July 11   Issued 1,000 shares of $100 par value preferred stock for cash at $105 per share.

Instructions

    (a) Journalize the transactions.

    (b) Explain the nature of the cost involved in the March 2 transaction, in terms of how it would be classified in the financial statements.

Journalize non-cash common stock transactions.
(SO 3)

E14–3   As an auditor for the CA firm of Bell and Heft, you encounter the following situations when auditing different clients:

    1. The Ruth Corporation is a closely held corporation whose stock is not publicly traded. On December 5, the corporation acquired land by issuing 5,000 shares of its no par value common stock. The owner's asking price for the land was $120,000 and the fair market value of the land was $110,000.

2. The Hand Corporation is a publicly held corporation whose common stock is traded on the securities markets. On June 1, it acquired land by issuing 20,000 shares of its no par value stock. At the time of the exchange, the land was advertised for sale at $250,000 and the stock was selling at $12 per share.

Instructions

Prepare the journal entries for each of the situations above.

E14–4 Talley Corporation is authorized to issue both preferred and common stock. The preferred dividend rate is $4 per year. During the first year of operations, the following events and transactions pertained to the preferred stock:

Allocate dividends between preferred and common stock.
(SO 4)

Feb. 1 Issued 30,000 shares for cash at $53 per share.

June 30 Paid semi-annual dividends totalling $100,000.

July 15 Issued 10,000 shares for cash at $57 per share.

Dec. 31 Paid semi-annual dividends totalling $140,000.

Instructions

Indicate how each of the dividends would be allocated between the preferred and common stock.

E14–5 Karen Kerr Corporation has 10,000 shares of no par value preferred stock outstanding, which had been issued at $100 per share. Each share is convertible into five shares of no par value common stock. When the market values of the two classes of stock are $110 and $25, respectively, 3,000 shares of preferred stock are converted into common stock.

Journalize conversion of preferred stock.
(SO 3, 4)

Instructions

(a) Journalize the conversion of the 3,000 shares.

(b) Repeat (a) assuming that market values at conversion are $95 and $25, respectively.

(c) Repeat (a) assuming each share is convertible into eight shares of no par value common stock.

[handwritten: 3000 × 100 = 300,000
Dr. Cash
Cr. P/S
Dr. P/S
Cr. C/S]

E14–6 The shareholders' equity section of Kimbria Shumway Corporation at December 31 is as follows:

Answer questions about shareholders' equity section.
(SO 3, 4, 5)

Contributed capital

  Capital stock

Preferred stock, cumulative, no par, 10,000 shares authorized, 6,000 shares issued and outstanding	$ 600,000
Common stock, no par, 750,000 shares authorized, 600,000 shares issued and outstanding	1,500,000
Additional contributed capital	300,000
Total contributed capital	2,400,000
Retained earnings	1,158,000
Total shareholders' equity	$3,558,000

Instructions

From a review of the shareholders' equity section, answer the following questions:

(a) Assuming there is a stated value, what is the stated value of the common stock?

(b) What was the average issuance price per share of the common stock?

(c) If the annual dividend on preferred stock is $48,000, what is the dividend rate on preferred stock?

(d) If dividends of $96,000 were in arrears on preferred stock, what would be the balance reported for Retained Earnings?

E14–7 In a recent year, the shareholders' equity section of a company showed the following (in alphabetical order): Additional contributed capital $680.5, Common stock $88.3, Preferred stock $66.0, and Retained earnings $3,750.2. All dollar data are in millions.

Prepare a shareholders' equity section and compute book value.
(SO 5, 7)

The preferred stock has 660,000 shares authorized, with a par value of $100 and an annual $3.75 per share cumulative dividend preference. At December 31, all authorized preferred stock is issued and outstanding. There are 300 million shares of no par value common stock authorized, of which 88.3 million are outstanding at December 31.

Instructions

(a) Prepare the shareholders' equity section, including disclosure of all relevant data.

(b) Compute the book value per share of common stock, assuming there are no preferred dividends in arrears. (Round to two decimals.)

Compute the book value per share with preferred stock.
(SO 7)

E14–8 At December 31, Kilgora Corporation has total shareholders' equity of $3,000,000. Included in this total are Preferred stock $500,000 and Contributed capital in excess of par value—Preferred stock $50,000. There are 10,000 shares of $50 par value 10% cumulative preferred stock outstanding. At year end, 200,000 shares of common stock are outstanding.

Instructions

Compute the book value per share of common stock, under each of the following assumptions:

(a) There are no preferred dividends in arrears, and the preferred stock does not have a redemption (call) price.

(b) Preferred dividends are one year in arrears (that is, the dividends for the current year have not been paid), and the preferred stock has a redemption (call) price of $60 per share.

PROBLEMS
··

Journalize and post stock transactions; prepare contributed capital section.
(SO 3, 4, 5)

P14–1 The Wetland Corporation was organized on January 1, 1999. It is authorized to issue 10,000 shares of 8%, $100 par value preferred stock and 500,000 shares of no par common stock with a stated value of $2 per share. The following stock transactions were completed during the first year:

Jan. 10 Issued 80,000 shares of common stock for cash at $3 per share.

Mar. 1 Issued 5,000 shares of preferred stock for cash at $104 per share.

Apr. 1 Issued 24,000 shares of common stock for land. The asking price of the land was $90,000; the fair market value of the land was $80,000.

June 20 Issued 80,000 shares of common stock for cash at $4 per share.

Aug. 1 Issued 10,000 shares of common stock to lawyers in payment of their bill of $48,750 for services rendered in helping the company organize.

Sept. 1 Issued 10,000 shares of common stock for cash at $5 per share.

Nov. 1 Issued 1,000 shares of preferred stock for cash at $108 per share.

Instructions

(a) Journalize the transactions.

(b) Post to the shareholders' equity accounts.

(c) Prepare the contributed capital section of shareholders' equity at December 31, 1999.

Prepare contributed capital section of shareholders' equity.
(SO 3, 4, 5)

P14–2   The Brazil Corporation was organized on January 1, 1999. It is authorized to issue 20,000 shares of no par value preferred stock with a $3 dividend rate, and 500,000 shares of no par common stock. The following stock transactions were completed during the first year:

Jan. 10 Issued 100,000 shares of common stock for cash at $3 per share.

Mar. 1 Issued 10,000 shares of preferred stock for cash at $51 per share.

Apr. 1 Issued 25,000 shares of common stock for land. The asking price of the land was $90,000; the fair market value of the land was $85,000.

May 1 Issued 75,000 shares of common stock for cash at $4 per share.

July 24 Issued 10,000 shares of common stock to lawyers in payment of their bill of $50,000 for services rendered in helping the company organize.

Sept. 1 Issued 5,000 shares of common stock for cash of $5 per share plus used equipment that had originally cost $10,000 and now has a net book value of $4,000 and a fair market value of $5,000.

Nov. 1 Issued 2,000 shares of preferred stock for cash at $53 per share.

Instructions

Prepare the contributed capital section of shareholders' equity at December 31, 1999. (Hint: You may find T accounts helpful in organizing the data.)

P14–3 The shareholders' equity accounts of Chung Corporation on January 1, 1999, were as follows:

Journalize and post transactions; prepare shareholders' equity section; compute the book value. (SO 3, 4, 5, 7)

Preferred Stock (no par, $10 noncumulative; 5,000 shares authorized, 3,000 shares issued)	$ 315,000
Common Stock (no par value; 300,000 shares authorized, 200,000 shares issued)	1, 400,000
Retained Earnings	488,000

During 1999, the corporation had the following transactions and events pertaining to its shareholders' equity:

Feb. 1 Issued 4,000 shares of common stock for $25,000.

July 20 Issued 1,000 shares of preferred stock for $107,000.

Sept. 3 Issued 2,000 shares of common stock for a patent valued at $13,000.

Dec. 31 Determined that net income for the year was $215,000.

Instructions

(a) Journalize the transactions and the closing entry for net income.

(b) Enter the beginning balances in the accounts and post the journal entries to the shareholders' equity accounts.

(c) Prepare a shareholders' equity section at December 31, 1999.

(d) Compute the book value per share of common stock at December 31, 1999, assuming the preferred stock does not have a redemption (call) price.

P14–4 The shareholders' equity accounts of the Capozza Corporation on January 1, 1999, were as follows:

Post transactions and prepare a shareholders' equity section; compute the book value and return on equity. (SO 3, 4, 5, 6, 7)

Preferred Stock (no par value, $6 cumulative;10,000 shares authorized and 8,000 issued)	$ 480,000
Common Stock (no par value; 2,000,000 shares authorized and 1,000,000 issued)	2,400,000
Retained Earnings	1,816,000

During 1999, the corporation had the following transactions and events pertaining to its shareholders' equity:

Feb. 1 Issued 28,000 shares of common stock for $100,000.

Sept. 3 Issued 5,000 shares of common stock for equipment valued at $25,000.

Dec. 31 Determined that net income for the year was $377,000.

The preferred stock has a redemption (call) price of $55 per share, and the current year's dividends are in arrears.

Instructions

(a) Enter the beginning balances in T accounts and post the above items to the shareholders' equity accounts.

(b) Prepare a shareholders' equity section at December 31, 1999, including the disclosure of the preferred dividends in arrears.

(c) Compute the book value per share of common stock at December 31, 1999. (Round to two decimals.)

(d) Compute the return on equity for 1999.

Journalize shareholders' equity transactions.
(SO 3, 4)

P14–5 Jackie Remmers Corporation is authorized to issue 10,000 shares of $100 par value, 10% convertible preferred stock and 200,000 shares of no par value common stock. On January 1, 1999, the ledger contained the following shareholders' equity balances:

Preferred Stock (4,000 shares)	$ 400,000
Contributed Capital in Excess of Par Value—Preferred	40,000
Common Stock (70,000 shares)	1,050,000
Retained Earnings	300,000

During 1999, the following transactions occurred:

Feb. 1 Issued 1,050 shares of preferred stock for land having a fair market value of $125,000.

Mar. 1 Issued 1,000 shares of preferred stock for cash at $120 per share.

July 1 Holders of 1,000 shares of preferred stock purchased at $110 per share converted the shares into common stock. Each share of preferred was convertible into 10 shares of common stock. Market values were: preferred stock $122 and common stock $15.

Sept. 1 Issued 400 shares of preferred stock for a patent. The asking price of the patent was $60,000. Market values were: preferred stock $125 and patent indeterminable.

Dec. 1 Holders of 1,000 shares of preferred stock purchased at $115 per share converted the shares into common stock. Each share of preferred was convertible into 10 shares of common stock. Market values were: preferred stock $125 and common stock $16.

Instructions

(a) Prior to 1999, what was the average price at which the preferred stock was issued?

(b) Journalize the transactions that occurred during 1999.

Journalize and post stock trans-
actions; prepare shareholders'
equity section; calculate the
return on equity.
(SO 3, 4, 5, 6)

P14–6 Shirley Denison Corporation is authorized to issue 10,000 shares of no par value, $10 convertible preferred stock and 125,000 shares of no par value common stock. On January 1, 1999, the ledger contained the following shareholders' equity balances:

Preferred Stock (5,000 shares)	$ 550,000
Common Stock (70,000 shares)	1,050,000
Retained Earnings	300,000

During 1999, the following occurred:

Feb. 1 Issued 1,000 shares of preferred stock for land having a fair market value of $120,000.

July 1 Holders of 2,000 shares of preferred stock purchased at $110 per share converted the shares into common stock. Each share of preferred was convertible into eight shares of common stock. Market values were: preferred stock $122 and common stock $17.

Sept. 1 Issued 440 shares of preferred stock for a patent. The asking price of the patent was $60,000. Market values were: preferred stock $125 and patent indeterminable.

Dec. 1 Holders of 1,000 shares of preferred stock purchased at $120 per share converted the shares into common stock. Each share of preferred was convertible into eight shares of common stock. Market values were: preferred stock $125 and common stock $16.

Dec. 31 Net income for the year was $260,000. No dividends were declared.

Instructions

(a) Journalize the transactions and the closing entry for net income.

(b) Enter the beginning balances in the accounts and post the journal entries to the shareholders' equity accounts. (Use J2 for the posting reference.)

(c) Prepare a shareholders' equity section at December 31, 1999.

(d) Calculate the company's return on equity for 1999.

Prepare shareholders' equity sec-
tion and compute book value.
(SO 5, 7)

P14–7 The following shareholders' equity accounts, arranged alphabetically, are in the ledger of Dublin Corporation at December 31, 1999:

Common Stock (no par value; 150,000 shares issued)	$2,400,000
Contributed Capital in Excess of Par Value—Preferred Stock	280,000
Preferred Stock ($100 par, 8% noncumulative)	400,000
Retained Earnings	1,134,000

Instructions

   (a) Prepare a shareholders' equity section at December 31, 1999.

   (b) Compute the book value per share of the common stock, assuming the preferred stock has a redemption (call) price of $110 per share.

   (c) Repeat part (b) assuming no redemption (call) or liquidation price is stated.

P14–8 The following shareholders' equity accounts, arranged alphabetically, are in the ledger of Hussain Corporation at December 31, 1999:

Compute book values; compare to amounts paid in.
(SO 3, 7)

Common Stock—no par (500,000 shares issued)	$4,000,000
Preferred Stock—no par, $4 cumulative (16,000 shares issued)	1,492,000
Retained Earnings	158,000

Instructions

   (a) Compute the book value per share of the common stock, assuming the preferred stock has a redemption (call) price of $60 per share and dividends are two years (i.e., the current year and one previous year) in arrears.

   (b) Repeat part (a) using a redemption (call) price of $100 per share and five years of dividends in arrears.

   (c) How does the book value compare to the average price paid, per share of common stock, when the shares were issued?

*B*roadening *Your Perspective*

FINANCIAL REPORTING PROBLEM

The shareholders' equity section for The Second Cup Ltd. is shown in the Consolidated Balance Sheets in Appendix A. You will also find data related to this problem on other pages of the appendix.

Instructions

Answer the following questions:

   (a) Does The Second Cup have preferred shares?

   (b) How many shares of common stock is the company authorized to issue?

   (c) How many shares of common stock were outstanding at June 28, 1997?

   (d) What was the average issue price of the shares outstanding as at June 24, 1995, and June 29, 1996?

   (e) What was the average price of the shares that were issued during the year ended June 28, 1997?

   (f) Calculate the book value per share at June 29, 1996, and June 28, 1997. (You can confirm the latter amount by referring to Illustration 14-16 in the chapter.)

DECISION CASE

The shareholders' meeting for Mantle Corporation has been in progress for some time. The chief financial officer for Mantle is presently reviewing the company's financial statements and is explaining the items that make up the shareholders' equity section of the balance sheet for the current year. The shareholders' equity section of Mantle Corporation at December 31, 1999, is as follows:

Contributed capital
  Capital stock
    Preferred stock, authorized 1,000,000 shares cumulative,
      no par value, $8 per share, 6,000 shares issued
      and outstanding $ 600,000
    Common stock, authorized 5,000,000 shares, $1 stated value,
      3,000,000 shares issued and outstanding   3,000,000

      Total capital stock   3,600,000
  Additional contributed capital
    Contibuted capital in excess of stated value—common stock   25,050,000
      Total contributed capital   28,650,000
Retained earnings   900,000

      Total shareholders' equity $29,550,000

A number of questions regarding the shareholders' equity section of Mantle Corporation's balance sheet have been raised at the meeting.

Instructions

Answer the following questions as if you were the chief financial officer for Mantle Corporation:

(a) "What does the cumulative provision related to the preferred stock mean?"

(b) "I thought the common stock was presently selling at $29.75, and yet the company has the stock stated at $1 per share. How can that be?"

(c) "Why is it necessary to show additional contributed capital? Why not just show common stock at the total amount paid or contributed?"

COMMUNICATION ACTIVITY

Louis P. Brady, your uncle, is an inventor who has decided to incorporate. Uncle Lou knows that you are an accounting major, and hopes that you can help him set up his business. In a recent letter to you, he ends with the question, "I'm filling out an incorporation application; can you tell me the differences in the following terms: (1) authorized stock, (2) issued stock, (3) preferred stock?"

Instructions

In a brief note, differentiate these different stock terms for Uncle Lou. Write the letter as friendly yet professional.

GROUP ACTIVITY

You are employed as an auditor for the firm of Honest and Accurate. On the last two engagements, you encountered the following situations:

1. Larry D. Beaty Corporation is a closely held corporation whose stock is not publicly traded. The most recent issuance of the company's stock was last year, at $12.50 per share. On May 15 the corporation acquired property (land and building) by issuing 20,000 shares of its $10 par value common stock. The day before the exchange, the property was advertised for sale at $260,000. This listing was based somewhat on a qualified independent appraisal of $240,000, with 25% of the amount attributed to the land and 75% to the building.

2. Nea B. Wood Corporation is a publicly held corporation whose common stock is traded on the Toronto Stock Exchange. On September 10, it acquired land by issuing 8,000 shares of no par value common stock. At the date of the exchange, the land was listed with a real estate firm at an advertised selling price of $175,000; it was assessed (for property tax purposes) at a value of $150,000 and the stock was selling at $20 a share. The company intended to improve the land, at a cost of $25,000, and then sell it for $210,000.

Instructions

In groups of five or six people:

(a) Discuss the approach that should be taken or the basis used when recording the above situations.

(b) Prepare the journal entry for each situation.

ETHICS CASE
....

The R & D division of Simplex Chemical Corp. has just developed a chemical for sterilizing the vicious Brazilian "killer bees" that are invading most of Central America, Mexico, and the southern states of the United States. The president of Simplex is anxious to get the chemical on the market, because Simplex's profits need a boost and his job is in jeopardy because of decreasing sales and profits. Simplex has an opportunity to sell this chemical in several Central American countries, where the laws are much more relaxed than in North America.

The director of Simplex's R & D division strongly recommends further laboratory testing for side effects of this chemical on other insects, birds, animals, plants, and even humans. He cautions the president, "We could be sued from all sides if the chemical has tragic side effects that we didn't even test for in the labs." The president answers, "We can't wait an additional year for your lab tests. We can avoid losses from such lawsuits by establishing a separate wholly-owned corporation to shield Simplex Corp. from such lawsuits. We can't lose any more than our investment in the new corporation, and we'll invest just the patent covering this chemical. We'll reap the benefits if the chemical works and is safe, and avoid the losses from lawsuits if it's a disaster."

The following week Simplex creates a new wholly-owned corporation called Zoebee Inc., sells the chemical patent to it for $10, and watches the spraying begin.

Instructions

(a) Who are the stakeholders in this situation?

(b) Are the president's motives and actions ethical?

(c) Can Simplex shield itself against losses of Zoebee Inc.?

CRITICAL THINKING
►*A Real-World Focus: Barrister Information Systems Corporation*
....

BARRISTER
INFORMATION SYSTEMS CORPORATION

Barrister Information Systems Corp. develops, assembles, markets, and services computer systems and local area networks for law firms.

Barrister Information Systems has two classes of preferred stock—A and C—in addition to its common stock. The 1,300 shares of Series A preferred stock are non-voting, have a 12% cumulative dividend, have liquidation preference rights over the Series C preferred stock and the common stock, and are redeemable (callable) by the company at any time for $1,000 per share plus cumulative unpaid dividends. Each share of Series A preferred stock is convertible into 500 shares of common stock. At one point, the cumulative unpaid dividends on the Series A preferred stock totalled $254,000.

Instructions

(a) If the par value of the Class A preferred stock is $100 per share, what dollar amount in dividends can the shareholders expect annually on the Class A preferred stock?

(b) Estimate the number of years the dividends are in arrears, on the Class A preferred stock.

(c) Should the $254,000 in dividends not paid be reported as a liability on the balance sheet?

(d) What can you conclude about the dividends on Barrister's common stock?

(e) Are there any features that Barrister's preferred shares do not possess?

ACCOUNTING ON THE WEB

Incorporated in 1878, the Toronto Stock Exchange is the second-largest stock exchange in North America and among the top 10 in the world. The TSE is Canada's largest capital market, accounting for over 80% of the value of shares traded on Canadian exchanges. This case explores the TSE web site, to learn more about the TSE, its indices, and processes. We also learn how to use this website to obtain current stock quotes for listed companies.

Instructions
Specific requirements of this Internet case are available on-line at www.wiley.com/canada/weygandt.

Answers to Self-Study Questions
1. c 2. b 3. d 4. b 5. c 6. d 7. b 8. d

Concepts for Review

Standing on Guard for High-Tech Business

GUELPH, Ont. — "In the early part of this century, entrepreneurs made fortunes by seeking out valuable resources such as forests or mines," explains Brian Cox, Chief Executive Officer of GUARD, Inc., in Guelph, Ontario. "Today's route to wealth is finding valuable processes."

GUARD, Inc., exemplifies the new knowledge- and process-based corporation of the information age. Its mission is to bridge the gap between worthy inventions and profitable commercial concerns. It is a management company that establishes new, advanced technology businesses based on scientific breakthroughs made at the University of Guelph and elsewhere. "The University supplies the good ideas, then leaves it up to us, as a business, to do what business does best: exploit those ideas, and run the businesses that are based on them," says Dr. Cox.

GUARD was incorporated in 1994, the brainchild of a group of business people from science-driven industries and, as Dr. Cox calls them, "a few visionary professors" from the University of Guelph. In 1996 it became a publicly traded company, floating an initial public stock offering that yielded nearly $6.6 million. It

then separated itself formally from the University of Guelph, although the University still has a close business relationship with GUARD. GUARD is listed on the Alberta Stock Exchange.

GUARD is a young company. Though it has over a half-dozen potentially profitable projects under development, in its first few years its only income was interest from short-term investments. Thus, GUARD's 1996 Annual Report showed a net loss of $843,397 on its income statement and total shareholders' equity of $5,838,502 on its balance sheet—comprising $6,711,326 in capital stock and a deficit of $872,824. Its shareholders

receive no dividends. Rather, says Dr. Cox, "they are playing a game of long-term capital gains. A high-tech company can often take 12 to 15 years to mature. The shareholders' reward will be through rapid capital appreciation during this period."

So far, GUARD seems to be delivering this promised reward. Its shares appreciated from $2 to about $3.75 apiece in 15 months. And as long as it is successful, a company like GUARD creates sophisticated, top-quality jobs in Canada for high-tech professionals and managers who might otherwise go to the United States. ◀

CHAPTER · 15

CORPORATIONS: DIVIDENDS, RETAINED EARNINGS, AND INCOME REPORTING

▶ STUDY OBJECTIVES ◀

After studying this chapter, you should be able to:

1. *Prepare the entries for cash dividends, stock dividends, and stock splits, and compare their financial impact.*
2. *Identify the items that are reported in a statement of retained earnings.*
3. *Prepare a comprehensive shareholders' equity section.*
4. *Describe the form and content of corporation income statements.*
5. *Explain the concept of intraperiod tax allocation.*
6. *Indicate the statement presentation of material items not typical of regular operations.*
7. *Compute earnings per share and the price-earnings ratio.*

A profitable corporation distributes a portion of its earnings to its shareholders by declaring and paying dividends. A young corporation, like Guard, Inc., in the opening story, often incurs losses in its early years. As it matures, it will normally retain all of its earnings until it accumulates sufficient equity to sustain its operations.

This chapter discusses dividends, retained earnings, corporation income statements, and key earnings ratios. The organization of the chapter is as follows:

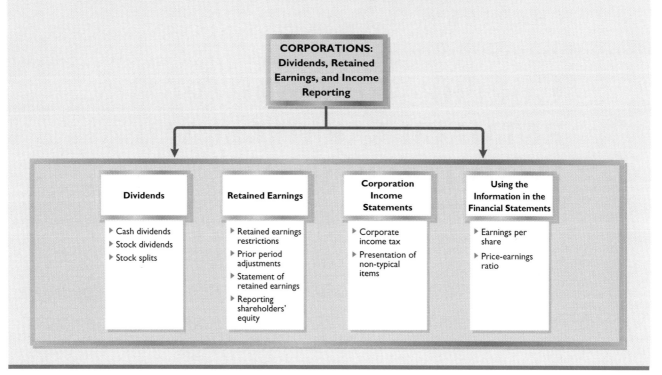

Dividends

A **dividend** is a pro rata (equal) distribution by a corporation to its shareholders. Potential buyers and sellers of a corporation's stock are very interested in a company's dividend policies and practices. Dividends can be cash, property, scrip (promissory note to pay cash), or (capital) stock. Cash dividends, which are the most common, and stock dividends, which are fairly common, will be the focus of discussion in this chapter.

Dividends may be expressed as a dollar amount per share, or as a percentage of the par or stated value of the stock if stock has been issued with par or stated values. In the financial press, **dividends are generally reported as a dollar amount per share**. For example, BC Tel has an annual dividend rate of $6 per share on one of its classes of preferred shares, and Hudson's Bay Company has a dividend rate of 72¢ on its common shares.

Cash Dividends

A **cash dividend** is a pro rata distribution of cash to shareholders. For a cash dividend to occur, a corporation must have:

1. **Retained earnings**. Dividends are normally paid out of retained earnings, which represents the accumulated income and losses of the corporation. Although laws governing cash dividends vary by jurisdiction, in general a deficit cannot be created by the declaration of the dividend. A dividend declared out of contributed capital is sometimes called a **liquidating dividend**, because the amount originally paid in by shareholders is being reduced or liquidated.

2. **Adequate cash**. Sufficient retained earnings does not indicate a company's ability to pay a dividend. For example, a sport and leisure company such as the Forzani Group Ltd., with a cash balance of $1.1 million and retained earnings of $9.6 million, could legally declare a dividend of $9.6 million. However, if it attempted to pay the dividend, in order to continue operating, it would need to raise additional cash through the sale of other assets or through additional financing. Before declaring a cash dividend, the board of directors must carefully consider both current and future demands on the company's cash resources. In some cases, current liabilities may make a cash dividend inappropriate; in other cases, a major expansion program may permit only a relatively small dividend.

3. **Declared dividends**. The board of directors has full authority to determine the amount of income to be distributed in the form of a dividend and the amount to be retained in the business. Unlike interest, dividends do not accrue on a note payable, and they are not a liability until declared.

Case in point The board of directors is not obligated to declare dividends.

The amount and timing of a dividend are important issues for management to consider. The payment of a large cash dividend could lead to liquidity problems for the enterprise. Conversely, a small dividend—or a missed dividend—may cause unhappiness among shareholders, who expect a reasonable cash payment from the company on a periodic basis. Many companies declare and pay cash dividends quarterly.

►*International note*

In Brazil, companies are required by law to distribute 50% of their net income annually as dividends.

►Accounting in Action ► *Business Insight*

In order to remain in business, companies must honour their interest payments to creditors, bankers, and bondholders. But the payment of dividends to shareholders is another matter. Many companies can survive, even thrive, without such payouts. In fact, management might consider dividend payments unnecessary, even harmful to the company. Pay your creditors, by all means. But fork over perfectly good cash to shareholders as dividends? "Why give money to those strangers?" is the response of one company president.

Investors must keep an eye on the company's dividend policy. For most companies, increased dividends despite irregular earnings can be a warning signal. So can the refusal of management to lower dividends when earnings fall or capital requirements rise. Companies with high dividends and rising debt may be borrowing money to pay shareholders. For investors who are seeking high returns on their stock investments, no, or low, dividends may mean high returns through capital appreciation of the stock.

Entries for Cash Dividends

Three dates are important for dividends: (1) the declaration date, (2) the record date, and (3) the payment date. Normally, there is a time span of two to four weeks between each date. Accounting entries are required on two of the dates—the declaration date and the payment date.

On the declaration date, the board of directors formally declares (authorizes) the cash dividend and announces it to shareholders. The declaration of a cash dividend

commits the corporation to a binding legal obligation that cannot be rescinded. Thus, an entry is required to recognize the decrease in retained earnings and the increase in the current liability, Dividends Payable.

To illustrate, assume that on December 1, 1999, the directors of Media General declare a 50¢ per share cash dividend on 100,000 shares of no par value common stock. The dividend record date is December 22; the payment date is January 20, 2000. The dividend is $50,000 (100,000 x 50¢), and the entry to record the declaration is:

Declaration Date

Dec. 1	Cash Dividends—Common	50,000	
	Dividends Payable		50,000
	(To record declaration of cash dividend)		

Dividends Payable is a current liability because it will normally be paid within the next month or so. Instead of debiting Cash Dividends, some accountants debit the Retained Earnings account directly, in order to avoid a later closing entry. While this is not incorrect, use of the Dividends account provides additional information in the ledger. For example, a company may have separate dividend accounts for each class of stock or for each type of dividend, as in this case. When a dividend account is used, its balance is transferred to Retained Earnings at the end of the year by a closing entry. Consequently, the effect of the declaration is the same—retained earnings is decreased and current liability is increased. For assignment problems, you should use a Dividends account for recording dividend declarations.

Case in point The record date is important in determining the dividend to be paid to each shareholder but not the total dividend.

On the record date ownership of the outstanding shares is determined so that the corporation knows who to pay the dividend to. The shareholders' records maintained by the corporation supply this information. The time interval between the declaration date and the record date enables the corporation to update its stock ownership records. Between the declaration date and record date, the number of shares outstanding should remain the same. Thus, the purpose of the record date is to identify the persons or entities that will receive the dividend, not to determine the amount of the dividend liability. For Media General, the record date is December 22. No entry is required on this date because the corporation's liability recognized on the declaration date is unchanged.

On the payment date, dividend cheques are mailed to shareholders and the payment of the dividend is recorded. The entry on January 20, the payment date, is:

Payment Date

Jan. 20	Dividends Payable	50,000	
	Cash		50,000
	(To record payment of cash dividend)		

Note that payment of the dividend reduces both current assets and current liabilities but has no effect on shareholders' equity. In a company's financial statements the cumulative effect of the **declaration and payment** of a cash dividend is to **decrease both shareholders' equity and total assets**.

▸Technology in Action

A casual glance at the *Financial Post* reveals the vast amount of stock traded on national and international stock exchanges. Thousands of shares of a single company's stock may change hands each day. Companies must rely on agents or trust companies who use computers, to track the volume of transactions for both ownership and dividend purposes.

Allocating Cash Dividends between Preferred and Common Stock

As explained in Chapter 14, preferred stock has priority over common stock in regard to dividends. That is, cash dividends must be paid to preferred shareholders before any dividends are paid to common shareholders.

To illustrate, assume that IBR Inc. has 1,000 shares of 8%, $100 par value cumulative preferred stock and 50,000 shares of no par value common stock outstanding at December 31, 1999. The dividend per share for preferred stock is $8 ($100 par value x 8%), and the required annual dividend for preferred stock is $8,000 (1,000 x $8). At December 31, 1999, the directors declare a $6,000 cash dividend. In this case, the entire dividend amount goes to preferred shareholders because of their dividend preference. The entry to record the declaration of the dividend is:

Dec. 31	Cash Dividends—Preferred	6,000	
	Dividends Payable		6,000
	(To record partial cash dividend to preferred		
	shareholders)		

Because of the cumulative feature, dividends of $2 per share are in arrears on preferred stock for 1999. These dividends must be paid to preferred shareholders before any future dividends can be paid to common shareholders. As explained in Chapter 14, dividends in arrears are not recorded as a liability (until declared), but should be disclosed in the financial statements.

At December 31, 2000, IBR declares a $50,000 cash dividend. The allocation of the dividend to the two classes of stock is as follows:

Total dividend		$50,000
Allocated to preferred stock		
Dividends in arrears, 1999 (1,000 x $2)	$2,000	
2000 dividend (1,000 x $8)	8,000	10,000
Remainder allocated to common stock		$40,000

Illustration 15-1

Allocating dividends to preferred and common stock

The entry to record the declaration of the dividend is:

Dec. 31	Cash Dividends—Preferred	10,000	
	—Common	40,000	
	Dividends Payable		50,000
	(To record declaration of cash dividends)		

If the preferred stock were not cumulative, preferred shareholders would have received only $8,000 in dividends in 2000 and common shareholders would have received $42,000.

Stock Dividends

A stock dividend is a pro rata distribution of the corporation's own stock to shareholders. Whereas a cash dividend is paid in cash, a stock dividend is paid in shares. **A stock dividend results in a decrease in retained earnings and an increase in contributed capital**. Unlike a cash dividend, a stock dividend does not decrease total shareholders' equity or total assets.

To illustrate a stock dividend, assume that you have a 2% ownership interest in IBR Inc. because you own 1,000 of its 50,000 shares of common stock. In a 10% stock dividend, 5,000 shares (50,000 x 10%) of stock would be issued. You would receive 100 shares (2% x 5,000), but your ownership interest would remain at 2% (1,100 ÷ 55,000).

Case in point Dividends were declared by 24% of the companies surveyed by *Financial Reporting in Canada*. Of these, only 4% were stock dividends.

You now own more shares of stock, but your ownership interest has not changed. Moreover, no cash is given out, and no liabilities have been assumed by the corporation.

What, then, are the purposes and benefits of a stock dividend? A corporation generally issues stock dividends for one or more of the following reasons:

1. To satisfy shareholders' dividend expectations without spending cash.
2. To increase the marketability of its stock by increasing the number of shares outstanding: this will likely decrease the market price per share. Decreasing the market price of the stock, makes it easier for smaller investors to purchase the shares.
3. To emphasize that a portion of shareholders' equity has been permanently retained in the business and is therefore unavailable for cash dividends.

Case in point   Because of its effects, declaring a stock dividend is also referred to as capitalizing retained earnings.

The size of the stock dividend and the value to be assigned to each dividend share are determined by the board of directors when the dividend is declared. The *Canada Business Corporations Act* recommends that directors of federally incorporated companies assign the **fair market value per share** for stock dividends. This directive is based on the assumption that a stock dividend will have little effect on the market price of the shares previously outstanding. Thus, many shareholders consider stock dividends to be distributions of earnings equal to the fair market value of the shares distributed. While the stock dividend value can be decided by the directors in some provincial jurisdictions, it is widespread practice to use fair market values. This text will follow this common practice.

Entries for Stock Dividends

To illustrate the accounting for stock dividends, assume that Medland Corporation has a balance of $300,000 in retained earnings and declares a 10% stock dividend on its 50,000 shares of no par value common stock. The current fair market value of its stock is $15 per share. The number of shares to be issued is 5,000 (10% x 50,000), and the total amount to be debited to Stock Dividends is $75,000 (5,000 x $15). The entry to record this transaction at the declaration date is as follows:

Helpful hint   The capitalization of retained earnings occurs at the declaration date.

Stock Dividends	75,000	
Common Stock Dividends Distributable		75,000
(To record declaration of 10% stock dividend)		

If the common stock had a par value of, say, $10 per share, the account Stock Dividends would be debited for the fair market value of the stock issued (5,000 x $15). Common Stock Dividends Distributable would be credited for the par value of the dividend shares (5,000 x $10), and the excess over par (5,000 x $5) would be credited to an additional contributed capital account.

Case in point   Note that the dividend account title is distributable, not payable.

Common Stock Dividends Distributable is a shareholders' equity account; it is not a liability, because assets will not be used to pay the dividend. If a balance sheet is prepared before the dividend shares are issued, the distributable account is reported in contributed capital: it is as an addition to common stock issued, as shown below:

Illustration 15-2

Statement presentation of common stock dividends distributable

Contributed capital		
Common stock	$500,000	
Common stock dividends distributable	75,000	$575,000

When the stock dividend shares are issued on the "payment" date, Common Stock Dividends Distributable is debited and Common Stock is credited, as follows:

	75,000	
Common Stock Dividends Distributable		
Common Stock		75,000
(To record issuance of 5,000 shares in a stock dividend)		

Effects of Stock Dividends

How do stock dividends affect shareholders' equity? They **change the composition of shareholders' equity** because a portion of retained earnings is transferred to contributed capital. However, **total shareholders' equity remains the same**. Stock dividends also have no effect on the legal capital per share, but the number of shares outstanding increases and the book value per share decreases. These effects are shown below for Medland Corporation:

Illustration 15-3

Stock dividend effects

	Before Stock Dividend	After Stock Dividend
Shareholders' equity		
Contributed capital		
Common stock, no par	$500,000	$575,000
Retained earnings	300,000	225,000
Total shareholders' equity	$800,000	$800,000
Outstanding shares	50,000	55,000
Book value per share	$ 16	$ 14.55

In this example, total contributed capital is increased by $75,000 and retained earnings is decreased by the same amount. Total shareholders' equity remains unchanged.

Stock Splits

A stock split, like a stock dividend, involves the issuance of additional shares of stock to shareholders according to their percentage ownership. However, **a stock split results in a reduction in the legal capital per share**. The purpose of a stock split is to increase the marketability of the stock by lowering its market value per share. This, in turn, increases investor interest and makes it easier for the corporation to issue additional stock. The effect of a split on market value is generally inversely proportional to the size of the split (see the example on the following page). Sometimes, due to increased investor interest, the share price rises beyond its intended split value.

    For example, after a 2-for-1 stock split (one share before the split equals two shares after the split), the market value of Scotiabank common stock fell from approximately $70 to $35. In announcing the split, Robert Chisholm, Scotiabank Vice-Chair, said, "This share split makes the Bank's shares more affordable for the average Canadian investor."

    In a stock split, the number of shares is increased in the same proportion that legal capital per share is decreased. For example, in a 2-for-1 split, one share of no par value stock is exchanged for two shares of no par value stock. If the stock has a par value of $10, then one share of $10 par value is exchanged for two shares of $5 par value stock. **A stock split does not have any effect on total contributed capital, retained earnings, or total shareholders' equity**. However, the number of shares outstanding increases and book value per share decreases.

    These effects are shown in Illustration 15-4 for Medland Corporation. Assume that, instead of a 10% stock dividend, Medland splits its 50,000 shares of no par value common stock on a 2-for-1 basis.

Case in point Some companies never split their stock, no matter how high their stock price gets. For example, Berkshire Hathaway's Class A stock, which sells for a pricey $100,000 per share, is definitely not in the average investor's price range!

Illustration 15-4

Stock split effects

	Before Stock Split	After Stock Split
Shareholders' equity		
Contributed capital		
Common stock	$500,000	$500,000
Retained earnings	300,000	300,000
Total shareholders' equity	$800,000	$800,000
Outstanding shares	50,000	100,000
Book value per share	$ 16	$ 8

Because a stock split does not affect the balances in any shareholders' equity accounts, **it is not necessary to journalize a stock split**. A memo entry noting the details of the split is sufficient.

Significant differences between stock splits, stock dividends, and cash dividends (after payment) are shown in Illustration 15-5. NE means no effect.

Item	Stock Split	Stock Dividend	Cash Dividend
Total assets	NE	NE	↓
Total liabilities	NE	NE	NE
Total shareholders' equity	NE	NE	↓
Total contributed capital	NE	↑	NE
Total retained earnings	NE	↓	↓
Legal capital per share	↓	NE	NE
Number of shares	↑	↑	NE
% of shareholder ownership	NE	NE	NE

Before You Go On . . .

▶Review It

1. What entries are made for cash dividends on: (a) the declaration date, (b) the record date, and (c) the payment date?

2. Contrast the effects of a stock dividend and a 2-for-1 stock split on: (a) shareholders' equity, (b) outstanding shares, and (c) book value per share.

▶Do It

Due to five years of record earnings at Sing CD Corporation, the market price of its 500,000 shares of no par value common stock tripled from $15 to $45 per share. During this period, common stock remained the same, at $2,000,000, but retained earnings increased from $1,500,000 to $10,000,000. President Diane Wood is considering either: (1) a 10% stock dividend, or (2) a 2-for-1 stock split. She asks you to show the before and after effects of each option on: (a) retained earnings, and (b) book value per share.

Reasoning: A stock dividend decreases retained earnings and increases contributed capital, but total shareholders' equity remains the same. Because additional shares of stock are issued in the dividend, book value per share is decreased. A stock split changes only legal capital per share and the number of shares outstanding. Thus, this event has no effect on the retained earnings balance, and it decreases book value per share.

Solution:

(a) (1) The stock dividend amount is $2,250,000 [(500,000 × 10%) × $45]. The new balance in retained earnings is $7,750,000 ($10,000,000 − $2,250,000).

(2) The Common Stock and Retained Earnings account balances after the stock split are the same as they were before the split: $2,000,000 and $10,000,000, respectively. The legal capital per share is $4 before the split ($2,000,000 ÷ 500,000); it is $2 after the split ($2,000,000 ÷ 1,000,000).

(b) The book value effects are as follows:

	Original Balances	After Stock Dividend	After Stock Split
Common stock	$ 2,000,000	$ 4,250,000	$ 2,000,000
Retained earnings	10,000,000	7,750,000	10,000,000
Total shareholders' equity	$12,000,000	$12,000,000	$12,000,000
Shares outstanding	500,000	550,000	1,000,000
Book value per share	$ 24	$ 21.82	$ 12

Related exercise material: BE15–1, BE15–2, BE15–3, E15–2, E15–4, E15–5, and E15–7.

Retained Earnings

···

As discussed in Chapter 14, **retained earnings** is the cumulative total of net income (loss)—since incorporation—that has been retained in the business. The balance in retained earnings is part of the shareholders' claim on the total assets of the corporation. It does not, however, represent a claim on any specific asset. Nor can the amount of retained earnings be associated with the balance of any individual asset account. For example, a $100,000 balance in retained earnings does not mean that there should be $100,000 in cash. The reason is that the cash resulting from the excess of revenues over expenses and dividends may have been used to purchase buildings, equipment, and other assets. Illustration 15-6 shows the relationship of cash (and temporary investments, where applicable) to retained earnings in selected companies:

STUDY OBJECTIVE

·········· 2 ··········

Identify the items that are reported in a statement of retained earnings.

Illustration 15-6

Retained earnings and cash balances

Company	(In Millions) Retained Earnings	Cash
Canadian Tire Corp., Ltd.	$1,059	$ 195
Imasco	2,882	57
Noranda Inc.	910	2,098
George Weston Limited	1,672	651

When expenses exceed revenues, a **net loss** results, as was the case in the opening story about GUARD, Inc. In contrast to net income, a net loss is debited to Retained Earnings when preparing closing entries. This is done even if a debit balance results in Retained Earnings, as it did in GUARD's case. A debit (or negative) balance in retained earnings is identified as a deficit and is reported as a deduction in the shareholders' equity section, as shown in illustration 15–7:

Illustration 15-7

Shareholders' equity with deficit

Shareholders' equity	
Contributed capital	
Common stock	$800,000
Retained earnings (deficit)	(50,000)
Total shareholders' equity	$750,000

Retained Earnings Restrictions

Case in point *Financial Reporting in Canada* reported in a recent year that 10% of the companies surveyed have restrictions.

The balance in retained earnings is generally available for dividend declarations. In some cases, however, there may be **retained earnings restrictions** that make a portion of the balance currently unavailable for dividends. Restrictions generally are one or more of the following types:

1. **Contractual restrictions**. Long-term debt contracts may impose a restriction on retained earnings as a condition for the loan. The restriction limits the use of corporate assets for the payment of dividends. Thus, it enhances the likelihood that the corporation will be able to meet required loan payments.
2. **Voluntary restrictions**. The board of directors of a corporation may voluntarily create retained earnings restrictions for specific purposes. For example, the board may authorize a restriction for the purpose of future plant expansion. By reducing the amount of retained earnings available for dividends, they may make more cash available for the planned expansion.

Retained earnings restrictions are generally disclosed in the notes to the financial statements. For example, Norcen Energy Resources Limited, an oil and gas company headquartered in Calgary, included the following note in a recent financial statement:

Illustration 15-8

Disclosure of restriction

NORCEN ENERGY RESOURCES LIMITED

Note 10 Shareholders' Equity
(vii) Dividend Restrictions

Covenants respecting certain of Norcen's non-convertible long-term debt impose a limit on dividend payments by Norcen, such limit being related in part to consolidated net earnings, as defined. Under the most restrictive of these covenants, retained earnings in the amount of $86 million were available for the payment of dividends at December 31.

Prior Period Adjustments

An adjustment of financial results for prior periods is only appropriate in two circumstances: (1) correcting an error related to a prior period, and (2) changing an accounting principle. When a correction of an error or a change in accounting principle results, the accounting treatment is similar.

1. The corrected amount or new principle should be used in reporting the results of operations of the current year.
2. The cumulative effect of the correction or change should be disclosed net of (after subtracting) applicable taxes, as an adjustment of opening retained earnings.
3. All prior period financial statements should be corrected or restated to facilitate comparison.
4. The effects of the change should be detailed and disclosed in a footnote.

Let's look at the accounting for correction of errors and for changes in accounting principle.

Correction of Prior Period Errors

Suppose that after the books have been closed and the financial statements have been issued, a corporation discovers that a material error has been made in reporting net income of a prior year. How should a correction of a prior period error be recorded in the accounts and reported in the financial statements? The correction is made directly to Retained Earnings, because the effect of the error is now in this account. The net income for the previous period has been recorded in retained earnings through the journalizing and posting of closing entries.

If a correction affects net income, then income tax expense will also be in error. That is, if a revenue or expense account is incorrect, then income before taxes is incorrect, as is income tax expense (which was based on income before taxes).

To illustrate, assume that General Microwave Corp. discovers in 1999 that it overstated cost of goods sold in 1998 by $30,000 as a result of computational errors in counting inventory. These errors overstated expenses and understated income before income taxes by $30,000 for 1998. If we assume an income tax rate of 45%, the overall effect on net income is $16,500. That is, if cost of goods sold is $30,000 more than it should be, then there will be $30,000 less income before tax on which to compute income tax. Therefore, net income was understated by the difference after taxes [$30,000 x (1-45%)]. The following illustration details this effect, using assumed data for revenues and expenses:

	Incorrect (overstated CGS)	Correct (should be)	Difference
Revenues	$200,000	$200,000	$ –
Less: Expenses	125,000	95,000	(30,000)
Income before tax	75,000	105,000	30,000
Less: Income tax (45%)	33,750	47,250	13,500
Net income	$ 41,250	$ 57,750	$ 16,500

Illustration 15-9

Income effects of overstating cost of goods sold

If cost of goods sold is overstated, then inventory is also in error. On the balance sheet, current assets and retained earnings are also understated. The entry for the correction is as follows:

Inventory	30,000	
Income Tax Payable		13,500
Retained Earnings		16,500
(To adjust for overstatement of cost of goods sold		
in a prior period)		

Prior period corrections are reported in the statement of retained earnings, net of associated income taxes. Corrections are added (or deducted) from the beginning retained earnings balance to show the adjusted beginning balance. Assuming General Microwave has a beginning balance of $800,000 in retained earnings, the correction is reported as follows:

(Partial) Statement of Retained Earnings	
Balance, January 1, 1999, as previously reported	$800,000
Add: Correction for overstatement of cost of goods sold	
in 1998, net of income tax expense of $13,500	16,500
Balance, January 1, 1999, as corrected	816,500

Illustration 15-10

Statement presentation of prior period correction

Case in point What would be the impact on the 1999 financials if this error was not corrected in 1998? Cost of goods sold expense would be understated (because beginning inventory was understated), and net income would be overstated. Retained earnings has self-corrected on the balance sheet at the end of the period.

▸*Ethics note*

Changes in accounting principles should result in financial statements that are more informative for statement users. They should not be used to artificially improve the reported performance and financial position of the corporation.

Reporting either the correction or the related income tax amounts in the current year's income statement would be incorrect, because they apply to the prior year's income.

If 1998 financial results are presented with the 1999 financial statements for comparative purposes, 1998 amounts would be restated using the correct cost of goods sold expense and inventory amounts. An appropriately cross-referenced footnote should show the impact of the correction and the fact that the prior year's statements have been restated.

Change in Accounting Principle

To make comparisons easier, financial statements from the current period should be prepared using the same bases that were that used for the preceding period. That is, if a choice of generally accepted accounting principles is available, the principle initially chosen should be consistently applied from period to period. A **change in an accounting principle** (also known as accounting policy) occurs when the principle used in the current year is different from the one used in the preceding year.

A change is permitted when management thinks that the new generally accepted accounting principle results in a more appropriate presentation than the old generally accepted accounting principle. Examples of a change in accounting principle include a change in amortization methods (e.g., declining-balance to straight-line) and a change in inventory costing methods (e.g., FIFO to average cost). Since the new principle must be applied retroactively, the effect of a change in an accounting principle on retained earnings may be significant.

▸Accounting in Action ▸ *Business Insight*

 BCE changed the way amortization expense is calculated in response to regulatory changes. They anticipated that this change would improve their comparability to their competitors. This change in accounting principle decreased 1997 retained earnings by $2.9 billion.

Like the correction of a prior period error, the cumulative income effects of a change in accounting principle is reported, net of applicable taxes, as an adjustment to the opening balance of retained earnings. To illustrate, we will assume that at the beginning of 1999 St. Onge Limited changes from the straight-line method of amortization to the declining-balance method for equipment which had been purchased on January 1, 1996. The cumulative effect of this change is to increase amortization expense and decrease net capital assets (because of the increase accumulated amortization) for the years 1996–1998.

Retained earnings is affected by the change in amortization expense and income tax expense, both of which affect net income. Assume that the total increase in amortization expense during the period 1996–1998 amounts to $24,000, which decreases income before income taxes by $24,000. If the company had a 30% tax rate, the after tax effect of the change would be $16,800 [$24,000 x (1–30%)]. The entry to record this change in accounting principle is:

Before You Go On ...

►*Review It*

1. How are retained earnings restrictions generally reported?
2. Distinguish between a correction of a prior period error and a change in accounting principle.
3. What are the principal sources of debits and credits to Retained Earnings?

►*Do It*

Vega Corporation has retained earnings of $5,130,000 on January 1, 1999. During the year, the company earns $2,000,000 of net income and declares and pays a $250,000 cash dividend. In 1999, Vega records an adjustment of $180,000, net of applicable income taxes, for an overstatement of 1998 ending inventory due to a mathematical error. Prepare a statement of retained earnings for 1999.

Reasoning: The $180,000 correction of 1998 inventory is a prior period adjustment, which should be reported as a deduction from the beginning retained earnings balance. That is, if ending inventory is overstated, then cost of goods sold is understated. If expenses (CGS) are understated, then net income is overstated. Net income is shown as an addition in the statement and dividends are deducted in the statement.

Solution:

VEGA CORPORATION
Statement of Retained Earnings
For the Year Ended December 31, 1999

Balance, January 1, as previously reported	$5,130,000
Less: Correction for overstatement of ending inventory, net of applicable income taxes	(180,000)
Balance, January 1, as corrected	4,950,000
Add: Net income	2,000,000
	6,950,000
Less: Cash dividends	250,000
Balance, December 31	$6,700,000

Related exercise material: BE15–4, BE15–7, E15–1, E15–3, E15–6, E15–8, and E15–9.

▼Corporation Income Statements

The income statement helps users to evaluate the past performance of managers and estimate future cash flows. **Income statements for corporations are the same as the statements for proprietorships or partnerships except for the reporting of income taxes.**

STUDY OBJECTIVE
········ 4 ··········
Describe the form and content of corporation income statements.

Accounting in Action ▸ *Business Insight*

   Net income and its components, as reported in the income statement, measure a company's performance. The amount and trend of net income (earnings) are, therefore, of vital importance to management, shareholders, and creditors, among others. Net income results in an increase in retained earnings, and it provides an indication of the amount of dividends that a company may distribute.

Although financial theories state that reported net income should not affect a company's value, in reality net income has a major effect on the market price of a company's stock. For example, when Markham-based Geac Computer Corp. announced a record quarterly profit of $20.5 million, the price of its stock skyrocketed 25% in one day.

Corporate Income Tax

For income tax purposes, a corporation is considered a separate legal entity. As a result, **income tax expense** is reported in a separate section of the corporation income statement, located before net income. The condensed income statement for Leads Inc. in Illustration 15-15 shows a typical presentation. Note that income before income taxes is reported before income tax expense.

Illustration 15-15

Income statement with income taxes

Helpful hint Corporations may also use the single-step form of income statement discussed in Chapter 5.

LEADS INC. Income Statement For the Year Ended December 31, 1999	
Sales	$800,000
Cost of goods sold	600,000
Gross profit	200,000
Operating expenses	50,000
Income from operations	150,000
Other revenues and gains	10,000
Other expenses and losses	4,000
Income before income taxes	156,000
Income tax expense	46,800
Net income	$109,200

As discussed in Chapter 11, income tax expense and the related liability for income taxes payable are recorded as part of the adjusting process which precedes financial statement preparation.

 Accounting in Action ▸ *Ethics Insight*

A recent Statistics Canada report, *The Size of the Underground Economy in Canada*, speculates that many small businesses hide some of their income to avoid income tax. The underground economy, which includes unreported transactions in addition to other illegal activities, is estimated to total about 5% of GDP. This translates to $5–$15 billion in lost government revenue.

Revenue Canada's reaction indicates how concerned the government is about the underground economy. They are now devoting 1,200 members of their current staff to the reduction of tax-avoidance transactions related to the underground economy. They also hired 800 additional staff members to ensure that self-employed and unincorporated businesses comply with income reporting requirements.

Source: Atlantic Progress, January/February 1997, 9.

Interperiod Tax Allocation

Income taxes are, in reality, far more complicated than the preceding presentation implies. As discussed in earlier chapters, the accounting objectives for revenues and expenses for GAAP purposes differ from the accounting objectives for revenues and expenses for Revenue Canada's purposes. Because of this, timing differences often occur, as transactions must be recorded in one period for accounting purposes (in order to determine income tax expense) and in another period for income tax purposes (to determine the amount owed to Revenue Canada). These timing differences result in **deferred taxes**.

Deferred taxes are discussed at length in intermediate accounting courses. For now, it should be said that the income tax expense amount presented in many financial statements is usually divided between the amount currently due (**current**) and the amount due in the future (**deferred**). The act of dividing the amounts is called interperiod tax allocation. An illustration of interperiod income tax allocation is presented in the income statement of The Second Cup Ltd. in Appendix A.

Intraperiod Tax Allocation (Net of Tax)

Intraperiod tax allocation refers to the procedure of associating income taxes in a specified period with their related item of income. This can be contrasted with **interperiod tax allocation**, in which income taxes are allocated between two or more periods. Under intraperiod tax allocation, the income tax expense or tax saving is shown for income before income taxes; it is also identified for each non-typical item, as discussed in the next section of this chapter.

Earlier in the chapter, this concept was applied to the adjustments made to opening retained earnings (to corrections of prior period errors, and to changes in accounting principle). Intraperiod tax allocation provides statement users with informative disclosure of the income tax effects of these components. The general concept is "let the tax follow the income or loss."

Presentation of Non-Typical Items

The income statements we have studied so far provide considerable insight into a company's income-related activities. In studying such statements, the user may ask: (1) are the results typical for this company? and (2) are the results a reasonable indicator of the company's future earnings?

To provide answers to these questions, accountants recommend additional sections in the income statement to **report material items not typical of regular operations**. These items are reported in the income statement immediately before net income. The non-typical items include: (1) discontinued operations, and (2) extraordinary items. Each item reported in the income statement should be carefully explained in the notes to the financial statements. The income statement should also apply intraperiod tax allocation, reporting the income tax expense or savings applicable to each item.

Discontinued Operations

Many Canadian companies have been restructuring their organizations in recent years. For example, Cara Operations Limited sold Grand & Toy, Canada's largest office products company, to Boise Cascade Corporation for $146 million. This divesture allowed Cara "to refocus on what we know best: food service." In their income statement, Cara reported this sale in a separate section entitled "discontinued operations."

Discontinued operations refers to the disposal of a **significant segment** of a business, such as the cessation of an entire activity or the elimination of a major class of customers. Thus, John Labatt Limited's decision to terminate its interest in its dairy business was reported as discontinued operations. On the other hand, the phasing out of a model such as the Ford Thunderbird, or part of a product line, is not considered a disposal of a segment.

When the disposal of a significant segment occurs, the income statement should report both income from continuing operations and income (or loss) from discontinued operations. **The income (loss) from discontinued operations consists of the income (loss) from these operations and the gain (loss) on disposal of the segment: both items are presented net of applicable income taxes.**

To illustrate, assume that Hwa Energy Inc. has revenues of $2.5 million and expenses of $1.7 million from continuing operations in 1999. The company, therefore, has income before income taxes of $800,000. During 1999 the company discontinued and sold its unprofitable chemical division. The loss in 1999 from chemical operations was $140,000 ($200,000 net of $60,000 taxes), and the loss on disposal of the chemical division was $70,000 ($100,000 net of $30,000 taxes). The income statement presented below applies intraperiod tax allocation, and assumes a 30% tax rate:

Illustration 15-16

Statement presentation of discontinued operations

Helpful hint   Observe the dual disclosures: (1) the results of operations of the discontinued division (which must be eliminated from the results of continuing operations), and (2) the disposal of the operation.

HWA ENERGY INC. Partial Income Statement For the Year Ended December 31, 1999		
Income before income taxes		$800,000
Income tax expense		240,000
Income from continuing operations		560,000
Discontinued operations		
Loss from operations of chemical division, net of $60,000		
income tax saving	$140,000	
Loss from disposal of chemical division, net of $30,000		
income tax saving	70,000	210,000
Net income		$350,000

Note that the caption "Income from continuing operations" is used, and that a section called "Discontinued operations" is added. Income tax expense is allocated between these two sections. This presentation clearly indicates the separate effects of continuing operations and discontinued operations on net income.

Intraperiod tax allocation.   To illustrate the importance of intraperiod tax allocation, introduced earlier in this chapter, let's demonstrate the misleading results that may occur when intraperiod tax allocation is not followed. Without intraperiod tax allocation, Hwa's income statement would show:

Illustration 15-17

Partial income statement without intraperiod tax allocation

Partial Income Statement Without Tax Allocation		
Income before income taxes		$800,000
Income tax expense ($240,000 – $60,000 – $30,000)		150,000
Income from continuing operations		650,000
Discontinued operations		
Loss from operations of chemical division	$200,000	
Loss from disposal of chemical division	100,000	300,000
Net income		$350,000

This presentation is misleading, because income taxes are not directly related to the income or loss. The tax effects of income before taxes and income from discontinued operations have been combined in the reported income tax expense of $150,000. Income from continuing operations is distorted and not a faithful representation of events.

Note that net income remains unchanged at $350,000, whether intraperiod tax allocation is applied or not. However, **intraperiod tax allocation matches the tax to the items that affect the tax**, and the presentation in Illustration 15-16 does not have the weakness found in Illustration 15-17.

Extraordinary Items

Extraordinary items are events and transactions that meet three conditions. They are:

1. not expected to occur frequently
2. not typical of normal business activities
3. not subject to management's discretion

To be regarded as infrequent, the event or transaction should not be expected again in the foreseeable future. To be considered atypical, the item should be only incidentally related to the normal activities of the entity. To be judged outside of management's discretion, it should not depend primarily on decisions by management, including owners' directives.

In reality, extraordinary items are rare. Illustration 15-18 shows the appropriate classification of extraordinary and ordinary items.

► *International note*

Canada, Australia, the U.S., and the U.K. segregate extraordinary items (they are called exceptional in the U.K.). Other countries, however, do not distinguish between ordinary and extraordinary items.

Illustration 15-18

Examples of extraordinary and ordinary items

Extraordinary items

1. Effects of major casualties (acts of God) if rare in the area.

2. Expropriation (takeover) of property by a government.

3. Effects of a newly enacted law or regulation, such as a condemnation action.

Ordinary items

1. Effects of major casualties (acts of God) if frequent in the area.

2. Write-down of inventories or write off of receivables.

3. Losses attributable to labour disputes.

4. Gains or losses from sale of capital assets.

To evaluate all three criteria necessary to determine whether an item is extraordinary or not (on previous page), one must consider the environment in which the entity operates. Thus, Weyerhaeuser Co.—a paper, pulp, and packaging company—reported the $36 million in damages to its timberland caused by the nearby volcanic eruption of Mount St. Helens as an extraordinary item because the event was infrequent, atypical, and not determined by management. In contrast, Canada West Tree Fruits Ltd. in the Okanagan Valley does not report frost damage to its fruit crop as an extraordinary item because frost damage is not infrequent there.

Extraordinary items are reported net of taxes in a separate section of the income statement, immediately below discontinued operations. To illustrate, assume that in 1999 the government expropriated property held by Hwa Energy Inc., to facilitate the construction of a highway. If the loss is $70,000 before applicable income taxes of $21,000, the income statement presentation will show a deduction of $49,000, as shown in Illustration 15-19.

Illustration 15-19

Statement presentation of extraordinary items

HWA ENERGY INC. Partial Income Statement For the Year Ended December 31, 1999		
Income before income taxes		$800,000
Income tax expense		240,000
Income from continuing operations		560,000
Discontinued operations		
Loss from operations of chemical division, net of $60,000 income tax saving	$140,000	
Loss from disposal of chemical division, net of $30,000 income tax saving	70,000	210,000
Income before extraordinary item		350,000
Extraordinary item		
Expropriation of property, net of $21,000 income tax saving		49,000
Net income		$301,000

As illustrated, the caption "Income before extraordinary item" is added immediately before the section for the extraordinary item. This presentation clearly indicates the effect of the extraordinary item on net income. If there are no discontinued operations, the third line of the income statement in Illustration 15-19 would be labelled "Income before extraordinary item."

If a transaction or event meets one or more (but not all) of the criteria for an extraordinary item, it is reported under either "Other revenues and gains" or "Other expenses and losses" at its gross amount (without tax effect). This is true, for example, of gains (losses) resulting from the sale of capital assets, as explained in Chapter 10.

►Accounting in Action ► *Business Insight*

Catastrophic losses in Canada reached a record high of $600 million in 1996. This figure included losses resulting from flooding in the Saguenay region of Quebec, a severe hailstorm in Calgary, and winter storms on the west coast. The year 1997 wasn't much better: the Red River Valley flood in Manitoba was hailed as the flood of the century. Flood damage to public and private property exceeded $450 million; the economic loss from business interruptions alone totalled tens of millions of dollars.

In 1998 Canadians continued to reel from the effects of El Niño: the ice storm in Quebec and neighbouring provinces was hailed as the storm of the century. The ice storm was the most costly natural disaster in Canadian history, with losses in the range of $2 billion.

Before You Go On . . .
►*Review It*

1. What is the unique feature of a corporation income statement?
2. What is the primary objective of intraperiod tax allocation?
3. What are the similarities and differences in reporting material items not typical of regular operations?

►*Do It*

In its proposed 1998 income statement, W. Laws Co. Ltd. reported income before income taxes of $400,000, including a $75,000 loss incurred from closing six of 30 stores, extraordinary loss from fire of $100,000, and an income tax rate of 45%. Prepare a correct income statement, using intraperiod tax allocation, beginning with income before income taxes.

Reasoning: The $75,000 loss is correctly reported as part of continuing income. It is not a loss from discontinued operations, because Laws continues to operate other stores in the same line of business. The extraordinary loss should be disclosed separately from continuing income. Under intraperiod tax allocation, the income tax effect of each non-typical component is disclosed in the income statement. Thus, the extraordinary loss should be reported net of income taxes.

Solution:

W. LAWS CO. LTD.
(Partial) Income Statement

Income before income taxes	$400,000
Income tax expense (45%)	180,000
Income before extraordinary item	220,000
Extraordinary loss from fire, net of $45,000 income tax saving	55,000
Net income	$165,000

Related exercise material: BE15–5, BE15–6, E15–10, and E15–11.

Using the Information in the Financial Statements

STUDY OBJECTIVE

7

Compute earnings per share and the price-earnings ratio.

Two ratios related to income are frequently reported in the financial press and are widely used by shareholders and potential investors in evaluating the profitability of a company. The **earnings per share ratio** is one of the most significant pieces of information provided by the accounting system for the benefit of users. Earnings per share disclosures are required for publicly held companies and recommended for private companies. Investors, and others, link earnings per share to the market price per share. This linkage produces the **price-earnings ratio**.

Earnings Per Share

Case in point It might seem logical to call it net income per share. However, only earnings per share is used in the business world.

Earnings per share (EPS) indicates the net income earned by each share of outstanding common stock. Thus, **earnings per share is reported only for common stock**. The formula for computing earnings per share when there has been no change in outstanding shares during the year is as follows:

Illustration 15-20

Earnings per share formula —no change in outstanding shares

For example, if Skateboard Co. has net income of $200,000 and 50,000 shares of common stock outstanding for the year, earnings per share is $4 ($200,000 ÷ 50,000).

Because of the importance of earnings per share, most companies report it directly on the face of their income statement, rather than by a note to the statements. Generally, this amount is simply reported below net income on the statement. For Skateboard Co. the presentation would be:

Illustration 15-21

Basic earnings per share disclosure

Net Income	$200,000
Earnings per share	$ 4

When the income statement contains an item from the two additional sections described earlier in the chapter—discontinued operations or extraordinary items—EPS should be disclosed for each component. Assume that Hwa Energy had 100,000 shares of common stock outstanding during the year; the additional EPS disclosures for the income statement shown in Illustration 15-19 would be as shown below:

Illustration 15-22

Additional earnings per share disclosures

Net income	$301,000
Earnings per share	
Income from continuing operations	$5.60
Loss from discontinued operations	(2.10)
Income before extraordinary item	3.50
Extraordinary loss	(.49)
Net income	$3.01

These disclosures enable decision makers to recognize the effects on EPS of income from continuing operations, as distinguished from income or loss from material items not typical of regular operations. **Earnings per share from continuing operations is generally the most useful per share amount**, because it represents the results of continuing and ordinary business activity. Thus, it provides the best basis for predicting future operating results.

The computation of earnings per share may involve one or all of the following: (1) weighted average shares outstanding, (2) preferred stock dividends, and (3) complex capital structures.

Weighted Average Shares Outstanding

If there has been any change in the number of shares of common stock outstanding during the year, the weighted average shares outstanding should be used in computing EPS. The **weighted average shares** are computed by determining the time a given number of shares is outstanding during the period. To illustrate, assume that Rally Inc. had 100,000 shares of common stock outstanding on January 1 and issued an additional 10,000 shares of stock on October 1. The weighted average number of shares of stock for the year is computed as follows:[1]

100,000	shares x 12/12 of a year	100,000	shares outstanding for a full year
10,000	shares x 3/12 of a year	2,500	shares outstanding for three months
		102,500	Weighted average shares outstanding

Illustration 15-23

Computation of weighted average shares outstanding

The weighted average is used because the issuance of stock changes the amount of net assets that is available during the period for revenues.

Preferred Stock Dividends

Earnings per share relates to earnings per share of **common stock**. When a corporation has both preferred and common stock outstanding, the current year's dividend declared on preferred stock is subtracted from net income to determine **income available to common shareholders**. Assuming weighted average common stock is involved, the formula for computing EPS is:

Illustration 15-24

Expanded earnings per share formula

To illustrate, assume that Rally Inc. reports net income of $211,000 on its 102,500 weighted average common shares. During the year it also declares a $6,000 dividend

---

[1] An alternative acceptable computation of weighted average shares outstanding is:

100,000 shares outstanding for the last 3 months of the year (100,000 × 9/12) =	75,000 shares
110,000 shares outstanding for the first 9 months of the year (110,000 × 3/12) =	27,500 shares
	102,500 Total weighted average shares

on its preferred stock. Therefore, Rally has $205,000 ($211,000 − $6,000) available for common stock dividends. Earnings per share is $2 ($205,000 ÷ 102,500). If the preferred stock is cumulative, the dividend for the current year is deducted, whether or not it is declared.

Complex Capital Structure

When a corporation has securities that may be converted into common stock—which, if converted, would reduce or dilute the earnings per share—the corporation has a complex capital structure. Two examples of such securities are convertible bonds (discussed in Chapter 16) and convertible preferred stock (discussed in Chapter 14). The adverse effect that these securities can have on EPS is significant. More importantly, the effect of convertible securities on EPS would be unexpected unless financial statements call attention to the potential effect.

Two earnings per share figures are computed and reported when convertible securities have a material effect on EPS.[2] The first EPS figure is called basic earnings per share. It is based on the weighted average common shares outstanding, plus shares referred to as common stock equivalents. Common stock equivalents are securities that will probably be converted into common shares. For example, convertible preferred stock would be classified as a common stock equivalent if it is likely to be converted into common stock.

The second EPS figure, referred to as fully diluted earnings per share, assumes the maximum dilution (reduction) possible. It reflects the dilution in earnings per share that would occur if *all* dilutive securities were converted into common shares. Potentially dilutive securities that are not considered a common stock equivalent (and so are not used for computing basic earnings per share) are included for computing fully diluted earnings per share. Thus, **fully diluted earnings per share is lower than basic earnings per share**. The following excerpt from the income statement of the Bank of Montreal illustrates the statement presentation of basic and fully diluted earnings per share.

Case in point   Recently, Coca-Cola Beverages Ltd., Sears Canada Inc., and George Weston Limited were among the many major companies that reported only basic EPS data.

Illustration 15-25

Basic and fully diluted earning per share disclosure

BANK OF MONTREAL	
Net Income (in millions of dollars except per share amounts)	$ 1,305
Preferred dividends	$ 83
Net income available to common shareholders	$ 1,222
Average common shares outstanding (in thousands)	260,410
Net Income Per Common Share (note 14)	
Basic	$ 4.69
Fully diluted	$ 4.62

Some companies with net losses, such as GUARD, Inc., in the opening story and Second Cup in 1996, report a loss per share. If only one figure is reported for earnings (loss) per share, it is assumed to be basic earnings per share. Either no fully diluted earnings per share exist, or they are not materially different from basic.

The computations for determining basic and fully diluted earnings per share are complex. They include additional earnings per share computations known as adjusted basic earnings per share and pro forma earnings per share. Earnings per share will be discussed extensively in future accounting courses.

---

[2] The accounting profession considers a material dilutive effect to exist when the potential reduction to earnings per share is 3% or more. Thus, $0.31 per share would be considered materially different than $0.32 ($0.01 ÷ $0.32 = 3.1%), but $9.75 per share would not be considered materially different than $10.00 ($0.25 ÷ $10.00 = 2.5%).

Price-Earnings Ratio

The **price-earnings (P/E) ratio** helps investors determine whether the stock is a good investment in relation to earnings. It is a per share calculation, computed by dividing the market price of the stock by its earnings per share.

To illustrate, we will calculate the price-earnings ratio for the Bank of Montreal, assuming a market price of $60.85 and using the basic earnings per share figure presented in Illustration 15-25.

Illustration 15-26

Computation of price-earnings ratio

This ratio would be read as indicating that the Bank of Montreal stock is trading 13 times earnings. A high P/E ratio can be one indicator that the market believes the company has future growth potential.

Before You Go On . . .
►Review It

1. Explain the components of the formula for computing earnings per share when there is only common stock, and outstanding shares are unchanged during the year.
2. How are weighted average shares outstanding computed?
3. What effect does preferred stock have on the formula for computing earnings per share?
4. What is the difference between basic and fully diluted earnings per share?
5. How is the price-earnings ratio computed?

Related exercise material: BE15–8, BE15–9, BE15–10, and E15–12.

►A Look Back at GUARD, Inc.

To answer the following questions, refer to the opening story.
1. Although GUARD has chosen not to pay cash dividends to its shareholders in the past, would it be permitted to pay a cash dividend in the upcoming year if management chose that option?
2. If GUARD is unable to declare a cash dividend, would a stock dividend be a suitable option instead?
3. Prepare the closing journal entry that GUARD would make to close its net loss to retained earnings. Assume revenues and expenses have already been closed.
4. GUARD had a 2,984,185 weighted average number of common shares outstanding in 1996. Compute the loss per share for 1996. Do you have enough information to compute GUARD'S price-earnings ratio?

Solution:

1. In order for GUARD to pay a cash dividend, it must have sufficient retained earnings, adequate cash, and a formal declaration of the dividend by the Board of Directors. All three criteria must be met. GUARD does not have any retained earnings, and it is not permitted to create (or increase) a deficit through the payment of dividends. Therefore, no dividend can be declared.

2. As discussed in (1), GUARD has insufficient retained earnings to declare or pay any type of dividend—whether cash or stock.

3.

Deficit	843,397	
Income Summary		843,397
(To close net loss)		

4.

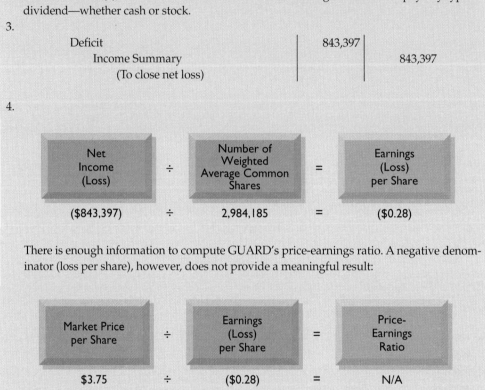

Net Income (Loss)	÷	Number of Weighted Average Common Shares	=	Earnings (Loss) per Share
($843,397)	÷	2,984,185	=	($0.28)

There is enough information to compute GUARD's price-earnings ratio. A negative denominator (loss per share), however, does not provide a meaningful result:

Market Price per Share	÷	Earnings (Loss) per Share	=	Price-Earnings Ratio
$3.75	÷	($0.28)	=	N/A

▼*Summary of Study Objectives*
....

1. *Prepare the entries for cash dividends, stock dividends, and stock splits, and compare their financial impact.* Entries for both cash and stock dividends are required at the declaration date and the payment or distribution date. There is no entry for a stock split. Cash dividends reduce assets and shareholders' equity (retained earnings). Stock dividends reduce retained earnings and increase common stock, but have no impact on total shareholders' equity. Stock splits reduce the market price of the stock and its legal capital per share, and increase the number of shares issued, but overall have no impact on the financial position of the firm.

2. *Identify the items that are reported in a statement of retained earnings.* Additions to retained earnings include net income, corrections of understatements of prior years' net income, and increases due to the cumulative effect of a change in accounting principle. Deductions consist of net loss, correc-

tions of overstatements of prior years' net income, decreases due to the cumulative effect of a change in accounting principle, and cash and stock dividends.

3. *Prepare a comprehensive shareholders' equity section.* A comprehensive shareholders' equity section includes all shareholders' equity accounts. It consists of two sections: contributed capital and retained earnings. It should also include notes to the financial statements that explain adjustments to opening retained earnings, restrictions on retained earnings, and dividends in arrears, if any.

4. *Describe the form and content of corporation income statements.* The form and content of corporation income statements are similar to the statements of proprietorships and partnerships with one exception: income tax expense must be reported in a separate section before net income in the corporation's income statement.

5. *Explain the concept of intraperiod tax allocation.* Intraperiod tax allocation refers to the procedure of associating income taxes with the specific item that directly affects the income taxes for the period.

6. *Indicate the statement presentation of material items not typical of regular operations.* Material items not typical of regular operations are reported net of taxes in sections on the income statement immediately before net income. These items include: (a) discontinued operations, and (b) extraordinary items.

7. *Compute earnings per share and the price-earnings ratio.* Earnings (loss) per share is computed by dividing net income (loss) by the number of common shares outstanding during the period. Additional complications arise when shares outstanding must be weighted and when preferred stock dividends and complex capital structures are involved. The price-earnings ratio is computed by dividing the market price per share by the earnings per share.

GLOSSARY

Basic earnings per share   The amount of earnings (or loss) per share based on the weighted average common shares outstanding plus common stock equivalents. (p. 638).

Cash dividend   A pro rata equal distribution of cash to shareholders. (p. 616).

Change in accounting principle   The use of a generally accepted accounting principle in the current year that is different from the one used in the preceding year. (p. 626).

Complex capital structure   A situation in which a corporation has securities outstanding that may be converted into common stock, which, if converted, would reduce or dilute earnings per share. (p. 638).

Correction of a prior period error   The correction of an error in previously issued financial statements. (p. 625).

Declaration date   The date the board of directors formally declares the dividend and announces it to shareholders. (p. 617).

Deficit   A debit (negative) balance in retained earnings. (p. 623).

Discontinued operations   The disposal of a significant segment of a business. (p. 632).

Dividend   A distribution of cash, property, scrip, or shares by a corporation to its shareholders on a pro rata (equal) basis. (p. 616).

Earnings per share (EPS)   The net income (or loss) earned by each share of outstanding common stock. (p. 636).

Extraordinary items   Events and transactions that are infrequent, atypical, and not at the discretion of management. (p. 633).

Fully diluted earnings per share   An amount that shows the maximum dilution possible in earnings (loss) per share. (p. 638).

Interperiod tax allocation   The allocation of income tax expense between two or more periods to record the amount which is currently due and the amount which is due in the future (deferred). (p. 631).

Intraperiod tax allocation   The procedure of associating income taxes with the specific item that directly affects the income taxes for the period. (p. 631).

Payment date   The date cash dividend cheques are mailed to shareholders. For a stock dividends, the date the shares are distributed to shareholders. (p. 618).

Price-earnings (P/E) ratio   The ratio of the market price of a common share to earnings per common share. (p. 639).

Record date   The date when ownership of outstanding shares is determined for dividend purposes. (p. 618).

Retained earnings restrictions   Circumstances that make a portion of retained earnings currently unavailable for dividends. (p. 624).

Statement of retained earnings   A financial statement that shows the changes in retained earnings during the year. (p. 627).

Stock dividend   A pro rata equal distribution of the corporation's own shares to shareholders. (p. 619).

Stock split   The issuance of additional shares of stock to shareholders according to their percentage ownership, accompanied by a reduction in the legal value per share. (p. 621).

DEMONSTRATION PROBLEM

The events and transactions of the Dever Corporation for the year ending December 31, 1999, resulted in the following data:

Cost of goods sold	$2,600,000
Net sales	4,400,000
Other expenses and losses	9,600
Other revenues and gains	5,600
Selling and administrative expenses	1,100,000
Dividends declared	40,000
Income from operations of plastics division	70,000
Gain on sale of plastics division	500,000
Retained earnings, January 1, 1999	700,000
Loss from tornado disaster (extraordinary loss)	600,000
Cumulative effect of changing from straight-line amortization to double-declining-balance (increase in amortization expense)	300,000

Analysis reveals that:

1. All items are before the applicable income tax rate of 30%.
2. The plastics division was sold on July 1.
3. All operating data for the plastics division have been segregated.
4. There were 100,000 shares of common stock outstanding during the year.

Instructions

Prepare an income statement for the year, including the presentation of earnings per share data, and a statement of retained earnings.

Solution to Demonstration Problem

DEVER CORPORATION
Income Statement
For the Year Ended December 31, 1999

Net sales		$4,400,000
Cost of goods sold		2,600,000
Gross profit		1,800,000
Selling and administrative expenses		1,100,000
Income from operations		700,000
Other revenues and gains	$ 5,600	
Other expenses and losses	9,600	4,000
Income before income taxes		696,000
Income tax expense ($696,000 x 30%)		208,800
Income from continuing operations		487,200
Discontinued operations		
Income from operations of plastics division, net of $21,000 income taxes ($70,000 x 30%)	$ 49,000	
Gain on sale of plastics division, net of $150,000 income taxes ($500,000 x 30%)	350,000	399,000
Income before extraordinary item		886,200
Extraordinary item		
Tornado loss, net of income tax saving $180,000 ($600,000 x 30%)		420,000
Net income		$ 466,200
Earnings per share		
Income from continuing operations		$4.87
Income from discontinued operations		3.99
Income before extraordinary item		8.86
Extraordinary loss		(4.20)
Net income		$4.66

DEVER CORPORATION
Statement of Retained Earnings
For the Year Ended December 31, 1999

Retained earnings, January 1, 1999—as previously reported	$ 700,000
Less: Effect on prior years of change in accounting principle (method of amortization) $300,000, net of 30% income tax saving, $90,000	210,000
Retained earnings, January 1, 1999—as adjusted	490,000
Add: Net income for 1999	466,200
	956,200
Less: Dividends declared	40,000
Retained earnings, December 31, 1999	$ 916,200

SELF-STUDY QUESTIONS

Answers are at the end of the chapter.

(SO 1)   1. Entries for cash dividends are required on the:

     a. declaration date and the payment date.

     b. record date and the payment date.

     c. declaration date, record date, and payment date.

     d. declaration date and the record date.

(SO 1)   2. Which of the following statements about stock dividends is true?

     a. A debit to Retained Earnings for the par value (if any) of the shares issued should be made.

     b. A stock dividend decreases total shareholders' equity.

     c. Market value per share is usually assigned to the dividend shares.

     d. A stock dividend ordinarily will have no effect on book value per share of stock.

(SO 2)   3. Which one of the following is *not* reported in a statement of retained earnings.

     a. cash and stock dividends.

     b. net income and net loss.

     c. corrections of errors in prior periods' income.

     d. sales of stock above stated value.

(SO 2, 6)   4. A prior period adjustment is:

     a. reported in the income statement as a non-typical item.

     b. made directly to retained earnings.

     c. reported directly in the shareholders' equity section.

     d. reported in the statement of retained earnings as an adjustment of the ending balance of retained earnings.

5. In the balance sheet, Stock Dividends Distributable is reported as: (SO 1)

     a. a deduction from total contributed capital and retained earnings.

     b. an addition to contributed capital.

     c. a deduction from retained earnings.

     d. a current liability.

6. Corporation income statements may be the same as the income statements for unincorporated companies, except for: (SO 4)

     a. gross profit.

     b. income tax expense.

     c. operating income.

     d. net sales.

7. Intraperiod tax allocation refers to the: (SO 5)

     a. association of income taxes with the items that directly affect the income taxes for the period.

     b. allocation of income taxes to different accounting periods.

     c. system of deferring income taxes to later accounting periods.

     d. reporting of income taxes by interim accounting periods.

8. In reporting discontinued operations, the income statement should have a special section that shows: (SO 4, 6)

     a. gains and losses from the disposal of the discontinued segment.

     b. gains and losses from operations of the discontinued segment.

     c. Both (a) and (b).

     d. Neither (a) nor (b).

(SO 6)   9. The Rand Corporation has income before taxes of $400,000 and an extraordinary loss of $100,000. If the income tax rate is 25% on all items, the income statement should show income before extraordinary items and after extraordinary items, respectively, of:

    a. $325,000 and $100,000.

    b. $325,000 and $75,000.

    c. $300,000 and $100,000.

    d. $300,000 and $75,000

10. The income statement for Nadeen, Inc., shows income before income taxes $700,000, income tax expense $210,000, and net income $490,000. If Nadeen has 100,000 shares of common stock outstanding throughout the year, earnings per share is: (SO 7)

    a. $7.00.

    b. $4.90.

    c. $2.10.

    d. No correct answer is given.

QUESTIONS

1. (a) What is a dividend? (b) "Dividends must be paid in cash." Do you agree? Explain.

2. Robin O'Malley maintains that adequate cash is the only requirement for the declaration of a cash dividend. Is Robin correct? Explain.

3. (a) Three dates are important in connection with cash dividends. Identify the dates, and explain their significance to the corporation and its shareholders.

    (b) Identify the accounting entries that are made for a cash dividend and the date of each entry.

4. NVC Inc. declares a $45,000 cash dividend on December 31, 1999. The required annual dividend on preferred stock is $12,000. Determine the allocation of the dividend to preferred and common shareholders, assuming the preferred stock is cumulative and dividends are one year in arrears.

5. Contrast the effects of a cash dividend and a stock dividend on a corporation's balance sheet.

6. Jill Simmons asks, "Since stock dividends don't change anything, why declare them?" What is your answer to Jill?

7. Pella Corporation has 10,000 shares of common stock outstanding when they announce a 2-for-1 split. Before the split, the stock had a market price of $140 per share. After the split, how many shares of stock will be outstanding, and what will be the approximate market price per share?

8. The board of directors is considering a stock split or a stock dividend. They understand that total shareholders' equity will remain the same under either action. However, they are not sure of the different effects of the two types of actions on other aspects of shareholders' equity. Explain the differences to the directors.

9. What is a prior period adjustment, and how is it reported in the financial statements?

10. ABC Corporation has a retained earnings balance of $240,000 on January 1. During the year, a prior period adjustment of $90,000 is recorded because of the understatement of amortization in the prior period. Show the presentation of these data in the statement of retained earnings.

11. What is the purpose of a retained earnings restriction? Identify the possible causes of retained earnings restrictions.

12. How are retained earnings restrictions generally reported in the financial statements?

13. Identify the events that result in credits and debits to retained earnings.

14. Omar Radhah believes that both the beginning and ending balances in retained earnings are shown in the shareholders' equity section. Is Omar correct? Discuss.

15. Ellen Nels, who owns many investments in common stock, says, "I don't care what a company's net income is. The balance sheet tells me everything I need to know!" How do you respond to Ellen?

16. What is the unique feature of a corporation income statement? Illustrate this feature, using assumed data.

17. Define the term "intraperiod tax allocation." Why is this type of allocation important?

18. Why is it important to report discontinued operations separately from income from continuing operations?

19. You are considering investing in Tracey Transportation, which reports 1999 earnings per share of $6.50 on income before extraordinary items and $4.75 on net income. Which EPS figure would you consider more relevant to your investment decision? Why?

20. Iron Inc. reported 1998 earnings per share of $3.26 and had no extraordinary items. In 1999, EPS on income before extraordinary items was $2.99 and EPS on net income was $3.49. Is this a favourable trend?

21. Indicate which of the following items would be reported as an extraordinary item in Corus Corporation's income statement.

    (a) Loss from damages caused by earthquake tremors.

    (b) Loss from sale of temporary investments.

    (c) Loss attributable to a labour strike.

    (d) Loss caused when manufacture of a product was prohibited by the federal government.

(e) Loss from flood damage. (The nearby Black River floods every two to three years.)

(f) Write-down of obsolete inventory.

(g) Expropriation of a factory by a foreign government.

22. When studying for an accounting test, a fellow student says, "Changes in accounting principles are reported in the statement of retained earnings." Is your friend correct, or should he study harder?

23. Why must preferred dividends be subtracted from net income when computing earnings per share?

24. Jean Marin owns 100 shares of Redlands Corporation. She tells you, "The corporation earned net income of $1,000,000 and had 200,000 shares of common stock outstanding. That should be earnings per share of $5.00. But they reported basic earnings per share of $4.10 and fully diluted earnings per share of $3.69." Explain how these figures could be correct.

BRIEF EXERCISES

BE15–1 The C-B Corporation has 10,000 shares of common stock outstanding. It declares a $2 per share cash dividend on November 1 to shareholders in the records on December 1. The dividend is paid on December 31. Prepare the entries on the appropriate dates to record the declaration and payment of the cash dividend.

Prepare the entries for a cash dividend.
(SO 1)

BE15–2 Patina Corporation has 100,000 shares of no par value common stock outstanding. It declares a 10% stock dividend on December 1, when the market value per share is $15. The dividend shares are issued on December 31. Prepare the entries for the declaration and distribution of the stock dividend.

Prepare the entries for a stock dividend.
(SO 1)

BE15–3 The shareholders' equity section of Mertz Corporation consists of common stock (no par) $1,000,000 and retained earnings $400,000. A 10% stock dividend (10,000 shares) is declared when the market value per share is $16. Show the before-and-after effects of the dividend on: (a) the components of shareholders' equity, (b) shares outstanding, and (c) book value per share.

Show the before and after effects of a stock dividend.
(SO 1)

BE15–4 For the year ending December 31, 1999, Maddy Inc. reports net income $182,000 and dividends $85,000. Prepare the statement of retained earnings for the year, assuming the balance in retained earnings on January 1, 1999, was $220,000.

Prepare a statement of retained earnings.
(SO 2)

BE15–5 An inexperienced accountant for Lima Corporation showed the following in the income statement: Income before income taxes and extraordinary item $300,000 and extraordinary loss from flood (before taxes) $80,000. The extraordinary loss and taxable income are both subject to a 30% tax rate. Prepare a correct income statement using intraperiod tax allocation.

Show correct intraperiod tax allocation.
(SO 4, 5)

BE15–6 On June 30, Osbern Corporation discontinued its operations in Mexico. During the year, the operating loss on these operations was $400,000 before taxes. On September 1, Osbern disposed of the Mexico facility at a pretax loss of $160,000. The applicable tax rate is 30%. Show the discontinued operations section of the income statement.

Prepare a discontinued operations section of the income statement.
(SO 5, 6)

BE15–7 On January 1, 1999, Shirli, Inc., changed from the straight-line method of amortization to the declining-balance method. The cumulative effect of the change was to increase prior years' amortization by $50,000 and 1999 amortization by $8,000. Explain how the company should report the effects of this change on: (a) prior years, and (b) the current year. The income tax rate is 30%.

Explain how the effects of a change in accounting principle are reported.
(SO 2)

BE15–8 Genoa Corporation's income statement shows: Income from continuing operations $580,000, Loss from discontinued operations $200,000, and Extraordinary loss $80,000. Show the earnings per share data that should be presented in the income statement, assuming there are 100,000 shares of common stock outstanding throughout the year, and no preferred shares.

Show earnings per share data in the income statement.
(SO 7)

BE15–9

(a) Darlin Corporation reports net income of $380,000 and a weighted average of 200,000 shares of common stock outstanding for the year. Compute the earnings per share of common stock.

(b) Assume also that Darlin has cumulative preferred dividends for the current year of $20,000 that were declared and paid. Compute the earnings per share of common stock.

(c) Assume that the preferred dividends referred to in part (b) were not declared and paid. What difference would this make, in computing the earnings per share of common stock?

Compute earnings per share, with and without preferred shares.
(SO 7)

BE15–10 Lake Company reports basic earnings per share of $5.00, and its common stock is currently selling at $52.50 per share. Explain how its price-earning ratio would be affected by: (a) a 2% stock dividend and (b) a 2-for-1 stock split.

Explain effects of stock dividend and stock splits on price-earnings ratio.
(SO 1, 7)

EXERCISES

••

Journalize cash dividends and indicate statement presentation.
(SO 1, 2)

E15–1   On January 1, Tara Corporation had 75,000 shares of no par value common stock issued and outstanding. During the year, the following occurred:

Apr. 1 Issued 5,000 additional shares of common stock.
June 15 Declared a cash dividend of $1 per share to shareholders in the records on June 30.
July 10 Paid the $1 cash dividend.
Dec. 1 Issued 2,000 additional shares of common stock.
     15 Declared a cash dividend on outstanding shares of $1.50 per share to shareholders of record on December 31.

Instructions

(a) Prepare the entries required to record the dividends.
(b) How are dividends and dividends payable reported in the financial statements prepared at December 31?

Allocate cash dividends to preferred and common stock.
(SO 1)

E15–2   The Oshawa Corporation was organized on January 1, 1997. During its first year, the corporation issued 2,000 shares of no par value preferred stock and 100,000 shares of no par value common stock. At December 31, the company declared the following cash dividends: 1997 $6,000, 1998 $12,000, and 1999 $30,000.

Instructions

(a) Show the allocation of dividends to each class of stock assuming the preferred stock dividend is $4.50 and not cumulative.
(b) Show the allocation of dividends to each class of stock assuming the preferred stock dividend is $5.00 and cumulative.
(c) Journalize the declaration of the cash dividend at December 31, 1999, under part (b).

Journalize stock dividend; prepare a shareholders' equity section.
(SO 1, 3)

E15–3   On January 1, 1999, Kenya Corporation had $1,500,000 of common stock outstanding that was issued at $10, and retained earnings of $750,000. The company issued 50,000 shares of common stock at $14 on July 1, and earned net income of $400,000 for the year.

Instructions

(a) Journalize the declaration of a 10% stock dividend on December 10, 1999, when the market value is $16 per share.
(b) Prepare the shareholders' equity section at December 31, 1999, assuming that the stock dividend has not yet been distributed.

Compare the effects of a stock dividend and a stock split.
(SO 1)

E15–4   On October 31, the shareholders' equity section of Sarah Laine Company consists of Common stock $800,000 and Retained earnings $400,000. The company is considering the following two courses of action: (1) declaring a 10% stock dividend on the 80,000 $10 par value shares outstanding, or (2) effecting a 2-for-1 stock split that will reduce par value to $5 per share. The current market price is $14 per share.

Instructions

Prepare a tabular summary of the effects that the alternative actions would have on the components of shareholders' equity, outstanding shares, and book value per share. Use the following column headings: Before Action, After Stock Dividend, and After Stock Split.

Compute book value per share; indicate account balances after a stock dividend.
(SO 1)

E15–5   On October 1, Valentino Corporation's shareholders' equity is as follows:

Common stock, no par value (20,000 shares)	$225,000
Retained earnings	175,000
Total shareholders' equity	$400,000

On October 1, Valentino declares and distributes a 10% stock dividend when the market value of the stock is $18 per share.

Instructions

(a) Compute the book value per share: (1) before the stock dividend, and (2) after the stock dividend. (Round to two decimals.)
(b) Indicate the balances in the shareholders' equity accounts after the stock dividend shares have been distributed.

Indicate various effects on share-holders' equity components.
(SO 1, 2, 3)

E15–6 During 1999, Kettle Corporation had the following transactions and events:

1. Declared a cash dividend.
2. Issued no par value common stock for cash.
3. Completed a 3-for-1 stock split.
4. Declared a stock dividend.
5. Made a prior period adjustment for overstatement of net income.
6. Issued the shares of common stock required by the stock dividend declaration in (4) above.
7. Paid the cash dividend declared in (1) above.

Instructions

Indicate the effect(s) of each of the foregoing items on the subdivisions of shareholders' equity. Present your answer in tabular form with the following columns. Use I for increase, D for decrease, and NE for no effect. Item 1 is given as an example.

	Contributed Capital		
Item	**Capital Stock**	**Additional**	**Retained Earnings**
1.	NE	NE	D

Prepare correcting entries for dividends and a stock split.
(SO 1)

E15–7 Before preparing financial statements for the current year, the chief accountant for DeVito Company discovered the following errors in the accounts:

1. The declaration and payment of a $25,000 cash dividend was recorded as a debit to Interest Expense $25,000 and a credit to Cash $25,000.
2. A 10% stock dividend (1,000 shares) was declared on the no par value common stock when the market value per share was $10. The only entry made was: Retained Earnings (Dr.) $10,000 and Dividend Payable (Cr.) $10,000. The shares have not been issued.
3. The company declared a 4-for-1 stock split involving the issue of 400,000 shares of $5 stated value common stock for 100,000 shares of $20 stated value common stock. It was recorded as a debit to Retained Earnings $2,000,000 and a credit to Common Stock $2,000,000.

Instructions

Prepare the correcting entries at December 31.

Prepare a statement of retained earnings.
(SO 2)

E15–8 On January 1, 1999, Windsor Corporation had Retained Earnings of $580,000. During the year, Windsor had the following selected transactions:

1. Declared cash dividends $120,000.
2. Corrected overstatement of 1998 net income because of amortization error $20,000.
3. Earned net income $310,000.
4. Declared stock dividends $60,000.

Instructions

Prepare a statement of retained earnings for the year.

Prepare the shareholders' equity section.
(SO 3)

E15–9 The following accounts appear in the ledger of Ozabal Inc. after the books are closed at December 31:

Common Stock, no par, 400,000 shares authorized; 300,000 shares issued	$ 866,000
Common Stock Dividends Distributable	75,000
Preferred Stock, $5 par value, 8%, 40,000 shares authorized; 30,000 shares issued	150,000
Retained Earnings	900,000
Contributed Capital in Excess of Par Value—Preferred Stock	244,000

Instructions

Prepare the shareholders' equity section of the balance sheet at December 31, assuming $100,000 of retained earnings is restricted for plant expansion.

Prepare a corrected income statement.
(SO 4, 5, 6)

E15–10 For its fiscal year ending October 31, 1999, Dave Grometer Corporation reports the following partial data:

Income before income taxes	$640,000
Income tax expense (30% x $500,000)	150,000
Income before extraordinary items	490,000
Extraordinary loss from firestorm	140,000
Net income	$350,000

The fire loss is an extraordinary item. The income tax rate is 30% on all items.

Instructions

(a) Prepare a corrected income statement, beginning with income before income taxes.
(b) ◁▦▦▦▷ Explain, in memo form, why the original income statement data are misleading.

Prepare an income statement with non-typical items.
(SO 4, 5, 6)

E15–11   Dasola Corporation has income from continuing operations of $240,000 for the year ended December 31, 1999. It also has the following items (before considering income taxes): (1) an extraordinary loss of $60,000, (2) a gain of $50,000 on the discontinuation of a division, (3) a change in an accounting principle that resulted in an increase in prior years' amortization of $30,000, and (4) a correction of an error in last year's financial statements that resulted in a $20,000 understatement of 1998 net income. Assume all items are subject to income taxes at a 30% tax rate.

Instructions

(a) Prepare an income statement, beginning with income from continuing operations.
(b) Indicate the statement presentation of any items not included in (a) above.

Compute earnings per share under various assumptions.
(SO 7)

E15–12   The Morse Corporation has a simple capital structure. At December 31, 1999, the company has 2,000 shares of no par value, $8 cumulative preferred stock outstanding and 100,000 shares of no par value common stock issued. Morse's net income for the year is $600,000.

Instructions

Compute the earnings per share of common stock for each of the following separate situations. (Round to two decimals.)

(a) The dividend to preferred shareholders was declared, and there has been no change in the number of shares of common stock outstanding during the year.
(b) The dividend to preferred shareholders was declared, and 20,000 shares of common stock were issued on April 1, 1999.
(c) The dividend to preferred shareholders was not declared, and 20,000 shares of common stock were issued on April 1.

PROBLEMS

* *

Prepare dividend entries and a shareholders' equity section.
(SO 1, 3)

P15–1   On January 1, 1999, O'Brien Corporation had the following shareholders' equity accounts:

Common Stock (no par value, 80,000 shares issued and outstanding)	$1,000,000
Retained Earnings	540,000

During the year, the following transactions occurred:

Jan. 15 Declared a $1 cash dividend per share to shareholders of record on January 31, payable February 15.
Feb. 15 Paid the dividend declared in January.
Apr. 15 Declared a 10% stock dividend to shareholders of record on April 30, distributable May 15. On April 15, the market price of the stock was $13 per share.
May 15 Issued the shares for the stock dividend.
July 1 Announced a 2-for-1 stock split. The market price per share prior to the announcement was $15.
Dec. 1 Declared a $0.50 per share cash dividend to shareholders of record on December 15, payable January 10, 2000.
      31 Determined that net income for the year was $250,000.

Instructions

(a) Journalize the transactions and the closing entries for net income and dividends.
(b) Enter the beginning balances and post the entries in part (a) to the shareholders' equity accounts. (Note: Open additional shareholders' equity accounts as needed.)
(c) Prepare the shareholders' equity section of the balance sheet at December 31, 1999.

Prepare the shareholders' equity section, reflecting dividends and stock split.
(SO 1, 2, 3)

P15–2   On January 1, 1999, Stengel Corporation had the following shareholders' equity accounts:

Common Stock (no par value, 60,000 shares issued and outstanding)	$1,400,000
Retained Earnings	500,000

During the year, the following transactions occurred:
  Feb. 1 Declared a $1 cash dividend per share to shareholders of record on February 15, payable March 1.
  Mar. 1 Paid the dividend declared in February.
  Apr. 1 Announced a 4-for-1 stock split. Prior to the split, the market price per share was $36.
  July 1 Declared a 5% stock dividend to shareholders of record on July 15, distributable July 31. On July 1, the market price of the stock was $13 per share.
      31 Issued the shares for the stock dividend.
  Dec. 1 Declared a $0.50 per share dividend to shareholders of record on December 15, payable January 5, 2000.
      31 Determined that net income for the year was $350,000.

Instructions
Prepare the shareholders' equity section of the balance sheet at: (a) March 31, (b) June 30, (c) September 30, and (d) December 31, 1999.

P15–3   On January 1, 1999, Cedeno Inc. had the following shareholders' equity balances:

Common Stock, no par value (500,000 shares issued)	$1,500,000
Stock Dividends Distributable	200,000
Retained Earnings	600,000

Prepare the shareholders' equity section, reflecting various events.
(SO 1, 3)

During 1999, the following transactions and events occurred:
  1. Issued 50,000 shares of common stock as a result of a 10% stock dividend declared on December 15, 1998.
  2. Issued 30,000 shares of common stock for cash at $5 per share.
  3. Corrected an error that had understated the net income for 1997 by $70,000.
  4. Declared and paid a cash dividend of $100,000.
  5. Earned net income of $300,000.

Instructions
Prepare the shareholders' equity section of the balance sheet at December 31, 1999.

P15–4   The shareholders' equity accounts of Fryman Company at January 1, 1999, are as follows:

Preferred Stock, no par, 6000 shares issued	$300,000
Common Stock, no par, 250,000 shares issued	500,000
Retained Earnings	600,000

Journalize and post transactions; prepare the shareholders' equity section.
(SO 1, 3, 6)

During 1999, the company had the following transactions and events:
  July 7 Declared a $0.50 cash dividend on common stock.
  Aug. 1 Discovered a $45,000 understatement of 1998 amortization. (Ignore income taxes.)
  Sept. 1 Paid the cash dividend declared on July 1.
  Dec. 1 Declared a 10% stock dividend on common stock when the market value of the stock was $18 per share.
      15 Declared a $4.50 cash dividend on preferred stock, payable January 15, 2000. This was the full regular annual dividend on the preferred shares; there are no dividends in arrears.
      31 Determined that net income for the year was $385,000.
      31 Recognized a $200,000 restriction of retained earnings for plant expansion.

Instructions
  (a) Journalize the transactions, events, and closing entries.
  (b) Enter the beginning balances in the accounts and post to the shareholders' equity accounts. (Note: Open additional shareholders' equity accounts as needed.)
  (c) Prepare the shareholders' equity section of the balance sheet at December 31, 1999.

P15–5   The shareholders' equity accounts of Rodriguez, Inc., at January 1, 1999, are as follows:

Preferred Stock, no par, 4,000 shares issued	$400,000
Common Stock, no par, 180,000 shares issued	900,000
Retained Earnings	500,000

Prepare a statement of retained earnings, reflecting dividends and correction of error.
(SO 1, 2, 6)

During 1999, the company had the following transactions and events:

July 1 Declared a $0.50 cash dividend on common stock.

Aug. 1 Discovered a $72,000 overstatement of 1998 amortization. (Ignore income taxes.)

Sept. 1 Paid the cash dividend declared on July 1.

Dec. 1 Declared 10% stock dividend on common stock when the market value of the stock was $12 per share.

15 Declared a $9 per share cash dividend on preferred stock, payable January 31, 2000.

31 Determined that net income for the year was $350,000.

Instructions

Prepare a statement of retained earnings for the year. There are no preferred dividends in arrears.

Prepare the shareholders' equity section, reflecting various events.
(SO 1, 2, 3)

P15–6 After the books have been closed, the ledger of Reno Corporation at December 31, 1999, contains the following shareholders' equity accounts:

Preferred Stock (10,000 shares issued)	$1,000,000
Common Stock (400,000 shares issued)	2,000,000
Contributed Capital in Excess of Stated Value—Common	1,200,000
Common Stock Dividends Distributable	140,000
Retained Earnings	2,540,000

A review of the accounting records reveals the following:

1. No errors have been made in recording 1999 transactions or in preparing the closing entries.
2. Preferred stock is no par value, non-cumulative, $10 dividend, and redeemable at $125. Since January 1, 1998, 10,000 shares have been outstanding; 20,000 shares are authorized.
3. Common stock is no par value, with a stated value of $5 per share; 600,000 shares are authorized.
4. The January 1 balance in Retained Earnings was $2,200,000.
5. A cash dividend of $400,000 was declared and properly allocated to preferred and common stock on November 1. No dividends were paid to preferred shareholders in 1998.
6. On December 31, a 5% common stock dividend was declared on common stock when the market price per share was $7.
7. Net income for the year was $880,000.
8. On December 31, 1999, the directors authorized a $100,000 restriction of retained earnings for plant expansion. (Use Note 3 to disclose this matter.)

Instructions

(a) Compute the allocation of the cash dividend to preferred and common stock.

(b) Prepare a statement of retained earnings for the year ended December 31, 1999.

(c) Prepare the shareholders' equity section of the balance sheet at December 31.

Prepare a statement of retained earnings; compute earnings per share data and price-earnings ratio.
(SO 1, 2, 7)

P15–7 The post-closing trial balance of Maggio Corporation at December 31, 1999 contains the following shareholders' equity accounts:

Preferred Stock (15,000 shares issued)	$ 750,000
Common Stock (250,000 shares issued)	3,000,000
Common Stock Dividends Distributable	320,000
Retained Earnings	743,000

A review of the accounting records reveals the following:

1. No errors have been made in recording 1999 transactions or in preparing the closing entries.
2. Preferred stock is no par, with cumulative dividends of $5 per share; 15,000 shares have been outstanding since January 1, 1998.
3. Authorized stock is 20,000 shares of preferred, 500,000 shares of common with no par value.
4. The January 1 balance in Retained Earnings was $920,000.
5. On July 1, 20,000 shares of common stock were sold for cash at $16 per share.
6. On September 1, the company discovered an understatement error of $60,000 for amortization in 1998. The net of tax effect of $42,000 was properly debited to Retained Earnings.
7. A cash dividend of $250,000 was declared and properly allocated to preferred and common stock on October 1. No dividends were paid to preferred shareholders in 1998.
8. On December 31, an 8% common stock dividend was declared on common stock when the

market price per share was $16.
9. Net income for the year was $435,000.
10. On December 31, 1999, the directors authorized disclosure of a $200,000 restriction of retained earnings for plant expansion. (Use Note X.)

Instructions

(a) Compute the allocation of the cash dividend to preferred and common stock.
(b) Prepare a statement of retained earnings for the year.
(c) Compute the earnings per share of common stock, using the weighted average shares outstanding for the year.
(d) Calculate the price-earnings ratio for the company's common stock, as of December 31, 1999.

P15–8 Coquitlam Corporation owns a number of travel agencies and a chain of motels in western Canada. Its condensed operating results for 1999 show the following:

Prepare an income statement with non-typical items; show earnings per share data.
(SO 4, 5, 6, 7)

Operating revenues	$14,580,000
Operating expenses	10,600,000
Income from operations	3,980,000

An additional analysis of the data indicates that the travel agencies are very profitable but that the motel chain has been unprofitable. During the first nine months of 1999, the motels lost $500,000 from operating revenues of $4,200,000 and operating expenses of $4,700,000. Consequently, on October 1, the motel operation was discontinued and sold at a loss of $1,200,000 before taxes. The motel operating results are included in income from operations, but the loss on disposal is not included in the operating results shown above.

In November, an expropriation action was taken against the company to obtain property for a new national park. As a result, the corporation suffered an extraordinary loss of $800,000 before taxes, which is not included in the operating results.

During the year, Coquitlam had other expenses and losses of $80,000, which are not included in the operating results. The corporation is in a 30% tax bracket. At December 31, Coquitlam has 480,000 shares of common stock outstanding, of which 120,000 were issued on September 1, 1999.

Instructions

Prepare an income statement for the year, including the earnings per share presentations.

P15–9 The ledger of Gala Corporation at December 31, 1999, contains the following summary data:

Prepare an income statement, including earnings per share data, with non-typical items.
(SO 4, 5, 6, 7)

Net sales	$1,500,000
Cost of goods sold	800,000
Selling expenses	110,000
Administrative expenses	140,000
Other revenues and gains	40,000
Other expenses and losses	30,000

Your analysis reveals the following additional information that is *not included in the above data*:
1. The entire ceramics division was discontinued on August 31. The loss from operations for this division before income taxes was $150,000. The ceramics division was sold at a gain of $60,000 before income taxes.
2. On July 12, an airplane crashed into one of the company's plants, resulting in an extraordinary loss of $70,000 before income taxes.
3. During the year, Gala changed its amortization method from straight-line to declining-balance. The cumulative effect of the change on prior years' net income was a decrease of $30,000 before taxes. (Assume that amortization under the new method is correctly included in the ledger data for the current year.)
4. The income tax rate on all items is 30%.

Instructions

(a) Prepare an income statement for the year ended December 31, 1999.

(b) Prepare the earnings per share data that should appear in the income statement, assuming there were 100,000 shares of common stock outstanding throughout the year.

Prepare an income statement and statement of retained earnings, with non-typical items.
(SO 2, 4, 5, 6, 7)

P15–10 The ledger of Zurich Corporation at December 31, 1999, contains the following summary data:

Net sales	$1,800,000
Cost of goods sold	1,000,000
Selling expenses	120,000
Administrative expenses	130,000
Other revenues and gains	20,000
Other expenses and losses	28,000

Your analysis reveals the following additional information that is *not included in the above data*:

1. The entire Personal Communication Devices division was discontinued on August 31. The gain from operations for this division before income taxes was $50,000. The Personal Communication Devices division was sold at a loss of $70,000 before income taxes.
2. On May 15, company property was expropriated for a highway. The settlement resulted in an extraordinary gain of $90,000 before income taxes.
3. During the year, Zurich changed its amortization method from double-declining-balance to straight-line. The cumulative effect of the change on prior years' net incomes was an increase of $40,000 before taxes. Amortization under the new method is correctly included in the ledger data for the current year.
4. The income tax rate on all items is 30%.
5. The retained earnings balance at the beginning of the year was $340,000.
6. Dividends declared during the year totalled $25,000.
7. There were 100,000 shares of common stock outstanding throughout the year.

Instructions

(a) Prepare an income statement for the year, including earnings per share data.
(b) Prepare a statement of retained earnings for the year ended December 31, 1999.

Broadening Your Perspective

FINANCIAL REPORTING PROBLEM

Refer to the consolidated financial statements, and the notes that accompany them, for The Second Cup Ltd., which are reproduced in Appendix A.

Instructions
Answer the following questions:

(a) How many shares were issued under the Directors, Officer and Employee Stock Option Plan during the year ended June 28, 1997?

(b) As at June 28, 1997, what percentage of the company assets was financed by shareholders' equity?

(c) Did the company report any discontinued operations or extraordinary items during the years ended June 29, 1996, and June 28, 1997?

(d) How much were the earnings (loss) per share for the years ended June 29, 1996, and June 28, 1997?

(e) How much (if anything) was paid in dividends during the years ended June 29, 1996, and June 28, 1997?

DECISION CASE

ITI Education Corporation, through its Information Technology Institute, is Canada's leading career-oriented postgraduate information technology education organization. Through its programs, university graduates become highly skilled, versatile information technology professionals.

The company's annual report for the year ended October 31, 1997, included the following (note that the company had negative retained earnings, which are referred to as a deficit):

	1997	1996
Deficit, beginning of year		
As previously reported	$(1,413,352)	$ NIL
Adjustment of prior periods (Note 3)	(1,236,803)	(385,059)
As restated	(2,650,155)	(385,059)
Net loss for the year	(844,307)	(2,265,096)
Deficit, end of year	$(3,494,462)	$(2,650,155)

Note 3 to the consolidated financial statements was as follows:

3. Change in method of accounting for pre-operating period costs

During the year, ITI Information Technology Institute Incorporated, a subsidiary company, changed its method of accounting from deferring and amortizing pre-operating period costs to expensing these costs in the year incurred. The effects of this change in accounting policy have been applied retroactively, and result in the following changes to accounts reported on in prior years:

- Depreciation and amortization expense for 1996 decreased $112,656, operating expenses increased $964,400, with a corresponding increase in net loss and deficit of $851,744 for the year.
- As at October 31, 1996 the financial position of the company has changed as follows:

Decrease in pre-operating period costs	$1,399,217
Decrease in contributed surplus (See note on p. 654)	162,414
Increase in opening deficit at November 1, 1995	385,059

Contributed surplus

Balance, beginning of year	
As previously reported	$162,414
Adjustment of prior periods	(162,414)
Balance, end of year (as restated)	NIL

As noted in Chapter 14, Contributed Surplus is an alternative term for Additional Contributed Capital.

Instructions

(a) Summarize how ITI's financial statements for the year ended October 31, 1996, were affected by this change in accounting policy. Be sure that you account for the entire $1,399,217 involved.

(b) Why, do you think, was contributed surplus involved in this?

(c) How would this change in accounting policy affect how a shareholder or creditor would assess the company?

(d) The balance in the company's capital stock account at the end of the 1996 fiscal year was $1,389,103. Calculate the company's total shareholders' equity, as restated, at that time. How do you think you would have felt if you had been a shareholder or a creditor of ITI at that time?

(e) What prediction could one make about the company's capital stock account during the 1997 fiscal year?

COMMUNICATION ACTIVITY

In the past year, Alameda Corporation declared a 10% stock dividend and Butte, Inc., announced a 2-for-1 stock split. Your parents own 100 shares of each company's common stock. During a recent phone call, your parents ask you, as an accounting student, to explain the difference between the two events.

Instructions

Write a letter to your parents explaining the effects of the two events for shareholders, and the effects of each event on the financial statements of each corporation.

GROUP ACTIVITY

The topics explained in this chapter include: (1) corrections of prior period errors, (2) retained earnings restrictions, (3) intraperiod tax allocation, (4) discontinued operations, (5) extraordinary items, and (6) changes in accounting principles.

Instructions

With the class divided into six groups, each group should choose one of the above topics. Each group is to explain its assigned topic to the class, and to illustrate how the topic is reported in the financial statements of a corporation.

ETHICS CASE

Flambeau Corporation has paid 60 consecutive quarterly cash dividends (15 years). The last six months, however, have been a real cash drain on the company, as profit margins have been greatly narrowed by increasing competition. With a cash balance sufficient to meet only day-to-day operating needs, the president, Vince Ramsey, has decided that a stock dividend instead of a cash dividend should be declared. He tells Flambeau's financial vice-president, Janice Rahn, to issue a press release stating that the company is extending its consecutive dividend record with the issuance of a 5% stock dividend. "Write the press release to convince the shareholders that the stock dividend is just as good as a cash dividend," he orders. "Just watch our stock rise when we announce the stock dividend; it must be a good thing if that happens."

Instructions

(a) Who are the stakeholders in this situation?

(b) Is there anything unethical about Ramsey's intentions or actions?

(c) Which would you rather receive as a shareholder—a cash dividend or a stock dividend? Why?

CRITICAL THINKING
►*A Real-World Focus: BFGoodrich Company*

•••

The BFGoodrich Company is a diversified manufacturer of tires, vinyl products, specialty chemicals, and aerospace products. Selected financial data, in millions of dollars, for a recent two-year period were as follows.

	Current Year	Prior Year
Sales	$2,416.7	$2,023.5
Total operating expenses	2,118.7	1,822.8
Total operating income	298.0	200.7
Income from continuing operations	209.9	83.6
Loss from discontinued operations (net of taxes)	16.9	4.4
Extraordinary gain (net of taxes)	–	25.8
Cumulative effect on prior years' incomes of change in method of accounting for taxes	2.7	–
Dividends on preferred stock	8.8	9.8
Dividends on common stock	43.3	37.0
Income retained in the business at end of year	548.9	405.3

The notes to the company's financial statements indicate that the weighted average number of common shares outstanding were 25,179,000 for the current year and 23,651,000 for the prior year.

Instructions

(a) Explain the difference between total operating income and income from continuing operations.

(b) Present the earnings per share data for the company for each year.

(c) Comment on the relative importance of the non-typical items in each year.

(d) Prepare a retained earnings statement for the current year.

ACCOUNTING ON THE WEB

•••

SEDAR (System for Electronic Document Analysis and Retrieval) contains all securities filings by Canadian public companies. This includes financial statements, annual reports, prospectuses, press releases, and other public company filings. This case views a selection of public documents available on this web site.

Instructions

Specific requirements of this Internet case are available on-line at www.wiley.com/canada/weygandt.

Answers to Self-Study Questions
1. a 2. c 3. d 4. b 5. b 6. b 7. a 8. c 9. d 10. b

• • • • • • ▶ **Concepts for Review**

Before studying this chapter, you should understand or, if necessary, review:

a. *What a current liability and a long-term liability are. (Ch. 4, pp. 154-155 and Ch. 11, p. 462).*

b. *How to record adjusting entries for interest expense. (Ch. 3, pp. 102-103).*

c. *How to record entries for the issuance of notes payable and related interest expense. (Ch. 11, p. 464-465).*

d. *How to compute the present value of bonds. (Appendix B, pp. B7–B9).*

Confederation Bridge Is Attractive to Both Travellers and Bondholders

CAPE JOURIMAIN, N. B.—A link to the mainland was a condition of the deal through which Prince Edward Island joined Confederation in 1873. For nearly 125 years, this provision had been fulfilled through a ferry service subsidized by the federal government. But since the spring of 1997, travellers to the land made famous by Anne of Green Gables can arrive without risk of seasickness, via the Confederation Bridge.

At 13 kilometres long, the structure is one of the longest bridges in the world. Building it was a complex engineering feat. Raising the capital to build it was equally complex, explains Chad King, Liability and Trust Fund Advisor to the New Brunswick Department of Finance. The bridge was developed and built by Strait Crossing Development, a private company, which now has the right to operate the bridge (and keep any proceeds from tolls) for 35 years. To raise the capital needed up front for this huge project, the Province of New Brunswick created Strait Crossing Financial Inc. This crown corporation, wholly owned by the province, issued bonds for $661,542,612 on October 7, 1993. The bond proceeds were then loaned to Strait Crossing Development, with the same interest rates and repayment terms.

The bonds mature on April 1, 2032, and have a principal value of $661 million, with an interest rate of 4.5%. Annual payments to bondholders of principal, interest, and accrued interest began May 31, 1997.

"Even though the payments didn't begin for a few years, the bonds were very attractive to investors and sold quickly," explains Mr. King, who also serves as secretary-treasurer of Strait Crossing Financial. For one thing, they are indexed, so if inflation goes up they won't lose any of their value. Second, they are secured by a legal obligation of the Government of Canada to make annual subsidy payments (essentially, the federal money that formerly went to subsidize the ferry lines now goes towards paying the bondholders). Finally, the bonds were given an Aaa rating by Moody's Investors Service, which signals that they are of the very best investment quality. Moody's is one of two major bond rating agencies in the U.S. (Standard and Poor's is the other). They provide ratings for some Canadian bond issues, particularly if they are also sold in the U.S.

At the end of 35 years, about the time the bonds mature, ownership of the bridge reverts to Canada.◀

CHAPTER • 16

LONG-TERM LIABILITIES

As you can see from the opening story, Strait Crossing Financial chose to issue bonds to fund the construction of the Confederation Bridge. When the bond proceeds were lent to Strait Crossing Development, a note payable resulted. The portion of the bonds and note payable not due within the next year are classified as **long-term liabilities**. In this chapter we will explain the accounting for the major types of long-term liabilities reported on the balance sheet. These liabilities include bonds, long-term notes, or lease obligations. The organization of the chapter is as follows:

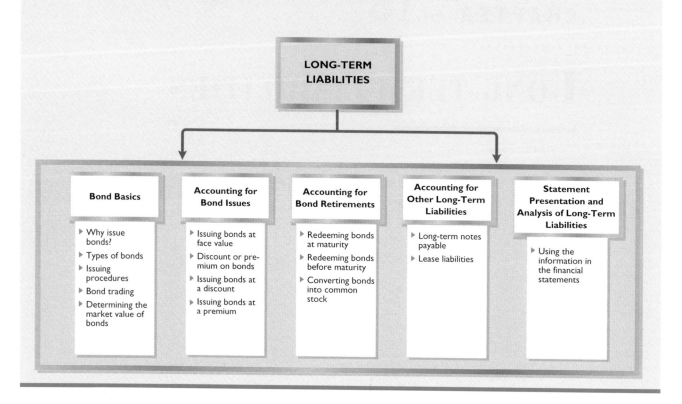

▼Bond Basics

•••

STUDY OBJECTIVE
•••••••••▼••••••••••
Describe the advantages of issuing bonds instead of common stock.

Bonds are a form of interest-bearing notes payable issued by corporations, governments, and government agencies such as Strait Crossing Financial. Bonds are usually sold in denominations of a thousand dollars (or multiples of a thousand dollars). As a result, bonds attract many investors.

Why Issue Bonds?

A corporation may use long-term financing other than bonds, such as notes payable and leasing. However, these other forms of financing involve one individual, one company, or a financial institution. Notes payable and leasing rarely provide enough money for plant expansion and major projects like new buildings. To obtain **large amounts of long-term capital**, corporate management usually must decide whether to issue bonds or to use equity financing (common stock).

From the standpoint of the corporation seeking long-term financing, bonds offer the following advantages over common stock:

Illustration 16-1

Advantages of bond financing over common stock

Bond Financing	Advantages
	1. **Shareholder control is not affected.** Bondholders do not have voting rights, so current owners (shareholders) retain full control of the company.
	2. **Tax savings result.** Bond interest is deductible for tax purposes; dividends on stock are not.
	3. **Earnings per share on common stock may be higher.** Although bond interest expense reduces net income, earnings per share on common stock often is higher under bond financing, because no additional shares of common stock are issued.

To illustrate the potential effect on earnings per share, assume that Microsystems, Inc., is considering two plans for financing the construction of a new $5-million plant. Plan A involves the issuance of 200,000 shares of common stock at the current market price of $25 per share. Plan B involves the issuance of $5-million, 6% bonds at face value. Income before interest and taxes on the new plant will be $1.5 million; income taxes are expected to be 45%. Microsystems currently has 100,000 shares of common stock outstanding. The alternative effects on earnings per share for each plan are shown in Illustration 16-2.

Illustration 16-2

Effects on earnings per share—shares vs. bonds

	Plan A Issue Stock	Plan B Issue Bonds
Income before interest and taxes	$1,500,000	$1,500,000
Interest (6% x 5,000,000)	–	300,000
Income before income taxes	1,500,000	1,200,000
Income tax expense (45%)	675,000	540,000
Net income	$ 825,000	$ 660,000
Outstanding shares	300,000	100,000
Earnings per share	$ 2.75	$ 6.60

Note that net income is $165,000 lower with long-term debt financing (bonds). However, earnings per share is higher, because there are 200,000 fewer shares of common stock outstanding. In addition, because the issue of shares (Plan A) leads to higher net income, it may result in increased dividend requirements, which are an after-tax cost as opposed to bond interest.

The major disadvantages of issuing bonds are the interest that must be paid on a periodic basis and the principal (face value) of the bonds that must be paid at maturity. A company with fluctuating earnings and a relatively weak cash position may have difficulty paying interest requirements in periods of low earnings.

Accounting in Action ► *Business Insight*

Our discussion of long-term liabilities in this chapter is relatively traditional. However, it is important to understand how the corporate world uses leveraging (debt financing). An obscure firm at one time, U.S.-based Kohlberg Kravis Roberts & Co. (KKR) learned the intricacies of leveraged buyouts (in which management or a third party takes over a company, financing it with debt) so well that it now is routinely involved in takeovers of large corporations.

Why the use of debt? The approach is relatively simple—buy a company's shares using debt, sell off assets or shares to pay off the debt, restructure the company, and sell off the restructured company at a handsome profit. Consider the example of Duracell, the world's leader in alkaline batteries. KKR bought Duracell from the Kraft food giant in 1988 with $500 million of its own money and $2 billion of borrowed money. In 1991, it sold just enough Duracell shares to reduce its debt and recoup its original investment. In 1996, KKR sold Duracell to Gillette for nearly $10 billion.

KKR recognized the value of Duracell, patiently waited for the right time to sell, and reaped a bonanza. KKR bought with 80% borrowed money. Even after servicing the cost of debt, KKR earned a phenomenal return on its investment.

Although this strategy sometimes works, in other cases the acquired company has an enormous debt load that has been difficult, if not impossible, to pay off from operations. The collapse of the Canadian real estate company Campeau Corporation is one such illustration. Their ill-fated purchase of two U.S. retail empires, Allied Stores Corp. and Federated Department Stores Inc., resulted in a multibillion-dollar debacle and bankruptcy.

Types of Bonds

Bonds may have many different features. Some types of commonly issued bonds are described in the following sections. Note that a bond can have more than one of the following features (e.g., it can be secured, term, registered, and convertible):

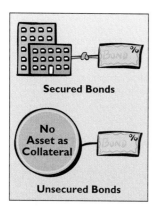

Secured Bonds

Unsecured Bonds

Secured and Unsecured Bonds

Secured bonds are considered secure because specific assets of the issuer are used as collateral for the bonds. There are different types of secured bonds. A bond secured by real estate, for example, is called a mortgage bond. A bond secured by assets set aside to retire the bonds is called a sinking fund bond. Debenture bonds are issued against the general credit of the borrower. There are no assets used as collateral. These bonds, also called **unsecured bonds**, are used extensively by large corporations with good credit ratings. For example, in a recent annual report Noranda reported almost $1.5 billion of debenture bonds outstanding.

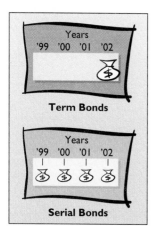

Term Bonds

Serial Bonds

Term and Serial Bonds

Bonds that are due for payment (mature) at a single specified future date are called term bonds. In contrast, bonds that mature in instalments are called serial bonds. For example, the Confederation Bridge bonds referred to in the opening story are serial bonds, since annual payments include both principal and interest. If none of the principal was due to be repaid until April 1, 2032, the bonds would be considered term bonds.

Registered and Bearer Bonds

Bonds issued with the name of the owner are called registered bonds; interest payments on registered bonds are made by cheque or direct deposit to registered bondholders. Canada Savings Bonds, issued by the federal government each fall, are an example of registered bonds. Interest is generally paid annually on Canada Savings Bonds. Bonds that are not registered are called bearer (or coupon) bonds; holders are required to send in coupons to receive interest payments. Bearer bonds may be transferred directly to another party. In contrast, the transfer of registered bonds requires cancellation of the bonds by the institution and the issuance of new bonds. With minor exceptions, most bonds issued today are registered bonds.

Convertible and Redeemable/Retractable Bonds

Bonds that can be converted into shares by the bondholder called convertible bonds. Bonds which the issuer can retire at a stated dollar amount prior to maturity are known as redeemable bonds or **callable bonds**. Retractable bonds are bonds which can be redeemed prior to maturity, at the option of the holder. Ivaco has debentures which are convertible into Class A shares and which are retractable at the option of the bondholder at any time prior to maturity. These debentures are also redeemable by Ivaco in specified circumstances.

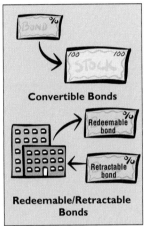

▶ Accounting in Action ▶ *Business Insight*

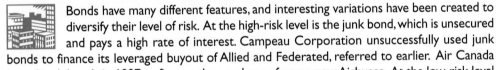

Bonds have many different features, and interesting variations have been created to diversify their level of risk. At the high-risk level is the junk bond, which is unsecured and pays a high rate of interest. Campeau Corporation unsuccessfully used junk bonds to finance its leveraged buyout of Allied and Federated, referred to earlier. Air Canada issued junk bonds in 1997 to finance the purchase of seven new Airbuses. At the low-risk level is the deep discount or zero interest (also known as stripped) bond, which pays very little or no interest.

Canadian bond-rating agencies, such as Canadian Bond Rating Service and Dominion Bond Rating Service, help investors assess the risk level or credit worthiness of bonds. The highest quality bonds are graded as AAA bonds; superior quality, AA; good quality, A; medium grade, BBB; and so on.

Issuing Procedures

Within a corporation, formal approval by the board of directors (and sometimes the shareholders) is required before bonds can be issued. **In authorizing the bond issue, the board of directors must state the total number of bonds to be authorized, total face value, and the contractual interest rate.**

The face value is the amount of principal due at the maturity date. The contractual interest rate is the rate stated on the bond certificate; it is used to determine the amount of cash interest the borrower pays and the investor receives. The contractual rate is stated as an annual rate, and interest is generally paid semi-annually.

Alternative terminology
Face value is also called *par value*, or *maturity value*. The contractual interest rate is commonly known as the *coupon*, or *stated*, *interest rate*.

Helpful hint Do not confuse the terms *indenture* and *debenture*. Indenture refers to the formal bond document (contract). Debenture bonds are unsecured bonds.

The terms of the bond issue are stated in a legal document called a bond indenture. In addition to the terms, the indenture summarizes the respective rights and privileges of the bondholders and their trustees, as well as the obligations and commitments of the issuing company. The **trustee** (usually a financial institution) keeps records of each bondholder, maintains custody of unissued bonds, and holds conditional title to any pledged property (collateral).

After the bond indenture is prepared, **bond certificates** are printed. The indenture and the certificate are separate documents. Bombardier Inc., headquartered in Montreal, is a world leader in transportation, motorized consumer products, and aerospace. They use bonds to help finance their operations in five continents. Illustration 16-3 shows a bond certificate for one of Bombardier's bond issues. As shown

Illustration 16-3

Bond certificate

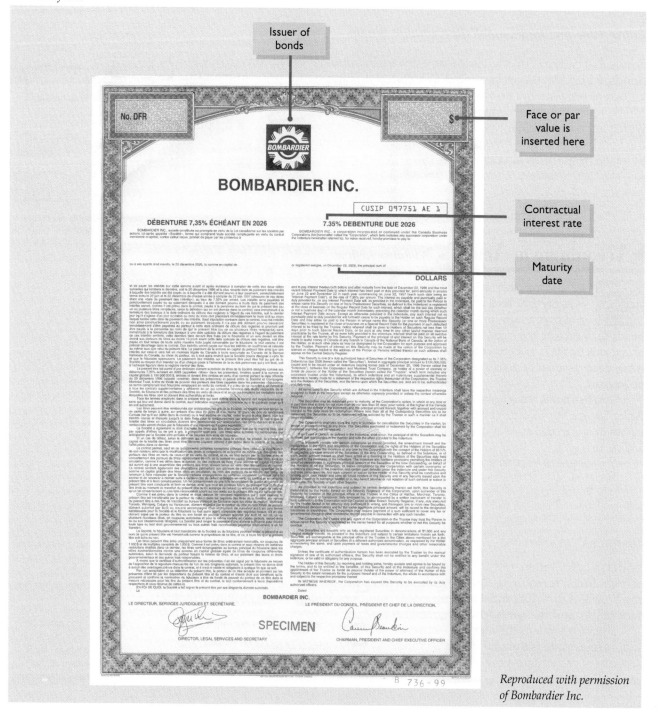

Reproduced with permission of Bombardier Inc.

in this illustration, a bond certificate provides information such as the following: name of issuer, face value of the bonds, contractual interest rate, and maturity date. Bonds are generally sold through an investment company that specializes in selling securities. In most cases, the issue is underwritten by the investment company. Under an underwriting arrangement, the company sells the bonds to the investment company, which, then, sells the bonds to individual investors.

Bond Trading

Corporate bonds, like capital stock, are traded on organized securities markets. Thus, bondholders have the opportunity to convert their bonds into cash at any time by selling the bonds at the current market price. The following illustration shows bond prices and yields which are published daily in newspapers and the financial press.

	Coupon	Mat. date	Bid $	Yld %
Bombardier	7.350	Dec 22/26	113.12	6.35

Illustration 16-4

Market information for bonds

The information in Illustration 16-4 indicates that Bombardier has issued 7.35% bonds that mature on December 22, 2026. They are currently yielding a 6.35% return on the bid price. **The bid or bond price is quoted as a percentage of the face value of the bond, which is usually $1,000.** Thus, a $1,000 bond with a quoted price of 103.12 means that the selling price of the bond is 103.12% of face value, or $1,031.20.

Transactions between a bondholder and other investors **are not journalized by the issuing corporation**. If Vinod Thakkar sells his Bombardier bonds to Julie Tarrel, the issuing corporation, Bombardier, does not journalize the transaction (although it does keep records of the names of bondholders). A corporation makes journal entries only when it issues or buys back bonds and when bondholders convert bonds into common stock.

Case in point The face value of most marketable bonds is $1,000, but it can be any value, such as $100 or $5,000 or $10,000.

Determining the Market Value of Bonds

If you were an investor interested in purchasing a bond, how would you determine how much to pay? To be more specific, assume that Thibodeau, Inc., issues a zero-interest bond (pays no interest) with a face value of $1,000,000 due in 20 years. For this bond, the only cash you receive is a million dollars at the end of 20 years. Would you pay a million dollars for this bond? We hope not, because a million dollars received 20 years from now is not the same as a million dollars received today. The reason you would not pay a million dollars relates to the **time value of money**. If you had a million dollars today, you would invest it and earn interest so that at the end of 20 years your investment would be worth much more than a million dollars. Thus, if someone is going to pay you a million dollars 20 years from now, you would want to find out its equivalent today, or its **present value**. In other words, you would want to determine how much must be invested today at current interest rates to have a million dollars in 20 years.

The market value (present value) of a bond is, therefore, a function of three factors: (1) the dollar amounts to be received, (2) the length of time until the amounts are received, and (3) the market rate of interest. The market interest rate is the rate investors demand for loaning funds to a corporation. This rate is also commonly known as the **effective interest rate** or **yield**. The process of finding the present value is called **discounting** the future amounts.

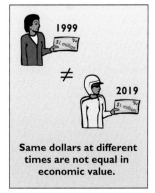

Same dollars at different times are not equal in economic value.

To illustrate, assume that Kimmel Company on January 1, 1999, issues $100,000 of 4% bonds, due in five years, with interest payable semi-annually. The purchaser of the bonds would receive the following two cash payments: (1) **principal** $100,000 to be paid at maturity, and (2) ten $2,000 **interest payments** ($100,000 × 4% × ⁶⁄₁₂ mos.) over the term of the bonds. The time diagram for both cash flows is shown below:

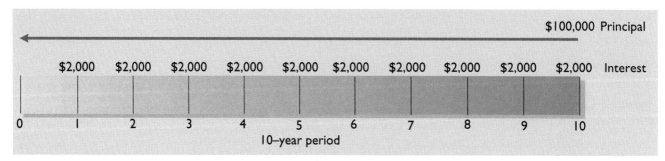

Illustration 16-5

Time diagram depicting cash flows

The present values of these amounts, assuming investors are satisfied with a 4% rate, are as shown in Illustration 16-6:

Illustration 16-6

Computing the present value of bonds

Present value of $100,000 received in 10 periods	
$100,000 × 0.82035 (Table B-1: *n*=10, *i*=2%)	$ 82,035
Present value of $2,000 received annually for 10 periods	
$2,000 × 8.98259 (Table B-2: *n*=10, *i*=2%)	17,965
Present (market) value of bonds	$100,000

Helpful hint   The price of a bond is equal to the present value of all the future cash payments related to the bond.

The present value of the bonds always equals the principal when the effective interest rate is the same as the contractual interest rate, as it is in this case. Present value tables on pages B3 and B5 in Appendix B provide the present value numbers to be used, or these values can be determined mathematically. You need to apply the following important principles are when you compute the present value of bonds:

1. Table B-1 is *always* used to compute the present value of the principal (single sum).
2. Table B-2 is *always* used to compute the present value of the interest (annuity).
3. The face value of the bonds and the contractual interest rate are used to compute the interest payment.
4. The same effective interest rate (*i*) and number of periods (*n*) are used to determine the discount (present value) factors for the present value of the principal and interest.
5. When interest is paid semi-annually, don't forget to halve your annual interest rates (*i* = annual interest rate × 6/12 months for both the contractual and effective interest rates) and to double the number of periods (*n* = years × 2).

Further discussion of the concepts and the mechanics of the time value of money computations is provided in Appendix B at the end of the book.

Before You Go On...
▸*Review It*

1. What are the advantages of bond versus common stock financing?
2. What are secured versus unsecured bonds, term versus serial bonds, registered versus bearer bonds, and redeemable versus retractable bonds?

3. Explain the terms face value, contractual interest rate, and effective interest rate.

4. Explain why you would prefer to receive $1 million today rather than five years from now.

Related exercise material: BE16–1 and E16–1.

Accounting for Bond Issues

Bonds may be issued at face value, below face value (at a discount), or above face value (at a premium). They also are sometimes issued between interest dates.

Issuing Bonds at Face Value

To illustrate the accounting for bonds, assume that Desjardins Corporation issues 1,000, 10-year, 5%, $1,000 bonds dated January 1, 1999, at 100 (100% of face value). The entry to record the sale is:

Jan. 1	Cash	1,000,000	
	Bonds Payable		1,000,000
	(To record sale of bonds at face value)		

> **STUDY OBJECTIVE**
> ········ **2** ········
>
> *Prepare the entries for the issuance of bonds and the recording of interest expense.*

Over the term (life) of the bonds, entries are required for bond interest. Interest on bonds payable is computed in the same manner as interest on notes payable, as explained in Chapter 11, with one exception. It is important to use the exact number of days in the period when calculating short-term interest in order to get the correct total. For example, if you use 3/12 months as the duration on a short-term note, when it should have been 90/365 days, you get the wrong total interest. With bonds, and a much longer time frame, months are more commonly used. You may record slightly more interest in one period than another, but the difference between periods is not important because the total amount is not affected.

Assume that interest is payable semi-annually on January 1 and July 1 on the bonds described above. Interest of $25,000 ($1,000,000 × 5% × 6/12) must then be paid on July 1, 1999. The entry for the payment, assuming no previous accrual of interest, is:

> ► *International note*
>
> The priority of bondholders' versus shareholders' rights varies across countries. In Japan, Germany, and France, shareholders and employees are given priority, with liquidation of the company to pay creditors seen as a last resort. In Britain, creditors' interests are put first—the courts are quick to give control of the company to creditors.

July 1	Bond Interest Expense	25,000	
	Cash		25,000
	(To record payment of bond interest)		

At December 31, an adjusting entry is required to recognize the $25,000 of interest expense incurred since July 1. The entry is:

Dec. 31	Bond Interest Expense	25,000	
	Bond Interest Payable		25,000
	(To accrue bond interest)		

Bond interest payable is classified as a current liability, because it is scheduled for payment within the next year (in fact, it is due the next day). When the interest is paid on January 1, 2000, Bond Interest Payable is debited and Cash is credited for $25,000.

Issuing Bonds Between Interest Dates

Bonds are often issued between interest payment dates. **When this occurs, the investor must pay the market price for the bonds plus accrued interest since the last interest date.** At the next interest date, the corporation will return the accrued interest to the investor by paying the full amount of interest due since the last interest payment date.

To illustrate, assume that Desjardins Corporation sells its $1,000,000, 5% bonds at face value plus accrued interest on March 1. Interest is payable semi-annually on July 1 and January 1. The accrued interest is $8,333 ($1,000,000 × 5% × 2/12). The total proceeds on the sale of the bonds, therefore, are $1,008,333, and the entry to record the sale is:

Mar. 1	Cash	1,008,333	
	Bonds Payable		1,000,000
	Bond Interest Payable		8,333
	(To record sale of bonds at face		
	value plus accrued interest)		

At the first interest date, it is necessary to eliminate the bond interest payable balance and to recognize interest expense for the four months (March 1–June 30) that the bonds have been outstanding. Interest expense in this example is, therefore, $16,667 ($1,000,000 x 5% x 4/12). The entry on July 1 for the $25,000 interest payment is:

July 1	Bond Interest Payable	8,333	
	Bond Interest Expense	16,667	
	Cash		25,000
	(To record payment of bond interest)		

Case in point For a short time, the issuer now has some additional funds (the accrued interest collected) for which no interest is charged.

Why does Desjardins Corporation collect interest at the time of issuance, then return this interest at the time of payment? Collection of accrued interest at the issuance date allows the company to pay a full period's interest to all bondholders at the next interest payment date. Desjardins Corporation does not have to determine the individual amount of interest due each holder based on the time each bond has been held by the investor.

In other words, if bonds were not sold "with accrued interest," Desjardins Corporation would have to keep track of the purchaser and the dates that the bonds were purchased. This procedure would be necessary to ensure that each bondholder received the correct amount of interest. By selling the bonds "with accrued interest," Desjardins does not have to pay an employee to maintain detailed records.

In the opening story, the Confederation Bridge bonds also had accrued interest at the first interest payment date, May 31, 1997. However, this interest did not result from selling the bonds between interest dates. It resulted because interest had not been paid for the period from the date of issue, October 7, 1993, until the first payment date, May 31, 1997.

Discount or Premium on Bonds

The previous illustrations assumed that the contractual (coupon) interest rate paid on bonds and the market (effective) interest rate of the bond were the same. The contractual interest rate is the rate applied to the face (par) value to determine the interest paid in a year. The market interest rate is the rate investors demand for loaning funds to a corporation. When the contractual interest rate and the market interest rate are the same, bonds sell at face value.

However, market interest rates change daily. They are influenced by the type of bond issued, the state of the economy, current industry conditions, and the company's individual performance. As a result, the contractual and market interest rates often differ; bonds therefore sell below or above face value.

To illustrate, suppose that investors have two options: purchase bonds that have just been issued with a contractual interest rate (equal to today's market interest rate) of 6%, or purchase bonds issued at an earlier date with a lower contractual interest rate of 5%. If the bonds are of equal risk, investors will select the 6% investment. To make the investments equal, investors need a way to get a 6% return from the 5% bonds. As investors cannot change the contractual interest rate, they will therefore pay less than the face value for the bonds. By paying less for the bonds, they can obtain the current or market rate of interest, 6%. In these cases, **bonds sell at a discount**.

Conversely, if the market interest rate is **lower** than the contractual interest rate, investors will have to pay more than face value for the bonds. That is, if the market interest rate is 4%, but the contractual interest rate is 5%, investors will find these bonds attractive, and bid the price up. In these cases, **bonds sell at a premium**. The Confederation Bridge bonds were issued at a premium.

These relationships are shown graphically in Illustration 16-7:

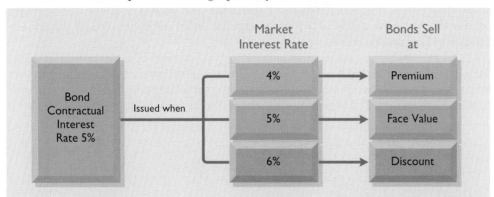

Illustration 16-7

Interest rates and bond prices

Issuance of bonds at an amount different from face value is quite common. By the time a company prints the bond certificates and markets the bonds, it will be a coincidence if the market rate and the contractual rate are the same. Thus, the issuance of bonds at a discount does not mean that the financial strength of the issuer is suspect. Conversely, the sale of bonds at a premium does not indicate that the financial strength of the issuer is exceptional.

Helpful hint Bonds can also sell between interest dates at a discount or a premium.

Issuing Bonds at a Discount

To illustrate the issuance of bonds at a discount, assume that on January 1, 1999, Candlestick, Inc., sells $1-million five-year, 5% bonds at 95.7345 (95.7345% of face value) with interest payable on July 1 and January 1. The entry to record the issuance is:

Jan. 1	Cash	957,345	
	Discount on Bonds Payable	42,655	
	Bonds Payable		1,000,000
	(To record sale of bonds at a discount)		

Although Discount on Bonds Payable has a debit balance, it is not an asset. Rather, it is a **contra account**, which is **deducted from bonds payable** on the balance sheet, as illustrated on the next page:

Alternative terminology The balance in the Discount on Bonds Payable account is often referred to as Unamortized Discount on Bonds Payable.

Illustration 16-8

Statement presentation of discount on bonds payable

Long-term liabilities		
Bonds payable	$1,000,000	
Less: Discount on bonds payable	42,655	$957,345

The $957,345 represents the **carrying (or book) value** of the bonds. On the date of issue, this amount equals the market price of the bonds.

Helpful hint   Amortization of the bond discount is charged to Interest Expense, not to Amortization Expense.

The issuance of bonds below face value makes the total cost of borrowing higher than the bond interest paid. That is, the issuing corporation must pay not only the contractual interest rate over the term of the bonds, but also the face value (rather than the issuance price) at maturity. Therefore, the difference between the issuance price ($957,345) and the face value ($1,000,000) of the bonds—the discount ($42,655)—is an **additional cost of borrowing that should be recorded as bond interest expense over the life of the bonds**.

Amortizing Bond Discount

To comply with the **matching principle**, the bond discount must be allocated to each accounting period that benefits from the use of the cash proceeds. There are two methods for allocating this discount to interest expense: the straight-line and effective interest methods of amortization.

Straight-Line Method of Amortization.   The straight-line method of amortization is the simpler of the two methods. It allocates the same amount to interest expense in each interest period. The amount is determined as shown in Illustration 16-9:

Illustration 16-9

Formula for straight-line method of bond discount amortization

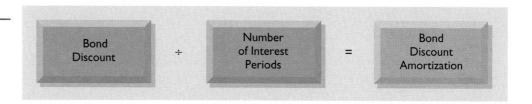

In this example, the bond discount amortization is $4,265.50 ($42,655 ÷ 10 six-month periods). The entry to record the payment of bond interest and the amortization of bond discount on the first interest date (July 1, 1999) is:

July 1	Bond Interest Expense	29,265.50	
	Discount on Bonds Payable		4,265.50
	Cash		25,000.00
	(To record payment of bond interest and amortization of bond discount)		

At December 31, the adjusting entry is:

Dec. 31	Bond Interest Expense	29,265.50	
	Discount on Bonds Payable		4,265.50
	Bond Interest Payable		25,000.00
	(To record accrued bond interest and amortization of bond discount)		

Over the term of the bonds, the balance in Discount on Bonds Payable will decrease annually by the same amount until it reaches zero at the maturity date of the bonds. Thus, the carrying value of the bonds at maturity will be equal to the face value of the bonds.

A bond discount amortization schedule, as shown in Illustration 16-10, helps to determine interest expense, discount amortization, and the carrying value of the bond. In the illustration, the interest expense recorded each period is $29,265.50. This is the total period interest expense which includes both the interest payment ($25,000) and the discount amortization ($4,265.50). Note also that the carrying value of the bond increases by $4,265.50 each period until it reaches its face value $1,000,000 at the end of period 10.

Illustration 16-10

Bonds discount amortization schedule—straight-line method

Semi-annual Interest Period	(A) Interest Payment (2.5% × $1,000,000)	(B) Interest Expense (A) + (C)	(C) Discount Amortization ($42,655 ÷ 10)	(D) Unamortized Discount (D) − (C)	(E) Bond Carrying Value ($1,000,000 − D)
Issue date				$42,655.00	$ 957,345.00
1	$ 25,000	$ 29,265.50	$ 4,265.50	38,389.50	961,610.50
2	25,000	29,265.50	4,265.50	34,124.00	965,876.00
3	25,000	29,265.50	4,265.50	29,858.50	970,141.50
4	25,000	29,265.50	4,265.50	25,593.00	974,407.00
5	25,000	29,265.50	4,265.50	21,327.50	978,672.50
6	25,000	29,265.50	4,265.50	17,062.00	982,938.00
7	25,000	29,265.50	4,265.50	12,796.50	987,203.50
8	25,000	29,265.50	4,265.50	8,531.00	991,469.00
9	25,000	29,265.50	4,265.50	4,265.50	995,734.50
10	25,000	29,265.50	4,265.50	-0-	1,000,000.00
	$250,000	$292,655.00	$42,655.00		

Column (A) remains constant because the face value of the bonds ($1,000,000) is multiplied by the semi-annual contractual interest rate (5% 3 6/12 = 2.5%) each period.

Column (B) is computed as the interest paid (Column A) plus the discount amortization (Column C).

Column (C) indicates the discount amortization each period.

Column (D) decreases each period by the same amount until it reaches zero at maturity.

Column (E) increases each period by the same amount of discount amortization until it equals the face value at maturity.

Effective Interest Method of Amortization. The straight-line method of amortization has a conceptual weakness. It does not completely satisfy the matching principle. With the straight-line method, if interest expense is calculated as a percentage of the carrying value of the bonds, it varies each interest period. This can be seen by using data from the first three interest periods of the bond amortization schedule shown in Illustration 16-10:

Illustration 16-11

Interest percentage rates under straight-line method

Semi-annual Interest Period	Interest Expense to Be Recorded (A)	Bond Carrying Value (B)	Interest Expense as a Percentage of Carrying Value (A) ÷ (B)
1	$29,265.50	$957,345.00	3.06%
2	29,265.50	961,610.50	3.04%
3	29,265.50	965,876.00	3.03%

Helpful hint The straight-line method results in a constant amount of interest expense each period. The effective interest method results in a different interest expense for each period: this is because a different constant percentage is applied to a changing carrying value.

Note that with a bond discount, interest expense as a percentage of carrying value declines in each interest period. However, to completely comply with the matching principle, interest expense as a percentage of carrying value should not change over the life of the bonds. This percentage, referred to as the **effective** or **market interest rate**, is established when the bonds are issued, and remains constant in each interest period. Only the effective interest method of amortization gives a constant percentage.

Under the effective interest method of amortization, the amortization of bond discount (or bond premium) results in a periodic interest expense which is equal to a constant percentage of the carrying value of the bonds. The effective interest method contains these three steps:

1. At the beginning of the interest period (or end of preceding period) compute the **bond interest expense** by multiplying the carrying value of the bonds by the effective interest rate.
2. Compute the **bond interest paid** (or accrued) by multiplying the face value of the bonds by the contractual interest rate.
3. Compute the **amortization amount** by determining the difference between the amounts computed in steps (1) and (2).

These steps are shown in Illustration 16-12:

Illustration 16-12

Computation of amortization—effective interest method

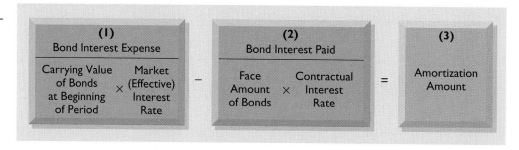

To illustrate the effective interest method of bond discount amortization, we will continue to use Candlestick, Inc., as an example. As you recall, Candlestick issued $1 million of five-year, 5% bonds. Assume that instead of being given a selling price, you are asked to determine the market value or selling price of the bonds. The selling price should enable the bonds to give an effective interest rate of 6%, because the market rate for similar bonds was 6%. Interest continues to be payable semi-annually on July 1 and January 1. Computation of the selling price of the bonds is therefore as follows:

Illustration 16-13

Computation of bond selling price

Present value of principal	
$1,000,000 × 0.74409 (Table B-1: *n*=10, *i*=3%)	$744,090
Present value of interest	
$1,000,000 × 5% × 6/12 mos	
= $25,000 × 8.53020 (Table B-2: *n*=10, *i*=3%)	213,255
Present (market) value of bonds	$957,345

The bonds will sell for $957,345 (95.7345% of face value), which results in a bond discount of $42,655 ($1,000,000 − $957,345). This is the same selling price used earlier in the chapter. However, instead of being told that the bonds were sold at 95.7345, you have calculated the selling price just as interested bond investors must do in real life.

Preparing a bond discount amortization schedule as shown in Illustration 16-14 makes it easier to record the interest expense and the discount amortization. For simplicity, amounts have been rounded to the nearest dollar in this schedule.

Semi-annual Interest Period	(A) Interest Payment (2.5% × $1,000,000)	(B) Interest Expense (3% × preceding bond carrying value)	(C) Discount Amortization (B − A)	(D) Unamortized Discount (D − C)	(E) Bond Carrying Value ($1,000,000 − D)
Issue date				$42,655	$ 957,345
1	$ 25,000	$ 28,720	$ 3,720	38,935	961,065
2	25,000	28,832	3,832	35,103	964,897
3	25,000	28,947	3,947	31,156	968,844
4	25,000	29,065	4,065	27,091	972,909
5	25,000	29,187	4,187	22,904	977,096
6	25,000	29,313	4,313	18,591	981,409
7	25,000	29,442	4,442	14,149	985,851
8	25,000	29,576	4,576	9,573	990,427
9	25,000	29,713	4,713	4,860	995,140
10	25,000	29,860*	4,860	-0-	1,000,000
	$250,000	$292,655	$42,655		

Column (A) remains constant because the face value of the bonds ($1,000,000) is multiplied by the semi-annual contractual interest rate (5% 3 6/12 = 2.5%) each period.

Column (B) is computed as the preceding bond carrying value times the semi-annual effective interest rate (6% 3 6/12 = 3%).

Column (C) indicates the discount amortization each period.

Column (D) decreases each period by the same amount until it reaches zero at maturity.

Column (E) increases each period until it equals the face value at maturity.

* $6 difference due to rounding.

Note that interest expense as a percentage of carrying value remains constant at 3%.
For the first interest period, the entry to record the payment of interest and amortization of bond discount by Candlestick is:

Illustration 16-14
Bond discount amortization schedule—effective interest method

July 1	Bond Interest Expense ($957,345 × 3%)	28,720	
	Discount on Bonds Payable		3,720
	Cash ($1,000,000 × 2.5%)		25,000
	(To record payment of bond interest and amortization of bond discount)		

For the second interest period, the following adjusting entry is made:

Dec. 31	Bond Interest Expense ($961,065 × 3%)	28,832	
	Discount on Bonds Payable		3,832
	Bond Interest Payable ($1,000,000 × 2.5%)		25,000
	(To record accrued bond interest and amortization of bond discount)		

Total bond interest expense for 1999 is $57,552 ($28,720 + $28,832). In contrast, total interest expense using the straight-line amortization method was $58,531 ($29,265.50 + $29,265.50) for the same period.

►Technology in Action

The amortization schedule is an excellent example of an accounting computation which can be efficiently and effectively performed by an electronic spreadsheet. Once the selling price, face amount, contractual rate of interest, effective rate of interest, and number of interest periods are determined and entered into the spreadsheet, all of the computations until maturity can be performed by the computer. Note that all data needed for the adjusting entries can be taken directly from the amortization schedule.

Issuing Bonds at a Premium

The issuance of bonds at a premium can be illustrated by assuming the Candlestick, Inc., bonds described above are sold at 104.4915 (104.4915% of face value) rather than at 95.7345.

The entry to record the sale is:

Jan. 1	Cash	1,044,915	
	Bonds Payable		1,000,000
	Premium on Bonds Payable		44,915
	(To record sale of bonds at a premium)		

Premium on bonds payable is **added to bonds payable** on the balance sheet, as shown below:

Illustration 16-15

Statement presentation of bond premium

Long-term liabilities		
Bonds payable	$1,000,000	
Add: Premium on bonds payable	44,915	$1,044,915

Helpful hint Both discount and premium accounts are valuation accounts. A discount account is a contra-type valuation account (its balance is deducted from Bonds Payable), whereas a premium account is an adjunct-type valuation account (its balance is added to the balance of Bonds Payable).

The sale of bonds above face value causes the total cost of borrowing to be **less than the bond interest paid**, because the borrower is not required to repay the bond premium at the maturity date of the bonds. Thus, the premium is considered to be **a reduction in the cost of borrowing** that should be credited to Bond Interest Expense over the life of the bonds.

Amortizing Bond Premium

The same two methods—straight-line and effective interest—used to amortize a bond discount can also be used to amortize a bond premium and compute interest expense.

Straight-Line Method of Amortization. The formula for determining bond premium amortization under the straight-line method is to divide the bond premium by the number of interest periods. Thus, the premium amortization for each interest period is $4,491.50 ($44,915 ÷ 10). The entry to record the first payment of interest on July 1 is:

Helpful hint Amortization of the bond premium is effectively credited to Interest Expense, not to Amortization Expense or to a revenue account.

July 1	Bond Interest Expense	20,508.50	
	Premium on Bonds Payable	4,491.50	
	Cash		25,000.00
	(To record payment of bond interest		
	and amortization of bond premium)		

At December 31, the adjusting entry is:

Dec. 1	Bond Interest Expense	20,508.50	
	Premium on Bonds Payable	4,491.50	
	Bond Interest Payable		25,000.00
	(To record accrued bond interest		
	and amortization of bond premium)		

Over the term of the bonds, the balance in Premium on Bonds Payable will decrease semi-annually by the same amount until it reaches zero at maturity.

A bond premium amortization schedule, as shown in Illustration 16-16, helps to determine interest expense, premium amortized, and the carrying value of the bond. The illustration shows that the interest expense recorded each period is $20,508.50 under the straight-line method: this is the amount of the interest payment ($25,000) reduced by the premium amortization ($4,491.50). Note also that the carrying value of the bond decreases by $4,491.50 each period until it reaches its face value of $1,000,000 at the end of period 10.

Helpful hint Carrying values *increase* to maturity value with a bond discount and *decrease* to maturity value with a bond premium.

Semi-annual Interest Period	(A) Interest Payment (2.5% × $1,000,000)	(B) Interest Expense (A − C)	(C) Premium Amortization ($44,915 ÷ 10)	(D) Unamortized Premium (D − C)	(E) Bond Carrying Value ($1,000,000 + D)
Issue date				$44,915.00	$1,044,915.00
1	$ 25,000	$ 20,508.50	$ 4,491.50	40,423.50	1,040,423.50
2	25,000	20,508.50	4,491.50	35,932.00	1,035,932.00
3	25,000	20,508.50	4,491.50	31,440.50	1,031,440.50
4	25,000	20,508.50	4,491.50	26,949.00	1,026,949.00
5	25,000	20,508.50	4,491.50	22,457.50	1,022,457.50
6	25,000	20,508.50	4,491.50	17,966.00	1,017,966.00
7	25,000	20,508.50	4,491.50	13,474.50	1,013,474.50
8	25,000	20,508.50	4,491.50	8,983.00	1,008,983.00
9	25,000	20,508.50	4,491.50	4,491.50	1,004,491.50
10	25,000	20,508.50	4,491.50	-0-	1,000,000.00
	$250,000	$205,085.00	$44,915.00		

Column (A) remains constant because the face value of the bonds ($1,000,000) is multiplied by the semi-annual contractual interest rate (5% 3 6/12 = 2.5%) each period.

Column (B) is computed as interest paid (Column A) less the premium amortization (Column C).

Column (C) indicates the premium amortization each period.

Column (D) decreases each period by the same amount until it reaches zero at maturity.

Column (E) decreases each period by the same amount of premium amortization until it equals the face value at maturity.

Illustration 16-16

Bond premium amortization schedule—straight-line method

Effective Interest Method of Amortization. The amortization of bond premium by the effective interest method is similar to the procedures described for bond discount. As an example, assume that Candlestick, Inc., issues its $1-million, 5%, five-year bonds on January 1, 1999, with interest payable on July 1 and January 1. In this case, the bonds are issued to yield an effective interest rate of 4% (the competitive market rate). The bonds will sell at a premium of $44,915.

Illustration 16-17

Computation of bond selling price

Present value of principal	
$1,000,000 × 0.82035 (Table B-1: *n*=10, *i*=2%)	$ 820,350
Present value of interest	
$1,000,000 × 5% × 6/12 mos	
= $25,000 × 8.98259 (Table B-2: *n*=10, *i*=2%)	224,565
Present value of bonds	$1,044,915

The bond premium amortization schedule is shown in Illustration 16-18. Figures have been rounded to the nearest dollar for simplicity.

Semi-annual Interest Period	(A) Interest Payment (2.5% × $1,000,000)	(B) Interest Expense (2% × preceding bond carrying value)	(C) Premium Amortization (A − B)	(D) Unamortized Premium (D − C)	(E) Bond Carrying Value ($1,000,000 + D)
Issue date				$44,915	$1,044,915
1	$ 25,000	$ 20,898	$ 4,102	40,813	1,040,813
2	25,000	20,816	4,184	36,629	1,036,629
3	25,000	20,733	4,267	32,362	1,032,362
4	25,000	20,647	4,353	28,009	1,028,009
5	25,000	20,560	4,440	23,569	1,023,569
6	25,000	20,471	4,529	19,040	1,019,040
7	25,000	20,381	4,619	14,421	1,014,421
8	25,000	20,288	4,712	9,709	1,009,709
9	25,000	20,194	4,806	4,903	1,004,903
10	25,000	20,097*	4,903	-0-	1,000,000
	$250,000	$205,085	$44,915		

Column (A) remains constant because the face value of the bonds ($1,000,000) is multiplied by the semi-annual contractual interest rate (5% 3 6/12 = 2.5%) each period.

Column (B) is computed as the preceding bond carrying value times the semi-annual effective interest rate (4% 3 6/12 = 2%).

Column (C) indicates the premium amortization each period.

Column (D) decreases each period by the same amount until it reaches zero at maturity.

Column (E) decreases each period until it equals the face value at maturity.

* $1 difference due to rounding.

Illustration 16-18

Bond premium amortization schedule—effective interest method

The entry on the first interest date is:

July 1	Bond Interest Expense ($1,044,915 × 2%)	20,898	
	Premium on Bonds Payable	4,102	
	Cash ($1,000,000 × 2.5%)		25,000
	To record payment of bond interest and		
	amortization of bond premium)		

For the second interest period, interest expense will be $20,816 and the premium amortization will be $4,184. Total bond interest expense for 1999 is $41,714 ($20,898 + $20,816) using the effective interest method of amortization. In contrast, interest expense is $41,017 ($20,508.50 + $20,508.50) using straight-line amortization.

STUDY OBJECTIVE

· · · · · · · · · · ▼ 3 · · · · · · · · · ·

Contrast the effects of the straight-line and effective interest methods of amortizing bond discount and premium.

Comparing the Straight-Line and Effective Interest Methods of Amortization. Whether amortizing a bond discount or a bond premium, the effective interest method results in varying amounts of amortization and interest expense per period but a constant interest percentage rate in relation to the carrying value. The straight-line method results in constant amounts of amortization and interest expense per period but a varying interest percentage rate. **The straight-line and effective interest methods of amortization result in the same total amount of interest expense over the term of the bonds.** Furthermore, the interest expense amount for each interest period is generally comparable. **However, when the periodic amounts are materially different, the effective interest method is required under generally accepted accounting principles (GAAP).** For the assignments in this book, unless otherwise told, you should use the effective interest method of amortizing any bond discount or premium.

Before You Go On...

►Review It

1. What entry is made to record the issuance of bonds payable of $1 million at 100? At 96? At 102?
2. Explain the accounting for bonds sold between interest dates.
3. Why do bonds sell at a discount? At a premium? At face value?
4. Distinguish between the straight-line and effective interest methods of amortization.

►Do It

A bond amortization table shows: (a) interest to be paid, $50,000, (b) interest expense to be recorded, $52,000, and (c) amortization, $2,000. Answer the following questions: (1) Were the bonds sold at a premium or at a discount? (2) After recording the interest expense, will the bond carrying value increase or decrease?

Reasoning: To answer the questions, you need to know the effects that the amortization of bond discount and bond premium have on bond interest expense and on the carrying value of the bonds. Bond discount amortization increases both bond interest expense and the carrying value of the bonds. Bond premium amortization has the reverse effect.

Solution: The bond amortization table indicates that interest expense is $2,000 greater than the interest paid. This difference is equal to the amortization amount. Thus, the bonds were sold at a discount. The interest entry will decrease Discount on Bonds Payable and increase the carrying value of the bonds.

Related exercise material: BE16–2, BE16–3, BE16–4, BE16–5, BE16–10, E16–2, E16–5, E16–10, and E16–11.

▼Accounting for Bond Retirements

Bonds may be retired either when they are purchased (redeemed) by the issuing corporation or when they are converted into common stock by bondholders. These transactions are explained in the following sections.

STUDY OBJECTIVE
............4............
Prepare the entries when bonds are retired.

Redeeming Bonds at Maturity

Regardless of the issue price of bonds, the book value of the bonds at maturity will equal their face value. This can be seen in Illustrations 16-10, 14, 16, and 18 where the carrying value of the bonds at the end of their five-year life ($1 million) is equal to the face value of the bonds.

Assuming that the interest for the last interest period is paid and recorded separately, the entry to record the redemption of the Candlestick bonds at maturity is:

Bonds Payable	1,000,000	
Cash		1,000,000
(To record redemption of bonds at maturity)		

Redeeming Bonds before Maturity

Bonds may be redeemed before maturity. A company may decide to retire bonds before maturity to reduce interest cost or to remove debt from its balance sheet. When bonds are retired before maturity, it is necessary to: (1) eliminate the carrying value of the bonds at the redemption date, (2) record the cash paid, and (3) recognize the gain or loss on redemption. The carrying value of the bonds is the face value of the bonds less unamortized bond discount or plus unamortized bond premium at the redemption date.

To illustrate, assume that at the end of the eighth period Candlestick, Inc. (having sold its bonds at a premium and using the effective interest method of amortization as shown in Illustration 16-18), retires its bonds at 103, after paying the semi-annual interest. The carrying value of the bonds at the redemption date, as shown in the bond premium amortization schedule, is $1,009,709. The entry to record the redemption at the end of the eighth interest period (January 1, 2003) is:

Jan. 1	Bonds Payable	1,000,000	
	Premium on Bonds Payable	9,709	
	Loss on Bond Redemption	20,291	
	Cash ($1,000,000 × 103%)		1,030,000
	(To record redemption of bonds at 103)		

Note that the loss of $20,291 is the difference between the cash paid of $1,030,000 and the carrying value of the bonds of $1,009,709. This is very similar to the calculation of a loss or gain on the sale of capital assets: in both cases, cash is compared to carrying value. However, the determination of whether a loss or a gain results naturally differs, depending on whether you are selling capital assets (assets) or purchasing bonds (liabilities). For example, when you sell an asset, you gain when the cash received is **greater than** the carrying value. When you retire a liability, you gain when the cash paid is **less than** the carrying value.

Illustration 16-19

Comparison of asset and liability gain and loss

Capital Assets	**Bonds Payable**
Sale price (proceeds)	Purchase price
− Carrying value	− Carrying value
Gain (loss)	Loss (gain)

Losses (gains) on bond redemption are reported in the income statement as Other Losses or Gains.

Converting Bonds into Common Stock

Convertible bonds have features that are attractive both to bondholders and to the issuer. The conversion gives bondholders an opportunity to benefit if the market price of the common stock increases substantially. Furthermore, until conversion, the bondholder receives interest on the bond. For the issuer, the bonds sell at a higher price and pay a lower rate of interest than similar debt securities that do not have a conversion option. Many corporations, such as Air Canada, Inco, Magna International, and Noranda, have convertible bonds outstanding.

A convertible bond essentially consists of two components. The first component is a liability, with the agreement to repay the principal upon maturity of the bond. The second component is equity, since the bondholder has the right to convert the bonds to shares. These two elements—liability and equity—must be recorded and presented separately on the balance sheet.

This is another accounting example of recognizing **substance over form**. The allocation of the selling price of convertible bonds between the liability and equity accounts, and accounting for convertible bonds and other financial instruments, is left for an intermediate accounting course.

▶Accounting in Action ► *International Insight*

Now that you have read about bonds, you may be beginning to realize how significant bond financing can be. A dramatic example of bond financing that literally changed the course of history is seen in Britain's struggle for supremacy in the 18th and 19th centuries. With only a fraction of the population and wealth of France, Britain ultimately humbled its mightier foe through the use of bonds. Because of its effective central bank and a fair system of collecting taxes, Britain developed the capital markets that enabled its government to issue bonds. Britain was able to borrow money at almost half the cost paid by France, and was able to incur more debt as a proportion of the economy than France could. Britain thus could more than match the French navy, raise an army of its own, and lavishly subsidize other armies, eventually destroying Napoleon and his threat to Europe.

Source: "How British Bonds Beat Back Bigger France," Forbes, March 13, 1995.

Before You Go On...
▶*Review It*

1. Explain the accounting for redemption of bonds at maturity, and before maturity, by payment in cash.
2. Distinguish between gains (losses) from the sale of capital assets and repurchase of bonds.

▶*Do It*

R & B Inc. issued $500,000, 10-year bonds at a premium. Prior to maturity, when the carrying value of the bonds is $508,000, the company retires the bonds at 101. Prepare the entry to record the redemption of the bonds.

Reasoning: To record the redemption of bonds before maturity, it is necessary to: (1) eliminate the carrying value of the bonds, (2) recognize the cash paid, and (3) recognize the gain or loss equal to the difference between (1) and (2).

Solution: There is a $3,000 gain on redemption, because the cash paid, $505,000 is lower than the carrying value of $508,000 ($500,000 + $8,000). The entry is:

Bonds Payable	500,000	
Premium on Bonds Payable	8,000	
Gain on Bond Redemption		3,000
Cash ($500,000 × 101%)		505,000
(To record redemption of bonds at 101)		

Related exercise material: BE16-6, E16-3, E16-4, and E16-6.

▼Accounting for Other Long-Term Liabilities

Other common types of long-term obligations are notes payable and capital lease liabilities. The accounting for these liabilities is explained in the following sections.

Long-Term Notes Payable

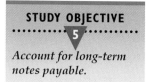

STUDY OBJECTIVE

·········· **5** ··········

Account for long-term notes payable.

The use of notes payable in long-term debt financing is quite common. Long-term notes payable are similar to short-term interest-bearing notes payable except that the terms of the notes exceed one year. In periods of unstable interest rates, the interest rate on long-term notes may change as the market rate for comparable loan changes. An example of this is the $1.2 billion of floating rate long-term debt issued by Hudson's Bay.

A long-term note may be unsecured or secured. The Strait Crossing Development note payable referred to in the chapter vignette is unsecured and bears interest at 4.5%, the same interest rate as the bonds. A secured note includes terms such as a **mortgage**, which pledges title to specific assets as security for the loan. Mortgage notes payable are widely used by individuals to purchase homes and by many small, and some large, companies to acquire capital assets. For example, approximately 52% of the Forzani Group's long-term debt relates to mortgage notes on land and buildings.

Like other long-term notes payable, mortgage loan terms (conditions) may include either a fixed or an adjustable interest rate. Typically, the terms require the borrower to make instalment payments over the term (duration) of the loan. Each payment consists of: (1) interest on the unpaid balance of the loan, and (2) a reduction of loan principal. The interest decreases each period (as the principal decreases), while the portion applied to the loan principal increases.

Mortgage notes payable are initially recorded at face value, and entries are subsequently required for each instalment payment. To illustrate, assume that Porter Technology Inc. issues a $500,000, 7%, 10-year mortgage note on December 1, 1999, to obtain needed financing for the construction of a new research laboratory. The terms provide for monthly instalment payments of $5,805. The instalment payment schedule for the first few months, rounded to the nearest dollar, is as follows:

Illustration 16-20

Mortgage instalment payment schedule—effective interest method

Monthly Interest Period	(A) Cash Payment	(B) Interest Expense (D × 7% × 1/12)	(C) Reduction of Principal (A − B)	(D) Principal Balance (D − C)
Issue date (01/12/99)				$500,000
1 (31/12/99)	$5,805	$2,917	$2,888	497,112
2 (31/01/00)	5,805	2,900	2,905	494,207
3 (28/02/00)	5,805	2,883	2,922	491,285

Helpful hint The periodic amount of interest expense decreases because the principal balance is decreasing. In the last years of the term of the mortgage most of each monthly payment will go to reducing the principal balance; only a small portion is required to cover interest expense.

The entries to record the mortgage loan and first instalment payment are as follows:

Dec. 1	Cash	500,000	
	Mortgage Notes Payable		500,000
	(To record mortgage loan)		
Dec. 31	Interest Expense	2,917	
	Mortgage Notes Payable	2,888	
	Cash		5,805
	(To record monthly payment on mortgage)		

In the balance sheet, the reduction in principal for the next year is reported as a current liability, and the remaining unpaid principal balance is classified as a long-term liability. The total liability at December 31, 1999, for Porter Technology is $497,112. If you added one year to the mortgage schedule (not shown), you could determine that the principal will be reduced to $461,110 by December 31, 2000. Consequently, $36,002 ($497,112 − $461,110) of this liability is current, and $461,110 (the principal balance at December 31, 2000) is long-term.

►Technology in Action

Electronic spreadsheet programs can create a schedule of instalment loan payments. This allows you to put in the data for your own mortgage or car loan to get an illustration that really "drives home."

Lease Liabilities

As indicated in Chapter 10, a lease is a contractual arrangement between a **lessor** (owner of a property) and a **lessee** (renter of a property) that grants the right to use specific property for a period of time in return for cash payments. The two main types of lease are operating lease and capital leases.

STUDY OBJECTIVE
•••••••••• ▼ ••••••••••
6
Contrast the accounting for operating leases and capital leases.

►Accounting in Action ► *Business Insight*

Leasing is big business in Canada. How big? 16% of the machinery and equipment purchased in a recent year was financed by lease. The combined equipment and vehicle industry is estimated by the Canadian Finance & Leasing Association to total between $50 and $60 billion. The reasons often stated for leasing include favourable tax treatment, increased flexibility, and increased cash flow.

Operating Leases

Rental of an apartment and rental of a car are examples of operating leases. **An operating lease intends temporary use of the property by the lessee with continued ownership of the property by the lessor.** The lease (or rental) payments are recorded as an expense by the lessee and as revenue by the lessor. For example, assume that a sales representative for Western Inc. leases a car from Hertz Car Rental at the airport and that Hertz charges a total of $275. The entry by the lessee, Western Inc., would be:

Case in point *Financial Reporting in Canada* notes that 149 companies reported operating leases and 75 companies reported capital leases in a recent year.

Car Rental Expense	275	
Cash		275
(To record payment of lease rental charge)		

In addition, the lessee may have other costs during the lease period. For example, in the case above, the lessee may be required to pay for gas and insurance. These costs are also reported as an expense.

Capital Leases

In most lease contracts, a periodic payment is made by the lessee and is recorded as rent expense in the income statement. However, in some cases the lease contract transfers all the benefits and risks of ownership to the lessee. In these cases, the lease is, in effect, a purchase of the property. This type of lease is called a capital lease, because the present value of the cash payments for the lease are capitalized and recorded as an asset.

The lessee must record the lease **as an asset**—that is, as a capital lease—if any **one** of the following conditions exists:

1. **The lease transfers ownership of the property to the lessee.** *Rationale:* If, during or at the end of the lease term, the lessee receives ownership of the asset, the leased asset should be reported as an asset on the lessee's books.
2. **The lease contains a bargain purchase option.** *Rationale:* If, during the term of the lease, the lessee can purchase the asset at a price substantially below its fair market value, the lessee will obviously exercise this option. Thus, the lease should be reported as a leased asset on the lessee's books.
3. **The lease term is equal to 75% or more of the economic life of the leased property.** *Rationale:* If the lease term is for much of the asset's useful life, the asset has effectively been purchased and should be recorded by the lessee.
4. **The present value of the lease payments equals or exceeds 90% of the fair market value of the leased property.** *Rationale:* If the present value of the lease payments is equal to, or almost equal to, the fair market value of the asset, the lessee has essentially purchased the asset. As a result, the leased asset should be recorded on the books of the lessee.

To illustrate, assume that Fortune Company decides to lease new equipment. The lease period is four years and the economic life of the leased equipment is estimated to be five years. The present value of the lease payments is $190,000 and the fair market value of the equipment is $200,000. There is no transfer of ownership during the lease term, nor is there any bargain purchase option.

In this example, Fortune has essentially purchased the equipment. Conditions (3) and (4) have been met. First, the lease term is 80% (≥75%) of the economic life of the asset, and second, the present value of cash payments is 95% (≥ 90%) of the equipment's fair market value. The entry to record the transaction is as follows:

Leased Asset—Equipment	190,000	
Lease Liability		190,000
(To record leased asset and lease liability)		

Case in point In a recent year, Canadian National Railway reported $291 million on their balance sheet as capital lease obligations.

Case in point Off balance sheet financing is a major reporting problem. Some other off balance sheet items are guarantees and unfunded pensions obligations.

The leased asset is reported on the balance sheet under capital assets. **The portion of the lease liability expected to be paid in the next year is reported as a current liability. The remainder is classified as a long-term liability.**

Most lessees do not like to report leases on their balance sheets. The reason is that the lease liability increases the company's total liabilities. This, in turn, may make it more difficult for the company to obtain needed funds from lenders. As a result, companies attempt to keep leased assets and lease liabilities off the balance sheet by not meeting any of the four conditions listed above. This procedure of keeping liabilities off the balance sheet is often called **off balance sheet financing**.

Statement Presentation and Analysis of Long-term Liabilities

STUDY OBJECTIVE

7

Explain the methods for the financial statement presentation and analysis of long-term liabilities.

Long-term liabilities are reported in a separate section of the balance sheet, immediately after current liabilities. Summary data are usually presented in the balance sheet and detailed data (such as interest rates, maturity dates, conversion privileges, and assets pledged as collateral) is shown in a supporting schedule. The current maturities of long-term debt should be reported under current liabilities if they will be paid from current assets.

Illustration 16-21 shows selected extracts of long-term debt presentation from the Forzani Group Ltd.'s financial statements:

The Forzani Group Ltd.	
Liabilities (in thousands)	
Current	
...	...
Current portion of obligations under capital leases	290
Current portion of long-term debt	897
	61,337
Obligations under capital leases (*Note 4*)	228
Long-term debt (*Note 6*)	3,809

Illustration 16-21

Balance sheet presentation of long-term liabilities

Using the Information in the Financial Statements

Long-term creditors and shareholders are interested in a company's long-run solvency, particularly its ability to pay interest when it is due and to repay its debt at maturity. Two ratios evaluate a company's ability to meet its debt obligations: the times interest earned ratio and the debt to total assets ratio.

Times Interest Earned

The times interest earned ratio measures the ability of a company to meet interest payments when they are due. It is calculated by dividing income before interest expense and income taxes by interest expense. The computation of the times interest earned ratio for Second Cup is as follows:

Illustration 16-22

Computation of times interest earned

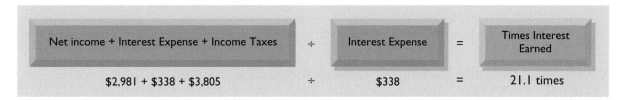

Net income + Interest Expense + Income Taxes	÷	Interest Expense	=	Times Interest Earned
$2,981 + $338 + $3,805	÷	$338	=	21.1 times

Second Cup has no long-term debt and little short-term debt. It is therefore able to provide a substantial cushion of safety for its debtors.

Debt to Total Assets

Earlier in the chapter, we mentioned leveraged buyouts—transactions that are financed primarily with debt. The concept of **leverage** is borrowing at one rate and investing it at a higher rate; in other words, using other people's money to make money. While some leverage is good, too much leverage may endanger a company if it cannot meet heavy interest and debt payments. This is especially problematic during a recession, when many corporations find that leveraging magnifies their losses and contributes significantly to their financial problems.

► *International note*

In many Commonwealth countries, the concept of leverage is referred to as *gearing*.

▶Accounting in Action ▶ *Business Insight*

One company that has successfully used leverage is Montreal-based Unican Security Systems Ltd., the world's largest manufacturer of keys and electronic locks. It financed its recent European expansion with debt borrowed at a cost of 9%. With this money, Unican has been able to earn a return on its equity of 14%. The difference between these two numbers—14% and 9%—is called positive leverage, or spread.

Source: Globe and Mail, March 22, 1997, B24.

The **debt to total assets ratio** indicates the percentage of total assets is owed to creditors, providing one measure of leverage. Second Cup's debt to total assets ratio is:

Illustration 16-23

Computation of debt to total assets

Total Debt	÷	Total Assets	=	Debt to Total Assets
$11,173	÷	$112,389	=	9.9%

Second Cup's debt to total assets ratio is very low. As mentioned before, their assets are primarily financed by equity, rather than debt.

▶*International note*

The amount of debt borrowed by a country can affect its creditworthiness and ability to borrow funds. One measure of the degree of debt financing is the ratio of national debt to gross national product. In a recent survey, Canada's ratio was 69%, second only to Italy at 107%. The U.S., Germany, France, and Britain's ratios are close together, ranging between 40% and 50%. At that time, Japan won the debt race with the smallest ratio of 16%. Subsequently, Japan's debt ratio has risen to nearly 100% of its gross national product as the country deals with currency chaos and financial turmoil.
Source: The Globe and Mail, June 5, 1997, B4.

Before You Go On...

▶*Review It*

1. Explain the accounting for long-term mortgage notes payable.
2. What is the difference in accounting for an operating lease and for a capital lease?
3. How would you measure a company's capacity to meet its debt obligations?

Related exercise material: BE16-7, BE16-8, BE16-9, E16-7, E16-8, and E16-9.

A Look Back at the Confederation Bridge Bonds
• •

Refer to the opening story and answer the following questions:

1. The Confederation Bridge bonds, with a principal value of $661 million, were issued for proceeds of $661,542,612. What was the amount of the bond premium or discount? Was the contractual interest rate likely higher or lower than the market (effective) interest rate at the date of issue?
2. Annual payments to bondholders began in 1997, and included accrued interest. Why do you suppose interest payments were deferred until 1997? Would Strait Crossing have made any journal entry(ies) to recognize this interest before 1997? If so, provide the entry(ies) they would have made.
3. The Strait Crossing Financial Inc. (Confederation Bridge) bonds are rated Aaa by Moody's Investor Service. Why is it important to this crown corporation that its bonds have a high bond rating?

Solution:
1. The bonds were issued at a premium of $542,612. Bondholders were willing to pay more than the principal value of the bonds, since the contractual interest rate (4.5%) was higher than what they could earn in the marketplace.
2. Interest payments were likely deferred until 1997 in order to coincide with the bridge opening, awaiting the cash flow from bridge receipts and the federal government subsidy that used to go to the ferry lines. Note that this point relates only to the timing of the cash flows, not to the recognition—or matching—of expenses.

> Because interest payments did not begin until May 31, 1997, interest for the period October 7, 1993, to May 31, 1997, accrued. At each interest payment date, Strait Crossing would recognize the expense and make the following journal entry:
>
> | May 31, 1994; 1995; 1996 | Interest Expense | |
> |---|---|---|
> | | Interest Payable | |
> | | (To record accrued interest) | |
>
> Additionally, the bond premium would be amortized at these dates.
>
> 3. Having a high-quality bond rating is as important to a crown corporation as it is to a business corporation. A high bond rating indicates that the bonds are less risky, and thus more attractive to purchasers of the bonds. They are generally referred to as "gilt edged" bonds, with a lower interest rate and lower cost to the issuer.

▼Summary of Study Objectives

1. *Describe the advantages of issuing bonds instead of common stock.* Bonds may be sold to many investors, and they offer the following advantages over common stock: (a) shareholder control is not affected, (b) tax savings result, (c) the borrower may benefit from leverage, and (d) earnings per share of common stock may be higher.

2. *Prepare the entries for the issuance of bonds and the recording of interest expense.* When bonds are issued, Cash is debited for the cash proceeds and Bonds Payable is credited for the face value of the bonds. In addition, Bond Interest Payable is credited if there is accrued interest, and the accounts Premium on Bonds Payable and Discount on Bonds Payable are used to show the bond premium and bond discount. The effective interest method or straight-line method of amortization is used to allocate any bond discount and bond premium to interest expense.

3. *Contrast the effects of the straight-line and effective interest methods of amortizing bond discount and premium.* The straight-line method of amortization results in a constant amount of amortization and interest expense per period but a varying percentage rate of interest. In contrast, the effective interest method results in varying amounts of amortization and interest expense per period but a constant percentage rate of interest. The effective interest method results in a better matching of expenses with revenues. When the difference between the straight-line method and the effective interest method is material, the use of the effective interest method is

required under GAAP.

4. *Prepare the entries when bonds are retired.* When bonds are redeemed at maturity, Cash is credited and Bonds Payable is debited for the face value of the bonds. When bonds are redeemed before maturity, it is necessary to: (a) eliminate the carrying value of the bonds at the redemption date, (b) record the cash paid, and (c) recognize the gain or loss on redemption.

5. *Accounting for long-term notes payable.* Each payment consists of: (1) interest on the unpaid balance of the loan, and (2) a reduction of loan principal. The interest decreases each period, while the portion applied to the loan principal increases each period.

6. *Contrast the accounting for operating leases and capital leases.* For an operating lease, lease (or rental) payments are recorded as an expense by the lessee (renter). For a capital lease, the lessee records the asset and related obligation at the present value of the future lease payments.

7. *Explain the methods for the financial statement presentation and analysis of long-term liabilities.* The nature and amount of each long-term debt should be reported in the balance sheet or in schedules in the notes accompanying the statements. The long-run solvency of a company may be analysed by computing two ratios. The times interest earned ratio measures a company's ability to meet its interest payments as they come due. The debt to total assets ratio indicates what proportion of company assets have been financed by debt.

Glossary

Bearer (coupon) bonds Bonds that are not registered. (p. 661).

Bond certificate A legal document indicating the name of the issuer, the face value of the bonds, and other data such as the contractual interest rate and maturity date of the bonds. (p. 662).

Bond indenture A legal document that states the terms of the bond issue. (p. 662).

Bonds A form of interest-bearing notes payable issued by corporations, governments, and government entities. (p. 658).

Capital lease A contractual arrangement that transfers all the benefits and risks of ownership to the lessee, so that the lease is, in effect, a purchase of the property. (p. 679).

Contractual interest rate Rate used to determine the amount of interest the borrower pays and the investor receives. (p. 661).

Convertible bonds Bonds that permit bondholders to convert them into common stock. (p. 661).

Debenture bonds Bonds issued against the general credit of the borrower. Also called unsecured bonds. (p. 660).

Debt to total assets ratio   The ratio of total liabilities to total assets. Indicates the proportion of assets that are financed by debt. (p. 682).

Discount (on bonds payable)   The difference that results when the selling price of the bonds is less than the face value of the bonds. This occurs when the market interest rate is greater than the contractual interest rate. (p. 667).

Effective interest method of amortization   A method of amortizing bond discount or bond premium that results in periodic interest expense equal to a constant percentage of the carrying value of the bonds. (p. 670).

Face value   Amount of principal due at the maturity date of the bond. (p. 661).

Market (effective) interest rate   The rate investors require for loaning funds to the corporation. (p. 663).

Mortgage bonds   Bonds secured by capital assets. (p. 660).

Mortgage note payable   A long-term note that pledges title to specific units of property as security for the loan. (p. 678).

Operating lease   A contractual arrangement that gives the lessee temporary use of the property, with continued ownership of the property by the lessor. (p. 679).

Premium (on bonds payable)   The difference that results when the selling price of the bonds is greater than the face value of the bonds. This occurs when the market interest rate is less than the contractual interest rate. (p. 667).

Redeemable bonds   Bonds that the issuer can redeem at a stated dollar amount prior to maturity. Also known as callable bonds. (p. 661).

Registered bonds   Bonds issued in the name of the owner. (p. 661).

Retractable bonds   Bonds that the bondholder can redeem at a stated dollar amount prior to maturity. (p. 661).

Secured bonds   Bonds that have specific assets of the issuer pledged as collateral. (p. 660).

Serial bonds   Bonds that mature in instalments. (p. 660).

Sinking fund bonds   Bonds secured by specific assets set aside to retire them. (p. 660).

Straight-line method of amortization   A method of amortizing bond discount or bond premium that allocates the same amount to interest expense in each interest period. (p. 668).

Term bonds   Bonds that mature at a single specified future date. (p. 660).

Times interest earned ratio   A measure of a firm's ability to meet its interest obligations. It is computed by dividing income before interest expense and income taxes by interest expense. (p. 681).

DEMONSTRATION PROBLEM 1

Snyder Software Inc. successfully developed a new spreadsheet program. However, to produce and market the program, the company needed $2 million of additional financing. On December 31, 1999, Snyder borrowed money as follows:

1. Snyder issued $500,000, 11%, 10-year bonds. The bonds sold at face value and pay semi-annual interest on January 1 and July 1.

2. Snyder issued $1 million, 10%, 10-year bonds for $885,301. Interest is payable semi-annually, on January 1 and July 1. Snyder uses the straight-line method of amortization.

3. Snyder also issued a $500,000, 12%, 15-year mortgage note payable. The terms provide for semi-annual instalment payments of $36,324 on June 30 and December 31.

Instructions

1. For the 10-year, 11% bonds, prepare journal entries for:
    (a) the issuance of the bonds on January 1, 2000.
    (b) interest expense on July 1 and December 31, 2000.
    (c) the payment of interest on January 1, 2001.

2. For the 10-year, 10% bonds:
    (a) journalize the issuance of the bonds on January 1, 2000.
    (b) prepare a bond discount amortization schedule for the first six interest periods.
    (c) prepare the journal entries for interest expense and amortization of bond discount in 2000.
    (d) prepare the entry for the redemption of the bonds at 101 on January 1, 2003, after paying the interest due on this date.

3. For the mortgage note payable:
    (a) prepare the entry for the issuance of the note on December 31, 1999.
    (b) prepare a payment schedule for the first four instalment payments.
    (c) indicate the current and noncurrent amounts for the mortgage note payable at December 31, 2000.

Solution to Demonstration Problem 1

1. (a) 2000

Jan. 1	Cash	500,000	
	Bonds Payable		500,000
	(To record issue of 11%, 10-year bonds at face value)		

(b) 2000

July 1	Bond Interest Expense	27,500	
	Cash ($500,000 x 0.055)		27,500
	(To record payment of semi-annual interest)		
Dec. 31	Bond Interest Expense	27,500	
	Bond Interest Payable		27,500
	(To record accrual of semi-annual bond interest)		

(c) 2001

Jan. 1	Bond Interest Payable	27,500	
	Cash		27,500
	(To record payment of accrued interest)		

2. (a) 2000

Jan. 1	Cash	885,301	
	Discount on Bonds Payable	114,699	
	Bonds Payable		1,000,000
	(To record issuance of bonds at a discount)		

(b)

Semi-annual Interest Period	Interest to Be Paid	Interest Expense to Be Recorded	Discount to Be Amortized	Unamortized Discount	Bond Carrying Value
Issue Date				$114,699	$885,301
1	$50,000	$55,735	$5,735	108,964	891,036
2	50,000	55,735	5,735	103,229	896,771
3	50,000	55,735	5,735	97,494	902,506
4	50,000	55,735	5,735	91,759	908,241
5	50,000	55,735	5,735	86,024	913,976
6	50,000	55,735	5,735	80,289	919,711

(c) 2000

July 1	Bond Interest Expense	55,735	
	Discount on Bonds Payable		5,735
	Cash		50,000
	(To record payment of semi-annual interest and amortization of bond discount)		
Dec. 31	Bond Interest Expense	55,735	
	Discount on Bonds Payable		5,735
	Bond Interest Payable		50,000
	(To record accrual of semi-annual interest and amortization of bond discount)		

(d) 2003

Jan. 1	Bonds Payable			1,000,000	
	Loss on Bond Redemption			90,289*	
		Discount on Bonds Payable			80,289
		Cash			1,010,000
		(To record redemption of bonds at 101)			
		*($1,010,000–$919,711)			

3. (a) 1999

Dec. 31	Cash			500,000	
		Mortgage Notes Payable			500,000
		(To record issuance of mortgage note payable)			

(b)

Semi-annual Interest Period	Cash Payment	Interest Expense	Reduction of Principal	Principal Balance
Issue Date				$500,000
1	$36,324	$30,000	$6,324	493,676
2	36,324	29,621	6,703	486,973
3	36,324	29,218	7,106	479,867
4	36,324	29,792	7,532	472,335

(c) Current liability　$14,638 ($7,106 + $7,532)
　　Long-term liability　$472,335.

DEMONSTRATION PROBLEM 2

Gardner Corporation issues $1,750,000, 10-year, 12% bonds on January 1, 1999, at $1,968,100 to yield 10%. The bonds pay semi-annual interest July 1 and January 1. Gardner uses the effective interest method of amortization.

Instructions

(a) Prepare the journal entry to record the issuance of the bonds.

(b) Prepare the journal entry to record the payment of interest on July 1, 1999.

(c) Prepare the adjusting entry required on December 31, 1999.

Solution to Demonstration Problem 2

(a)

Jan. 1	Cash			1,968,100	
		Premium on Bonds Payable			218,100
		Bonds Payable			1,750,000
		(To record issuance of bonds at a premium)			

(b)

July 1	Bond Interest Expense			98,405*	
	Premium on Bonds Payable			6,595**	
		Cash			105,000
		(To record payment of semi-annual interest and amortization of bond premium)			
		*($1,750,000 + 218,100) × 5%			
		**$105,000 – $98,405			

(c)

Dec. 31	Bond Interest Expense	98,075*	
	Premium on Bonds Payable	6,925**	
	Interest Payable		105,000
	(To record payment of semi-annual interest and amortization of bond premium)		
	*($1,750,000 + 211,505) × 5%		
	**$105,000 − $98,075		

SELF-STUDY QUESTIONS

Answers are at the end of the chapter.

(SO 1) 1. The term used for bonds that are unsecured is:
   a. redeemable bonds.
   b. indenture bonds.
   c. debenture bonds.
   d. convertible bonds.

(SO 2) 2. If bonds are issued at a premium, it indicates that:
   a. the contractual interest rate exceeds the market interest rate.
   b. the market interest rate exceeds the contractual interest rate.
   c. the contractual interest rate and the market interest rate are the same.
   d. no predictable relationship exists between the two rates.

(SO 2) 3. On January 1, Hurley Corporation issues $500,000, five-year, 12% bonds at 96 with interest payable on July 1 and January 1. The entry on July 1 to record payment of bond interest and the amortization of bond discount using the straight-line method will include a:
   a. debit to Interest Expense, $30,000.
   b. debit to Interest Expense, $60,000.
   c. credit to Discount on Bonds Payable, $4,000.
   d. credit to Discount on Bonds Payable, $2,000.

(SO 2) 4. For the bonds issued in question 3, above, what is the carrying value of the bonds at the end of the third interest period?
   a. $486,000.
   b. $488,000.
   c. $472,000.
   d. $464,000.

(SO 2) 5. When the interest payment dates of a bond are May 1 and November 1, and a bond issue is sold on June 1, the amount of cash received by the issuer will be:
   a. decreased by accrued interest from June 1 to November 1.
   b. decreased by accrued interest from May 1 to June 1.
   c. increased by accrued interest from May 1 to June 1.
   d. increased by accrued interest from June 1 to November 1.

(SO 4) 6. Gester Corporation retires its $100,000 face value bonds at 105 on January 1, after following the payment of semi-annual interest. The carrying value of the bonds at the redemption date is $103,745. The entry to record the redemption will include a:
   a. credit of $3,745 to Loss on Bond Redemption.
   b. debit of $3,745 to Premium on Bonds Payable.
   c. credit of $1,255 to Gain on Bond Redemption.
   d. debit of $5,000 to Premium on Bonds Payable.

(SO 5) 7. Andrews Inc. issues a $497,000, 10%, three-year mortgage note on January 1. The note will be paid in three annual instalments of $200,000, each payable at the end of the year. What is the amount of interest expense that should be recognized by Andrews Inc. in the second year?
   a. $16,567.
   b. $49,740.
   c. $34,670.
   d. $347,600.

(SO 6) 8. Lease A does not contain a bargain purchase option, but the lease term is equal to 90% of the estimated economic life of the leased property. Lease B does not transfer ownership of the property to the lessee by the end of the lease term, but the lease term is equal to 75% of the estimated economic life of the leased property. How should the lessee classify these leases?

	Lease A	Lease B
a.	Operating lease	Capital lease
b.	Operating lease	Operating lease
c.	Capital lease	Operating lease
d.	Capital lease	Capital lease

(SO 3) 9. On January 1, Besalius Inc. issued $1,000,000, 9% bonds for $939,000. The market rate of interest for these bonds is 10%. Interest is payable *annually* on December 31. Besalius uses the effective interest method of amortizing bond discount. At the end of the first year, Besalius should report unamortized bond discount of:

a. $54,900.

b. $57,100.

c. $51,610.

d. $51,000.

(SO 3)   10. On January 1, Dias Corporation issued $2,000,000, 7%, five-year bonds with interest payable on July 1 and January 1. The bonds sold for $1,918,880. The

market rate of interest for these bonds was 8%. On the first interest date, using the effective interest method, the debit entry to Bond Interest Expense is for:

a. $67,161.

b. $70,000.

c. $76,755.

d. $80,000.

QUESTIONS

1. (a) What are long-term liabilities? Give three examples. (b) What is a bond?

2. (a) As a source of long-term financing, what are the major advantages of bonds over common stock? (b) What are the major disadvantages of using bonds for long-term financing?

3. Contrast the following types of bonds: (a) secured and unsecured, (b) term and serial, (c) convertible and redeemable.

4. The following terms are important in issuing bonds: (a) face value, (b) contractual interest rate, (c) bond indenture, and (d) bond certificate. Explain each of these terms.

5. Describe the two major obligations a company has when it issues bonds.

6. Assume that Stoney Inc. sold bonds with a face value of $100,000 for $104,000. Was the market interest rate equal to, less than, or greater than the bonds' contractual interest rate? Explain.

7. Barbara Secord and Jack Dalton are discussing how the market price of a bond is determined. Barbara believes that the market price of a bond is only affected by the amount of the principal payment at the end of its term. Is she right? Discuss.

8. If a 10%, 10-year, $600,000 bond is issued at face value and interest is paid semi-annually, what is the amount of the interest payment at the end of the first semi-annual period?

9. If the Bonds Payable account has a balance of $900,000 and the Discount on Bonds Payable account has a balance of $40,000, what is the carrying value of the bonds?

10. Explain the straight-line method of amortizing discount and premium on bonds payable.

11. Moby Corporation issues $200,000 of 8%, five-year bonds on January 1, 1999, at 104. Assuming that the straight-line method is used to amortize the pre-

mium, what is the total amount of interest expense for 1999?

12. Which accounts are debited and which are credited if a bond issue originally sold at a premium is redeemed before maturity at 97 and immediately after the payment of interest?

13. What is a convertible bond? Discuss the advantages of a convertible bond from the standpoint of: (a) the bondholders, and (b) the issuing corporation.

14. Doug Bareak, a friend of yours, has recently purchased a home for $125,000. He paid $25,000 down and financed the remainder with a 10.5%, 20-year mortgage, payable at $998.38 per month. At the end of the first month, Doug received a statement from the bank indicating that only $123.38 of principal was paid during the month. At this rate, he calculated that it will take over 67 years to pay off the mortgage. Explain why this is not the case.

15. (a) What is a lease agreement? (b) What are the two major types of lease? (c) Distinguish between the two types of lease.

16. Marshall Company rents a warehouse on a month-to-month basis for the storage of its excess inventory. Periodically the company must rent space when its production greatly exceeds actual sales. What is the nature of this type of lease agreement, and what accounting treatment should it receive?

17. Rodriguez Company entered into an agreement to lease computers from Elgin Electronics Inc. The present value of the lease payments is $186,300. Assuming that this is a capital lease, what entry would Rodriguez Company make on the date of the lease agreement?

18. In general, what are the requirements for the financial statement presentation of long-term liabilities?

19. Julia Amant is explaining the advantages of the effective interest method of bond amortization to her accounting staff. What should Julia be saying?

20. Summit Corporation issues $400,000 of 9%, five-year bonds on January 1, 1999, at 104. If Summit uses the effective interest method to amortize the premium, will the annual interest expense increase or decrease over the life of the bonds? Explain.

BRIEF EXERCISES

BE16–1 Olga Inc. is considering two alternatives to finance its construction of a new $2-million plant:

(a) Issuance of 200,000 shares of common stock at the market price of $10 per share.
(b) Issuance of $2-million, 8% bonds at face value.

Complete the following table, and indicate which alternative is preferable.

	Issue Shares	Issue Bonds
Income before interest and taxes	$ 1,000,000	$ 1,000,000
Interest expense from bonds	_____	_____
Income before income taxes		
Income tax expense (30%)	_____	_____
Net income	$ _____	$ _____
Outstanding shares	_____	700,000
Earnings per share	_____	_____

Comparison of bond versus stock financing.
(SO 1)

BE16–2 Keystone Corporation issued 1,000, 9%, five-year, $1,000 bonds dated January 1, 1999, at 100. (a) Prepare the journal entry to record the sale of these bonds on January 1, 1999. (b) Prepare the journal entry to record the first interest payment on July 1, 1999 (interest payable semi-annually). Assume no previous accrual of interest. (c) Prepare the adjusting journal entry on December 31, 1999, to record interest expense.

Journal entries for bonds issued at face value.
(SO 2)

BE16–3 Dominic Company issues $2-million, 10-year, 9% bonds at 98, with interest payable on July 1 and January 1. The straight-line method is used to amortize bond discount. (a) Prepare the journal entry to record the sale of these bonds on January 1, 1999. (b) Prepare the journal entry to record interest expense and bond discount amortization on July 1, 1999. Assume no previous accrual of interest.

Journal entries for bonds issued at a discount, using the straight-line method of amortization.
(SO 2)

BE16–4 Hercules Inc. issues $5-million, five-year, 10% bonds at 103, with interest payable on July 1 and January 1. The straight-line method is used to amortize bond premium. (a) Prepare the journal entry to record the sale of these bonds on January 1, 1999. (b) Prepare the journal entry to record interest expense and bond premium amortization on July 1, 1999. Assume no previous accrual of interest.

Journal entries for bonds issued at a premium, using the straight-line method of amortization.
(SO 2)

BE16–5 Goodland Inc. has $1-million, 10-year, 12% bonds outstanding with interest payable on July 1 and January 1. The bonds were dated January 1, 1999, but were issued on May 1, 1999, at face value plus accrued interest. (a) Prepare the journal entry to record the sale of the bonds on May 1, 1999. (b) Prepare the journal entry to record the interest payment on July 1, 1999.

Journal entries for bonds issued between interest dates.
(SO 2)

BE16–6 The balance sheet for Hathaway Company reports the following information on July 1, 1999:

Long-term liabilities

Bonds payable	$ 1,000,000	
Less: Discount on bonds payable	60,000	$940,000

Journal entry for redemption of bonds.
(SO 4)

Hathaway decides to redeem these bonds at 102 after paying semi-annual interest. Prepare the journal entry to record the redemption on July 1, 1999.

BE16–7 Escobar Inc. issues a $300,000, 10%, 10-year mortgage note on December 31, 1999, to obtain financing for a new building. The terms provide for semi-annual instalment payments of $24,073. Prepare the entry to record the mortgage loan on December 31, 1999, and the first two instalment payments.

Accounting for long-term notes payable.
(SO 5)

Contrast accounting for operating and capital leases.
(SO 6)

BE16–8   Prepare the journal entries that the lessee should make to record the following transactions:

1. The lessee makes a lease payment of $80,000 to the lessor in an operating lease transaction.
2. Goldbaum Company leases a new building from Bracer Construction, Inc. The present value of the lease payments is $600,000. The lease is a capital lease.

Financial statement presentation of long-term liabilities.
(SO 7)

BE16–9   Long-term liability items are presented below for Warner Company at December 31, 1999. Prepare the long-term liabilities section of the balance sheet for Warner Company.

Bonds payable, due 2004	$900,000
Lease liability	50,000
Notes payable, due 2006	80,000
Discount on bonds payable	45,000

Effective interest method of bond amortization.
(SO 3)

BE16–10   The partial bond discount amortization schedule for Lodge Corp. is presented below uses the effective interest method of amortization.

Semi-annual Interest Period	Interest to Be Paid	Interest Expense to Be Recorded	Discount to Be Amortized	Unamortized Discount	Bond Carrying Value
Issue Date				$62,311	$937,689
1	$45,000	$46,884	$1,884	60,427	939,573
2	45,000	46,979	1,979	58,448	941,552

Instructions

(a) Prepare the journal entry to record the payment of interest and the discount amortization at the end of period 1.
(b) Explain why interest expense is greater than interest paid.
(c) Explain why interest expense will increase each period.

EXERCISES

Compare financing alternatives—issuance of common stock versus bonds.
(SO 1)

E16–1   Sundown Airlines is considering two alternatives to finance the purchase of a fleet of airplanes. These alternatives are:

1. Issue 60,000 shares of common stock at $45 per share. (Cash dividends have not been paid and are not foreseen).
2. Issue 13%, 10-year bonds at face value for $2,700,000.

It is estimated that the company will earn $900,000 before interest and taxes as a result of this purchase. The company has an estimated tax rate of 30%, and has 90,000 shares of common stock outstanding prior to the new financing.

Instructions

Determine the effect on net income and earnings per share for these two methods of financing.

Journal entries for issuance of bonds, payment, and accrual of interest.
(SO 2)

E16–2   On January 1, Laramie Company issued $90,000, 10%, 10-year bonds at face value. Interest is payable semi-annually, on July 1 and January 1. Interest is not accrued on June 30.

Instructions

Present journal entries to record:

(a) The issuance of the bonds.
(b) The payment of interest on July 1.
(c) The accrual of interest on December 31.

Journal entries for bonds, payment of interest, straight-line amortization, and redemption at maturity.
(SO 2, 4)

E16–3   Salameh Company issued $240,000, 9%, 20-year bonds on January 1, 1999, at 103. Interest is payable semi-annually, on July 1 and January 1. Salameh uses straight-line amortization for bond premium or discount. Interest is not accrued on June 30.

Instructions

Prepare the journal entries to record:

(a) The issuance of the bonds.
(b) The payment of interest and the premium amortization on July 1, 1999.
(c) The accrual of interest and the premium amortization on December 31, 1999.
(d) The redemption of the bonds at maturity, assuming interest for the last interest period has been paid and recorded.

E16–4   Cotter Company issued $180,000, 11%, 10-year bonds on December 31, 1998, for $172,000. Interest is payable semi-annually, on June 30 and December 31. Cotter uses the straight-line method to amortize bond premium or discount.

Journal entries for issuance of bonds, payment of interest, straight-line amortization, and redemption at maturity.
(SO 2, 4)

Instructions

Prepare the journal entries to record:

(a) The issuance of the bonds.
(b) The payment of interest and the discount amortization on June 30, 1999.
(c) The payment of interest and the discount amortization on December 31, 1999.
(d) The redemption of the bonds at maturity, assuming interest for the last interest period has been paid and recorded.

E16–5   On April 1, Varma Company issued $72,000, 10%, 10-year bonds dated January 1 at face value plus accrued interest. Interest is payable semi-annually, on July 1 and January 1.

Journal entries for issuance of bonds between interest dates; payment and accrual of interest.
(SO 2)

Instructions

Present journal entries to record:

(a) The issuance of the bonds.
(b) The payment of interest on July 1. Interest is not accrued on June 30.
(c) The accrual of interest on December 31.

E16–6   Two separate situations presented below are:

1. Ernst Corporation retired $120,000 face value, 12% bonds on June 30, 1999, at 102. The carrying value of the bonds at the redemption date was $107,500. The bonds pay semi-annual interest, and the interest payment due on June 30, 1999, has been made and recorded.

2. Young, Inc., retired $150,000 face value, 12.5% bonds on June 30, 1999, at 98. The carrying value of the bonds at the redemption date was $151,000. The bonds pay semi-annual interest, and the interest payment due on June 30, 1999, has been made and recorded.

Journal entries for redemption of bonds.
(SO 4)

Instructions

For each independent situation above, prepare the appropriate journal entry for the redemption of the bonds.

E16–7   Peyton Co. receives $110,000 when it issues a $110,000, 10% mortgage note payable to finance the construction of a building at December 31, 1999. The terms provide for semi-annual instalment payments of $7,500 on June 30 and December 31.

Journal entries to record mortgage note and instalment payments.
(SO 5)

Instructions

Prepare the journal entries to record the mortgage loan and the first two instalment payments.

E16–8   Two separate situations are presented below:

1. Ready Car Rental leased a car to Rockefeller Company for one year. Terms of the operating lease agreement call for monthly payments of $500, commencing on May 21.

2. On January 1, 1999, Wizard Inc. entered into an agreement to lease 60 computers from Hi-Tech Electronics. The terms of the lease agreement require three annual rental payments of $120,000 (including 10% interest) beginning December 31, 1999. The present value of the three rental payments is $298,422. Wizard considers this a capital lease.

Journal entries for an operating lease and a capital lease.
(SO 6)

Instructions

(a) Prepare the appropriate journal entry to be made by Rockefeller Company for the first lease payment.

(b) Prepare the journal entry to record the lease agreement on the books of Wizard Inc. on January 1, 1999.

Financial statement presentation of long-term liabilities.
(SO 7)

E16–9   The adjusted trial balance for Viola Corporation at the end of the current year contained the following accounts:

Bond interest payable	$ 9,000
Lease liability	59,500
Bonds payable, due 2007	120,000
Premium on bonds payable	32,000

Of the amount shown as lease liability, $11,000 is due within the next year.

Instructions

(a) Prepare the long-term liabilities section of the balance sheet.

(b) Indicate the proper balance sheet classification for the account(s) listed above that do not belong in the long-term liabilities section.

Journal entries for issuance of bonds and payment of interest; amortization using the effective-interest method.
(SO 3)

E16–10   Quebec Corporation issued $260,000, 9%, 10-year bonds on January 1, 1999, for $243,799. This price resulted in an effective interest rate of 10% on the bonds. Interest is payable semi-annually, on July 1 and January 1. Quebec uses the effective interest method to amortize bond premium or discount. Interest is not accrued on June 30.

Instructions

Prepare the journal entries (rounded to the nearest dollar) to record:

(a) the issuance of the bonds.

(b) the payment of interest and the discount amortization on July 1, 1999.

(c) the accrual of interest and the discount amortization on December 31, 1999.

Journal entries for issuance of bonds and payment of interest; amortization using the effective interest method.
(SO 3)

E16–11   Cumberland Company issued $180,000, 11%, 10-year bonds on January 1, 1999, for $191,216. This price resulted in an effective interest rate of 10% on the bonds. Interest is payable semi-annually, on July 1 and January 1. Cumberland uses the effective interest method to amortize bond premium or discount. Interest is not accrued on June 30.

Instructions

Prepare the journal entries (rounded to the nearest dollar) to record:

(a) the issuance of the bonds.

(b) the payment of interest and the premium amortization on July 1, 1999.

(c) the accrual of interest and the premium amortization on December 31, 1999.

PROBLEMS

$\cdots\cdots\cdots\cdots\cdots\cdots\cdots\cdots\cdots\cdots\cdots\cdots\cdots\cdots\cdots\cdots\cdots\cdots\cdots\cdots\cdots\cdots\cdots\cdots\cdots\cdots\cdots\cdots\cdots$

Prepare journal entries for issuance of bonds, interest and straight-line amortization for two years.
(SO 2)

P16–1   Montego Electric sold $3,000,000, 10%, 10-year bonds on January 1, 1999. The bonds were dated January 1 and pay interest July 1 and January 1. Montego Electric uses the straight-line method to amortize bond premium or discount. The bonds were sold at 104. Assume no interest is accrued on June 30.

Instructions

(a) Prepare the journal entry to record the issuance of the bonds on January 1, 1999.

(b) Prepare a bond premium amortization schedule for the first four interest periods.

(c) Prepare the journal entries for interest and amortization of the premium in 1999 and 2000.

(d) Show the balance sheet presentation of the bond liability at December 31, 2000.

P16–2   Beatrice Corporation sold $1,500,000, 8%, 10-year bonds on January 1, 1999. The bonds were dated January 1, 1999, and pay interest on July 1 and January 1. Beatrice Corporation uses the straight-line method to amortize bond premium or discount. Assume no interest is accrued on June 30.

Prepare journal entries for issuance of bonds, interest, and straight-line amortization of premium and discount.
(SO 2)

Instructions

(a) Prepare all the necessary journal entries to record the issuance of the bonds and bond interest expense for 1999, assuming that the bonds sold at 102.

(b) Prepare journal entries as in part (a) assuming that the bonds sold at 97.

(c) Show balance sheet presentation for each bond issue at December 31, 1999.

P16–3   The following is taken from the Bermuda Corp. balance sheet at December 31, 1999:

Prepare journal entries for payment of interest, straight-line amortization of discount, and redemption of bonds.
(SO 2, 4)

Current liabilities		
Bond interest payable (for six months		
from July 1 to December 31)		$ 132,000
Long-term liabilities		
Bonds payable, 11%, due		
January 1, 2010	$2,400,000	
Less: Discount on bonds payable	84,000	2,316,000

Interest is payable semi-annually, on January 1 and July 1. The bonds are redeemable on any semi-annual interest date. Bermuda uses straight-line amortization for any bond premium or discount. From December 31, 1999, the bonds will be outstanding for an additional 10 years. Assume no interest is accrued on June 30.

Instructions

(Round all computations to the nearest dollar.)

(a) Journalize the payment of bond interest on January 1, 2000.

(b) Prepare the entry to amortize bond discount and to pay the interest due on July 1, 2000.

(c) Assume that, after paying interest on July 1, 2000, Bermuda Corp. redeems bonds that have a face value of $800,000. Record the redemption of the bonds, at a price of 102.

P16–4   The following is taken from the Walenda Oil Company balance sheet at December 31, 1999:

Calculate interest rate on bonds; record partial redemption; prepare adjusting entry using straight-line amortization.
(SO 2, 4)

Current liabilities		
Bond interest payable (for six		
months, from July 1 to December 31)		$ 216,000
Long-term liabilities		
Bonds payable, due January 1, 2010	$3,600,000	
Add: Premium on Bonds Payable	300,000	3,900,000

Interest is payable semi-annually, on January 1 and July 1. The bonds are redeemable on any semi-annual interest date. Walenda uses straight-line amortization for any bond premium or discount. From December 31, 1999, the bonds will be outstanding for an additional 10 years. Assume no interest is accrued on June 30.

Instructions

(a) Calculate the contractual rate of interest on these bonds.

(b) Assume that, after paying interest on July 1, 2000, Walenda Company redeems bonds having a face value of $1,800,000. The redemption price paid is 101. Record the redemption of the bonds.

(c) Prepare the adjusting entry at December 31, 2000, to amortize bond premium and to accrue interest on the remaining bonds.

P16–5   Nankin Electronics issues a $900,000, 10%, 10-year mortgage note on December 31, 1998, to help finance a plant expansion program. The terms provide for semi-annual instalment payments (not including real estate taxes and insurance) of $72,218. Payments are due June 30 and December 31.

Prepare instalment payments schedule and journal entries for a mortgage note payable.
(SO 5)

Instructions

(a) Prepare an instalment payments schedule for the first two years.
(b) Prepare the entries for: (1) the mortgage loan, and (2) the first two instalment payments.
(c) Show how the total mortgage liability should be reported on the balance sheet at December 31, 1999. (Hint: Remember to divide the liability between long-term and any current portions.)

Prepare journal entries for a mortgage note payable; show balance sheet presentation.
(SO 5, 7)

P16–6 Elite Electronics issues an $800,000, 12%, 10-year mortgage note on December 31, 1998. The proceeds from the note will be used to finance a new research laboratory. The terms of the note provide for semi-annual instalment payments, exclusive of real estate taxes and insurance, of $69,748. Payments are due June 30 and December 31.

Instructions

(a) Prepare the entries for the first two instalment payments.
(b) Show how the mortgage liability should be reported on the balance sheet at December 31, 1999. (Hint: Remember to report any current portions separately from the long-term liability.)

Anaylse various lease situations and prepare journal entries.
(SO 6)

P16–7 Three different lease transactions are presented below for Manitoba Enterprises. Assume that all lease transactions start on January 1, 1999. Manitoba does not receive title to the properties leased during or at the end of the lease term.

	Lessor		
	Lornegren Associates	Potter Co.	Haskins Inc.
Type of property	Bulldozer	Truck	Furniture
Bargain purchase option	None	None	None
Lease term	4 years	6 years	3 years
Estimated economic life	8 years	7 years	5 years
Yearly rental	$13,000	$ 6,000	$ 4,500
Fair market value of leased asset	$80,000	$29,000	$27,500
Present value of the lease rental payments	$48,000	$27,000	$12,000

Instructions

(a) Are the leases above operating or capital leases? Explain your reasoning for each.
(b) What would appear on the balance sheet for Manitoba Enterprises with respect to the bulldozer and lease contract with Lornegren Associates?
(c) How should the lease transaction for Potter Co. be recorded on January 1, 1999?
(d) How should the lease transaction for Haskins Inc. be recorded in 1999?

Prepare journal entries for issuance of bonds and payment of interest, with amortization, using the effective interest method.
(SO 3)

P16–8 On July 1, 1999, Global Satellites issued $1,200,000 face value, 9%, 10-year bonds at $1,125,227. This price resulted in an effective interest rate of 10% on the bonds. Global uses the effective interest method to amortize bond premium or discount. The bonds pay semi-annual interest July 1 and January 1.

Instructions

(Round all computations to the nearest dollar.)

(a) Prepare the journal entry to record the issuance of the bonds on July 1, 1999.
(b) Prepare an amortization table through December 31, 2000 (three interest periods), for this bond issue.
(c) Prepare the journal entry to record the accrual of interest and the amortization of the discount on December 31, 1999.
(d) Prepare the journal entry to record the payment of interest and the amortization of the discount on July 1, 2000.
(e) Prepare the journal entry to record the accrual of interest and the amortization of the discount on December 31, 2000.

Prepare effective interest amortization schedule; explain income statment impact; show balance sheet presentation.
(SO 3, 7)

P16–9 On July 1, 1999, Mt. Champlain Corporation issued $1,500,000 face value, 12%, 10-year bonds at $1,686,934. This price resulted in an effective interest rate of 10% on the bonds. Mt. Champlain uses the effective interest method to amortize bond premium or discount. The bonds pay semi-annual interest July 1 and January 1.

Instructions

(Round all computations to the nearest dollar.)

- (a) Prepare an amortization table until December 31, 2000 (three interest periods), for this bond issue.
- (b) Explain how the amortization of the bond premium affects the income statement.
- (c) Show how the total bond liability would be presented on the balance sheet as of December 31, 2000.

P16–10 On July 1, 1999, Saudi Chemical Company issued $2,000,000 face value, 12%, 10-year bonds at $2,249,245. This price resulted in a 10% effective interest rate on the bonds. Saudi uses the effective interest method to amortize bond premium or discount. The bonds pay semi-annual interest on each July 1 and January 1.

Prepare journal entries for issuance of bonds and payment of interest, with amortization using the effective interest method; answer analytical questions.
(SO 3, 7)

Instructions

- (a) Prepare the journal entries to record the following transactions:
    1. The issuance of the bonds on July 1, 1999.
    2. The accrual of interest and the amortization of the premium on December 31, 1999.
    3. The payment of interest and the amortization of the premium on July 1, 2000.
    4. The accrual of interest and the amortization of the premium on December 31, 2000.
- (b) Show the proper balance sheet presentation for the liability for bonds payable on the December 31, 2000, balance sheet.
- (c) Provide answers to the following questions:
    1. Would the bond interest expense reported in 2000 be the same, greater, or less if the straight-line method of amortization were used?
    2. What is the total cost of borrowing over the life of the bonds?
    3. Would the total bond interest expense be greater, the same, or less if the straight-line method of amortization were used?

P16–11 On July 1, 1999, Cheree Company issued $2,200,000 face value, 10%, 10-year bonds at $1,947,651. This price resulted in an effective interest rate of 12% on the bonds. Cheree uses the effective interest method to amortize bond premium or discount. The bonds pay semi-annual interest July 1 and January 1.

Answer analytical questions regarding bonds; show balance sheet presentation.
(SO 3, 7)

Instructions

- (a) Determine the total cost of borrowing over the life of the bonds.
- (b) Determine the amount of interest expense that should be reported for the year ending December 31, 2000.
- (c) Would the bond interest expense reported in 2000 be the same, greater, or less if the straight-line method of amortization were used?
- (d) Show the proper balance sheet presentation for the liability for bonds payable on the December 31, 2000, balance sheet.

Broadening Your Perspective

FINANCIAL REPORTING PROBLEM

In its annual report for the year ended June 28, 1997, The Second Cup Ltd. reported no long-term borrowing in the form of notes, bonds, or debentures. Its only long-term debt was labelled "other deferred liabilities" and consisted primarily of deferred income taxes. A similar situation existed at the end of its 1996 fiscal year.

As mentioned in the chapter, the Second Cup also had a very low Debt to Total Assets ratio and a high Times Interest Earned ratio.

Instructions

(a) 1. If very little of a company's overall financing is in the form of long-term debt, most of it must be in the form of short-term debt or shareholders' equity. Calculate each of these components as a percentage of the company's total financing (liabilities plus shareholders' equity) as of June 28, 1997.

2. What type of short-term debt did The Second Cup have as of June 28, 1997?

2. How risky is The Second Cup's apparent financing strategy?

(b) 1. Access The Second Cup's most recent financial statements and determine whether the company has issued any long-term notes, bonds, or debentures since the end of its 1997 fiscal year.

2. Calculate the Debt to Total Assets ratio and the Times Interest Earned ratio, based upon the The Second Cup's most recent financial statements.

3. Determine whether these ratios have increased, decreased, or remained essentially the same since the end of its 1997 fiscal year, and comment upon these results.

DECISION CASE

The condensed balance sheet is presented below is for Construction, Inc., as of December 31, 1999:

CONSTRUCTION, INC.
Balance Sheet
December 31, 1999

Current assets	$ 800,000	Current liabilities	$1,200,000
Capital assets	1,600,000	Long-term liabilities	700,000
		Common stock	400,000
		Retained earnings	100,000
Total	$2,400,000	Total	$2,400,000

Construction has decided that it needs to purchase a new crane for its operations. The new crane costs $900,000 and has a useful life of 15 years. However, Construction's bank has refused to provide any help in financing the purchase of the new equipment, even though the company is willing to pay an above-market interest rate for the financing.

The chief financial officer for Construction, Lisa Colder, meets with the manufacturer of the crane and discusses the possibility of a lease arrangement. After some negotiation, the manufacturer agrees to lease the crane to Construction under the following terms: length of the lease, seven years; payments, $100,000 per year. The present value of the lease payments is $548,732.

The board of directors at Construction is delighted with this new lease because they have the use of the crane for the next seven years at what they regard as a reasonable cost. In addition, Lisa Colder notes that this type of financing is good because it keeps debt off the balance sheet.

Instructions

    (a) Why do you think the bank decided not to lend money to Construction, Inc.?

    (b) How should this lease transaction be reported in the financial statements?

    (c) What does Lisa Colder mean when she says, "leasing keeps debt off the balance sheet"?

COMMUNICATION ACTIVITY

Finn Berg, president of the Blue Marlin, is thinking of issuing bonds to finance an expansion of his business. He has asked you to: (1) discuss the advantages of bonds over common stock financing, (2) indicate the type of bonds he might issue, and (3) explain the issuing procedures used in bond transactions.

Instructions

Write a memorandum to the president, answering his request.

GROUP ACTIVITY

As described in the text, the possibilities for the issuance of bonds include: (1) bonds issued at face value, between interest dates, (2) bonds issued at a discount, on an interest date, and (3) bonds issued at a premium, on an interest date.

Instructions

With the class divided into groups, each group is to choose one of the three bond issuance scenarios listed above. Each group is then to explain the following, using dollar amounts that are different from those used in the text: (a) the entry to record the sale of the bonds, (b) the entry at the end of the first interest period after the sale, and (c) the financial statement presentation of the bond liability and interest expense at the end of the first interest period.

ETHICS CASE

Andy Vicks is the president, founder, and majority owner of Custom Medical Corporation, an emerging medical technology products company. Custom is in dire need of additional capital to keep operating and to bring several promising products to final development, testing, and production. Andy, as owner of 51% of the outstanding stock, manages the company's operations. He places heavy emphasis on research and development and long-term growth. The other principal stockholder is Jill Caterino, who, as a nonemployee investor, owns 40% of the stock. Jill would like to de-emphasize the R&D functions and emphasize the marketing function, to maximize short-run sales and profits from existing products. She believes this strategy will raise the value of Custom's stock.

    All of Andy's personal capital and borrowing power is tied up in his 51% stock ownership. He knows that any offering of additional shares of stock will dilute his controlling interest, because he won't be able to participate in such an issuance. Jill, however, has money and would likely buy enough shares to gain control of Custom. She would then dictate the company's future direction, even if it meant replacing Andy as president and CEO.

The company already has considerable debt. Raising additional debt will be costly, will adversely affect Custom's credit rating, and will increase the company's reported losses (due to the growth in interest expense). Jill and the other minority stockholders express opposition to the assumption of additional debt, fearing the company will be pushed to the brink of bankruptcy.

Wanting to maintain his control and to preserve the direction of "his" company, Andy is doing everything possible to avoid a stock issuance. He is contemplating a large issuance of bonds, even if it means the bonds are issued with a high effective interest rate.

Instructions

(a) Who are the stakeholders in this situation?
(b) What are the ethical issues in this case?
(c) What would you do if you were Andy?

CRITICAL THINKING
▸A Real-World Focus: Bond Quotations in the Financial Press

Below is a sample of how bond market data is frequently presented in newspapers.

Canadian Bonds

Provided by RBC Dominion Securities

Selected quotations, with changes since the previous day, on actively traded bond issues. Yield are calculated to full maturity, unless marked C to indicate callable date. Price is the midpoint between final bid and ask quotations Apr. 20, 1998.

Issuer	Coupon	Maturity	Price	Yield $	Chg
CANADA	6.500	AUG 01/99	101.35	5.17	-0.01
CANADA	7.750	SEP 01/99	102.80	5.20	-0.01
CANADA	4.750	SEP 15/99	99.52	5.16	-0.01
CANADA	9.250	DEC 01/99	105.36	5.22	-0.02
CANADA	5.500	FEB 01/00	100.43	5.21	-0.01
CANADA	8.500	MAR 01/00	105.12	5.21	-0.02
CANADA	5.000	MAR 15/00	99.78	5.13	-0.01
CANADA	10.500	JUL 01/00	109.77	5.24	-0.03
CANADA	7.500	SEP 01/00	104.53	5.24	-0.02
CANADA	5.000	DEC 01/00	99.65	5.16	-0.01
CANADA	10.500	MAR 01/01	112.80	5.25	0.00
CANADA	7.500	MAR 01/01	105.50	5.25	0.02
CANADA	9.750	JUN 01/01	111.93	5.26	0.02
CANADA	7.000	SEP 01/01	105.01	5.25	0.03
CANADA	9.750	DEC 01/01	113.79	5.26	0.03
CANADA	8.500	APR 01/02	110.85	5.25	0.03
CANADA	5.500	SEP 01/02	101.02	5.22	0.05
CANADA	11.750	FEB 01/03	126.02	5.26	0.05
CANADA	7.250	JUN 01/03	108.49	5.26	0.06
CANADA	5.250	SEP 01/03	100.15	5.21	0.06
CANADA	7.500	DEC 01/03	110.39	5.26	0.07
CANADA	6.500	JUN 01/04	106.18	5.27	0.04
CANADA	9.000	DEC 01/04	120.02	5.27	0.04
CANADA	8.750	DEC 01/05	121.04	5.28	0.08
CANADA	14.000	OCT 01/06	157.41	5.30	0.05
CANADA	7.000	DEC 01/06	111.55	5.28	0.10
CANADA	7.250	JUN 01/07	113.80	5.28	0.12
CANADA	6.000	JUN 01/08	105.49	5.28	0.13
CANADA	10.000	JUN 01/08	135.85	5.30	0.14
CANADA	9.500	JUN 01/10	136.42	5.33	0.18
CANADA	9.000	MAR 01/11	133.30	5.34	0.20
CANADA	10.250	MAR 15/14	151.12	5.38	0.30
CANADA	9.750	JUN 01/21	155.61	5.46	0.43
CANADA	8.000	JUN 01/23	134.35	5.46	0.40
CANADA	9.000	JUN 01/25	149.52	5.46	0.45
CANADA	8.000	JUN 01/27	136.82	5.45	0.44
CANADA	5.750	JUN 01/29	105.62	5.37	0.37
CMHC	5.500	SEP 03/02	100.69	5.31	0.05
ALBERTA	6.250	MAR 01/01	102.39	5.27	0.02
ALBERTA	6.375	JUN 01/04	105.16	5.34	0.04
B C	9.000	JAN 09/02	111.33	5.40	0.04
B C	7.750	JUN 16/03	110.04	5.40	0.06
B C	9.000	JUN 21/04	117.96	5.43	0.03
B C	6.000	JUN 09/08	103.74	5.50	0.12
B C	8.500	AUG 23/13	128.99	5.63	0.20
B C	6.150	NOV 19/27	105.05	5.79	0.35
B C MUN FIN	7.750	DEC 01/05	113.51	5.50	0.08
B C MUN FIN	5.500	MAR 24/08	99.95	5.50	0.12
HYDRO QUEBEC	10.875	JUL 25/01	115.08	5.43	0.02
HYDRO QUEBEC	5.500	MAY 15/03	100.05	5.49	0.05
HYDRO QUEBEC	7.000	JUN 01/04	107.29	5.53	0.00
HYDRO QUEBEC	10.250	JUN 16/12	142.73	5.77	0.14
HYDRO QUEBEC	9.625	JUL 15/22	147.25	5.92	0.45
MANITOBA	7.875	APR 07/03	110.38	5.36	0.06
MANITOBA	5.750	JUN 02/08	102.07	5.47	0.12
MANITOBA	7.750	DEC 22/25	128.45	5.69	0.40
NEW BRUNSWIC	8.000	MAR 17/03	110.66	5.39	0.06
NEW BRUNSWIC	5.700	JUN 02/08	101.85	5.45	0.20
NEW BRUNSWIC	6.000	DEC 27/17	103.90	5.67	0.26
NEWFOUNDLAND	6.150	APR 17/28	103.20	5.92	0.34
NOVA SCOTIA	5.250	JUN 02/03	99.32	5.41	0.06
NOVA SCOTIA	6.600	JUN 01/27	110.55	5.84	0.36
ONTARIO	10.875	JAN 10/01	112.78	5.35	0.01
ONTARIO	8.000	MAR 11/03	110.63	5.39	0.06
ONTARIO	8.750	APR 22/03	113.93	5.40	0.06
ONTARIO	7.750	DEC 08/03	110.92	5.40	0.06
ONTARIO	9.000	SEP 15/04	118.61	5.42	0.04
ONTARIO	8.250	DEC 01/05	116.89	5.44	0.08
ONTARIO	7.500	JAN 19/06	112.55	5.45	0.08
ONTARIO	7.750	JUL 24/06	114.75	5.46	0.08
ONTARIO	6.125	SEP 12/07	104.72	5.46	0.12
ONTARIO	9.500	JUL 13/22	148.07	5.77	0.41
ONTARIO	7.600	JUN 02/27	125.42	5.78	0.40
ONTARIO	6.500	MAR 08/29	110.24	5.78	0.37
ONTARIO HYD	10.000	MAR 19/01	111.50	5.36	0.01
ONTARIO HYD	8.625	FEB 06/02	110.38	5.39	0.05
ONTARIO HYD	9.000	JUN 24/02	112.68	5.40	0.05
ONTARIO HYD	5.375	JUN 02/03	99.91	5.39	0.06
ONTARIO HYD	7.750	NOV 03/05	113.76	5.44	0.08
ONTARIO HYD	5.600	JUN 02/08	100.86	5.48	0.12
ONTARIO HYD	8.250	JUN 22/26	133.96	5.78	0.41
QUEBEC	10.000	APR 26/00	107.82	5.37	-0.03
QUEBEC	10.250	OCT 15/01	114.20	5.44	0.00
QUEBEC	5.250	APR 01/02	99.30	5.46	0.05
QUEBEC	7.500	DEC 01/03	109.19	5.51	0.05
QUEBEC	7.750	MAR 30/06	113.38	5.59	0.08
QUEBEC	6.500	OCT 01/07	106.25	5.62	0.15
QUEBEC	11.000	APR 01/09	142.50	5.66	0.20
QUEBEC	8.500	APR 01/26	134.70	5.93	0.40
QUEBEC	6.000	OCT 01/29	100.91	5.94	0.36
SASKATCHEWAN	6.125	OCT 10/01	102.28	5.35	0.00
SASKATCHEWAN	5.500	JUN 02/08	100.37	5.45	0.12
SASKATCHEWAN	8.750	MAY 30/25	140.65	5.76	0.45
TORONTO -MET	6.100	AUG 15/07	103.99	5.53	0.12
TORONTO -MET	6.100	DEC 12/17	103.09	5.83	0.26
AGT LIMITED	8.800	SEP 22/25	137.23	6.00	0.41
ASSOCIATES	5.400	SEP 04/01	99.45	5.59	0.03
AVCO FINS.	750	JUN 02/03	100.25	5.69	0.00
BANK OF MONT	6.900	OCT 16/01	104.10	5.51	0.03
BANK OF MONT	6.400	APR 09/02	102.95	5.51	0.03
BANK OF MONT	5.550	AUG 27/02	100.02	5.54	0.05
BANK OF MONT	5.650	DEC 01/03	100.40	5.56	0.07
BANK OF MONT	8.150	MAY 09/06	115.74	5.64	0.08
BANK OF N S	6.000	DEC 04/01	101.44	5.53	0.03
BANK OF N S	6.250	JUN 12/02	102.45	5.54	0.04
BANK OF N S	8.100	MAR 24/03	110.43	5.55	0.06
BANK OF N S	5.400	APR 01/03	99.34	5.56	0.06
BANK OF N S	7.400	FEB 08/06	110.76	5.64	0.08
BANK OF N S	6.250	JUL 16/07	104.09	5.66	0.12
BELL CDA ENT	8.950	APR 01/02	111.28	5.55	0.03
BELL CDA ENT	6.200	AUG 28/07	103.99	5.63	0.12
CAN CRED TST	5.625	MAR 24/05	99.85	5.65	-0.02
CAN TRUST M	5.450	DEC 03/01	99.63	5.57	0.04
CAN TRUST M	5.650	SEP 13/02	100.27	5.57	0.04
CARDS TRUST	5.420	SEP 21/01	99.65	5.54	0.00
CARDS TRUST	5.630	DEC 21/05	100.02	5.63	0.00
CDN IMP BANK	4.500	DEC 06/99	98.83	5.37	-0.01
CDN OCC PET	6.300	JUN 02/08	99.05	6.43	0.12
CRESTAR EN	6.450	OCT 01/07	98.73	6.63	0.11
DOMTAR INC	10.000	APR 15/11	120.97	7.43	0.16
GRTR TTO AIR	5.400	DEC 03/02	99.53	5.52	0.05
GRTR TTO AIR	5.950	DEC 03/07	102.27	5.63	0.12
GRTR TTO AIR	6.450	DEC 03/27	106.84	5.95	-0.09
GTC TRANS	6.200	JUN 01/07	101.88	5.92	0.11
IMPERIAL OIL	9.875	DEC 15/99	105.97	5.49	-0.02
INTERPRV PIP	8.200	FEB 15/24	128.99	5.97	0.38
LEGACY	5.930	NOV 15/02	99.76	5.99	0.05
LOBLAWS CO	6.650	NOV 08/27	107.41	6.10	0.35
LOEWEN	6.100	OCT 01/02	98.09	6.62	0.05
LONDON INS	9.375	JAN 08/02	111.98	5.56	0.03
MORGUARD RET	6.600	OCT 09/07	98.73	6.78	0.11
MSTR CR TRUS	5.760	AUG 21/02	100.64	5.58	0.01
MSTR CR TRUS	5.700	NOV 21/03	100.61	5.57	0.02
MSTR CR TRUS	6.150	DEC 21/04	102.88	5.61	-0.03
NAV CANADA	7.560	MAR 01/27	119.96	6.08	0.22
OXFORD	6.860	JUL 21/04	98.37	7.20	0.04
RENAISSANCE	6.850	FEB 06/07	105.37	6.04	0.04
ROGERS CABLE	8.750	JUL 15/07	101.65	8.48	0.10
ROGERS CANT	10.500	JUN 01/06	112.91	8.24	0.07
ROYAL BANK	11.000	JAN 11/02	117.22	5.53	0.03
ROYAL BANK	5.400	SEP 03/02	99.47	5.54	0.05
ROYAL BANK	5.400	APR 07/03	99.46	5.53	0.06
ROYAL BANK	6.500	SEP 12/06	105.58	5.64	0.09
ROYAL BANK	6.750	JUN 04/07	107.57	5.65	0.12
ROYAL BANK	5.600	APR 22/08	99.84	5.62	0.12
SASK WHEAT	6.600	JUL 18/07	102.35	6.25	0.11
STRAIT CROSS	6.170	SEP 15/31	100.72	6.12	0.34
T D BANK	5.600	SEP 05/01	100.25	5.51	0.03
T D BANK	6.450	OCT 17/01	102.74	5.52	0.03
TRIZEC HAHN	7.950	JUN 01/07	103.76	7.36	0.11
UNION GAS	8.650	NOV 10/25	134.13	6.07	0.40
WEST FRASER	6.800	NOV 19/07	100.78	6.68	0.11
WESTON GEO	7.450	FEB 09/04	108.58	5.64	-0.17
WSTCOAST ENE	6.750	DEC 15/27	109.07	6.08	0.35
REAL RETURN	4.250	DEC 01/21	105.80	3.87	0.10
REAL RETURN	4.250	DEC 01/26	106.59	3.87	0.09

The information contained herein has been obtained from sources which we believe to be reliable but we cannot guarantee its accuracy or completeness. Clients should consult their own advisors prior to acting on this information. This report is not and under no circumstances is to be construed as an offer to sell or the solicitation of an offer to buy any securities. This report is furnished on the basis and understanding that RBC Dominion Securities Inc. is to have no responsibility or liability whatsoever in respect thereof. The inventories of RBC Dominion Securities Inc. may from time to time include securities mentioned herein.

Dates such as "15 Mar 99" indicate that the bonds mature on March 15, 1999. Notice that, within each subcategory, the bonds are listed in order of ascending maturity date (or "term to maturity").

Instructions

Based upon these data, answer the following questions:

1. There are two sets of interest rates given, labelled "Coupon" and "Yield." Which of these is the nominal or contractual rate of interest and which is the effective rate?
2. Look at the range of interest rates listed under "Coupon" and "Yield." Which column of rates has the widest range? Why, do you think, is this so?
3. As the term to maturity gets longer, does the yield rate tend to get higher or lower? Explain why this may be logical.
4. Compare the yields for the Government of Canada bonds, the Provincial bonds, and the Corporate bonds, and determine which category has the lowest yield rates. Explain why this may be logical.
5. Are most of the bonds listed selling at a premium or at a discount?

 **ACCOUNTING ON THE WEB**

There are two Internet cases available for this chapter. The first reviews Bonds OnLine, which provides a glossary of bond terms. The second case reviews the Dominion Bond Rating Sevice, one of the agencies that rate companies issuing debt securities, by evaluating their relative credit quality. Other bond rating services are briefly introduced.

Instructions

Specific requirements of this Internet case are available on-line at www.wiley.com/canada/weygandt.

Answers to Self-Study Questions
1. c 2. a 3. d 4. a 5. c 6. b 7. c 8. d 9. b 10. c

They Play the Market for Fun, Profit, and an Education

MISSION, B.C.—In many ways, A.J. and Ben Shewan, two brothers from Mission, British Columbia, are typical investors. In managing their diversified portfolio, they consult with a few trusted advisers, try to learn from their mistakes, show a preference for companies they know something about, and, in the end, trust their gut feelings.

In other ways, however, the Shewan brothers are a little unusual. For one thing, their average rate of return is over 30% per annum. For another, they're still in junior high school.

A.J. and Ben, aged 14 and 12, respectively, have been investing in the stock market for seven years. Starting with $1,000 earned through odd jobs such as delivering papers and collecting pop bottles, they made their first few investments with help from their parents. With continued contributions—the boys now have seven paper routes—and successful stock trades, they have amassed over $90,000.

The brothers choose companies that relate to their daily experience. For example, they recently purchased shares in a B.C. juice company because "you see their drinks in stores and people bring them to school." Five years ago, following an airplane trip to New York, they bought into Boeing Co. at $19 a share. Recently they sold at over $50 per share. Other holdings include CP Rail (A.J. is a model-railway buff), Wall Financial, and Imperial Metals.

They also own shares in tobacco and food giant RJR Nabisco. As they see it, "it's better than wasting your money on cigarettes and candy bars." ◀

CHAPTER 17

INVESTMENTS

After studying this chapter, you should be able to:

1. *Distinguish between temporary and long-term investments.*
2. *Explain the accounting for debt investments.*
3. *Explain the accounting for stock investments.*
4. *Describe the purpose and usefulness of consolidated financial statements.*
5. *Indicate how debt and stock investments are valued and reported on the financial statements.*
6. *Prepare a consolidated balance sheet (appendix).*

Stock investments, such as those made by the Shewan brothers, are just one of many types of investments available for purchase. Investments can include bonds as well as stocks, and can be made by mutual funds, banks, pension funds, or corporate financial managers. Investments can be purchased for a short or a long period of time, and as either a passive investment or with the intention of controlling a company. As you will see in this chapter, the way in which a company accounts for its investments is determined by a number of factors. The organization of this chapter is as follows:

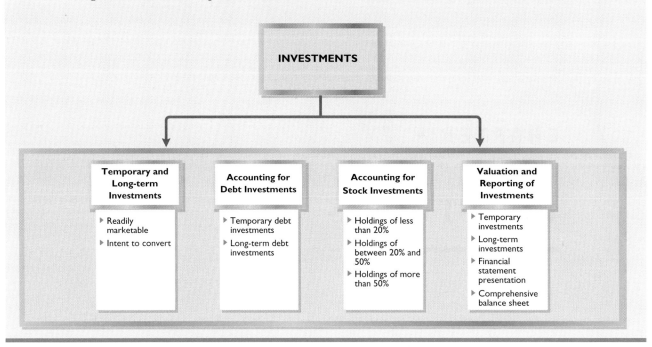

Temporary and Long-Term Investments

STUDY OBJECTIVE
⋯⋯⋯ **1** ⋯⋯⋯

Distinguish between temporary and long-term investments.

Many companies experience seasonal fluctuations in sales. A Victoria marina, for example, will have higher sales in the spring, summer, and fall than in the winter, whereas the reverse will be true for a Banff ski shop. Thus, many companies may have cash on hand, at the end of their operating cycles which is not needed until the start of another operating cycle. As a result, these companies may invest the excess funds to earn interest and dividends. The relationship of temporary investments to the operating cycle is shown in Illustration 17-1:

Illustration 17-1

Temporary investments and the operating cycle

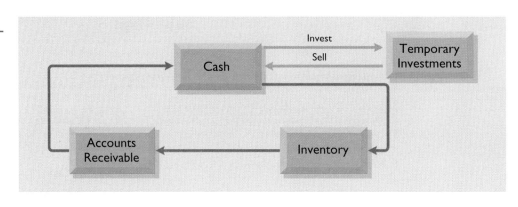

Temporary investments are securities, held by a company, that are: (1) **readily marketable**, and (2) **intended to be converted into cash** in the near future. Investments that do not meet **both** criteria are classified as long-term investments. These securities ordinarily include **short-term paper** (certificates of deposit, treasury bills, and commercial paper), **debt securities** (government and corporate bonds), and **equity securities** (preferred and common shares), such as those purchased by the Shewan brothers. When short-term paper, debt, and/or equity securities of several different corporations or institutions are held, the group of securities is identified as an **investment portfolio**.

Readily Marketable

An investment is readily marketable when it can be sold easily, whenever the need for cash arises. Short-term paper meets this criterion because it can easily be sold to other investors. Stocks and bonds that are traded on organized securities markets, such as the Toronto Stock Exchange, are readily marketable because they can be bought and sold daily. In contrast, there may be only a limited market for the securities issued by small corporations and no market at all for the securities of a privately held company.

Intent to Convert

Intent to convert means that management intends to sell the investment if and when the need for cash arises. It is the intention of selling that determines whether or not the investment is classified as temporary, not the length of time it is held. For example, an Intrawest ski resort may invest idle cash during the summer months with the intent to sell the securities to buy supplies and equipment before the next winter season. This investment is considered temporary even if lack of snow cancels the next ski season and eliminates the need to convert the securities into cash as intended.

Accounting for Debt Investments

Debt investments are investments in debt securities such as government and corporation bonds. These investments may be classified as temporary or long-term.

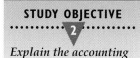

STUDY OBJECTIVE

2

Explain the accounting for debt investments.

Temporary Debt Investments

In accounting for debt investments, entries are required to record: (1) the acquisition, (2) the interest revenue, and (3) the sale.

Entries at Acquisition

At acquisition, the cost principle applies. Cost includes all expenditures made to acquire these investments, such as the price paid plus brokerage fees (commissions), if any. If bonds are purchased between interest payment dates, as discussed in Chapter 16, the accrued interest that is paid by the purchaser does not form part of the Investment account, but is recorded separately as a current asset, Interest Receivable.

Assume that Kuhl Corporation acquires 50 Doan Inc. 8%, 10-year, $1,000 bonds on January 1, 1999, for $54,000, including brokerage fees of $1,000. The bonds pay interest semi-annually, on July 1 and January 1. The entry to record the investment is:

Jan. 1	Investment in Doan Bonds	54,000	
	Cash		54,000
	(To record purchase of 50 Doan Inc. bonds)		

Entries for Bond Interest

The entry for the receipt of interest on July 1 is:

<table>
<tr><td>July 1</td><td>Cash ($50,000 × 8% × 6/12)</td><td>2,000</td><td></td></tr>
<tr><td></td><td>   Interest Revenue</td><td></td><td>2,000</td></tr>
<tr><td></td><td>   (To record receipt of interest on Doan Inc. bonds)</td><td></td><td></td></tr>
</table>

Helpful hint Remember that interest receipts (or payments) are always calculated using the bond's face or principal value, which is $50,000 (50 × $1,000) in this case.

If Kuhl Corporation's fiscal year ends on December 31, it is necessary to accrue the interest of $2,000 earned since July 1. The adjusting entry is:

Dec. 31	Interest Receivable	2,000	
	Interest Revenue		2,000
	(To accrue interest on Doan Inc. bonds)		

Interest Receivable is reported as a current asset in the balance sheet; Interest Revenue is reported under Other Revenues and Gains in the income statement. When the interest is received on January 1, the entry is:

Jan. 1	Cash	2,000	
	Interest Receivable		2,000
	(To record receipt of accrued interest)		

A credit to Interest Revenue at this time would be incorrect, because the interest revenue was earned and accrued in the preceding accounting period.

Entries for Sale of Bonds

When the bonds are sold, it is necessary to update any unrecorded interest up to the date of sale, and credit the investment account for the cost of the bonds. Any difference between the net proceeds from sale of the bonds (sales price less brokerage fees) and their original cost is recorded as a gain or loss. Assume, for example, that Kuhl Corporation receives net proceeds of $58,000 on the sale of the Doan Inc. bonds on January 1, 2000, after receiving (and recording) the interest due. Since the securities cost $54,000, a gain of $4,000 has been realized. The entry to record the sale is:

Jan. 1	Cash	58,000	
	Investment in Doan Bonds		54,000
	Gain on Sale of Investment in Doan Bonds		4,000
	(To record sale of Doan Inc. bonds)		

The gain on sale of debt investments is reported under Other Revenues and Gains in the income statement.

Long-Term Debt Investments

The accounting for temporary debt investments and for long-term debt investments is similar. The major exception is when bonds are purchased at a premium or discount. As we saw in Chapter 16, this results when a bond is purchased above (premium) or below (discount) its face value.

For temporary investments, the bond premium or discount is not recorded separately from the principal investment. Nor is any bond premium or discount amortized to interest revenue: this is because the bonds are held for a short period of time and a misstatement of interest revenue for short period is not considered important.

For long-term investments, however, any bond premium or discount is amortized to interest revenue over the remaining term of the bonds. Like the issuer of the bonds, the investor uses either the straight-line or the effective interest method of amortization. The effective interest method is required under generally accepted accounting principles when the difference between the annual amounts of the two amortization methods is significant.

Accounting for a long-term investment in bonds is essentially the inverse of accounting for long-term bonds payable, discussed in Chapter 16. Using the Kuhl Corporation example introduced earlier, the following illustration compares the entries for Kuhl to record the acquisition of 50 Doan 8%, 10-year, $1,000 bonds as a long-term investment and Doan's recording of the bonds as a long-term liability. The entries for the first interest period are also included. For the purpose of this illustration, it has been assumed that the bonds yield an effective interest rate of 7%.

Illustration 17-2

Comparison of long-term bond investment and liability

Date	Kuhl Corporation (Investor)				Doan Inc. (Investee)		
Jan. 1	Investment in Doan Bonds	50,000			Cash	54,000	
	Premium on Bonds[1]	4,000			Premium on Bonds		4,000
	Cash		54,000		Bonds Payable		50,000
	(To record purchase of 50				(To record issue of 8%, 10-year		
	Doan Bonds)				bonds)		
July 1	Cash ($50,000 x 8% x 6/12)	2,000			Interest Expense ($54,000 x 7% x 6/12)	1,890	
	Premium on Bonds		110		Premium on Bonds	110	
	Interest Revenue ($54,000 x 7%		1,890		Cash ($50,000 x 8% x 6/12)		2,000
	x 6/12)				(To record interest expense and		
	(To record receipt of semi-				and payment of semi-annual		
	annual interest and amor-				interest)		
	tization of bond premium)						

Before You Go On . . .

►Review It

Helpful hint Contrast the accounts used with those demonstrated in Chapter 16.

1. What criteria must be met for an investment to be classified as temporary?
2. What entries are required for an investment in bonds?
3. How does the accounting for a temporary debt investment differ from that for a long-term debt investment?

Kuhl: Investor (Bondholder)	Doan: Investee (Issuer)
Investment in Bonds	Bonds Payable
Interest Revenue	Interest Expense

►Do It

The Wang Corporation had the following transactions for temporary debt investments:
Feb. 1 Purchased 30, 5%, $1,000 Hillary Co. bonds for $29,500, plus accrued interest of $125 and brokerage fees of $900. Interest is payable semi-annually, on July 1 and January 1.

---

[1] Note that, for the investor, Premium on Bonds is a **debit** balance account, because the premium represents part of the cost of the investment.

July 1　Received semi-annual interest on Hillary Co. bonds.

July 1　Sold 15 Hillary Co. bonds for $14,650 less $400 brokerage fees.

(a) Journalize the transactions, and (b) prepare the adjusting entry for the accrual of interest on December 31.

Reasoning: Bond investments are recorded at cost. If bonds are purchased between interest dates, any interest accruing from the last interest payment date is paid to the seller of the bonds. This interest will be recovered by the investor, from the investee, at the next semi-annual interest payment date. Interest receivable is computed using the face value of the bonds, not the net carrying value.

Since these are temporary investments, the discount (or premium) is neither recorded separately nor amortized. When bonds are sold, the investment account is credited for the cost of the bonds. Any difference between the cost and the net proceeds is recorded as a gain or loss.

Solution:

(a) Feb. 1	Interest Receivable ($30,000 × 5% × 1/12)		125	
	Investment in Hillary Bonds ($29,500 + $900)		30,400	
	Cash ($29,500 + $900 + $125)			30,525
	(To record purchase of 30 Hillary Co. bonds)			
July 1	Cash ($30,000 × 5% × 6/12)		750	
	Interest Receivable			125
	Interest Revenue			625
	(To record receipt of interest on Hillary Co. bonds)			
July 1	Cash ($14,650 − $400)		14,250	
	Loss on Sale of Investment in Hillary Bonds		950	
	Investment in Hillary Bonds ($30,400 × 15/30)			15,200
	(To record sale of 15 Hillary Co. bonds)			
(b) Dec. 31	Interest Receivable		375	
	Interest Revenue ($15,000 × 5% × 6/12)			375
	(To accrue interest on Hillary Co. bonds)			

Related exercise material: BE17–1 and E17–1.

Accounting for Stock Investments

STUDY OBJECTIVE

3

Explain the accounting for stock investments.

▶ *International note*

A recent study demonstrated the peril of investing overseas. For the same company under different reporting systems, income was $240,600, $260,600, $84,600, and $10,402 in Australia, the United Kingdom, the United States, and Germany respectively.

Stock investments are investments in the equity securities (capital stock) of corporations. Although a company may purchase the stock of another company for many reasons, usually its primary reason is to **increase its own income**. This may be achieved through: (1) earning dividend income, (2) realizing gains by selling share investments at a higher price than originally paid, or (3) expanding, diversifying, or otherwise creating a profitable operating relationship. Usually preferred stock is held to earn dividend income; either common or preferred stock is held for share price appreciation, and common shares are also held to influence intercorporate relationships.

The accounting for investments in stock is based on how much influence the investor has over the operating and financial affairs of the issuing corporation (commonly called the **investee**), as shown in Illustration 17-3. On the following pages we will explain and illustrate the application of each guideline.

Illustration 17-3

Accounting guidelines for stock investments

Investor's Ownership Interest in Investee's Common Stock	Presumed Influence on Investee	Accounting Guidelines
Less than 20%	Insignificant	Cost method
Between 20% and 50%	Significant	Equity method
More than 50%	Controlling	Equity method for accounting; Consolidated financial statments for financial reporting

►Accounting in Action ► *Business Insight*

A corporation may have a variety of motives in purchasing the capital stock of another corporation. Not the least of these reasons is to influence or control a major supplier, customer, or otherwise-related company. Take, for example, Noranda Inc., a diversified natural resources company headquartered in Toronto. Noranda's investments in common stock include the following in each of its three primary operations:

Mining and Metals	Forest Products	Oil and Gas
Heath Steele (100%)	Noranda Forest Inc. (66%)	Canadian HunterExploration Ltd. (100%)
Noranda Aluminum, Inc. (100%)	CSC Forest Products Ltd. (50%)	Norcen Energy Resources Limited (49%)
American Racing Equipment, Inc. (100%)	Fraser Papers Inc. (100%)	Superior Propane Inc. (50%)
Falconbridge Limited (46%)	James Maclaren Industries Inc. (100%)	
Battle Mountain Gold Company (28%)	Norbord Industries Inc. (100%)	
Wire Rope Industries Ltd. (85%)	Northwood Pulp and Timber Limited (50%)	

In addition to other long-term investments, Noranda's investment portfolio included, for the same year, temporary investments in shares and debentures of $194 million.

Holdings of Less Than 20%

In accounting for stock investments of less than 20%, the cost method is used. Under the cost method, the investment is recorded at cost and revenue is recognized only when cash dividends are received. The entries for stock investments under the cost method follow.

Entries at Acquisition

At acquisition, the cost principle applies. Cost includes all expenditures made to acquire these investments, such as the price paid plus brokerage fees (commissions), if any. Assume, for example, that on July 1, 1999, St. Amand Corporation acquires 1,000 shares (10% ownership) of Beal Corporation common stock at $40 per share plus brokerage fees of $500. The entry for the purchase is:

July 1	Investment in Beal Common Shares	40,500	
	Cash [(1,000 × $40) + $500]		40,500
	(To record purchase of 1,000 shares of Beal Corporation common stock)		

Entries for Dividends

During the time the stock is held, entries are required for any cash dividends received. Thus, if a $2 per share dividend is received by St. Amand Corporation on December 1, the entry is:

Dec. 1	Cash (1,000 x $2)	2,000	
	Dividend Revenue		2,000
	(To record receipt of a cash dividend)		

Dividend Revenue is reported under Other Revenues and Gains in the income statement. Unlike interest on notes and bonds, dividends do not accrue until declared, and so they are not recognized until they are declared. When dividends are declared, Dividend Receivable should be debited and Dividend Revenue credited. When the dividend is subsequently received, Cash is debited and Dividend Receivable credited. Typically, however, the investor uses a Dividend Receivable account only when financial statements are prepared between the declaration date and the payment date.

Entries for Sale of Stock

When stock is sold, the difference between the net proceeds from the sale of the stock (sales price less brokerage fees) from the sale and the cost of the stock is recognized as a gain or a loss. Assume, for instance, that St. Amand Corporation receives net proceeds of $39,500 on the sale of its Beal stock on February 10, 2000. Because the stock cost $40,500, a loss of $1,000 has been incurred. The entry to record the sale is:

Feb. 10	Cash	39,500	
	Loss on Sale of Investment in Beal Common Shares	1,000	
	Investment in Beal Common Shares		40,500
	(To record sale of Beal common stock)		

The loss account is reported under Other Expenses and Losses in the income statement.

Holdings of between 20% and 50%

When an investor owns 20% to 50% of the common stock of a corporation, it is generally presumed that the investor has significant influence over the financial and operating activities of the investee. It is important to understand that **this presumed influence may be negated by extenuating circumstances**. For example, a company that acquires a 25% interest in another company in a hostile takeover may not have any significant influence over the investee.[2] In other words, companies are required to use judgement instead of blindly following the guidelines.

If an investor has significant influence, the investor should record its share of the net income of the investee in the year when it is earned. To delay recognizing the investor's share of net income until a cash dividend is declared ignores the fact that the investor is better off because the investee has earned income. Additionally, by using its influence an investor could force a dividend payment from the investee even when the investee reports a net loss. Using dividends as a basis for recognizing income does not properly indicate the economics of the situation.

This type of investment in common stock requires the use of the equity method. Under the equity method, the investment in common stock is initially recorded at cost, and the investment account is adjusted annually to show the investor's equity in the investee. Each year, the investor: (1) debits the investment account and credits revenue for its share of the investee's net income, and (2) credits the investment account when dividends are received[3]. The investment account is reduced for dividends received, because the net assets of the investee are decreased when a dividend is paid.

Case in point Cara Operations operates Swiss Chalet, Harvey's, and Beaver Foods, among other businesses. In 1996, it purchased 37% of The Second Cup Ltd.'s shares. Cara accounts for its investment in Second Cup using the equity method of accounting.

Entries at Acquisition

Assume that Milar Corporation acquires 30% of the common stock of Beck Company for $120,000 on January 1, 1999. Milar is assumed to have significant influence over Beck. The entry to record this transaction is:

Jan. 1	Investment in Beck Common Shares	120,000	
	Cash		120,000
	(To record purchase of Beck common stock)		

Entries for Revenue and Dividends

For 1999, Beck reports net income of $100,000 and declares and pays a $40,000 cash dividend. Milar is required to record: (1) its share of Beck's income, $30,000 (30% × $100,000), and (2) the reduction in the investment account for the dividends received, $12,000 ($40,000 × 30%). The entries are:

(1)

Dec. 31	Investment in Beck Common Shares	30,000	
	Revenue from Investment in Beck Company		30,000
	(To record 30% equity in Beck's 1999 net income)		

(2)

Dec. 31	Cash	12,000	
	Investment in Beck Common Shares		12,000
	(To record dividends received)		

---

[2] Among the factors that should be considered in determining an investor's influence are whether: (1) the investor has representation on the investee's board of directors, (2) the investor participates in the investee's policy-making process, (3) there are material transactions between the investor and the investee, and (4) the common stock held by other shareholders is concentrated or dispersed.

[3] Conversely, the investor debits a loss account and credits the investment account for its share of the investee's net loss.

After the transactions for the year have been posted, the investment and revenue accounts will show the following:

Illustration 17-4

Investment and revenue accounts after posting

Investment in Beck Common Shares				Revenue from Investment in Beck Company	
Jan. 1	120,000	Dec. 31	12,000		Dec. 31 30,000
Dec. 31	30,000				
Dec. 31	Bal. 138,000				

During the year, the investment account has increased by $18,000 ($138,000 − $120,000). This $18,000 is Milar's 30% equity in the $60,000 increase in Beck's retained earnings ($100,000 − $40,000). In addition, Milar will report $30,000 of revenue from its investment, which is 30% of Beck's net income of $100,000.

The difference between income reported under the cost method and reported under the equity method can be significant. For example, if Milar were assumed not to have significant influence, they would report only $12,000 of dividend revenue (30% × $40,000) using the cost method. Illustration 17-5 compares the journal entries used to record these investment transactions, first, by assuming that the cost method (no significant influence) was used by Milar, and then by assuming that the equity method (as discussed in this section) was used.

Illustration 17-5

Comparison of cost and equity method journal entries

Cost Method			Equity Method		
Acquisition					
Investment in Beck			Investment in Beck		
Common Shares	120,000		Common Shares	120,000	
Cash		120,000	Cash		120,000
Investee reports earnings					
No entry			Investment in Beck		
			Common Shares	30,000	
			Revenue from Investment		30,000
Investee pays dividends					
Cash	12,000		Cash	12,000	
Dividend Revenue		12,000	Investment in Beck		
			Common Shares		12,000

▶Accounting in Action ▸ *Business Insight*

Ottawa-based Corel Corp. sold its entertainment and educational CD business to Toronto-based I. Hoffmann and Associates Inc. Instead of a cash purchase price, Corel requested an equity interest of 22% in the small multimedia development and training company. Corel needed to focus its resources on the next generation of office software but also wanted to retain a piece of the pie in what is sometimes called the *edutainment* business. Corel's CEO, Michael Cowpland, was given a seat on the company's board of directors.

Source: Globe and Mail, April 7, 1997, B4.

Holdings of More Than 50%

A company that owns more than 50% of the common stock of another entity is known as the **parent company**. The entity whose stock is owned by the parent company is called the **subsidiary (affiliated) company**. Because of its stock ownership, the parent company has a controlling interest in the subsidiary company. Voting control can also occur with stock ownership of less than 50%, depending on how widely dispersed share ownership is and other factors mentioned previously.

►Accounting in Action ► *Business Insight*

Hudson's Bay Company owns 100% of the common stock of Zellers Inc. The common shareholders of Hudson's Bay elect its board of directors, who, in turn, select the Hudson's Bay's officers and managers. The board of directors controls the property owned by the corporation, which includes the common stock of Zellers. Thus, the Hudson's Bay board of directors can elect the board of directors of Zellers and, in effect, control Zellers' operations.

When a company **controls** the common stock of another company, the parent obviously oversees the financial and operating activities of the subsidiary. For the same reasons that the equity method is used to account for investments where significant influence exists, the equity method is used by the parent company for investment accounting purposes where control exists. In addition, **for financial reporting purposes only**, consolidated financial statements are prepared.

Consolidated financial statements present the assets and liabilities controlled by the parent company and the combined profitability of the subsidiary companies. They are prepared in addition to the financial statements for each of the individual parent and subsidiary companies. **Consolidated statements are especially useful to the shareholders, board of directors, and management of the parent company.** Moreover, consolidated statements inform creditors, prospective investors, and regulatory agencies of the size and range of operations of the companies that operate under common control.

Provided below are examples of two companies that prepare consolidated statements, and some of their subsidiary companies.

Case in point The operating relationship between a parent company and a subsidiary is similar to the operating relationship between parents and their teenagers. The parent may exercise tight or relatively little control.

STUDY OBJECTIVE
·········· 4 ··········

Describe the purpose and usefulness of consolidated financial statements.

Bombardier Inc.	Canadian Pacific
Auburn Technology Inc.	Canadian Pacific Hotels & Resorts Inc.
Bombardier Eurorail	Contship Holdings NV
Bombardier Motor Corporation of America	Fording Inc.
Bombardier Transit Corporation	Delta Hotels and Resort
De Havilland Inc.	PanCanadian Petroleum Limited
Learjet Inc.	St. Lawrence & Hudson Railway Company Limited

Illustration 17-6

Selected subsidiary companies

Another example of a consolidated company is The Second Cup Ltd. Second Cup owns 69.5% of Coffee People (which recently merged with Gloria Jean's, the second-largest chain of specialty coffee stores in the U.S.). The accounting for consolidated financial statements is discussed in the appendix to this chapter.

Before You Go On . . .

▶*Review It*

1. Compare the accounting entries for investments in stock for which ownership is: (a) less than 20% with no significant influence, and (b) more than 20% with significant influence.
2. What is the purpose of consolidated financial statements?

▶*Do It*

Two separate situations are presented below.
1. CJW Inc. acquired 5% of the 400,000 shares of common stock of Stillwater Corp. at a total cost of $6 per share on May 18, 1999. On August 30, Stillwater declared and paid a $0.10 per share dividend. On December 31, Stillwater reported net income of $244,000 for the year.
2. Dumas, Inc., obtained significant influence over North Sails by buying 40% of North Sails' 60,000 outstanding shares of common stock at a cost of $12 per share on January 1, 1999. On April 15, North Sails declared and paid a cash dividend of $0.75 per share. On December 31, North Sails reported a net income of $120,000 for the year.

Prepare all necessary journal entries for 1999 for: (1) CJW Inc., and (2) Dumas, Inc.

   Reasoning: When an investor owns less than 20% of the common stock of another corporation, it is presumed that the investor has relatively little influence over the investee and the cost method should be used. As a result, net income earned by the investee cannot be recognized as income by the investor. For investments of 20% or more, significant influence is presumed. The equity method should be used and therefore the investor's share of the net income of the investee should be recorded.

   Solution:

(1) CJW Inc.: Cost Method

May	18	Investment in Stillwater Common Shares	120,000	
		(400,000 × 5% x $6)		
		Cash		120,000
		(To record purchase of 20,000 shares of		
		Stillwater Corp. stock)		
Aug.	30	Cash	2,000	
		Dividend Revenue ($0.10 × 20,000)		2,000
		(To record receipt of cash dividend)		
Dec.	31	No entry to record investee's net income		

(2) Dumas, Inc.: Equity Method

Jan.	1	Investment in North Sails Common Shares	288,000	
		(60,000 × 40% × $12)		
		Cash		288,000
		(To record purchase of 24,000 shares of		
		North Sails' stock)		
Apr.	15	Cash	18,000	
		Investment in North Sails Common Shares		18,000
		($0.75 × 24,000)		
		(To record receipt of cash dividend)		
Dec.	31	Investment in North Sails Common Shares	48,000	
		($120,000 × 40%)		
		Revenue from Investment in North Sails		48,000
		(To record 40% equity in North Sails' net income)		

Related exercise material: BE17–2, BE17–3, E17–3, and E17–5.

Valuation and Reporting of Investments

The value of debt and stock investments may fluctuate greatly during the time they are held. The Scotia McLeod Universe Bond Index and the Toronto Stock Exchange (TSE) 300 composite index are two indices that track the volatile nature of debt and stock prices. These indices, based on Canadian bond and stock prices, may drop drastically with unfavourable economic developments and jump dramatically with favourable economic events. If prices fluctuate so much, how should investments be valued at the balance sheet date? Valuation could be at cost, at market value, or at the lower of cost and market value. The quality of **conservatism** makes it necessary to use the lower of cost and market (LCM) rule.

You were introduced to the lower of cost and market rule in Chapter 9, with respect to inventories. Just as inventories have a relevant market value, so too do investments. If the market value of the investments falls below their cost, this potential loss should be recognized at the earliest possible time, to minimize any negative impact on decision makers. Application of the LCM rules varies depending upon whether the investment is temporary or long-term.

STUDY OBJECTIVE

5

Indicate how debt and stock investments are valued and reported on the financial statements.

▶ ***International note***

The oldest and most widely quoted stock market index in the U.S. is the Dow Jones Industrial Average. In Britain, it is the FT-SE; in Germany, the DAX; and in Japan, the Nikkei.

Temporary Investments

To illustrate the valuation of temporary investments, assume that on December 31, 1999, Plano Corporation has the following costs and market values:

Investments	Cost	Market Value	Unrealized Gain (Loss)
Yorkville Company bonds	$ 50,000	**$ 48,000**	$(2,000)
Wu Company shares	**90,000**	99,000	9,000
Total	$140,000	$147,000	$ 7,000

Illustration 17-7

Valuation of temporary investments

▶ ***Ethics note***

Some managers would like to avoid writing down temporary investments that have experienced losses, arguing that the decline is only due to short-term fluctuations in the market value. This would improve income. Do you think this is ethical?

The lower of cost and market rule can be applied to each individual investment or to the portfolio as a whole. If the LCM rule was applied on a total portfolio basis, Plano Corporation would note an unrealized gain of $7,000, because total market value ($147,000) is $7,000 greater than total cost ($140,000). Remember that while conservatism allows losses to be recognized in advance of realization, gains are not recognized in advance. No entry would be required until the investments are sold.

If the LCM rule is applied to individual securities, only the Yorkville Company bonds will be written down. Therefore, the Yorkville bonds will be reported at their market value of $48,000, while the Wu shares will be reported at their cost of $90,000. The investment portfolio will be reported at an LCM value of $138,000 ($48,000 + $90,000) on the balance sheet.

The adjusting entry for Plano Corporation is:

Dec. 31	Unrealized Loss	2,000	
	Allowance to Reduce Cost to Market Value		2,000
	(To record unrealized loss on Yorkville bonds)		

The LCM rule is normally applied to the total portfolio and not to individual investments. Applying LCM individually would result in an overly conservative valuation for what is already a conservative rule.

Whether the total portfolio or the individual investment approach is used, the decline in value from cost to market is reported as an **unrealized loss,** because the securities have not been sold. The unrealized loss is reported on the income statement (in the Other Expenses and Losses section), because of the likelihood that the securities will be sold at market value since they are a short-term investment.

A valuation allowance account, Allowance to Reduce Cost to Market Value, is used to record the difference between the cost and market value of the securities. The use of this contra asset account, Allowance to Reduce Cost to Market Value, enables the company to maintain a record of its investment cost. Actual cost is needed to determine the gain or loss realized when the securities are sold. The Allowance account balance is deducted from the cost of the investments to arrive at the lower of cost and market valuation reported on the balance sheet for the temporary investments.

The Allowance account is carried forward into future accounting periods, in a manner similar to that for the Allowance for Doubtful Accounts, which offsets Accounts Receivable. No entries are made to the Allowance to Reduce Cost to Market Value account during the period. At the end of each reporting period, the balance in the account is adjusted to the difference between cost and market value. If the market value rises above the cost, the Allowance account can be adjusted to a zero balance. The valuation allowance should never have a debit balance; this would result in the recognition of an unrealized gain.

Some companies do not use an Allowance account for their temporary investments, since they plan to dispose of the securities in the near future. Therefore, if the difference between cost and market is considered immaterial, the journal entry to adjust cost to a lower market value is often ignored.

Long-Term Investments

Because long-term investments have longer maturities than temporary investments, their carrying values should not be adjusted to reflect temporary fluctuations in market values. If market falls substantially below cost and the drop is not due to temporary fluctuations, the investment must be reduced to its market value. This value becomes the investment's new cost base. Any write-down to market value is accounted for on the income statement as a **realized** (not an unrealized) loss, with no subsequent recovery in value anticipated or recorded.

To illustrate, assume that Hébert Corporation purchased 10,000 shares of Bre-X Minerals Ltd. at a cost of $20 per share, as a long-term investment. These shares are now worthless. The adjusting entry for Hébert to record the realized loss of $200,000 is as follows:

Dec.	31	Realized Loss	200,000	
		Investment in Bre-X Minerals Shares		200,000
		(To record permanent, realized loss on		
		long-term investment in Bre-X shares)		

Financial Statement Presentation

Case in point *Financial Reporting in Canada* indicates that 67% of the companies surveyed reported temporary investments, and that 67% also reported long-term investments.

Because of their high liquidity, **temporary investments** are either listed immediately below cash or combined with cash in the current asset section of the balance sheet. Temporary investments are reported at the lower of cost and market value. Because of the importance of market value to the reader of the financial statements, the market value is also disclosed, usually in parentheses or by footnote. For example, if Plana applied LCM to its total portfolio, temporary investments would be reported at their cost of $140,000, as follows:

Illustration 17-8

Presentation of temporary investments–at cost

Current assets	
Cash	$xx,xxx
Temporary investments, at cost (market $147,000)	140,000

If Plano Corporation applied the LCM rule to individual securities, its temporary investments, carried at market rather than cost, could be presented as follows:

Illustration 17-9

Presentation of temporary investments—at market

Current assets		
Cash		$xx,xxx
Temporary investments, at cost	$140,000	
Less: Allowance to reduce cost to market value	2,000	
Temporary investments, at market		138,000

More often, however, the allowance is not reported separately. Temporary investments are simply stated to be at the lower of cost and market and presented in one line, similar to the presentation style indicated in Illustration 17-8.

Long-term investments are generally reported in a separate section of the balance sheet, immediately below current assets, as shown in Illustration 17-11. Also note how The Second Cup Ltd., presents its investment in Great Canadian Bagel, Ltd., on its balance sheet, reproduced in Appendix A.

In the income statement, the following items are reported in the nonoperating section:

Illustration 17-10

Nonoperating items related to investments

Alternative terminology
Interest revenue is also called *interest income*, and dividend revenue may be called *dividend income*.

Other Revenue and Gains	**Other Expenses and Losses**
Interest Revenue	Loss on Sale of Investments
Dividend Revenue	Realized Loss
Gain on Sale of Investments	Unrealized Loss

Comprehensive Balance Sheet

Numerous examples of sections of classified balance sheets have been presented in this and preceding chapters. The balance sheet shown in Illustration 17-11 includes such topics from previous chapters as issuance of long-term bonds, issuance of no par value common stock, organization costs, and restrictions of retained earnings. From this chapter, the statement includes (highlighted in red) temporary and long-term investments (reported at cost and at equity), and descriptive notations within the statement.

Illustration 17-11

Comprehensive balance sheet

ZABOSCHUK CORPORATION
Balance Sheet
December 31, 1999

Assets

Current assets		
Cash		$ 21,000
Temporary investments, at lower of cost and market (market $75,000)		60,000
Accounts receivable	$84,000	
Less: Allowance for doubtful accounts	4,000	80,000
Merchandise inventory, at FIFO cost		130,000
Prepaid insurance		23,000

Illustration 17-11 (continued)

Comprehensive balance sheet

Total current assets			314,000
Investments			
Investments in stock of less than 20% owned companies, at cost		$ 50,000	
Investments in stock of more than 20% owned companies, at equity		250,000	
Total long-term investments			300,000
Capital assets			
Land		$200,000	
Buildings	$800,000		
Less: Accumulated amortization	200,000	600,000	
Equipment	180,000		
Less: Accumulated amortization	54,000	126,000	
Goodwill		100,000	
Organization costs		70,000	
Total capital assets			1,096,000
Total assets			$1,710,000

Liabilities and Shareholders' Equity

Current liabilities			
Accounts payable			$ 185,000
Bond interest payable			10,000
Income taxes payable			60,000
Total current liabilities			255,000
Long-term liabilities			
Bonds payable, 7%, due 2010		$300,000	
Less: Discount on bonds		10,000	
Total long-term liabilities			290,000
Total liabilities			545,000
Shareholders' equity			
Common stock, no par value, 200,000 shares authorized, 80,000 shares issued and outstanding		$900,000	
Retained earnings (of which $100,000 is restricted for plant expansion)		265,000	
Total shareholders' equity			1,165,000
Total liabilities and shareholders' equity			$1,710,000

Before You Go On . . .

▶Review It

1. What is the proper valuation and reporting of temporary and long-term investments on a balance sheet?

2. Explain how temporary and long-term investments are reported on a balance sheet.

Related exercise material: BE17–4, BE17–5, BE17–6, BE17–7, BE17–8, E17–2, E17–4, E17–6, E17–7, and E17–8.

A Look Back at the Shewan Brothers

Refer back to the opening story about A.J. and Ben Shewan and answer the following questions:
1. The Shewans have averaged a 30% rate of return over the last seven years. Is it more likely that this return has been earned from dividends or from appreciation in share value? Why?

2. If they want to make their investment income look good, which securities should they sell and which ones should they keep?

3. What investment strategies do the two brothers use?

Solution:

1. Firms could not consistently pay anywhere near a 30% dividend; thus most of the Shewans' return must be coming from appreciation in share value.

2. In order to maximize reported income, the Shewan brothers could choose at year end to sell all securities that have experienced gains, and to hold all such securities that have unrealized losses.

3. They use financial information from advisors to evaluate factors such as a security's safety, industry rank, and volatility. In addition, they use good, sound common sense by looking for new products that they understand, relate to, and think have promising futures.

*S*ummary of Study Objectives

1. *Distinguish between temporary and long-term investments.* Temporary investments are securities held by a company that are readily marketable and intended to be exchanged for cash in the near future as the need for cash arises. Investments that do not meet both criteria are classified as long-term investments.

2. *Explain the accounting for debt investments.* Entries for investments in debt securities are required when the bonds are purchased, when interest is received or accrued, and the bonds are sold. The accounting for long-term investments in bonds is the same as for temporary investments in bonds, except that bond premium and bond discount must be recorded and amortized.

3. *Explain the accounting for stock investments.* Entries for investments in stock are required when the stock is purchased, when dividends are received, and when the stock is sold. When the investor company is not able to exert significant influence (ownership usually less than 20%) over the operating and financial policies of the investee company, the cost method is used. When significant influence exists (ownership usually 20%

or more), the equity method should be used. When control is exercised (ownership usually greater 50%), consolidated financial statements should be prepared for financial reporting purposes.

4. *Describe the purpose and usefulness of consolidated financial statements.* When a company controls the common stock of another company, consolidated financial statements detailing the financial position of the combined entity must be prepared. These statements are especially useful to the shareholders, board of directors, and management of the parent company.

5. *Indicate how debt and stock investments are valued and reported on the financial statements.* Temporary investments in debt and stock securities are valued at the lower of cost and market, with market values separately disclosed. Long-term investments are valued at cost. If market value is anticipated to be less than cost on a permanent basis, the investment should be written down to market, which now becomes its new cost base.

*A*PPENDIX ▸ *Preparing Consolidated Financial Statements*

*P*reparing a Consolidated Balance Sheet

Consolidated balance sheets are prepared from the individual balance sheets of the affiliated companies. They are not prepared from ledger accounts kept by the consolidated entity, because only the separate legal entities (the affiliated companies) maintain accounting records.

All items in the individual balance sheets are included in the consolidated balance sheet except amounts for transactions between the affiliated companies. Transactions between the affiliated companies are identified as **intercorporate transactions**. The process of excluding these transactions when preparing consolidated statements is

STUDY OBJECTIVE
6

Prepare a consolidated balance sheet.

Helpful hint Eliminations are aptly named because they eliminate duplicate data. They are not adjustments.

called **intercorporate eliminations**. These eliminations are necessary to avoid overstating assets, liabilities, and shareholders' equity in the consolidated balance sheet. For example, amounts payable by a subsidiary to a parent company and the related receivable reported by the parent company would be eliminated. The objective in a consolidated balance sheet is to show only obligations to, and receivables from, parties who are not part of the affiliated group of companies.

To illustrate, assume that on January 1, 1999, Powers Construction Company pays $150,000 in cash for 100% of Serto Brick Company's common stock. Powers Construction Company records the investment in their own accounting records using the equity method of accounting. Powers purchases the shares directly from the shareholders of Serto Brick Company; therefore, no journal entry is made by Serto.

Illustration 17A-1

Recording controlling investment

Powers Construction Company (Parent)			Serto Brick Company (Subsidiary)
Investment in Serto Company Common Stock	150,000		No entry
Cash		150,000	

The Investment in Serto Brick Company common stock that appears on the balance sheet of Powers Construction Company represents an interest in the net assets of Serto. If one simply combined the items in the separate balance sheets of the affiliated companies, there would be a double counting of assets. That is, the combined data would show an Investment in Serto Brick Company Common Stock. However, the consolidated entity cannot own an investment in itself. Similarly, there would be a double counting in shareholders' equity because the common stock of Serto Brick Company is completely owned by the shareholders of Powers Construction Company. This double counting must be eliminated in the preparation of a consolidated balance sheet, by showing the Investment in Serto Brick Company at zero and reporting only the common stock and retained earnings of Powers Construction Company as shareholders' equity.

Use of a Work Sheet—Cost Equal to Book Value

Helpful hint   Like the work sheets described earlier in this textbook, consolidated work sheets are optional.

A work sheet usually makes it easier to prepare consolidated balance sheets. As shown in Illustration 17A-2,[4] the work sheet for a consolidated balance sheet contains columns for: (1) the balance sheet data for the separate legal entities, (2) intercorporate eliminations, and (3) consolidated data. All data in the work sheet is for to the preceding example in which Powers Construction Company acquires 100% ownership of Serto Brick Company for $150,000. In this case, the cost of the investment, $150,000, is equal to the book value, $150,000 ($100,000 + $50,000), of the subsidiary's net assets. The intercorporate elimination results in a credit to the Investment account maintained by Powers for its balance, $150,000, and debits to the Common Stock and Retained Earnings accounts of Serto for their respective balances, $100,000 and $50,000.

Note that because intercorporate eliminations are only used for the calculation of correct consolidated data, they are only presented on the work sheet. They are not journalized or posted by either of the affiliated companies, and therefore do not affect the ledger accounts. Powers Construction Company's investment account and Serto Brick Company's common stock and retained earnings accounts are reported separately by each of these entities when they prepare their own financial statements.

---

[4] Condensed data are used throughout this material to keep details at a minimum.

POWERS COMPANY AND SUBSIDIARY
Work Sheet—Consolidated Balance Sheet
January 1, 1999 (Acquisition Date)

Assets	Powers Construction Company	Serto Brick Company	Eliminations Dr.	Eliminations Cr.	Consolidated Data
Current assets	50,000	80,000			130,000
Investment in Serto Brick Company common stock	150,000			150,000	–0–
Capital assets (net)	325,000	145,000			470,000
Totals	525,000	225,000			600,000
Liabilities and Shareholders' Equity					
Current liabilities	50,000	75,000			125,000
Common stock—Powers Construction Company	300,000				300,000
Common stock—Serto Brick Company		100,000	100,000		–0–
Retained earnings—Powers Construction Company	175,000				175,000
Retained earnings—Serto Brick Company		50,000	50,000		–0–
Totals	525,000	225,000	150,000	150,000	600,000

Illustration 17A-2

Work sheet—Cost equals book value

▶Technology in Action

The consolidated work sheet is another good spreadsheet application. Computer programs are available that can merge multiple general ledgers for consolidated entities. All you need to do is supply the eliminating information and enter a few command keystrokes, and the consolidated financial statements will come off the printer, ready for distribution.

Use of a Work Sheet—Cost Above Book Value

The cost of acquiring the common stock of another company may be above or below its book value. The management of the parent company may pay more than book value because it believes: (1) the fair market values of identifiable assets such as land, buildings, and equipment are higher than their recorded book values, and/or (2) the subsidiary's future earnings prospects warrant a payment for goodwill.

To illustrate, assume the same data used above, except that Powers Construction Company pays $165,000 in cash for 100% of Serto's common stock. The **excess of cost over book value** is $15,000 ($165,000–$150,000). This excess is first reallocated to specific assets, such as inventory and land, if their fair market values on the acquisition date exceed their book values. Any remainder is considered to be goodwill.

Assume that the fair market value of Serto's property and equipment is $155,000, whereas their cost was $145,000. Thus, $10,000 of the excess of cost over book value is allocated to property and equipment, and the remainder, $5,000, is allocated to goodwill. The working paper eliminating entry would be:

Capital assets: Property and equipment	10,000	
Capital assets: Goodwill	5,000	
Common stock—Serto Brick Company	100,000	
Retained earnings—Serto Brick Company	50,000	
Investment in Serto Brick Company Common Stock		165,000

Total assets and total liabilities and shareholders' equity are the same as in the preceding example ($600,000). However, in this case total assets includes: a $15,000 excess of cost over book value that has been reallocated to the capital asset accounts of property and equipment ($10,000) and goodwill ($5,000).

POWERS CONSTRUCTION COMPANY AND SUBSIDIARY
Work Sheet—Consolidated Balance Sheet
January 1, 1999 (Acquisition Date)

Assets	Powers Construction Company	Serto Brick Company	Eliminations Dr.	Cr.	Consolidated Data
Current assets	35,000	80,000			115,000
Investment in Serto Brick Company common stock	165,000			165,000	–0–
Capital assets (net)	325,000	145,000	10,000 5,000		485,000
Totals	525,000	225,000			600,000
Liabilities and Shareholders' Equity					
Current liabilities	50,000	75,000			125,000
Common stock—Powers Construction Company	300,000				300,000
Common stock—Serto Brick Company		100,000	100,000		–0–
Retained earnings—Powers Construction Company	175,000				175,000
Retained earnings—Serto Brick Company		50,000	50,000		–0–
Totals	525,000	225,000	165,000	165,000	600,000

Illustration 17A-3

Work sheet—cost above book value

Content of a Consolidated Balance Sheet

The condensed consolidated balance sheet of Powers Construction Company, based on the data presented in Illustration 17A-3, is shown in Illustration 17A-4. At the end of each reporting period, as explained in Chapter 10, goodwill would be amortized by the straight-line method over the period benefited, but not in excess of 40 years.

Illustration 17A-4

Consolidated balance sheet

POWERS CONSTRUCTION COMPANY
Consolidated Balance Sheet
January 1, 1999

Assets

Current assets		$115,000
Capital assets (net)		485,000
Total assets		$600,000

Liabilities and Shareholders' Equity

Current liabilities		$125,000
Shareholders' equity		
Common stock	$300,000	
Retained earnings	175,000	475,000
Total liabilities and shareholders' equity		$600,000

▶Accounting in Action ▶ *International Insight*

In addition to one company (parent) acquiring another company (subsidiary), companies can merge or combine operations for the same purposes. Low interest rates, a strong economy, and globalization have provided the right climate for mergers and acquisitions. 1997 was a record year, with more than $1.4 trillion of corporate marriages as companies combined to add new markets, reduce costs, and increase profits. In Canada, the proposed combination of the Royal Bank of Canada and the Bank of Montreal will (if approved) be the largest merger in Canadian business history.

Source: Globe and Mail, July 2, 1997, B9.

Consolidated Income Statement

A consolidated income statement is also prepared for affiliated companies. This statement shows the results of operations of affiliated companies as though they were one economic unit. This means that the statement shows only revenue and expense transactions between the consolidated entity and companies and individuals that are outside the affiliated group. Consequently, all intercorporate revenue and expense transactions must be eliminated. Intercorporate transactions such as sales between affiliates and interest on loans charged by one affiliate to another must be eliminated. A work sheet facilitates the preparation of consolidated income statements in the same manner as it does for the balance sheet.

> **Case in point** Earnings per share data are based on consolidated net income.

The preparation of consolidated income statements is more complex than the preparation of consolidated balance sheets. This, and other more complicated consolidation topics (such as what happens when there is less than 100% ownership), will be discussed in advanced accounting courses.

Before You Go On . . .
▶*Review It*

1. Why are eliminations needed when preparing consolidated financial statements?
2. What eliminations are made for the parent company's investment in the common stock of a subsidiary company?
3. How is the excess of cost over book value reported in a consolidated balance sheet?

Related exercise material: BE17-9, BE17-10, E17-9, and E17-10.

▼*Summary of Study Objective*

6. *Prepare a consolidated balance sheet.* Consolidated balance sheets are similar in form and content to the financial statements of an individual corporation. A consolidated balance sheet shows only the assets and liabilities controlled by the parent company, excluding all intercorporate transactions.

GLOSSARY

Consolidated financial statements Financial statements that present the assets and liabilities controlled by the parent company, and the combined profitability of the affiliated companies. (p. 711).

Controlling interest Ownership of more than 50%, or voting control, of the common stock of another entity. (p. 711).

Cost method An accounting method in which the investment in stock is recorded at cost and investment revenue is recognized only when cash dividends are received. (p. 707).

Debt investments   Investments in government and corporation bonds. (p. 703).

Equity method   An accounting method in which the investment in common stock is initially recorded at cost, and the investment account is then adjusted annually to show the investor's equity in the investee. (p. 709).

Goodwill   The amount paid to purchase a business in excess of the fair market value of its net identifiable assets. Goodwill often occurs because of a favourable record of past or anticipated future performance. (p. 719).

Long-term investments   Investments that are not readily marketable or that management does not intend to convert into cash in the near future. (p. 703).

Lower of cost and market (LCM)   A conservative rule that states that investments must be carried at the lower of their cost or market value. (p. 713).

Stock investments   Investments in the capital stock of corporations. (p. 706).

Temporary investments   Investments that are readily marketable and intended to be exchanged for cash in the near future when the need for cash arises. (p. 703).

DEMONSTRATION PROBLEM

In its first year of operations, the DeMarco Company had the following selected transactions in temporary equity investments.

June 1 Purchased for cash 600 shares of Sanburg common stock at $24 per share plus $300 brokerage fees.

July 1 Purchased for cash 800 shares of Cey common stock at $33 per share plus $600 brokerage fees.

Sept. 1 Received a $1 per share cash dividend from Cey Corporation.

Nov. 1 Sold 200 shares of Sanburg common stock for cash at $27 per share less $150 brokerage fees.

Dec. 15 Received a $0.50 per share cash dividend on Sanburg common stock.

At December 31, the market values per share were: Sanburg $25 and Cey $30.

Instructions

(a) Journalize the transactions.

(b) Prepare the adjusting entry at December 31 to report the securities at the appropriate value.

Solution to Demonstration Problem

(a)	June	1	Investment in Sanburg Co.	14,700	
			Cash		14,700
			(To record purchase of 600 shares of Sanburg common stock)		
	July	1	Investment in Cey Corp.	27,000	
			Cash		27,000
			(To record purchase of 800 shares of Cey common stock)		
	Sept.	1	Cash	800	
			Dividend Revenue		800
			(To record receipt of $1 per share cash dividend from Cey Corporation)		
	Nov.	1	Cash	5,250	
			Investment in Sanburg Co.		4,900
			Gain on Sale of Stock Investments		350
			(To record sale of 200 shares of Sanburg common stock)		
	Dec.	15	Cash	200	
			Dividend Revenue		200
			(To record receipt of $0.50 per share dividend from Sanburg)		

(b) The following table shows the relevant values at the end of the fiscal year:

Investment	Cost	Market Value	Unrealized Gain (Loss)
Sanburg common stock	$ 9,800	$10,000	$ 200
Cey common stock	27,000	24,000	(3,000)
Totals	$36,800	$34,000	$(2,800)

Although the lower of cost and market valuation could be applied to each individual security, it is usually applied to the portfolio as a whole. This results in the following adjusting journal entry:

Dec.	31	Unrealized Loss on Temporary Investments	2,800	
		Allowance to Reduce Cost to Market Value		2,800
		(To record unrealized loss on temporary investments)		

Note: All **asterisked** Questions, Exercises, and Problems relate to material contained in the Appendix to this chapter.

SELF-STUDY QUESTIONS

••

Answers are at the end of the chapter.

(SO 1)

1. Temporary investments must be readily marketable and be expected to be sold:
   a. within the operating cycle.
   b. within the next year or operating cycle, whichever is shorter.
   c. within the next year or operating cycle, whichever is longer.
   d. whenever the need for cash arises.

(SO 2)

2. Hanes Company has debt investments costing $26,000 and sells for $28,000 plus accrued interest (which has been recorded). In journalizing the sale, credits are:
   a. Debt Investments, Loss on Sale of Debt Investments, and Bond Interest Receivable.
   b. Debt Investments, Gain on Sale of Debt Investments, and Bond Interest Receivable.
   c. Debt Investments, Gain on Sale of Debt Investments, and Bond Interest Revenue.
   d. Debt Investments and Bond Interest Receivable.

(SO 2, 3)

3. Pryor Company receives net proceeds of $42,000 on the sale of investments that cost $39,500. This transaction should be reported in the income statement as:
   a. loss of $2,500 under Other Expenses and Losses.
   b. loss of $2,500 under Operating Expenses.
   c. gain of $2,500 under Other Revenues and Gains.
   d. gain of $2,500 under Operating Revenues.

(SO 3)

4. The equity method of accounting for long-term investments in stock should be used when the investor has significant influence over an investee and owns:
   a. between 20% and 50% of the investee's common stock.
   b. 20% or more of the investee's common stock.
   c. more than 50% of the investee's common stock.
   d. less than 20% of the investee's common stock.

(SO 4)

5. Which of the following statements is false? Consolidated financial statements are useful to determine the:
   a. profitability of specific subsidiaries.
   b. combined profitability of enterprises under common control.
   c. range of a parent company's operations.
   d. full extent of combined obligations of enterprises under common control.

(SO 5)

6. At the end of the first year of operations, the total cost of the temporary investments portfolio is $120,000, and total market value is $115,000. The financial statements should show:
   a. a reduction of an asset of $5,000 in the balance sheet and a realized loss of $5,000 in the income statement.
   b. a reduction of an asset of $5,000 and an unrealized loss of $5,000 in the shareholders' equity section.
   c. a reduction of an asset of $5,000 in the current asset section and an unrealized loss in Other Expenses and Losses of $5,000.
   d. a reduction of an asset of $5,000 in the current asset section and a realized loss of $5,000 in Other Expenses and Losses.

(SO 5)

7. An unrealized loss on temporary investments is reported as a:
   a. contra asset account.
   b. contra shareholders' equity account.
   c. loss in the income statement.
   d. loss in the retained earnings statement.

(SO 6)

*8. Pate Company pays $175,000 for 100% of Sinko's common stock when Sinko's shareholders' equity consists of Common Stock $100,000 and Retained Earnings $60,000. In the work sheet for the consolidated balance sheet, the eliminations will include a:

a. credit to Investment in Sinko Common Stock $160,000.

b. credit to Goodwill $15,000.

c. debit to Retained Earnings $75,000.

d. debit to Goodwill $15,000.

(SO 6)   * 9. Which of the following statements about intercompany eliminations are *true*?

a. They are not journalized or posted by any of the subsidiaries.

b. They do not affect the ledger accounts of the parent company.

c. Intercompany eliminations are made only on the work sheet to help arrive at correct consolidated data.

d. All of these statements are true.

*10. Which of the following statements about consolidated income statements is *false*?   (SO

a. A work sheet facilitates the preparation of the statement.

b. The consolidated income statement shows the results of operations of affiliated companies as a single economic unit.

c. All revenue and expense transactions between parent and subsidiary companies are eliminated.

d. When a subsidiary is wholly owned, the form and content of the statement will differ from the income statement of an individual corporation.

QUESTIONS

1. Kirk Wholesale Supply owns stock in Xerox Corporation, which it intends to hold indefinitely because of some negative tax consequences if they sell it. Should the investment in Xerox be classified as a temporary investment? Why?

2. (a) What is the cost of an investment in bonds?
   (b) When is interest on bonds recorded?

3. Ann Adler is confused about losses and gains on the sale of debt investments. Explain to Ann: (a) how the gain or loss is computed, and (b) the statement presentation of the gains and losses.

4. Clio Company sells an investment in bonds for $45,000, including $3,000 of accrued interest. The bonds originally cost $40,000. In recording the sale, Clio books a $5,000 gain. Is this correct? Explain.

5. What is the cost of an investment in stock?

6. To acquire Mega Corporation stock, R. L. Duran pays $65,000 in cash plus $1,500 broker's fees. Assuming the stock is readily marketable and the company intends to sell it when the need for cash arises, how should this stock be reported on Duran's balance sheet?

7. (a) When should a long-term investment in common stock be accounted for by the equity method? (b) When is revenue recognized under this method?

8. Malon Corporation uses the equity method to account for its ownership of 35% of the common stock of Flynn Packing. During 1999, Flynn reports a net income of $80,000 and declares and pays cash dividends of $10,000. What recognition should Malon Corporation give to these events?

9. What constitutes "significant influence" when an investor's financial interest is below the 50% level?

10. Distinguish between the cost and equity methods of accounting for investments in shares.

11. What are consolidated financial statements?

12. What are the valuation guidelines for reporting investments at a balance sheet date?

13. Wendy Walner is the controller of G-Products, Inc. At December 31, the company's temporary investments cost $74,000 and have a market value of $70,000. Indicate how Wendy would report these data in the financial statements prepared on December 31.

14. Using the data in question 13, how would Wendy report the data if the investments were long-term?

15. What is the proper statement presentation of the account Unrealized Loss on Temporary Investments?

16. What is the purpose of reporting unrealized losses on temporary investments?

*17. (a) What asset and equity balances are eliminated in preparing a consolidated balance sheet for a parent and a wholly owned subsidiary? (b) Why are they eliminated?

*18. Weller Company pays $320,000 to purchase all the outstanding common stock of Wood Corporation. At the date of purchase the net assets of Wood have a book value of $290,000. Weller's management allocates $20,000 of the excess cost to undervalued land on the books of Wood. What should be done with the rest of the excess?

BRIEF EXERCISES

••

BE17–1   Phelps Corporation purchased debt investments for $41,500 on January 1, 1999. On July 1, 1999, Phelps received cash interest of $2,075. Journalize the purchase and the receipt of interest. Assume that no interest has been accrued.

Journalize entries for debt investments.
(SO 2)

BE17–2   On August 1, McLain Company buys 1,000 shares of ABC common stock for $35,000 cash plus brokerage fees of $600. On December 1, the shares are sold for $38,000 in cash. Journalize the purchase and sale of the common stock.

Journalize entries for stock investments.
(SO 3)

BE17–3   Harmon Company owns 30% of Hook Company. For the current year Hook reports net income of $150,000 and declares and pays a $50,000 cash dividend. Record Harmon's equity in Hook's net income and the receipt of dividends from Hook.

Journalize entries under the equity method of accounting.
(SO 3)

BE17–4   Cost and market value data for the temporary investments of Michele Company at December 31, 1999, are $62,000 and $59,000, respectively. Prepare the adjusting entry to record the securities at the lower of cost and market value.

Prepare adjusting entry to reflect lower of cost and market value.
(SO 5)

BE17–5   For the data presented in BE17–4, show the financial statement presentation of the temporary investments and related accounts.

Indicate statement presentation using lower of cost and market value.
(SO 5)

BE17–6   Duggen Corporation holds stock securities costing $72,000 as a long-term investment. At December 31, 1999 the market value of the securities is $65,000. Assuming the decline in value is not due to temporary market fluctuations, prepare the adjusting entry to record the securities at market value.

Prepare adjusting entry to reflect lower of cost and market.
(SO 5)

BE17–7   For the data presented in BE17–6, show the financial statement presentation of the long-term investments and related accounts.

Indicate statement presentation using lower of cost and market value.
(SO 5)

BE17–8   Saber Corporation has the following long-term investments: common stock of Sword Co. (10% ownership), original cost $108,000, current market value $113,000; common stock of Epee Inc. (30% ownership), original cost $210,000, equity method valuation $250,000, current market value $253,000. Prepare the investments section of the balance sheet.

Prepare investments section of balance sheet.
(SO 5)

*BE17–9   Provo Company acquires 100% of the common stock of Stanton Company for $180,000 cash. On the acquisition date, Stanton's ledger shows Common Stock $120,000 and Retained Earnings $60,000. Complete the work sheet for the following accounts: Provo Company—Investment in Stanton Common Stock; Stanton Company—Common Stock; and Stanton Company—Retained Earnings.

Prepare partial consolidated work sheet, when cost equals book value.
(SO 6)

*BE17–10   Data for the Provo and Stanton companies are given in BE17–9. Assume that Provo, instead of paying $180,000, pays $200,000 to acquire the 100% interest in Stanton Company. Complete the work sheet for the accounts identified in BE17–9, and for the Goodwill account.

Prepare partial consolidated work sheet, when cost exceeds book value.
(SO 6)

EXERCISES

••

E17–1   Piper Corporation had the following transactions with debt investments:

Journalize debt investment transactions and accrue interest.
(SO 2)

Jan. 1   Purchased 60 $1,000 Harris Co. 10% bonds for $60,000 cash plus brokerage fees of $900. Interest is payable semi-annually on July 1 and January 1.

July 1   Received semi-annual interest on Harris Co. bonds.

July 1   Sold 30 Harris Co. bonds for $32,000 less $400 brokerage fees.

Instructions

(a)   Journalize the transactions.

(b)   Prepare the adjusting entry for the accrual of interest at December 31.

E17–2   Malea Company had the following transactions with stock investments:

Journalize stock investment transactions; explain income statement presentation.
(SO 3, 5)

Feb. 1   Purchased 800 shares of ABC common stock (2% of the total number of shares) for $8,200 cash plus brokerage fees of $200.

July 1 Received cash dividends of $1 per share on ABC common stock.

Sept. 1 Sold 300 shares of ABC common stock for $4,000 less brokerage fees of $100.

Dec. 1 Received cash dividends of $1 per share on ABC common stock.

Instructions

(a) Journalize the transactions.

(b) Explain how dividend revenue and the gain (loss) on sale should be reported in the income statement.

Journalize stock investment transactions.
(SO 3)

E17–3 McCormick Inc. had the following transactions with investments in common stock:

Jan. 1 Purchased 1,000 shares of Starr Corporation common stock (5% of the total number of shares) for $70,000 cash plus $1,400 broker's commission.

July 1 Received a cash dividend of $9 per share.

Dec. 1 Sold 500 shares of Starr Corporation common stock for $37,000 cash less $800 broker's commission.

Dec.31 Received a cash dividend of $9 per share.

Instructions

Journalize the transactions.

Journalize and post transactions; determine balance sheet presentation.
(SO 3, 5)

E17–4 On January 1 Ranier Corporation purchased 25% of the voting shares of Bellingham Corporation for $150,000. At December 31 Bellingham declared and paid a $60,000 cash dividend and reported net income of $200,000.

Instructions

(a) Journalize the transactions.

(b) Determine the amount to be reported for the investment in Bellingham stock at December 31.

Journalize entries under cost and equity methods.
(SO 3)

E17–5 Presented below are two independent situations:

1. Karen Cosmetics acquired 10% of the 200,000 shares of common stock of Bell Fashion at a total cost of $12 per share on March 18, 1999. On June 30, Bell declared and paid a $75,000 dividend. On December 31, Bell reported net income of $122,000 for the year. At December 31, the market price of Bell Fashion was $15 per share. The stock is classified as a temporary investment.

2. Ismail, Inc., obtained significant influence over Diner Corporation by buying 30% of Diner's 30,000 outstanding shares of common stock at a total cost of $9 per share on January 1, 1999. On June 15, Diner declared and paid a cash dividend of $35,000. On December 31, Diner reported a net income of $80,000 for the year.

Instructions

Prepare all the necessary journal entries for 1999 for: (a) Karen Cosmetics, and (b) Ismail, Inc.

Prepare year-end adjustment and show statement presentation.
(SO 5)

E17–6 At December 31, 1999, the temporary investments for Nielson, Inc., are as follows:

Security	Cost	Market Value
A	$17,500	$15,000
B	12,500	14,000
C	23,000	21,000
Totals	$53,000	$50,000

Instructions

(a) Prepare the adjusting entry at December 31, 1999 to report the portfolio of securities at the lower of cost and market value.

(b) Show the balance sheet and income statement presentation at December 31, 1999.

Prepare year-end adjustment; show and explain statement presentation.
(SO 5)

E17–7 Data for temporary stock investments are presented in E17–6. Assume instead that the investments are classified as long-term investments, and that any declines in value are not considered to be due to temporary market fluctuations.

Instructions

(a) Prepare the adjusting entry at December 31, 1999, to report the securities in the appropriate manner.

(b) Show the statement presentation at December 31, 1999.

(c) ◁▭▭▭▷ J. Arnet, a member of the board of directors, does not understand the reporting of the loss. Write a letter to Mr. Arnet explaining the calculation of the loss and the reasons for reporting it.

E17–8 Felipe Company has the following data at December 31, 1999:

Prepare year-end adjustments and show statement presentations; two types of investments.
(SO 5)

	Cost	Market value
Temporary Investments	$120,000	$100,000
Long-term Investments	125,000	90,000

Additional information: (1) In previous periods, the market value of Temporary Investments was always higher than their cost. Consequently, the company does not yet have an Allowance to Reduce Cost to Market Value. (2) The decline in the market value of the Long-term Investments is not considered to be attributable to temporary market fluctuations.

Instructions

(a) Prepare the adjusting entries to report each class of securities appropriately.

(b) Indicate the statement presentation of each class of securities and the related loss accounts.

*E17–9 On January 1, Swiss Corporation acquires 100% of Arco Inc. for $200,000 in cash. The condensed balance sheets of the two corporations immediately after the acquisition are as follows:

Prepare consolidated work sheet when cost equals book value.
(SO 6)

	Swiss Corporation	Arco Inc.
Current assets	$ 60,000	$ 40,000
Investment in Arco Inc. common stock	200,000	–
Capital assets (net)	300,000	210,000
	$560,000	$250,000
Current liabilities	$180,000	$ 50,000
Common stock	225,000	75,000
Retained earnings	155,000	125,000
	$560,000	$250,000

Instructions

Prepare a work sheet for a consolidated balance sheet.

*E17–10 Data for the Swiss and Arco corporations are presented in E17–9. Assume that instead of paying $200,000 in cash for Arco Inc., Swiss Corporation pays $215,000 in cash. Thus, at the acquisition date the assets of Swiss Corporation are: Current assets $45,000, Investment in Arco Inc. Common Stock $215,000, and Capital Assets (net) $300,000.

Prepare consolidated work sheet when cost exceeds book value.
(SO 6)

Instructions

Prepare a work sheet for a consolidated balance sheet.

PROBLEMS

P17–1 The following transactions related to a temporary debt investment occurred for Lund Corporation:

Journalize investment transactions and show financial statement presentation.
(SO 2, 5)

1999
Jan. 1   Purchased $50,000 RAM Corporation 10% bonds for $50,000.
July 1   Received interest on RAM bonds.
Dec. 31 Accrued interest on RAM bonds.

2000
Jan. 1   Received interest on RAM bonds.
Jan. 1   Sold $25,000 RAM bonds for $27,500.
July 1   Received interest on RAM bonds.

Instructions

(a) Journalize the transactions.

(b) Assume that the market value of the bonds at December 31, 1999, was $47,000. Prepare the adjusting entry to record these bonds at the lower of cost and market value.

(c) Show the balance sheet presentation of the bonds and interest receivable at December 31, 1999, and indicate where any unrealized gain or loss is reported in the financial statements.

Journalize investment transactions, prepare adjusting entry, and show statement presentation.

(SO 2, 3, 5)

P17–2   In January 1999 the management of Reed Company concludes that it has sufficient cash to purchase some temporary investments in debt and equity securities. During the year, the following transactions occurred:

Feb. 1	Purchased 800 shares of IBF common stock for $32,000 plus brokerage fees of $800.
Mar. 1	Purchased 500 shares of RST common stock for $15,000 plus brokerage fees of $500.
Apr. 1	Purchased 60 $1,000, 12% CRT bonds for $60,000 plus $1,200 brokerage fees. Interest is payable semi-annually on April 1 and October 1.
July 1	Received a cash dividend of $0.60 per share on the IBF common stock.
Aug. 1	Sold 200 shares of IBF common stock at $42 per share less brokerage fees of $350.
Sept. 1	Received a $1 per share cash dividend on the RST common stock.
Oct. 1	Received the semi-annual interest on the CRT bonds.
Oct. 1	Sold the CRT bonds for $63,000 less $1,000 brokerage fees.

At December 31, the market values of the IBF and RST common shares were $39 and $30 respectively, per share.

Instructions

(a) Journalize the transactions.

(b) Prepare the adjusting entry at December 31, 1999, to report the investments at the lower of cost and market value.

(c) Show the balance sheet presentation of the temporary investments at December 31, 1999.

(d) Identify the income statement accounts involved, and give the statement classification of each account.

Journalize transactions and adjusting entry for stock investments; show statement presentation.

(SO 3, 5)

P17–3   On December 31, 1998, Harmon Associates owned the following securities that were being held as long-term investments:

Common Stock	Shares	Cost
A Co.	1,000	$50,000
B Co.	6,000	36,000
C Co.	1,200	24,000

The securities are not held for influence or control over the investees. In 1999, the following transactions occurred:

July 1	Received $1 per share semi-annual cash dividend on B Co. common stock.
Aug. 1	Received $0.50 per share cash dividend on A Co. common stock.
Sept. 1	Sold 500 shares of B Co. common stock for cash at $8 per share less brokerage fees of $100.
Oct. 1	Sold 400 shares of A Co. common stock for cash at $54 per share less brokerage fees of $600.
Nov. 1	Received $1 per share cash dividend on C Co. common stock.
Dec. 15	Received $0.50 per share cash dividend on A Co. common stock.
31	Received $1 per share semi-annual cash dividend on B Co. common stock.

At December 31, the market values per share of the common stocks were: A Co. $47, B Co. $6, and C Co. $18.

Instructions

(a) Journalize the 1999 transactions and post to the account Long-term Investments.

(b) Prepare the adjusting entry at December 31, 1999, to show the securities at the lower of cost and market value, assuming that any declines are not due to temporary market fluctuations.

(c) Show the balance sheet presentation of the investments at December 31, 1999.

P17–4 On December 31, 1999, Karen Associates owned the following securities that are held as long-term investments. The securities are not held for influence or control of the investees.

Journalize transactions and adjusting entry for stock investments; two scenarios.
(SO 3, 5)

Common Stock	Shares	Cost
X Co.	2,000	$90,000
Y Co.	5,000	45,000
Z Co.	1,500	30,000

In 2000, the following transactions occurred.

July 1 Received $1 per share semi-annual cash dividend on Y Co. common stock.

8 Received 4,000 shares of X Co. common stock in a 3-for-1 stock split.

Aug. 1 Received $0.50 per share cash dividend on X Co. common stock.

Sept. 1 Sold 700 shares of Y Co. common stock for cash at $8 per share less brokerage fees of $200.

Oct. 1 Sold 600 shares of X Co. common stock for cash at $18 per share less brokerage fees of $500.

Dec.15 Received $0.50 per share cash dividend on X Co. common stock.

31 Received $1 per share semi-annual cash dividend on Y Co. common stock.

At December 31, the market values per share were: X Co. $16, Y Co. $8, and Z Co. $17.

Instructions

(a) Journalize the 2000 transactions and post to the account Long-term Investments.

(b) Prepare the adjusting entry at December 31, 2000, to show the securities at the lower of cost and market value, assuming that any declines are not due to temporary market fluctuations.

(c) How would your answer to part (b) differ if the declines *are* considered to be due to temporary market fluctuations?

P17–5 Cardinal Concrete acquired 20% of the outstanding common stock of Edra, Inc., on January 1, 1999, by paying $1,200,000 for 50,000 shares. Edra declared and paid an $0.80 per share cash dividend on June 30 and again on December 31, 1999. Edra reported net income of $700,000 for the year.

Prepare journal entries using cost and equity methods; explain differences.
(SO 3)

Instructions

(a) Prepare the journal entries for Cardinal Concrete for 1999 assuming Cardinal cannot exercise significant influence over Edra. (Use the cost method.)

(b) Prepare the journal entries for Cardinal Concrete for 1999 assuming Cardinal can exercise significant influence over Edra. (Use the equity method.)

(c) ⬅ The board of directors of Cardinal Concrete is confused about the differences between the cost and equity methods. Prepare a memorandum for the board that: (1) explains each method, and (2) shows the account balances for both the investment and the related revenue under each method at December 31, 1999.

P17–6 DFM Services acquired 30% of the outstanding common stock of BNA Company on January 1, 1999, by paying $800,000 for 40,000 shares. BNA declared and paid $0.40 per share cash dividends on March 15 and September 15, 1999. BNA reported net income of $350,000 for the year.

Determine whether cost or equity method should be used; prepare journal entries.
(SO 3)

Instructions

(a) Prepare the journal entries for DFM Services for 1999, assuming DFM can exercise significant influence over BNA.

(b) Prepare the journal entries for DFM Services for 1999 assuming DFM cannot exercise significant influence over BNA.

(c) Explain why a different method of accounting should be used in part (a) and part (b).

Journalize investment transactions and show financial statement presentation.
(SO 3, 5)

P17–7   The following are in Hi-Tech Company's portfolio of long-term securities at December 31, 1998:

	Cost
500 shares of Awixa Corporation common stock	$26,000
700 shares of HAL Corporation common stock	42,000
400 shares of Renda Corporation preferred stock	16,800

Hi-Tech had the following transactions related to the securities during 1999:

Jan.	7	Sold 500 shares of Awixa Corporation common stock at $56 per share less brokerage fees of $700.
Jan.	10	Purchased 200 common shares of Mintor Corporation at $78 per share plus brokerage fees of $240.
	26	Received a cash dividend of $1.15 per share on HAL Corporation common stock.
Feb.	2	Received cash dividends of $0.40 per share on Renda Corporation preferred stock.
	10	Sold all 400 shares of Renda Corporation preferred stock at $28 per share less brokerage fees of $180.
Apr.	30	Received 700 shares of HAL Corporation common stock as a result of a 2-for-1 stock split.
July	1	Received a cash dividend of $1 per share on HAL Corporation common stock.
Aug.	3	Received 20 shares of Mintor Corporation common stock as the result of a 10% stock dividend.
Sept.	1	Purchased an additional 400 shares of the common stock of Mintor Corporation at $82 per share plus brokerage fees of $400.
Dec.	15	Received a cash dividend of $1.50 per share on Mintor Corporation common stock.

At December 31, 1999, the market values of the securities were:

HAL Corporation common stock	$32 per share
Mintor Corporation common stock	$70 per share

Hi-Tech uses separate account titles for each investment, such as Investment in HAL Corporation Common Stock.

Instructions

(a) Prepare journal entries to record the transactions.

(b) Post to the investment accounts. (Use T accounts.)

(c) Prepare the adjusting entry at December 31, 1999, to report the individual securities at the lower of cost and market value, assuming that any declines are not due to temporary market declines.

(d) Show the balance sheet presentation of the investments at December 31, 1999.

Prepare balance sheet, including various investments.
(SO 5)

P17–8   The following data, presented in alphabetical order, are taken from the records of Ocelot Corporation.

Accounts payable	$ 70,000
Accounts receivable	110,000
Accumulated amortization—building	180,000
Accumulated amortization—equipment	52,000
Allowance for doubtful accounts	6,000
Bonds payable (10%, due 2012)	400,000
Buildings	900,000
Cash	92,000
Common stock (500,000 shares authorized; 300,000 issued)	1,700,000
Discount on bonds payable	20,000
Dividends payable	50,000
Equipment	275,000
Goodwill	200,000
Income taxes payable	120,000
Investment in Indira Inc, stock, at equity	240,000
Investment in Manitoulin Company, at cost	110,000
Land	500,000
Merchandise inventory, at average cost	360,000
Notes payable (due 2000)	70,000
Organization costs	50,000
Preferred stock (no par value; $5 cumulative; 5,000 shares authorized and issued)	200,000
Prepaid insurance	16,000
Retained earnings	300,000
Temporary investment, at cost (market value $193,000)	185,000
Trademark (net of accumulated amortization)	90,000

Instructions

Prepare a balance sheet at December 31, 1999.

P17–9 The following data, presented in alphabetical order, are taken from the records of Alameda Corporation:

Prepare balance sheet, including various investments.
(SO 5)

Accounts payable	250,000
Accounts receivable	120,000
Accumulated amortization - building	180,000
Accumulated amortization - equipment	62,000
Allowance for doubtful accounts	6,000
Allowance to reduce temporary investments from cost to market value	20,000
Bonds payable (10%, due 2010)	500,000
Buildings	950,000
Cash	72,000
Common stock (500,000 shares authorized; 220,000 issued)	1,500,000
Dividends payable	80,000
Equipment	275,000
Goodwill	200,000
Income taxes payable	100,000
Investment in Dion common stock (10% ownership)	278,000
Investment in Huston common stock (30% ownership)	230,000
Land	676,000
Merchandise inventory, at FIFO cost (which is lower than market value)	170,000
Notes payable (due 2000)	70,000
Organization costs	60,000
Premium on bonds payable	40,000
Prepaid insurance	10,000
Retained earnings ($100,000 restricted for expansion)	413,000
Temporary investments, at cost	180,000

Instructions

Prepare a balance sheet at December 31, 1999.

*P17–10 Linger Corporation purchased all the outstanding common stock of Chrissy Foods, Inc., on December 31, 1999. Just before the purchase, the condensed balance sheets of the two companies appeared as follows:

Prepare consolidated work sheet and balance sheet, when cost exceeds book value.
(SO 6)

	Linger Corporation	Chrissy Foods, Inc.
Current assets	$1,480,000	$ 439,500
Property, plant, and equipment (net)	2,100,000	672,000
	$3,580,000	$1,111,500
Current liabilities	$ 578,000	$ 92,500
Common stock	1,950,000	525,000
Retained earnings	1,052,000	494,000
	$3,580,000	$1,111,500

Linger used current assets of $1,200,000 to acquire the stock of Chrissy Foods. The excess of this purchase price over the book value of Chrissy Foods' net assets is allocated as follows: $81,000 to Chrissy Foods' property, plant, and equipment and the remainder to goodwill.

Instructions

(a) Prepare the entry for Linger's acquisition of Chrissy Foods, Inc., stock.

(b) Prepare a consolidated work sheet at December 31, 1999.

(c) Prepare a consolidated balance sheet at December 31, 1999.

Broadening Your Perspective

FINANCIAL REPORTING PROBLEM

Refer to the financial statements and accompanying notes for The Second Cup Ltd., which are presented in Appendix A.

Instructions

1. Notice, on the balance sheet, that Short-term Investments has been combined with Cash. What type of investments are these? (Hint: Refer to the notes to the consolidated financial statements.)
2. Also notice, on the balance sheet, the company's Investment in Great Canadian Bagel, Ltd.
    (a) Is this a debt investment or a stock investment?
    (b) Has this investment been made to simply earn investment income, or to establish a business relationship? (Refer to management's discussion and analysis of the operating results.)
    (c) Is this investment being accounted for by the cost method or the equity method?
3. Explain the meaning of the terms "consolidated" financial statements and "subsidiary" company.
4. Refer to Note 2: Acquisition and Divestiture
    (a) As of June 29, 1996, The Second Cup had substantial investments in Coffee Plantation, Inc.,
        and Edglo Enterprises, Inc. Why were these not listed as investments on the June 29, 1996, balance sheet?
    (b) What percentage of the total purchase price paid for the Edglo acquisition was designated as Goodwill?
    (c) With reference to the figures provided in Note 2, explain what Goodwill is and how it arises.
5. What percentage of the total assets on the consolidated balance sheet is Goodwill?

DECISION CASE

At the beginning of the question-and-answer portion of the annual shareholders' meeting of Revell Corporation, shareholder Carol Finstrom asks, "Why did management sell the holdings in AHM Company at a loss when this company was very profitable during the period its stock was held by Revell?"

Since president Larry Wisdom has just concluded his speech on the recent success and bright future of Revell, he is taken aback by this question and responds, "I remember we paid $1,100,000 for that stock some years ago, and I am sure we sold that stock at a much higher price. You must be mistaken."

Finstrom retorts, "Well, right here in footnote number 7 to the annual report it shows that 240,000 shares, a 30% interest in AHM, was sold on the last day of the year. Also, it states that AHM earned $550,000 this year and paid out $150,000 in cash dividends. Further, a summary statement indicates that in past years, while Revell held AHM stock, AHM earned $1,240,000 and paid out $440,000 in dividends. Finally, the income statement for this year shows a loss on the sale of AHM stock of $180,000. So, I doubt that I am mistaken."

Red-faced, president Wisdom turns to you.

Instructions

What dollar amount did Revell receive upon the sale of the AHM stock? Explain why both shareholder Finstrom and president Wisdom are correct.

COMMUNICATION ACTIVITY

Chapperal Corporation has purchased two securities for its portfolio. The first is a stock investment in Sting Ray Corporation, one of its suppliers. Chapperal purchased 10% of Sting Ray with the intention of holding it for a number of years, but has no intention of purchasing more shares.

The second investment is a purchase of debt securities. Chapperal purchased the debt securities because its analysts believe that changes in market interest rates will cause these securities to increase in value in a short period of time. Chapperal intends to sell the securities as soon as they have increased in value.

Instructions

Write a memo to Gil Stiles, the Chief Financial Officer, explaining how to account for each of these investments, and what the implications of this accounting treatment are for reported income.

GROUP ACTIVITY

Finland Corporation holds a portfolio of debt and equity investments. Although some of the securities in the portfolio have increased in value, the total market value of the portfolio is below its total cost. Finn Berge, Finland Corporation's president, has decided to classify all securities in the portfolio that have decreased in value as long-term investments, and to assume that the declines are due to temporary fluctuations in market values. He will classify all securities that have increased in value as temporary investments.

Instructions

In groups of four or five, discuss the following:

(a) What impact will this classification approach have on Finland Corporation's reported results?

(b) Is this an appropriate approach for classifying these securities?

(c) What are the implications of this approach for subsequent years?

ETHICS CASE

Scott Kreiter Financial Services Company holds a large portfolio of debt and equity securities as an investment. The total market value of the portfolio at December 31, 1999, is greater than total cost, with some securities having increased in value and others having decreased. Vicki Lemke, the financial vice-president, and Ula Greenwood, the controller, are in the process of classifying the securities in the portfolio for the first time.

Lemke suggests selling all the securities that have increased in value, in order to increase net income for the year. She also wants to classify the securities that have decreased in value as long-term investments, and to attribute the declines to temporary fluctuations in market values, so that the decreases in value will not affect 1999 net income.

Greenwood disagrees. She recommends selling all the securities that have decreased in value. Greenwood argues that the company is having a good earnings year and that recognizing the losses now will help to smooth income for this year.

Instructions

(a) Is there anything unethical in what Lemke and Greenwood propose?

(b) Who are the stakeholders affected by their proposals?

CRITICAL THINKING
▶*A Real-World Focus: SPS Technologies, Inc.*

SPS Technologies, Inc., was formed in 1903 as Standard Pressed Steel. Today the company is engaged in the design, manufacture, and marketing of high-strength mechanical fasteners, superalloys, and magnetic materials for the aerospace, automotive, and off-highway equipment industries. The company owns plants in the United States, the United Kingdom, Ireland, Australia, and Spain, and has minority interests in facilities in Brazil and India.

The following note to the financial statements appears in a recent SPS annual report:

Investments: The Company's investments in affiliates consist of a 16.75% interest in Precision Fasteners Ltd., Bombay, India; a 46.49% interest in Metalac S.A. Industria e Comercio, Sao Paulo, Brazil; a 51.0% interest in Pacific Products Limited, Guernsey, Channel Islands; and a 51.0% interest in National-Arnold Magnetics Company, Adelanto, California. Dividends received from these companies were $42,000, $44,000, and $66,000 during the past three years.

Instructions

(a) Do the investments in these companies represent short- or long-term investments? Are these investments in shares or in bonds of these companies?

(b) The ownership percentages in these companies vary. Based upon the information given, which accounting method would appear appropriate for each company? What other information would you like to know before deciding how to account for each investment?

(c) How would SPS account for dividends received from Precision Fasteners Ltd.? From National-Arnold Magnetics Company?

ACCOUNTING ON THE WEB

There are two interesting Internet cases related to the topic of investments.

The first case is about two brothers—one an English major, the other a girls basketball coach. They had an interest in investing and created a chat group on AOL, a light-hearted place they called The Motley Fool. This permanent site, with its motto, "to educate, amuse, and enrich," is now one of the most popular investment sites on the Internet. We review the educational component of this site—including the basics of the stock market, what corporate financial information is useful when assessing a stock, and a model portfolio.

The second case reviews analysts' investment ratings over time, and across companies, in the same industry. Most publicly traded companies are analysed by numerous analysts. These analysts often don't agree about a company's future prospects. This case reviews analysts' recommendations and determines to what extent the analysts experienced "earnings surprises," which can cause changes in stock prices.

Instructions

Specific requirements of these Internet cases are available on-line at www.wiley.com/canada/weygandt.

Answers to Self-Study Questions
1. d   2. b   3. c   4. b*   5. a   6. c   7. c   8. d   9. d   10. d

*a and c are also correct; however, neither of these choices is as complete as b.

Getting It There

MISSISSAUGA, Ont.—United Parcel Service, a giant in the package and document delivery business, keeps a steady flow of packages moving all over the world. Meanwhile, at UPS Canada Ltd.'s Mississauga, Ontario, headquarters, Shivani Chakravorty pays attention to the steady flow of cash moving in and out of the company.

"During our start-up period as a subsidiary company here in Canada," explains Ms. Chakravorty, a UPS Strategic Financial Analyst, "we would sometimes borrow funds from our U.S. parent if need be. Now we are operating self-sufficiently."

In both situations, forecasting of cash flow is very important.

For example, UPS recently expanded its facilities at the airport in Hamilton, Ontario. One component of this major project was the construction of an automated conveyor belt to move packages through the facility. The schedule

originally called for building this belt, at a cost of about $2.5 million, in January 1998. But because of changes in volume flow in the summer of 1997, "we built it in March instead," says Ms. Chakravorty.

A company's Statement of Cash Flows facilitates decisions of this kind. It can also be useful to reassure outside parties of a company's finan-

cial stability in cases where unusual events, such as strikes or large purchases, reduce revenues or margins.

As a privately held company, UPS does not publish its financial statements. But a 1997 *Fortune* magazine survey ranked it #1 in its industry for the second year in a row—and #3 among all other companies in terms of financial soundness! ◄

CHAPTER 18

THE STATEMENT OF CASH FLOWS

After studying this chapter, you should be able to:

1. *Indicate the primary purpose of the statement of cash flows.*
2. *Distinguish among operating, investing, and financing activities.*
3. *Prepare a statement of cash flows using the indirect method.*
4. *Prepare a statement of cash flows using the direct method.*
5. *Distinguish between cash flow per share and earnings per share.*
6. *Explain the procedural steps in using a work sheet to prepare the statement of cash flows (appendix).*

As the story about UPS indicates, the statement of cash flows provides information for decision making that is not always available from the balance sheet, income statement, and statement of retained earnings. In fact, if a thoughtful investor were to look at the three traditional financial statements of some well-known companies, he or she might have questions like the following: How did Andrés Wines pay cash dividends of $2.7 million in a year in which it had no cash, only bank indebtedness? How did Air Canada purchase new planes costing $607 million in a year in which it reported net income of only $149 million? How did Seagram's finance its $8 billion purchase of U.S. entertainment giant MCA? Answers to these and similar questions can be found in this chapter, which presents the statement of cash flows. The organization of this chapter is as follows:

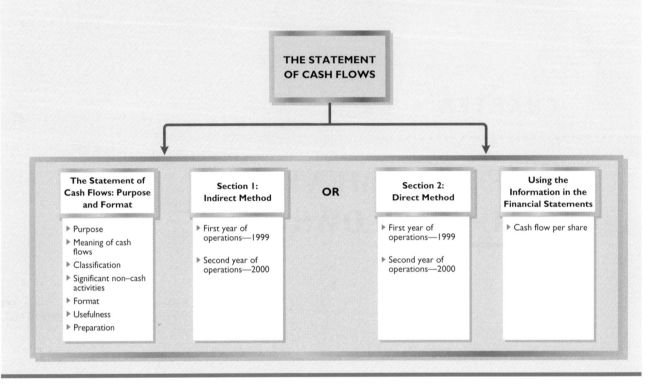

▼he Statement of Cash Flows: Purpose and Format

The three basic financial statements we've studied so far present only partial information about a company's cash flows (cash receipts and cash payments). For example, comparative balance sheets show the increase in capital assets during the year, but they do not show how the additions were financed or paid for. The income statement shows net income, but it does not indicate the amount of cash generated by operating activities. Similarly, the statement of retained earnings shows cash dividends declared but not the cash dividends paid during the year. None of these statements presents a detailed summary of the net change in cash as a result of operating, investing, and financing activities during the period.

Accounting in Action ▶ International Insight

Libbey-Owens-Ford (LOF), a member of the Pilkington Group, is a world leader in glass products for the building, transport, and electronics markets. The Company's mission statement in its annual report emphasizes the importance of cash flow as follows: "LOF stresses the importance of cash flow measurement and performance. Individual companies must analyse the cash flow effects of running their business. Where cash comes from and what cash is used for must be simply and clearly set forth."

Purpose of the Statement of Cash Flows

The primary purpose of the statement of cash flows is to provide information about the cash receipts and cash payments of an entity during a period. A secondary objective is to provide information about the operating, investing, and financing activities of the entity during the period. The statement of cash flows reports the cash receipts, cash payments, and net change in cash that result from the operating, investing, and financing activities of an enterprise during a period. The statement's format explains the change between the beginning and ending cash balances.

Reporting the causes of changes in cash is useful because investors, creditors, and other interested parties want to know what is happening to a company's most liquid resource—its cash. As the opening story about UPS demonstrates, a statement of cash flows helps us understand what is happening. It provides answers to the following simple, but important, questions about the enterprise:

STUDY OBJECTIVE
⋯⋯⋯⋯▽⋯⋯⋯⋯
1
Indicate the primary purpose of the statement of cash flows.

1. Where did the cash come from during the period?
2. What was the cash used for during the period?
3. What was the change in the cash balance during the period?

Meaning of "Cash Flows"

The statement of cash flows is generally prepared using **cash and cash equivalents** as its basis. Cash equivalents are short-term, highly liquid investments that are both:

1. Readily convertible to known amounts of cash, and
2. So near to their maturity that their market value is relatively unaffected by changes in interest rates.

Generally, only investments with original maturities of three months or less qualify under this definition. Examples of cash equivalents are treasury bills, commercial paper (short-term corporate notes), and money market funds. All are typically purchased with cash that is not immediately needed. Note that since cash and cash equivalents are viewed as the same, transfers between cash and cash equivalents are not treated as cash receipts and cash payments—i.e., they are not reported in the statement of cash flows. The term *cash* when used in this chapter includes cash and cash equivalents. It is recommended, for clarity, that this term be specifically defined within the statement of cash flows.

Classification of Cash Flows

The statement of cash flows classifies cash receipts and cash payments according to the operating, investing, and financing activities that produced them. Transactions and other events characteristic of each kind of activity are as follows:

STUDY OBJECTIVE
⋯⋯⋯⋯▽⋯⋯⋯⋯
2
Distinguish among operating, investing, and financing activities.

1. **Operating activities** include the cash effects of transactions that create revenues and expenses and thus affect net income.
2. **Investing activities** include: (a) acquiring and disposing of investments and productive long-lived assets, and (b) lending money and collecting the loans.
3. **Financing activities** include: (a) obtaining cash from issuing debt and repaying the amounts borrowed, and (b) obtaining cash from shareholders and providing them with a return on their investment.

Operating activities is the most important category, because it shows the cash that is provided by company operations. This source of cash is generally considered to be the best measure of a company's ability to generate sufficient cash to continue as a going concern.

Illustration 18-1 lists typical cash receipts and cash payments within each of the three classifications:

Illustration 18-1

Typical receipts and payments classified by activity

Types of Cash Inflows and Outflows

Operating activities
    Cash inflows:
        From sale of goods or services.
        From returns on loans (interest received) and on equity securities (dividends received).
    Cash outflows:
        To suppliers for inventory.
        To employees for services.
        To governments for taxes.
        To lenders for interest.
        To others for expenses.
Investing activities
    Cash inflows:
        From sale of capital assets.
        From sale of investments (debt or equity securities of other entities).
        From collection of principal on loans to other entities.
    Cash outflows:
        To purchase capital assets.
        To purchase investments (debt or equity securities of other entities).
        To make loans to other entities.
Financing activities
    Cash inflows:
        From sale of equity securities (company's own stock).
        From issuance of debt (bonds and notes).
    Cash outflows:
        To shareholders as dividends.
        To redeem long-term debt.

As you can see, some cash flows relating to investing or financing activities are classified as operating activities. For example, receipts of investment revenue (interest and dividends) and payments of interest to lenders are classified as operating activities, because these items are reported in the income statement.

Note that, generally: (1) operating activities involve income determination (income statement) items and usually affect non-cash working capital (current assets and current liability) accounts, (2) investing activities involve cash flows resulting from changes in investments and long-term asset items (noncurrent items on the left-hand side of the balance sheet), and (3) financing activities involve cash flows resulting from changes in long-term liability and shareholders' equity items (noncurrent items on the right-hand side of the balance sheet).

Significant Non-cash Activities

Not all of a company's significant activities involve cash. Examples of significant non-cash activities are:

1. Issuance of common stock to purchase assets.
2. Conversion of bonds into common stock.
3. Issuance of debt to purchase assets.
4. Exchanges of capital assets.

Significant financing and investing activities that do not affect cash are not reported in the body of the statement of cash flows. However, these activities are reported in a separate note to the financial statements.

The reporting of these activities in a separate note satisfies the **full disclosure principle**, because it identifies significant non-cash investing and financing activities of the enterprise. (For assignments, you should include the note disclosure for any significant non-cash investing and financing activities. See lower section of Illustration 18-2 for an example.)

Format of the Statement of Cash Flows

The three activities discussed above (operating, investing, and financing)—plus the significant non-cash investing and financing activities—constitute the general format of the statement of cash flows. A widely used condensed form of the statement of cash flows is shown in Illustration 18-2:

COMPANY NAME Statement of Cash Flows Period Covered		
Cash flows from operating activities		
(List of individual items)	XX	
Net cash provided (used) by operating activities		XXX
Cash flows from investing activities		
(List of individual inflows and outflows)	XX	
Net cash provided (used) by investing activities		XXX
Cash flows from financing activities		
(List of individual inflows and outflows)	XX	
Net cash provided (used) by financing activities		XXX
Net increase (decrease) in cash		XXX
Cash at beginning of period		XXX
Cash at end of period		XXX
Note x:		
Non-cash investing and financing activities		
(List of significant non-cash investing and financing transactions)		XXX

Illustration 18-2

Format of statement of cash flows

The statement of cash flows covers the same period of time as the income statement (e.g., for the year ended). The cash flows from the operating activities section always appears first, followed by the investing activities and the financing activities sections. **Individual inflows and outflows from investing and financing activities are reported separately**. Thus, the cash outflow for the purchase of capital assets is reported separately from the cash inflow from the sale of capital assets. Similarly, the cash inflow from the issuance of debt securities is reported separately from the cash outflow for the retirement of debt. If a company did not report the inflows and outflows separately, the investing and financing activities of the enterprise would be obscured and thus assessment of future cash flows made more difficult.

The reported operating, investing, and financing activities result in net cash being either provided or used by each activity. The net cash provided or used by each activity is totalled to show the net increase (decrease) in cash for the period. The net increase (decrease) in cash for the period is then added to, or subtracted from, the beginning of the period cash balance to obtain the end-of-period cash balance. Finally, any significant non-cash investing and financing activities are reported in a note to the statement.

Usefulness of the Statement of Cash Flows

The information in a statement of cash flows should help investors, creditors, and others assess various aspects of the firm's financial position:

1. **The entity's ability to generate future cash flows**. Investors and others examine the relationships between items such as sales and net cash provided by operating activities, or cash provided by operations and increases or decreases in cash. This helps them make predictions of the amounts, timing, and uncertainty of future cash flows better than from accrual basis data. Such predictions allow readers to compare the present value of future cash flows of other companies and thus make investment or divestment decisions. By focusing on cash, companies are easier to compare since the arbitrary effects of using different accounting policies are eliminated.

2. **The entity's liquidity and solvency**. Simply put, if a company does not have adequate cash, employees cannot be paid, debts settled, or dividends paid. Employees, creditors, and shareholders are particularly interested in this statement, because it alone shows the flows of cash in a business. Readers can use this statement to evaluate the changes in the financial position and structure of the firm.

3. **The reasons for the difference between net income and cash provided (used) by operating activities**. Net income is important because it provides information on the success or failure of a business enterprise. However, some are critical of accrual-based net income because it requires many estimates. As a result, the reliability of the number is often challenged. Such is not the case with cash. Thus, many readers of the financial statements want to know the reasons for the difference between net income and net cash provided by operating activities. Then they can assess for themselves the reliability of the income number.

> **Helpful hint**   Income from operations and cash flow from operating activities are different. Income from operations is based on accrual accounting; cash flow from operating activities is prepared on a cash basis.

4. **The cash investing and financing transactions during the period**. By examining a company's investing activities and its financing transactions, a financial statement reader can better understand why assets and liabilities increased or decreased during the period.

 ▸**Accounting in Action** ▸ *Business Insight*

Wide variations between net income and cash provided by operating activities are illustrated by the following results for two companies, engaged in similar types of retail merchandising, for the same fiscal year (all data are in millions of dollars):

Company	Net Income	Cash Provided from Operations
Hudson's Bay Company	$ 36.1	$ 241.1
Sears Canada Inc.	8.8	278.2

Preparation of the Statement of Cash Flows

The statement of cash flows is prepared differently from the three other basic financial statements. First, it is not prepared from an adjusted trial balance. Because the statement requires detailed information concerning the changes in account balances that occurred between two periods of time, an adjusted trial balance will not provide the necessary data for the statement. Second, the statement of cash flows deals with cash receipts and payments. As a result, **the accrual concept is not used in the preparation of a statement of cash flows**.

The information to prepare this statement usually comes from three sources:

Comparative balance sheet. Information in this statement indicates the amount of the changes in assets, liabilities, and shareholders' equity from the beginning to the end of the period.

Current income statement. Information in this statement helps the reader to determine the amount of cash provided, or used, by operations during the period.

Additional information. Additional information includes transaction data that are needed to determine how cash was provided or used during the period.

Preparing the statement of cash flows from these data sources involves three major steps, explained in Illustration 18-3.

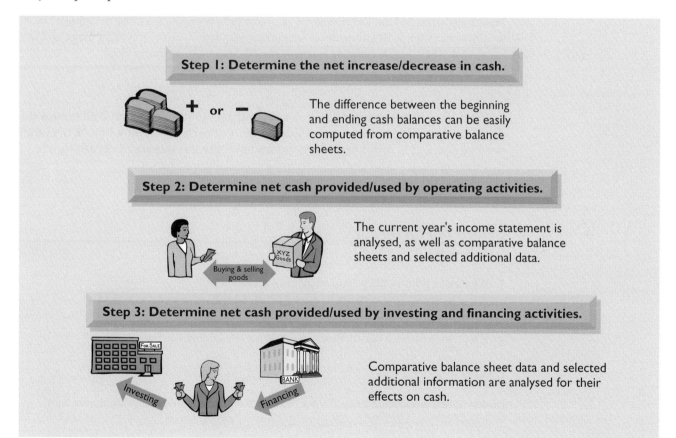

Step 1: Determine the net increase/decrease in cash.

The difference between the beginning and ending cash balances can be easily computed from comparative balance sheets.

Step 2: Determine net cash provided/used by operating activities.

The current year's income statement is analysed, as well as comparative balance sheets and selected additional data.

Step 3: Determine net cash provided/used by investing and financing activities.

Comparative balance sheet data and selected additional information are analysed for their effects on cash.

Illustration 18-3

Three major steps in preparing the statement of cash flows

►*International note*

International accounting requirements are quite similar in most respects for the statement of cash flows. Some interesting exceptions: in Australia, the direct method is mandatory; in Japan, operating and investing activities are combined; and in Spain, the indirect method is mandatory. Also, in a number of European and Scandinavian countries a cash flow statement is not required at all, although in practice most publicly traded firms provide one.

Indirect and Direct Methods

In order to perform step 2, **the operating activities section of the statement of cash flows must be converted from an accrual basis to a cash basis**. This conversion may be done by either of two methods: (1) the indirect method, or (2) the direct method. **Both methods arrive at the same total amount** for "Net cash provided (used) by operating activities," but the disclosed items that make up the total amount differ.

The indirect method is used more extensively. Companies favour the indirect method because it focuses on the differences between net income and cash flow from operating activities. Others, however, prefer the direct method. The direct method shows operating cash receipts and payments. Thus, it is more consistent with the objective of a statement of cash flows. The CICA encourages the direct method of reporting cash flows but permits the use of the indirect method.

►Accounting in Action ► *International Insight*

The statement of cash flows is an excellent example of the harmonization of accounting standards to facilitate international comparison of global financial statements. The CICA, which in the past required the indirect method, recently amended its *Handbook* section Statement of Changes in Financial Position. The section has been retitled Cash Flow Statements, and the direct method of preparation is encouraged. The recommendations are now consistent with International Accounting Standard 7, Cash Flow Statements, and U.S. Statement of Financial Accounting Standard No. 95, Statement of Cash Flows.

Section 1 of this chapter illustrates the **indirect method**; Section 2 illustrates the **direct method**. These sections are independent of each other; only one or the other need be covered in order to understand and prepare the statement of cash flows.

Before You Go On . . .
►*Review It*

1. What is the primary purpose of a statement of cash flows?
2. What are the major classifications of cash flows in the statement of cash flows?
3. What are the three major steps in the preparation of a statement of cash flows?
4. Why is the statement of cash flows useful? What key information does it convey?

►*Do It*

During its first week of existence, Carrier Molding Company had the following transactions:

1. Issued 100,000 shares of no par value common stock for $800,000 cash.
2. Borrowed $200,000 from the National Bank, signing a five-year note at prime plus 1% interest.
3. Purchased two semi-trailer trucks for $170,000 cash.
4. Paid employees $12,000 for salaries and wages.
5. Collected $20,000 cash for services rendered.

Classify, by type of cash flow activity, each of these transactions. Indicate whether the transaction would be reported as a source, or a use, of cash.

Reasoning:

All cash flows are classified into three types of activities for the purposes of reporting cash inflows and outflows: operating activities, investing activities, and financing activities. Operating activities include the cash effects of transactions that create revenues and expenses and thus affect net income. Investing activities include: (a) acquiring and disposing of investments and productive long-lived assets, and (b) lending money and collecting on the loans. Financing activities include: (a) obtaining cash from issuing debt and repaying the amounts borrowed, and (b) obtaining cash from shareholders and providing them with a return on their investment.

Solution:

1. Financing activity; source of cash.
2. Financing activity; source of cash.
3. Investing activity; use of cash.
4. Operating activity; use of cash.
5. Operating activity; source of cash.

Related exercise material: BE18–3, BE18–5, BE18–10, E18–1, and E18–6.

SECTION 1 ► Indirect Method

To explain and illustrate the indirect method, we will use the transactions of the Computer Services Corporation for two years, 1999 and 2000. Annual statements of cash flows will be prepared. Basic transactions will be used in the first year; additional transactions will be added in the second year.

STUDY OBJECTIVE
•••••••••• 3 ••••••••••
Prepare a statement of cash flows using the indirect method.

First Year of Operations—1999

Computer Services Corporation started operations on January 1, 1999, when it issued 50,000 shares of no par value common stock for $50,000 cash. The company rented its office space and equipment and performed consulting services throughout the first year. The comparative balance sheets at the beginning and end of 1999, showing increases or decreases, appear in Illustration 18-4:

COMPUTER SERVICES CORPORATION Comparative Balance Sheet			
Assets	Dec. 31, 1999	Jan. 1, 1999	Change Increase/Decrease
Cash	$34,000	$ –0–	$34,000 Increase
Accounts receivable	30,000	–0–	30,000 Increase
Equipment	10,000	–0–	10,000 Increase
Total	$74,000	$ –0–	
Liabilities and Shareholders' Equity			
Accrued expenses payable	$ 4,000	$ –0–	$ 4,000 Increase
Common stock	50,000	–0–	50,000 Increase
Retained earnings	20,000	–0–	20,000 Increase
Total	$74,000	$ –0–	

Illustration 18-4

Comparative balance sheet, 1999

Helpful hint Note that although each of the balance sheet items of Computer Services increased, their individual effects are not the same. Some of these increases are cash inflows and some are cash outflows.

The income statement and additional information for Computer Services Corporation are shown in Illustration 18-5:

Illustration 18-5

Income statement and additional information, 1999

COMPUTER SERVICES CORPORATION Income Statement For the Year Ended December 31, 1999		
Revenues		$85,000
Operating expenses		40,000
Income before income taxes		45,000
Income tax expense		10,000
Net income		$35,000

Additional information:
(a) Examination of selected data indicates that a dividend of $15,000 was declared and paid during the year.
(b) The equipment was purchased at the end of 1999. No amortization was taken in 1999.

Determining the Net Increase (Decrease) in Cash (Step 1)

Helpful hint   You may wish to insert the beginning and ending cash balances, and the increase (decrease) in cash necessitated by these balances, immediately into the statement of cash flows. The net increase (decrease) is the target amount. The net cash flows from the three classes of activity must equal the target amount.

To prepare a statement of cash flows, the first step is **determining the increase or decrease in cash**. This is a simple computation. For example, Computer Services Corporation had no cash on hand at the beginning of 1999 but had $34,000 on hand at the end of 1999. Thus, the change in cash for 1999 was an increase of $34,000.

Determining Net Cash Provided (Used) by Operating Activities (Step 2)

Helpful hint   Whether the indirect or direct method (Section 2) is used, total cash provided, or used, by operating activities will be the same.

To determine cash provided (or used) by operating activities under the indirect method, **net income is adjusted for items that did not affect cash**. A useful starting point is to understand **why** net income must be adjusted. Under generally accepted accounting principles, most companies use the accrual basis of accounting. As you have learned, this basis requires that revenue be recorded when earned and that expenses be recorded when incurred. Earned revenues may include credit sales that have not been collected in cash and expenses incurred that may not have been paid in cash. Thus, under the accrual basis of accounting, net income does not indicate the net cash provided by operating activities. Under the indirect method, net income must be adjusted to convert certain items to the cash basis.

The indirect method (or reconciliation method) starts with net income and converts it to net cash provided by operating activities. In other words, **the indirect method adjusts net income for items that affected reported net income but did not affect cash**, as shown in Illustration 18-6. That is, non-cash charges in the income statement are added back to net income, and non-cash credits are deducted to compute net cash provided by operating activities. A useful starting point for identifying the adjustments to net income is the current asset and current liability accounts other than cash. Those accounts—receivables, payables, prepayments, and inventories—should be analysed for their effects on cash.

Increase in Accounts Receivable. When accounts receivable increase during the year, revenues on an accrual basis are higher than revenues on a cash basis. In other words, operations of the period led to increased revenues, but **not all of these revenues resulted in an increase in cash**. Some of the increase in revenues resulted in an increase in accounts receivable.

The income statement in Illustration 18-5 shows that Computer Services Corporation had $85,000 in revenues. To determine how much cash was collected from sales revenues, it is useful to make a summary of changes during the year to the Accounts Receivable account. T accounts provide a useful structure, as detailed in Illustration 18-7:

Illustration 18-7

Analysis of accounts receivable

△ 30,000↑

ACCOUNTS RECEIVABLE				
1/1/99	Balance	–0–	Receipts from customers	55,000
	Revenues	85,000		
12/31/99	Balance	30,000		

The ending balance of Accounts Receivable is $30,000 and revenues (assumed to be on account) journalized during the period were $85,000 (dr. Accounts Receivable; cr. Revenues). It can be deduced mathematically ($85,000−$30,000) that receipts from customers must have been $55,000 in cash. Revenues reported on the accrual based income statement are higher than cash collections. Therefore, to convert net income to net cash provided by operating activities, the increase of $30,000 in accounts receivable must be deducted from net income ($85,000 accrual basis revenue−$30,000 increase in accounts receivable = $55,000 cash basis revenue).

Increase in Accrued Expenses Payable. In the first year, operating expenses on account were debited to Operating Expenses and credited to Accrued Expenses Payable.

Illustration 18-8

Analysis of accounts payable

△ 4,000 ↑

ACCRUED EXPENSES PAYABLE				
Payments to creditors	36,000	1/1/99	Balance	–0–
			Operating expenses	40,000
		12/31/99	Balance	4,000

When accrued expenses payables increase during the year, operating expenses on an accrual basis are higher than they are on a cash basis. For Computer Services Corporation, operating expenses reported in the income statement were $40,000. However, since Accrued Expenses Payable increased $4,000, only $36,000 ($40,000–$4,000) of the expenses were paid in cash. To adjust net income to net cash provided by operating activities, the increase of $4,000 in accrued expenses payable must be added to net income ($40,000 accrual basis expenses + $4,000 increase in accrued expenses payable = $36,000 cash basis expenses).

For Computer Services Corporation, the changes in accounts receivable and accrued expenses payable were the only changes in non-cash current asset and current liability accounts. This means that any other revenues or expenses reported in the income statement were received or paid in cash. Thus, Computer Services' income tax expense of $10,000 was paid in cash, and no further adjustment of net income is necessary.

The operating activities section of the statement of cash flows for Computer Services Corporation is shown in Illustration 18-9:

Illustration 18-9

Presentation of net cash provided by operating activities, 1999—indirect method

Cash flows from operating activities		
Net income		$35,000
Adjustments to reconcile net income to net cash provided by operating activities:		
Increase in accounts receivable	$(30,000)	
Increase in accrued expenses payable	4,000	(26,000)
Net cash provided by operating activities		9,000

Determining Net Cash Provided (Used) by Investing and Financing Activities (Step 3)

The third and final step in preparing the statement of cash flows begins with a study of the balance sheet to determine changes in noncurrent accounts. The changes in each noncurrent account are then analysed using selected transaction data to determine the effect, if any, the changes had on cash.

In Computer Services Corporation, the three noncurrent accounts are Equipment, Common Stock, and Retained Earnings, and all three have increased during the year. What caused these increases? No transaction data are given for the increases in Equipment of $10,000 and Common Stock of $50,000. In doing your assignments, you can conclude that **any unexplained differences in noncurrent accounts involve cash**. Thus, the increase in equipment is assumed to be a purchase of equipment for $10,000 cash. This purchase is reported as a cash outflow in the investing activities section. The increase in common stock resulted from the issuance of common stock for $50,000 cash. It is reported as an inflow of cash in the financing activities section of the statement of cash flows.

The reasons for the net increase of $20,000 in the Retained Earnings account are determined by analysis.

Illustration 18-10

Analysis of retained earnings

RETAINED EARNINGS					
12/31/99	Cash dividend	15,000	1/1/99	Balance	–0–
			12/31/99	Net income	35,000
			12/31/99	Balance	20,000

First, net income increased retained earnings by $35,000. Second, the additional information provided in Illustration in 18-5 indicates that a cash dividend of $15,000 was declared and paid. The $35,000 increase due to net income is reported in the operating activities section. The cash dividend paid is reported in the financing activities section.

The $20,000 increase in Retained Earnings in 1999 is a **net** change. When a net change in a noncurrent balance sheet account has occurred during the year, the causes of the net change are usually reported separately in the statement of cash flows.

Statement of Cash Flows

Having completed the three steps above, we can prepare the statement of cash flows. The statement starts with the operating activities section, followed by the investing activities section, and, finally, the financing activities section. The 1999 statement of cash flows for Computer Services is shown in Illustration 18-11:

COMPUTER SERVICES CORPORATION Statement of Cash Flows For the Year Ended December 31, 1999		
Cash flows from operating activities		
Net income		$35,000
Adjustments to reconcile net income to net cash provided by operating activities:		
Increase in accounts receivable	$(30,000)	
Increase in accrued expenses payable	4,000	(26,000)
Net cash provided by operating activities		9,000
Cash flows from investing activities		
Purchase of equipment	$(10,000)	
Net cash used by investing activities		(10,000)
Cash flows from financing activities		
Issuance of common stock	$50,000	
Payment of cash dividends	(15,000)	
Net cash provided by financing activities		35,000
Net increase in cash		34,000
Cash, January 1		–0–
Cash, December 31		$34,000

Illustration 18-11

Statement of cash flows, 1999—indirect method

Computer Services' statement of cash flows for 1999 shows that operating activities **provided** $9,000 cash; investing activities **used** $10,000 cash; and financing activities **provided** $35,000 cash. The increase in cash of $34,000 reported in the statement of cash flows agrees with the increase of $34,000 shown as the change in the cash account in the comparative balance sheet.

Notice how the statement of cash flows links the income statement with the beginning and ending balance sheets. Net income from the income statement is the starting point in determining operating activities. The changes in the balance sheet accounts are explained in terms of their impact on cash, and lead to the end-of-period cash balance on the balance sheet and on the statement of cash flows.

Second Year of Operations—2000

In Illustrations 18-12 and 18-13, there is information related to the second year of operations for Computer Services Corporation:

Illustration 18-12

Comparative balance sheet, 2000

COMPUTER SERVICES CORPORATION
Comparative Balance Sheet
December 31, 2000

Assets	2000	1999	Change Increase/Decrease	
Cash	$ 56,000	$34,000	$ 22,000	Increase
Accounts receivable	20,000	30,000	10,000	Decrease
Prepaid expenses	4,000	–0–	4,000	Increase
Land	130,000	–0–	130,000	Increase
Building	160,000	–0–	160,000	Increase
Accumulated amortization—building	(11,000)	–0–	11,000	Increase
Equipment	27,000	10,000	17,000	Increase
Accumulated amortization—equipment	(3,000)	–0–	3,000	Increase
Total	$383,000	$74,000		
Liabilities and Shareholders' Equity				
Accrued expenses payable	$ 59,000	$ 4,000	$ 55,000	Increase
Bonds payable	130,000	–0–	130,000	Increase
Common stock	50,000	50,000	–0–	
Retained earnings	144,000	20,000	124,000	Increase
Total	$383,000	$74,000		

Illustration 18-13

Income statement and additional information, 2000

COMPUTER SERVICES CORPORATION
Income Statement
For the Year Ended December 31, 2000

Revenues		$507,000
Operating expenses (excluding amortization)	$261,000	
Amortization expense	15,000	
Loss on sale of equipment	3,000	279,000
Income from operations		228,000
Income tax expense		89,000
Net income		$139,000

Additional information:
(a) In 2000, the company declared and paid a $15,000 cash dividend.
(b) The company obtained land through the issuance of $130,000 of long-term bonds.
(c) A building costing $160,000 was purchased for cash; equipment costing $25,000 was also purchased for cash.
(d) During 2000, the company sold for $4,000 cash, equipment with a book value of $7,000 (cost $8,000, less accumulated amortization $1,000).

Determining the Net Increase (Decrease) in Cash (Step 1)

To prepare a statement of cash flows from this information, the first step is to **determine the increase or decrease in cash**. As the information presented shows, cash increased $22,000 ($56,000−$34,000).

Determining Net Cash Provided (Used) by Operating Activities (Step 2)

As in step 2 in 1999, net income on an accrual basis must be adjusted to arrive at net cash provided (used) by operating activities. Explanations for the adjustments to net income for Computer Services in 2000 are as follows:

Decrease in Accounts Receivable. Accounts receivable decrease during the period because cash receipts are higher than revenues reported on an accrual basis. To adjust net income to net cash provided by operating activities, the decrease of $10,000 in accounts receivable must be added to net income.

Increase in Prepaid Expenses. Prepaid expenses increase during a period because cash paid for expenses is higher than expenses reported on an accrual basis. Cash payments have been made in the current period, but expenses (as charges to the income statement) have been deferred to future periods. To adjust net income to net cash provided by operating activities, the increase of $4,000 in prepaid expenses must be deducted from net income. An increase in prepaid expenses results in a decrease in cash during the period.

Increase in Accrued Expenses Payable. Like the increase in 1999, the increase of $55,000 in accrued expenses payable during the year 2000 must be added to net income to adjust to net cash provided by operating activities.

Amortization Expense. During 2000, Computer Services Corporation reported amortization expense of $15,000. Of this amount, $11,000 was related to the building and $4,000 to the equipment. These two amounts were determined by analysing the accumulated amortization accounts.

Increase in Accumulated Amortization—Building. As shown in Illustration 18-12, accumulated amortization increased $11,000. This change represents the amortization expense on the building for the year. **Because amortization expense is a noncash charge, it is added back to net income** in order to arrive at net cash provided by operating activities. It is important to recognize that this amount is not added to operating activities, as if it were a source of cash; amortization does not involve cash. It is added to cancel the net income deduction created by the (amortization) expense because this expense does not use actual cash.

Increase in Accumulated Amortization—Equipment. The increase in the Accumulated Amortization—Equipment account was $3,000. This amount does not represent the overall amortization expense for the year because the additional information indicates that this account was decreased (debited $1,000) as a result of the sale of some equipment. Thus, amortization expense for 2000 was $4,000 ($3,000 + $1,000). This amount is added to net income (in order to cancel the deduction created by the expense) to determine net cash provided by operating activities.

The T account below provides information about the changes that occurred in this account in 2000.

Helpful hint Amortization is similar to any other non-cash expense that reduces net income. If it does not involve a current cash outflow, it must be added back to net income to arrive at cash provided by operations.

ACCUMULATED AMORTIZATION—EQUIPMENT				
Accumulated amortization on equipment sold	1,000	1/1/00	Balance	–0–
			Amortization expense	4,000
		12/31/00	Balance	3,000

Illustration 18-14

Analysis of accumulated amortization—equipment

Other charges to expense that do not require the use of cash, such as the amortization of bond discounts, are treated in the same manner as amortization of capital assets.

Loss on Sale of Equipment.   On the income statement, Computer Services Corporation reported a $3,000 loss on the sale of equipment (book value $7,000 less cash proceeds $4,000). Like amortization, **the loss reduced net income but did not reduce cash**. Thus, the loss is **added to net income** in determining net cash provided by operating activities.

If there is a gain on sale, the reverse occurs. To not deduct a gain from net cash provided by operating activities would be to count the gain—once in the operating activities section (as part of net income), and again in the investing activities section (as part of the cash proceeds from sale). As a result, a gain is deducted from net income to calculate net cash provided by operating activities.

Other credits to income, such as the amortization of bond premiums and recognition of the investor's share of the investee's net income from an equity long-term investment, would also be deducted from accrual-based income in determining net cash provided by operating activities.

As a result of the previous adjustments, net cash provided by operating activities is $218,000, as computed in Illustration 18-15:

Illustration 18-15

Presentation of net cash provided by operating activities, 2000—indirect method

Cash flows from operating activities		
Net income		$139,000
Adjustments to reconcile net income to net cash provided by operating activities:		
Amortization expense	$15,000	
Loss on sale of equipment	3,000	
Decrease in accounts receivable	10,000	
Increase in prepaid expenses	(4,000)	
Increase in accrued expenses payable	55,000	79,000
Net cash provided by operating activities		218,000

Summary of Conversion to Net Cash Provided by Operating Activities—Indirect Method.   The statement of cash flows prepared by the indirect method starts with net income and adds (or deducts) items not affecting cash to arrive at net cash provided by operating activities. The additions and deductions consist of: (1) changes in specific non-cash current assets and current liabilities, and (2) non-cash items reported in the income statement. A summary of the adjustments for current assets and current liabilities is provided in Illustration 18-16:

Illustration 18-16

Adjustments for current assets and current liabilities

Helpful hint   Here is a useful aid to remember whether account changes should be deducted from, or added to, net income to determine the cash flow effect:

–	+
↑	↑
Current Assets	Current Liabilities
↓	↓
+	–

	Adjustments to Convert Net Income to Net Cash Provided (Used) by Operating Activities	
	Add to Net Income	**Deduct from Net Income**
Current Assets		
Accounts receivable	Decrease	Increase
Inventory	Decrease	Increase
Prepaid expenses	Decrease	Increase
Other current assets	Decrease	Increase
Current Liabilities		
Accounts payable	Increase	Decrease
Accrued expenses payable	Increase	Decrease
Other current liabilities	Increase	Decrease

Adjustments for the non-cash items reported in the income statement are made as shown in Illustration 18-17:

Non-cash Items	Adjustments to Convert Net Income to Net Cash Provided by Operating Activities
Amortization (of capital assets) expense	Add
Amortization of bond discount to interest expense	Add
Amortization of bond premium to interest expense	Deduct
Loss on sale of asset	Add
Gain on sale of asset	Deduct
Income from long-term equity investment	Deduct

Illustration 18-17

Adjustments for non-cash items

Helpful hint Non-cash expenses (debits) are added to net income; non-cash revenues (credits) are deducted.

Determining Net Cash Provided (Used) by Investing and Financing Activities (Step 3)

After finding net cash provided by operating activities, the remaining changes in balance sheet accounts are analysed to determine net cash provided (used) by investing and financing activities.

Increase in Land. As indicated from the change in the land account, land of $130,000 was purchased through the issuance of long-term bonds. Although the issuance of bonds payable for land has no effect on cash, it is a significant non-cash investing and financing activity that merits disclosure. As indicated earlier, these activities are disclosed in a footnote to the statement of cash flows.

Increase in Building. As specified in the additional data, a building was acquired using cash of $160,000. This transaction is a cash outflow reported in the investing section.

Increase in Equipment. The equipment account increased $17,000. Based on the additional information, this was a net increase resulting from two transactions: (1) purchase of equipment of $25,000, and (2) sale for $4,000 of equipment that cost $8,000. The T account below details the changes in this account during the year:

EQUIPMENT				
1/1/00	Balance	10,000	Cost of equipment sold	8,000
	Purchase of equipment	25,000		
12/31/00	Balance	27,000		

Illustration 18-18

Analysis of equipment

These transactions are classified as investing activities, and each transaction should be reported separately. Thus the purchase of equipment should be reported as an outflow of cash for $25,000 and the sale should be reported as an inflow of cash for $4,000.

Increase in Bonds Payable. The bonds payable account increased $130,000. As shown in the additional information, land was acquired from the issuance of these bonds. As indicated earlier, this non-cash transaction is reported in a separate schedule at the bottom of the statement.

Helpful hint When stocks or bonds are issued for cash, it is the amount of the issuance price (proceeds) that appears on the statement of cash flows as a financing inflow, not the amount of par value of the stocks or the face value of the bonds. Use the amount recorded in the Cash account.

Increase in Retained Earnings. Retained earnings increased $124,000 during the year. This increase can be explained by two factors: (1) net income of $139,000, increased retained earnings, and (2) dividends of $15,000 decreased retained earnings.

Helpful hint It is the **payment** of dividends, not the declaration, that appears on the cash flow statement.

Net income is adjusted to net cash provided by operating activities in the operating activities section. Payment of the dividends is a cash outflow that is reported as a financing activity.

Statement of Cash Flows

By combining the previous items, we obtain a statement of cash flows for the year 2000 for Computer Services Corporation, as presented in Illustration 18-19:

Illustration 18-19

Statement of cash flows, 2000—indirect method

Helpful hint   Note that in the investing and financing activities sections, positive numbers indicate cash inflows (receipts) and negative numbers indicate cash outflows (payments).

COMPUTER SERVICES CORPORATION Statement of Cash Flows For the Year Ended December 31, 2000		
Cash flows from operating activities		
Net income		$139,000
Adjustments to reconcile net income to net cash provided by operating activities:		
Amortization expense	$ 15,000	
Loss on sale of equipment	3,000	
Decrease in accounts receivable	10,000	
Increase in prepaid expenses	(4,000)	
Increase in accrued expenses payable	55,000	79,000
Net cash provided by operating activities		218,000
Cash flows from investing activities		
Purchase of building	$(160,000)	
Purchase of equipment	(25,000)	
Sale of equipment	4,000	
Net cash used by investing activities		(181,000)
Cash flows from financing activities		
Payment of cash dividends	$ (15,000)	
Net cash used by financing activities		(15,000)
Net increase in cash		22,000
Cash, January 1		34,000
Cash, December 31		$ 56,000
Note x:		
Non-cash investing and financing activities		
Issuance of bonds payable to purchase land		$130,000

In Appendix A, Second Cup also uses the indirect method to prepare their statement of cash flows. Note that Second Cup titles their statement the **statement of changes in financial position**. More than 60% of the companies surveyed by *Financial Reporting in Canada* use this title, rather than Statement of Cash Flows, to describe this statement. With the recent introduction of the new CICA recommendation, more companies will likely switch to the title Statement of Cash Flows in the future. Review the format of this statement in Appendix A for another illustration of how to present cash flow information.

Before You Go On . . .

▶Review It

1. What is the format of the operating activities section of the statement of cash flows for the indirect method?
2. Where is amortization expense shown on a statement of cash flows using the indirect method?
3. Where are significant non-cash investing and financing activities shown in a statement of cash flows? Give some examples.

▶Do It

Presented below is information related to Reynolds Company. Use the indirect method to prepare a statement of cash flows.

REYNOLDS COMPANY LTD.
Comparative Balance Sheet
December 31

Assets	2000	1999	Change Increase/Decrease	
Cash	$ 54,000	$ 37,000	$ 17,000	Increase
Accounts receivable	68,000	26,000	42,000	Increase
Inventories	54,000	–0–	54,000	Increase
Prepaid expenses	4,000	6,000	2,000	Decrease
Land	45,000	70,000	25,000	Decrease
Buildings	200,000	200,000	–0–	
Accumulated amortization—buildings	(21,000)	(11,000)	10,000	Increase
Equipment	193,000	68,000	125,000	Increase
Accumulated amortization—equipment	(28,000)	(10,000)	18,000	Increase
Totals	$569,000	$386,000		

Liabilities and Shareholders' Equity				
Accounts payable	$ 23,000	$40,000	$ 17,000	Decrease
Accrued expenses payable	10,000	–0–	10,000	Increase
Bonds payable	110,000	150,000	40,000	Decrease
Common stock (no par)	220,000	60,000	160,000	Increase
Retained earnings	206,000	136,000	70,000	Increase
Totals	$569,000	$386,000		

Helpful hint To prepare the statement of cash flows:
1. Determine the net increase (decrease) in cash.
2. Determine net cash provided (used) by operating activities.
3. Determine net cash provided (used) by investing and financing activities.
4. Operating activities generally relate to revenues and expenses, which are affected by changes in non-cash current assets and current liabilities and non-cash items in the income statement.
5. Investing activities generally relate to changes in noncurrent assets.
6. Financing activities generally relate to changes in noncurrent liabilities and shareholders' equity accounts.

REYNOLDS COMPANY LTD.
Income Statement
For the Year Ended December 31, 2000

Revenues		$890,000
Cost of goods sold	$465,000	
Operating expenses	221,000	
Interest expense	12,000	
Loss on sale of equipment	2,000	700,000
Income from operations		190,000
Income tax expense		65,000
Net income		$125,000

Additional information:

(a) Operating expenses include amortization expense of $33,000 and charges from prepaid expenses of $2,000.

(b) Land was sold at its book value for cash.

(c) Cash dividends of $55,000 were declared and paid in 2000.

(d) Interest expense of $12,000 was paid in cash.

(e) Equipment with a cost of $166,000 was purchased for cash. Equipment with a cost of $41,000 and a book value of $36,000 was sold for $34,000 cash.

(f) Bonds of $10,000 were redeemed at their book value for cash; bonds of $30,000 were converted into common stock.

(g) Common stock of $130,000 was issued for cash.

(h) Accounts payable pertain to merchandise suppliers.

Reasoning: As you have learned, the balance sheet and the income statement are prepared from an adjusted trial balance of the general ledger. The statement of cash flows is prepared from an analysis of the content and changes in the balance sheet and the income statement.

Solution:

REYNOLDS COMPANY LTD.
Statement of Cash Flows
For the Year Ended December 31, 2000

Cash flows from operating activities		
Net income		$125,000
Adjustments to reconcile net income to net cash provided		
by operating activities:		
Amortization expense	$ 33,000	
Increase in accounts receivable	(42,000)	
Increase in inventories	(54,000)	
Decrease in prepaid expenses	2,000	
Decrease in accounts payable	(17,000)	
Increase in accrued expenses payable	10,000	
Loss on sale of equipment	2,000	(66,000)
Net cash provided by operating activities		59,000
Cash flows from investing activities		
Sale of land	$ 25,000	
Sale of equipment	34,000	
Purchase of equipment	(166,000)	
Net cash used by investing activities		(107,000)
Cash flows from financing activities		
Redemption of bonds	$ (10,000)	
Sale of common stock	130,000	
Payment of dividends	(55,000)	
Net cash provided by financing activities		65,000
Net increase in cash		17,000
Cash, at January 1		37,000
Cash, at December 31		$ 54,000

Note x:
Non-cash investing and financing activities

Conversion of bonds into common stock	$ 30,000

Related exercise material: BE18–1, BE18–2, BE18–4, E18–2, E18–3, E18–4, and E18– 5.

Note: This concludes Section 1 on preparation of the statement of cash flows using the indirect method. Unless your instructor assigns Section 2, you should turn to the concluding section of the chapter, "Using the Information in the Financial Statements."

SECTION 2► Direct Method

To illustrate the direct method, we will use the transactions of Computer Services Corporation for two years, 1999 and 2000. Annual statements of cash flows will be prepared. Basic transactions will be used in the first year, with additional transactions added in the second year.

STUDY OBJECTIVE
·········· ▼ ··········
    4
Prepare a statement of cash flows using the direct method.

First Year of Operations—1999

Computer Services Corporation began business on January 1, 1999, when it issued 50,000 shares of no par value common stock for $50,000 cash. The company rented office and sales space along with equipment. The comparative balance sheet at the beginning and end of 1999, and the changes in each account, are shown in Illustration 18-20:

COMPUTER SERVICES CORPORATION
Comparative Balance Sheet

Assets	Dec. 31, 1999	Jan. 1, 1999	Change Increase/Decrease	
Cash	$34,000	$ –0–	$34,000	Increase
Accounts receivable	30,000	–0–	30,000	Increase
Equipment	10,000	–0–	10,000	Increase
Total	$74,000	$ –0–		
Liabilities and Shareholders' Equity				
Accrued expenses payable	$4,000	$ –0–	$4,000	Increase
Common stock (no par)	50,000	–0–	50,000	Increase
Retained earnings	20,000	–0–	20,000	Increase
Total	$74,000	$ –0–		

Illustration 18-20

Comparative balance sheet, 1999

The income statement and additional information for Computer Services Corporation are shown in Illustration 18-21:

COMPUTER SERVICES CORPORATION
Income Statement
For the Year Ended December 31, 1999

Revenues	$85,000
Operating expenses	40,000
Income before income taxes	45,000
Income tax expense	10,000
Net income	$35,000

Illustration 18-21

Income statement and additional information, 1999

Additional information:
(a) Examination of selected data indicates that a dividend of $15,000 was declared and paid during the year.
(b) The equipment was purchased at the end of 1999. No amortization was taken in 1999.

Determining the Net Increase (Decrease) in Cash (Step 1)

The comparative balance sheet for Computer Services Corporation shows a zero cash balance at January 1, 1999, and a cash balance of $34,000 at December 31, 1999. Thus, the change in cash for 1999 was a net increase of $34,000.

Helpful hint You may wish to insert the beginning and ending cash balances, and the increase (decrease) in cash necessitated by these balances, immediately into the statement of cash flows. The net increase (decrease) is the target amount. The net cash flows from the three classes of activities must equal the target amount.

Determining the Net Cash Provided (Used) by Operating Activities (Step 2)

Helpful hint   Whether the direct or indirect method (Section 1) is used, net cash provided by operating activities will be the same.

Under the direct method, **cash provided, or used, by operating activities is computed by adjusting each item in the income statement from the accrual basis to the cash basis.** To simplify and condense the operating activities section, **only major classes of operating cash receipts and cash payments are reported.** The difference between these major classes of cash receipts and cash payments is the net cash provided by operating activities, as shown in Illustration 18-22.

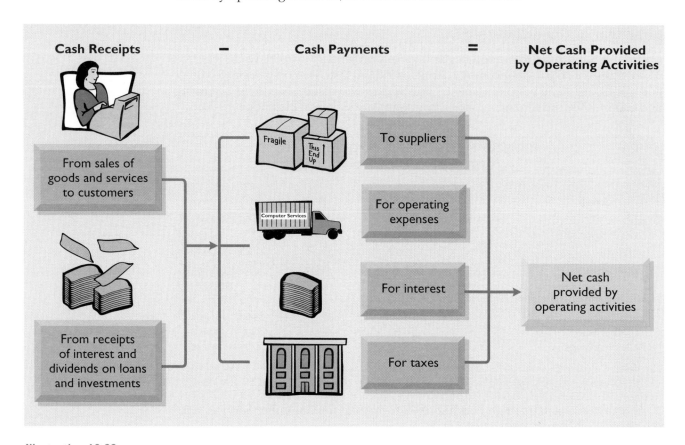

Illustration 18-22

Major classes of cash receipts and payments

   An efficient way to apply the direct method is to analyse the revenues and expenses reported in the income statement in the order in which they are listed. Cash receipts and cash payments related to these revenues and expenses are then determined. The direct method adjustments for Computer Services Corporation in 1999, to determine net cash provided by operating activities, are presented in the following sections.

Cash Receipts from Customers.   The income statement for Computer Services Corporation reported revenues from customers of $85,000. To determine cash receipts from customers, it is necessary to consider the change in accounts receivable during the year. When accounts receivable increase during the year, revenues on an accrual basis are higher than cash receipts from customers. In other words, operations led to increased revenues, but not all of these revenues resulted in cash receipts. To determine the amount of cash receipts, the increase in accounts receivable is deducted from sales revenues. Conversely, a decrease in accounts receivable is added to sales revenues, because cash receipts from customers then exceed sales revenues.

   For Computer Services Corporation, accounts receivable increased $30,000. Thus, cash receipts from customers were $55,000, computed as follows:

Revenues from sales	$85,000
Deduct: Increase in accounts receivable	30,000
Cash receipts from customers	$55,000

Illustration 18-23

Computation of cash receipts from customers

The relationship among cash receipts from customers, revenues from sales, and changes in accounts receivable is shown in Illustration 18-24:

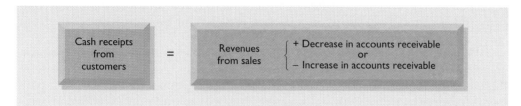

Cash Receipts from Interest and Dividends. Computer Services does not have cash receipts from any source other than customers. If an income statement details interest and/or dividend revenue, these amounts must be adjusted for any accrued interest and/or dividends receivable to determine actual cash receipts. As in Illustration 18-24, increases in accrued receivables would be deducted from accrual based revenues. Decreases in accrued receivable accounts would be added to accrual based revenues.

Cash Payments to Suppliers. Computer Services Corporation is a service corporation, not a merchandising corporation. When merchandising companies report cost of goods sold on their income statement, it is necessary to find purchases for the year before cash payments to suppliers can be determined. To find purchases, cost of goods sold is adjusted for the change in inventory. When inventory increases during the year, it means that purchases exceed cost of goods sold. As a result, the increase in inventory is added to cost of goods sold to arrive at purchases.

After purchases are computed, cash payments to suppliers are determined by adjusting purchases for the change in accounts payable. When accounts payable increase during the year, cash is conserved (i.e., not paid out). As a result, an increase in accounts payable is deducted from purchases to arrive at cash payments for goods. Conversely, a decrease in accounts payable is added to purchases, because cash payments to suppliers exceed purchases.

The relationship between cash payments to suppliers, cost of goods sold, changes in inventory, and changes in accounts payable is shown in the following formula:

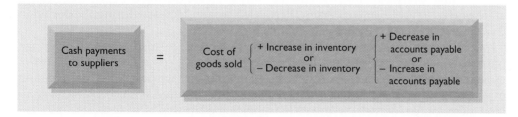

Cash Payments for Operating Expenses. Operating expenses of $40,000 were reported on Computer Services' income statement. To determine the cash paid for operating expenses (excluding interest and income taxes), this amount must be adjusted for any changes in prepaid expenses and accrued liabilities.

If prepaid expenses increase during the year, this will cause cash paid for operating expenses to be higher than operating expenses reported on the income statement. To adjust operating expenses to cash payments for services, the increase in any prepaids must be added to operating expenses. Conversely, if prepaid expenses decrease during the year, the decrease must be deducted from operating expenses in order to determine the effect upon cash.

Operating expenses must also be adjusted for changes in accrued liability accounts (e.g., accrued rent payable). While some companies record accrued liabilities separately; others combine them with accounts payable. In a merchandising company, the Accounts Payable account is often reserved for purchases on account and accrued liability accounts are used for all other payables.

When accrued expenses payable increase during the year, operating expenses on an accrual basis are higher than they are on a cash basis. As a result, an increase in these payable accounts is deducted from operating expenses to arrive at cash payments for services. Conversely, a decrease in these payable accounts is added to operating expenses because cash payments exceed operating expenses.

Computer Services Corporation's cash payments for operating expenses were $36,000, computed as follows:

Illustration 18-26

Computation of cash payments for operating expenses—direct method

Operating expenses	$40,000
Add: Increase in prepaid expenses	–0–
Deduct: Increase in accrued expenses payable	(4,000)
Cash payments for operating expenses	$36,000

The relationship among cash payments for operating expenses, operating expenses, changes in prepaid expenses, and changes in accrued expense payable is shown in the following formula:

Illustration 18-27

Formula to compute cash payments for operating expenses—direct method

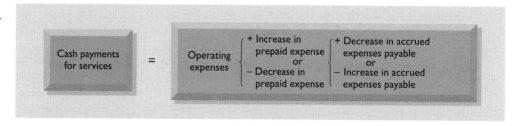

Some companies separately report payments to employees, removing these payments from operating expenses. To determine payments to employees, you would have to know the Salary (or Wage) Expense amount on the income statement and any Salaries and Benefits Payable on the balance sheet. Cash payments to employees would equal Salary Expense, increased by any decrease during the period in Salaries and Benefits Payable, or conversely, decreased by any increase during the period in Salaries and Benefits Payable.

Other companies condense their income statements in such a manner that cash payments to suppliers and employees (i.e., they do not separately disclose cost of goods sold or salary expense) cannot be separated from cash payments for operating expenses. Although the disclosure will not be as informative, it is acceptable to combine these sources of cash payments for reporting purposes.

Cash Payments for Interest and Income Taxes.   Computer Services has no interest expense. The income statement for Computer Services does show income tax expense of $10,000. This amount equals the cash paid, because the comparative balance sheet indicated no income taxes payable at either the beginning or the end of the year.

The relationship among cash payments for income taxes, income tax expense, and changes in income taxes payable (if any) is shown in the following formula:

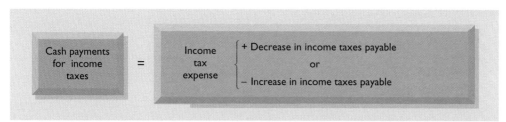

Illustration 18-28

Formula to compute cash payments for income taxes—direct method

A similar formula can be extended to interest expense, if applicable. Amounts for income taxes and interest, if any, should be reported separately.

All of the revenues and expenses in the 1999 income statement have now been adjusted to a cash basis. The operating activities section of the statement of cash flows is as follows:

Illustration 18-29

Operating activities section—direct method

Cash flows from operating activities		
Cash receipts from customers		$55,000
Cash payments:		
For operating expenses	$(36,000)	
For income taxes	(10,000)	(46,000)
Net cash provided by operating activities		9,000

Determining Net Cash Provided (Used) by Investing and Financing Activities (Step 3)

The first step for preparing the investing and financing activities sections of the statement of cash flows is to determine any changes in noncurrent accounts reported in the comparative balance sheet. The change in each account is then analysed using the additional information to determine the effect of the change on cash.

Increase in Equipment. No additional information is given for the increase in equipment. In such cases, you should assume that the increase affected cash. (You should make the same assumption in doing your assignments when the cause of a change in a noncurrent account is not explained.) The purchase of equipment is an investing activity. Thus, an outflow of cash of $10,000 for the purchase of equipment should be reported in the investing activities section.

Increase in Common Stock. The increase in common stock resulted from the issuance of common stock for $50,000 cash. It is reported as an inflow of cash in the financing activities section of the statement of cash flows.

Increase in Retained Earnings. The $20,000 increase in Retained Earnings in 1999 is a net change. When a net change in a noncurrent balance sheet account has occurred during the year, it is necessary to report the individual items that caused the net change.

For the Retained Earnings account, the reasons for the net increase of $20,000 are determined by analysis. First, net income increased retained earnings by $35,000. Second, the additional information section indicates that a cash dividend of $15,000 was declared and paid. The cash dividend paid is reported as an outflow of cash in the financing activities section.

Statement of Cash Flows

The statement of cash flows can now be prepared. The operating activities section is reported first, followed by the investing and financing activities sections. The statement of cash flows for Computer Services Corporation for 1999 is shown in Illustration 18-30:

Helpful hint Investing and financing activities are measured and reported in the same way under the direct and indirect methods.

Helpful hint It is the **payment** of dividends, not the declaration, that appears on the cash flow statement.

Illustration 18-30

Statement of cash flows, 1999—direct method

COMPUTER SERVICES CORPORATION
Statement of Cash Flows
For the Year Ended December 31, 1999

Cash flows from operating activities		
Cash receipts from customers		$55,000
Cash payments:		
For operating expenses	$(36,000)	
For income taxes	(10,000)	(46,000)
Net cash provided by operating activities		9,000
Cash flows from investing activities		
Purchase of equipment	$(10,000)	
Net cash used by investing activities		(10,000)
Cash flows from financing activities		
Issuance of common stock	$ 50,000	
Payment of cash dividends	(15,000)	
Net cash provided by financing activities		35,000
Net increase in cash		34,000
Cash, January 1		–0–
Cash, December 31		$34,000

Helpful hint Note that in the investing and financing activities sections, positive numbers indicate cash inflows (receipts) and negative numbers indicate cash outflows (payments)

The statement of cash flows shows that operating activities **provided** $9,000 of the net increase in cash of $34,000. Investing activities **used** $10,000 of cash, and financing activities **provided** $35,000 of cash. The net increase in cash of $34,000 agrees with the increase in cash of $34,000 reported in the comparative balance sheet, and financing activities **provided** $35,000 of cash.

Second Year of Operations—2000

Illustrations 18-31 and 18-32 present the comparative balance sheet, the income statement, and additional information pertaining to the second year of operations for Computer Services Corporation.

Illustration 18-31

Comparative balance sheet, 2000

COMPUTER SERVICES CORPORATION
Comparative Balance Sheet
December 31

Assets	2000	1999	Change Increase/Decrease
Cash	$ 56,000	$34,000	$ 22,000 Increase
Accounts receivable	20,000	30,000	10,000 Decrease
Prepaid expenses	4,000	–0–	4,000 Increase
Land	130,000	–0–	130,000 Increase
Building	160,000	–0–	160,000 Increase
Accumulated amortization—building	(11,000)	–0–	11,000 Increase
Equipment	27,000	10,000	17,000 Increase
Accumulated amortization—equipment	(3,000)	–0–	3,000 Increase
Total	$383,000	$74,000	
Liabilities and Shareholders' Equity			
Accrued expenses payable	$ 59,000	$ 4,000	$ 55,000 Increase
Bonds payable	130,000	–0–	130,000 Increase
Common stock	50,000	50,000	–0–
Retained earnings	144,000	20,000	124,000 Increase
Total	$383,000	$74,000	

Illustration 18-32

Income statement and additional information, 2000

COMPUTER SERVICES CORPORATION
Income Statement
For the Year Ended December 31, 2000

Revenues		$507,000
Operating expenses (excluding amortization)	$261,000	
Amortization expense	15,000	
Loss on sale of equipment	3,000	279,000
Income from operations		228,000
Income tax expenses		89,000
Net income		$139,000

Additional information:
(a) In 2000, the company declared and paid a $15,000 cash dividend.
(b) The company obtained land through the issuance of $130,000 of long-term bonds.
(c) A building costing $160,000 was purchased for cash; equipment costing $25,000 was also purchased for cash.
(d) During 2000, the company sold equipment with a book value of $7,000 (cost $8,000, less accumulated amortization $1,000) for $4,000 cash.

Determining the Net Increase (Decrease) in Cash (Step 1)

The comparative balance sheet shows a beginning cash balance of $34,000 and an ending cash balance of $56,000. Thus, there was a net increase of $22,000 in cash in 2000.

Determining Net Cash Provided (Used) in Operating Activities (Step 2)

Cash Receipts from Customers.   Revenues from sales were $507,000. Since accounts receivable decreased $10,000, cash receipts from customers were greater than sales revenues. Cash receipts from customers were $517,000, computed as follows:

Illustration 18-33

Computation of cash receipts from customers

Revenues from sales	$507,000
Add: Decrease in accounts receivable	10,000
Cash receipts from customers	$517,000

Cash Payments for Operating Expenses.   Operating expenses (exclusive of amortization expense) for 2000 were reported at $261,000. This amount is then adjusted for changes in prepaid expenses and accrued expenses payables to arrive at cash payments for operating expenses. You will recall that Computer Services made no cash payments to suppliers.

As indicated by the comparative balance sheet, prepaid expenses increased $4,000 during the year. This means that cash payments for expenses this year were greater than the operating expense amount shown (cash was paid for both operating and prepaid expenses). To arrive at cash payments for operating expenses, the increase in prepaid expenses is added to operating expenses.

Accrued liabilities increased $55,000 during the period, conserving cash for a short time. As a result, cash payments were less, by $55,000, than the amount reported for operating expenses. The increase in accrued expenses payable is deducted from operating expenses. Cash payments for operating expenses were $210,000, computed as follows:

Illustration 18-34

Computation of cash payments for operating expenses

Operating expenses, exclusive of amortization	$261,000
Add: Increase in prepaid expenses	4,000
Deduct: Increase in accrued expenses payable	(55,000)
Cash payments for operating expenses	$210,000

Amortization Expense and Loss on Sale of Equipment.   Operating expenses are shown without amortization. Amortization expense in 2000 was $15,000. Amortization expense is not shown on a statement of cash flows because it is a non-cash charge. If the amount for operating expenses includes amortization expense, operating expenses must be reduced by the amount of amortization to determine the cash payments for operating expenses.

The loss on sale of equipment of $3,000 is also a non-cash charge. The loss on sale of equipment reduces net income, but it does not reduce cash. Thus, the loss on sale of equipment is not reported on a statement of cash flows.

Other charges to expense that do not require the use of cash, such as the amortization of a bond discount, are treated in the same manner as amortization of capital assets.

Cash Payments for Income Taxes.   Income tax expense reported on the income statement was $89,000. No income taxes payable were reported. Cash payments for income taxes were, therefore, $89,000.

Summary of Conversion to Net Cash Provided by Operating Activities—Direct Method.   The direct method classifies operating activities into major categories of cash receipts (e.g., from customers, from investments) and cash payments (e.g., to suppliers, for operating expenses, for interest, for income taxes). To find cash receipts and payments, accrual-based revenues and expenses must be adjusted for changes in non-cash current asset and current liability accounts.

Increases in related current liability accounts and decreases in related current asset accounts are added to accrual based revenues to determine cash receipts. For example, decreases in accounts receivable and increases in unearned revenues are added to sales revenues. Conversely, increases in accounts receivable and decreases in unearned revenues are deducted from sales revenues.

Increases in related current asset accounts and decreases in related current liability accounts are added to accrual based expenses to determine cash payments. For example, increases in inventory and decreases in accounts payable must be added to cost of goods sold to determine the amount paid to suppliers during the period. Increases in income tax payable must be deducted from income tax expense to determine the cash paid for income taxes.

Non-cash items, such as amortization, do not affect cash and are therefore excluded from the statement of cash flows.

Determining Net Cash Provided (Used) by Investing and Financing Activities (Step 3)

Increase in Land.   Land increased $130,000. The additional information section indicates that bonds were issued to purchase the land. Although the issuance of bonds for land has no effect on cash, it is a **significant non-cash investing and financing transaction**. This transaction must be disclosed in a note to the statement of cash flows.

Increase in Building.   As specified in the additional data, a building was acquired using cash of $160,000. This transaction is a cash outflow reported in the investing section.

Increase in Equipment.   The comparative balance sheet shows that equipment increased $17,000 in 2000. The additional information in Illustration 18-32 indicates that the increase resulted from two investing transactions: (1) equipment costing $25,000 was purchased for cash, and (2) equipment costing $8,000 was sold for $4,000 cash when its book value was $7,000 ($8,000 cost, less accumulated amortization of

$1,000).

The relevant data for the statement of cash flows are the cash paid for the purchase and the cash proceeds from the sale. For Computer Services Corporation, the investing activities section will show purchase of equipment $25,000, as an outflow of cash; and sale of equipment $4,000, as an inflow of cash. **The two amounts should not be offset,** because one is an outflow of cash and the other is an inflow of cash. **Both flows should be shown.**

Increase in Bonds Payable. Bonds Payable increased $130,000. The additional information indicated that bonds were issued in exchange for land. As noted previously, this transaction is a **significant non-cash investing and financing transaction** that must be reported in a note to the statement.

Increase in Retained Earnings. The net increase in Retained Earnings of $124,000 resulted from net income of $139,000 and the declaration and payment of a cash dividend of $15,000. **Net income is not reported in the statement of cash flows under the direct method.** Instead, the individual components that make up net income are reported when they affect cash flows. Cash dividends paid of $15,000 are reported in the financing activities section as an outflow of cash.

Statement of Cash Flows

The statement of cash flows for Computer Services Corporation is shown in Illustration 18-35:

COMPUTER SERVICES CORPORATION Statement of Cash Flows For the Year Ended December 31, 2000		
Cash flows from operating activities		
Cash receipts from customers		$517,000
Cash payments:		
For operating expenses	$ (210,000)	
For income taxes	(89,000)	(299,000)
Net cash provided by operating activities		218,000
Cash flows from investing activities		
Purchase of building	$(160,000)	
Purchase of equipment	(25,000)	
Sale of equipment	4,000	
Net cash used by investing activities		(181,000)
Cash flows from financing activities		
Payment of cash dividends	$ (15,000)	
Net cash used by financing activities		(15,000)
Net increase in cash		22,000
Cash, January 1		34,000
Cash, December 31		$ 56,000
Note x:		
Non-cash investing and financing activities		
Issuance of bonds payable to purchase land		$130,000

Illustration 18-35

Statement of cash flows, 2000—direct method

Before You Go On...

▶Review It

1. What is the format of the operating activities section of the statement of cash flows, using the direct method?
2. Where is amortization expense shown on a statement of cash flows, using the direct method?
3. Where are significant non-cash investing and financing activities shown on a statement of cash flows? Give some examples.

▶Do It

Presented below is information related to Reynolds Company. Use the direct method to prepare a statement of cash flows.

Helpful hint To prepare the statement of cash flows:
1. Determine the net increase (decrease) in cash.
2. Determine net cash provided (used) by operating activities.
3. Determine net cash provided (used) by investing and financing activities.
4. Operating activities generally relate to cash receipts and cash payments from operations (income statement).
5. Investing activities generally relate to changes in noncurrent assets.
6. Financing activities generally relate to changes in noncurrent liabilities and shareholders' equity accounts.

REYNOLDS COMPANY LTD.
Comparative Balance Sheet
December 31

Assets	2000	1999	Change Increase/Decrease	
Cash	$ 54,000	$ 37,000	$ 17,000	Increase
Accounts receivable	68,000	26,000	42,000	Increase
Inventories	54,000	–0–	54,000	Increase
Prepaid expenses	4,000	6,000	2,000	Decrease
Land	45,000	70,000	25,000	Decrease
Buildings	200,000	200,000	–0–	
Accumulated amortization—buildings	(21,000)	(11,000)	10,000	Increase
Equipment	193,000	68,000	125,000	Increase
Accumulated amortization—equipment	(28,000)	(10,000)	18,000	Increase
Totals	$569,000	$386,000		

Liabilities and Shareholders' Equity				
Accounts payable	$ 23,000	$ 40,000	$ 17,000	Decrease
Accrued expenses payable	10,000	–0–	10,000	Increase
Bonds payable	110,000	150,000	40,000	Decrease
Common stock	220,000	60,000	160,000	Increase
Retained earnings	206,000	136,000	70,000	Increase
Totals	$569,000	$386,000		

REYNOLDS COMPANY LTD.
Income Statement
For the Year Ended December 31, 2000

Revenues		$890,000
Cost of goods sold	$465,000	
Operating expenses	221,000	
Interest expense	12,000	
Loss on sale of equipment	2,000	700,000
Income from operations		190,000
Income tax expense		65,000
Net income		$125,000

Additional information:
(a) Operating expenses include amortization expense of $33,000 and charges from prepaid expenses of $2,000.
(b) Land was sold at its book value for cash.
(c) Cash dividends of $55,000 were declared and paid in 2000.
(d) Interest expense of $12,000 was paid in cash.
(e) Equipment with a cost of $166,000 was purchased for cash. Equipment with a cost of $41,000 and a book value of $36,000 was sold for $34,000 cash.
(f) Bonds of $10,000 were redeemed at their book value for cash; bonds of $30,000 were converted into common stock.
(g) Common stock of $130,000 was issued for cash.
(h) Accounts payable pertain to merchandise suppliers.

Reasoning: The indirect and the direct methods differ primarily in their presentation of the cash flows from the operating activities. The direct method reports cash receipts less cash payments to arrive at net cash provided by operating activities.

Solution:

REYNOLDS COMPANY LTD.
Statement of Cash Flows
For the Year Ended December 31, 2000

Cash flows from operating activities		
Cash receipts from customers		$848,000[a]
Cash payments:		
To suppliers	$ (536,000)[b]	
For operating expenses	(176,000)[c]	
For interest expense	(12,000)	
For income taxes	(65,000)	(789,000)
Net cash provided by operating activities		59,000
Cash flows from investing activities		
Sale of land	$ 25,000	
Sale of equipment	34,000	
Purchase of equipment	(166,000)	
Net cash used by investing activities		(107,000)
Cash flows from financing activities		
Redemption of bonds	$ (10,000)	
Sale of common stock	130,000	
Payment of dividends	(55,000)	
Net cash provided by financing activities		65,000
Net increase in cash		17,000
Cash, January 1		37,000
Cash, December 31		$ 54,000

Note x:
Non-cash investing and financing activities

Conversion of bonds into common stock	$ 30,000

Computations:
[a] $848,000 = $890,000 − $42,000
[b] Payments to suppliers: $536,000 = $465,000 + $54,000 + $17,000
[c] Payments for operating expenses: $176,000 = $221,000 − $33,000 − $2,000 − $10,000

Related exercise material: BE18–6, BE18–7, BE18–8, BE18–9, E18–7, E18–8, E18–9, and E18–10.

Note: This concludes Section 2 on preparation of the statement of cash flows using the direct method. You should now turn to the next—and concluding—section of the chapter, "Using the Information in the Financial Statements."

Using the Information in the Financial Statements

The statement of cash flows provides information about a company's financial health that is not evident from analysis of the balance sheet or the income statement. Bankers, creditors, and other users of the statement of cash flows are often more concerned with cash flow from operations than they are with net income, because they are interested in a company's ability to pay its bills.

▶ Accounting in Action ▸ *Business Insight*

Noel Tichy, in his book *The Leadership Engine*, says, "I am a great believer in cash flow. Earnings is a man-made convention but cash is cash."

Source: *Globe and Mail*, October 23, 1997, B16.

STUDY OBJECTIVE

5

Distinguish between cash flow per share and earnings per share.

Because of the importance of the statement of cash flows to a wide variety of users, many people have recommended that the statement of cash flows include **cash flow per share** data, just as the income statement includes **earnings per share** data. Although the CICA does not require the inclusion of cash flow per share data in the statement of cash flows, companies often include the ratio on the face of the statement of cash flows, or in a note to the financial statements cross-referenced to this statement. Cash flow per share information is not a substitute for earnings per share. It should not be presented on the face of the income statement.

Cash Flow Per Share

Cash flow is an important measure of performance for companies. It is computed by determining cash flow from operating, investing, and financing activities, then dividing this result by the weighted average number of common shares outstanding. This is exactly how earnings per share are calculated (see Illustration 15-20) except that cash flow replaces net income. Just as for EPS, if preferred dividends have been declared for the period, they must be deducted to arrive at cash flow available for the common shareholders. Both the cash flow per share and EPS computations can be refined if complex capital structures exist. These calculations await further study in an intermediate accounting course.

The following illustration demonstrates the computation of cash flow per share for The Second Cup Ltd.:

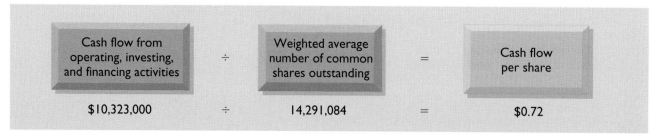

Cash flow from operating, investing, and financing activities	÷	Weighted average number of common shares outstanding	=	Cash flow per share
$10,323,000	÷	14,291,084	=	$0.72

Illustration 18-36

Computation of cash flow per share

Second Cup's cash flow per share is more than three times its reported earnings per share of $0.21. It is interesting to compare cash flow per share to earnings per share for selected companies in a recent year. Neither statistic on its own provides sufficient information for decision makers; however, taken together, earnings and cash provide two significant pieces of information needed to predict a company's future viability.

	Cash Flow Per Share	Earnings Per Share
Coca-Cola Beverages	$(0.22)	$0.29
Cott Corporation	0.05	0.56
Maple Leaf Foods	0.57	0.51
Molson Cos.	(4.30)	1.89
Seagram Co. Ltd.	0.26	(0.15)

Illustration 18-37

Comparison of cash flow and earnings per share for selected companies

► **Ethics note**

Many investors believe that "cash is cash and everything else is accounting"—that is, cash flow is less susceptible to management manipulation and fraud than traditional accounting measures such as net income. Although reliance on cash flows to the exclusion of accrual accounting is inappropriate, comparing cash from operations to net income can sometimes reveal important information about the quality of reported net income. It can show the extent to which net income provides a good measure of actual performance.

Before You Go On . . .

► **Review It**

1. Explain why cash flow per share can differ so much from reported earnings per share.

A Look Back at United Parcel Service

Refer to the opening story about UPS's deferral of cash needed to build an automated conveyor belt, and answer the following questions:
1. Why was the conveyor belt constructed in March rather than as originally intended in January?
2. Explain what information in the balance sheet, income statement, and statement of cash flows would have helped Ms. Chakravorty make this decision prior to January.
3. How would the construction of the airport, including the $2.5-million conveyor belt, be presented on the statement of cash flows?

Solution:

1. The construction of the conveyor belt was likely deferred until March because of reduced volumes. This reduction means less cash was available to pay the principal and interest payments on monies that had to be borrowed to finance this construction.
2. The balance sheet would provide information about the amount of cash on hand, the current asset and current liability (working capital) position of the company, and the amount of current debt load the company would have, before financing for this project. Net income, as presented on the income statement, would be helpful in predicting future earnings. The statement of cash flows would add to the ending cash position presented on the balance sheet, by explaining where cash came from and where cash went. This information is useful, in combination with net income, in predicting future cash flows. Future cash in(out)flows are essential to ensure that project financing can be obtained, maintained, and ultimately repaid.
3. The total cost of constructing the airport would be reported on the statement of cash flows as an outflow of cash and as an investing activity. Users would realize that one of the uses of cash was the construction of an airport that would have many years of life.

Summary of Study Objectives

1. *Indicate the primary purpose of the statement of cash flows.* The primary purpose of the statement of cash flows is to provide information about the cash receipts and cash payments of an entity during a period. A secondary objective is to provide information about the operating, investing, and financing activities of the entity during the period.

2. *Distinguish among operating, investing, and financing activities.* Operating activities include the cash effects of transactions that affect net income. Investing activities involve cash flows resulting from changes in investments and long-term asset items. Financing activities involve cash flows resulting from changes in long-term liability and shareholders' equity items.

3. *Prepare a statement of cash flows using the indirect method.* The preparation of a statement of cash flows involves three major steps: (1) determining the net increase or decrease in cash, (2) determining net cash provided (used) by operating

activities, and (3) determining net cash flows provided (used) by investing and financing activities. Under the indirect method, accrual-based net income is adjusted to net cash provided by operating activities.

4. *Prepare a statement of cash flows using the direct method.* The preparation of the statement of cash flows involves three major steps: (1) determining the net increase or decrease in cash, (2) determining net cash provided (used) by operating activities, and (3) determining net cash flows provided (used) by investing and financing activities. The direct method reports cash receipts less cash payments to arrive at net cash provided by operating activities.

5. *Distinguish between cash flow per share and earnings per share.* Cash flow per share measures the amount of cash provided by operating, investing, and financing activities, for each common share. Earnings per share measures the amount of accrual based net income, for each common share.

APPENDIX ▸ Using a Work Sheet to Prepare the Statement of Cash Flows—Indirect Method

STUDY OBJECTIVE

⬇ 6

Explain the procedural steps in using a work sheet to prepare the statement of cash flows.

When numerous adjustments of net income are necessary, **a work sheet is often used to assemble and classify the data that will appear on the statement of cash flows**. The work sheet helps prepare the statement, but its use is optional.

The following guidelines are important in using a work sheet:

1. In the balance sheet accounts section, **accounts with debit balances are listed separately from those with credit balances**. This means, for example, that Accumulated Amortization is listed under credit balances, not as a contra account under debit balances. The beginning and ending balances of each account are entered in the appropriate columns. The transactions that caused the change in the account balance during the year are entered as reconciling items in the two middle columns. After all reconciling items have been entered, each line pertaining to a balance sheet account should foot across. That is, the beginning balance plus or minus the reconciling item(s) must equal the ending balance. When all balance sheet accounts agree, all changes in account balances have been reconciled.

2. The bottom portion of the work sheet consists of the operating, investing, and financing activities sections. Accordingly, it provides the information necessary to prepare the formal statement of cash flows. **Inflows of cash are entered as debits in the reconciling columns, and outflows of cash are entered as credits in the reconciling columns.** Thus, in this section the sale of equipment for cash at book value is entered as a debit under investing activities. Similarly, the purchase of land for cash is entered as a credit under investing activities.

3. The reconciling items shown in the work sheet are not entered in any journal or posted to any account. They do not represent either adjustments or corrections of the balance sheet accounts. They are used only to facilitate the preparation of the statement of cash flows.

Preparing the Work Sheet

As with work sheets illustrated in earlier chapters, the preparation of a work sheet involves a series of steps. The steps in this case are:

1. Entering the balance sheet accounts and their beginning and ending balances in the balance sheet accounts section.
2. Entering the data that explain the changes in all balance sheet accounts other than cash—and their effects on the statement of cash flows—in the reconciling columns of the work sheet.
3. Entering the increase or decrease in cash on the cash line and at the bottom of the work sheet. This entry ensures that the totals of the reconciling columns are in agreement.

The work sheet can be used for either the indirect method or the direct method of determining operating activities. You will remember that use of the indirect or direct methods affects only the computation and presentation of operating cash flows, not investing and financing cash flows. To illustrate the preparation of a work sheet, we will use the 2000 data for Computer Services Corporation and the indirect method. Your familiarity with these data should help you understand the use of a work sheet. Refer to Illustrations 18-12 and 18-13 for the comparative balance sheets, income statement, and selected data for 2000.

The work sheet for Computer Services Corporation is shown in Illustration 18A-1.

 # Technology in Action

 The work sheet illustrates how easy it is to generate a statement of cash flows using a computer. The computer output must be carefully analysed, to ensure that changes in balance sheet accounts are not netted (that is, increases offset against decreases).

Determining the Reconciling Items

Several approaches may be used to determine the reconciling items. For example, the changes that affect net cash provided by operating activities could be completed first, and then the effects of financing and investing transactions could be calculated. Alternatively, the balance sheet accounts could be analysed in the order in which they are listed on the work sheet. We will follow this latter approach for Computer Services, except for cash. As indicated above, **cash is handled last**.

COMPUTER SERVICES CORPORATION
Work Sheet
Statement of Cash Flows
For the Year Ended December 31, 2000

Balance Sheet Accounts	Balance 12/31/99	Reconciling Items Debit	Reconciling Items Credit	Balance 12/31/00
Debits				
Cash	34,000	(l) 22,000		56,000
Accounts receivable	30,000		(a) 10,000	20,000
Prepaid expenses	–0–	(b) 4,000		4,000
Land	–0–	(c) 130,000 *		130,000
Building	–0–	(d) 160,000		160,000
Equipment	10,000	(e) 25,000	(f) 8,000	27,000
Total	74,000			397,000
Credits				
Accrued expenses payable	4,000		(g) 55,000	59,000
Bonds payable	–0–		(c) 130,000 *	130,000
Accumulated amortization—building	–0–		(h) 11,000	11,000
Accumulated amortization—equipment	–0–	(f) 1,000	(i) 4,000	3,000
Common stock	50,000			50,000
Retained earnings	20,000	(k) 15,000	(j) 139,000	144,000
Total	74,000			397,000
Statement of Cash Flows Effects				
Operating activities				
Net income		(j) 139,000		
Decrease in accounts receivable		(a) 10,000		
Increase in prepaid expenses			(b) 4,000	
Increase in accrued expenses payable		(g) 55,000		
Amortization expense—building		(h) 11,000		
Amortization expense—equipment		(i) 4,000		
Loss on sale of equipment		(f) 3,000		
Investing activities				
Purchase of building			(d) 160,000	
Purchase of equipment			(e) 25,000	
Sale of equipment		(f) 4,000		
Financing activities				
Payment of dividends			(k) 15,000	
Totals		583,000	561,000	
Increase in cash			(l) 22,000	
Totals		583,000	583,000	

* Significant non-cash investing and financing activity.

Illustration 18A-1

*Completed work sheet—
indirect method*

Accounts Receivable. The decrease of $10,000 in accounts receivable means that cash collections from revenues are higher than the revenues reported in the income statement. To convert net income to net cash provided by operating activities, the decrease of $10,000 is added to net income. The entry in the reconciling columns of the work sheet is:

| (a) | Operating Activity—Decrease in Accounts Receivable | 10,000 | |
| | Accounts Receivable | | 10,000 |

Helpful hint Note that the decrease in accounts receivable represents an inflow/increase in cash, and is therefore logically recorded as a debit.

Prepaid Expenses. An increase of $4,000 in prepaid expenses means that expenses deducted in determining net income are less than expenses that were paid in cash. Thus, the increase of $4,000 must be deducted from net income in determining net cash provided by operating activities. The work sheet entry is:

| (b) | Prepaid Expenses | 4,000 | |
| | Operating Activity—Increase in Prepaid Expenses | | 4,000 |

Helpful hint The increase in prepaid expenses represents an outflow/decrease in cash, and is therefore logically recorded as a credit.

Land. The increase in land of $130,000 resulted from a purchase through the issuance of long-term bonds. This transaction should be reported as a significant non-cash investing and financing activity. The work sheet entry is:

| (c) | Land | 130,000 | |
| | Bonds Payable | | 130,000 |

Building. The cash purchase of a building for $160,000 is an investing activity cash outflow. The entry in the reconciling columns of the work sheet is:

| (d) | Building | 160,000 | |
| | Investing Activity—Purchase of Building | | 160,000 |

Equipment. The increase in equipment of $17,000 resulted from a cash purchase of $25,000 and the sale of equipment costing $8,000. The book value of the equipment was $7,000, the cash proceeds were $4,000, and a loss of $3,000 was recorded. The work sheet entries are:

| (e) | Equipment | 25,000 | |
| | Investing Activity—Purchase of Equipment | | 25,000 |

(f)	Investing Activity—Sale of Equipment	4,000	
	Operating Activity—Loss on Sale of Equipment	3,000	
	Accumulated Amortization—Equipment	1,000	
	Equipment		8,000

Helpful hint Note that, in each case, we are reconstructing journal entries—except that cash is replaced by the appropriate activity (operating, investing, or financing).

Accrued Expenses Payable. The increase of $55,000 in accrued expenses payable must be added to net income to obtain net cash provided by operating activities. The following work sheet entry is made:

| (g) | Operating Activity—Increase in Accrued Expenses Payable | 55,000 | |
| | Accrued Expenses Payable | | 55,000 |

Bonds Payable. The increase of $130,000 in this account resulted from the issuance of bonds for land. This has already been dealt with in work sheet entry (c) above.

Accumulated Amortization—Building, and Accumulated Amortization—Equipment. The increases in these accounts of $11,000 and $4,000, respectively, resulted from amortization expense. Amortization expense is a **non-cash charge that must be added to net income** in determining net cash provided by operating activities. The work sheet entries are:

| (h) | Operating Activity—Amortization Expense—Building | 11,000 | |
| | Accumulated Amortization—Building | | 11,000 |

| (i) | Operating Activity—Amortization Expense—Equipment | 4,000 | |
| | Accumulated Amortization—Equipment | | 4,000 |

Retained Earnings. The $124,000 increase in retained earnings resulted from net income of $139,000 and the declaration of a $15,000 cash dividend that was paid in 2000. Net income is included in net cash provided by operating activities, and the dividends are a financing activity cash outflow. The entries in the reconciling columns of the work sheet are:

(j)	Operating Activity—Net Income	139,000	
	Retained Earnings		139,000

(k)	Retained Earnings	15,000	
	Financing Activity—Payment of Dividends		15,000

Disposition of Change in Cash. The firm's cash increased $22,000 in 2000. The final entry on the work sheet, therefore, is:

(l)	Cash	22,000	
	Increase in Cash		22,000

As shown in the work sheet, the increase in cash is entered in the reconciling credit column as a **balancing** amount. This entry should complete the reconciliation of the changes in the balance sheet accounts. In addition, it should ensure the totals of the reconciling columns agree. When all changes have been explained and the reconciling columns agree, the reconciling columns are ruled to complete the work sheet.

Preparing the Statement

The statement of cash flows is prepared directly from the data that appear in the work sheet under Statement of Cash Flows Effects. The reconciling columns should also be scanned for any asterisked items that designate significant non-cash activities. The formal statement was shown in Illustration 18-19.

Before You Go On . . .

▸Review It

1. Explain how the worksheet facilitates the preparation of the statement of cash flows.

Related exercise material: BE18–11 and E18–11.

◤ummary of Study Objective
••

6. *Explain the procedural steps in using a work sheet to prepare the statement of cash flows.* When there are numerous adjustments, a work sheet can be a helpful tool in preparing the statement of cash flows. Key guidelines for using a work sheet are: (1) list accounts with debit balances separately from those with credit balances, (2) in the reconciling columns in the bottom portion of the work sheet, show cash inflows as debits and cash outflows as credits, (3) do not enter reconciling items in any journal or ledger, but use them only to help prepare the statement of cash flows.

The steps in preparing the work sheet are: (1) entering beginning and ending balances of balance sheet accounts, (2) entering debits and credits in reconciling columns, and (3) entering the increase or decrease in cash in two places as a balancing amount.

GLOSSARY
••

Cash flow per share Cash flow from operations divided by the weighted average number of common shares outstanding. (p. 768).

Direct method A method of determining the net cash provided by operating activities by adjusting each item in the income statement from the accrual basis to the cash basis. (p. 758).

Financing activities Cash flow activities that include obtaining cash from issuing debt and repaying the amounts borrowed, and obtaining cash from shareholders and providing them with a return on their investment. (p. 740).

Indirect method A method of preparing a statement of cash flows in which net income is adjusted for items that did not affect cash, to determine net cash provided by operating activities. (p. 746).

Investing activities Cash flow activities that include acquiring and disposing of investments and productive long-lived assets, and lending money and collecting on those loans. (p. 740).

Operating activities Cash flow activities that include the cash effects of transactions that create revenues and expenses, and thus affect net income. (p. 740).

Statement of cash flows A basic financial statement (also known as statement of changes in financial position) that provides information about the cash receipts and cash payments of an entity during a period, classified as operating, investing, and financing activities, in a format that reconciles the beginning and ending cash balances. (p. 739).

DEMONSTRATION PROBLEM

The income statement for the year ended December 31, 1999, for John Kosinski Manufacturing Company contains the following condensed information:

Revenues		$6,583,000
Cost of goods sold	$3,427,000	
Operating expenses (excluding amortization)	1,469,000	
Amortization expense	880,000	
Loss on sale of machinery	24,000	5,800,000
Income before income taxes		783,000
Income tax expense		353,000
Net income		$ 430,000

Machinery was sold (at a loss of $24,000) for $270,000 cash. Other machinery was purchased at a cost of $750,000. The following balances are reported on Kosinski's comparative balance sheet at December 31:

	1999	1998
Cash	$672,000	$130,000
Accounts receivable	775,000	610,000
Inventories	834,000	867,000
Accounts payable	521,000	501,000

Income tax expense of $353,000 equals the amount paid in 1999. Dividends declared and paid in 1999 totalled $200,000.

Instructions

(a) Prepare the statement of cash flows using the indirect method.
(b) Prepare the statement of cash flows using the direct method.

Solution to Demonstration Problem

JOHN KOSINSKI MANUFACTURING COMPANY
Statement of Cash Flows
For the Year Ended December 31, 1999

(a) <u>Indirect Method</u>

Cash flows from operating activities		
Net income		$ 430,000
Adjustments to reconcile net income to net cash provided by operating activities:		
Amortization expense	$880,000	
Loss on sale of machinery	24,000	
Increase in accounts receivable	(165,000)	
Decrease in inventories	33,000	
Increase in accounts payable	20,000	792,000
Net cash provided by operating activities		1,222,000
Cash flows from investing activities		
Sale of machinery	$270,000	
Purchase of machinery	(750,000)	
Net cash used by investing activities		(480,000)
Cash flows from financing activities		
Payment of cash dividends		(200,000)
Net increase in cash		542,000
Cash at beginning of period (January 1, 1999)		130,000
Cash at end of period (December 31, 1999)		$ 672,000

Problem-Solving Strategies

1. Only the Operating Activities section of the Statement of Cash Flows differs between the indirect and the direct methods.

2. Although the details differ between the indirect and direct methods, the final total under Operating Activities is the same under both methods.

3. Both methods report identical information under Investing and Financing Activities.

4. Operating Activities relate to revenues and expenses (as well as gains and losses) and changes in current assets and current liabilities.

5. Investing Activities relate to long-term assets.

6. Financing Activities relate to long-term liabilities and shareholders' equity.

(b)   Direct Method

Cash flows from operating activities	
Cash collections from customers	$6,418,000*
Cash payments to suppliers	(3,374,000)**
Cash payments for operating expenses	(1,469,000)
Cash payment for income taxes	(353,000)
Net cash provided by operating activities	1,222,000
Cash flows from investing activities	
Sale of machinery	$270,000
Purchase of machinery	(750,000)
Net cash used by investing activities	(480,000)
Cash flows from financing activities	
Payment of cash dividends	(200,000)
Net increase in cash	542,000
Cash at beginning of period (January 1, 1999)	130,000
Cash at end of period (December 31, 1999)	$ 672,000

Direct Method Computations

* Cash collections from customers:	
Revenues per the income statement	$6,583,000
Less increase in accounts receivable	165,000
Cash collections from customers	$6,418,000
** Cash payments to suppliers:	
Cost of goods sold per the income statement	$3,427,000
Deduct decrease in inventories	(33,000)
Deduct increase in accounts payable	(20,000)
Cash payments for operating expenses	$3,374,000

Note: All **asterisked** Questions, Exercises, and Problems relate to material contained in the appendix to the chapter.

SELF-STUDY QUESTIONS
••

Answers are at the end of the chapter.

(SO 1)   1. Which of the following about the statement of cash flows is incorrect?
   a. It is a fourth basic financial statement.
   b. It provides information about cash receipts and cash payments of an entity during a period.
   c. It reconciles the ending cash account balance to the bank statement balance.
   d. It provides information about the operating, investing, and financing activities of the business.

(SO 2)   2. The statement of cash flows classifies cash receipts and cash payments by the following activities:
   a. operating and nonoperating.
   b. investing, financing, and operating.
   c. financing, operating, and nonoperating.
   d. investing, financing, and nonoperating.

(SO 2)   3. An example of a cash flow from an operating activity is:

   a. payment of cash to lenders for interest.
   b. receipt of cash from the sale of capital stock.
   c. payment of cash dividends to the company's shareholders.
   d. none of the above.

(SO 2)   4. An example of a cash flow from an investing activity is:
   a. receipt of cash from the issuance of bonds payable.
   b. payment of cash to repurchase outstanding capital stock.
   c. receipt of cash from the sale of equipment.
   d. payment of cash to suppliers for inventory.

(SO 2)   5. Cash dividends paid to shareholders are classified on the statement of cash flows as:
   a. operating activities.
   b. investing activities.
   c. a combination of the above.
   d. financing activities.

SO 2)

6. An example of a cash flow from a financing activity is:
   a. receipt of cash from sale of land.
   b. issuance of debt for cash.
   c. purchase of equipment for cash.
   d. none of the above.

SO 2)

7. Which of the following about the statement of cash flows is *incorrect*?
   a. The direct method may be used to report cash provided by operations.
   b. The statement shows the cash provided (used) for three categories of activity.
   c. The operating section is the last section of the statement.
   d. The indirect method may be used to report cash provided by operations.

Questions 8 and 9 apply only to the indirect method.

SO 3)

8. Net income is $132,000, accounts payable increased $10,000 during the year, inventory decreased $6,000 during the year, and accounts receivable increased $12,000 during the year. Under the indirect method, net cash provided by operations is:
   a. $102,000.
   b. $112,000.
   c. $124,000.
   d. $136,000.

SO 3)

9. In determining cash provided by operations under the indirect method, non-cash charges that are added to net income do not include :
   a. amortization expense.
   b. an increase in inventory.
   c. an increase in accounts payable.
   d. loss on sale of equipment.

Questions 10 and 11 apply only to the direct method.

10. The beginning balance in accounts receivable is $44,000 and the ending balance is $42,000. Sales during the period are $129,000. Cash receipts from customers is:
    a. $127,000.
    b. $129,000.
    c. $131,000.
    d. $141,000.

(SO 4)

11. Which of the following items is reported on a cash flow statement prepared by using the direct method?
    a. loss on sale of building.
    b. increase in accounts receivable.
    c. amortization expense.
    d. cash payments to suppliers.

(SO 4)

12. The statement of cash flows should not be used to evaluate an entity's ability to:
    a. earn net income.
    b. generate future cash flows.
    c. pay dividends.
    d. meet obligations.

(SO 5)

*13. In a work sheet for the statement of cash flows, a decrease in accounts receivable is entered in the reconciling columns as a credit to Accounts Receivable and a debit in the:
    a. investing activities section.
    b. operating activities section.
    c. financing activities section.
    d. none of the above.

(SO 6)

QUESTIONS

1. (a) What is the statement of cash flows? (b) Alice Weiseman maintains that the statement of cash flows is an optional financial statement. Do you agree? Explain.

2. What questions about cash are answered by the statement of cash flows?

3. What are "cash equivalents"? How do cash equivalents affect the statement of cash flows?

4. Distinguish among the three types of activities reported in the statement of cash flows.

5. What are the major sources (inflows) of cash in a statement of cash flows? What are the major uses (outflows) of cash?

6. Why is it important to disclose certain non-cash transactions? How should they be disclosed?

7. Wilma Flintstone and Barny Kublestone were discussing the presentation format of the statement of cash flows of Rock Candy Co. At the bottom of Rock Candy's statement of cash flows was a separate section entitled "Non-cash investing and

financing activities." Give three examples of significant non-cash transactions that would be reported in this section.

8. Why is it necessary to use comparative balance sheets, a current income statement, and certain transaction data in preparing a statement of cash flows?

9. Contrast the advantages and disadvantages of the direct and indirect methods. Are both methods acceptable? Which method is preferred by the CICA?

10. When the total cash inflows exceed the total cash outflows in the statement of cash flows, how and where is this excess identified?

11. Describe the indirect method for determining net cash provided by operating activities.

12. Why is it necessary to convert accrual-based net income to cash-basis income when preparing a statement of cash flows?

13. The president of Aerosmith Company is puzzled. During the last year, the company experienced a net loss of $800,000, yet its cash increased $300,000 during the same period of time. Explain to the president how this situation could occur.

14. Identify five items that are adjustments to reconcile net income to net cash provided by operating activities, under the indirect method.

15. Why and how is amortization expense reported in a statement prepared using the indirect method?

16. Why is the statement of cash flows useful?

17. During 1999, Johnny Carson Company converted $1,700,000 of its total $2,000,000 of bonds payable into common stock. Indicate how the transaction would be reported on a statement of cash flows, if at all.

18. Describe the direct method for determining net cash provided by operating activities.

19. Give the formulas under the direct method for computing: (a) cash receipts from customers, and (b) cash payments to suppliers.

20. Cindy Crawford Inc. reported sales of $2 million for 1999. Accounts receivable decreased $100,000 and accounts payable increased $300,000. Compute cash receipts from customers, assuming that the receivable and payable transactions related to operations.

21. Why is amortization expense not reported in the cash flow from operating activities section, under the direct method?

*22. Why is it advantageous to use a work sheet when preparing a statement of cash flows? Is a work sheet required in preparing a statement of cash flows?

BRIEF EXERCISES

Compute cash from operating activities—indirect method.
(SO 3)

BE18–1   Crystal, Inc., reported net income of $2.5 million in 1999. Amortization for the year was $260,000, accounts receivable decreased $350,000, and accounts payable decreased $310,000. Compute net cash provided by operating activities, using the indirect approach.

Compute cash from operating activities—indirect method.
(SO 3)

BE18–2   The net income for Sterling Engineering Co. for 1999 was $280,000. For 1999, amortization on capital assets was $60,000, and the company incurred a loss on sale of capital assets of $9,000. Compute net cash provided by operating activities, under the indirect method.

Indicate statement presentation of selected transactions.
(SO 2)

BE18–3   Each of the following items must be considered in preparing a statement of cash flows for Murphy Co. for the year ended December 31, 1999. For each item, state how it should be shown in the statement of cash flows:

(a) Issued bonds for $200,000 cash.

(b) Purchased equipment for $150,000 cash.

(c) Sold land costing $20,000 for $20,000 cash.

(d) Declared and paid a $50,000 cash dividend.

Compute cash from operating activities—indirect method.
(SO 3)

BE18–4   The comparative balance sheet for the Rolex Company shows the following changes in non-cash current asset accounts: accounts receivable decrease $80,000, prepaid expenses increase $12,000, and inventories increase $30,000. Compute net cash provided by operating activities, using the indirect method, assuming that net income is $200,000.

Classify items by activity.
(SO 2)

BE18–5   Classify the following items as an operating, investing, or financing activity. Assume all items involve cash.

(a) Purchase of equipment.

(b) Sale of building.

(c) Redemption of bonds.

(d) Payment of dividends.

(e) Issuance of capital stock.

BE18–6 Billy Idol Corporation has accounts receivable of $14,000 at 1/1/99 and $24,000 at 12/31/99. Sales revenues were $480,000 for the year. What is the amount of cash receipts from customers in 1999?

Compute cash receipts from customers—direct method.
(SO 4)

BE18–7 Depeche Mode Corporation reported income taxes of $70,000 on its 1999 income statement and income taxes payable of $12,000 at December 31, 1998, and $9,000 at December 31, 1999. What amount of cash payments were made for income taxes during 1999?

Compute cash payments for income tax—direct method.
(SO 4)

BE18–8 Excel Corporation reports operating expenses of $90,000, excluding amortization expense of $15,000, for 1999. During the year, prepaid expenses decreased $6,600 and accrued expenses payable increased $4,400. Compute the cash payments for operating expenses in 1999.

Compute cash payments for operating expenses—direct method.
(SO 4)

BE18–9 The T accounts for Equipment and the related Accumulated Amortization for Cindy Trevis Company at the end of 1999 are as follows:

Determine cash received from sale of equipment.
(SO 3, 4)

Equipment			
Beg. bal.	80,000	Disposals	22,000
Acquisitions	41,600		
End. bal.	99,600		

Accumulated Amortization			
Disposals	5,500	Beg. bal.	44,500
		Amort.	12,000
		End. bal.	51,000

In addition, Cindy Trevis Company's income statement reported a loss on the sale of equipment of $6,700. What amount was reported on the statement of cash flows as "cash flow from sale of equipment"?

BE18–10 The following T account is a summary of the cash account of Anita Baker Company:

Identify financing activity transactions.
(SO 2)

Cash (Summary Form)

Balance, 1/1/99	8,000		
Receipts from customers	364,000	Payments to suppliers	200,000
Dividends on stock investments	6,000	Payments operating expenses	140,000
Proceeds from sale of equipment	36,000	Interest paid	10,000
Proceeds from issuance of bonds		Taxes paid	8,000
payable	100,000	Dividends paid	40,000
Balance, 12/31/99	116,000		

For Anita Baker Company, what amount of net cash provided (used) by financing activities should be reported in the statement of cash flows?

*BE18–11** Using the data in BE18–8, indicate how the changes in prepaid expenses and accrued expenses payable should be entered in the reconciling columns of a work sheet. Assume that beginning balances were: prepaid expenses, $18,600, and accrued expenses payable, $8,200. (Hint: Under the direct method of presenting cash flows from operations, revenues and expenses are listed on the work sheet, rather than net income. The changes in prepaids and accruals are entered as adjustments to the operating expenses, to convert them to the amount of cash paid.)

Indicate cash flow work sheet entries.
(SO 6)

EXERCISES

E18–1 Li Eng Corporation had the following transactions during 1999:

Classify transactions by type of activity.
(SO 2)

1. Purchased a machine for $30,000, giving a long-term note in exchange.

2. Issued common stock for cash, $50,000.

3. Collected $16,000 of accounts receivable.

4. Declared and paid a cash dividend of $25,000.

5. Sold a long-term investment with a cost of $15,000 for $15,000 cash.

6. Issued $200,000 of common stock from the conversion of bonds having a face value of $200,000.

7. Paid $18,000 on accounts payable.

Instructions

Analyse the transactions above and indicate whether each transaction resulted in a cash flow from: (a) operating activities, (b) investing activities, (c) financing activities, or (d) non-cash investing and financing activities.

Prepare an operating activities section—indirect method.
(SO 3)

E18–2   Joe Pesci Company reported net income of $195,000 for 1999. Pesci also reported amortization expense of $35,000 and a loss of $5,000 on the sale of equipment. The comparative balance sheet shows an increase in accounts receivable of $15,000 for the year, an $8,000 increase in accounts payable, and a decrease in prepaid expenses $4,000.

Instructions

Prepare the operating activities section of the statement of cash flows for 1999. Use the indirect method.

Prepare an operating activities section—indirect method.
(SO 3)

E18–3   The current sections of Barth Inc.'s balance sheets at December 31, 1998 and 1999, are presented below.

	1999	1998
Current assets		
Cash	$105,000	$ 99,000
Accounts receivable	110,000	89,000
Inventory	171,000	186,000
Prepaid expenses	27,000	32,000
Total current assets	$413,000	$406,000
Current liabilities		
Accrued expenses payable	$ 15,000	$ 5,000
Accounts payable	85,000	92,000
Total current liabilities	$100,000	$ 97,000

Barth's net income for 1999 was $122,000. Amortization expense was $24,000.

Instructions

Prepare the net cash provided by operating activities section of Barth Inc.'s statement of cash flows for the year ended December 31, 1999, using the indirect method.

Prepare a partial statement of cash flows—indirect method.
(SO 3)

E18–4   Presented below are three accounts that appear in the general ledger of Roberta Dupré Corp. during 1999:

Equipment

Date		Debit	Credit	Balance
Jan. 1	Balance			160,000
July 31	Purchase of equipment	70,000		230,000
Sept. 2	Cost of equipment constructed	53,000		283,000
Nov. 10	Cost of equipment sold		45,000	238,000

Accumulated Amortization—Equipment

Date		Debit	Credit	Balance
Jan. 1	Balance			71,000
Nov. 10	Accumulated amortization on equipment sold	30,000		41,000
Dec. 31	Amortization for year		24,000	65,000

Retained Earnings

Date		Debit	Credit	Balance
Jan. 1	Balance			105,000
Aug. 23	Dividends (cash)	14,000		91,000
Dec. 31	Net income		47,000	138,000

Instructions

From the postings in the accounts above, indicate how the information is reported on a statement of cash flows, by preparing a partial statement of cash flows using the indirect method. The loss on sale of equipment was $6,000.

E18–5 A comparative balance sheet for Winfrey Company is presented below:

Prepare a statement of cash flows—indirect method.
(SO 3)

December 31

Assets	1999	1998
Cash	$ 63,000	$ 22,000
Accounts receivable	85,000	76,000
Inventories	180,000	189,000
Land	75,000	100,000
Equipment	260,000	200,000
Accumulated amortization	(66,000)	(42,000)
Total	$597,000	$545,000

Liabilities and Shareholders' Equity		
Accounts payable	$ 34,000	$ 47,000
Bonds payable	150,000	200,000
Common stock	214,000	164,000
Retained earnings	199,000	134,000
Total	$597,000	$545,000

Additional information:

1. Net income for 1999 was $105,000.
2. Cash dividends of $40,000 were declared and paid.
3. Bonds payable amounting to $50,000 were redeemed for cash $50,000.
4. Common stock was issued for $50,000 cash.
5. Land was sold at a gain of $5,000.

Instructions

Prepare a statement of cash flows for 1999 using the indirect method.

E18–6 An analysis of comparative balance sheets, the current year's income statement, and the general ledger accounts of Brosnan Corp. uncovered the following items. Assume all items involve cash unless there is information to the contrary.

Classify transactions by type of activity.
(SO 2)

(a) Purchase of land.
(b) Payment of dividends.
(c) Sale of building at book value.
(d) Exchange of land for patent.
(e) Conversion of bonds into common stock.
(f) Redemption of bonds.
(g) Receipt of interest on notes receivable.
(h) Issuance of capital stock.
(i) Amortization of patent.
(j) Issuance of bonds for land.
(k) Payment of interest on notes payable.
(l) Loss on sale of land.
(m) Receipt of dividends on investment in stock.

Instructions

Indicate how the above items should be classified in the statement of cash flows using these major classifications: operating activity (indirect method), investing activity, financing activity, and significant non-cash investing and financing activity.

Compute cash from operating activities—direct method.
(SO 4)

E18–7   Kelly McGillis Company has just completed its first year of operations on December 31, 1999. Its initial income statement showed that Kelly McGillis had revenues of $157,000 and operating expenses of $78,000. Accounts receivable and accounts payable at year end were $42,000 and $33,000, respectively. Assume that accounts payable related to operating expenses. Ignore income taxes.

Instructions

Compute net cash provided by operating activities, using the direct method.

Compute cash payments—direct method.
(SO 4)

E18–8   The income statement for the Garcia Company shows cost of goods sold $355,000 and operating expenses (without amortization) $230,000. The comparative balance sheet for the year shows that inventory increased $6,000, prepaid expenses decreased $6,000, accounts payable (merchandise suppliers) decreased $8,000, and accrued expenses payable increased $8,000.

Instructions

Using the direct method, compute (a) cash payments to suppliers and (b) cash payments for operating expenses.

Compute cash flow from operating activities—direct method.
(SO 2, 4)

E18–9   The year 2000 accounting records of Flypaper Airlines reveal the following transactions and events:

Payment of interest	$ 6,000	Collection of accounts receivable	$180,000
Cash sales	48,000	Payment of salaries and wages	68,000
Receipt of dividend revenue	14,000	Amortization expense	16,000
Payment of income taxes	16,000	Proceeds from sale of aircraft	812,000
Net income	38,000	Purchase of equipment for cash	22,000
Payment of accounts payable		Loss on sale of aircraft	3,000
for merchandise	90,000	Payment of dividends	14,000
Payment for land	74,000	Payment of other expenses	20,000

Instructions

Prepare the cash flows from operating activities section, using the direct method. (Not all of the above items will be used.)

Calculate operating cash flows—direct method.
(SO 4)

E18–10   The following information is taken from the general ledger of Joan Robinson Company:

Rent	Rent expense	$ 31,000
	Prepaid rent, January 1	5,900
	Prepaid rent, December 31	3,000
Salaries	Salaries expense	$ 54,000
	Salaries payable, January 1	5,000
	Salaries payable, December 31	8,000
Sales	Revenue from sales	$180,000
	Accounts receivable, January 1	12,000
	Accounts receivable, December 31	9,000

Instructions

In each of the above cases, compute the amount that should be reported in the operating activities section of the statement of cash flows, applying the direct method.

Prepare a cash flow work sheet—indirect method.
(SO 6)

*E18–11   Refer to Exercise E18–5 (Winfrey Company) and use these data to prepare a work sheet for a statement of cash flows for 1999. Enter the reconciling items directly on the work sheet, identifying the entries alphabetically.

PROBLEMS

••

P18–1 The income statement of Breckenridge Company is shown below:

BRECKENRIDGE COMPANY
Income Statement
For the Year Ended November 30, 1999

Sales		$6,900,000
Cost of goods sold		
Beginning inventory	$1,900,000	
Purchases	4,400,000	
Goods available for sale	6,300,000	
Ending inventory	1,600,000	
Cost of goods sold		4,700,000
Gross profit		2,200,000
Operating expenses		
Selling expenses	$ 450,000	
Administrative expenses	700,000	1,150,000
Net income		$1,050,000

Additional information:

1. Accounts receivable decreased $300,000 during the year.
2. Prepaid expenses increased $150,000 during the year.
3. Accounts payable to suppliers of merchandise decreased $300,000 during the year.
4. Accrued expenses payable decreased $100,000 during the year.
5. Administrative expenses include amortization expense of $60,000.

Instructions

(a) Prepare the operating activities section of the statement of cash flows for the year ended November 30, 1999, for Breckenridge Company, using the indirect method.

(b) Prepare the operating activities section of the statement of cash flows, using the direct method.

P18–2 The income statement of Hanalei International Inc. for the year ended December 31, 1999, reported the following condensed information:

Revenue from fees	$430,000
Operating expenses	280,000
Income from operations	150,000
Income tax expense	47,000
Net income	$103,000

Hanalei's balance sheet contained the following comparative data at December 31:

	1999	1998
Accounts receivable	$50,000	$40,000
Accounts payable	30,000	41,000
Income taxes payable	6,000	4,000

Hanalei has no amortizable assets.

Instructions

Prepare the operating activities section of the statement of cash flows using the direct method.

*Prepare an operating activities
section—indirect method.*
(SO 3)

P18–3   Using the data from Problem 18–2, prepare the operating activities section of the statement of cash flows using the indirect method.

*Prepare an operating activities
section—direct method.*
(SO 4)

P18–4   Vail Company's income statement for the year ended December 31, 1999, contained the following condensed information:

Revenue from fees		$840,000
Operating expenses (excluding amortization)	$624,000	
Amortization expense	60,000	
Loss on sale of equipment	26,000	710,000
Income before income taxes		130,000
Income tax expense		40,000
Net income		$ 90,000

Vail's balance sheet contained the following comparative data at December 31:

	1999	1998
Accounts receivable	$47,000	$55,000
Accounts payable	41,000	33,000
Income taxes payable	4,000	9,000

Instructions

Prepare the operating activities section of the statement of cash flows, using the direct method.

*Prepare an operating activities
section—indirect method.*
(SO 3)

P18–5   Using the data from Problem 18–4, prepare the operating activities section of the statement of cash flows, using the indirect method.

*Prepare a statement of cash
flows—indirect method and
direct method.*
(SO 3, 4)

P18–6   The financial statements of Sean Seymor Company appear below:

SEAN SEYMOR COMPANY
Comparative Balance Sheet
December 31

Assets	1999		1998	
Cash		$ 26,000		$ 13,000
Accounts receivable		18,000		14,000
Merchandise inventory		38,000		35,000
Capital assets	$70,000		$78,000	
Less: accumulated amortization	(30,000)	40,000	(24,000)	54,000
Total		$122,000		$116,000

Liabilities and Shareholders' Equity				
Accounts payable		$ 29,000		$ 33,000
Income taxes payable		15,000		20,000
Bonds payable		20,000		10,000
Common stock		25,000		25,000
Retained earnings		33,000		28,000
Total		$122,000		$116,000

SEAN SEYMOR COMPANY
Income Statement
For the Year Ended December 31, 1999

Sales		$240,000
Cost of goods sold		180,000
Gross profit		60,000
Selling expenses	$ 28,000	
Administrative expenses	6,000	34,000
Income from operations		26,000
Interest expense		2,000
Income before income taxes		24,000
Income tax expense		7,000
Net income		$ 17,000

The following additional data were provided:

1. Dividends of $12,000 were declared and paid.
2. Equipment was sold during the year for $10,000 cash. This equipment cost $15,000 originally and had a book value of $10,000 at the time of sale.
3. All amortization expenses, $11,000, are in the selling expenses category.
4. All sales and purchases are on account.
5. Additional equipment was purchased for $7,000 cash.

Instructions

(a) Prepare a statement of cash flows, using the indirect method.
(b) Further analysis reveals the following:
   1. Accounts payable pertains solely to merchandise creditors.
   2. All operating expenses, except for amortization, are paid in cash.

   Prepare a statement of cash flows using the direct method.

P18–7 The financial statements of Swayze Company appear below:

Prepare a statement of cash flows—indirect method.
(SO 3)

SWAYZE COMPANY
Comparative Balance Sheet
December 31

Assets	1999	1998
Cash	$ 29,000	$ 13,000
Accounts receivable	28,000	14,000
Merchandise inventory	25,000	35,000
Capital assets	60,000	78,000
Accumulated amortization	(20,000)	(24,000)
Total	$122,000	$116,000

Liabilities and Shareholders' Equity		
Accounts payable	$ 29,000	$ 23,000
Income taxes payable	5,000	8,000
Bonds payable	27,000	33,000
Common stock	18,000	14,000
Retained earnings	43,000	38,000
Total	$122,000	$116,000

SWAYZE COMPANY
Income Statement
For the Year Ended December 31, 1999

Sales		$220,000
Cost of goods sold		180,000
Gross profit		40,000
Selling expenses	$18,000	
Administrative expenses	6,000	24,000
Income from operations		16,000
Interest expense		2,000
Income before income taxes		14,000
Income tax expense		4,000
Net income		$ 10,000

The following additional data were provided:

1. Dividends declared and paid were $5,000.
2. During the year, equipment was sold for $8,500 cash. This equipment had cost $18,000 originally and had a book value of $8,500 at the time of sale.
3. All amortization expenses are in the selling expenses category.
4. All sales and purchases are on account.

Instructions

Prepare a statement of cash flows, using the indirect method.

Prepare a statement of cash flows —direct method.
(SO 4)

P18–8 Data for the Swayze Company are presented in P18–7. Further analysis reveals the following:

1. Accounts payable pertain entirely to merchandise suppliers.
2. All operating expenses except for amortization were paid in cash.

Instructions

Prepare a statement of cash flows for Swayze Company, using the direct method.

Prepare a statement of cash flows —indirect method.
(SO 3)

P18–9 Condensed financial data of Norway Company appear below:

NORWAY COMPANY
Comparative Balance Sheet
December 31

Assets	1999	1998
Cash	$ 96,700	$ 47,250
Accounts receivable	86,800	57,000
Inventories	121,900	102,650
Investments	84,500	87,000
Capital assets	250,000	205,000
Accumulated amortization	(49,500)	(40,000)
	$590,400	$458,900

Liabilities and Shareholders' Equity	1999	1998
Accounts payable	$ 52,700	$ 48,280
Accrued expenses payable	12,100	18,830
Bonds payable	100,000	70,000
Common stock	250,000	200,000
Retained earnings	175,600	121,790
	$590,400	$458,900

NORWAY COMPANY
Income Statement Data
For the Year Ended December 31, 1999

Sales		$297,500
Gain on sale of capital assets		1,750
		299,250
Less:		
Cost of goods sold	$ 99,460	
Operating expenses (excluding amortization expense)	14,670	
Amortization expense	42,700	
Income taxes	7,270	
Interest expense	2,940	167,040
Net income		$132,210

Additional information:

1. New capital assets costing $92,000 were purchased for cash during the year.
2. Investments were sold at cost.
3. Capital assets costing $47,000 were sold for $15,550, resulting in a gain of $1,750.
4. A cash dividend of $78,400 was declared and paid during the year.

Instructions

Prepare a statement of cash flows, using the indirect method.

P18–10 Data for Norway Company are presented in P18–9. Further analysis reveals that accounts payable pertains exclusively to merchandise creditors.

Prepare a statement of cash flows —direct method (SO 4)

Instructions

Prepare a statement of cash flows for Norway Company using the direct method.

P18–11 Condensed financial data of Fern Galenti, Inc., appear below.

Prepare a statement of cash flows —indirect method (SO 3)

FERN GALENTI, INC.
Comparative Balance Sheet
December 31

Assets	1999	1998
Cash	$ 97,800	$ 38,400
Accounts receivable	90,800	33,000
Inventories	112,500	102,850
Prepaid expenses	18,400	16,000
Investments	108,000	94,000
Capital assets	270,000	242,500
Accumulated amortization	(50,000)	(52,000)
	$647,500	$474,750

Liabilities and Shareholders' Equity		
Accounts payable	$ 92,000	$ 67,300
Accrued expenses payable	16,500	17,000
Bonds payable	85,000	110,000
Common stock	220,000	175,000
Retained earnings	234,000	105,450
	$647,500	$474,750

FERN GALENTI, INC.
Income Statement Data
For the Year Ended December 31, 1999

Sales		$342,780
Less:		
Cost of goods sold	$115,460	
Operating expenses	12,410	
(excluding amortization)		
Amortization expense	46,500	
Income taxes	7,280	
Interest expense	2,730	
Loss on sale of capital assets	7,500	191,880
Net income		$150,900

Additional information:

1. New capital assets costing $85,000 were purchased for cash during the year.
2. Old capital assets with an original cost of $57,500 were sold for $1,500 cash.
3. Bonds matured and were paid off at face value for cash.
4. A cash dividend of $22,350 was declared and paid during the year.

Instructions

Prepare a statement of cash flows, using the indirect method.

Prepare a statement of cash flows
—direct method.
(SO 4)

P18–12   Data for Fern Galenti, Inc., are presented in P18–11. Further analysis reveals that accounts payable pertains solely to merchandise creditors.

Instructions

Prepare a statement of cash flows for Fern Galenti, Inc., using the direct method.

Prepare a statement of cash flows
—indirect method.
(SO 3)

P18–13   Presented below is the comparative balance sheet for Cousin Tommy's Toy Company as of December 31:

COUSIN TOMMY'S TOY COMPANY
Comparative Balance Sheet
December 31

Assets	1999	1998
Cash	$ 41,000	$45,000
Accounts receivable	47,500	52,000
Inventory	151,450	142,000
Prepaid expenses	16,780	21,000
Land	100,000	130,000
Equipment	228,000	155,000
Accumulated amortization—equipment	(45,000)	(35,000)
Building	200,000	200,000
Accumulated amortization—building	(60,000)	(40,000)
	$679,730	$670,000
Liabilities and Shareholders' Equity		
Accounts payable	$ 43,730	$ 40,000
Bonds payable	250,000	300,000
Common stock	200,000	150,000
Retained earnings	186,000	180,000
	$679,730	$670,000

Additional information:

1. Operating expenses include amortization expense of $42,000 and charges from prepaid expenses of $4,220.

2. Land was sold for cash at cost.
3. Cash dividends of $32,000 were paid.
4. Equipment was purchased for $95,000 cash. In addition, equipment costing $22,000 with a book value of $10,000 was sold for $8,100 cash.
5. Bonds were converted at face value by issuing common stock.

Instructions

Prepare a statement of cash flows for the year ended December 31, 1999, using the indirect method.

P18–14   Presented below is the comparative balance sheet for Cortina Company at December 31:

Prepare a statement of cash flows —indirect method.
(SO 3)

CORTINA COMPANY
Comparative Balance Sheet
December 31

	1999	1998
Cash	$ 40,000	$ 57,000
Accounts receivable	77,000	64,000
Inventory	132,000	140,000
Prepaid expenses	12,140	16,540
Land	125,000	150,000
Equipment	200,000	175,000
Accumulated amortization—equipment	(60,000)	(42,000)
Building	250,000	250,000
Accumulated amortization—building	(75,000)	(50,000)
	$701,140	$760,540
Accounts payable	$ 33,000	$ 45,000
Bonds payable	235,000	265,000
Common stock	280,000	250,000
Retained earnings	153,140	200,540
	$701,140	$760,540

Additional information:

1. Net income for 1999 was $26,890.
2. Operating expenses include amortization expense of $70,000 and charges from prepaid expenses of $4,400.
3. Equipment was purchased for cash. In addition, equipment costing $40,000, with a book value of $13,000, was sold for $14,000 cash.
4. Land was sold for cash at cost.
5. Bonds were converted at face value by issuing common stock.
6. Cash dividends were paid during the year.

Instructions

Prepare a statement of cash flows for 1999 using the indirect method.

*P18–15   Refer to Problem 18–9 (Norway Company) and use these data to prepare a work sheet for a statement of cash flows. Enter the reconciling items directly in the work sheet columns, identifying the entries alphabetically.

Prepare a cash flows work sheet—indirect method.
(SO 6)

*P18–16   Refer to Problem 18–11 (Fern Galenti, Inc.) and use these data to prepare a work sheet for a statement of cash flows for 1999. Enter the reconciling entries directly on the work sheet, identifying the entries alphabetically.

Prepare a cash flows work sheet—indirect method.
(SO 6)

Broadening Your Perspective

FINANCIAL REPORTING PROBLEM

Refer to the consolidated financial statements for The Second Cup Ltd., which are reproduced in Appendix A.

Instructions

1. Answer the following basic questions regarding the "statement of cash flows":
   (a) What title does The Second Cup use for this statement?
   (b) Does The Second Cup use the direct or the indirect method? Explain your reasoning.

2. Refer to the line in the Operating Activities section of the statement that reads "Loss (Gain) on Disposal of Capital Assets." Explain why the gain in fiscal 1997 was subtracted, and the loss on disposal of capital assets in 1996 was added, in calculating the cash provided by operations.

3. Compare the company's cash flows related to Investing Activities during fiscal 1997 versus 1996, and comment upon anything significant that you observe.

4. Notice the huge increase in cash and short-term investments that occurred during the year ended June 29, 1996. What was the primary cause of this increase?

5. Comment upon the change in cash and short-term investments during fiscal 1997 and the company's balance of cash and short-term investments at June 28, 1997.

DECISION CASE

Greg Rhoda and Debra Sondgeroth are examining the following statement of cash flows for Tuktoyaktuk Trading Company for the year ended January 31, 2000.

TUKTOYAKTUK TRADING COMPANY
Statement of Cash Flows
For the Year Ended January 31, 2000

Sources of cash		
From sales of merchandise	$370,000	
From sale of capital stock	420,000	
From sale of investment (purchased below)	80,000	
From amortization	55,000	
From issuance of note for truck	20,000	
From interest on investments	6,000	
Total sources of cash		$951,000
Uses of cash		
For purchase of fixtures and equipment	$340,000	
For merchandise purchased for resale	268,000	
For operating expenses (including amortization)	160,000	
For purchase of investment	75,000	
For purchase of truck by issuance of note	20,000	
For interest on note payable	3,000	
Total uses of cash		866,000
Net increase in cash		$ 85,000

Greg claims that Tuktoyaktuk's statement of cash flows is an excellent portrayal of a superb first year, because cash increased $85,000. Debra replies that it was not a superb first year, that the year was an operating failure, that the statement was incorrectly presented, and that $85,000 is not the actual increase in cash. The cash balance at the beginning of the year was $140,000.

Instructions

(a) With whom do you agree, Greg or Debra? Explain your position.

(b) Using the data provided, prepare a statement of cash flows in proper form using the **indirect method**. The only non-cash items in the income statement are amortization and the gain from the sale of the investment, and there were no changes in any current accounts other than cash.

(c) Prepare the operating activities section of the statement of cash flows using the **direct method**.

(d) Would you recommend the payment of a cash dividend this year?

COMMUNICATION ACTIVITY

Arnold Byte, the owner-president of Computer Services Corporation, is unfamiliar with the statement of cash flows which you, as his accountant, prepared. He asks for further explanation.

Instructions

Write Mr. Byte a brief memo explaining the form and content of the statement of cash flows for Computer Services Corp., as shown in Illustration 18-35.

GROUP ACTIVITY

In groups of four or five, discuss what you would expect to observe in the operating, investing, and financing sections of a statement of cash flows of:

(a) a severely financially troubled firm.

(b) a recently formed firm that is experiencing rapid growth.

Develop a list of what you would expect to see, in each section of the statement, for each of these two situations.

ETHICS CASE

Portage Corporation is a wholesaler of automotive parts. It has 10 shareholders who have been paid a total of $1 million in cash dividends for eight consecutive years. The Board of Directors' policy requires that in order for this dividend to be declared, net cash provided by operating activities as reported in Portage's current year's statement of cash flows must be in excess of $1 million. President and CEO Phil Monat's job is secure so long as he produces annual operating cash flows to support the usual dividend.

At the end of the current year, controller Rick Rodgers presents President Monat with some disappointing news—the net cash provided by operating activities is calculated by the indirect method to be only $970,000. The president says to Rick, "We must get that amount above $1 million. Isn't there some way to increase operating cash flow by another $30,000?" Rick answers,

"These figures were prepared by my assistant. I'll go back to my office and see what I can do." The president replies, "I know you won't let me down, Rick."

Upon close scrutiny of the statement of cash flows, Rick concludes that he can get the operating cash flows above $1 million by reclassifying a $60,000, two-year note payable that is listed in the financing activities section as "Proceeds from bank loan—$60,000." He will report the note instead as "Increase in payables—$60,000" and treat it as an adjustment of net income in the operating activities section. He returns to the president, saying, "You can tell the Board to declare their usual dividend. Our net cash flow provided by operating activities is $1,030,000." "Good man, Rick! I knew I could count on you," exults the president.

Instructions

(a) Who are the stakeholders in this situation?

(b) Was there anything unethical about the president's actions? Was there anything unethical about the controller's actions?

(c) Are the Board members or anyone else likely to discover the misclassification?

CRITICAL THINKING
▸*A Real-World Focus: Praxair Incorporated*

Praxair was founded in 1907 as Linde-Air Products Company and was a pioneer in separating oxygen from air. It was purchased and run as a subsidiary of Union Carbide. In 1992, Praxair became an independent public company. Today, the company is one of the top three suppliers of industrial gases worldwide. Praxair has operations in all regions of the world.

The following management discussion was included in one of Praxair's recent annual reports:

> **Liquidity, Capital Resources and Other Financial Data**—Praxair changed its presentation of the Statement of Cash Flows to the direct method to report major classes of cash receipts and payments from operations. Praxair believes the direct method more clearly presents its operating cash flows. Prior years' cash flow information has been reclassified to conform to the current year presentation.

Instructions

(a) What method has Praxair changed from?

(b) What will the newly prepared cash flow statement show that the former one did not?

(c) Will the cash flows from investing and financing appear any differently under the new method of preparation from how they appeared under the old method?

 # ACCOUNTING ON THE WEB

The software industry presents some unique challenges regarding cash flow. The industry is highly competitive, with a practice of providing free, or heavily discounted, products as a market-entry technique. This case reviews the sources and uses of cash flows of a major company in the software industry. The changing stock price of this company is evaluated against its cash and income (loss) position.

Instructions

Specific requirements of this Internet case are available on-line at www.wiley.com/canada/weygandt.

Answers to Self-Study Questions
1. c 2. b 3. a 4. c 5. d 6. b 7. c 8. d 9. b 10. c 11. d 12. a 13. b

• • • • • ▶ **Concepts for Review**

Before studying this chapter, you should understand or, if necessary, review:

a. *The various types of users of financial statement information. (Ch. 1, pp. 3–5)*

b. *The content and classification of a corporate income statement. (Ch. 15, pp. 629–634)*

c. *Weighted average number of outstanding shares. (Ch. 15, p. 637)*

d. *The content and classification of a corporate balance sheet. (Ch. 17, pp. 715–716)*

e. *The ratios briefly introduced in previous chapters: Current (Ch. 4, pp. 156–157); acid test, receivables turnover, collection period (Ch. 8, pp. 350–352); inventory turnover, days sales in inventory (Ch. 9, pp. 394–395); asset turnover, return on assets (Ch. 10, pp. 443–444); return on equity, book value (Ch. 14, p. 597–599); earnings per share, price-earnings (Ch. 15, p. 639); times interest earned, debt to total assets (Ch. 16, pp. 681–682); and cash flow per share (Ch. 18, p. 768) ratios.*

Students Vote Yes to Finance Student Centre

TORONTO, Ont.—Would you be willing to pay an extra yearly fee to finance a new student centre on your campus? In 1987, a referendum at York University asked students exactly that question, and they responded with a definite "yes."

York has long been a respected institution and home to a number of highly prestigious programs. But its vast, largely undeveloped campus on the northwestern outskirts of Toronto didn't provide a very vibrant atmosphere. The now-completed student centre was a definite improvement. Today, instead of having to settle for unremarkable cafeterias scattered across campus, students can choose from a row of well-loved fast-food options, or eat at the more upscale Underground restaurant, which also boasts a concert stage. The centre also includes meeting rooms and offices for student organizations and a student day-care centre.

How did York get the $24.5 million in capital needed for this project? Explains Brenda Blackstock, York's internal auditor, "The univer-

sity established a separate corporation to build and run the student centre. They took out a loan for most of the needed funds, guaranteed by York, to be paid back over time with the income from the student levy."

"Like most big schools, we have a long-term contract to do all our business at one bank," says Ms. Blackstock, "and they receive a copy of our audited financial statements every year." Before handing out such a large sum of money—even to Canada's third-largest university—the bank analysed these financial

statements closely.

"The bank assured itself that York was financially able to shoulder such a loan: that its cash flow was reliable enough to make the payments, that its debt-to-assets ratio was not excessive, etc.," says Ms. Blackstock.

Rob Castle, the Student Centre Manager, adds: "The levy was also a major factor in securing the loan. We had to supply proof that it had passed, and the bank has first call on those revenues under our agreement." ◀

CHAPTER 19

FINANCIAL STATEMENT ANALYSIS

▶ STUDY OBJECTIVES ◀

After studying this chapter, you should be able to:

1. *Discuss the need for comparative analysis.*
2. *Identify the tools of financial statement analysis.*
3. *Explain and apply horizontal analysis.*
4. *Describe and apply vertical analysis.*
5. *Identify and compute ratios and describe their purpose and use in analysing a firm's liquidity, profitability, and solvency.*
6. *Recognize the limitations of financial statement analysis.*

If you had excess cash to invest, how would you invest it? The most popular choices are stocks or bonds. If stocks are your choice, should you invest in conservative financial institution stock, such as the Canadian Western Bank, or in more speculative oil and gas exploration stock, such as Gulf Canada Resources? If you choose to buy bonds, should you invest in Bell Canada's quality bonds, which generally have greater stability, less risk, and lower yields, or in Consumers Gas bonds, which offer higher rates of return but may be considered less stable and of greater risk? To answer these types of questions, it is helpful for you to understand how to analyse financial statement information.

Financial statement analysis, the topic of this chapter, enhances the usefulness of published financial statements in making decisions about a company. The organization of this chapter is as follows:

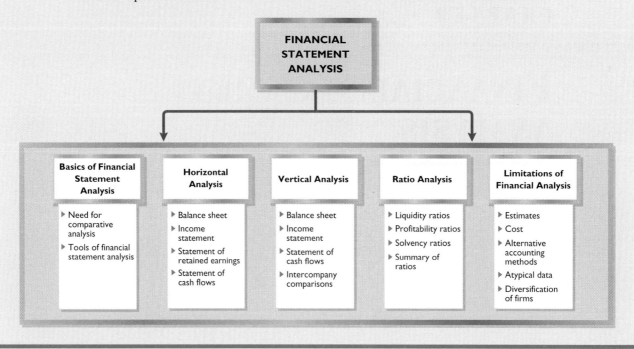

▼ Basics of Financial Statement Analysis

To analyse financial statements, three characteristics of a company are evaluated: its liquidity, its profitability, and its solvency. For example, a **short-term creditor**, such as a bank, is primarily interested in the ability of the borrower to pay obligations when they come due. The liquidity of the borrower in such a case is extremely important because it helps the bank in evaluating the safety of a loan. A **long-term creditor,** such as a bondholder, however, looks to indicators such as profitability and solvency that indicate the firm's ability to survive over a long period of time. Long-term creditors, such as the bank that financed York University's student centre in the opening vignette, consider such measures as the amount of debt in the company's capital structure and its ability to meet interest payments. Similarly, **shareholders** are interested in the profitability and solvency of the enterprise when they assess the likelihood of dividends and the growth potential of the stock.

Need for Comparative Analysis

Every item reported in a financial statement has significance. For example, when Corel Corporation reports cash of $10 million on its balance sheet, we know that the company had that amount of cash on the balance sheet date. However, we do not know whether the amount represents an increase over prior years, or whether the amount is adequate for the company's cash needs. To obtain this information, it is necessary to compare the amount of cash with other financial statement data.

Comparisons can be made on a number of different bases—three are illustrated in this chapter:

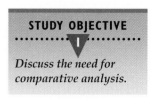

STUDY OBJECTIVE
▼
1
Discuss the need for comparative analysis.

1. **Intracompany basis**. This basis compares an item or financial relationship **within a company** in the current year with the same item or relationship in one or more prior years. For example, a comparison of Corel's cash balance at the end of the current year with last year's balance will show the amount of the increase or decrease. Likewise, Corel can compare the percentage of cash to current assets at the end of the current year with the percentage in one or more prior years. Intracompany comparisons are useful in detecting changes in significant trends.

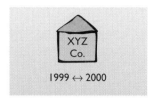

2. **Intercompany basis**. This basis compares an item or financial relationship of one company with the same item or relationship in **one or more competing companies**. The comparisons are made on the basis of the published financial statements of the individual companies. For example, Corel's total sales for the year can be compared with the total sales of one of its major competitors, such as Microsoft Corporation. Intercompany comparisons are useful in understanding a company's competitive position.

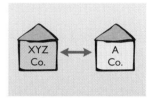

3. **Industry averages**. This basis compares an item or financial relationship of a company with **industry averages** (or **norms**). Annually, Dun & Bradstreet Canada publishes *Key Business Ratios*, *The Financial Post* publishes *Industry Reports*, and Statistics Canada publishes *Financial Performance Indices for Canadian Business*. Comparisons with industry averages provide information about a company's relative performance within the industry. For example, Corel's net income can be compared with the average net income of all companies in the software industry.

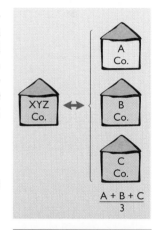

Tools of Financial Statement Analysis

Various tools are used to evaluate the significance of financial statement data. Three commonly used tools are:

Horizontal analysis: a technique for evaluating a series of financial statement data *over a period of time*.

Vertical analysis: a technique for evaluating financial statement data that expresses each item in a financial statement as of a percent of a base amount *for the same period of time*.

Ratio analysis: expresses the relationship among selected items of financial statement data.

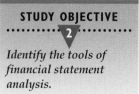

STUDY OBJECTIVE
▼
2
Identify the tools of financial statement analysis.

Horizontal analysis is used primarily in intracompany comparisons. Two features in published financial statements facilitate this type of comparison. First, each of the basic financial statements is presented on a comparative basis for a minimum of two years. Second, a summary of selected financial data is presented for a series of five to 10 years or more.

Vertical analysis is used in both intracompany and intercompany comparisons. Ratio analysis is used in all three types of comparison. In the following sections, we will explain and illustrate each of the three types of analysis.

Case in point In its annual report, The Second Cup Ltd. presents five years of comparative data selected from operating results, financial position, and operating statistics to help shareholders and other interested parties make intracompany comparisons (see Appendix A).

Horizontal Analysis

STUDY OBJECTIVE

3

Explain and apply horizontal analysis.

Horizontal analysis, also called **trend analysis**, is a technique for evaluating a series of financial statement data over a period of time. Its purpose is to determine the increase or decrease that has taken place, expressed as either an amount or a percentage. For example, assume the net sales figures of Kellogg Company are as follows:

Illustration 19-1

Kellogg's net sales

KELLOGG COMPANY				
Net Sales (in millions)				
2000	1999	1998	1997	1996
$6,562.8	$6,295.4	$6,190.6	$5,786.6	$5,181.4

If we assume that 1996 is the base year, we can measure all percentage increases or decreases from this base period amount as follows:

$$\frac{\text{Current year amount} - \text{Base year amount}}{\text{Base year amount}}$$

For example, we can determine that net sales for Kellogg Company increased approximately 12% [($5,786.6−$5,181.4)÷$5,181.4] from 1996 to 1997. Similarly, we can determine that net sales increased 27% [($6,562.8−$5,181.4)÷$5,181.4] from 1996 to 2000. The percentage of the base period for each of the five years, assuming 1996 is the base period, is shown in Illustration 19-2:

Illustration 19-2

Horizontal analysis of Kellogg's net sales

KELLOGG COMPANY				
Net Sales (in millions)				
Base Period 1996				
2000	1999	1998	1997	1996
$6,562.8	$6,295.4	$6,190.6	$5,786.6	$5,181.4
127%	121%	119%	112%	100%

Balance Sheet

To further illustrate horizontal analysis, we will use the financial statements of Quality Department Store, a hypothetical full-line department store located in a small city. Its two-year condensed balance sheets for 2000 and 1999, showing dollar and percentage changes, are presented in Illustration 19-3.

The comparative balance sheet in Illustration 19-3 shows that a number of significant changes have occurred in Quality Department Store's financial structure from 1999 to 2000. In the assets section, capital assets (net) increased $165,000, or 25.4%. In the liabilities section, current liabilities increased $41,500, or 13.7%. In the shareholders' equity section, we find that retained earnings increased $202,600, or 38.6%. This suggests that the company expanded its asset base during 2000. They did this primarily by keeping income in the business, rather than by adding more long-term debt.

QUALITY DEPARTMENT STORE INC.
Condensed Balance Sheet
December 31

Illustration 19-3

Horizontal analysis of a balance sheet

Helpful hint It is difficult to understand how significant a change is when only the dollar amount of the change is examined. When the change is expressed as a percentage, it is easier to grasp the true magnitude of the change.

	2000	1999	Increase or (Decrease) during 2000	
			Amount	Percentage
Assets				
Current assets	$1,020,000	$ 945,000	$ 75,000	7.9%
Capital assets (net)	815,000	650,000	165,000	25.4%
Total assets	$1,835,000	$1,595,000	$240,000	15.0%
Liabilities				
Current liabilities	$ 344,500	$ 303,000	$ 41,500	13.7%
Long-term liabilities	487,500	497,000	(9,500)	(1.9%)
Total liabilities	832,000	800,000	32,000	4.0%
Shareholders' Equity				
Common stock, no par	275,400	270,000	5,400	2.0%
Retained earnings	727,600	525,000	202,600	38.6%
Total shareholders' equity	1,003,000	795,000	208,000	26.2%
Total liabilities and shareholders' equity	$1,835,000	$1,595,000	$240,000	15.0%

Income Statement

Illustration 19-4 presents a two-year comparative income statement for Quality Department Store for the years 2000 and 1999, in a condensed format:

QUALITY DEPARTMENT STORE INC.
Condensed Income Sheet
For the Years Ended December 31

Illustration 19-4

Horizontal analysis of an income statement

	2000	1999	Increase or (Decrease) during 2000	
			Amount	Percentage
Sales	$2,195,000	$1,960,000	$235,000	12.0%
Sales returns and allowances	98,000	123,000	(25,000)	(20.3%)
Net sales	2,097,000	1,837,000	260,000	14.2%
Cost of goods sold	1,281,000	1,140,000	141,000	12.4%
Gross profit	816,000	697,000	119,000	17.1%
Selling expenses	253,000	211,500	41,500	19.6%
Administrative expenses	104,000	108,500	(4,500)	(4.1%)
Total operating expenses	357,000	320,000	37,000	11.6%
Income from operations	459,000	377,000	82,000	21.8%
Other revenues and gains				
Interest and dividends	9,000	11,000	(2,000)	(18.2%)
Other expenses and losses				
Interest expense	36,000	40,500	(4,500)	(11.1%)
Income before income taxes	432,000	347,500	84,500	24.3%
Income tax expense	168,200	139,000	29,200	21.0%
Net income	$ 263,800	$ 208,500	$ 55,300	26.5%

Helpful hint Note that while the amount column is additive (the total is $55,300), the percentage column is not additive (the total is not 26.5%). A separate percentage has been calculated for each item.

Horizontal analysis of the income statements shows the following changes:

1. Net sales increased $260,000, or 14.2% ($260,000÷$1,837,000).
2. Cost of goods sold increased $141,000, or 12.4% ($141,000÷$1,140,000).
3. Total operating expenses increased $37,000, or 11.6% ($37,000÷$320,000).

Overall, gross profit and net income were up substantially. Gross profit, for example, increased 17.1%, and net income 26.5%. It appears, therefore, that Quality's profit trend is favourable.

Statement of Retained Earnings

Quality Department Store's comparative statement of retained earnings for the years 2000 and 1999 is presented in Illustration 19-5. Analysed horizontally, net income increased $55,300, or 26.5%, whereas dividends on the common stock increased only $1,200, or 2%. Ending retained earnings, as shown in the horizontal analysis of the balance sheet, increased 38.6%. As indicated earlier, Quality Department Store kept a significant portion of its net income to pay for additional capital assets.

Illustration 19-5

Horizontal analysis of a statement of retained earnings

QUALITY DEPARTMENT STORE INC. Statement of Retained Earnings For the Years Ended December 31				
			Increase or (Decrease) during 2000	
	2000	1999	Amount	Percentage
Retained earnings, Jan. 1	$525,000	$376,500	$148,500	39.4%
Add: Net income	263,800	208,500	55,300	26.5%
	788,800	585,000	203,800	
Deduct: Dividends	61,200	60,000	1,200	2.0%
Retained earnings, Dec. 31	$727,600	$525,000	$202,600	38.6%

The measurement of changes from period to period in terms of percentages is relatively straightforward and is quite useful. However, complications can result in making the computations. For example, if an item has no value in a base year or preceding year and a value in the next year, no percentage change can be computed. Similarly, if a negative amount appears in the base or preceding period and a positive amount exists the following year, or vice versa, no percentage change can be computed.

Statement of Cash Flows

Horizontal analysis can also be performed on the statement of cash flows, as shown in Illustration 19-6.

Quality's cash flow from operating activities has declined 17.3%. An analysis of the detail provided in the operating activities section of the statement indicates that this decline is primarily due to increased payments for the income taxes resulting from increased profitability.

Horizontal analysis is not as useful when performed on the investing and financing activities sections of the statement. The amounts presented in these sections detail the change between two periods (opening and ending balance sheets). Computing percentage changes of changes does not provide very meaningful information.

QUALITY DEPARTMENT STORE INC.
Condensed Statement of Cash Flows
For the Years Ended December 31

	2000	1999	Increase or (Decrease) during 2000 Amount	Percentage
Cash flows from operating activities				
Cash receipts:				
From customers	$2,047,000	$2,000,000	$ 47,000	2.4%
From interest and dividends	9,000	11,000	(2,000)	(18.2%)
Cash payments:				
To suppliers	(1,369,500)	(1,327,000)	(42,500)	(3.2%)
For operating expenses	(357,000)	(353,000)	(4,000)	(1.1%)
For interest	(36,000)	(40,500)	4,500	11.1%
For income taxes	(168,200)	(139,000)	(29,200)	(21.0%)
Net cash provided by operating activities	125,300	151,500	(26,200)	(17.3%)
Cash flows from investing activities				
Purchase of capital assets	(165,000)	0	(165,000)	N/A
Net cash used by investing activities	(165,000)	0	(165,000)	N/A
Cash flows from financing activities				
Reduction of long-term debt	(9,500)	(8,000)	(1,500)	N/A
Issuance of common stock	5,400	0	5,400	N/A
Payment of cash dividends	(61,200)	(60,000)	(1,200)	N/A
Net cash used by financing activities	(65,300)	(68,000)	2,700	N/A
Net increase (decrease) in cash and temporary investments	(105,000)	83,500	(188,500)	N/A
Cash and temporary investments, January 1	225,000	141,500	83,500	59.0%
Cash and temporary investments, December 31	$ 120,000	$ 225,000	$(105,000)	(46.7%)

Vertical Analysis

Vertical analysis, sometimes referred to as **common size analysis**, is a technique for evaluating financial statement data that expresses each item within a financial statement as a percentage of a base amount. For example, on a balance sheet we might say that current assets are 22% of total assets (total assets being the base amount), or on an income statement we might say that selling expenses are 16% of net sales (net sales being the base amount).

STUDY OBJECTIVE
4

Describe and apply vertical analysis.

Balance Sheet

Presented in Illustration 19-7 is the comparative balance sheet for Quality Department Store for 2000 and 1999, analysed vertically. The base for the asset items is **total assets**, and the base for the liability and shareholders' equity items is **total liabilities and shareholders' equity** (equals total assets).

In addition to showing the relative size of each category on the balance sheet, vertical analysis may show the **percentage change** in the individual asset, liability, and shareholders' equity items. In this case, even though current assets increased $75,000 from 1999 to 2000, they decreased from 59.2% to 55.6% of total assets. Capital assets (net) increased from 40.8% to 44.4% of total assets, and retained earnings increased from 32.9% to 39.7% of total liabilities and shareholders' equity. These results reinforce the earlier observation that Quality is choosing to finance its growth through retention of earnings, rather than through the issuance of additional debt.

Alternative terminology
Horizontal analysis is also known as *dynamic* analysis, since it spans years. Vertical analysis is also known as *static* analysis, since it incorporates only one year.

Illustration 19-7

Vertical analysis of a balance sheet

Helpful hint   The formula for calculating these balance sheet percentages is:

$$\frac{\text{Each item on B/S}}{\text{Total assets}} = \%$$

QUALITY DEPARTMENT STORE INC. Condensed Balance Sheet For the Years Ended December 31				
	2000		**1999**	
Assets	Amount	Percentage	Amount	Percentage
Current assets	$1,020,000	55.6%	$ 945,000	59.2%
Capital assets (net)	815,000	44.4%	650,000	40.8%
Total assets	$1,835,000	100.0%	$1,595,000	100.0%
Liabilities				
Current liabilities	$ 344,500	18.8%	$ 303,000	19.0%
Long-term liabilities	487,500	26.5%	497,000	31.2%
Total liabilities	832,000	45.3%	800,000	50.2%
Shareholders' Equity				
Common stock, no par	275,400	15.0%	270,000	16.9%
Retained earnings	727,600	39.7%	525,000	32.9%
Total shareholders' equity	1,003,000	54.7%	795,000	49.8%
Total liabilities and shareholders' equity	$1,835,000	100.0%	$1,595,000	100.0%

Income Statement

Vertical analysis of the comparative income statements of Quality, shown in Illustration 19-8, reveals that cost of goods sold as a percentage of net sales declined 1% (62.1% versus 61.1%) and that total operating expenses declined 0.4% (17.4% versus 17.0%). As a result, it is not surprising to see income from operations as a percentage of net sales increase from 20.5% to 21.9%. As indicated by the horizontal analysis, Quality appears to be a profitable enterprise that is becoming even more successful.

Illustration 19-8

Vertical analysis of an income statement

Helpful hint   The formula for calculating these income statement percentages is:

$$\frac{\text{Each item on I/S}}{\text{Net sales}} = \%$$

QUALITY DEPARTMENT STORE INC. Condensed Income Statement For the Years Ended December 31				
	2000		**1999**	
	Amount	Percentage	Amount	Percentage
Sales	$2,195,000	104.7%	$1,960,000	106.7%
Sales returns and allowances	98,000	4.7%	123,000	6.7%
Net sales	2,097,000	100.0%	1,837,000	100.0%
Cost of goods sold	1,281,000	61.1%	1,140,000	62.1%
Gross profit	816,000	38.9%	697,000	37.9%
Selling expenses	253,000	12.0%	211,500	11.5%
Administrative expenses	104,000	5.0%	108,500	5.9%
Total operating expenses	357,000	17.0%	320,000	17.4%
Income from operations	459,000	21.9%	377,000	20.5%
Other revenues and gains Interest and dividends	9,000	0.4%	11,000	0.6%
Other expenses and losses Interest expense	36,000	1.7%	40,500	2.2%
Income before income taxes	432,000	20.6%	347,500	18.9%
Income tax expense	168,200	8.0%	139,000	7.5%
Net income	$ 263,800	12.6%	$ 208,500	11.4%

Statement of Cash Flows

Vertical analysis can also be performed on the statement of cash flows. However, this is seldom done, since each statement already provides comparative detail of the change between two periods (opening and ending balance sheets). The value of this statement comes from the analysis it allows of where cash came from and what it was used for, not from the preparation of percentage comparisons of these changes against a base amount.

Intercompany Comparisons

Another benefit of vertical analysis is that it enables you to compare companies of different sizes. For example, Quality's main competitor is Sears. Using vertical analysis, the condensed balance sheet (or the income statement, statement of retained earnings, or statement of cash flows) of the small local retail enterprise Quality Department Store can be more meaningfully compared with the balance sheet (or respective financial statement) of the giant retailer Sears Canada, as shown in Illustration 19-9:

Illustration 19-9

Intercompany balance sheet comparison—vertical analysis

CONDENSED BALANCE SHEETS

(in thousands)	Quality Department Store Inc.		Sears Canada Inc.	
	Dollars	Percentage	Dollars	Percentage
Current assets	$1,020.0	55.6%	$1,811,800	66.3%
Investments and other assets		0.0%	177,800	6.5%
Capital assets (net)	815.0	44.4%	744,400	27.2%
Total assets	$1,835.0	100.0%	$2,734,000	100.0%
Current liabilities	$ 344.5	18.8%	$1,070,800	39.2%
Long-term liabilities	487.5	26.5%	714,500	26.1%
Total liabilities	832.0	45.3%	1,785,300	65.3%
Common stock	275.4	15.0%	448,300	16.4%
Retained earnings	727.6	39.7%	500,400	18.3%
Total shareholders' equity	1,003.0	54.7%	948,700	34.7%
Total liabilities and shareholders' equity	$1,835.0	100.0%	$2,734,000	100.0%

Although Sears's total assets are 1,490 times greater than the total assets of the smaller Quality Department Store, vertical analysis eliminates this difference in size. The percentages show that Quality's and Sears's current assets are somewhat dissimilar, at 55.6% and 66.3%.

The percentages related to capital assets are also significantly different, at 44.4% and 27.2%. A number of factors contribute to this disparity. For example, Quality owns its own facilities, whereas Sears often leases facilities in malls or elsewhere. Sears also generates a significant portion of its revenues from catalogue sales. Although Sears has 110 department stores, it has more than 1,700 catalogue pick-up locations, which do not require capital-intensive facilities. It also has 60 independent, locally owned and operated stores, which generate additional revenue.

While Sears's retained earnings are 688 times larger than those for Quality, Sears's retained earnings as a percentage of total liabilities and shareholders' equity (18%) are much lower than Quality's (39.7%). This could be because Sears reduced its retained earnings by paying more dividends, in proportion to its shareholders, than did Quality. In fact, we have seen that Quality has been retaining a substantial portion of its earnings to finance growth. Quality paid out only 23.2% ($61,200 ÷ $263,800) of its net income as dividends in 2000, while Sears paid out 259% of its net income (Sears reported net income of $8.8 million, and paid dividends of $22.8 million). This is known as the dividend payout ratio, discussed later in this chapter.

Before You Go On . . .

▸*Review It*

1. What are the different tools that might be used to compare financial information?
2. What is horizontal analysis?
3. What is vertical analysis?

▸*Do It*

Summary financial information for Bonora Company is as follows:

	December 31, 1999	December 31, 1998
Current assets	$234,000	$180,000
Capital assets (net)	756,000	420,000
Total assets	$990,000	$600,000

Compute the amount and percentage changes in 1999, using: (a) horizontal analysis, assuming 1998 is the base year, and (b) vertical analysis, assuming total assets is the base.

Reasoning: For horizontal analysis, since 1998 is the base year, the percentage change is found by dividing the amount of the increase by the 1998 amount. For vertical analysis, since total assets is the base, the percentage amount is found by dividing each respective account balance (i.e., current assets, capital assets) by total assets, for each of 1998 and 1999.

Solution:

(a) Horizontal analysis:	Increase in 1999	Percentage
Current assets	$ 54,000	30% [($234,000−$180,000)÷$180,000]
Capital assets (net)	336,000	80% [($756,000−$420,000)÷$420,000]
Total assets	$ 390,000	65% [($990,000−$600,000)÷$600,000]

(b) Vertical analysis:	1999		1998	
Current assets	23.6%	($234,000÷$990,000)	30%	($180,000÷$600,000)
Capital assets (net)	76.4%	($756,000÷$990,000)	70%	($420,000÷$600,000)
Total assets	100.0%		100%	

Related exercise material: BE19–1, BE19–2, BE19–3, BE19–4, BE19–5, BE19–6, E19–1, E19–2, E19–3, and E19–4.

▾**R**atio Analysis

STUDY OBJECTIVE

5

Identify and compute ratios and describe their purpose and use in analysing a firm's liquidity, profitability, and solvency.

Ratio analysis expresses the relationships between selected items of financial statement data. A **ratio** expresses the mathematical relationship between one quantity and another. The relationship is expressed as either a percentage, a rate, or a simple proportion. To illustrate, recently Le Château had current assets of $37.3 million and current liabilities of $12.5 million. The relationship is determined by dividing current assets by current liabilities. The alternative means of expression are:

Percentage: Current assets are 298% of current liabilities.
Rate: Current assets are 2.98 times greater than current liabilities.
Proportion: The relationship of current assets to liabilities is 2.98:1.

►Technology in Action

Many accounting computer programs routinely generate financial ratios. All the ratio computations presented in this chapter can be done with electronic spreadsheets as well. There are also many programs written specifically for financial statement analysis. These packages are written for both general purpose use and use in specific industries. For example, financial institutions routinely use over 60 ratios, some of which are used specifically by the banking industry.

For analysis of the primary financial statements, ratios can be classified as follows:

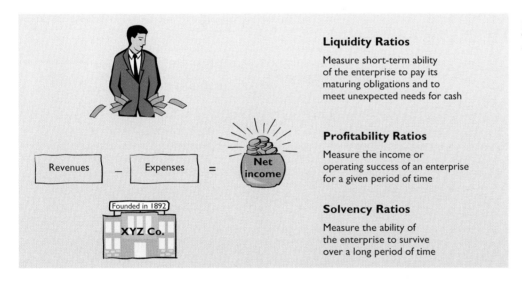

Liquidity Ratios

Measure short-term ability of the enterprise to pay its maturing obligations and to meet unexpected needs for cash

Profitability Ratios

Measure the income or operating success of an enterprise for a given period of time

Solvency Ratios

Measure the ability of the enterprise to survive over a long period of time

Illustration 19-10

Financial ratio classifications

Ratios can provide clues about underlying conditions that may not be apparent from inspection of the individual components of a particular ratio. However, a single ratio by itself is not very meaningful. Accordingly, in the following discussion we will use:

1. **Intracompany comparisons** covering two years for the Quality Department Store.
2. **Intercompany comparisons** of Quality Department Store and Sears Canada, Quality's principal competitor.
3. **Industry average comparisons** based on The Financial Post's *Industry Reports* for the wholesale and retail industry.

A number of these ratios have been introduced in previous chapters. They are included again in this chapter for completeness and further discussion.

Case in point Data for the years 2000 and 1999 for Sears and the department store industry was not available at the time of publication. Comparable real-life data from these sources have been used in this chapter, but the dates have been advanced for illustration purposes.

Liquidity Ratios

Liquidity ratios measure the short-term ability of the enterprise to pay its maturing obligations and to meet unexpected needs for cash. Short-term creditors such as bankers and suppliers are particularly interested in assessing **liquidity**. The ratios that can be used to determine the enterprise's short-term debt-paying ability are the current ratio, acid test ratio, current debt cash coverage ratio, receivables turnover, and inventory turnover.

1. Current Ratio

Case in point

	Co. A	Co. B
Current assets	$100,000	$500,000
Current liabilities	50,000	450,000
Working capital	$ 50,000	$ 50,000
Current ratio	2.0:1	1.1:1

The current ratio is a widely used measure of a company's liquidity and short-term debt-paying ability. The ratio is computed by dividing current assets by current liabilities. It is sometimes referred to as the **working capital ratio** because **working capital** is the excess of current assets over current liabilities. The current ratio is a more dependable indicator of liquidity than working capital. Two companies with the same amount of working capital may have significantly different current ratios. The 2000 and 1999 current ratios for Quality Department Store and comparative data are shown in Illustration 19-11:

Illustration 19-11

Current ratio

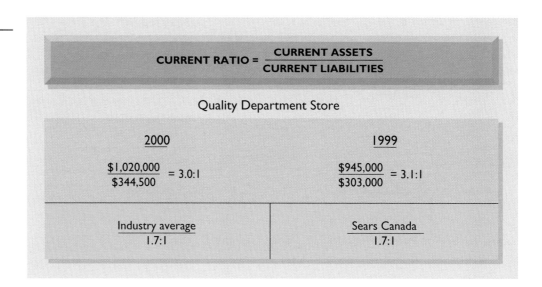

What does the ratio actually mean? The 2000 ratio of 3.0:1 means that for every dollar of current liabilities, Quality has $3 of current assets. Quality's current ratio has decreased slightly in the current year. However, compared to the industry average and Sears Canada's 1.7:1 current ratio, Quality appears to be highly liquid.

The current ratio is only one measure of liquidity. It does not take into account the composition of the current assets. For example, a satisfactory current ratio does not disclose the fact that a portion of the current assets may be tied up in uncollectible accounts receivable or in slow-moving inventory. A dollar of cash is more readily available to pay the bills than is a dollar of slow-moving inventory that has yet to be sold and collected.

Case in point   Can any corporation operate successfully without much working capital? Yes, if it has very predictable cash flows and solid earnings. A surprising number of companies are pursuing this goal. The rationale: less money tied up in working capital means more money to invest in more productive/profitable assets.

Accounting in Action ► *Business Insight*

The apparent simplicity of the current ratio can have real-world limitations, because an addition of equal amounts to both the numerator and the denominator causes the ratio to decrease. Assume, for example, that a company has $2,000,000 of current assets and $1,000,000 of current liabilities; its current ratio is 2:1. If it purchases $1,000,000 of inventory on account, it will have $3,000,000 of current assets and $2,000,000 of current liabilities; its current ratio will decrease to 1.5:1. If, instead, the company pays off $500,000 of its current liabilities, it will have $1,500,000 of current assets and $500,000 of current liabilities, and its current ratio will increase to 3:1. Thus, any trend analysis should be done with care, since the ratio is susceptible to quick changes and is easily influenced by management.

2. Acid Test Ratio

The acid test ratio is a measure of a company's immediate short-term liquidity; it is computed by dividing the sum of cash, temporary investments, and net receivables by current liabilities. Thus, it is an important complement to the current ratio. For example, assume that the current assets of Quality Department Store for 2000 and 1999 consist of the following items:

Alternative terminology
The acid test ratio is also called the *quick* ratio.

	2000	1999
Current assets		
Cash	$ 100,000	$155,000
Temporary investments	20,000	70,000
Receivables (net)	230,000	180,000
Inventory	620,000	500,000
Prepaid expenses	50,000	40,000
Total current assets	$1,020,000	$945,000

Illustration 19-12

Current assets of Quality Department Store

Cash, temporary investments, and receivables are highly liquid compared to inventory and prepaid expenses. The inventory may not be readily saleable, and the prepaid expenses may not be recoverable. Thus, the acid test ratio measures **immediate** liquidity. The 2000 and 1999 acid test ratios for Quality Department Store and comparative data are as follows:

Illustration 19-13

Acid test ratio

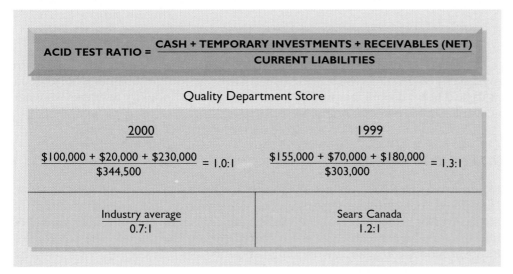

ACID TEST RATIO = $\dfrac{\text{CASH + TEMPORARY INVESTMENTS + RECEIVABLES (NET)}}{\text{CURRENT LIABILITIES}}$

Quality Department Store

2000	1999
$\dfrac{\$100,000 + \$20,000 + \$230,000}{\$344,500} = 1.0:1$	$\dfrac{\$155,000 + \$70,000 + \$180,000}{\$303,000} = 1.3:1$
Industry average 0.7:1	Sears Canada 1.2:1

Is an acid test ratio of 1.0:1 adequate? The ratio has declined in 2000. However, when compared to the industry median of 0.7:1 and Sears 1.2:1, Quality's acid test ratio appears adequate, with sufficient near-term liquidity to satisfy all current obligations in full.

3. Current Debt Cash Coverage Ratio

A disadvantage of the current and acid test ratios is that they employ year-end balances of current assets and current liability accounts. These year-end balances may not be representative of what the company's current position was during most of the year. A ratio that partially corrects for this problem is the ratio of net cash provided by operating activities to average current liabilities: this is called the **current debt cash coverage ratio**. Because it uses net cash provided by operating activities and an average of the current liabilities, rather than a balance at a point in time, it may provide a better representation of liquidity.

To illustrate the computation of this ratio, refer back to Illustration 19-6 to determine that Quality Department Store's net cash flows provided by operating activities were $125,300 in 2000 and $151,500 in 1999. Current liabilities at January 1, 1999, were $290,000.

Illustration 19-14

Current debt cash coverage ratio

Helpful hint   Whenever an end-of-period (e.g., balance sheet) figure is compared to a period figure (e.g., income statement or statement of cash flows), the end-of-period figure must be averaged so that it approximates the same period of time. Comparison of end-of-period figures to end-of-period figures, or period figures to period figures, do not require averaging.

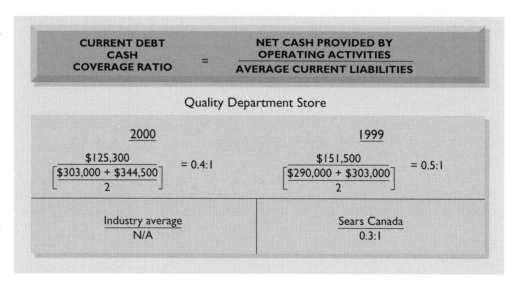

The ratio has declined slightly in 2000. Is the coverage adequate? It is difficult to say. Quality's operating cash flow coverage of average current liabilities is not as good as its acid test ratio, but it is slightly better than Sears's. Industry averages were not available for this particular ratio.

4. Receivables Turnover

Liquidity may be measured by how quickly certain assets can be converted to cash. How liquid, for example, are the receivables? The ratio used to assess the liquidity of the receivables is the **receivables turnover ratio**. This ratio measures the number of times, on average, receivables are collected during the period. The receivables turnover ratio is computed by dividing net credit sales (net sales less cash sales) by the average net receivables during the year. Unless seasonal factors are significant, average net receivables outstanding can be computed from the beginning and ending balance of the net receivables.[1]

Assuming that all sales are credit sales and the balance of accounts receivable (net) at the beginning of 1999 is $200,000, the receivables turnover ratio for Quality Department Store and comparative data are shown in Illustration 19-15. Quality's receivables turnover improved in 2000. The turnover of 10.2 times compares quite favourably with Sears's 7.7 times, although it is significantly slower than the industry's median of 54.8 times. In general, the faster the turnover, the greater the reliability of the current and acid test ratios for assessing liquidity.

Illustration 19-15

Receivables turnover

$$\text{RECEIVABLES TURNOVER} = \frac{\text{NET CREDIT SALES}}{\text{AVERAGE NET RECEIVABLES}}$$

Quality Department Store

2000	1999
$\dfrac{\$2,097,000}{\left[\dfrac{\$180,000 + \$230,000}{2}\right]} = 10.2 \text{ times}$	$\dfrac{\$1,837,000}{\left[\dfrac{\$200,000 + \$180,000}{2}\right]} = 9.7 \text{ times}$
Industry average 54.8 times	Sears Canada 7.7 times

In some cases, the receivables turnover may be misleading. Some companies, especially large retail chains, encourage credit and revolving charge sales, and they slow collections in order to earn a healthy return on the outstanding receivables in the form of interest (at rates of up to 28.8%). This may explain why Sears's turnover is only 7.7 times.

Care must also be taken in interpreting this ratio, as credit sales were assumed to equal net sales. Although this was an assumption (and likely an erroneous one, since many department stores do have a significant amount of cash sales), intracompany, intercompany, and industry comparisons can still be made, as the same assumption (total sales approximates credit sales) was applied to Sears and the industry average.

A popular variant of the receivables turnover ratio is the average collection period in days. This conversion is done by dividing 365 days by the turnover ratio. For example, in 2000 the receivables turnover of 10.2 times for Quality is divided into 365 days to obtain 35.8 days. This means that the average collection period for receivables is approximately 36 days. The average collection period is frequently used to assess the effectiveness of a company's credit and collection policies. The general rule is that the collection period should not greatly exceed the credit term period (i.e., the time allowed for payment).

▶ *International note*
Average collection periods are usually longer in Japan than in other countries. Due dates are frequently extended during business downturns to ensure that a stable workforce can be maintained.

5. Inventory Turnover

The inventory turnover ratio measures the average number of times the inventory is sold during the period. Its purpose is to measure the liquidity of the inventory. The inventory turnover is computed by dividing cost of goods sold by the average

Helpful hint Inventory is compared to cost of goods sold, not sales, because inventory is recorded at cost.

---

[1] If seasonal factors are significant, the average receivables balance might be determined by using monthly amounts.

inventory during the period. Unless seasonal factors are significant, average inventory can be computed from the beginning and ending inventory balances. Assuming that the inventory balance for Quality Department Store at the beginning of 1999 was $450,000, its inventory turnover and comparative data are shown in Illustration 19-16.

Illustration 19-16

Inventory turnover

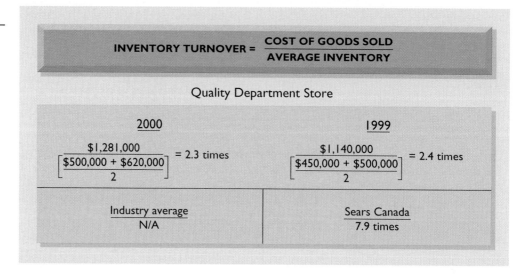

Quality's inventory turnover declined slightly in 2000. The turnover ratio of 2.3 times is low compared to Sears's inventory turnover of 7.9. Not suprisingly, the industry average is not available for this ratio. Few companies disclose their cost of goods sold in their financials. An industry ratio of 9.4 is available for sales divided by average inventory, however. This compares to a much slower 3.7 for Quality ($2,097.00 ÷ [($500,000 + $620,000) ÷ 2]). Generally, the faster the inventory turnover, the less cash that is tied up in inventory and the less chance of inventory obsolescence. As mentioned before, however, it is important to use judgement in interpreting these ratios. Remember that Quality is only one store, while Sears has hundreds.

A variant of the inventory turnover ratio is the average **days sales in inventory**. For example, the inventory turnover in 2000 of 2.3 times divided into 365 is approximately 159 days. An average selling time of 159 days is also very slow compared to Sears's rapid average of 46 days.

One possible explanation for the significant variance between Sears and the industry ratios is that the industry ratios are greatly affected by giant retailers such as Wal-Mart and the Bay, in addition to Sears, who are large enough to take advantage of just-in-time or other computerized inventory management techniques. Sears's year-end inventory balance, for example, is only 27.0% of its total current assets, whereas Quality's is 60.8%. Quality, as an independent department store, may not have access to many sophisticated inventory options. Nonetheless, Quality must keep a close eye on its inventory. It runs the very real financial risk of being left with unsaleable inventory that is out of season or out of fashion, not to mention the additional costs of financing and carrying this inventory for an extended period of time.

▶Accounting in Action ▸ *Business Insight*

Inventory turnover ratios vary considerably among industries. For example, grocery store chains have a turnover of eight times and an average selling period of 46 days. In contrast, jewellery stores have an average turnover of 1.7 times and an average selling period of 215 days. Within a company there may be significant differences in inventory turnover among different types of products. Thus, in a grocery store the turnover of perishable items such as produce, meats, and dairy products will be faster than the turnover of soaps and detergents.

Profitability Ratios

Profitability ratios measure the income or operating success of an enterprise for a specific period of time. Income, or the lack of it, affects the company's ability to obtain debt and equity financing, the company's liquidity position, and the company's ability to grow. As a consequence, creditors and investors alike are interested in evaluating earning power (profitability). Profitability is frequently used as the ultimate test of management's operating effectiveness. Profitability ratios include the profit margin, cash return on sales, asset turnover, return on assets, return on common shareholders' equity, book value per share, cash flow per share, earnings per share, price-earnings, and payout ratios.

6. Profit Margin

The profit margin ratio is a measure of the percentage of each dollar of sales that results in net income. It is computed by dividing net income by net sales for the period. Quality Department Store's profit margin ratios and comparative data are shown in Illustration 19-17.

Alternative terminology
The profit margin ratio is also called the *rate of return on sales.*

Illustration 19-17

Profit margin ratio

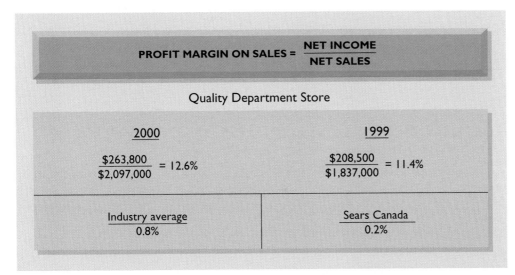

PROFIT MARGIN ON SALES = $\dfrac{\text{NET INCOME}}{\text{NET SALES}}$

Quality Department Store

2000	1999
$\dfrac{\$263,800}{\$2,097,000} = 12.6\%$	$\dfrac{\$208,500}{\$1,837,000} = 11.4\%$
Industry average 0.8%	Sears Canada 0.2%

Quality experienced an increase in its profit margin from 1999 to 2000. Its profit margin is unusually high in comparison with the industry average of 0.8% and Sears's 0.2%. One possible explanation for this is that Quality may sell higher-quality merchandise, with correspondingly higher prices and higher margins, than other companies such as Sears.

When you compare intercompany amounts, **it is also important for you to identify and segregate the impact of any unusual or extraordinary items**. For example, Sears's income was unusually low in the year in question, reduced by unusual restructuring costs of $45 million.

In the absence of any abnormal revenues or expenses, high-volume (high inventory turnover) enterprises such as grocery stores (Loblaws or Safeway) and discount stores (Zellers or Wal-Mart) generally experience low profit margins, whereas low-volume enterprises such as jewellery stores (Cartier) or airplane manufacturers (Bombardier) have high profit margins.

7. Cash Return on Sales Ratio

The profit margin ratio discussed above is an accrual based ratio, which uses net income as the numerator. The cash counterpart to that ratio is the cash return on sales ratio (or cash profit margin), which uses net cash provided by operating activities (from the statement of cash flows) as the numerator and net sales as the denominator. The difference between these two ratios can be explained as the difference between accrual accounting and cash basis accounting (i.e., differences in the timing of revenue and expense recognition). Using net cash provided by operating activities of $125,300 in 2000 and $151,500 in 1999, Quality Department Store's cash return on sales is computed as follows:

Illustration 19-18

Cash return on sales

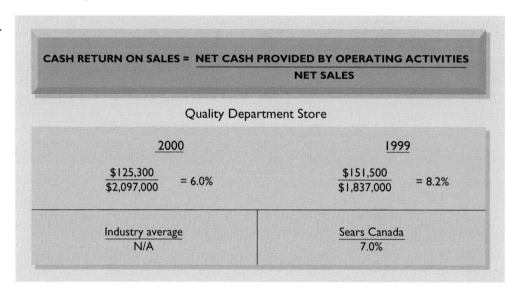

Quality's cash return on sales (6.0%) is considerably lower than its profit margin on sales (12.6%). The statement of cash flows presented in Illustration 19-6 details the sources (and uses) of cash provided by operating activities. The primary differences between net income and cash provided by operating activities were caused by increased receivables (which increased accrual based sales but not cash receipts from customers) and decreased payables (which increased cash payments to suppliers and cash payments for operating expenses).

In comparison to its competition, Quality appears to have a reasonable, although declining, cash return on sales.

8. Asset Turnover

The asset turnover ratio measures how efficiently a company uses its assets to generate sales. It is determined by dividing net sales by average total assets for the period. The resulting number shows the dollars of sales produced by each dollar of assets. Unless seasonal factors are significant, average total assets can be computed from the beginning and ending balance of total assets. Assuming that the total assets at the beginning of 1999 were $1,446,000, the 2000 and 1999 asset turnover ratios for Quality Department Store and comparative data are as follows:

Illustration 19-19

Asset turnover

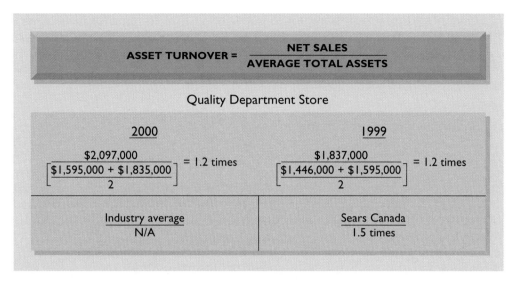

The asset turnover ratio shows that in 2000 Quality generated sales of $1.20 for each dollar it had invested in assets. The ratio is unchanged from 1999 to 2000. Quality's asset turnover ratio is somewhat below Sears's ratio of 1.5 times.

Asset turnover ratios vary considerably among industries. For example, a large natural resource company like Noranda has a ratio of 0.7 times, and the large grocery chain George Weston has a ratio of 2.4 times. Zellers and the Bay, two other competitors of Quality have asset turnover ratios of 1.5 times, similar to Sears.

9. Return on Assets

An overall measure of profitability is return on assets. This ratio is computed by dividing net income by average total assets. The 2000 and 1999 return on assets for Quality Department Store and comparative data are shown below:

Illustration 19-20

Return on assets

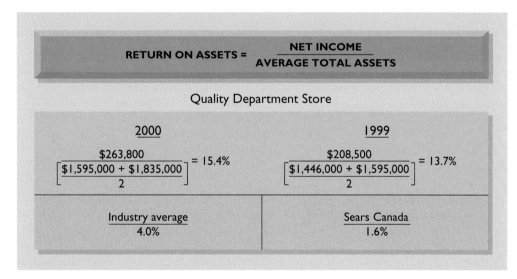

Quality's return on assets improved from 1999 to 2000. Its return of 15.4% is very high compared to the industry median of 4.0% and Sears's 1.6%. Although the percentage is high, it must be seen in perspective. Quality's earnings improved, and they were strong to begin with. However, they are being compared to a relatively small asset base, so small dollar increases result in large percentage increases.

10. Return on Common Shareholders' Equity

Another widely used ratio that measures profitability, from the common shareholder's viewpoint, is return on common shareholders' equity. In Chapter 15 we computed a basic return on total shareholders' equity. This ratio is usually refined further to show how many dollars of net income were earned for each dollar invested by the owners (i.e., common shareholders). It is computed by dividing net income by average common shareholders' equity. Assuming that common shareholders' equity at the beginning of 1999 was $667,000, the 2000 and 1999 ratios for Quality Department Store and comparative data are shown in Illustration 19-21:

Illustration 19-21

Return on common shareholders' equity— no preferred stock

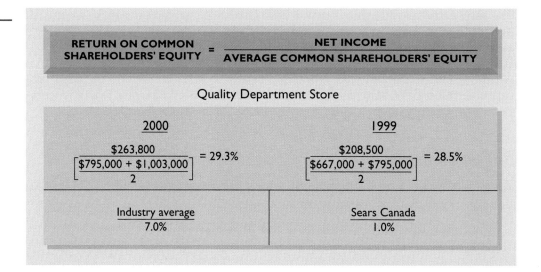

Quality's rate of return on common shareholders' equity is unusually high, at 29.3%, considering an industry average of 7.0% and a rate of 1.0% for Sears.

When **preferred stock** is present, preferred dividend requirements are deducted from net income to compute income available to common shareholders. Similarly, the legal capital of preferred stock (or call price, if applicable) must be deducted from total shareholders' equity to arrive at the amount of common shareholders' equity used in this ratio.

Alternative terminology
Trading on the equity is also called *leveraging*.

Note that Quality's rate of return on shareholders' equity (29.3%) is substantially higher than its rate of return on assets (15.4%). The reason is that Quality has made effective use of leverage or trading on the equity at a gain. Trading on the equity at a gain means that the company has borrowed money at a lower rate of interest than it is able to earn by using the borrowed money. Leverage is simply trying to use money supplied by nonowners to increase the return to the owners. A comparison of the rate of return on total assets with the rate of interest paid for borrowed money indicates the profitability of trading on the equity. Note, however, that trading on the equity is a two-way street. For example, if you borrow money at 7% and earn only 4% on it, you are trading on the equity at a loss. Quality Department Store earns more on its borrowed funds than it has to pay in the form of interest. Thus, the return to share-holders exceeds the return on assets, which indicates that shareholders are benefiting from the positive leveraging.

11. Book Value Per Share

Book value per share represents **the equity a common shareholder has in the net assets of the corporation** from owning one share of stock. Assuming that the number of common shares outstanding for Quality Department Store at December 31 was 272,700 for 2000 and 270,000 for 1999, book value per share is computed as follows:

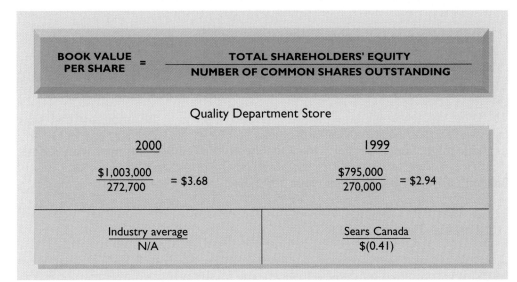

Illustration 19-22

Book value per share— no preferred stock

If there is **preferred stock** outstanding, since preferred shareholders have a prior claim on net assets over common shareholders, their equity (or call price) must be deducted from total shareholders' equity to determine the shareholders' equity that applies to the common stock.

Quality's book value per share has increased, reflecting their increased retention of earnings. Bear in mind, however, that book value per share is not a measure of the worth of a company. It reflects historical costs, not anticipated earnings.

Note that no industry data are presented. In addition, the Sears book value per share amount is presented for information only. Such comparisons are not meaningful because of the wide variations in the number of shares of outstanding stock among companies and differences in the fair values of the shares.

12. Cash Flow Per Share

Cash flow per share is an important measure of performance for companies. It is computed by dividing cash flow from operating, investing, and financing activities by the weighted average number of common shares outstanding.[2] The 2000 and 1999 ratios for Quality Department Store and comparative data are shown in Illustration 19-23.

---

[2] The weighted average number of common shares is assumed to equal the year end numbers, supplied above, for simplicity. You will recall that this term was introduced in Chapter 15, with basic computations demonstrated in Illustration 15-23.

Illustration 19-23

Computation of cash flow per share

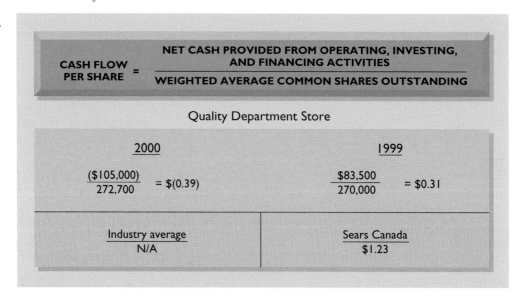

CASH FLOW PER SHARE =	NET CASH PROVIDED FROM OPERATING, INVESTING, AND FINANCING ACTIVITIES
	WEIGHTED AVERAGE COMMON SHARES OUTSTANDING

Quality Department Store

2000	1999
$\frac{(\$105,000)}{272,700} = \$(0.39)$	$\frac{\$83,500}{270,000} = \$0.31$
Industry average N/A	Sears Canada $1.23

When the term cash flow per share is used, it refers to the amount of cash flow applicable to each share of **common stock**.

One might conclude that while Quality's profitability is stronger than Sears's, Sears's cash flow is far superior to Quality's. However, such comparisons are not meaningful—just as with book value per share.

13. Earnings Per Share (EPS)

▶ *International note*

The most-often quoted measure of shareholder profitability is earnings per share. Only in a few countries, such as Germany and Italy, is EPS not disclosed.

Earnings per share is a measure of the net income earned on each share of common stock. It is computed by dividing net income by the weighted average number of common shares outstanding during the year.

Shareholders usually think in terms of the number of shares they own or plan to buy or sell. Reducing net income earned to a per share basis provides a useful measure of profitability. The net income per share for Quality Department Store for 2000 and 1999 is computed as shown in Illustration 19-24.

Illustration 19-24

Earnings per share— no preferred stock

EARNINGS PER SHARE =	NET INCOME
	WEIGHTED AVERAGE COMMON SHARES OUTSTANDING

Quality Department Store

2000	1999
$\frac{\$263,800}{272,700} = \$0.97$	$\frac{\$208,500}{270,000} = \$0.77$
Industry average N/A	Sears Canada $0.09

Quality's earnings per share increased 20 cents per share in 2000. This represents a 26% increase over the 1999 earnings per share of 77 cents. As with return on common shareholders' equity preferred dividends must be deducted from net income to arrive at income available to the common shareholders. Computing earnings per share can be complex. These intricacies will be studied in an intermediate accounting course.

14. Price-Earnings Ratio

The price-earnings ratio is an often-quoted statistic that measures the ratio of the market price of each share of common stock to the earnings per share. The price-earnings (PE) ratio reflects investors' assessments of a company's future earnings. It is computed by dividing the market price per share of the stock by earnings per share. Assuming that the market price of Quality Department Store stock is $12 in 2000 and $8 in 1999, the price-earnings ratio is computed as follows:

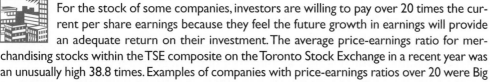

$$\text{PRICE-EARNINGS RATIO} = \frac{\text{MARKET PRICE PER SHARE OF STOCK}}{\text{EARNINGS PER SHARE}}$$

Quality Department Store

2000	1999
$\dfrac{\$12.00}{\$0.97} = 12.4 \text{ times}$	$\dfrac{\$8.00}{\$0.77} = 10.4 \text{ times}$
Industry average 15.4 times	Sears Canada 97.8 times

Illustration 19-25

Price-earnings ratio

In 2000, each share of Quality's stock sold for 12.4 times the amount that was earned on each share. Sears's price-earnings ratio of 97.8 times is an extraordinarily high ratio. This ratio was affected when earnings were reduced by an unusual charge of $45 million related to restructuring costs. A more representative price-earnings ratio for Sears Canada is its current PE ratio of 20.9, still higher than the industry average of 15.4 times.

▶Accounting in Action ▸ *Business Insight*

For the stock of some companies, investors are willing to pay over 20 times the current per share earnings because they feel the future growth in earnings will provide an adequate return on their investment. The average price-earnings ratio for merchandising stocks within the TSE composite on the Toronto Stock Exchange in a recent year was an unusually high 38.8 times. Examples of companies with price-earnings ratios over 20 were Big Rock Brewery (89), Bonavista Petroleum (88), Cambior (99), Pegasus Gold (66), Rogers Cantel (75), and Seagram (35). Examples of companies with low price-earnings ratios were Denison Mines (2), Dylex (6), Far West (6), National Bank (8), and Provigo (9).

15. Payout Ratio

Helpful hint   Companies must be cautious about changing their payout ratio too dramatically, Why? Because shareholders buy and hold stock on the basis of the company's historical and expected dividend-paying practices.

The **payout ratio** measures the percentage of earnings distributed as cash dividends. It is computed by dividing cash dividends by net income. Companies that have high growth rates are usually characterized by low payout ratios, because they reinvest most of their net income in the business. The 2000 and 1999 payout ratios for Quality Department Store are computed as follows:

Illustration 19-26

Payout ratio

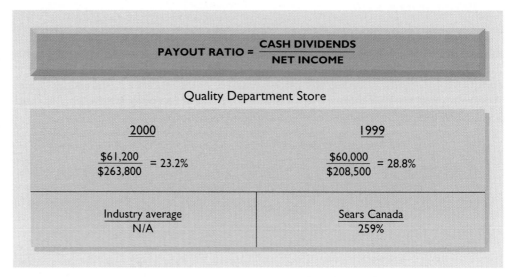

Quality's payout ratio is low when compared to Sears's unusual payout ratio of 259%. As indicated earlier, Quality has apparently decided to fund its purchase of capital assets through retention of earnings. Sears's payout ratio is due more to its strong cash position than its accrual based income.

Many companies with stable earnings have high payout ratios. For example, BCE has an 81% payout ratio. Conversely, companies that are expanding rapidly, such as Alliance Atlantis Communications, Biochem Pharma, and Corel, have never paid a cash dividend.

Solvency Ratios

Solvency ratios measure the ability of the enterprise to survive over a long period of time. Long-term creditors and shareholders are interested in a company's long-run solvency, particularly its ability to pay interest as it comes due and to repay the face value of the debt at maturity. Total debt to total assets, times interest earned, and cash total debt coverage are three ratios that provide information about debt-paying ability.

16. Total Debt to Total Assets Ratio

Case in point   A popular variant of this ratio is the debt to equity ratio, computed by dividing total debt by shareholders' equity. It compares the percentage of assets provided by creditors to that provided by shareholders.

The **total debt to total assets ratio** measures the percentage of the total assets provided by creditors, which is another indicator of the degree of leveraging. It is computed by dividing total debt (both current and long-term liabilities) by total assets. This ratio provides some indication of the company's ability to absorb losses without hurting the interests of creditors. The higher the percentage of total debt to total assets, the greater the risk that the company may be unable to meet its maturing obligations. The 2000 and 1999 ratios for Quality Department Store and comparative data are as follows:

Illustration 19-27

Total debt to total assets

$$\text{TOTAL DEBT TO TOTAL ASSETS} = \frac{\text{TOTAL DEBT}}{\text{TOTAL ASSETS}}$$

Quality Department Store

2000	1999
$\dfrac{\$832,000}{\$1,835,000} = 45.3\%$	$\dfrac{\$800,000}{\$1,595,000} = 50.2\%$
Industry average N/A	Sears Canada 65.3%

A ratio of 45.3% means that creditors have provided 45.3% of Quality Department Store's total assets. Or, conversely, that shareholders have financed 54.7% (100% – 45.3%) of the total assets. Quality's 45.3% is below Sears's ratio of 65.3%. The lower the ratio, the more equity "buffer" there is for creditors if the company becomes insolvent. Thus, from the creditors' point of view a low ratio of total debt to total assets is usually desirable.

The adequacy of this ratio is often judged in light of the company's earnings. Generally, companies with relatively stable earnings, such as utilities, have higher total debt to total assets ratios than cyclical companies with widely fluctuating earnings, such as many high-tech companies.

17. Times Interest Earned Ratio

The times interest earned ratio provides an indication of the company's ability to meet interest payments as they come due. It is computed by dividing **income before interest expense and income taxes** by interest expense. The 2000 and 1999 ratios for Quality Department Store and comparative data are shown in Illustration 19-28.

Alternative terminology
The times interest earned ratio is also called the *interest coverage* ratio.

Illustration 19-28

Times interest earned

$$\text{TIMES INTEREST EARNED} = \frac{\text{INCOME BEFORE INCOME TAXES AND INTEREST EXPENSE}}{\text{INTEREST EXPENSE}}$$

Quality Department Store

2000	1999
$\dfrac{\$468,000}{\$36,000} = 13 \text{ times}$	$\dfrac{\$388,000}{\$40,500} = 9.6 \text{ times}$
Industry average 32.1	Sears Canada 1.3 times

Note that the times interest earned ratio uses income before income taxes and interest expense, because this represents the amount available to cover interest. For Quality Department Store, the 2000 amount of $468,000 is computed by taking the income before income taxes of $432,000 and adding back the $36,000 interest expense. The interest expense of Quality is very well covered, at 13 times, relative to Sears at 1.3 times, although not as safe as the industry, in general.

18. Total Debt Cash Coverage Ratio

The ratio of net cash provided by operating activities to average total liabilities, referred to as the total debt cash coverage ratio, is a cash basis measure of solvency. Earlier (see ratio #3), we calculated a short-term version of this ratio using *current* liabilities. We now use *total* liabilities to expand the horizon.

This ratio demonstrates a company's ability to repay its liabilities from cash generated from operating activities, without having to liquidate the assets used in its operations. Using Quality's net cash provided by operating activities of $125,300 in 2000 and $151,500 in 1999, and assuming total liabilities of $779,000 on January 1, 1999, the total debt cash coverage ratios are computed as follows:

Illustration 19-29

Total debt cash coverage ratio

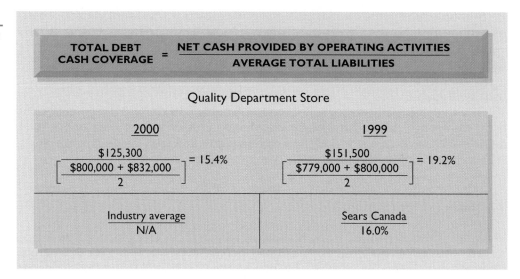

Based on net cash generated from operations in 2000, it would take Quality more than six years (100% ÷ 15.4%) to generate enough cash to pay off all its liabilities (assuming that all of the net cash generated was used for that purpose only). Quality's ratio is comparable to Sears's.

Summary of Ratios

Illustration 19-30

Summary of liquidity, profitability, and solvency ratios

A summary of the ratios discussed in the chapter is presented in Illustration 19-30, including the formula and purpose or use of each ratio.

Ratio	Formula	Purpose or Use
Liquidity Ratios		
1. Current ratio	$\dfrac{\text{Current assets}}{\text{Current liabilities}}$	Measures short-term debt-paying ability
2. Acid test or quick ratio	$\dfrac{\text{Cash + temporary investments + receivables (net)}}{\text{Current liabilities}}$	Measures immediate short-term liquidity
3. Current debt cash coverage ratio	$\dfrac{\text{Net cash provided by operating activities}}{\text{Average current liabilities}}$	Measures short-term debt-paying ability (cash basis)

4.	Receivables turnover	$\dfrac{\text{Net credit sales}}{\text{Average net receivables}}$	Measures liquidity of receivables
	Collection period	$\dfrac{365 \text{ days}}{\text{Receivables turnover}}$	Measures number of days receivables are outstanding
5.	Inventory turnover	$\dfrac{\text{Cost of goods sold}}{\text{Average inventory}}$	Measures liquidity of inventory
	Days sales in inventory	$\dfrac{365 \text{ days}}{\text{Inventory turnover}}$	Measures number of days stock is on hand

Profitability Ratios

6.	Profit margin	$\dfrac{\text{Net income}}{\text{Net sales}}$	Measures net income generated by each dollar of sales
7.	Cash return on sales ratio	$\dfrac{\text{Net cash provided by operating activities}}{\text{Net sales}}$	Measures the net cash flow generated by each dollar of sales
8.	Asset turnover	$\dfrac{\text{Net sales}}{\text{Average total assets}}$	Measures how efficiently assets are used to generate sales
9.	Return on assets	$\dfrac{\text{Net income}}{\text{Average total assets}}$	Measures overall profitability of assets
10.	Return on common shareholders' equity	$\dfrac{\text{Net income}}{\text{Average common shareholders' equity}}$	Measures profitability of shareholders' investment
11.	Book value per share	$\dfrac{\text{Total shareholders' equity}}{\text{Number of common shares outstanding}}$	Measures the equity in net assets of each share of common stock
12.	Cash flow per share	$\dfrac{\text{Net cash provided by all activities}}{\text{Weighted average common shares outstanding}}$	Measures the amount of cash flow generated by each share of common stock
13.	Earnings per share	$\dfrac{\text{Net income}}{\text{Weighted average common shares outstanding}}$	Measures net income earned on each share of common stock
14.	Price-earnings ratio	$\dfrac{\text{Market price per share of stock}}{\text{Earnings per share}}$	Measures ratio of the market price per share to earnings per share
15.	Payout ratio	$\dfrac{\text{Cash dividends}}{\text{Net income}}$	Measures percentage of earnings distributed in the form of cash dividends

Solvency Ratios

16.	Total debt to total assets	$\dfrac{\text{Total debt}}{\text{Total assets}}$	Measures percentage of total assets provided by creditors
17.	Times interest earned	$\dfrac{\text{Income before income taxes and interest expense}}{\text{Interest expense}}$	Measures ability to meet interest payments as they come due
18.	Total debt cash coverage ratio	$\dfrac{\text{Net cash provided by operating activities}}{\text{Average total liabilities}}$	Measures the long-term debt paying ability (cash basis)

Illustration 19-30 (continued)

Summary of liquidity, profitability, and solvency ratios

▶Technology in Action

In terms of the types of financial information that are available and the ratios used by various industries, you should be aware that what is covered in this textbook gives you only the "Titanic approach." That is, you are seeing only the tip of the iceberg compared to the vast databases and different types of ratio analysis that are available on computers. The availability of information is not a problem. The real trick is to be discriminating enough to select pertinent comparative data, perform relevant analyses, and interpret them correctly.

Before You Go On . . .

▶*Review It*

1. What are liquidity ratios? Explain the current ratio, acid test ratio, current debt cash coverage ratio, receivables turnover ratio, and inventory turnover ratio.

2. What are profitability ratios? Explain profit margin, the cash return on sales ratio, asset turnover, return on assets, return on common shareholders' equity, book value per share, cash flow per share, earnings per share, price-earnings ratio, and payout ratio.

3. What are solvency ratios? Explain total debt to total assets, times interest earned, and total debt cash coverage ratio.

▶*Do It*

Selected financial data for Drummond Company at December 31, 1999, are as follows: net cash provided by operating activities $315; total assets $2,350; total liabilities December 31, 1999, $1,300; and total liabilities December 31, 1998, $1,500. Compute the total debt to total assets ratio and the total debt cash coverage ratio.

   Reasoning: The formula for the total debt to total assets ratio is: total debt ÷ total assets. The formula for the total debt cash coverage ratio is: net cash provided by operating activities ÷ average total liabilities.

   Solution:

   Total debt to total assets   = 55.3% [$1,300 ÷ $2,350]
   Total debt cash coverage   = 22.5% [$315 ÷ (($1,300 + $1,500) ÷ 2)]

Related exercise material: BE19–7, BE19–8, BE19–9, BE19–10, BE19–11, E19–5, E19–6, E19–7, E19–8, E19–9, and E19–10.

▼imitations of Financial Analysis

STUDY OBJECTIVE
▾
6

Recognize the limitations of financial statement analysis.

Significant business decisions are frequently made by using one or more of the three analytical tools illustrated in this chapter. However, you should be aware of some of the limitations of these tools, and of the financial statements on which they are based.

Estimates

Financial statements contain numerous estimates. Estimates, for example, are used to determine the allowance for uncollectible receivables, periodic amortization, the costs of warranties, and contingencies. To the extent that these estimates are inaccurate or biased, the financial ratios and percentages are inaccurate or biased.

Cost

Traditional financial statements are based on cost and are not adjusted for price-level changes. Comparisons of unadjusted financial data from different periods may be invalid due to significant inflation or deflation. For example, a 10-year comparison of Sears's revenues might show growth of 1%. But this growth trend would be misleading if the general price-level had increased, or decreased, significantly during the same 10-year period.

Alternative Accounting Methods

Variations among companies in the application of generally accepted accounting principles may hamper comparability. For example, one company may use the FIFO method of inventory costing, whereas another company in the same industry may use average. If inventory is a significant asset to both companies, it is unlikely that their current ratios are comparable. In addition to differences in inventory costing methods, differences exist in reporting such items as amortization. Although these differences in accounting methods might be detectable from reading the notes to the financial statements, adjusting the financial data to compensate for the different methods is difficult, if not impossible, in some cases.

▸ *International note*

In an increasing number of industries, competition is global. To evaluate a firm's standing, an investor or analyst must make comparisons to firms from other countries. However, due to the many differences in accounting practices, these comparisons can be both difficult and misleading.

Atypical Data

Fiscal year-end data may not be typical of the financial condition during the year. Firms frequently establish a fiscal year end that coincides with the low point in operating activity or in inventory levels. Therefore, certain account balances (cash, receivables, payables, and inventories) at year end may not be representative of the balances in the accounts during the year.

Diversification of Firms

Diversification in Canadian industry also limits the usefulness of financial analysis. Many firms today are so diversified that they cannot be classified by industry. Others appear to be comparable but are not. You might think, for example, that PepsiCo and Coca-Cola are comparable, as soft drink industry competitors. But are they really comparable when PepsiCo owns food enterprises such as Pizza Hut, Kentucky Fried Chicken, Taco Bell, and Frito-Lay, in addition to Tropicana beverages, and Coca-Cola focusses more on beverage products such as Hi-C, Minute Maid, and Cadbury Schweppes. Industry averages provided by the *Financial Post* combined both wholesale and retail companies. Are these averages comparable to those of a retailer? Consolidated financial statements also hinder comparisons. For example, the ratios computed for Sears (and compared to Quality Department Store) were based on consolidated results, which may very well be skewed by the inclusion of subsidiary-company results.

▸ *Ethics note*

When investigating diversified firms, investors often are most interested in learning about the results of particular divisions. Firms are required to disclose the results of distinct lines of business separately if they are a material part of operations. Unfortunately, shifting revenues and expenses across divisions to achieve desired results reduces the usefulness of this information for financial statement analysis.

▸Accounting in Action ▸ *Business Insight*

 Many people would argue that non-financial performance measures are more important than financial measures in assessing success. Financial measures can evaluate only past performance; non-financial measures may be better predictors of future perform-ance. Non-financial performance measures include factors such as customer service, customer satisfaction, and market performance. Knowledge resources also contribute to a firm's success. These include innovation, information systems, employee satisfaction and abilities, and company and product reputation.

Before You Go On . . .

►Review It

1. What are some limitations of financial analysis?
2. Give examples of alternative accounting methods that hamper comparability.
3. In what way does diversification limit the usefulness of financial statement analysis?

►*A Look Back at York University*

Refer to the opening story and answer the following questions:

1. What financial ratio(s) helped York University acquire financing for the student centre? What other ratios or data are provided by a university when borrowing funds? What relevant information is provided by these ratios or data?
2. What are the sources of funds for a university or college?
3. Educational institutions are being held to higher standards of accountability than ever before. What other financial and non-financial measures might a university or college use to account for its performance?

Solution:

1. The bank reviewed York University's cash flow, including its cash debt coverage ratios and total debt to total assets ratio. These ratios helped the bank in assessing York's ability to meet both its interest and its principal loan repayments, in case the guarantee was exercised. The bank also would have been very interested in York's projected student enrolment, in order to determine how long it would take York to repay the loan through student fees. They likely also would have asked to review the projected revenues and costs of operating the student centre.
2. A university obtains funds from tuition; contributions, gifts, and bequests from alumni, friends, and corporations; grants from government, foundations, and companies; earnings from endowment investments and operating funds; and borrowings. In York's case, it also receives funds from students to finance the student centre.
3. Other ratios might include endowment ratios, student GPA scores, and student-teacher ratios. The endowment ratio is the ratio of gifts the university has received relative to the number of students; the larger its endowment, the less pressure a school has to generate money from other sources. The higher the GPA scores, the more demand there is to attend that institution. The lower the student-teacher ratio, or class size, the more personal attention and assistance there is for each student.

◢*Summary of Study Objectives*

1. *Discuss the need for comparative analysis.* There are three bases of comparison: (1) intracompany, which compares an item or financial relationship with other data within a company, (2) intercompany, which compares an item or financial relationship of a company with data of one or more competing companies, and (3) industry, which compares company data with industry averages.

2. *Identify the tools of financial statement analysis.* Financial statements may be analysed horizontally, vertically, and with ratios.

3. *Explain and apply horizontal analysis.* Horizontal analysis is a technique for evaluating a series of data over a period of time to determine the increase or decrease that has taken place, expressed as either an amount or a percentage.

4. *Describe and apply vertical analysis.* Vertical analysis is a technique for expressing each item within a financial statement as a percentage of a relevant total or a base amount.

5. *Identify and compute ratios and describe their purpose and use in analysing a firm's liquidity, profitability, and solvency.* The formula and purpose of each ratio are presented in Illustration 19-30.

6. *Recognize the limitations of financial statement analysis.* The usefulness of analytical tools is limited by the use of estimates, the cost basis of accounting, the application of alternative accounting methods, atypical data at year end, and the diversification of firms.

GLOSSARY

Acid test ratio   A measure of a company's immediate short-term liquidity, computed by dividing the sum of cash, temporary investments, and (net) receivables by current liabilities. (p. 807).

Asset turnover ratio   A measure of how efficiently a company uses its assets to generate sales, computed by dividing net sales by average total assets. (p. 812).

Book value per share   The equity a common shareholder has in the net assets of the corporation from owning one share of stock, computed by dividing shareholders' equity by the number of common shares outstanding. (p. 815).

Cash flow per share   The flow produced by each share of common stock, computed by dividing net cash provided by operating, investing, and financing activities by the weighted average number of common shares outstanding. (p. 815).

Cash return on sales ratio   A measure of the cash generated by every dollar of sales, computed by dividing net cash provided by operating activities by net sales. (p. 812).

Collection period   365 days divided by the receivables turnover. Determines average number of days for which receivables are outstanding. (p. 809).

Current debt cash coverage ratio   A cash basis measure of short-term debt-paying ability, computed by dividing net cash provided by operating activities by average current liabilities. (p. 808).

Current ratio   A measure of a company's liquidity and short-term debt-paying ability, computed by dividing current assets by current liabilities. (p. 806).

Days sales in inventory   The number of days that stock is on hand, computed by dividing 365 days by the inventory turnover ratio. (p. 810).

Earnings per share   The net income earned by each share of common stock, computed by dividing net income by the weighted average common shares outstanding. (p. 816).

Horizontal analysis   A technique for evaluating a series of financial statement data over a period of time to determine the increase (decrease) that has taken place, expressed as either an amount or a percentage. (p. 798).

Inventory turnover ratio   A measure of the liquidity of inventory, computed by dividing cost of goods sold by average inventory. (p. 809).

Liquidity ratios   Measures of the short-term ability of the enterprise to pay its maturing obligations and to meet unexpected needs for cash. (p. 806).

Payout ratio   Measures the percentage of earnings distributed as cash dividends, computed by dividing cash dividends by net income. (p. 818).

Price-earnings ratio   The ratio of the market price of each share of common stock to the earnings per share, computed by dividing the market price of the stock by earnings per share. (p. 817).

Profitability ratios   Measures of the income or operating success of an enterprise for a specific period of time. (p. 811).

Profit margin ratio   Measures the percentage of each dollar of sales that results in net income, computed by dividing net income by net sales. (p. 811).

Ratio analysis   A technique for evaluating financial statements that expresses the relationship between selected financial statement data. (p. 804).

Receivables turnover ratio   A measure of the liquidity of receivables, computed by dividing net credit sales by average net receivables. (p. 808).

Return on assets   An overall measure of profitability, computed by dividing net income by average total assets. (p. 813).

Return on common shareholders' equity   Measures the dollars of net income earned for each dollar invested by the owners, computed by dividing net income by average common shareholders' equity. (p. 814).

Solvency ratios   Measures of the ability of the enterprise to survive over a long period of time. (p. 818).

Times interest earned ratio   Measure of a company's ability to meet interest payments as they come due, computed by dividing income before interest expense and income taxes by interest expense. (p. 819).

Total debt cash coverage ratio   A cash basis measure of total debt-paying ability, computed by dividing net cash provided by operating activities by average total liabilities. (p. 820).

Total debt to total assets ratio   Measures the percentage of total assets provided by creditors, computed by dividing total debt by total assets. (p. 818).

Trading on the equity (leverage)   Borrowing money at a lower rate of interest than can be earned by using the borrowed money. (p. 814).

Vertical analysis   A technique for evaluating financial statement data that expresses each item within a financial statement as a percentage of a base amount. (p. 801).

DEMONSTRATION PROBLEM

The condensed financial statements of Kellogg Company for the years 1998-2000 are presented below:

KELLOGG COMPANY
Balance Sheet
December 31

	(In millions)		
	2000	1999	1998
Assets			
Current assets			
Cash and short-term investments	$ 266.3	$ 98.1	$ 126.7
Accounts receivable (net)	564.5	536.8	526.3
Inventories	396.3	403.1	416.4
Prepaid expenses and other current assets	206.4	207.1	201.9
Total current assets	1,433.5	1,245.1	1,271.3
Capital assets (net)	3,033.8	2,992.0	2,743.7
Total assets	$4,467.3	$4,237.1	$4,015.0
Liabilities and Shareholders' Equity			
Current liabilities	$1,185.2	$1,214.6	$1,034.7
Long-term liabilities	1,474.6	1,309.1	1,035.1
Shareholders' equity—common	1,807.5	1,713.4	1,945.2
Total liabilities and shareholders' equity	$4,467.3	$4,237.1	$4,015.0

KELLOGG COMPANY
Income Statement
For the Year Ended December 31

	(In millions)		
	2000	1999	1998
Sales (all on account)	$6,562.0	$6,295.4	$6,190.6
Cost and expenses:			
Cost of goods sold	2,950.7	2,989.0	2,897.5
Selling and administrative expenses	2,448.7	2,237.5	2,188.3
Interest expense	32.6	34.8	34.0
Total costs and expenses	5,432.0	5,261.3	5,119.8
Income before income taxes	1,130.0	1,034.1	1,070.8
Income tax expense	424.6	353.4	381.1
Net income	$ 705.4	$ 680.7	$ 689.7

Instructions

Compute the following ratios for Kellogg for 2000 and 1999:

(a) Current ratio.
(b) Quick (acid test) ratio.
(c) Receivables collection period.
(d) Inventory turnover.
(e) Profit margin ratio.
(f) Total asset turnover.
(g) Return on assets.
(h) Return on common shareholders' equity.
(i) Debt to total assets.
(j) Times interest earned.

Solution to Demonstration Problem

	2000	1999
(a) Current ratio:		
$1,433.5 ÷ $1,185.2 =	1.2:1	
$1,245.1 ÷ $1,214.6 =		1.0:1
(b) Quick (acid test) ratio:		
($266.3 + 564.5) ÷ $1,185.2 =	0.7:1	
($ 98.1 + 536.8) ÷ $1,214.6 =		0.5:1
(c) First, we need to calculate the receivables turnover rate:		
$6,562.0 ÷ ([564.5 + 536.8] ÷ 2) =	11.9 times	
$6,295.4 ÷ ([536.8 + 526.3] ÷ 2) =		11.8 times
Then, we use it to calculate the average collection period:		
365 days ÷ 11.9 =	30.7 days	
365 days ÷ 11.8 =		30.9 days
(d) Inventory turnover:		
$2,950.7 ÷ [($396.3 + $403.1) ÷ 2] =	7.4 times	
$2,989.0 ÷ [($403.1 + $416.4) ÷ 2] =		7.3 times
(e) Profit margin:		
$705.4 ÷ $6,562.0 =	10.7%	
$680.7 ÷ $6,295.4 =		10.8%
(f) Total asset turnover:		
$6,562.0 ÷ ([$4,467.3 + 4,237.1] ÷ 2) =	1.5 times	
$6,295.4 ÷ ([$4,237.1 + 4,015.0] ÷ 2) =		1.5 times
(g) Return on assets:		
$705.4 ÷ [($4,467.3 + $4,237.1) ÷ 2] =	16.2%	
$680.7 ÷ [($4,237.1 + $4,015.0) ÷ 2] =		16.5%
(h) Return on common shareholders' equity:		
$705.4 ÷ [($1,807.5 + $1,713.4) ÷ 2] =	40.1%	
$680.7 ÷ [($1,713.4 + $1,945.2) ÷ 2] =		37.2%
(i) Debt to total assets:		
$2,659.8 ÷ $4,467.3 =	59.5%	
$2,523.7 ÷ $4,237.1 =		59.6%
(j) Times interest earned:		
($705.4 + $424.6 + $32.6) ÷ $32.6 =	35.7 times	
($680.7 + $353.4 + $34.8) ÷ $34.8 =		30.7 times

Problem-Solving Strategies

1. Only the most liquid of the current assets should be included in the calculation of the quick (or acid test) ratio. Inventories and Prepaid Expenses are, therefore, usually excluded.
2. For ratios that involve both income statement amounts and balance sheet amounts (such as rates of return and turnover rates), remember that the balance sheet amounts should be based upon averages.
3. When the Return on Common Shareholders' Equity is higher than the Return on Assets, this indicates that the shareholders' are benefitting from the positive effects of leverage.
4. The calculation of the Times Interest Earned ratio must be based upon income before interest expense and income taxes (since this represents the amount of income available to cover the interest charges).

SELF-STUDY QUESTIONS

••

Answers are at the end of the chapter.

(SO 1, 2)

1. Comparisons of data within a company are an example of the following comparative basis:
   a. Industry averages.
   b. Intracompany.
   c. Intercompany.
   d. Both (b) and (c).

2. In horizontal analysis, each item is expressed as a percentage of the: (SO 3)
   a. net income amount.
   b. shareholders' equity amount.
   c. total assets amount.
   d. base year amount.

(SO 4)   3. In vertical analysis, the base amount for amortization expense is generally:

    a. net sales.

    b. amortization expense in a previous year.

    c. gross profit.

    d. fixed assets.

(SO 4)   4. The following schedule is a display of what type of analysis?

	Amount	Percentage
Current assets	$200,000	25%
Capital assets	600,000	75%
Total assets	$800,000	

    a. Horizontal analysis.

    b. Differential analysis.

    c. Vertical analysis.

    d. Ratio analysis.

(SO 3)   5. Leland Corporation reported net sales of $300,000, $330,000, and $360,000 in the years 1997, 1998, and 1999, respectively. If 1997 is the base year, what is the trend percentage for 1999?

    a. 77%.

    b. 108%.

    c. 120%.

    d. 130%.

(SO 5)   6. Which of the following measures is an evaluation of a firm's ability to pay current liabilities?

    a. Acid test ratio.

    b. Current ratio.

    c. Both (a) and (b).

    d. None of the above.

(SO 5)   7. A measure that is useful for evaluating the efficiency in managing inventories is:

    a. inventory turnover ratio.

    b. average days to sell inventory.

    c. both (a) and (b).

    d. none of the above.

(SO 5)   8. Which of the following is not a liquidity ratio?

    a. Current ratio.

    b. Total asset turnover.

    c. Inventory turnover.

    d. Receivables turnover.

(SO 5)   9. Plano Corporation reported net income $24,000, net sales $400,000, and average assets $600,000 for 1999. The 1999 profit margin was:

    a. 6%.

    b. 12%.

    c. 40%.

    d. 200%.

(SO 6)   10. Which of the following is generally not considered to be a limitation of financial analysis?

    a. Use of estimates.

    b. Use of ratio analysis.

    c. Use of cost.

    d. Use of alternative accounting methods.

QUESTIONS

1. (a) Tia Kim believes that the analysis of financial statements is directed at two characteristics of a company: liquidity and profitability. Is Tia correct? Explain.

    (b) Are short-term creditors, long-term creditors, and shareholders interested primarily in the same characteristics of a company? Explain.

2. (a) Distinguish among the following bases of comparison: (1) intracompany, (2) intercompany, and (3) industry averages.

    (b) Give the principal value of using each of the three bases of comparison.

3. Two popular methods of financial statement analysis are horizontal analysis and vertical analysis. Explain the difference between these two methods.

4. (a) If Roe Company had net income of $540,000 in 1999 and it experienced a 24.5% increase in net income for 2000, what is its net income for 2000?

    (b) If six cents of every dollar of Roe's revenue is net income in 1999, what is the dollar amount of 1999 revenue?

5. What is a ratio? What are the different ways of expressing the relationship of two amounts? What information does a ratio provide?

6. Name the major ratios useful in assessing (a) liquidity, and (b) solvency.

7. Tony Robins is puzzled. His company had a profit margin of 10% in 1999. He feels that this is an indication that the company is doing well. Joan Graham, his accountant, says that more information is needed to determine the firm's financial well-being. Who is correct? Why?

8. What do the following classes of ratios measure? (a) Liquidity ratios. (b) Profitability ratios. (c) Solvency ratios.

9. What is the difference between the current ratio and the acid test ratio?

10. Bullock Company, a retail store, has a receivables turnover ratio of 4.5 times. The industry average is 12.5 times. Does Bullock have a collection problem with its receivables?

11. Which ratios should be used to help answer the following questions?

   (a) Is the company efficient in using its assets to produce sales?

   (b) How near to sale is the inventory on hand?

   (c) How many dollars of net income were earned for each dollar invested by the owners?

   (d) Is the company able to meet interest charges as they come due?

12. The price-earnings ratio of McDonnell Douglas (aircraft builder) was 5, and the price-earnings ratio of Microsoft (computer software) was 43. Which company did the stock market favour? Explain.

13. What is the formula for computing the payout ratio? Would you expect this ratio to be high or low for a growth company?

14. With all other factors constant, indicate whether each of the following changes generally signals good or bad news about a company:

   (a) Increase in profit margin.

   (b) Decrease in inventory turnover.

   (c) Increase in current ratio.

   (d) Decrease in earnings per share.

   (e) Increase in price-earnings ratio.

   (f) Increase in debt to total assets ratio.

   (g) Decrease in times interest earned.

   (h) Increase in book value per share.

15. The return on total assets for Windsor Corporation is 7.6%. During the same year Windsor's return on shareholders' equity is 12.8%. What is the explantion for the difference in the two rates?

16. Which two ratios do you think should be of greatest interest to:

   (a) A pension fund considering the purchase of 20-year bonds?

   (b) A bank contemplating a short-term loan?

   (c) A common shareholder?

17. (a) What is meant by trading on the equity?

   (b) How would you determine the profitability of trading on the equity?

18. (a) Khris Inc. has net income of $270,000, weighted average shares of common stock outstanding of 50,000, and preferred dividends for the period of $40,000. What is Khris's earnings per share of common stock?

   (b) Phil Remmers, the president of Khris Inc., believes the computed EPS of the company is high. Comment.

19. Identify and briefly explain five limitations of financial analysis.

20. Unlike most retailers, whose fiscal year ends a month into the following year, Sears's year end is December 31.

   (a) What effect does Sears's nonstandard year end (for a retailer) have on the comparability of Sears's ratios with those of other large retailers?

   (b) What effect does Sears's year end have on the inventory turnover and receivables turnover ratios?

BRIEF EXERCISES

BE19–1 Using the following data from the comparative balance sheet of All-Province Company, prepare a horizontal analysis:

Prepare a horizontal analysis. (SO 3)

	December 31, 2000	December 31, 1999
Accounts receivable	$ 600,000	$ 400,000
Inventory	$ 780,000	$ 600,000
Total assets	$3,220,000	$2,800,000

BE19–2 Using the same data presented above in BE19-1 for All-Province Company, prepare a vertical analysis.

Prepare a vertical analysis. (SO 4)

BE19–3 Net income was $500,000 in 1998, $420,000 in 1999, and $504,000 in 2000. What is the percentage of change from: (1) 1998 to 1999, and (2) 1999 to 2000? Is the change an increase or a decrease?

Calculate the percentage of change. (SO 3)

BE19–4 If in 2000 Cavalier Company had net income of $672,300 and experienced a 25% increase in net income over 1999, what was its 1999 net income?

Use growth rate to calculate net income. (SO 3)

BE19–5 Vertical analysis (common size) percentages for Waubons Company's sales, cost of goods sold, and expenses are shown below:

Use vertical analysis to determine change in net income. (SO 4)

Vertical Analysis	2000	1999	1998
Sales	100.0	100.0	100.0
Cost of goods sold	59.2	62.4	64.5
Expenses	25.0	26.6	29.5

Did Waubons's net income as a percent of sales increase, decrease, or remain unchanged over the three-year period presented above? Use numbers to support for your answer.

Use horizontal analysis to determine change in net income.
(SO 3)

BE19–6 Horizontal analysis (trend analysis) percentages for Tilden Company's sales, cost of goods sold, and expenses are shown below:

Horizontal Analysis	2000	1999	1998
Sales	96.2	106.8	100.0
Cost of goods sold	102.0	97.0	100.0
Expenses	110.6	95.4	100.0

Did Tilden's net income increase, decrease, or remain unchanged over the three-year period presented above?

Calculate liquidity ratios.
(SO 5)

BE19–7 Selected condensed data taken from a recent balance sheet of Bob Evans Farms are as follows:

Cash	$ 8,241,000
Temporary investments	1,947,000
Accounts receivable	12,545,000
Inventories	14,814,000
Other current assets	5,371,000
Total current assets	$42,918,000
Total current liabilities	$44,844,000

What are the: (1) working capital, (2) current ratio, and (3) acid test ratio?

Calculate profitability ratios.
(SO 5)

BE19–8 Patriot Corporation has net income of $15 million and net revenue of $100 million in 1999. Its assets were $12 million at the beginning of the year and $14 million at the end of the year. What are: (a) Patriot's asset turnover ratio, and (b) profit margin ratio? (Round to two decimals.)

Evaluate collection of accounts receivable.
(SO 5)

BE19–9 The following data are taken from the financial statements of Diet-Mite Company:

	2000	1999
Accounts receivable (net), end of year	$ 560,000	$ 540,000
Net sales on account	5,500,000	4,100,000
Terms for all sales are n/30.		

Compute for each year: (1) the receivables turnover, and (2) the average collection period. What conclusions about the management of accounts receivable can be drawn from these data? At the end of 1998, accounts receivable (net) were $490,000.

Evaluate management of inventory.
(SO 5)

BE19–10 The following data are taken from the income statements of Clearwater Company:

	2000	1999
Sales	$6,420,000	$6,240,000
Beginning inventory	980,000	837,000
Purchases	4,640,000	4,661,000
Ending inventory	1,020,000	980,000

Compute for each year: (1) the inventory turnover ratio, and (2) the average days to sell the inventory. What conclusions concerning the management of the inventory can be drawn from these data?

Use profitability ratios.
(SO 5)

BE19–11 Haymark Products Company has shareholders' equity of $200,000 and net income of $50,000. It has a payout ratio of 20% and a rate of return on assets of 16%. How much did Haymark Products pay in cash dividends, and what were its average assets?

EXERCISES

E19–1 Financial information for Merchandise Inc. is presented below:

Prepare a horizontal analysis.
(SO 3)

	December 31, 1999	December 31, 1998
Current assets	$120,000	$100,000
Capital assets (net)	400,000	330,000
Current liabilities	91,000	70,000
Long-term liabilities	144,000	95,000
Common stock	150,000	115,000
Retained earnings	135,000	150,000

Instructions
Prepare a schedule showing a horizontal analysis for 1999, using 1998 as the base year.

E19–2 Operating data for Fleetwood Corporation are presented below:

Prepare a vertical analysis.
(SO 4)

	2000	1999
Sales	$800,000	$600,000
Cost of goods sold	472,000	390,000
Selling expenses	120,000	72,000
Administrative expenses	80,000	54,000
Income tax expense	38,400	25,200
Net income	89,600	58,800

Instructions
Prepare a schedule showing a vertical analysis for 2000 and 1999.

E19–3 The comparative balance sheets of British Columbia Corporation are presented below:

Prepare both horizontal and vertical analyses.
(SO 3, 4)

BRITISH COLUMBIA CORPORATION
Comparative Balance Sheets
As of December 31

	2000	1999
Assets		
Current assets	$ 72,000	$ 80,000
Capital assets (net)	123,000	130,000
Total assets	$ 195,000	$210,000
Liabilities & Shareholders' equity		
Current liabilities	40,800	$ 48,000
Long-term liabilities	138,000	150,000
Shareholders' equity	16,200	12,000
Total liabilities & shareholders' equity	$195,000	$210,000

Instructions
(a) Prepare a horizontal analysis of the balance sheet data for British Columbia Corporation using 1999 as a base. (Show the amount of increase or decrease as well.)

(b) Prepare a vertical analysis of the balance sheet data for British Columbia Corporation in column form for 2000.

E19–4 The comparative income statements of Olympic Corporation are shown on the following page:

Prepare both horizontal and vertical analyses.
(SO 3, 4)

OLYMPIC CORPORATION
Comparative Income Statements
For the Years Ended December 31

	2000	1999
Net sales	$550,000	$550,000
Cost of goods sold	440,000	450,000
Gross profit	110,000	100,000
Operating expenses	57,200	54,000
Net income	$ 52,800	$ 46,000

Instructions

(a) Prepare a horizontal analysis of the income statement data for Olympic Corporation using 1999 as a base. (Show the amounts of increase or decrease.)

(b) Prepare a vertical analysis of the income statement data for Olympic Corporation in columnar form for both years.

Compute liquidity ratios and compare results.
(SO 5)

E19–5   Nordstrom, Inc., operates department stores in several provinces. Selected financial statement data in millions of dollars for a recent year are as follows:

	End-of-Year	Beginning-of-Year
Cash and cash equivalents	$ 33	$ 91
Receivables (net)	676	586
Merchandise inventory	628	586
Prepaid expenses	61	52
Total current assets	$1,398	$1,315
Total current liabilities	$ 690	$ 627

For the year, net sales were $3,894 and cost of goods sold was $2,600.
The net cash provided by operating activities during the year was $500.

Instructions

(a) Compute the five liquidity ratios at the end of the current year.

(b) Using the data in the chapter, compare Nordstrom's liquidity with: (1) Sears Canada Inc., and (2) the industry averages for the wholesale and retail industry.

Determine the effects of transactions on current and acid test ratios.
(SO 5)

E19–6   Firpo Incorporated had the following transactions, involving current assets and current liabilities, during February 1999:

Feb.	3	Accounts receivable of $15,000 are collected.
	7	Equipment is purchased for $25,000 cash.
	11	$3,000 is paid for a one-year insurance policy.
	14	Accounts payable of $14,000 are paid.
	18	Cash dividends are declared, $6,000.

Additional information:

1. As of February 1, 1999, current assets were $140,000 and current liabilities were $50,000.
2. As of February 1, 1999, current assets included $15,000 of inventory and $5,000 of prepaid expenses.

Instructions

(a) Compute the current ratio at the beginning of the month and after each transaction.

(b) Compute the acid test ratio at the beginning of the month and after each transaction.

Compute selected ratios.
(SO 5)

E19–7   Georgette Company has the following comparative balance sheet data:

	December 31, 1999	December 31, 1998
Cash	$ 20,000	$ 30,000
Receivables (net)	65,000	60,000
Inventories	60,000	50,000
Capital assets (net)	200,000	180,000
	$345,000	$320,000

Accounts payable	$ 50,000	$ 60,000
Mortgage payable	100,000	100,000
Common stock	140,000	120,000
Retained earnings	55,000	40,000
	$345,000	$320,000

Additional information for 1999:
1. Net income was $25,000.
2. Sales on account were $420,000. Sales returns and allowances amounted to $20,000.
3. Cost of goods sold was $198,000.

Instructions

Compute the following ratios at December 31, 1999:
(a) Current.
(b) Acid test.
(c) Receivables turnover.
(d) Inventory turnover.

E19–8 Selected comparative statement data for Mighty Products Company are presented below. All balance sheet data are as of December 31.

Compute selected ratios. (SO 5)

	1999	1998
Net sales	$800,000	$720,000
Cost of goods sold	480,000	40,000
Interest expense	7,000	5,000
Net income	56,000	42,000
Accounts receivable	120,000	100,000
Inventory	85,000	75,000
Total assets	600,000	500,000
Total common shareholders' equity	450,000	310,000

Instructions

Compute the following ratios for 1999:
(a) Profit margin.
(b) Asset turnover.
(c) Return on assets.
(d) Return on common shareholders' equity.

E19–9 The income statement for the year ended December 31, 1999, of Jean LeFay, Inc., appears below.

Compute selected ratios. (SO 5)

Sales	$400,000
Cost of goods sold	230,000
Gross profit	170,000
Expenses (including $20,000 interest and $24,000 income taxes)	100,000
Net income	$ 70,000

Additional information:
1. Common stock outstanding January 1, 1999, was 30,000 shares. On July 1, 1999, 10,000 more shares were issued.
2. The market price of Jean LeFay, Inc., stock was $15 at the end of 1999.
3. Cash dividends of $21,000 were paid, $5,000 of which were to preferred shareholders.

Instructions

Compute the following ratios for 1999:
(a) Earnings per share.
(b) Price-earnings.
(c) Payout.
(d) Times interest earned.

Compute amounts from ratios.
(SO 5)

E19–10   Shaker Corporation experienced a fire on December 31, 1999, in which its financial records were partially destroyed. It has been able to salvage some of the records and has figured out the following balances:

	December 31, 1999	December 31, 1998
Cash	$ 30,000	$ 10,000
Receivables (net)	72,500	126,000
Inventory	200,000	180,000
Accounts payable	50,000	90,000
Notes payable	30,000	60,000
Common stock	400,000	400,000
Retained earnings	113,500	101,000

Additional information:
1. The inventory turnover is 3.6 times.
2. The return on common shareholders' equity is 22%. The company had no additional contributed capital.
3. The receivables turnover is 9.4 times.
4. The return on assets is 20%.
5. Total assets at December 31, 1998, were $605,000.

Instructions
Compute the following for Shaker Corporation:
  (a) Cost of goods sold for 1999.
  (b) Net sales for 1999.
  (c) Net income for 1999.
  (d) Total assets at December 31, 1999.

PROBLEMS

···

Prepare a vertical analysis and comment on profitability ratios.
(SO 4, 5)

P19–1   Comparative statement data for Chen Company and Couric Company, two competitors, appear below. All balance sheet data are as of December 31, 1999, and December 31, 1998.

	Chen Company		Couric Company	
	1999	**1998**	**1999**	**1998**
Net sales	$1,549,035		$339,038	
Cost of goods sold	1,080,490		238,006	
Operating expenses	302,275		79,000	
Interest expense	6,800		1,252	
Income tax expense	47,840		7,740	
Current assets	325,975	$312,410	83,336	$ 79,467
Capital assets (net)	521,310	500,000	139,728	125,812
Current liabilities	66,325	75,815	35,348	30,281
Long-term liabilities	108,500	90,000	29,620	25,000
Common stock	500,000	500,000	120,000	120,000
Retained earnings	172,460	146,595	38,096	29,998

Instructions
  (a) Prepare a vertical analysis of the 1999 income statement data for Chen Company and Couric Company in columnar form.

  (b) Comment on the relative profitability of the companies by computing the return on assets and the return on common shareholders' equity ratios for both companies.

Prepare a vertical analysis, compute rates of return, and comment on differences in profitability.
(SO 4, 5)

P19–2   Comparative statement data for Brooks Company and Shields Company, two competitors, appear on the following page. All balance sheet data are as of December 31, 1999, and December 31, 1998.

	Brooks Company		Shields Company	
	1999	1998	1999	1998
Net sales	$250,000		$1,200,000	
Cost of goods sold	160,000		720,000	
Operating expenses	51,000		252,000	
Interest expense	3,000		10,000	
Income tax expense	11,000		65,000	
Current assets	130,000	$110,000	700,000	$650,000
Capital assets (net)	305,000	270,000	800,000	750,000
Current liabilities	60,000	52,000	250,000	275,000
Long-term liabilities	50,000	68,000	200,000	150,000
Common stock	260,000	210,000	750,000	700,000
Retained earnings	65,000	50,000	300,000	275,000

Instructions
(a) Prepare a vertical analysis of the 1999 income statement data for Brooks Company and Shields Company.
(b) Compute the return on assets, the asset turnover, and the return on common shareholders' equity ratios for both companies.
(c) Comment on the relative profitability of these companies.
(d) Identify two main reasons for the difference in profitability.

P19–3   The comparative statements of Johnson Company are presented below.

Compute various types of ratio.
(SO 5)

JOHNSON COMPANY
Income Statement
For the Year Ended December 31

	1999	1998
Net sales (all on account)	$1,818,500	$1,750,500
Cost of goods sold	1,005,500	996,000
Gross profit	813,000	754,500
Selling and administrative expense	506,000	479,000
Income from operations	307,000	275,500
Other expenses and losses		
Interest expense	18,000	19,000
Income before income taxes	289,000	256,500
Income tax expense	86,700	77,000
Net income	$ 202,300	$ 179,500

JOHNSON COMPANY
Balance Sheet
December 31

Assets	1999	1998
Current assets		
Cash	$ 60,100	$ 64,200
Temporary investments	54,000	50,000
Accounts receivable (net)	107,800	102,800
Inventory	123,000	115,500
Total current assets	344,900	332,500
Capital assets (net)	625,300	520,300
Total assets	$970,200	$852,800

Liabilities and Shareholders' Equity

Current liabilities		
Accounts payable	$150,000	$145,400
Income taxes payable	43,500	42,000
Total current liabilities	193,500	187,400
Bonds payable	210,000	200,000
Total liabilities	403,500	387,400
Shareholders' equity		
Common stock	280,000	300,000
Retained earnings	286,700	165,400
Total shareholders' equity	566,700	465,400
Total liabilities and shareholders' equity	$970,200	$852,800

There were 60,000 common shares outstanding on December 31, 1998. On April 1, 1999, 4,000 shares were repurchased and cancelled.

Instructions

Compute the following ratios for 1999:

(a) Earnings per share.
(b) Return on common shareholders' equity.
(c) Return on assets.
(d) Current ratio.
(e) Acid test ratio.

(f) Receivables turnover.
(g) Inventory turnover.
(h) Times interest earned.
(i) Asset turnover.
(j) Debt to total assets.

Perform various types of ratio analysis and discuss results.
(SO 5)

P19–4 Condensed balance sheet and income statement data for Pitka Corporation appear below.

PITKA CORPORATION
Balance Sheet
December 31

	1999	1998	1997
Cash	$ 25,000	$ 20,000	$ 18,000
Receivables (net)	50,000	45,000	48,000
Merchandise inventory	90,000	85,000	64,000
Investments	75,000	70,000	45,000
Capital assets (net)	400,000	370,000	358,000
	$640,000	$590,000	$533,000
Current liabilities	$ 75,000	$ 80,000	$ 70,000
Long-term debt	80,000	85,000	50,000
Common stock	340,000	300,000	300,000
Retained earnings	145,000	125,000	113,000
	$640,000	$590,000	$533,000

PITKA CORPORATION
Income Statement
For the Years Ended December 31

	1999	1998
Sales	$740,000	$700,000
Less: Sales returns and allowances	40,000	50,000
Net sales	700,000	650,000
Cost of goods sold	420,000	400,000
Gross profit	280,000	250,000
Operating expenses (including income taxes)	236,000	218,000
Net income	$ 44,000	$ 32,000

Additional information:
1. All sales were on account.
2. All dividends were paid in cash.
3. There were 30,000 common shares outstanding throughout 1997 and 1998. On July 1, 1999, 4,000 shares of common stock were issued.
4. The market price of Pitka's common stock was $4.00, $5.00, and $7.95 for 1997, 1998, and 1999, respectively.

Instructions
(a) Compute the following ratios for 1998 and 1999:
   1. Receivables turnover.
   2. Inventory turnover.
   3. Profit margin.
   4. Asset turnover.
   5. Return on assets.
   6. Book value per share.
   7. Earnings per share.
   8. Price-earnings.
   9. Payout ratio.
   10. Debt to total assets.
(b) Based on the ratios calculated, discuss briefly the change in financial position and operating results of Pitka Corporation from 1998 to 1999.

P19–5 Condensed balance sheet and income statement data for Los Colinas Corporation appear below.

Perform ratio analysis and discuss results.
(SO 5)

LOS COLINAS CORPORATION
Balance Sheet
December 31

	1999	1998	1997
Cash	$ 40,000	$ 24,000	$ 20,000
Receivables (net)	70,000	45,000	48,000
Inventory	80,000	75,000	62,000
Investments	90,000	70,000	50,000
Capital assets (net)	450,000	400,000	360,000
	$730,000	$614,000	$540,000
Current liabilities	$ 98,000	$ 75,000	$ 70,000
Long-term debt	97,000	75,000	65,000
Common stock	400,000	340,000	300,000
Retained earnings	135,000	124,000	105,000
	$730,000	$614,000	$540,000

LOS COLINAS CORPORATION
Income Statement
For the Years Ended December 31

	1999	1998
Sales	$700,000	$750,000
Less: Sales returns and allowances	40,000	50,000
Net sales	660,000	700,000
Cost of goods sold	420,000	400,000
Gross profit	240,000	300,000
Operating expenses (including interest and income taxes)	194,000	237,000
Net income	$ 46,000	$ 63,000

Additional information:

1. All sales were on account.
2. Interest expense was $8,000 in 1999 and $7,000 in 1998.
3. Income taxes were $35,000 in 1999 and $45,000 in 1998.
4. All dividends were paid in cash.
5. There were 30,000 common shares outstanding on December 31, 1997. On July 1, 1998, 4,000 shares of common stock were issued, and on July 1, 1999, 6,000 shares were issued.
6. The market price of Los Colinas's common stock was $5.00, $4.50, and $2.30 for 1997, 1998, and 1999, respectively.

Instructions

(a) Compute the following ratios for 1998 and 1999:

1. Collection period.
2. Days sales in inventory.
3. Profit margin.
4. Asset turnover.
5. Return on common shareholders' equity.
6. Earnings per share.
7. Price-earnings.
8. Payout ratio.
9. Debt to total assets.
10. Times interest earned.

(b) Based on the ratios calculated, discuss briefly the change in financial position and operating results of Los Colinas Corporation from 1998 to 1999.

Compute various types of ratio, including effects of selected transactions.
(SO 5)

P19–6   Financial information for Caroline Company is presented below:

CAROLINE COMPANY
Balance Sheet
December 31

Assets	1999	1998
Cash	$ 70,000	$ 65,000
Short-term investments	45,000	40,000
Receivables (net)	94,000	90,000
Inventories	130,000	125,000
Prepaid expenses	25,000	23,000
Land	130,000	130,000
Building and equipment (net)	190,000	175,000
	$684,000	$648,000
Liabilities and Shareholders' Equity		
Notes payable	$100,000	$100,000
Accounts payable	45,000	42,000
Accrued liabilities	40,000	40,000
Bonds payable, due 1998	150,000	150,000
Common stock (20,000 shares)	200,000	200,000
Retained earnings	149,000	116,000
	$684,000	$648,000

CAROLINE COMPANY
Income Statement
For the Years Ended December 31

	1999	1998
Sales	$850,000	$790,000
Cost of goods sold	620,000	575,000
Gross profit	230,000	215,000
Operating expenses	194,000	180,000
Net income	$ 36,000	$ 35,000

Additional information:
1. All sales were on account.
3. Inventory at the beginning of 1998 was $115,000.
2. Receivables at the beginning of 1998 were $88,000.
4. Total assets at the beginning of 1998 were $630,000.

Instructions
(a) Indicate, by using ratios, the change in liquidity and profitability of Caroline Company from 1998 to 1999. (Note: Not all of the ratios can be computed.)
(b) Below there are three *independent* situations and a ratio that may be affected. For each situation, compute the affected ratio: (1) as of December 31, 1999, and (2) as of December 31, 2000. Net income for 2000 was $40,000. Total assets on December 31, 2000, were $700,000.

Situation	Ratio
1. 18,000 shares of common stock were sold at $10.00 each on July 1, 2000.	Return on common shareholders' equity
2. All of the notes payable were paid in 2000.	Debt to total assets
3. Market price of common stock was $9.00 and $12.80 on December 31, 1999 and 2000, respectively.	Price-earnings ratio

P19–7 Recent selected financial data of two intense competitors are presented below, in millions of dollars.

Compute various types of ratio for two companies and comment on results.
(SO 5)

	Bethlehem Steel Corporation	Inland Steel Company
Income Statement Data for Year		
Net sales	$4,819	$4,497
Cost of goods sold	4,548	3,991
Selling and administrative expenses	137	265
Interest expense	46	72
Other income (net)	7	0
Income taxes	14	62
Net income	$ 81	$ 107
Statement of Cash Flows Data for Year		
Net cash inflow from operating activities	$ 191	$ 171
Balance Sheet Data (End-of-Year)		
Current assets	$1,569	$1,081
Property, plant, and equipment (net)	2,759	1,610
Other assets	1,454	662
Total assets	$5,782	$3,353
Current liabilities	$1,011	$ 565
Long-term debt	3,615	2,056
Total shareholders' equity	1,156	732
Total liabilities and shareholders' equity	$5,782	$3,353

Beginning-of-Year Balances

Total assets	$5,877	$3,436
Total shareholders' equity	697	623

Other Data

Average net receivables	$ 511	$ 515
Average inventory	868	403

Instructions

(a) For each company, compute the following ratios:

1. Current ratio.	6. Return on assets.
2. Receivables turnover.	7. Return on common shareholders' equity.
3. Inventory turnover.	8. Debt to total assets.
4. Profit margin.	9. Times interest earned.
5. Asset turnover.	10. Total debt cash coverage.

(b) Compare the liquidity, profitability, and solvency of the two companies.

Compare liquidity, profitability and solvency for two companies. (SO 5)

P19–8 Recent selected financial data of two intense competitors are presented below, in millions of dollars. Note: Kmart Canada has since been purchased by the Hudson's Bay Company, and merged with Zellers.

	Kmart Corporation	Wal-Mart Stores, Inc.
Income Statement Data for Year		
Net sales	$34,025	$82,494
Cost of goods sold	25,992	65,586
Selling and administrative expenses	7,701	12,858
Interest expense	494	706
Other income (net)	572	918
Income taxes	114	1,581
Net income	$ 296	$ 2,681
Statement of Cash Flows Data for Year		
Net cash inflow from operating activities	$ 688	$ 3,555
Balance Sheet Data (End-of-Year)		
Current assets	$ 9,187	$15,338
Capital assets (net)	7,842	17,481
Total assets	$17,029	$32,819
Current liabilities	$ 5,626	$ 9,973
Long-term debt	5,371	10,120
Total shareholders' equity	6,032	12,726
Total liabilities and shareholders' equity	$17,029	$32,819
Beginning-of-Year Balances		
Total assets	$17,504	$ 26,441
Total shareholders' equity	6,093	10,753
Other Data		
Average net receivables	$ 1,570	$ 695
Average inventory	7,317	12,539

Instructions

Compare the liquidity, profitability, and solvency of the two companies.

Compute various types of ratio. (SO 5)

P19–9 The comparative statements of Ultra Vision Company are as follows:

ULTRA VISION COMPANY
Income Statement
For the Years Ended December 31

	1999	1998
Net sales (all on account)	$600,000	$520,000
Expenses		
Cost of goods sold	415,000	354,000
Selling and administrative expenses	120,800	114,800
Interest expense	7,200	6,000
Income tax expense	18,000	14,000
Total expenses	561,000	488,800
Net income	$ 39,000	$ 31,200

UTLRA VISION COMPANY
Balance Sheet
December 31

Assets	1999	1998
Current assets		
Cash	$ 21,000	$ 18,000
Temporary investments	18,000	15,000
Accounts receivable (net)	92,000	74,000
Inventory	84,000	70,000
Total current assets	215,000	177,000
Capital assets (net)	423,000	383,000
Total assets	$638,000	$560,000

Liabilities and Shareholders' Equity	1999	1998
Current liabilities		
Accounts payable	$112,000	$110,000
Income taxes payable	23,000	20,000
Total current liabilities	135,000	130,000
Long-term liabilities		
Bonds payable	130,000	80,000
Total liabilities	265,000	210,000
Shareholders' equity		
Common stock (30,000 shares)	150,000	150,000
Retained earnings	223,000	200,000
Total shareholders' equity	373,000	350,000
Total liabilities and shareholders' equity	$638,000	$560,000

Additional data:
1. The common stock recently sold at $19.50 per share.
2. The net cash provided by operating activities during 1999 was $29,000.

Instructions
Compute the following ratios for 1999:

(a) Current ratio.
(b) Acid test.
(c) Current debt cash coverage.
(d) Receivables turnover.
(e) Inventory turnover.
(f) Profit margin.
(g) Cash return on sales ratio.
(h) Asset turnover.
(i) Return on assets.

(j) Return on common shareholders' equity.
(k) Book value per share.
(l) Cash flow per share.
(m) Earnings per share.
(n) Price-earnings.
(o) Payout ratio.
(p) Debt to total assets.
(q) Times interest earned.
(r) Total debt cash coverage.

Use ratios to compute missing data.
(SO 5)

P19–10   Presented below is an incomplete income statement and an incomplete comparative balance sheet of Vienna Corporation:

VIENNA CORPORATION
Income Statement
For the Year Ended December 31, 1999

Sales	$11,000,000
Cost of goods sold	?
Gross profit	?
Operating expenses	1,665,000
Income from operations	?
Other expenses and losses	
Interest expense	?
Income before income taxes	?
Income tax expense	560,000
Net income	$?

VIENNA CORPORATION
Balance Sheet
December 31

Assets	1999	1998
Current assets		
Cash	$ 450,000	$ 375,000
Accounts receivable (net)	?	950,000
Inventory	?	1,720,000
Total current assets	?	3,045,000
Capital assets (net)	4,620,000	3,955,000
Total assets	$?	$7,000,000

Liabilities and Shareholders' Equity	1999	1998
Current liabilities	$?	$ 825,000
Long-term notes payable	?	2,800,000
Total liabilities	?	3,625,000
Common stock	3,000,000	3,000,000
Retained earnings	400,000	375,000
Total shareholders' equity	3,400,000	3,375,000
Total liabilities and shareholders' equity	$?	$7,000,000

Additional information:
1. The receivables turnover for 1999 is 10 times.
2. All sales are on account.
3. The profit margin for 1999 is 14.5%.
4. Return on assets is 22% for 1999.
5. The current ratio on December 31, 1999, is 3:1.
6. The inventory turnover for 1999 is 4.8 times.

Instructions
Use the ratios above to compute the missing information. Show computations. (Note: Start with one ratio and derive as much information as possible from it before trying another ratio. You will not be able to compute the missing amounts in the same sequence as they are presented above.)

*B*roadening Your Perspective

FINANCIAL REPORTING PROBLEM
....

Refer to the 1997 annual report and consolidated financial statements for The Second Cup Ltd., which are reproduced in Appendix A.

Instructions

1. Prepare vertical analysis (common-size) balance sheets and income statements for The Second Cup for fiscal years 1997 and 1996, and comment on any significant features that you observe in these. Hint: Use the Total Revenue figures as the base for your income statement calculations. (Systemwide Sales includes the revenues of all Second Cup franchises).

2. Prepare a ratio analysis of the company's financial statements, and comment on any significant results that you observe. (You may recall that many of these ratios have already been calculated in previous chapters.) For some of the ratio calculations, you will also need to refer to the following balance sheet amounts (in thousands of dollars) which the company reported for its fiscal year ended June 24, 1995:

ASSETS		
Current assets		
Cash and short-term investments	$ 190	
Account receivable	886	
Inventories	605	
Prepaid expenses and sundry assets	428	
		$ 2,109
Capital assets		6,109
Deferred income taxes		180
Goodwill, less accumulated amortization of $1,917		13,110
		$21,508
LIABILITIES		
Current liabilities		
Accounts payable and accrued liabilities	$ 1,957	
Deposits	180	
Income taxes payable	198	
		$ 2,335
SHAREHOLDERS' EQUITY		
Share capital (6,107,754 shares outstanding)	13,977	
Retained earnings	5,160	
Cumulative foreign exchange translation adjustment	36	
		19,173
		$21,508

3. Review the section of the report titled "Management's Discussion and Analysis of Operating Results." Using management's comments provided in this section, plus the points you noted in parts 1 and 2 above, write a one-page report summarizing your views regarding The Second Cup's financial position and performance. Hint: You should refer to qualitative information (such as the general state of the economy, the competitive environment in the industry, etc.) at the same time as you interpret the quantitative data.

DECISION CASE

As the accountant for J. Martinez Manufacturing Inc., you have been requested to develop some key ratios from the comparative financial statements. This information is to be used to convince creditors that J. Martinez Manufacturing Inc. is solvent, and to support the use of going-concern valuation procedures in the financial statements.

The data requested and the computations developed from the financial statements follow:

	2000	**1999**
Current ratio	3.1 times	2.1 times
Acid test ratio	0.8 times	1.4 times
Asset turnover	2.8 times	2.2 times
Net income	Up 32%	Down 8%
Earnings per share	$3.30	$2.50
Book value per share	Up 8%	Up 11%

Instructions

(a) J. Martinez Manufacturing Inc. asks you to prepare a list of brief comments stating how each of these items supports the solvency and going-concern potential of the business. The company wishes to use these comments to support its presentation of data to its creditors. You are to prepare the comments as requested, giving the implications and the limitations of each item separately, and then the general conclusion that may be drawn from them about J. Martinez's solvency and going-concern potential.

(b) What warnings should you offer these creditors about the limitations of ratio analysis for the purposes stated here?

COMMUNICATION ACTIVITY

L. R. Stanton is the Chief Executive Officer of Hi-Tech Electronics. Stanton is an expert engineer but a novice in accounting. Stanton asks you, as an accounting student, to explain: (1) the bases for comparison in analysing Hi-Tech's financial statements, and (2) the limitations, if any, in financial statement analysis.

Instructions

Write a letter to L. R. Stanton explaining the bases for comparison and the limitations of financial statement analysis.

GROUP ACTIVITY

Three types of analysis are explained in the chapter: horizontal, vertical, and ratio. The latter type (ratio analysis) is subdivided into liquidity, profitability, and solvency measures.

Instructions

The class should be divided into five groups. Each group will take one of the following topics: horizontal analysis; vertical analysis; ratio analysis—liquidity; ratio analysis—profitability; and ratio analysis—solvency.

For horizontal analysis and vertical analysis, the group should explain the analysis and illustrate its application to the balance sheet and income statement. For each category of ratio analysis, the group should state the formula and purpose of each ratio.

ETHICS CASE

Vern Fairly, president of Fairly Industries, wishes to issue a press release to bolster his company's image and maybe even its stock price, which has been gradually falling. As controller, you have been asked to provide a list of 20 financial ratios along with some other operating statistics relative to Fairly Industries' first quarter financials and operations.

Two days after you provide the ratios and data requested, you are asked by Roberto Sanchez, the public relations director of Fairly, to prove the accuracy of the financial and operating data contained in the press release written by the president and edited by Roberto. In the news release, the president highlights the sales increase of 25% over last year's first quarter and the positive change in the current ratio from 1.5:1 last year to 3:1 this year. He also emphasizes that production was up 50% over the prior year's first quarter. You note that the release contains only positive or improved ratios, and none of the negative or weakened ratios. For instance, no mention is made that the debt to total assets ratio has increased from 35% to 55%, that inventories are up 89%, and that, while the current ratio improved, the acid test ratio fell from 1:1 to 0.5:1. Roberto emphasized, "The Pres wants this release by early this afternoon."

Instructions

(a) Who are the stakeholders in this situation?

(b) Is there anything unethical in President Fairly's actions?

(c) Should you as controller remain silent? Does Roberto have any responsibility?

CRITICAL THINKING
►*A Real-World Focus: The Coca-Cola Company and PepsiCo, Inc.*

The Coca-Cola Company provides refreshments to every corner of the world. Four of its brands are among the five best-selling soft drinks in the world, and it ships nearly 11 billion cases of carbonated soft drinks per year. Despite its success, the company believes that great potential still exists—its top 16 markets account for 80% of its sales, but only 20% of the world's population.

Selected data from the consolidated financial statements for the Coca-Cola Company are presented below. (All dollars are in millions.)

Total current assets (including cash, accounts receivable, and temporary investments totaling $3,056)	$ 5,205
Total current liabilities	6,177
Net sales	16,172
Cost of goods sold	6,167
Net income	2,554
Average receivables	1,384
Average inventories	1,048
Average total assets	12,947
Average common shareholders' equity	4,910

Following are selected ratios for Coke's rival, PepsiCo, Inc.:

Current ratio	1:1
Acid test ratio	0.7:1
Receivables turnover	14.5 times
Inventory turnover	14.5 times
Profit margin	6.3%
Total asset turnover	1.2 times
Return on assets	7.4%
Return on common shareholders' equity	27%

Instructions

   (a) Compute the same ratios for the Coca-Cola Company as are shown above for PepsiCo, Inc.

   (b) Comment on the relative liquidity of these two competitors.

   (c) Comment on the relative profitability of the two companies.

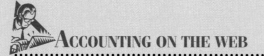

ACCOUNTING ON THE WEB

There are three Internet cases available for this important, seminal chapter.

The first case reviews IBM's *Guide to Understanding Financials,*which provides basic information to enable investors to understand the different financial statements.

The second case assesses the effectiveness of annual reports in presenting information to users. A company is selected from the Financial Post Annual Report Awards competition, and its annual report is reviewed to identify the key components of effective financial reporting.

The third case involves a comprehensive financial analysis of Big Rock Brewery, a young craft brewing company located in Calgary. In addition to reviewing the company home page and filings with the Securities Commission, you will hotlink to various related sites to study the company's business environment, investment climate, and current news. Financial ratios and other financial information will be gathered and studied. The reasons for the company's changing stock price are then assessed in light of the qualitative and quantitative analysis performed.

Instructions

Specific requirements of these Internet cases are available on-line at www.wiley.com/canada/weygandt.

CUMULATIVE COVERAGE — CHAPTERS 18 AND 19

Part I

Refer to the Demonstration Problem for Chapter 18, and its solution, in which a statement of cash flows was prepared for Kosinski Manufacturing Company.

Instructions

   1. Review the company's statement of cash flows, think about the information it conveys, and comment upon any significant points that you observe.

   2. The following data, together with that given in the Demonstration Problem, complete the balance sheet data for the company:

	1999	1998
Machinery (net)	$1,626,000	$2,050,000
Share capital	1,920,000	1,920,000
Retained earnings	1,466,000	1,236,000

   (a) Prepare a ratio analysis of Kosinski Manufacturing's balance sheets and income statement.

   (b) Interpret the ratio results and comment upon any significant points that you observe from them.

Part II

Refer to the Demonstration Problem for Chapter 19, and its solution, in which various ratios were calculated for Kellogg Company.

Instructions

1. Review the company's ratio results, think about the information they convey, and comment upon any significant points that you observe.

2. The following assumed data (in millions), together with that given in the Demonstration Problem, complete the data needed to prepare a statement of cash flows for the company:

   - Amortization expense was $330 in 2000 and $300 in 1999.
   - Capital assets worth $100 (net of accumulated amortization) were sold, at their book value, in 2000; none were sold in 1999.
   - New capital assets were acquired in both years.
   - Long-term debt of $200 was retired, at face value, in 2000; none was retired in 1999.
   - New long-term debt was issued in both years.
   - Share capital was unchanged during 2000, but it was reduced by $290 in 1999 when shares were repurchased and cancelled.
   - Dividends of $611.3 were paid in 2000, and $622.5 in 1999.

   (a) Prepare a statement of cash flows for Kellogg Company for the years 2000 and 1999.
   (b) Review the company's statement of cash flows and comment upon any significant points that you observe from it.

Answers to Self-Study Questions

1. b   2. d   3. a   4. c   5. c   6. c   7. c   8. b   9. a   10. b

SPECIMEN FINANCIAL STATEMENTS

The Annual Report

Once each year, corporations communicate to shareholders and other interested parties by issuing a complete set of audited financial statements. The **annual report**, the name of this communication for public corporations, summarizes the financial results of operations for the year and presents the corporation's plans for the future. Many annual reports have become attractive, multicoloured, glossy public relations pieces containing pictures of corporate officers and directors, as well as photos and descriptions of new products and buildings. Yet the basic function of every annual report is to report financial information, almost all of which is a product of the corporation's accounting system.

The content and organization of corporate annual reports have become fairly standardized. Excluding the public relations part of the report (pictures, products, and propaganda), the following items are traditionally included:

Financial Highlights
Letter to Shareholders
Management's Discussion and Analysis of Operating Results
Comparative Financial Statements
    Management Report
    Auditors' Report
    Balance Sheet
    Statement of Operations and Retained Earnings
    Statement of Changes in Financial Position
    Notes to the Financial Statements
Supplementary Financial Information
Directors and Officers
Corporate Information

In this appendix, we illustrate current financial reporting with a comprehensive set of corporate financial statements prepared in accordance with generally accepted accounting principles and audited by an independent chartered accounting firm. We are grateful for permission to use the actual financial statements and other accompanying financial information from the annual report of The Second Cup Ltd., a rapidly growing, publicly held company.

Financial Highlights

The financial highlights section of an annual report is usually presented inside the front cover or on the first page. This section generally reports the total or per share amounts for five to 10 financial items for the current year, and for one or more previous years. Financial items from the income statement and the balance sheet that are typically presented include sales, income from continuing operations, net income (or loss), earnings (or loss) per share, dividends per share, capital expenditures (if any), and the amount of cash flow from operations. The financial highlights section from the 1997 annual report for The Second Cup Ltd. is shown below:

Delivering the Ultimate Customer Experience

FINANCIAL HIGHLIGHTS

(MILLIONS OF CANADIAN DOLLARS, EXCEPT PER SHARE AMOUNTS)	**1997**	1996
OPERATING RESULTS		
SYSTEMWIDE SALES	$260.9	$214.4
REVENUE	73.1	63.3
EBITDA*	6.1	8.2
GAIN ON DISPOSITION OF COFFEE PLANTATION	2.2	—
PROVISION FOR COFFEE PLANTATION STORE CLOSURES	—	(4.9)
NET EARNINGS (LOSS)	3.0	(2.4)
EARNINGS (LOSS) PER SHARE	$ 0.21	$(0.25)
FINANCIAL POSITION		
CASH AND SHORT-TERM INVESTMENTS	$ 46.1	$ 35.8
SHAREHOLDERS' EQUITY	101.2	97.4
NUMBER OF STORES AT END OF PERIOD		
FRANCHISED	514	453
CORPORATE	53	59
TOTAL	567	512

*EBITDA represents earnings before interest, taxes, depreciation, amortization and unusual items.

The Second Cup Ltd. is a North American leader in the specialty coffee market. We are the market leader with 299 stores in Canada.

Our Gloria Jean's Coffee operation includes more than 240 stores in the United States, as well as 27 international stores in countries including Japan, Mexico and Ireland.

Letter to Shareholders

Nearly every annual report contains a letter to the shareholders from the Chair of the Board of Directors (normally also called the Chief Executive Officer), or the President (also called the Chief Operating Officer), or both. This letter typically discusses the company's accomplishments during the preceding year and highlights significant events such as mergers and acquisitions, new products, operating achievements, business philosophy, changes in officers or directors, financing commitments, expansion plans, and future prospects. The letter to the shareholders of The Second Cup Ltd., signed by Michael Bregman, Chair and Chief Executive Officer, is shown below:

LETTER TO OUR SHAREHOLDERS

Uncompromising Commitment to

COMMUNITY ●

We do not deserve honours on our report card for Second Cup's performance over the past year. Second Cup shareholders did not participate in the appreciation enjoyed by North American equities over the past year and we are fully accountable for creating value. Though fiscal 1997 was full of positive achievements, our U.S. operations produced disappointing results and we have not yet deployed our growing cash resources. Yet, I feel extraordinarily upbeat about our Company's future prospects.

While I believe it is important to acknowledge that we were tested, I am proud of our achievements over the past year. Our financial performance for fiscal 1997 improved materially over the prior year. Systemwide sales rose to $261 million and net earnings totalled $3.0 million or 21¢ per share. A $2.2 million gain on the sale of Coffee Plantation's core Arizona stores in May was offset by a comparable provision related to under-performing stores at Gloria Jean's Gourmet Coffees.

In Canada, we enjoyed an excellent year of growth and the momentum continues. Systemwide sales rose by 19% to $108 million. In spite of an increased competitive environment in our core markets, same-store sales increased by 5.8% for the year. I view this as one of many important indicators of our building strength with Canadian consumers. We added a total of 56 new stores and ended the year with 299 outlets. Included were the first 13 units opened with our partners at Cara. Increasingly, we are managing Second Cup as a supremely valuable brand with a view to capitalizing on our leadership in Canada's growing specialty coffee market. For the first time, Second Cup's brand can be found in selectively placed markets outside of Second Cup stores. Today, Second Cup coffee is proudly served on all Air Canada flights. In addition, after a highly successful test, we have entered a new partnership to offer Second Cup coffee in Eaton's department stores across Canada. We are exploring many other creative initiatives that are designed to profitably build the Second Cup brand while

enhancing the success of our core stores and franchisees. Our rapid pace of growth has created a need to continually strengthen our management team. To this end, Randy Powell has recently assumed the presidency of our Canadian Operations. Randy is an accomplished leader and brings to our Company an outstanding record of marketing success. He knows how to build brands.

We expect to deliver another year of record growth in Canadian sales, earnings, store openings and cash flow in fiscal 1998. Though the story has been most impressive for some time, we see even greater opportunities to build additional value in Canada.

The situation in the U.S. is quite different. We are leading Gloria Jean's Gourmet Coffees through a period of fundamental change in values and culture to position the company to prosper in the future. Though the earnings last year do not yet reflect the changes, Gloria Jean's is a much better company

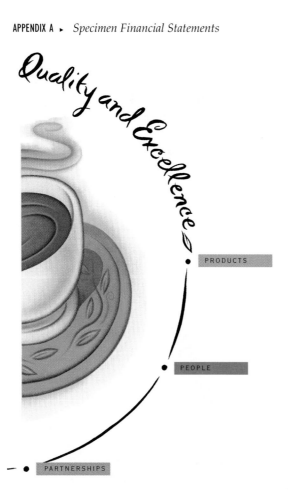

Quality and Excellence

PRODUCTS

PEOPLE

PARTNERSHIPS

today than one year ago. Alton McEwen, our President of U.S. Operations, has been building a foundation with an uncompromising commitment to quality and excellence at all levels. Much like our early experience at Second Cup, some of these changes take time. We expect materially improved results in the coming year. Already we are seeing encouraging signs, including record franchisee pre-orders for our innovative line of Holiday coffee gifts.

We successfully completed two notable transactions in fiscal 1997. Last October we invested $6.5 million in The Great Canadian Bagel, Ltd., principally in the form of a convertible debenture. This company has grown explosively and with 150 units, is by far the leader in Canada's bagel segment. From our base position, we will watch the company's progress and will consider whether to further invest in the future.

At Coffee Plantation, when we realized that our initial investment aspirations for scale would not be met, our

disciplined approach called for action. Our successful divestiture in May of Coffee Plantation's Arizona stores for $11.7 million generated a gain of $2.2 million and reflected the quality of the operations we had built there. We have now closed all but one of the seven stores in Texas and California, for which we had taken a provision last year. We intend to close the remaining store shortly. We continue to believe that there may emerge an opportunity to pursue a consolidation strategy in North America's specialty coffee segment. However, we must carefully assess the quality of available properties and ensure that values will prove attractive for the creation of shareholder value.

Kathy Welsh joined us as Executive Vice-President and Chief Financial Officer last fall and together, we have focused much of our attention on the above-mentioned internal activities. We believe this was time well spent and better secures our foundation for the future. We are now concentrating on identifying new opportunities to build value for Second Cup shareholders.

Why am I so enthusiastic about Second Cup's future? The reasons are many. We have strengthened our senior management team. We have effectively managed our way through some difficult issues. Second Cup in Canada occupies a position of growing leadership in an extraordinarily attractive business segment and we are poised to build brand equity. Gloria Jean's is improving after a very challenging first 18 months under Second Cup ownership. We have divested Coffee Plantation, which was not producing shareholder value. Our balance sheet is even stronger than before with net cash of approximately $46 million at year end. Finally, we have great confidence in our management team and we enjoy strong sponsorship and support from our key shareholders and directors.

Though we do not deserve honours on our report card for the past year's performance, we have definitely passed numerous tests and have emerged stronger than ever before. Looking ahead, we will aggressively pursue internal and external opportunities through which we will strive to maximize shareholder value.

MICHAEL BREGMAN

Chairman and Chief Executive Officer

Management's Discussion and Analysis of Operating Results

In this portion of the annual report, management analyses the operating results presented in the financial statements. In addition, it usually sheds light on its competition, market position, and market share. Because the majority of the annual report is based on historical information—which is dated by the time the reader receives it—the MD&A (as it is commonly called) attempts to be more forward-looking. It therefore includes a management discussion about the future directions and prospects of the company. Ideally, management's comments are expressed in a frank and forthright manner, with no concealment or bias.

MANAGEMENT'S DISCUSSION AND ANALYSIS OF OPERATING RESULTS

This discussion and analysis should be read in conjunction with the consolidated financial statements and related notes included in the Annual Report to Shareholders of The Second Cup Ltd. ("Second Cup" or the "Company").

RESULTS OF OPERATIONS

On a consolidated basis, systemwide sales increased 22% to $261 million for the 52 weeks ended June 28, 1997 ("1997") from $214 million for the 53 weeks ended June 29, 1996 ("1996"). Total revenue rose 15% to $73.1 million in 1997. These increases were driven by continued growth in Canadian Operations and the inclusion of a full year of activity for Gloria Jean's Gourmet Coffees ("Gloria Jean's") in U.S. Operations.

Consolidated operating earnings before interest, taxes, depreciation, amortization and unusual items ("EBITDA") were $6.1 million in 1997 compared to $8.2 million a year ago. Substantial growth in Canadian Operations' EBITDA was offset by disappointing results in Gloria Jean's. Included in 1997 EBITDA are write-downs and provisions totalling $2.2 million related to under-performing Gloria Jean's corporate stores. After interest, taxes and a $2.2 million gain on disposition of the Arizona Coffee Plantation stores, the net earnings for the period were $3.0 million (21¢ per share). This compares

to a loss, after a $4.9 million provision for Coffee Plantation store closures, of $2.4 million (25¢ per share) in the prior year.

Canadian Operations

Systemwide sales increased 19% to $108 million for 1997 from $90.8 million for 1996. Net growth in new Second Cup locations contributed $12.5 million of the increase and comparable store sales increases of 5.8% for the 52 week period added $4.7 million. In 1996, systemwide sales included an additional week's sales of $1.8 million.

The pace of store development accelerated with 61 openings in 1997, but fell short of the 80 to 100 locations originally planned, primarily due to a shortfall in stores opened (13 versus 50 planned) under the license agreement with Cara Operations Limited ("Cara"). Potential locations have now been identified and Cara expects to open 64 Second Cup stores in fiscal 1998. Overall, the Company expects to open more than 100 new stores in the next fiscal year.

Franchise revenue advanced $2.4 million or 23% to $12.7 million, reflecting increased royalties arising from higher systemwide sales and a $0.5 million master license fee with Cara.

Retail sales of corporate stores increased 58% to $6.8 million, largely due to more stores in 1997. An 8.9% comparable store sales increase contributed $0.5 million of additional sales. There were 21 corporate stores at June 28, 1997 (June 29, 1996 – 15 stores). While

CONSOLIDATED NUMBER OF STORES

■ FRANCHISE STORES
■ CORPORATE STORES

512   567

453

514

59   53

1996   **1997**

16

CANADIAN OPERATIONS

(MILLIONS OF CANADIAN DOLLARS)	**1997**	1996	PERCENT CHANGE
SYSTEMWIDE SALES	**$108.0**	$90.8	19%
REVENUE			
FRANCHISE REVENUE	**$12.7**	$10.3	23%
SALES FROM CORPORATE STORES	6.8	4.3	58%
	19.5	14.6	34%
EBITDA – CANADIAN OPERATIONS	8.1	6.2	31%
CORPORATE OFFICE ADMINISTRATION	(1.4)	(0.5)	
EBITDA – CANADA	$ 6.7	$ 5.7	18%
NUMBER OF STORES			
OPENED	61	29	
CLOSED	5	6	
NUMBER OF STORES AT YEAR END			
FRANCHISED	278	228	
CORPORATE	21	15	
TOTAL NUMBER OF STORES	299	243	

these stores are generally profitable, they do not represent an attractive return on capital for the shareholder and Second Cup is planning to reduce the total number of corporate stores in fiscal 1998.

EBITDA for the Canadian Operations increased by 31% to $8.1 million in 1997, reflecting earnings associated with new stores and increased systemwide sales. During the year, the Company invested in additional infrastructure costs, principally management, to provide support for accelerated store growth.

Effective February 1997, Second Cup became the exclusive coffee supplier for all Air Canada flights. While this arrangement did not contribute significantly to earnings in the year, the exposure of the Second Cup brand through this alliance has been beneficial.

Corporate office administration costs include all public company expenses together with the costs associated with the Chairman and Chief Executive Officer and the Executive Vice-President and Chief Financial Officer. These costs were $1.4 million in 1997 compared to $0.5 million in the prior year. Corporate office administration costs are not expected to change materially in fiscal 1998.

U.S. Operations

Systemwide sales for U.S. Operations increased 24% to $153 million in 1997 from $124 million in 1996. Systemwide sales in Coffee Plantation declined as a result of the divestiture prior to year end and store closures during the year (refer to Divestiture and Provision for Store Closures following). Gloria Jean's systemwide sales increased to $140 million from $109 million last year, reflecting the impact of a full year of reported results in 1997 versus nine months in 1996. Comparable store sales at Gloria Jean's for 1997 were flat. In the next year, 20 to 30 new Gloria Jean's stores are planned.

Revenues increased 10% to $53.6 million for 1997 from $48.7 million in 1996. Franchise revenue rose to $8.1 million from $6.8 million a year ago, relating to a full year's royalty income and increased new store openings.

The number of Gloria Jean's corporate stores increased to 31 at June 28, 1997 from 22 at June 29, 1996. These additional outlets and the full year's results included in 1997 increased corporate store

U.S. OPERATIONS	**1997**			1996			
(MILLIONS OF CANADIAN DOLLARS)	GLORIA JEAN'S	COFFEE PLANTATION	TOTAL	GLORIA JEAN'S	COFFEE PLANTATION	TOTAL	PERCENT CHANGE
SYSTEMWIDE SALES	$140.4	$12.5	**$152.9**	$108.9	$14.7	$123.6	24%
REVENUE							
PRODUCT SALES	$ 22.4	$ —	**$ 22.4**	$ 19.0	$ —	$ 19.0	18%
FRANCHISE REVENUE	8.1	—	**8.1**	6.8	—	6.8	19%
SALES FROM CORPORATE							
STORES	10.6	12.5	**23.1**	8.2	14.7	22.9	1%
	41.1	12.5	**53.6**	34.0	14.7	48.7	10%
EBITDA –							
U.S. OPERATIONS	$(0.6)	—	**$(0.6)**	$4.1	$(1.6)	$2.5	
NUMBER OF STORES							
OPENED	29	1	**30**	17	12	29	
ACQUIRED	—	—	**—**	236	—	236	
CLOSED/DISPOSED	9	22	**31**	6	—	6	
NUMBER OF STORES AT							
YEAR END							
FRANCHISED	236		**236**	225		225	
CORPORATE	31	1	**32**	22	22	44	
TOTAL NUMBER OF STORES	267	1	**268**	247	22	269	

CONSOLIDATED SYSTEMWIDE SALES

IN MILLIONS OF DOLLARS

214.4   260.9

108.0

90.8

139.9

108.9

14.7   12.5

0.5

1996   **1997**

■ SECOND CUP STORES
■ GLORIA JEAN'S STORES
■ COFFEE PLANTATION STORES
■ WHOLESALE PRODUCT SALES
  TO THIRD PARTIES

17

sales to $10.6 million from $8.2 million last year. These corporate store operations generated a loss of $0.7 million in addition to requiring a significant investment of administration and support. Also, the corporate store carrying values were written down by $1.0 million to their estimated net realizable value and a provision of $1.2 million was taken in respect of potential lease termination costs. Future earnings will continue to reflect the ongoing operating results of these stores. Stabilizing corporate store operations and resolving under-performing locations are key priorities for fiscal 1998.

U.S. Operations incurred an EBITDA loss of $0.6 million in 1997, compared to EBITDA of $2.5 million a year ago, reflecting disappointing results at Gloria Jean's and reduced losses at Coffee Plantation. In the first quarter, which is typically a slow sales period and for which there was no comparable period in 1996, Gloria Jean's reported an EBITDA loss of $0.5 million.

The operating results for Coffee Plantation include store operating losses of $1.1 million (1996: $1.7 million) arising from the non-Arizona stores which were slated for closure or sale at the end of fiscal 1996 (refer to Divestiture and Provision for Store Closures following). Infrastructure costs at Coffee Plantation were scaled back in 1997, reducing losses at this subsidiary.

1997 represented a year of investment at Gloria Jean's. Key priorities in the year included building a new management team, implementing improved systems, standards and controls throughout the organization, establishing credibility with the franchise community, upgrading store standards and modernizing store assets. Many of the initiatives begun in fiscal 1997 are expected to positively impact results beginning in fiscal 1998.

The costs associated with these management priorities, including the reorganization expenses incurred in building the management team, are reflected in 1997 EBITDA. Due to the Company's commitment to sell only the best quality coffees and its refusal to compromise on freshness standards, an inventory write-down of $0.8 million was incurred in 1997, primarily related to overproduction of seasonal products. Management has implemented a new system for holiday season product orders to eliminate exposure to excess stock in fiscal 1998.

Depreciation and Amortization

The increases in depreciation of capital assets and amortization of goodwill relate to the impact of a full year of costs for Gloria Jean's in 1997 compared to a partial year reflected for 1996.

Divestiture and Provision for Store Closures

As described in note 2 to the consolidated financial statements, the Company divested its 15 Arizona Coffee Plantation stores, effective May 21, 1997 for proceeds of $11.7 million. After taking into account the write-off of all remaining Coffee Plantation assets, and providing for all known exposures, this transaction resulted in a gain on sale of $2.2 million. While the Arizona stores were profitable, the prospect of future growth outside Arizona was not encouraging and the contribution they provided to overall shareholder value, after infrastructure costs, was not meaningful. Consequently, the Company decided to divest these stores at a reasonable value.

In 1996, the Company made a provision of $4.9 million for the closure or divestiture of its seven non-Arizona Coffee Plantation locations. This provision included a write-down of capital assets of $4.0 million to estimated net realizable value, as well as a write-off of the deferred store opening costs and a provision for estimated lease termination costs. At June 28, 1997 one of these stores, in Texas, remained open and is expected to be closed or sold in fiscal 1998. All known exit costs for this store have been fully provided.

Interest Income (Expense)

The Company earned $1.8 million interest income in 1997 compared to a net interest expense of $0.4 million in fiscal 1996. In 1996, the Company incurred $0.9 million interest expense relating to the costs of bank debt used to finance a portion of the acquisition cost of Gloria Jean's and for expansion within Coffee Plantation. A portion of the proceeds from the private placement of common stock in May 1996 was used to discharge bank debt, and interest income of $0.6 million was earned on the investment of the remaining cash proceeds to the end of the 1996 fiscal year.

Interest income in 1997 included $0.4 million relating to the convertible debenture, bearing interest at 10%, which the Company invested in The Great Canadian Bagel, Ltd. on October 4, 1996. The remaining cash resources of the Company are invested in highly liquid, high quality instruments with a maturity of three months or less at the time of purchase.

Income Taxes

The Company has net operating loss carryforwards of $19.4 million in the U.S. available to shelter future taxable earnings. Of this amount, $5.2 million has been recognized in the consolidated financial statements as a long-term deferred tax asset of $2.0 million. The

18

tax benefit of the remaining net operating loss carryforwards will be reflected in income when they are applied.

INVESTMENT IN THE GREAT CANADIAN BAGEL, LTD.

As a means to participate in the rapidly expanding retail bagel sector, in October 1996, the Company invested $6.5 million in The Great Canadian Bagel, Ltd., Canada's leader in this category. This investment, described in note 4 to the consolidated financial statements, provides the Company with an attractive base rate of return on investment and the opportunity to realize substantial upside value through an optional equity participation upon conversion of the debenture and exercise of share purchase warrants. Additionally, it has solidified a strategic alliance between the two companies. At June 28, 1997 four twin Second Cup – Great Canadian Bagel stores were in operation, with encouraging results. Additional twin sites are planned for fiscal 1998.

LIQUIDITY AND CAPITAL RESOURCES

Cash and short-term investments increased $10.3 million to $46.1 million at June 28, 1997 largely as a result of continuing strong operating cash flows. As discussed earlier, $11.7 million was generated from the proceeds on disposition of the Arizona Coffee Plantation stores and $6.5 million was invested in The Great Canadian Bagel, Ltd. during the year.

The Company invested $5.6 million in capital assets during the year, compared to $7.8 million in 1996. The 1996 investment included $5.9 million for capital attributable to the expansion of Coffee Plantation. Future capital expenditures and working capital requirements are expected to be met by internally generated funds and are not material to the Company's overall cash flow.

The Company does not consider financial resources to be a constraint and is confident that financing from internal cash flows, existing cash resources and external financing sources are readily available should an attractive investment opportunity arise.

RISKS AND UNCERTAINTIES

Competition is expected to increase in the specialty coffee retailing industry because it is an attractive sector with low barriers to entry. During 1997 the Company faced increased competitive presence in its core Toronto market. Despite this, comparable store sales for this area were up solidly, in line with national averages. The quality of execution at store level remains critical to continued success.

The price of coffee is subject to fluctuation and may be affected by a variety of factors. At store level, because the Company's total cost of coffee is modest compared to systemwide sales and overall cost of sales, significant increases in the price of coffee have a limited impact on overall store profitability. Retail price increases associated with highly publicized world coffee cost increases have been successfully implemented with no measurable loss in unit volume. In addition, because much of the Company's income stream is royalty based, it is generally insulated from the variability in store level earnings arising from changes in the price of coffee. Gloria Jean's roasts and distributes coffee to its franchisees on a cost-plus basis which includes the actual cost of coffee.

The Company hedges the risk of fluctuations in coffee prices for the stores by buying forward contracts to lock in acceptable margins at store level. This policy of forward purchasing enabled the Company, in a period of escalating costs which began in January 1997, to delay the implementation of a full retail price increase until June 1997 in Canada and July 1997 in the United States.

OUTLOOK

In Canada, we expect continued growth at an accelerated pace as we pursue additional opportunities to build value and increase both top and bottom line results. We will also concentrate on building our brand equity through carefully selected new partnerships. In the United States, our key priority is to stabilize our corporate store operations and to resolve the under-performing stores. In addition, we will continue to emphasize improved store operating standards and entrench the culture of an uncompromising commitment to product quality and superior customer service. In so doing, we will improve store sales and profitability. We expect to deliver a material improvement in earnings at Gloria Jean's in fiscal 1998. Corporately, we will seek to deploy the Company's cash resources to provide a meaningful enhancement of shareholder value.

Comparative Financial Statements

Management Report

A relatively recent addition to corporate annual reports is the statement made by management about its role in, and responsibility for, the accuracy and integrity of the financial statements. Second Cup's management letter is entitled **Management's Responsibility for Financial Reporting**. In it, the Chairman and Chief Executive Officer, along with the Executive Vice-President and Chief Financial Officer, do the following on behalf of management: (1) assume primary responsibility for the financial statements and the related notes, (2) outline and assess the company's internal control system, (3) declare the financial statements to be in conformity with generally accepted accounting principles, and (4) comment on the audit and the composition and role of the Audit Committee of the Board of Directors. Second Cup's management report is presented below:

MANAGEMENT'S RESPONSIBILITY FOR FINANCIAL REPORTING

The management of The Second Cup Ltd. is responsible for the integrity of the financial statements and all other information contained within this annual report. The financial statements were prepared by management in accordance with generally accepted accounting principles which involve the use of informed judgements and estimates. All financial information in the annual report is consistent with the financial statements.

The Company maintains systems of internal control which have been designed to provide reasonable assurance that accounting records are reliable and assets are safeguarded. The independent audit firm of Price Waterhouse have audited the financial statements on behalf of the shareholders and have expressed an opinion based upon their audit which was conducted in accordance with generally accepted auditing standards.

The Board of Directors oversees management's responsibility for financial reporting primarily through its Audit Committee, the majority of the members of which are outside directors, and to which the independent auditors have free access.

MICHAEL BREGMAN
Chairman and Chief Executive Officer

KATHY A. WELSH
Executive Vice-President and Chief Financial Officer

Toronto, Canada
August 27, 1997

Auditors' Report

All publicly held corporations, as well as many other enterprises and organizations (both profit and not-for-profit, large and small), hire independent public accountants to have an objective, expert report on their financial statements. Based on a comprehensive examination of the company's accounting system and records, and the financial statements, the external auditor issues the auditors' report.

The standard auditors' report consists of three paragraphs: (1) an introductory paragraph, (2) a scope paragraph, and (3) the opinion paragraph. In the **introductory paragraph**, the auditor identifies who and what was audited and indicates the responsibilities of management and the auditor relative to the financial statements. In the scope paragraph, the auditor states that the audit was conducted in accordance with generally accepted auditing standards and discusses the nature and limitations of the audit. In the opinion paragraph, the auditor expresses an informed opinion as to: (1) the fairness of the financial statements, and (2) their conformity with generally accepted accounting principles. The Auditors' Report of Price Waterhouse, Chartered Accountants, addressed to the shareholders of The Second Cup Ltd., is shown below:

AUDITORS' REPORT

To the Shareholders of The Second Cup Ltd.

We have audited the consolidated balance sheets of The Second Cup Ltd. as at June 28, 1997 and June 29, 1996 and the consolidated statements of operations and retained earnings and changes in financial position for the fiscal periods then ended. These financial statements are the responsibility of the Company's management. Our responsibility is to express an opinion on these financial statements based on our audits.

We conducted our audits in accordance with generally accepted auditing standards. Those standards require that we plan and perform an audit to obtain reasonable assurance whether the financial statements are free of material misstatement. An audit includes examining, on a test basis, evidence supporting the amounts and disclosures in the financial statements. An audit also includes assessing the accounting principles used and significant estimates made by management, as well as evaluating the overall financial statement presentation.

In our opinion, these consolidated financial statements present fairly, in all material respects, the financial position of the Company as at June 28, 1997 and June 29, 1996 and the results of its operations and the changes in its financial position for the fiscal periods then ended in accordance with generally accepted accounting principles.

Toronto, Canada
August 27, 1997

Price Waterhouse

Chartered Accountants

The auditor's report issued on Second Cup's financial statements is **unqualified; or "clean"**; that is, it contains no qualifications or exceptions. In other words, the auditor conformed completely with generally accepted auditing standards in performing the audit, and the financial statements conformed in all significant respects with generally accepted accounting principles. If the financial statements do not conform with generally accepted accounting principles, or if the scope of the audit has been restricted, the auditor must issue a **qualified** opinion and describe the exception. If the lack of conformity with GAAP is significant, the auditor is obliged to issue an **adverse** opinion or denial. An adverse opinion means that the financial statements do not present fairly the company's financial condition and/or the results of the company's operations at the dates and for the periods reported.

Companies do their best to obtain an unqualified auditor's report. Hence, you will rarely encounter anything other than this type of opinion on the financial statements.

Financial Statements and Accompanying Notes

The standard set of financial statements consists of: (1) a comparative balance sheet for two years, (2) a comparative income statement for two years, (3) a statement of retained earnings (sometimes combined with the statement of income) for two years, (4) a comparative statement of cash flow (also called changes in financial position) for two years, and (5) a set of accompanying notes that are considered an integral part of the financial statements. Some companies present comparative figures for three years. The auditors' report, unless stated otherwise, covers the financial statements and the accompanying notes. The financial statements and accompanying notes for Second Cup for the years ended June 28, 1997, and June 29, 1996, appear on the following pages. They are **consolidated financial statements**, which means that the statements include the financial results for Second Cup's Canadian and U.S. operations combined.

CONSOLIDATED BALANCE SHEETS

(THOUSANDS OF DOLLARS)	JUNE 28 **1997**	JUNE 29 1996
ASSETS		
CURRENT ASSETS		
CASH AND SHORT-TERM INVESTMENTS	$ 46,083	$ 35,760
ACCOUNTS RECEIVABLE	5,436	5,662
INVENTORIES (NOTE 3)	5,489	6,439
INCOME TAXES RECOVERABLE	—	739
PREPAID EXPENSES AND SUNDRY ASSETS	1,368	792
DEFERRED INCOME TAXES	—	1,735
	58,376	51,127
CAPITAL ASSETS (NOTE 5)	10,858	14,330
OTHER ASSETS	15	667
INVESTMENT IN THE GREAT CANADIAN BAGEL, LTD. (NOTE 4)	6,495	—
DEFERRED INCOME TAXES	2,722	1,056
GOODWILL, LESS ACCUMULATED AMORTIZATION OF $3,514 (1996 – $2,777)	33,923	37,571
	$112,389	$104,751
LIABILITIES		
CURRENT LIABILITIES		
ACCOUNTS PAYABLE AND ACCRUED LIABILITIES	$ 9,020	$ 6,289
DEPOSITS	371	534
INCOME TAXES PAYABLE	1,106	—
	10,497	6,823
OTHER DEFERRED LIABILITIES	676	556
SHAREHOLDERS' EQUITY		
SHARE CAPITAL (NOTE 6)	94,432	94,294
RETAINED EARNINGS	5,775	2,794
CUMULATIVE FOREIGN EXCHANGE TRANSLATION ADJUSTMENT	1,009	284
	101,216	97,372
	$112,389	$104,751

See accompanying notes to Consolidated Financial Statements.

Approved by the Board

MICHAEL BREGMAN
Chairman

ROY SUGDEN
Director

CONSOLIDATED STATEMENTS OF OPERATIONS AND RETAINED EARNINGS

(THOUSANDS OF DOLLARS, EXCEPT PER SHARE DATA)	FIFTY-TWO WEEKS ENDED **JUNE 28 1997**	FIFTY-THREE WEEKS ENDED JUNE 29 1996
SYSTEMWIDE SALES	$260,881	$214,358
REVENUE		
PRODUCT SALES	$ 22,412	$ 19,040
FRANCHISE REVENUE	20,783	17,030
SALES FROM CORPORATE STORES	29,868	27,232
TOTAL REVENUE	$ 73,063	$ 63,302
EBITDA*	$ 6,055	$ 8,221
DEPRECIATION OF CAPITAL ASSETS	2,258	2,006
AMORTIZATION OF GOODWILL	1,011	860
EARNINGS BEFORE THE UNDERNOTED	2,786	5,355
GAIN ON DISPOSITION OF COFFEE PLANTATION (NOTE 2)	2,222	—
PROVISION FOR COFFEE PLANTATION STORE		
CLOSURES (NOTE 8)	—	(4,900)
EARNINGS BEFORE INTEREST AND TAXES	5,008	455
INTEREST INCOME (EXPENSE) (NOTE 7)	1,778	(389)
EARNINGS BEFORE INCOME TAXES	6,786	66
INCOME TAXES (NOTE 9)		
CURRENT	3,500	2,216
DEFERRED	305	216
	3,805	2,432
NET EARNINGS (LOSS)	2,981	(2,366)
RETAINED EARNINGS, BEGINNING OF PERIOD	2,794	5,160
RETAINED EARNINGS, END OF PERIOD	$ 5,775	$ 2,794
WEIGHTED AVERAGE SHARES OUTSTANDING		
DURING THE FISCAL PERIOD	14,291,084	9,450,937
EARNINGS (LOSS) PER SHARE	$0.21	$(0.25)

*EBITDA represents earnings before interest, taxes, depreciation, amortization and unusual items.

See accompanying notes to Consolidated Financial Statements.

CONSOLIDATED STATEMENTS OF CHANGES IN FINANCIAL POSITION

(THOUSANDS OF DOLLARS)	FIFTY-TWO WEEKS ENDED **JUNE 28 1997**	FIFTY-THREE WEEKS ENDED JUNE 29 1996
CASH PROVIDED BY (USED IN)		
OPERATING ACTIVITIES		
NET EARNINGS (LOSS) FOR THE FISCAL PERIOD	$ 2,981	$ (2,366)
ITEMS NOT INVOLVING CASH		
AMORTIZATION AND DEPRECIATION	3,269	2,866
WRITE-DOWN OF GLORIA JEAN'S STORE ASSETS	1,030	—
DEFERRED INCOME TAXES	91	216
LOSS (GAIN) ON DISPOSAL OF CAPITAL ASSETS	(70)	105
PROVISION FOR COFFEE PLANTATION STORE CLOSURES (NOTE 8)	—	4,900
GAIN ON DISPOSITION OF COFFEE PLANTATION (NOTE 2)	(2,222)	—
CASH FLOW FROM OPERATIONS	5,079	5,721
DECREASE (INCREASE) IN NONCASH WORKING CAPITAL	3,435	(1,403)
	8,514	4,318
INVESTING ACTIVITIES		
PURCHASE OF CAPITAL ASSETS	(5,645)	(7,834)
PROCEEDS FROM DISPOSAL OF CAPITAL ASSETS	1,139	263
INVESTMENT IN THE GREAT CANADIAN BAGEL, LTD. (NOTE 4)	(6,495)	—
ACQUISITION OF GLORIA JEAN'S GOURMET COFFEES (NOTE 2)	—	(40,000)
PROCEEDS ON DISPOSITION OF COFFEE PLANTATION (NOTE 2)	11,747	—
CUMULATIVE FOREIGN EXCHANGE TRANSLATION ADJUSTMENTS	153	45
	899	(47,526)
FINANCING ACTIVITIES		
PROCEEDS ON ISSUANCE OF SHARES (NOTE 6)	138	79,226
OTHER ASSETS	652	(575)
OTHER DEFERRED LIABILITIES	120	127
	910	78,778
INCREASE IN CASH DURING THE FISCAL PERIOD	10,323	35,570
CASH AND SHORT-TERM INVESTMENTS, BEGINNING OF FISCAL PERIOD	35,760	190
CASH AND SHORT-TERM INVESTMENTS, END OF FISCAL PERIOD	$46,083	$35,760

See accompanying notes to Consolidated Financial Statements.

NOTES TO CONSOLIDATED FINANCIAL STATEMENTS

JUNE 28, 1997 AND JUNE 29, 1996 (TABULAR AMOUNTS IN THOUSANDS OF DOLLARS)

1. SUMMARY OF SIGNIFICANT ACCOUNTING POLICIES

Principles of consolidation

The consolidated financial statements include the accounts of the Company and its wholly-owned subsidiaries. All significant inter-company accounts and transactions have been eliminated on consolidation.

Cash and short-term investments

The short-term investments are recorded at cost and represent highly liquid instruments with a maturity of three months or less at the time of purchase.

Inventories

Inventories are valued at the lower of cost and net realizable value with cost being determined substantially on a first-in, first-out basis.

Investment in The Great Canadian Bagel, Ltd.

The Company's investments in The Great Canadian Bagel, Ltd. are carried at cost, as the Company does not exercise significant influence or control.

Capital assets

Capital assets are recorded at cost. Depreciation is calculated using the straight-line basis at the following rates, which are based on the expected useful life of the asset:

Manufacturing equipment,

furniture, fixtures and other	7 years
Leasehold improvements	lesser of 10 years and remaining term of the lease.

Goodwill

The excess of the purchase price over the estimated fair value of identifiable net assets acquired represents goodwill. Goodwill is amortized over 40 years on a straight-line basis.

The Company reviews the carrying value of goodwill on an annual basis to determine if an impairment in value has occurred. The Company measures the potential impairment of goodwill by comparing the undiscounted value of expected future earnings before income taxes, interest and amortization of goodwill to the current carrying value of goodwill. Any permanent impairment in the value of goodwill is written off against earnings. The Company is of the opinion that there has been no permanent impairment in the value of goodwill.

Foreign currency translation

The accounts of the Company's foreign subsidiaries operating in the United States are translated using the current rate method. Under this method, assets and liabilities are translated into Canadian dollars at the year-end exchange rate. Revenue and expenses are translated at the average exchange rates in effect during the year. Exchange gains or losses on translation are deferred and included as a separate component of shareholders' equity.

Foreign denominated unhedged short-term monetary items, principally short-term investments, are translated into Canadian dollars at year-end exchange rates; exchange gains and losses are

recognized in the same period as the foreign currency revenues to which they relate.

Financial instruments

Financial instruments, including short-term investments, accounts receivable, investment in The Great Canadian Bagel, Ltd., accounts payable and accrued liabilities are initially recorded at historical cost. If subsequent circumstances indicate a decline in the fair value of a financial asset which is other than temporary, the financial asset would be written down to its fair value. Unless otherwise indicated, the fair values of financial instruments approximate their recorded amounts. With the exception of the investment in The Great Canadian Bagel, Ltd., fair values of financial instruments approximate recorded amounts because of the short period to receipt or payment of cash.

The Company has entered into a forward foreign exchange contract to hedge its exposure to changes in the value of the Canadian dollar related to a U.S. dollar denominated short-term investment. Gains and losses on the forward exchange contract are recognized in the same period as the foreign currency revenues to which they relate.

Systemwide sales

Systemwide sales includes retail sales of all corporate and franchised stores, based on sales information reported by store operators, and product sales to third parties.

Franchise revenue

Initial franchise fees for stores are recognized as income when the store has opened. Master franchise fees are recognized as income when the agreement has been signed and any material conditions have been met. Franchise royalties are recognized as earned.

Store pre-opening costs

Certain costs incurred in connection with the opening of new corporate-owned stores are capitalized and expensed over the stores' first year of operations.

Fiscal year end

The Company's fiscal year end is the last Saturday in June.

Comparative figures

Certain comparative figures have been reclassified to conform with the financial statement presentation adopted in the current year.

2. ACQUISITION AND DIVESTITURE

On May 21, 1997, the Company sold the assets of its 15 Arizona-based Coffee Plantation stores to Coffee People, Inc., a public company based in Portland, Oregon for proceeds of $11.7 million. The transaction resulted in a gain of $2.2 million. The net book value of all goodwill and capital assets of Coffee Plantation, Inc. has been expensed as a cost of the sale. At June 28, 1997, one Coffee Plantation store remained open in Houston, Texas. This store has been slated for closure (refer to note 8, Provision for Coffee Plantation Store Closures).

On November 10, 1995, the Company, through a wholly-owned subsidiary, completed the acquisition of 100% of the issued and outstanding shares of Edglo Enterprises, Inc. ("Edglo") effective September 30, 1995. Edglo operates the Gloria Jean's chain of gourmet coffee retail stores, primarily in the United States. The results of operations of Edglo have been consolidated with those of the Company from the effective date of acquisition. The acquisition has been accounted for by the purchase method of accounting. The following is a summary of net assets acquired at fair market value.

CURRENT ASSETS	$14,492
CAPITAL ASSETS	6,720
OTHER ASSETS	92
GOODWILL	25,150
	46,454
CURRENT LIABILITIES	(6,028)
OTHER LIABILITIES	(426)
	(6,454)
	$40,000
CONSIDERATION	
CASH	39,527
COSTS RELATED TO THE ACQUISITION	473
	$40,000

3. INVENTORIES

	1997	1996
COFFEE		
UNROASTED	$ 1,892	$ 2,209
ROASTED	1,388	1,641
OTHER MERCHANDISE HELD FOR RESALE	852	1,154
SUPPLIES	1,357	1,435
	$ 5,489	$ 6,439

4. INVESTMENT IN THE GREAT CANADIAN BAGEL, LTD.
The Company holds investments in The Great Canadian Bagel, Ltd. consisting of:

SUBORDINATED CONVERTIBLE DEBENTURE	$ 5,695
5% EQUITY INTEREST (1,000,591 COMMON SHARES)	800
	$ 6,495

The subordinated convertible debenture bears interest at 10%, payable quarterly in arrears, and was issued October 4, 1996. The debenture matures the earlier of October 4, 1999 or the date on which The Great Canadian Bagel, Ltd. receives a receipt from the Ontario Securities Commission for a final prospectus in connection with an initial public offering of its common shares. The debenture is convertible into 5,004,834 common shares at any time prior to maturity. After conversion of the debenture, the Company would hold a 24% equity interest in The Great Canadian Bagel, Ltd. Management believes that the carrying value of these investments approximates fair market value, based on internal analysis as no external market data is available.

The Company also holds warrants to purchase additional shares of The Great Canadian Bagel, Ltd. which expire on October 4, 1997 and October 4, 1998. On a proforma basis, the Company would own a 30% equity interest in The Great Canadian Bagel, Ltd. after the exercise of all warrants and conversion of the debenture.

5. CAPITAL ASSETS

	1997	1996
LEASEHOLD IMPROVEMENTS	$ 6,957	$11,807
FURNITURE, FIXTURES AND OTHER	5,544	6,543
MANUFACTURING EQUIPMENT	5,054	2,770
	17,555	21,120
LESS: ACCUMULATED DEPRECIATION	6,697	6,790
	$10,858	$14,330

Depreciation of capital assets for the fiscal period ended June 28, 1997 was $2,258,000 (June 29, 1996 – $2,006,000).

6. SHARE CAPITAL
Authorized share capital consists of an unlimited number of common shares and an unlimited number of first preference shares issuable in one or more series of which none are issued.

During the prior fiscal period, the shareholders of multiple voting shares converted their shares to subordinate voting shares and on May 13, 1996, the Company filed articles of amendment and restated articles of incorporation.

The changes in issued share capital after the conversion of the shares referred to above are as follows:

	UNLIMITED COMMON SHARES	
	SHARES	AMOUNT
BALANCE AS AT JUNE 24, 1995	6,107,754	$13,977
ISSUED ON PRIVATE PLACEMENTS, NET OF TAX-EFFECTED COSTS OF $2,603,000	8,134,650	80,077
ISSUED FOR CASH TO EMPLOYEES	34,300	240
BALANCE AS AT JUNE 29, 1996	14,276,704	$94,294
ISSUED FOR CASH TO EMPLOYEES AND DIRECTORS	18,995	138
BALANCE AS AT JUNE 28, 1997	14,295,699	$94,432

The Company has an Amended Director, Officer and Employee Stock Option Plan and two share purchase plans under which shares are reserved for future issue.

Up to 860,775 shares have been authorized for issue under the Amended Director, Officer and Employee Stock Option Plan (the "Option Plan"). To June 28, 1997, 51,600 shares have been issued upon exercise of stock options under the Option Plan. Options granted under the Option Plan are exercisable commencing three years after the date granted and expire seven years thereafter. At June 28, 1997, 419,729 options are issued and outstanding (June 29, 1996 – 355,700 options). Options to purchase 389,446 remain available to be granted in the future. A summary of activity under the Option Plan is as follows:

NOTES TO CONSOLIDATED FINANCIAL STATEMENTS *(continued)*

JUNE 28, 1997 AND JUNE 29, 1996 (TABULAR AMOUNTS IN THOUSANDS OF DOLLARS)

	NUMBER	OPTION PRICE
OUTSTANDING AT JUNE 24, 1995	260,700	$6.75-$8.00
ISSUED	235,000	$8.25-$13.625
CANCELLED	(105,700)	$8.00-$8.25
EXERCISED	(34,300)	$7.00
OUTSTANDING AT JUNE 29, 1996	355,700	$6.75-$13.625
ISSUED	199,429	$9.97-$12.50
CANCELLED	(118,100)	$6.75-$13.625
EXERCISED	(17,300)	$6.75-$8.00
OUTSTANDING AT JUNE 28, 1997	419,729	$6.75-$13.625

Up to 147,876 shares may be issued under the Directors Share Plan, which was approved by the shareholders at the October 16, 1996 Annual and Special Meeting. During the year ended June 28, 1997, 1,695 shares at prices ranging from $9.25 to $11.01 were issued to Directors of the Company under this Plan. Also during the fiscal 1997 year, 7,554 shares have been allotted for future issue to Directors at prices ranging from $9.25 to $11.01. Under the Directors Share Plan, 138,627 shares remain available for future issue or allotment.

Under the Share Purchase Plan, which was approved by the Board of Directors on October 16, 1996, employees have an opportunity from time-to-time to elect to purchase shares at fair market value price from treasury. Up to 405,588 shares are reserved for future issue. To June 28, 1997 no shares have been issued under the Share Purchase Plan.

7. INTEREST INCOME (EXPENSE)

	1997	1996
INTEREST EARNED	$ 2,116	$ 600
INTEREST EXPENSE		
LONG-TERM DEBT	—	(941)
OTHER	(338)	(48)
	$ 1,778	$ (389)

8. PROVISION FOR COFFEE PLANTATION STORE CLOSURES

The Coffee Plantation, Inc., a United States subsidiary of the Company, planned to close or divest its stores in all states other than Arizona in fiscal 1997. The provision of $4.9 million made in fiscal 1996 for these stores included a write-down of capital assets in the amount of $4.0 million to estimated net realizable value, as well as a write-off of the deferred store opening costs and a provision for estimated lease termination costs.

During fiscal 1997, six of these Coffee Plantation stores were either closed or sold. The assets of the Arizona-based Coffee Plantation stores were also sold in fiscal 1997 (refer to note 2). At June 28, 1997, one Coffee Plantation store remained open in Texas. This store will be either closed or divested in fiscal 1998. All capital assets and expected costs relating to this store closure have been fully provided. Included in the earnings for the year ended June 28, 1997 are the operating results for Coffee Plantation until the disposition of the Arizona-based stores, including store operating losses of approximately $1.1 million arising from these non-Arizona stores.

9. INCOME TAXES

	1997	1996
COMBINED CANADIAN APPROXIMATE INCOME		
TAX RATES	45%	45%
INCOME TAXES AT COMBINED CANADIAN		
STATUTORY RATES	$3,054	$ 30
UNRECOGNIZED BENEFIT OF LOSS		
CARRYFORWARDS AND OTHER		
TIMING DIFFERENCES	1,616	2,433
FOREIGN TAX RATE REDUCTION	(1,503)	(525)
FOREIGN WITHHOLDING TAXES	410	213
NONDEDUCTIBILITY OF AMORTIZATION		
OF GOODWILL	374	315
MANUFACTURING AND PROCESSING		
PROFITS REDUCTION	(98)	(80)
OTHER	(48)	46
	$3,805	$2,432

The Company's United States subsidiaries have net operating loss carryforwards and other net timing differences of approximately $19.4 million available to reduce future taxable income and income taxes payable. The net operating loss carryforwards commence to expire in 2010. The potential benefit of $5.2 million of the net operating loss carryforwards has been reflected in the financial statements as a long-term deferred tax asset of $2.0 million.

10. CASH HELD IN TRUST

Cash held in trust on behalf of franchisees at June 28, 1997 amounted to $1,187,000 (June 29, 1996 – $2,136,000) and is not recorded on the Company's balance sheet.

11. MINIMUM LEASE COMMITMENTS AND CONTINGENT LIABILITIES

The Company has lease commitments for corporate-owned stores and office premises. The Company also, as the franchisor, is the lessee in most of the franchisees' lease agreements. The Company enters into sublease agreements with the individual franchisee, whereby the franchisee assumes responsibility for and makes lease payments directly to the landlord.

The Company's minimum lease commitments and contingent liabilities for any leases subject to a sublease agreement between the Company and a franchisee are as follows:

	MINIMUM LEASE COMMITMENTS	CONTINGENT LIABILITIES
1998	$ 3,764	$ 20,383
1999	3,847	19,745
2000	3,718	18,737
2001	3,358	16,427
2002	2,601	14,438
THEREAFTER	9,071	39,880
	$26,359	$129,610

12. RELATED PARTY TRANSACTIONS

During the year ended June 28, 1997, the Company recorded franchise income of $0.6 million from Cara Operations Limited, which owns approximately 35% of the Company's issued and outstanding common shares. The franchise income was earned in the normal course of business pursuant to the license agreement signed July 2, 1996.

Supplementary Financial Information

• •

In addition to the financial statements and the accompanying notes, two items of supplementary financial information typically are presented: business segment information and a five- or 10-year summary of related financial data.

Business Segment Information

Earlier we mentioned that Second Cup's financial statements were consolidated, or combined. To help financial statement users assess the performance of diversified companies that operate in several different countries, industries, and/or lines of business, segmented financial information is also required. The required information for each significant segment includes revenues, income (or loss) from operations, assets, and export sales. This information is generally included in the form of notes and schedules in the notes accompanying the financial statements. Second Cup's summary of its business segment information is shown below:

13. SEGMENTED INFORMATION

The following is a summary of the Company's operations and assets by geographic area:

	CANADA		UNITED STATES		CONSOLIDATED	
	JUNE 28 1997	JUNE 29 1996	**JUNE 28 1997**	JUNE 29 1996	**JUNE 28 1997**	JUNE 29 1996
REVENUE	$19,490	$14,602	$53,573	$48,700	$ 73,063	$ 63,302
EBITDA	$ 6,702	$ 5,732	$ (647)	$ 2,489	$ 6,055	$ 8,221
DEPRECIATION AND AMORTIZATION	659	525	2,610	2,341	3,269	2,866
EARNINGS BEFORE THE UNDERNOTED	$ 6,043	$ 5,207	$(3,257)	$ 148	$ 2,786	$ 5,355
GAIN ON DISPOSITION OF COFFEE PLANTATION					2,222	—
PROVISION FOR COFFEE PLANTATION STORE CLOSURES					—	(4,900)
EARNINGS BEFORE INTEREST AND TAXES					$ 5,008	$ 455
INTEREST INCOME (EXPENSE)					1,778	(389)
INCOME TAXES					(3,805)	(2,432)
NET EARNINGS (LOSS)					$ 2,981	$ (2,366)
TOTAL ASSETS	$49,824	$41,851	$62,565	$62,900	$112,389	$104,751

Five- or 10-Year Summary

A five- or 10-year summary of selected financial data is usually presented in close proximity to the audited financial statements. From such a summary, one can determine trends and growth patterns over a fairly long period of time. Second Cup presented the following five-year financial review, which includes operating results, financial position data, and selected operating statistics:

FIVE-YEAR FINANCIAL REVIEW

(THOUSANDS OF CANADIAN DOLLARS, EXCEPT PER SHARE AMOUNTS)	1997	1996	1995	1994	1993
OPERATING RESULTS					
SYSTEMWIDE SALES	$260,881	$214,358	$80,675	$64,297	$53,724
REVENUE	73,063	63,302	21,008	15,055	8,462
EBITDA	6,055	8,221	4,948	4,780	3,758
EARNINGS BEFORE INCOME TAXES	6,786	66	4,179	3,883	2,294
NET EARNINGS (LOSS) FOR THE PERIOD	2,981	(2,366)	2,249	2,112	1,169
CASH FLOW FROM OPERATIONS	5,079	5,721	3,182	2,764	1,726
EARNINGS (LOSS) PER SHARE	$0.21	$(0.25)	$0.37	$0.35	$0.26
FINANCIAL POSITION					
CASH AND SHORT-TERM INVESTMENTS	$ 46,083	$ 35,760	$ 190	$ 2,558	$ 6,723
TOTAL ASSETS	112,389	104,751	21,508	19,575	19,137
LONG-TERM DEBT	—	—	—	—	3,507
SHAREHOLDERS' EQUITY	101,216	97,372	19,173	17,054	14,129
OPERATING STATISTICS					
NUMBER OF STORES OPENED IN THE PERIOD	91	58	39	19	15
NUMBER OF STORES CLOSED/DISPOSED IN THE PERIOD	36	12	7	7	7
NUMBER OF STORES ACQUIRED IN THE PERIOD	—	236	2	2	0
NUMBER OF STORES AT END OF PERIOD	567	512	230	196	182

27

Directors and Officers

Every annual report includes a list (and sometimes photos) of the members of the Board of Directors and the officers of the company. The **Board of Directors** is elected annually at the company's annual general meeting by the common shareholders to serve as their representatives. The Board has the ultimate moral and legal responsibility to manage and direct the operations and affairs of the company with care and integrity. One of the more important committees of the Board is the Audit Committee, which communicates with the auditors and assumes overall responsibility for the scope of the audit, results of the audit, internal controls, and published financial information.

Second Cup's directors and officers follows:

DIRECTORS AND OFFICERS

Board of Directors

LOUIS BREGMAN
*Executive Vice-President
of the Corporation*

MICHAEL BREGMAN
*Chairman and Chief Executive Officer
of the Corporation*

DIAN COHEN
*President
Dian Cohen Productions Ltd.*

DALE LASTMAN [2]
*Co-Chairman and Partner
Goodman, Phillips & Vineberg
Barristers & Solicitors*

ALTON McEWEN
*President and Chief Operating Officer
U.S. Operations*

RANDY A. POWELL
*President and Chief Operating Officer
Canadian Operations*

ROY SUGDEN [1]
Retired Executive

M. BERNARD SYRON
*Chairman and Chief Executive Officer
Cara Operations Limited*

GABRIEL TSAMPALIEROS [1]
*President and Chief Operating Officer
Cara Operations Limited*

Corporate Officers
The Second Cup Ltd.

MICHAEL BREGMAN
*Chairman and
Chief Executive Officer*

LOUIS BREGMAN
Executive Vice-President

ALTON McEWEN
*President and Chief Operating Officer
U.S. Operations*

ROBERT M. HAFT [2]
Founder and Managing Partner
Hamilton Morgan
President
Vitamin Superstore

HUGH SEGAL [1][2]
Fellow in the School of Policy Studies
Queen's University; Associate
Gluskin Sheff & Associates Inc.

RANDY A. POWELL
President and Chief Operating Officer
Canadian Operations

KATHY A. WELSH
Executive Vice-President and
Chief Financial Officer
Secretary-Treasurer

(1) Member of the Audit Committee
(2) Member of the Governance,
    Nominating and Human Resources
    Committee

Corporate Information

· ·

Corporate information gives the location of the company's head office and of other entities associated with the company, such as the auditor and legal counsel. It also usually informs shareholders of the date, time, and location of its annual meeting. Second Cup's corporate information also includes capital stock information, such as its stock trading symbol (SKL), which you can refer to in determining Second Cup's current stock market price when reading the stock market pages.

CORPORATE INFORMATION

The Second Cup Ltd.
175 Bloor Street East
South Tower, Suite 801
Toronto, Ontario
Canada M4W 3R8
Tel: (416) 975-5541
Fax: (416) 975-5207

Gloria Jean's
Gourmet Coffees
11480 Commercial Parkway
Castroville, California
U.S.A. 95012
Tel: (408) 633-6300
Fax: (408) 633-5920

Registrar and Transfer Agent
Montreal Trust Company
of Canada
151 Front Street West, 8th Floor
Toronto, Ontario
Canada M5J 2N1
Tel: (416) 981-9500

Principal Bankers
The Toronto-Dominion Bank

Principal Solicitors
Goodman, Phillips & Vineberg
Barristers & Solicitors
Toronto, Ontario, Canada

Auditors
Price Waterhouse
Chartered Accountants
Toronto, Ontario, Canada

Stock Trading Symbol
SKL

Stock Exchange Listing
The Toronto Stock Exchange

Annual General Meeting
Notice
The Annual Meeting of
shareholders will be held on
Wednesday, October 29, 1997
at 11:00 a.m. at the Design
Exchange, 234 Bay Street,
Toronto, Ontario, Canada.

APPENDIX · B

PRESENT VALUE CONCEPTS

Business enterprises borrow and invest large sums of money. Both of these types of transactions involve the use of **present value computations**. A present value computation is based on the concept of the **time value of money**. For example, would you rather be given $1,000 today, or be given $1,000 a year from today? If you get the $1,000 today and invest it to earn 5% per year, the $1,000 will accumulate to $1,050 ($1,000 plus the $50 interest) one year from today. The $1,000 received today is the present value amount that is equivalent to $1,050 one year from now.

The present value, therefore, is based on three variables: (1) the dollar amount to be received (the future amount), (2) the length of time until the amount is received (the number of periods), and (3) the interest rate (the discount rate). The process of determining the present value is referred to as **discounting the future amount**. The word **discount** has many meanings in accounting, each of which varies with the context in which it is being used. Be careful not to confuse the use of this word.

In this textbook, present value computations are used to measure several items. For example, in Chapter 16 we determined the market price of a bond by computing the present value of the principal and interest payments. Calculating the amount to be reported for notes payable and capital lease liabilities also involves present value computations. And, in Chapter 27, the discounted cash flow technique and the net present value method are used to make capital budget decisions.

Present Value of a Single Future Amount

To illustrate present value concepts, assume that you are willing to invest a sum of money that will yield $1,000 at the end of one year. In other words, what amount would you need to invest today to have $1,000 one year from now? If you want a 5% rate of return, the investment or present value is $952.38 ($1,000 ÷ 1.05). The computation of this amount is shown in Illustration B-1:

Present value × (1 + interest rate)	= Future value
Present value × (1 + 5%)	= $1,000
Present value	= $1,000 ÷ 1.05
Present value	= $952.38

Illustration B-1

Present value computation — $1,000 discounted at 5% for one year

The future amount ($1,000), the discount rate (5%), and the number of periods (one) are known. The variables in this situation can be depicted in the following time diagram:

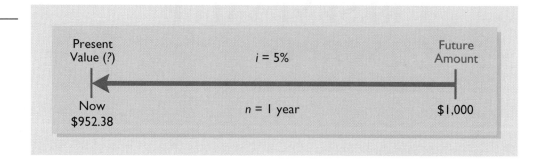

If the single future amount of $1,000 is to be received in two years and discounted at 5%, its present value is $907.03 [($1,000 ÷ 1.05) ÷ 1.05], depicted as follows:

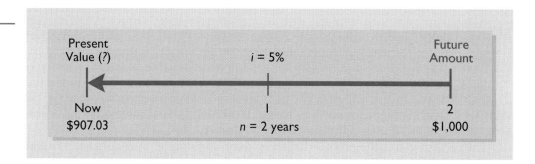

The present value of 1 may also be determined through tables that show the present value of 1 for n periods. In Table B-1 on page B3, n is the number of discounting periods involved. The percentages are the periodic interest rates or discount rates, and the five-digit decimal numbers in the respective columns are the factors for the present value of 1.

When Table B-1 is used, the future amount is multiplied by the present value factor specified at the intersection of the number of periods and the discount rate. For example, the present value factor for 1 period at a discount rate of 5% is .95238, which equals the $952.38 ($1,000 × .95238) computed in Illustration B-1. For two periods at a discount rate of 5%, the present value factor is .90703, which equals the $907.03 ($1,000 × .90703) computed previously.

Helpful hint
PV = FV × PV factor
FV = PV ÷ PV factor

If, instead of computing the present value, as in Illustration B-3, you know the present value and wish to determine the future amount, the present value amount can be *divided* by the present value factor specified at the intersection of the number of periods and the discount rate in Table B-1. For example, it can easily be determined that an initial investment of $907.03 will grow to yield a future amount of $1000 in two periods, at an annual discount rate of 5% ($1,000 = $907.03 ÷ .90703).

Note that **a higher discount rate produces a smaller present value**. For example, using an 8% discount rate, the present value of $1,000 due one year from now is $925.93 versus $952.38 at 5%. It should also be recognized that **the further removed from the present the future amount is, the smaller the present value**. For example, using the same discount rate of 5%, the present value of $1,000 due **in five years** is $783.53, versus the present value of $1,000 due in one year, which is $952.38.

TABLE B-I
PRESENT VALUE OF I
(Present Value of a Single Sum)

(n) Periods	2%	2½%	3%	4%	5%	6%	7%	8%	9%	10%	11%	12%	15%
1	.98039	.97561	.97087	.96154	.95238	.94340	.93458	.92593	.91743	.90909	.90090	.89286	.86957
2	.96117	.95181	.94260	.92456	.90703	.89000	.87344	.85734	.84168	.82645	.81162	.79719	.75614
3	.94232	.92860	.91514	.88900	.86384	.83962	.81630	.79383	.77218	.75131	.73119	.71178	.65752
4	.92385	.90595	.88849	.85480	.82270	.79209	.76290	.73503	.70843	.68301	.65873	.63552	.57175
5	.90573	.88385	.86261	.82193	.78353	.74726	.71299	.68058	.64993	.62092	.59345	.56743	.49718
6	.88797	.86230	.83748	.79031	.74622	.70496	.66634	.63017	.59627	.56447	.53464	.50663	.43233
7	.87056	.84127	.81309	.75992	.71068	.66506	.62275	.58349	.54703	.51316	.48166	.45235	.37594
8	.85349	.82075	.78941	.73069	.67684	.62741	.58201	.54027	.50187	.46651	.43393	.40388	.32690
9	.83676	.80073	.76642	.70259	.64461	.59190	.54393	.50025	.46043	.42410	.39092	.36061	.28426
10	.82035	.78120	.74409	.67556	.61391	.55839	.50835	.46319	.42241	.38554	.35218	.32197	.24718
11	.80426	.76214	.72242	.64958	.58468	.52679	.47509	.42888	.38753	.35049	.31728	.28748	.21494
12	.78849	.74356	.70138	.62460	.55684	.49697	.44401	.39711	.35553	.31863	.28584	.25668	.18691
13	.77303	.72542	.68095	.60057	.53032	.46884	.41496	.36770	.32618	.28966	.25751	.22917	.16253
14	.75788	.70773	.66112	.57748	.50507	.44230	.38782	.34046	.29925	.26333	.23199	.20462	.14133
15	.74301	.69047	.64186	.55526	.48102	.41727	.36245	.31524	.27454	.23939	.20900	.18270	.12289
16	.72845	.67362	.62317	.53391	.45811	.39365	.33873	.29189	.25187	.21763	.18829	.16312	.10686
17	.71416	.65720	.60502	.51337	.43630	.37136	.31657	.27027	.23107	.19784	.16963	.14564	.09293
18	.70016	.64117	.58739	.49363	.41552	.35034	.29586	.25025	.21199	.17986	.15282	.13004	.08081
19	.68643	.62553	.57029	.47464	.39573	.33051	.27651	.23171	.19449	.16351	.13768	.11611	.07027
20	.67297	.61027	.55368	.45639	.37689	.31180	.25842	.21455	.17843	.14864	.12403	.10367	.06110

Before You Go On . . .

▶ Review It

1. How is Table B-1 used to compute the present value of a single future amount?
2. How can Table B-1 be used to compute the future amount of a single present value?

▶ Do It

Suppose you have a winning lottery ticket and the lottery commission gives you the option of taking $10,000 three years from now, or taking the present value of $10,000 now. An 8% discount rate is used. How much will you receive if you accept your winnings now?

Reasoning: This problem illustrates the use of Table B-1 to determine the present value of 1.

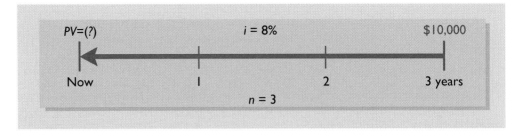

Solution: The present value factor from Table B-1 is .79383 (three periods at 8%). The present value of $10,000 to be received in three years, discounted at 8%, is $7,938.30 ($10,000 × .79383).

▶*Do It Again*

Determine the amount you must deposit now in your savings account, paying 3% interest, in order to accumulate $5,000 for a down payment on a Ford Escort four years from now, when you graduate.

Reasoning: This problem illustrates the use of Table B-1 to determine the present value of 1.

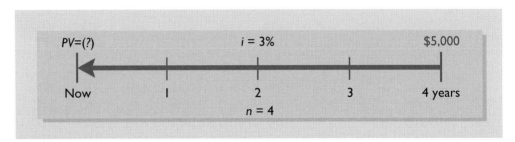

Solution: The present value factor from Table B-1 is .88849 (four periods at 3%). The present value of $5,000 to be received in four years, discounted at 3%, is $4,442.45 ($5,000 3 .88849).

Related exercise material: BEB–3, BEB–4, BEB–5, BEB–16, and BEB–17.

▼Present Value of a Series of Future Amounts (Annuities)

Alternative terminology
Payments at the end of each period are known as an *ordinary annuity* or *annuity in arrears.* Payments at the beginning of each period are known as an *annuity due* or *annuity in advance.* Unless otherwise indicated, this text assumes that all payments are made or received at the end of each period.

The preceding discussion involved the discounting of only a single future amount. Businesses and individuals frequently engage in transactions in which a series of equal dollar amounts are to be received or paid periodically. Examples of a series of periodic receipts or payments are loan agreements, instalment sales, mortgage notes, lease (rental) contracts, and pension obligations. These series of periodic receipts or payments are called **annuities**. In computing the present value of an annuity, it is necessary to know the (1) discount rate, (2) number of discount periods, and (3) amount of the periodic receipts or payments.

To illustrate the computation of the present value of an annuity, assume that you will receive $1,000 cash annually for three years, and that the discount rate is 4%. This situation is depicted in the following time diagram:

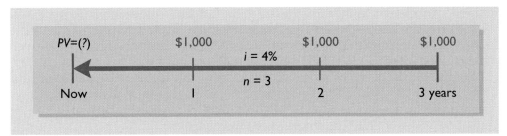

Illustration B-4

Time diagram for a three-year annuity

The present value in this situation may be computed as follows:

Illustration B-5

Present value of a series of future amounts computation

Future Amount	×	Present Value of 1 Factor at 4%	= Present Value
$1,000 (One year away)		.96154	$ 961.54
1,000 (Two years away)		.92456	924.56
1,000 (Three years away)		.88900	889.00
		2.77510	$2,775.10

This method of calculation is required when the periodic cash flows are not uniform in each period. However, when the future receipts are the same in each period, there are two other ways to compute present value. First, the annual cash flow can be

TABLE B-2
PRESENT VALUE OF AN ORDINARY ANNUITY OF 1

(n) Periods	2%	2½%	3%	4%	5%	6%	7%	8%	9%	10%	11%	12%	15%
1	.98039	.97561	.97087	.96154	.95238	.94340	.93458	.92593	.91743	.90909	.90090	.89286	.86957
2	1.94156	1.92742	1.91347	1.88609	1.85941	1.83339	1.80802	1.78326	1.75911	1.73554	1.71252	1.69005	1.62571
3	2.88388	2.85602	2.82861	2.77509	2.72325	2.67301	2.62432	2.57710	2.53129	2.48685	2.44371	2.40183	2.28323
4	3.80773	3.76197	3.71710	3.62990	3.54595	3.46511	3.38721	3.31213	3.23972	3.16987	3.10245	3.03735	2.85498
5	4.71346	4.64583	4.57971	4.45182	4.32948	4.21236	4.10020	3.99271	3.88965	3.79079	3.69590	3.60478	3.35216
6	5.60143	5.50813	5.41719	5.24214	5.07569	4.91732	4.76654	4.62288	4.48592	4.35526	4.23054	4.11141	3.78448
7	6.47199	6.34939	6.23028	6.00205	5.78637	5.58238	5.38929	5.20637	5.03295	4.86842	4.71220	4.56376	4.16042
8	7.32548	7.17014	7.01969	6.73274	6.46321	6.20979	5.97130	5.74664	5.53482	5.33493	5.14612	4.96764	4.48732
9	8.16224	7.97087	7.78611	7.43533	7.10782	6.80169	6.51523	6.24689	5.99525	5.75902	5.53705	5.32825	4.77158
10	8.98259	8.75206	8.53020	8.11090	7.72173	7.36009	7.02358	6.71008	6.41766	6.14457	5.88923	5.65022	5.01877
11	9.78685	9.51421	9.25262	8.76048	8.30641	7.88687	7.49867	7.13896	6.80519	6.49506	6.20652	5.93770	5.23371
12	10.57534	10.25776	9.95400	9.38507	8.86325	8.38384	7.94269	7.53608	7.16073	6.81369	6.49236	6.19437	5.42062
13	11.34837	10.98319	10.63496	9.98565	9.39357	8.85268	8.35765	7.90378	7.48690	7.10336	6.74987	6.42355	5.58315
14	12.10625	11.69091	11.29607	10.56312	9.89864	9.29498	8.74547	8.24424	7.78615	7.36669	6.98187	6.62817	5.72448
15	12.84926	12.38138	11.93794	11.11839	10.37966	9.71225	9.10791	8.55948	8.06069	7.60608	7.19087	6.81086	5.84737
16	13.57771	13.05500	12.56110	11.65230	10.83777	10.10590	9.44665	8.85137	8.31256	7.82371	7.37916	6.97399	5.95423
17	14.29187	13.71220	13.16612	12.16567	11.27407	10.47726	9.76322	9.12164	8.54363	8.02155	7.54879	7.11963	6.04716
18	14.99203	14.35336	13.75351	12.65930	11.68959	10.82760	10.05909	9.37189	8.75563	8.20141	7.70162	7.24967	6.12797
19	15.67846	14.97889	14.32380	13.13394	12.08532	11.15812	10.33560	9.60360	8.95011	8.36492	7.83929	7.36578	6.19823
20	16.35143	15.58916	14.87747	13.59033	12.46221	11.46992	10.59401	9.81815	9.12855	8.51356	7.96333	7.46944	6.25933

multiplied by the sum of the three present value factors. In the example above, $1,000 × 2.77510 equals $2,775.10. Second, annuity tables may be used. As illustrated in Table B-2 , these tables show the present value of 1 to be received periodically for a given number of periods.

From Table B-2, it can be seen that the present value factor of an annuity of 1 for three periods at 4% is 2.77509.[1] This present value factor is the total of the three individual present value factors, as shown in Illustration B-5. Applying this amount to the annual cash flow of $1,000 produces a present value of $2,775.09.

Interest Rates and Time Periods

In the preceding calculations, the discounting has been done on an annual basis using an annual interest rate obtained from a table. There are two situations where adjustments may be required to the interest rate, the time period, or both.

Interpolation

In situations where the factor for a certain interest rate is not available, it can be deduced or **interpolated** from the tables. For example, if you wished to find the factor to determine the present value of 1 for a $3\frac{1}{2}\%$ interest rate and five periods, it would be difficult to use Table B-1 to do so. Table B-1 (or Table B-2 for that matter) does not have a $3\frac{1}{2}\%$ interest rate column. We can, however, average the factors for the 3% and 4% interest rates to approximate the factor for a $3\frac{1}{2}\%$ interest rate.

Illustration B-6

Interpolation of $3\frac{1}{2}\%$ interest rate factor

	Factor, $n=5$, $i=3\%$	.86261
+	Factor, $n=5$, $i=4\%$	.82193
=	Sum of two factors	1.68454
÷	Average two factors	2
=	Factor, $n=5$, $i=3\frac{1}{2}\%$	.84227

Using Time Periods of Less Than One Year

Discounting may be done over shorter periods of time than one year — such as monthly, quarterly, or semi-annually. When the time frame is less than one year, it is necessary to convert the annual interest rate to the applicable time frame. Assume, for example, that the investor in Illustration B-5 received $500 **semi-annually** for three years instead of $1,000 annually. In this case, the number of periods becomes six (three annual periods × 2), the discount rate is 2% (4% × 6/12), the present value factor from Table B-2 is 5.60143, and the present value of the future cash flows is $2,800.72 (5.60143 × $500). This amount is slightly higher than the $2,775.10 computed in Illustration B-5 because interest is computed twice during the same year; therefore, interest is earned on the first half-year's interest. This is known as compound interest.

---

[1] The difference of .00001 between 2.77509 and 2.77510 is due to rounding.

Before You Go On . . .

▶Review It

1. What is an annuity?
2. How is Table B-2 used to compute the present value of an annuity?
3. How do you interpolate an interest rate?

▶Do It

Corkum Company has just signed a capitalizable lease contract for equipment that requires rental payments of $6,000 each, to be paid at the end of the next five years. The appropriate discount rate is 6%. What is the present value of the rental payments — that is, the amount used to capitalize the leased equipment?

Reasoning: This problem illustrates how to use Table B-2.

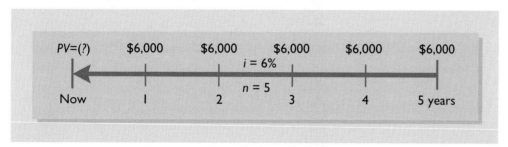

Solution: The present value factor from Table B-2 is 4.21236 (five periods at 6%). The present value of five payments of $6,000 each, discounted at 6%, is $25,274.16 ($6,000 × 4.21236).

Related exercise material: BEB–1, BEB–2, BEB–6, BEB–7, BEB–8, BEB–13, BEB–14, BEB–15, BEB–18, and BEB–19.

Computing the Present Value of a Bond

The present value (or market price) of a bond is a function of three variables: (1) the payment amounts, (2) the length of time until the amounts are paid, and (3) the discount rate.

The first variable (dollars to be paid) is made up of two elements: (1) the principal amount (a single sum), and (2) a series of interest payments (an annuity). To compute the present value of the bond, both the principal amount and the interest payments must be discounted — two different computations.

When the investor's discount rate is equal to the bond's contractual interest rate, the present value of the bonds will equal the face value of the bonds. To illustrate, assume a bond issue of 6%, five-year bonds with a face value of $100,000 with interest payable **semi-annually** on January 1 and July 1. If the discount rate is the same as the contractual rate, the bonds will sell at face value. In this case, the investor will receive: (1) $100,000 at maturity, and (2) a series of 10 $3,000 interest payments [($100,000 × 6%) × 6/12] over the term of the bonds. The length of time is expressed in terms of interest periods, in this case, 10, and the discount rate per interest period, 3%. The following time diagram depicts the variables involved in this discounting situation:

Illustration B-7

Time diagram for the present value of a 6%, five year bond paying interest semi-annually

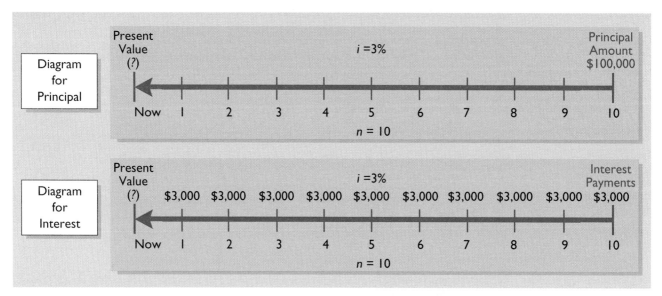

The computation of the present value of these bonds is shown below:

Illustration B-8

Present value of principal and interest (face value)

6% Contractual Rate — 6% Discount Rate	
Present value of principal to be received at maturity	
$100,000 × PV of 1 due in 10 periods at 3%	
$100,000 × .74409 (Table B-1)	$ 74,409
Present value of interest to be received periodically over the term of the bonds	
$3,000 × PV of 1 due periodically for 10 periods at 3%	
$3,000 × 8.53020 (Table B-2)	25,591*
Present value of bonds	$100,000

* Rounded

Now assume that the investor's required rate of return is 8%, not 6%. The future amounts are again $100,000 and $3,000, respectively. **These amounts are based on the bond contract, and do not vary with the investor's rate of return**. What does vary is the investor's rate of return, depending on available rates in the marketplace. In this case, a discount or effective interest rate of 4% (8% × 6/12) will be used. The present value of the bonds is $91,889, as computed in Illustration B–9:

6% Contractual Rate — 8% Discount Rate	
Present value of principal to be received at maturity $100,000 × PV of 1 due in 10 periods at 4% $100,000 × .67556 (Table B-1)	$67,556
Present value of interest to be received periodically over the term of the bonds $3,000 × PV of 1 due periodically for 10 periods at 4% $3,000 × 8.11090 (Table B-2)	24,333
Present value of bonds	$91,889

In this situation, the bonds will sell for $91,889, at a discount of $8,111. Bond discounts are discussed further in Chapter 16.

Conversely, if the discount rate is 5% and the contractual rate is 6%, the present value of the bonds is $104,376, computed as follows:

6% Contractual Rate — 5% Discount Rate	
Present value of principal to be received at maturity $100,000 × PV of 1 due in 10 periods at 2.5% $100,000 × .78120 (Table B-1)	$ 78,120
Present value of interest to be received periodically over the term of the bonds $3,000 × PV of 1 due periodically for 10 periods at 2.5% $3,000 × 8.75206 (Table B-2)	26,256
Present value of bonds	$104,376

These bonds will sell for $104,376, at a $4,376 premium.

The above discussion relied on present value tables to solve present value problems. Electronic calculators may also be used to compute present values without the use of these tables. Some calculators, especially financial calculators, have present value (PV) functions that allow you to calculate present values by merely punching in the proper amount, discount rate, periods, and pressing the PV key. Most computer spreadsheets and computer programs also have built-in formulas to perform the discounting functions given the basic information of the situation.

Before You Go On . . .

►*Review It*

1. Explain how the present value of a bond is determined.
2. If the bonds have interest payable semi-annually, should the *i* used to determine the appropriate discount factor be doubled or halved? The *n*?
3. What table is used to determine the present value of the bond principal? The bond interest?

Related exercise material: BEB–9, BEB–10, BEB–11, and BEB–12.

BRIEF EXERCISES

Use the present value tables.

BEB–1   For each of the following cases, indicate: (a) to what interest rate columns, and (b) to what number of periods you would refer in looking up the discount rate.

1. In Table B-1 (present value of 1):

	Annual Rate	Number of Years Involved	Discounts Per Year
a.	8%	1	Quarterly
b.	5%	10	Semi-annually
c.	6%	6	Annually

2. In Table B-2 (present value of an annuity of 1):

	Annual Rate	Number of Years Involved	Frequency of Payments
a.	8%	4	Quarterly
b.	5%	5	Semi-annually
c.	6%	20	Annually

Determine present values.

BEB–2   (a) What is the present value of $10,000 due eight periods from now, discounted at 8%? (b) What is the present value of $10,000 to be received at the end of each of six periods, discounted at 9%?

Compute the present value of a single-sum investment.

BEB–3   Smolinski Company is considering an investment that will return a lump sum of $500,000 five years from now. What amount should Smolinski Company pay for this investment in order to earn a 5% return?

Compute the present value of a single-sum investment.

BEB–4   Levesque Company earns 6% on an investment that will return $875,000 eight years from now. What is the amount Levesque should invest now in order to earn this rate of return?

Compute the future value of a single-sum investment, interest compounded annually.

BEB–5   On the joyous occasion of their granddaughter's birth, Kailynn's doting grandparents invest $5,000 in a 5 year guaranteed investment certificate (GIC) in her name. If the investment pays 6% annually, how much will the GIC yield when it matures 5 years from now? (Hint: You have learned that present value is determined by multiplying the future value by a factor from Table B-1 (PV × factor = FV). If future value is unknown, it can be determined by dividing the present value by the appropriate factor from Table B-1.)

Compute the future value of a single-sum investment, interest compounded semi-annually.

BEB–6   Assume the same information as BEB-5, except that the investment pays 6% twice a year; that is, interest is compounded semi-annually. How much will the GIC yield when it matures 5 years from now?

Compute the present value of an annuity investment.

BEB–7   Kilarny Company is considering investing in an annuity contract that will return $20,000 at the end of each year for 15 years. What amount should Kilarny Company pay for this investment, if it earns a 6% return?

Compute the present value of an annuity investment.

BEB–8   Deutsch Enterprises earns 9% on an investment that pays back $110,000 at the end of each of the next four years. What is the amount Deutsch Enterprises invested to earn the 9% rate of return?

Compute the present value of bonds.

BEB–9   Tek Railroad Co. is about to issue $100,000 of 10-year bonds that pay a 6% annual interest rate, with interest payable semi-annually. The discount or effective rate for such securities is 4%. How much can Tek expect to receive for the sale of these bonds?

Compute the present value of bonds.

BEB–10   Assume the same information as BEB-9, except that the discount rate is 8% instead of 4%. In this case, how much can Tek expect to receive from the sale of these bonds?

BEB–11 Caledonian Taco Company receives a $50,000, six-year note that bears interest of 4% (paid annually) from a customer at a time when the discount rate is 5%. What is the present value of the note received by Caledonian? (Hint: Calculate the present value of the principal and interest separately, similar to bonds.)

Compute the present value of a note.

BEB–12 Thibodeau Enterprises issued 5%, eight-year, $2,000,000 par value bonds that pay interest semi-annually on October 1 and April 1. The bonds are dated April 1, 1999, and are issued on that date. The discount rate of interest for such bonds on April 1, 1999, is 4%. What cash proceeds did Thibodeau receive from issuance of the bonds?

Compute the present value of bonds.

BEB–13 Barney Googal owns a garage and is contemplating purchasing a tire retreading machine for $16,280. After estimating costs and revenues, Barney projects a net cash flow from the retreading machine of $2,790 annually for eight years. Barney hopes to earn a return of 8% on such investments. What is the present value of the retreading operation? Should Barney Googal purchase the retreading machine?

Compute the value of a machine for purposes of making a purchase decision.

BEB–14 Hung-Chao Yu Company issues a 10%, six-year mortgage note on January 1, 1999 to obtain financing for new equipment. Land is used as collateral for the note. The terms provide for semi-annual instalment payments of $112,825. What were the cash proceeds received from the issuance of the note?

Compute the present value of a note.

BEB–15 Chang Company is considering purchasing equipment. The equipment will produce the following cash flows: Year 1, $30,000, Year 2, $40,000, Year 3, $50,000. Chang requires a minimum rate of return of 8%. What is the maximum price Chang should pay for this equipment?

Compute the maximum price to pay for a machine.

BEB–16 If Kerry Dahl invests $5,552.60 now, she will receive $10,000 at the end of 15 years. What annual rate of interest will Kerry earn on her investment? (Hint: Use Table B-1.)

Compute the interest rate on a single sum.

BEB–17 Maloney Cork has been offered the opportunity to invest $55,839 now. The investment will earn 6% per year, and at the end of that time will return Maloney $100,000. How many years must Maloney wait to receive $100,000? (Hint: Use Table B-1.)

Compute the number of periods of a single sum.

BEB–18 Annie Dublin purchased an investment for $11,469.92. From this investment, she will receive $1,000 annually for the next 20 years, starting one year from now. What rate of interest will Annie's investment be earning for her? (Hint: Use Table B-2.)

Compute the interest rate on an annuity.

BEB–19 André Bourque invests $8,851.37 now for a series of $1,000 annual returns, beginning one year from now. André will earn a return of 8% on the initial investment. How many annual payments of $1,000 will André receive? (Hint: Use Table B-2.)

Compute the number of periods of an annuity.

 # ACCOUNTING ON THE WEB

This problem illustrates the time value of money. The "Investing for Kids Java Goals Calculator" is used to see how long it will take to reach financial goals, using standard rates of return for bank deposits, T-bills, bonds, and shares.

Instructions

Specific requirements of this Internet case are available on-line at www.wiley.com/canada/weygandt.

COMPANY INDEX

SUBJECT INDEX

PHOTO CREDITS

All images copyright © 1997 PhotoDisc, Inc., unless otherwise noted.

WE WANT TO HEAR FROM YOU

By sharing your opinions about *Accounting Principles*, you will help us ensure that you are getting the most value for your textbook dollars. After you have used the book for a while, please fill out this form. Either fold, tape, and mail, or fax us toll free @ 1(800)565-6802!

Course name: _____ School name: _____

Your name: _____

I am using: ❑ Volume 1   ❑ Volume 2   ❑ Volume 3

1) Did you purchase this book (check all that apply):
   - ❑ From your campus bookstore
   - ❑ From a bookstore off-campus
   - ❑ New   ❑ Used   ❑ For yourself
   - ❑ For yourself and at least one other student

2) Was this text available at the bookstore when when you needed it?
   ❑ Yes   ❑ No

3) Was the study guide available at the bookstore when you needed it?
   ❑ Yes   ❑ No   ❑ Don't know

   If yes, did you purchase it?

   ❑ Yes   ❑ No   ❑ I intend to purchase it

4) Did you find the Study Guide to be a useful aid?
   ❑ Yes   ❑ No

Comments: _____

_____

_____

5) Did you purchase the working papers that are available with this book?
   ❑ Yes   ❑ No

   If yes, did you find them a useful study tool?
   ❑ Yes   ❑ No

Comments: _____

_____

_____

6) How far along are you in this course (put an X where you are now)?

   ❑———————————❑———————————❑
   Beginning   Midway   Completed

7) How much have you used this text (put an X where you are now)?

   ❑———————————❑———————————❑
   Skimmed   Read half   Read entire book

8) Have you read the introductory material (i.e., the Student Owner's Manual)?

   ❑   ❑   ❑
   Yes   No   Parts of it

9) Even if you have only skimmed this text, please rate the following features:

Features:	Very valuable/effective	Somewhat valuable/effective	Not valuable/effective
Value as a reference			
Readability			
Design & illustrations			
Study & review material			
Problems & exercises			
Relevant examples			
Overall perception			

10) What do you like most about this book? _____

_____

_____

_____

_____

11) How do you think we can improve future editions?

_____

_____

_____

_____

12) Do you have easy access to the WWW?
   ❑ Yes   ❑ No

   If yes, where do you access it?
   At home _____%   At School _____%

13) What kinds of things would you find useful on a website associated with this textbook?

   _____

   _____

   _____

   _____

14) At the end of the semester, what do you intend to do with this text?
   ❑ Keep it   ❑ Sell it   ❑ Unsure

15) May we quote you?   ❑ Yes   ❑ No

If you would like to receive information on other Wiley business books, please fill in the following information:

Name _____

Street _____ Apt. # _____

City _____ Prov. _____

Postal Code _____

Thank you for your time and feedback! You can contact us via e-mail at: cwells@wiley.com

 WILEY
Publishers Since 1807

-------------------------------------- (fold here) --------------------------------------

MAIL ➤ POSTE
Canada Post Corporation / Société canadienne des postes
Postage paid   **Port payé**
if mailed in Canada   si posté au Canada
Business   **Réponse**
Reply   **d'affaires**
0108529899   01

0108529899-M9W1L1-BR01

COLLEGE DIVISION
JOHN WILEY & SONS CANADA LTD
22 WORCESTER RD
PO BOX 56213 STN BRM B
TORONTO ON M7Y 9C1